Dogs of Velvet & Steel Productions

PRESENTS

Dogs of Velvet and Steel
Revised Edition

By Bob Stevens

The Supreme Court - Photo by my wife, Julie

The Stevens Family and Friend
(Julie, Lisa, Bob, Mike, Marla, Jubal, and T. Michael Riddle)

Victory in Freedom
United States Supreme Court
October 6, 2009

Copyright © 2012 by Robert John Stevens.

All rights reserved. Except as permitted under the United States Copyright Act of 1976, no part of this publication may be reproduced or distributed in any form or by any means, or stored in a data base or retrieval system, without the prior written permission of Robert Stevens.

Published by Pine Haven Press, Inc.
519 Main Street
Altavista, VA. 24517 - in association with Dogs of Velvet and Steel Productions.

Library of Congress Cataloging-in-Publication data: Stevens, Robert John
   Dogs of Velvet and Steel The Epilogue Includes biographical references
   - Supreme Court case - Pit Bull history and stories.

      ISBN 978-0-9857194-2-5
      ISBN 0-615-11835-6

      LCCN 2012942942

If you purchased this book without a cover you should be aware this book may have been stolen property and reported as "unsold and destroyed" to the publisher. In such case neither the author nor the publisher has received any payment for this "stripped book".

The scanning, uploading and distribution of this book via the internet or via any other means without the permission of Bob Stevens is illegal and punishable by law (including international law). Please do not participate in or encourage electronic piracy of copyrighted materials. Your support of the author's rights and his hard work in construction by purchasing only authorized editions directly from the author is appreciated.

Visit our website www.pitbullvictory.com

Front Cover Photo: Bob & Morochito's fourth generation, Victory's Secret (Vickie). Photo by wife Julie.

Ten Percent of the profits from all Dogs of Velvet and Steel Productions will be donated to Christian Ministries.

Contents

Acknowledgements 4
Dedication 6
The Epilogue 16
Chapter 1: Cast of Characters 18
Chapter 2: The Epilogue 81
Chapter 3: Bibliography 157
Dogs of Velvet and Steel 184

Dedication 185
Acknowledgements 186
Preface 191
Introduction 193
Chapter 1: History 207
Chapter 2: The Pit Bull Pet 272
Chapter 3: The Catch Dog 310
Chapter 4: The Schutzhund Dog 340
Chapter 5: The Competitive Weight-Pulling Dog 366
Chapter 6: Scientific Nutrition 380
Chapter 7: Scientific Conditioning 423
Chapter 8: Scientific Breeding 476
Chapter 9: Medicine Chest And Miscellaneous 532
Chapter 10: The Combat Dog 556
Chapter 11: Conclusion 627
Index 639

Acknowledgements

For seven years while I fought the fight for freedom of expression, my Julie suffered the fear she might lose her husband to a federal prison. She has been my wife and as such my partner through all of this – so her input and talents in making this book available cosmically extends back over a decade. 2003 pronounced a defining curve in our life pathway and her indescribable, fathomless, intuition and powers of observation that could not be replicated by anyone on this planet, helped put me on a straight path in travels long before but leading up to 2003. The experiences planted closer and deeper love, dependence and bonds that evolve only – and I do mean only – from striving together. Her dedication in this book captures and expresses more on this. Julie has been such a composite ingredient in the making of this book that I cannot list or adequately explain how she has helped me close my teeth and withdraw my pen as I am every bit as prone, left to myself, to trouble as our loved Pit Bulldogs.

And then there are my children and grandchildren. How can an author explain the inner security his children provide – keeps him running when his battery is on low charge – in ways that cannot be scripted. Along with my Julie my children Lisa Anne, Michael Scott, Michael Marsh, and grandson Jubal (and I cannot leave out little Rachael Emme born January 2010) all provided emotional support. Please don't glide over that acknowledgement, it is no insignificant thing.

For seven years many in the Pit Bull community helped enormously. Of course the Cast of Characters contains more description, but T. Michael Riddle and Gary Hammonds have been close for a long time. Many, many wrote protest letters to the government. Dick Stratton, Pat Patrick – even some military personnel wrote from the trenches fighting overseas, allowing they put their lives on the line for free America – and since they were all owners of Pit Bulldogs at home, they included their "American" Pit Bull Terriers. T. W. Williams helped. Bill Stewart used his *Pit Bull Reporter* magazine to help spread the word and garner protest letters from all across the nation. I saw Bill at a T. Michael wild boar hunt about a month or so before he passed.

The American Dog Breeders Association (ADBA), of course is central in all this. Your original *Dogs of Velvet and Steel* book promotes their conformation shows, weight pull competition and registry. The ADBA is without question at the core of preserving our breed, attenuating the outlaw stigmata and providing a quality registry, sanctioned conformation shows with certification of champion show dogs, and the sanctioned weight pulling competition, also with champion certification. This gives our breed credibility not only in our nation but in the world.

Special recognition, of course goes to my publisher Sonya Hightower Davis of Pine Haven Press, Inc. She walked me through the new, and to me, convoluted technological world of publishing and she plays a role in helping to glorify God with my teaching the Kingdom of God in this book.

Can't go without honorable mention to Patti Millett who represented us – and thus, on the bottom line, the APBT, and freedom of speech in America. With Supreme and I am convinced God-given (truly) legal talent, she established and settled VICTORY in Supreme Court.

Lastly I want to recognize my martial arts instructors. From them I found release, structure, focus and control. Grandmaster Bobby Taboada (Balintawak) is central. Grandmaster Daniel Pai (Kungfu), Grand Master Lawrence McSwain (karate), Grandmaster William Pierce (Aikikenjutsu), and Kent Eanes Kickboxing Champion. Moreover and importantly these warriors are all my close friends.

Ivan Carrillo did the Attack Team policeman over Bob. David Trujillo did the drawing of Bob focused on the policeman and Martin Moorefield did the drawings of the police terrorizing Julie, the State Trooper being a gunfighter, the free chickadee and the cross of Jesus on the hill.

Dedication

I would like to dedicate my Epilogue to the following people who have been strands in my life and who represent the fiber of my being and the essence of my life.

Like John Denver, I've seen desert storms. Drove through them on the California and Arizona desert on my Nighthawk motorcycle. I've been in the Colorado Mountains in the springtime with my daughter. Did my roadwork through the origins of our nation – Valley Forge, where my son resides. In the Navy, I've been on the high seas in the eye of a hurricane – and relaxed under a sleepy blue sky. I've smelled the sweat, blood, and testosterone of countless boxing and karate gyms and I have known the most tender, sweetest affection in all of human nature through my wife Julie and my children. It has been a good life. But still, the fat old lady has yet to begin singing God Bless America.

I have had Bulldogs been to the well and I have been to the well and it is the most alive feeling I know of short of an inspired Bible verse or prayer.

I am of the personal opinion that every man before he flies to the starry heaven, needs to have a beautiful wife that loves him and treats him right. I got that with my Julie. Perhaps it is because there is seven years between myself and my little sister, but there has never been any sibling rivalry with us. We have always loved and cared and helped each other out. Perhaps it is because our parents were kind, tender, unselfish, hard old fashioned New England work ethic parents as were our relatives. A blessing, all that, more valuable, far more valuable, than gold and silver. Every man should own and travel across and around the back roads of America in a midnight blue Dodge Van with his Bulldog in the back seat. And know the feeling of freedom in the wind slamming your hair by owning and breezing across our nation on his own motorcycle – or as Kris Kristofferson sang in "Leaving Her Was Easier" – "aching with the feeling of the freedom of an eagle when she flies." He should own at least one unique Bulldog and feel the fire. He should live the warrior and feel the high of kata (karate forms). Solidify all that by raising children that turn out to be good folks the world is better because of, and be an educator and impact and inspire young people to make a positive place in the world. To see yourself in your grandson and watch him grow to be a tender hearted but great (Krav Maga) warrior (his name is Jubal Smith (I call him Huckleberry) and the lion and the lamb dwell together within him) – this will fill your soul to the brim – almost. Almost because who can describe the birth of a granddaughter twenty years after your grandson's birth? But second that emotion. How can a man put it into words? I can't. Her name is Rachael Emme Stevens - I call her Rosebud and she taught me important lessons about our God because I prayed fervently and feverishly for her for twenty years and she came when I thought the prayers were denied. And finally – finally – to fulfill the ultimate reason for being – teach the Kingdom of God. I have been blessed that all of the above has been my life through the time of this writing, seventy plus years old. So - what is left? He who lives by the sword shall die by the sword.

My pen is my sword.

Next I present my wonderful wife Julie. She prepared the family collage. This book, my first after our win in Supreme Court, is dedicated to a long legged brunette. I first met her over thirty years ago. She was my dance instructor at Arthur Murray Dance Studio. This strikingly beautiful woman was a very talented graceful and natural dancer. She became my best friend. Now she is my business partner and she inspires me beyond words. I call her my full-time night time woman and I love her dearly. She has made all the difference in my life. And so I give you – my deeply loved wife - - - Julie Sheldon Marsh Stevens

And to you Julie, I say:

>Your love is my security
>Your smile is my day spring
>Your tender touch is my torch of tenacity.
>My tenacity is my truth
>Your pleasure is my purpose
>Your playthings are my pleasure
>Your love is my trust
>Your trust is my tenacity, my torch of truth
>
>Our togetherness is in the Lord
>The Lord is in our togetherness
>Together we survive
>Together we live
>Together we love

This is our family tree

Stevens Family – top left, clockwise: daughter Lisa, dad Bob and son Mike; granddaughter Rachel; Bob in Boston; wife Julie; stepdaughter Michael; grandson Jubal

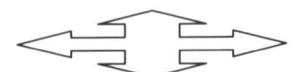

And - - - the book is dedicated to my Savior. I have no idea what the future holds for me, But I know WHO holds my future. Somewhere, out there, beyond the vast blue, blue sky – There is something greater than our daily issues, Deeper than our depression, more powerful than our poverty of spirit. My purpose is not my profession. It is not about my body, not a lot of lust and selfish desire. Somewhere out there - - - There IS something greater – and His name is Jesus Christ. And He IS the Son of God. Herein is reality. Herein is truth. The truest of TRUTH.

Love is a maybe, death is for sure
Sin is the curse; Christ is the cure (I forget the author).

It is better to seek refuge in the Lord than to trust in man –That is what it says in the very center of our Bible (Psalm 118:8) and I believe this with my heart because – GOD has shown me it is so. And I have found that at the edge of broken dreams there is an open door and its name is Salvation.

I'm a happy Christian. Is that okay? Should Christians be happy? Let us see what the Creator of our earth – the Creator of the whole universe for that matter - - - matter – has to say about it. We find it in Ecclesiastes 3: 1-15. Why not read all about it?

I suppose this aspect of the dedication may seem wordy and long. The way I view it – how can we say too much about our Creator, and I beg the reader to consider - the length and breadth of our Creator – can we say too much about Him? He has had much to say to us – to believers and to those He seeks to believe. I believe. I trust in the Lord. He is my belief system "Though He slay me, yet will I believe in Him." Said Job. I think you can only receive when you believe. Only then. Jesus said to the Centurion – not a Jewish man – upon his request for his child to be healed – Go – it will be done just as you believed it would. Our faith feeds on our belief system. And what you believe in your heart you tend to talk about. And so is the kingdom of God built. So I purpose to be a believer and a builder by trade. Every Dogs of Velvet and Steel Productions work shall express this.

It's all about faith. Faith sees the invisible. Faith believes the incredible, and faith receives the impossible. Believe then receive (Mark 11:24).

I don't know your story, dear reader. My story is – I look to Jesus and my walls come tumbling down. And if you cannot believe – you want to, you try, but you can't find it? I am not a preacher, so all I can say is I suggest you dig and dig and keep digging (and praying) until you get it. Like digging for pure gold in the mountain. Keep digging, defined as seeking, and asking, and knocking on heaven's door. After all it is about eternal life. Worth the dig. I don't know your story – but when you go – what will be your story? It is something to think about.

We all have questions. No one comprehends it all and sure sometimes it seems things don't work out. It sometimes seems we ask and do not seem to receive. And perhaps some things have been lost or misconstrued in translation – but – you cannot go wrong if you obey Christ Jesus. You can go very, very wrong when you don't. I say truly, it is a matter of life and death – and that is something to think about.

He knows our hunger. He knows our fears. He knows our longing. He knows what we need to be happy. He just has His own program guide. He deigns it, not us. Our perspective is here and now and linear. It is limited. His perspective is eternal and has no limits. We try to fathom Him, but we cannot. He is no great prophet who had a girlfriend named Mary. He is the Resurrection and the Life. So – what does God want from me you might ask? Read Micah 6:8, "He has told you, O man, what is good; and what does the Lord require of you but to do justice to love kindness and mercy and to walk humbly with your God." With. We have questions. The Bible has answers.

As mentioned, Dear Reader, I don't know your story, but personally, I mentioned to the Lord when I suffered through my tragic case – If He will restore my Dogs of Velvet and Steel Productions retirement business that I worked most of my adult life building – I will testify and glorify Him in that business for the rest of my days in this body. And so it goes, and so it goes. My story – I've got a ticket to ride – into eternity. I've been bought with a price, and I have a ticket to ride. I stand before you today, dear reader to testify, I've been redeemed, and I'm born again. I have a ticket to ride into eternity. A place of eternal bliss. Eternal security. Eternal peace – human words cannot adequately describe it – love comes to mind as the closest narrative. We cannot even portray a value system for it. How can this eternity be measured? No human can place a value there. I have a Kinsman Redeemer, I have an Advocate who is called the Resurrection and the Life (John 11:25). I don't mean to be wordy or flamboyant – this context is not to entertain, it is here to teach and to share.

Most folks in America can tell you what the very beginning of the Bible says – "In the beginning God created the heavens and the earth." How many can tell you – off the top of their hat – what the LAST words of the Bible say? You see I peeked at the end of the book – so I know how my story turns out. It reads: "The Grace of our Lord Jesus Christ be with you all, Amen (Rev. 22:21). Amen assures all of humanity whosoever reads these words that the whole Book is absolutely true and trustworthy – that's what AMEN means. AMEN IS THE MOST REMARKABLE WORD I KNOW OF. It is a universal word and translates directly from Hebrew into Greek and then Latin, and then English and a plethora of other languages. (I learned this from the Institute for Creation Research - Google them and check them out I strongly recommend). AMEN is also a title for Christ (Rev. 3:14). The Bible wraps up with:

"Look, I am coming quickly (not soon – quick when He arrives), and my reward is with Me. I am the Alpha and the Omega, the Beginning and the End. The First and the Last. Blessed are those who do His commandments, that they may have the right to the Tree of Life, and may enter through the gates into the City. I Jesus have sent my Angel to testify to you these things in the churches. I am the Root and the Offspring of David. The Bright and Morning Star. And the Spirit and the Bride say, "come! And let him who thirsts come. And WHOEVER desires let him take the water of life FREELY." Take nothing from this book and add nothing to this book. And lastly – "He who testifies to these things says "surely I am coming quickly." AMEN.

So I know how my story turns out and I hope you do to.

Some of The readers of this book may have been victimized. Maybe some readers can't get past their past. Then perhaps some readers can join me in my heart/soul testimony.

Thru many dangers, toils and snares, I have already come; 'tis grace that brought me safe thus far, and grace will lead me home. Moreover – when I've been there ten thousand years, bright shining as the sun – I've no less days to sing God's praise, than when I first begun. (From the famous hymn Amazing Grace by John Newton). John Newton, in his youth, was wild and a bad dude. He ended up in a cruel prison - in Africa I think. So cruel he was made to crawl on his knees and lap up his meals like a dog. Like the Count of Monte Christo his story reads. One day he escaped. While on the ship on the way back to England they hit a bad storm and he was terrified. Then he recalled his mother's prayers and he called out to God for mercy and begged for help and to be forgiven his evil life. Back in England he eventually became a famous preacher. He preached sermons when eighty years old and so fragile he could hardly hold up his sermon notes. It is said Amazing Grace is the most known and popular Christian hymn in existence today. Came from a bad dude prison inmate.

So – if you are reading this book and can't get past your past – and you think there is no way out - read on. Let us say, just as example, you are an inmate – with a long sentence. And in order to survive where you are you belong to a gang. No getting out. I have a book and story I suggest. Two books same genre, actually. First is *The Cross and the Switchblade* by the preacher David Wilkerson. God sent him on a mission to the Spanish Harlem aspect of Brooklyn, New York City. There he met Nicky Cruz, Warlord for the Mau Mau gang. This kid – a Cuban immigrant – was a crazy, bloodthirsty killer – from childhood. When he first met Mr. Wilkerson, he wanted to kill him. He told the man he wasted his time with him because he was way beyond redemption – and if the preacher didn't leave him alone and get off his turf he would kill him. Scary dude. The preacher persisted with Jesus loves you – and the rest – I leave you to read. The second book is entitled *Run Baby Run* – by that same Nicky Cruz who finally became born again – he not only found an open door to release – he became a nationally effective evangelist. The point of that story is not that God accepts gang members along with everyone and anyone else – although that is the case – the point is if you don't see any way out – God does - I have to say though – my experience is that sometimes His time frame is different than ours – so it might be a decade or decades – but if you are sincere He will do it with YOU.

Why does God allow things to happen to us? Even after – often even more after, we become saved? God wants us to learn. Learning takes time – and growth. We get pain. He lets us have our way – he lets us have our way up to a point – then – CONSEQUENCES. You see forgiveness is always there – but consequences remain. He allows us to go our own way and sin in order for us to learn. Without this process we can get pride. We can be like Lucifer who became Satan. He allows us our weakness. Pride is a stepping stone to fall. We learn to seek Him in ALL our decisions and choices - - and what happens when we don't. The consequences – He will turn it all into good, given time – if – we receive it. Takes time and a heart open to Him to learn this. We don't grow only by attending church and reading the Bible. We need experiential teaching. We grow by stumbling – mistakes – going down the wrong-way-paths – seeking poisonous Pastures. When we get old – we learn how much we depend on our Shepherd. We remember consequences - - and we don't want no more. He teaches us (over decades) how wide is His grace, mercy, loving instruction. And we learn from His forgive – to forgive others – that is – if we have a heart open to His instruction. GOD TEACHES US ABOUT HIMSELF. When the Word (the Bible) teaches us to acknowledge Him in everything - - - means - - - everything. But – we have to learn this - Romans 8:28 – "all things work for the good for those who love God, who have been called according to His purpose." Now look at verse 29 – "for those God foreknew, He also PREDESTINED to be conformed to the likeness of His Son." Predestined – those He called – and those He called He justified – and those He justified He also glorified. That resonates. Wanna be glorified? Come on! If you ask me if I believe in predestination, my answer is yes because God tells me it is so. If you ask me if I understand predestination, my answer is no – God is way beyond my comprehension – but when I go to Him I'll be glorified and then comprehend. My take on it – once we become born into Christ – if truly so born – we are predestined to become the human God envisioned when He created Adam and Eve – and he never quit that vision. So let the predestination begin. Be predestined to be shaped like clay to be like Jesus. We can be hurt by people. Jesus – Son of the Living God – was hurt by people. But people cannot make us bitter or vengeful – only we can choose that. Our circumstances cannot rob us of contentment and security. Paul said he LEARNED in every circumstance in prison out of prison, subject of betrayal, subject of friendship, rich and poor – to be content. He didn't look to this world for it – he looked to his everlasting world with Christ Jesus for this. It was his hope. It was his destiny. Now it is his reality. When Christ is our Rabbi – teacher – Sensei – and our Shepherd – we are led to peaceful secure pastures. My martial art "Sensei" are lead rams for my Shepherd – assigned by God to help me grow. I don't go with the Shinto or Buddhism – I go with Jesus. My martial Art is a draw to help me speak to folks about Jesus – salvation – and to teach the Kingdom of God. Jesus is my only true Sensei.

'Tis true – through many dangers, toils and snares, I have already come. So – what can wash away my sin? Nothing but the blood of Jesus. Our eternity will be pure. While in our physical body, in this world, we must have consequences – and they are indeed almost unbearable – almost – we must have consequences in order to learn and to be molded and shaped. I have experienced this. Now it is an integral aspect of my journalism.

And so I want to add to this dedication, an invitation. I know about love and I didn't take no time to think it over. I plunged right in and became soaked to the bone – baptized into eternal life. You come. Come swim in deep waters with the River of hope. The River of light. The River of transformation. The River of sanctification. Come and flow along the streams of happy freedom, exalted exuberance, the calling of God's telephone number, Jeremiah 33:3. Come go a-swimming. Lock and load and fire the gospel to others. This is what life is all about.

Christian Bibliography

I want to wrap this dedication with a bibliography for those who have pain and seek help – from the Creator of - Everything. The first one – is authored by the publisher of this book. She is an incredible example of what God can do for those who seek Him. She is a former very, very addicted Crack Cocaine addict – who found release and freedom in Christ and now she has her own ministry – she helps Crack addicts – very successfully. Her book:

Davis, Sonya Hightower. *From Drugs to God; What Now?* Virginia: Pine Haven Press, Inc. (that's her).
   This is a little booklet that has helped many addicts. You can order it from Pine Haven Press, Inc. P. O. Box 11893, Lynchburg Virginia, 24506 – or call 434-309-7248. If the book helps you she asks that you write her and give her your story and feedback.

Jeremiah, David. *When Your World Falls Apart*. Tennessee: Thomas Nelson, Inc. 2,000.

Scriptural Quotations in this book are from my *New King James Version Bible*, released as the *Possibility Thinkers Bible* by Robert Schuller. Thomas Nelson Publishers – and from my *NIV Study Bible*, Zondervan Publishing House – presented to me by my wife Julie. Are you in LOVE with God? Then search Him out – get a Study Bible.

Forgive others as Christ forgives you. This makes Jesus happy and warm. On the cross one criminal mocked Jesus. The other criminal asked forgiveness. Today that criminal has an eternal peace with Christ.

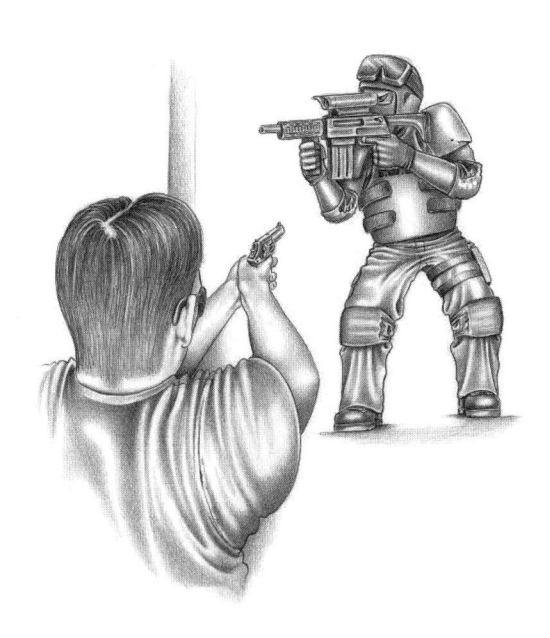

I came within a finger twitch of killing a policeman that fateful night, April 23, 2003, because of their senseless, absurd, preposterous – as well as illegal attack. The moment was shorter than an exclamation; and it defined a future for America, as had I not seen blue lights flashing through the trees from the corner of my eye – I had no idea what all that banging and childish screaming was about - I'd be gone and our constitutional freedom butchered by idiotic misinformation. The *Dogs of Velvet and Steel* book would no longer be available, nor would any other Pit Bull book. Your read came at a price.

The Epilogue

"Seven times down, eight times up."
That inscription appears on the karate/Kendo headbands sold by www.classicalfightingarts.org. In Japanese it is Nana Korobi Ya Oki.

Preface

The *Dogs of Velvet and Steel* (DVS) book was published in 1983. The world of the American Pit Bull Terrier (called Pit Bulls in today's America and so referred to in this epilogue) has changed drastically since. I would like to point out in this epilogue that the predictions and warnings made in the DVS book, in terms of the damage to the breed and our nation that animal activists could inculcate into our society, have been proven to be accurate prediction. The media breed representation the animal activists have since cultivated has grown to the level we are now facing, with almost extermination of the breed. The animal activists have been successful in making the breed illegal or near illegal along with any writing or journalism or films about the breed in some other countries. As predicted, the old "Doberman Craze" they started in the 1960's, has turned into a Pit Bull craze that far exceeds the nonsense they propagated back then. The Doberman craze began, as just one typical but relevant example, with widespread rumors (spread by the Humane Society of the United States) exemplified by such stories as folks who owned Doberman Pinschers fed them gun powder to make them mean (along with the same malarkey that they use today about Pit Bulls– that they take little dogs and kittens from the pound and let the Doberman's kill them to feed their blood lust). The result was that sickos and foolish people read this nonsense, believed it – and did it! They would acquire Dobermans, put spike collars on them, feed them gun powder (which weakens them, wreaking havoc with their nervous system and immune system and tremendously shortens their life and does absolutely nothing to make them tough). These foolish people would agitate their dogs to make them mean. What did not exist these crazy activists created. The animal activists have gone much further with the Pit Bull breed. According to Consumer Freedom and other HSUS exposes, they found it translated into millions of dollars in terms of donated funds they could keep with the expense of doing anything about the so-called killer Pit Bull kept to a minimum and pocket millions. Over and over again they have been caught doing this. I have reams of news articles and court recordings that show this and yet, they seem to retain the ability to defraud and bilk our citizens even convincing Hollywood, attorneys, and wealthy individuals to contribute to their fraudulent causes. They have been caught many times. They were caught soliciting millions to fight fur trapping and not spending any of the funds to eliminate fur trapping (documented in many sources such as Consumer Freedom). The court ordered them to repay a million dollars. They easily absorb these minor set backs. Spend thousands, keep millions. Today in the 21st century, news reporters (viewed in early 2010) have polled Americans randomly, asking them, "What do you think about the Pit Bull breed? Do you think they can be good family pets or do you think they cannot? Are they a threat to the nation?" The poll I saw (May 2010) indicated *one* citizen responded that they thought the Pit Bull breed, like any other canine, is the product of the owners and can be safe family pets. All of the others (I forget how many) responded, one way or the other, that they think Pit Bulls are killer dogs, a threat to the nation and should all be eliminated. This is so sad. And wrong.

The picture of Morochito was drawn by Joe Platzer of Ontario Canada

Chapter 1: Cast of Characters

> *"Balintawak"* – The name of my primary martial style, a reality combat style it is not sport. It means *"Cry of Freedom"* named after the Filipino revolution to gain freedom from the Spanish government that attempted to colonize the Philippines. The revolution was initiated from a province named Balintawak and there is a street named Balintawak in Cebu City, Philippines, where my grandmaster, Bobby Taboada grew up.

It is axiomatic, in today's America, that when you write about "Pit Bulls" it is difficult to avoid dialogue about the HSUS and PETA. I'd like to clarify a few things up front. Knitted throughout your book you will find a great deal of redundancy on this, which is my attempt at avoiding being taken out of context as I have been so many, many times. I will often recapitulate the following position:

You will find more negative comments concerning HSUS than I intended when I began writing, but the dialogue just went in that direction. The negative is the result of my journalism. I report as a fact-finder. You will find it all came from Consumer Reports, Humane Watch, and a plethora of canine periodicals. The wording and allegations are not mine; it is the result of research. The statement may appear based on gilding or affectation, but my intent is not to be polemical. It is true that the animal activists have painted their watercolor allegations forged in the crucible of that seven year battle with the HSUS induced federal government and my tears have splashed and attenuated their lies. But I don't seek to condemn the HSUS. What did our Lord say; forgive your enemies? I seek a metamorphosis. From animal activist to animal welfare. You will find what can be alleged to be positive comments about dog fighting. Please do not take me out of context without reading my track record promoting Schutzhund and the above noted healthy American alternatives for our breed. I don't seek to condemn dog fighters. I seek a metamorphosis from dog fighter to participation in the conformation show ring, the weight pulling competition, Schutzhund, and hunting. What I seek to accomplish from this truthful reporting is to negate the widespread misinformation about the American Pit Bull Terrier breed. They are not a vicious man-biting breed and I expose that like a fire alarm salesman seeking to instill shock so he can make a sale, exaggerated sensationalism about the breed, spread by activist organizations soliciting donations from the public by the hundred millions. This is not promoting or alleging dog fighting as a positive activity or that it is a mild sport that should be legalized. Rather I expose lies and deceit and that is all. So my journalism does expose the iconoclastic HSUS and their animal activist sinkholes and their irrational but powerful and nationally damaging polls. Their precedents are unequivocally harming animals and our freedom of expression. Or as Colin Dayan said in her book, *Law is a White Dog*, animals and people who are "disabled by law. Legal thought relied on a set of fictions." The animation of the metamorphosis mentioned above is a real challenge and at the core of my Epilogue. To my critics, before you quote me, quote this: I do not promote antagonism against animal activists and I do not promote degradation of dog fighters. I promote a metamorphosis and honesty.

With that in mind, the following "Cast of Characters" played a very central role in the development and what will in the future be considered significant history for the Pit Bull breed.

Gary Hammonds

That's Bobby Hall on my right and Gary Hammonds on my left at the ADBA nationals signing autographs.

Gary Hammonds leads the cast of characters I want to acknowledge in this book. There is a wind beneath the wings of every winner. Every athlete (human and canine) knows this. In this context it is fair to say that our breed would not have won my appeal nor would we have won in Supreme Court if it were not for Gary Hammonds. I say the breed and "we" because that case (including the trial) was never about me. It was about the American Pit Bull Terrier. They just wanted to use me because they thought they could use my match dog documentaries and my hunting video and booklet as a stepping stone to do to America what they did in our foundation nation, England; make the breed an outlaw and for the

HSUS and other criminal activists to prevail deleting our freedom of press about our breed.

Here is just one example of how Gary won this case for us (I could write a whole book about all he did). I was informed I could not have witnesses for the trial (long story). I fought that over and over and over again. I was told I could not communicate with any Bulldog folks and if I did I'd go to jail. I ended up, in effect telling them I can't get my witnesses unless I do and that I have a legal right under the constitution to my witnesses, so get your jail key ready, my letter to the bar is ready. But everybody I tried to contact was afraid of the government (and although they would not admit it every bit as afraid of HSUS as of the Mafia. I'm not finding fault. Everyone (involved with our breed and most animal breeders in America) knows how powerful the criminal HSUS is and how they can build a case out of nothing. No, I fault the animal activist terrorism, not the people, the families, or organizations that fear them. The comment about "criminal" HSUS is not my own. It is generated from countless documentation and commentary in over a decade of Pit Bull magazines, commentary from the Pit Bull fraternity (not dog fighters), other canine breeds, from Googling Consumer Freedom, Humane Watch, and other funded organizations that expose the criminal activities of HSUS and PETA, from my own witness in my trial who was an undercover agent for the FBI investigating the criminal activities of HSUS, and lastly from public pronouncements of the FBI about the criminal activities of HSUS.

You won't find Gary named in any of the news articles or NRA reports (in their periodicals) about the case, but Gary found the witnesses that made statements that became public record in that trial. Those statements could not be ignored in the appeal or by the Supreme Court Judges. Without the testimony of those witnesses, our first freedom of speech, insofar as our breed is concerned, would right now be erased. Actually it was called a "case of first impression." This means that in the entire history of American litigation, there had never been a case before any federal court involving the first amendment right to freedom of speech involving animal depiction. The free right to do documentaries on animals had never been a legal question in America. This, parenthetically, is one indication of the sheer power of the HSUS. They had the juice to get this nonsense all the way to Supreme Court.

Gary put me in touch with Glen Bui and the Animal Canine Foundation (I hope you will Google this organization. It will indicate many, many times where the criminal HSUS had been taken down in the courts, but just like the Mafia, they absorb it and keep moving on). Glenn Bui had worked five years undercover for the FBI investigating the criminal activities of

HSUS as the FBI has put HSUS and other animal activists high in their priorities. Glenn was not allowed to disclose his investigative findings in the trial, but he did stand up for the freedom of our breed and his testimony helped achieve justice. Glenn added Dr. Brisbin. Dr. Brisbin is featured in the "Catch Dog" chapter. See him also in the following "Cast of Characters." Although our American government took away my free right to call people, I called my good friend T. Michael Riddle anyway. T. Michael also follows in the cast of characters. Because of these people we now have the free right to documentaries for our breed. Dear reader, you have absolutely no idea, none, how very, very, close we came to having it taken away by our own government. Gary also worked relentlessly, behind the scenes, with people and organizations and support snowballed. I say again, not only the American Pit Bull Terrier, but our nation owes this man a lot. Nobody, *nobody*, can realize how much. But I have a pretty good idea.

> "Freedom is the sure possession of those alone who have the courage to defend it." - Pericles

This was cited on a unsigned, framed print, depicting a beautiful bald eagle with American flag background.

When I was a very new journalist for our breed, and countless dogmen would not give me their time, Gary Hammonds helped. Please notice the lion's share of pictures in your book was contributed by Gary Hammonds and he submitted several articles. Gary Hammonds was an internationally known and respected breeder and American Pit Bull Terrier expert when I first contacted him around 1980 or 81. When others had no time, he did.

You might notice in Gary's article below, he mentions a lot of the dog men when I first produced this book, used to gossip that I was a rookie and not qualified to write a book about the breed. The average male Pit Bull dogman will have ten times more stories and twenty times more gossip than a football fan, hunter, gun lover, and the local ladies gossip circle combined. Well, they were very correct on one point. I was very much a rookie and truth be known, still am. I am one of the few, perhaps the only, person in the world that learned and experienced all aspects on an advanced level of Schutzhund, weight pulling, catch dog training, and hunting and have years of hands on experience in all of it, but to this day I remain a rookie compared to Bobby Hall, Burton, Ralph Greenwood, the Plumbers (who I never met), Howard Teal, Crenshaw, Lester Hughes, Captain Ben, well I can't name them all, but you get the picture. I had only one dog when I wrote this book and over 25 years later, I've only owned his daughter, grandson, and great granddaughter. I'm still a journalist and a rookie.

Journalist and rookie I was then and am now. Gary has been there. The tiniest aspect of his brain knows more than I can learn in all my remaining years about our breed.

As I mentioned, twenty plus years ago when Gary helped me with your *Dogs of Velvet and Steel* book, he was one of the most respected and noted breeders of top quality in the world. Now, compound that. He doesn't just breed quality dogs he has a breeding program that utilizes every bit of modern as well as old school breeding concepts: inbreeding, linebreeding, and hybrid outcrossing. I recently recommended his bloodline to a newcomer who asked what breeder I recommend for a man starting out. When he asked why I responded, "Because his yard has stood the test of at least a third of a century, closer to half a century, and it isn't blind or sudden inspiration breeding. It is all based on the best of genetic concepts."

I tell you what. If you really want to know what it is like to own a true bred honest-to-goodness Pit Bull, I suggest you get Gary's book, mentioned. You see there is something no animal activist or supporter of these "humane" organizations can ever comprehend. That is the feeling of awe, respect, love, and companionship one gets from owning and working with a real gladiator bred dog. The best description I know of comes in Gary's book and the story about the dog Batima. As a postscript the type that owns and cuddles a cutsey, poopsey dog, fat as a butterbean and picks the dog up and carries it and puts a pretty diamond collar on the dog, well I guess they would be horrified by the story of Batima. They will never know the feeling of owning such a surreal animal. I want to say this: I don't agree with making a dog a cutsey, poopsey, butterball. If you want me to define canine cruelty, that is it. But I don't intend to make a law that it is illegal for these folks to engage in what they believe in. I am not getting on any bandwagon over it either. They have their way with dogs and the rest of us have ours. So I ask simply, leave us alone! Now, all you animal activists that read this paragraph are probably thinking, "Oh, got to get this book. This Batima pit dog is going to be all about animal cruelty; a dog fighting killer dog. Sorry. Horse manure. Batima was a farm dog. She watched over the property of a rural Texas family. She did catch work and protected the stock from local (and there were a lot) coyotes and wild dogs. Her story will show you what a real dog with gladiator genes is like. Great read and it may bring tears to your eyes. Even you tough dudes. And folks, you can't get a dog like that from a show pedigree. It comes from generations of working dogs.

I'd like to make it clear that all this is not said because Gary Hammonds is a friend. I have many Pit Bull friends that I never recommend their breeding. I just don't say anything about their breeding. Yes, Gary Hammonds is a friend, but I've actually only been to his home twice. And I mean it without exaggeration when I state that Gary Hammonds is a sui generis among Bulldog dogmen.

With all that said, I present Gary Hammonds' article to you. Gary also has a book entitled *A Half Century with the American Pit Bull Terrier*. If you want to know what the American Pit Bull Terrier and the now famous dogmen that formed them were about, I strongly recommend his book. It's a good read written in a folksy style that makes you feel you are there. You can get the book, or if you are a newcomer looking to begin your breeding program, for a pup or brood stock write to Gary Hammonds, 6520 Newt Patterson Rd. Mansfield, Texas, 76063 USA.

Reflections
By Gary Hammonds

My longtime friend, Bob Stevens, has asked me to do a short article about our affiliation, as well as my working with the breed, Catch Dog Enterprises, the American Dog Breeders Association, and the Endangered Breeds Association since the Dogs of Velvet and Steel, 1983.

To start with, Bob and I corresponded after he saw some of my articles and pictures of my dogs in the Bloodline Journal or Gazette. We were both interested in the working dogs and somewhat like minded in thinking that the breed could be trouble if not managed properly.

Bob's book, Dogs of Velvet and Steel, came about as Bob brainstormed and discovered how ignorant to the bulldog basics the newcomers to the breed were. Bob's passion for the bulldogs was obvious and "the bug" bit him bad. We discussed Dick Stratton's book, which would soon become several, and how well he had introduced the breed to the general public. We were in agreement that another book or two about basics of the breed could be helpful. While Bob may not have realized it, part of his impetus to writing the book, was to tell the truth about all aspects of the breed and debunk some of the outright lies told by the humaniacs. When he started his undertaking with the book, some of the dog people said he was a rookie and certainly had no background in the sporting aspect of the breed. Bob jumped in with both feet, doing his homework and was dead set on writing a book. I was only one of many he consulted with and I sent him pictures of my dogs as filler and an article or two. I honestly expected him to have his book ready in five years or so, but low and behold a little over two years and it was ready to go to the printers. It covered all bases and several people who were the first to read it had mostly positive comments on it, but some said there was some misinformation in it. I can only say there should have been with as much ground as he covered in a very short period of time. He still did a very good job and to this day, his book ranks up there with the Strattons, Farron, and Crenshaw books, and a very worthwhile read.

Bob's seven year journey through trials and tribulations came about by bogus charges brought by an equally bogus crush law. The feds were determined to see Bob do jail time behind an obviously unconstitutional law. Bob's innocence to any wrong doing was never a point of contention to them.

The book was considered by the humaniacs to be nothing more than a handbook for dog fighters. The three tapes and the book only told the truth, and I feel that the animal rights people saw them as direct exposure of some of their lies, not only about dog fighting, but to value the breed as an all-purpose dog. Bob's metal was tested to the max and his hanging tough through some incredibly hard times makes him a "living legend" as far as I am concerned. His doing so allowed "right to Prevail" and helped preserve a little of what should be our constitutional rights. Bob could have played the game, but chose not to. In doing this, he not only made a stand for the breed, but for the writers and authors who should never be censored by our government, the media, or any other special interest group.

Bob, at times, felt certain that he had been hung out to dry. To add insult to injury, he was not allowed to be in contact with dog people. For many of us wanting to help, hands were tied, but guess what, by networking with the right people you can get a lot done. So in essence, Bob did his part, and the people working on his behalf, up front and behind the scenes, did their part.

But to give credit where credit is due, I truly believe nothing short of divine intervention could have pulled it off for Bob. "Right" won in a case where all the cards were stacked against it. Thank the good Lord for a promise from His book: "If God is for us, who can be against us?"

Life's web, it seems, is far reaching and complex. I have been around the American Pit Bull Terrier all my life, and really appreciated the breed and how versatile they were. In the late 60's, well-bred bulldogs from working or sporting lines were hard to get if you weren't in with someone.

After about wearing out my Chevy Malibu in search of that right dog, I picked up the Bruno dog almost in my backyard. He is on the cover of my book, and many people have asked of all the good dogs, some of which are *famous, why in the world would you put the bat eared special on the cover? My answer was always simple, and to the point. "He was not only my favorite dog of all times, but a good one that clicked with me." Just like Mr. Bojangles and Teddy, after twenty years, I still miss him.* For me, it has been nearly forty years, and I still miss him as he was not only a great dog but one of my best friends. There was a lot of interest in those days for the American Pit Bull Terrier, and about everyone who saw Bruno, wanted a pup off him or to breed to him. He was quite impressive to say the least and one of the more intelligent animals that I have ever seen or known.

I never intended to breed or sell dogs, but since people were buying junk and getting ripped off in their bulldog endeavors, I decided to get a bitch that suited me and try my hand at breeding a few high caliber working dogs.

As it turned out, I have had over a thousand dogs come across this yard over the past forty plus years. My first love in the dogs has always been the working dogs. Thus the name, "Catch Dog Enterprises." It has become politically correct to not buy, sell, or breed dogs. Everyone from Ellen to Oprah has put a guilt trip on people breeding, showing, or working dogs, and make no mistake about it the dogs manipulations by man as a breeder has only made the animal more adaptable and truly man's best friend. For me, I refuse to apologize for my breeding efforts on behalf of the breeds I have used and improved over the years. My love of the APBT is obvious, and I plan to stand by the breed until my dying day, The Good Lord willing, I will not back down.

I put together a book several years ago that I hoped would lend itself to people being more conscientious when it came to their dogs. We know that the breed is not for everybody, so I hoped owners would educate themselves and my book is one that doesn't sugar coat it about any aspect of the breed. It is a different spin on the dogs, and one I feel will be beneficial to owners and would-be fanciers from all walks of life. In order to preserve and protect the breed, we must educate and police ourselves. The books I have mentioned along with many more are must reads for anyone who would like to save the most unique dog breed to ever live, from extinction.

I have worked with many organizations on behalf of the breed over the years and feel we must of necessity, "pull together in order to survive."

The ADBA is, in my mind, the number one supporter of the breed. Some have accused me of being "loyal to a fault" to the ADBA, and the EBA, and all I can say is, "I am guilty as charged." The ADBA, like any person or organization has worked tirelessly on behalf of the breed, and is the best registry I have ever used. Ralph and I saw eye to eye about the things we had to do to preserve the breed. Besides using their services to register my American Pit Bull Terriers and Patterdale Terriers, I write for the Gazette and have been judging their conformation shows for over 25 years.

I have been a supporter for the EBA for many years and sat on the board much of that time and was vilipended for one term. While doing this, I learned many things about breed specific laws and all the wrongs we as owners of the APBT have to deal with. The EBA is spread so thin it is a miracle that they have accomplished some of the things they have over the years.

I have also had the pleasure to work for the breed, and do judging and seminars in many countries besides ours. New Zealand was critical in the early nineties, as was Italy, Ecuador, and the Czech Republic. The breed is alive and well all over the world today and it is because of people with integrity and guts to take a stand. When you read this, make a pledge to be a better owner, support the folks who work for our dogs, and last but certainly not least, be prepared to do your part to preserve and protect the breed and never, never, quit!

I asked Gary to do an article for us to update his breeding and he provided the following:

THE DOGS OF THE CATCH DOG PLACE SINCE THE BOOK *DOGS OF VELVET AND STEEL*

You will see a lot of my old stuff pictured in Dogs of Velvet and Steel. *Most were the old Bruno-Heinzl bred dogs that were the foundation of my breeding program in those days. By the early 80's, I was making a transition to the Alligator family, which seemed to work well with my dogs and was more than just a name or pedigree to me. I had the pleasure to be personally affiliated with three of the dogs right off the "Nigger"- "Satin Lady" breeding during those years. I owned Alligator's sister, "Renee" for a while and knew both "Alligator" and his brother "Soko," a great trio of dogs that were impressive to say the least and produced dogs that were their equal or better.*

During those years I had many connections and almost like Maurice Carver himself, I had access to many good dogs. I have never been a perfectionist myself, but am very selective about what I decide to use in my breeding program, so some very well-bred dogs came across my yard and were never used.

In the early years, I had bred "Bruno" to "Katy Ann," which went back to "Texas Jack," who was a staff. This was done primarily for hybrid vigor and "Macho" was my favorite from the breeding. When he was bred to the "Rennee" bitch along came a litter of some of the best working dogs to ever come from the "Tonka"–"Red Barron" breeding. I had begun to get away from tight breeding in that period even though a lot of pure "Alligator" dogs had held together, surprisingly well for me.

I introduced the "Bully"- "Eli Jr.," stuff to mine when "Rufus" was bred to the "Black Sister" bitch, "Bullyson" bred to a daughter of "Eli Jr." while the "Bullyson"–"Eli Jr." stuff was on a roll, I saw it more valuable to me as a cross or catalyst breeding. My first impression came with me being somewhat certain that they were wound too tight to be smart and versatile enough to survive in working situations with hog, cattle, or man. To my surprise, some were amazingly controllable and focused enough to stay alive.

I was impressed enough with Crum's "China Boy" dog, who was off Garner's "Spike" and "Miss Molly," to feel it would be a perfect blend of the "Snooty" and "Bully" coming through Holt's "Jeremiah" to go good with my "Alligator"-"Bully," since my "Rufus" stuff was three quarter Carver through the "Satin Lady" bitch.

While the "Rufus" dog was the best of the "Alligator," for me, there were others that made their mark as producers. "Rufus" was off "Alligator" bred to his dam "Satin Lady" three quarter Carver through "Iron Head" and "Black Beauty" and one quarter Tudor's "Jeff" and "Baby" through the "Nigger" dog.

I also incorporated a dog, Garner's "Cajun Bull" off "Pedro" and "Black Widow." He was a grand producer of tall athletic dogs when mixed with mine. He produced "Lucan" off the "Princess" bitch that was down from Gilman's Alligator stuff. He was quite a producer and just a pleasure to own.

Of the Tudor blood, the "Panama Red" dogs were interesting and Red Dawson was a good friend of mine. We made several breedings of his family, which were near pure with "Alvin the Dog" as a kicker. He too had a little Staff in him, so you would expect some hybrid vigor in the old Tudor stuff which was the base. I had the "Sweet Red" bitch, which was a littermate to Mau Mau's "Stine." Both became tremendous producers and my "Dio" dog off "Andy B" and "Sweet Red" was a very good producer in his day. I also had some of the best of Tudor's old stuff bred by Jim Uselton. These dogs are gone now, but I figure had potential and enjoyed them while I had them.

Looking back, the dogs that did the most for me are almost too many to mention, but a few would have to be "Bruno," "Macho," "Willie Boy," "Andy L," "Kilroy," "J.M.," and "Pig (AKA "Snort"). Pig bred to "Rennie B" produced "Parkson" which I feel certain was as good a producer as "Rufus." "Pig" was off "Rufus" bred to Maurice, a "Stompanato" bitch directly from Maurice and Pat. "Parkson," in spite of being too big, was always one of my favorites. He is gone today as are most of his offspring, but definitely left his mark.

I have used the "Tonka"-"Red Barron" dogs over the past twenty years, not only because of their being good natural, but the tie into the "Bruno"-"Heinzl" and "Alligator" to a lesser degree.

I thank the good Lord for the good dogs and people I have known over the years. It has been nothing short of an adventure in life for me. As an afterthought, my friend Tom Lundberg had many of my dogs twenty or so years ago. Along the way, he got out of dogs, and then became reacquainted in 2006 as he wanted to get another one. He did and today, he has a very good kennel, with several American Dog Breeder Association Champions, and about as good a yard as there is in Texas. Tom paid me a huge compliment a few years back. He said he was pleasantly surprised in my yard's improvement during that time when he was out of the dogs. I asked how he thought they had improved and he said, "In structure, temperament, and certainly intelligence." It has been a labor of love for me and I could not have done it without my wife, Charlotte, my kids, Barry and Melanie, and then there are those friends and folks who just had faith in my dogs and gave me an "Atta Boy" from time to time. May the good Lord bless everyone who had a hand in making my Catch Dog dream come true.

T. Michael Riddle

T. Michael Riddle was an important witness in my trial. He gives guided hunts and catch dog work is his occupation. He joined Dr. Brisbin in getting a good many belly laughs at the sheer nonsense the "expert" government witness fed the jury. As you can see on the facing page, Michael owns a 1,000 acre ranch stocked with imported Eurasian Wild Boar, Fallow deer, feral hogs, buffalo, black tail deer, quail, dove, and turkey and his occupation is that of guided hunts on his ranch.

Native Hunt Enterprises Inc.
5669 Snell Ave. #357, San Jose, CA. 95123
toll free: (888) HUNT 3-2-1
www.nativehunt.com

FOR IMMEDIATE RELEASE: Aug 14, 2007

Hello fellow hunters! This has been a very productive and exciting year for Native Hunt Enterprises Inc.

We have just completed a brand new 4000 square foot dining/lounging area addition to our lodge at the Monterey county ranch and, we have also struck a deal with a local rancher who owns a 4600 acre parcel right across the road from Native Hunt.

We will be hunting the free ranging BUFFALO and EXOTICS at that ranch.

Native Hunt Enterprises Inc. has also acquired approximately 150 pure EURASIAN WILD BOAR as well as 100 FALLOW DEER for it's own 1000 acre high fence hunting facility.

We will still be offering our successful TYPICAL CALIFORNIA FERAL HOG hunts as well as our CALIFORNIA BLACK TAILED DEER hunts at the Fresno county open range ranch and the non-fenced areas of the Monterey county ranch.

Also, we seem to have gained a few resident CORSICAN RAMS who are currently enjoying our 200 acres of lush grain fields which they must feel we planted just for them. *(there's some big horns on them bad boys)*

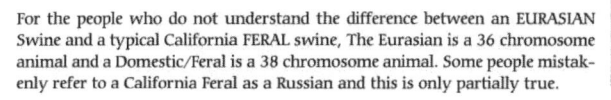

For the people who do not understand the difference between an EURASIAN Swine and a typical California FERAL swine, The Eurasian is a 36 chromosome animal and a Domestic/Feral is a 38 chromosome animal. Some people mistakenly refer to a California Feral as a Russian and this is only partially true.

The country of Russia had control of a few outposts along the California coast a couple hundred years ago and let loose several wild Eurasian swine along our northern coastline thus was born the term "Russian Boar." Today, those animal's bloodlines are severely watered down with DOMESTIC swine genetics and are called: Typical California Feral hogs. That is why you will see Belted, Spotted, Pug nosed and curly tailed hogs out on the cattle ranches which have hogs on them.

At Native Hunt Game Ranches we have been steadily eliminating the multi-colored pug nosed animals and you just simply will not see very many of these *(genetically faulted)* typical California feral hogs at our open range ranches.

Hunt with Michael and you will have the adventure
and memories of a lifetime.

To sign up for a hunt with Michael go to his website. He has exotic animals and the whole ambience you'll never, ever, forget.

This is T. Michael's foundation pure pit. He is Frankie, a super dog.
You generally find only one of these in a lifetime.

Michael's wife Sylvia with Frankie and Frankie's son Baron.

Baron's mother was ½ Great Dane for speed, endurance, and those long legs (the original Dane was a wild hog hunting dog) and ½ Neapolitan Mastiff. The Neo was a war dog that fought in the Grecian and Roman wars and in the Roman gladiator coliseum. They are fearless (not game – fearless). This blend bred back to many generations pure pit, produced, in my opinion a unique high octane blend of super dogs.

Michael is, to me, an incredible person and endemic of the many, many unique folks I have met through my beloved Bulldogs. He has really made a remarkable and awe-inspiring life for himself. His family foundation was country western in Southern Florida. But Michael aspired to be in the vanguard with the new age. He went to the hot spot, California, determined to become a rock star. A lot of people aspire, but Michael is one who lives that Bulldog persistence. He aspires, and then he *does*. His beginnings in California were in the hard-rock music world. He was a front man vocalist/guitarist for a three-piece ensemble in the California Bay Area. Michael has the ten hour work day ethic and surreal planning mind of Donald Trump. He followed his ten hour days with a quick shower and immediately heading for a Kenpo Karate studio where he became ranked in that highly street realistic style of martial arts. He became enormously popular and attracted the attention of nationally famous artists that sought him out for support playing artists such as Ronnie Montrose, Rick Derringer, John Butcher Axis, and Greg Howe. With the great Ronnie Montrose, he produced a full-length recording entitled "Psychotic Reaction" and a stirring ballad "Believe in My Love." Another touching ballad was "Only Your Heart." Michael's high-powered and energetic performances, as he would strut and sway across the stage, always brought the audience to their feet, screaming, or featured the audience stilled, silently soaking it. Media music magazines referred to his work as "reminiscent of early Van Halen and a unique and distinctive sound." Other quotes from media magazines include describing his work as "creative and flavorful, a mix of soulful hard rock and blues-style rifling." Along the way, Michael met his beautiful wife Sylvia, married and at the time of this writing has two impressionable children. And he built from the ground up and established his Native Hunt ranch and guided hunt business. I guess music must be akin to Bulldogs in the way it gets to the practitioner's blood. He has kept in touch with Ronnie Montrose and at the time of this writing, still jams with him. What a guy!

When we won the case in Supreme Court, Michael purchased me a ticket to go and visit him at his ranch and hunt with him and his catch dogs. I could not *believe* he would do this for me. What a wonderful friend. And I want to say it was one of the most memorable of experiences I've had in my life and I've had a lot. His dogs are specialty bred for catch work, inbred and line bred for many generations. Probably a thousand or close to it catches in his current breeding. He began by breeding a Great Dane to a Neapolitan Mastiff. The Great Dane gives size and athletic speed and endurance. The breed began in Germany used for hunting wild boar, was bred for speed and endurance and great courage. Of course many generations as a show dog or pet has attenuated most of that courage, but when you breed almost any breed to Pit Bull blood you tend to strengthen it and it can revert to its original performance. Originally the Dane was of the mastiff family; warrior dog. The Neo Mastiff is the ultimate in courage. They are fearless. It also adds a great deal of raw power. This breed is also quite different from the original, but again, when you breed a pit to it you bring out the original warrior. Both the Dane and the Mastiff also inculcated even temperament, helped dissolve dog aggression while keeping courage and the Neo also breeds in a calm focus that makes for a more effective catch dog. He bred his Dane/Neo to a pure Pit to get a catch dog he called Baron. Baron was beyond my description. Power like you would not believe. He would stay with and bring to its knees, any wild European hog or even a bear. Michael has pictures of it. He did not have the slow athleticism that the Neo carries. (Think of the Neo as like a Sumo fighter). He had the power of the Neo and the lean endurance of the Dane brought to the fore with the pure pit (his favorite Pit, named Frankie), along with pit gameness to hang with any animal of any size. Then he bred pit for many generations, in and out of Frankie and Baron until he had catch dogs that look identical to pure pit, have the gameness of pure pit, but way beyond in endurance and power and effective focus. His dogs have a very tough coat and a harder bite than the average pit. They are specialists. Catch is their game and you can't find any better. Pit Bull purists scoff. Go ahead. For me this Riddle breeding is one super surreal dog and a sui generis among Bulldogs.

My favorite was a large female named Rosie. She is a brown buckskin with a tail that curves up over her back when she is fired up. I noticed her right away and I felt something about her from the moment I laid eyes on her. So when we found hog I followed her and caught with her. When we arrived at the first possibility sight for hunting, Michael announced we should let the dogs loose. He had them in their crates on his truck. I opened the crates for the bay dogs and the young catch dogs and opened Rosie's crate last. Most hunters cut the dogs loose as I just described. I don't. I let Rosie out but I snatched her and straddled her, hands on her chest. Her eyes were like an eagle honing in on prey; golden and intense. I felt the warrior rise up in her chest. She began with a low moan and when I didn't release her it went to a loud cry. I felt the fire. I had not felt this for about a decade. I was so very alive at that moment. Nobody who has not felt this can comprehend. So I put my mouth to her ear, inhaled her essence and said, "Rosie, where's the pigs?" She exuded fire. I said, "Get 'em!" and lifted my hands. BAM she exploded like a torpedo. One of the hunters was standing at the edge of the bed and he had to duck as she sailed over his head. This ranch is on the California desert and it was hot and dry. Over a hundred in the shade if I recall. One dog had already gone into shock and needed to have an IV drip fluids in him and he had to be put up. Rosie, Michael, and I caught a hog at the bottom of a steep and slippery/sandy hill. It was not a good meat hog so we released it. But Rosie collapsed after that catch. The sand was too slippery and steep to put her on my shoulders and carry her, so Michael and I had to drag her up that steep hill. I put her on my lap on the back of a four wheeler while she panted in and out hard like a bellows with a very dry, raspy breathing pattern that would mean the end of most match dogs in a pit fight. She was close to shock, dehydration and collapse. It almost looked like she was a goner. We put her and the bay dogs back on the truck and went to another location. By the time we arrived, Rosie was revived and hunted out the rest of the day until dusk. That night she went out with us for another hunt. You don't get dogs like Rosie from a show pedigree. This dog is very, very special; the result of over twenty generations of specialty breeding. It is because there are hundreds of working catches in her blood. She has the above mentioned Baron and Frankie in her blood, probably twenty times. This is what it takes to make a working dog.

November 2009, Michael placed an article about the Supreme Court case in his nativehuntblog, and I'd like to share it with you. This was his article:

I first discovered Bob Stevens through a mutual friend named Bill Stewart about 24 years ago, and that was during the time when Bill was publishing a magazine called The Pit Bull Reporter. *Being an American Pit Bull Terrier fancier and utilizing them for my hunting business I would voraciously read anything that I could about the Pit Bull. I also found myself enjoying writing about and having published, many stories of my wild boar hunting exploits and adventure with them in various magazines also devoted to the breed.*

Through this relationship with The Pit Bull Reporter, *the American Dog Breeder's Association, and other publications, I continued to see advertisements for videos, Bulldog products, and a hardcover book about a breed called:* Dogs of Velvet and Steel, Pit Bulldogs a Manual for Owners. *That particular advertiser and expert about the American Pit Bull Terrier (Bulldawg) and author was Mr. Robert John Stevens, and I soon found myself sending $24 to the address indicated to get my copy of the book. (During the seven years of trial, Amazon was selling* Dogs of Velvet and Steel *for $500 and up!)*

The book arrived in the mail about 3 weeks later and I excitedly tore open the boxed wrappings and then grasped the red colored with black lettering prize between my fingers. I noticed that the author had scribbled something on the inside cover. It read, "To Thomas 'The Tracker' Riddle, Best Wishes, Bob Stevens."

Wow! I was immediately floored, this very much admired man knew me from my writings about hunting boar with my Bulldog's.

(Also note: They are called Bulldogs for a reason and that is due to the fact that early American settlers utilized the breed for helping to control unruly stock and especially cattle, henceforth the term, bulldog).

Of course I immediately sat down and wrote a letter thanking him for the autographed copy of his book and thus began a pen relationship with Bob that found us regaling each other over the next few years with wonderful hunting tales and especially with and about our Bulldogs.

About four years after that initial meeting with Bob I decided to venture out and enter into the magazine publishing business myself, and with my very first copy of Dogs Boars & 44's *proudly sporting a feature article written by Mr. Robert John Stevens, I was ecstatic and completely beside myself with pride in that first printing. Bob Stevens and I not only shared a mutual affection for the American Pit Bull Terrier breed and the hunting of wild boar with them, but we both also had developed a strong yearning to gain a deeper understanding knowledge of the dog, and to discover more about its illustrious history.*

To those who do not know anything more than what the popular news media has been spoon feeding the public concerning this wonderful animal, Mr. Stevens' book can fill you in quite elaborately on just what makes this most complicated and affectionate dog tick.

For the sake of brevity we will fast forward to the last year that President Clinton was in office and how the attack on our First Amendment, the Constitution itself and the whole fiasco here had gotten started. It seems while holding to their untruthful nature that Wayne Pacelle and Ingrid Newkirk, respectively heads of the Humane Society of the United States (HSUS) and People for the Ethical Treatment of Animals (PETA), had convinced our congress that a certain underground group of individuals were producing and catering to a small market of persons who enjoyed watching "Crush Videos." These videos allegedly depicted small animals that would be crushed underneath a sexily dressed woman's high-heel clad foot. The reason I charge "Untruthful" is because when asked to bring into evidence that these distasteful videos were around and being sold, not even one single alleged video could be brought forward to show that this horrible type of filming even exists.

HSUS and PETA also did the same thing with the hunting scheme, a "pay for the experience" computer game where a live animal is baited to within the camera and automated firearm range, and then with the click of a mouse, you can kill said animal. That scheme never even got off the ground because its origin received so much negative reaction from the public that he pulled the plug before even a single Internet item was even sold. Yet HSUS still cites in their propaganda material, that they were chiefly instrumental in the demise. They only jumped on the bandwagon after its creator shut the project down on its own volition. (Author's note– and they did the exact same thing with the so-called "crush videos"– that shut down on their own after a limited 2,000 run, but this time they were able to get it through legislation, into an unconstitutional law and brought it all the way to Supreme Court and even had one Supreme Court Judge convinced in the existence of these crush videos).

After getting a poorly written and ambiguous law into place and then signed by President Clinton, which made it illegal to transport for sale across state lines, any videos or other form of media depicting animal cruelty, the HSUS then vigorously went after Mr. Bob Stevens. This is when Bob called upon me to come and testify on his behalf at the original trial six years ago in Pennsylvania and my testimony can be viewed at page four of the brief as an expert witness on behalf of the defense.

Bob's defense, and rightly so, was that his videos fell under the exemptions to the law which were Religious, Political, Scientific, Educational, Journalistic, Historical, and Artistic Value. As far as Mr. Stevens' videos are concerned, they do fall into each and every exempted category and should not be viewed otherwise. The audacity of the HSUS and their megalomaniacal desire for power made them press on and with a flurry of propaganda laden with press releases funded by their large money coffers they were able to get a conviction against Mr. Stevens. The appeal was immediately filed and then the appellate court eventually overturned Bob's Pennsylvania conviction. The HSUS true to their form and not leaving things alone then filed their Amicus Brief with the Supreme Court of the United States of America.

Bob called and asked that I get anyone and everyone involved to file their own briefs in opposition and if you take a look at the Amicus Brief in Opposition you will see that even the Liberal Media like the New York Times and some Animal Rights advocate groups are in support of Mr. Robert John Stevens and his long standing fight against these tyrannical anti-constitutional groups like HSUS and PETA, Bob also informed me that as a witness to the original Pennsylvania trial, that I would not be able to file my own amicus brief.

When Bob called me and informed me of the Supreme Court date, October 6th 2009, I was excited and anxious to go. Although he informed me that he might not be able to get a seat for me I told him that it did not matter and that I would be there anyway. Bob called back a little while later and said that his lawyer, Ms. Patricia Millett had in fact obtained a seat for me. It was good news, but as I said, a little thing like not being able to sit in the gallery was not going to keep me away.

Later on the night of the 5th, we all met at a nice restaurant, all of Bob's family attended the feast as well as Bob's wife and two children. Life was so very tranquil at that point. Good food, good spirits, loved ones all around you and feeling very high in optimism pertaining to tomorrow's events about to take place. We all knew, for better or for worse, that history would be made on the very next day at the Supreme Court of the United States of America.

The next day we all met in the hotel lobby for the limo ride over to the court house and when we arrived it was such a fanfare of paparazzi you would have thought that a rock star or the President had arrived. We were met by the senior partner at Bob's public defender firm, Lisa Freeland and she informed us to not look at the cameras nor answer any questions that might be imposed by the media people. These camera toting media thugs were so rude as to shove their cameras right to within inches of our faces. When one in particular got a little too close for my comfort level, I gave him a hard elbow to his ribs and knocked him off balance, and I just kept walking on. You see, during my career as a rock and roll artist I became familiar with how to deal with these types of paparazzi, and I never even said one single word to them, knowing they will blow it completely out of proportion and in a very negative way just to sell a story.

We were led through a side entrance and into the court room and I have never seen so much marble in all my life as was in that building. Everything was made of marble, brass, and hard woods and thoroughly designed to make an individual feel small and intimidated. But it all was very beautiful nonetheless, while at the same time it felt cold and unforgiving, and it most certainly was designed to show all who entered through its hallowed walls just exactly who was the all seeing, all knowing and almighty boss of you!

As we sat there waiting for the nine Supreme Court Justices to enter I looked to my left and not more than few seats over was Mr. HSUS. Wayne Pacelle himself, in the flesh! Or should I say in the plastic as he appears to have had so many facelifts that he did not even bear the resemblance to a human being anymore. He looks much more like those marble statues standing cold and distant right out in the halls behind there. And shocker of shocks, right near him and seated closest to us was Ms. PETA Ingrid Newkirk, or someone who bears a very close resemblance to her. These Vegetarians and Vegans all look about the same to me so I might have been mistaken, but I don't think so. (If you care to find out if T. Michael or the author are making un-called for remarks, we suggest you Google

Consumer Freedom and Humane Watch and Activist Cash for exposure of these criminals).

It was Neil Katyal for the prosecution who started the proceeding and right out of the gate Ms. Sotomayor began grilling him and in the process uncovered many inconsistencies and contradictions within his diatribe. Ms. Sotomayor stated that there was not a discernible difference between Mr. Stevens' videos and the popular P.B.S. series about Pit Bulls filmed by David Roma. And in fact, David Roma's P.B.S. series contained more gruesome footage of pit bull fights than those of Mr. Stevens' videos! (Author's note – something that was not brought out in the appeal or in Supreme Court is that I had received a letter from David Roma giving high praise to my dog fighting documentaries and asking my permission to use them in his documentary, submitted at the Sundance Film Festival. I refused him, but I showed both my public defender and Ms. Millett copies of his letter. I begged them both to testify that my work could not be argued to have low social impact (when my work was invited to the Sundance Film Festival!) while David Roma's work, which as stated is way over the top more gruesome than mine, does have quality social impact. Does this make sense to you? Both attorneys seemed to feel that argument would not be tenable. I don't know why and nobody told me, but we won the case, so now, who cares!)

Justice Antonin Scalia then interjected by saying, "I really think that you should focus on the right under the first Amendment of people who like Bull Fighting, Cock Fighting, or Dog Fighting, to present their side of the argument. Justice Scalia continued by noting, "It is not up to the government to decide what people's worst instincts are. If the first amendment means anything, that's what it means."

The rest of the Justices all pretty much followed Ms. Sotomayor's lead and to the point that Mr. Katyal suddenly cut his speech short, and excused himself out of frustration towards the end of the hard line of questioning.

In bright contrast, Ms. Patricia Millett was in top form and eloquently handled all questions with poise and grace with the exception of one question, which was posed by Justice Alito that had something to do with human sacrifice and would she pay for a TV channel which aired such horrific things as that. This question caught everyone a little off guard but after the first few seconds of shock had passed, Ms. Millett said that although she personally would not give such television shows her patronage, to just let the public decide with their wallets whether such a thing as the humane sacrifice channel should exist or not. The First Amendment is about the freedom to express one's self through free speech *and the government has no business dictating what we chose to see or hear.*

(In preparing for her Supreme Court presentation, Patricia was "prepped" by many astute lawyers including the Sanford Law School. I also sent her piles of email "prepping" her. I know HSUS and how they think and argue. I told her I guarantee one of those Justices is going to ask you how you feel about horrific scenes on public TV and in the movies. I suggested that she could remind them that that very same court has already addressed that question in the "Deep Throat" case. Their famous colleague Alan Dershowitz argued that it is not the place of the government to dictate. He noted that the pornographic scenes disgusted him, but that it is the American wallet that should decide, not a controlling government. I informed Patti that there is no question, one of the Justices will ask the similar question and suggested she have her response calmly and immediately ready to fire like an index finger on a cocked revolver. When Justice Alito asked an almost identical question, there was this huge hush. Michael described it as a feeling of shock that pervaded the room. I guess my attorney didn't listen to me because it set her back for a bit. As Michael reports, she did recover and her response was almost identical to Dershowitz and resolved the issue like a huge period.)

Afterwards we all filed out of the courtroom and posed for a few pictures before retiring to our hotel rooms, exhausted, elated, and mentally numb from what we had just witnessed.

If that absolutely ludicrous and broad ranged law was upheld by the Supreme Court then we would all say goodbye to hunting videos and magazines depicting any animal legally harvested. Even cave drawings of historic man bringing down mammoth and wildebeest with their spears could be outlawed under that far-reaching piece of legislation.

All the way from that little Pennsylvania kangaroo court and the first court appointed lawyer, Michael Novara, who suggested that Bob take a plea bargain, and then on up to the Supreme Court of the Untied States of America, Bob Stevens has held true to his Christian beliefs and the United States Constitution all the while holding up his rights as a citizen therein. Mr. Robert John Stevens has fought a long and hard battle for that very freedom called the First Amendment and when the dust finally settles from this battle we will all owe a great debt of gratitude to him for having the dignity, loyalty, courage, devotion, and determination to hold true to his All-American beliefs.

Just the same as the American Pit Bull Terrier dogs which he loves so much, Bob Stevens is Game to the end.

Glen Bui

Glen Bui was an important witness in the trial. He was acting vice-President for the American Canine Foundation (ACF). I do wish you would Google this organization. They have done so much to expose and reveal the criminal actions of animal rights organizations such as HSUS and PETA. Their exposure is a matter of public record and easily documented in court transcripts across the nation. I also suggest the American Canine Foundation Education and Legislation website. This is just one of a plethora of sources that prove my comments and allegations regarding these criminal animal rights cabal are beyond allegations, proven facts.

ACF is a non-profit organization that depends on donations to help stop irresponsible and uninformed dog owners from harming themselves and their animals. ACF provides education and effective legislation to protect the public and *innocent* dogs from being victims of irresponsible owners and to protect dog owner's rights. In this capacity ACF engages in a lot of breed specific legislation and acts in a defense capacity to provide legal support and prevent innocent dogs and people from being harmed in court by humaniac animal rights prosecutors. ACF takes the position that breed bans are unconstitutional and based on flawed and erroneous data. ACF maintains its own accurate and easily verifiable data base to provide courts with factual material and expose fabricated studies and reports cited and used by animal rights attorneys to prosecute innocent people, resulting in innocent animals being killed en masse. For example, the amicus briefs filed in my case by animal rights groups included studies they cited. The Solicitor General (the prosecutor in my case at Supreme Court) also cited these studies. The Solicitor General is attorney Elena Kagen. She would not know anything about these animal rights studies so they had to have been provided to her by either HSUS or PETA, both of whom have used these same falsified studies in the past. I put in hours upon hours looking up these studies and seeking the confirmation and credibility of them. I did not find a single one of them that was not done on pure hearsay by a radical animal rights person. All of this is public record so I encourage you to seek this out and see for yourself. Google or otherwise follow up on every single study or report cited by the prosecution in my case, in the appeal and in Supreme Court. I speak primarily to those who support these animal activist organizations and have been misled by them for years. If you have put in hours writing up blogs about animal cruelty and support PETA, etc., then put in equal time to study them and see if my statements are my own or based on real facts. My examination found not one single credible citation. Not one. The problem is that neither of the justices nor the Solicitor General are going to study this and check on the integrity of the alleged studies. I sent my attorney pages and pages showing that some of the studies are downright falsified; some are based on news media reports by animal rights morons with huge imaginations and have no basis in reality whatsoever; obviously so if one were to merely take the time to read them. Some were based on actual studies, but cited sentences taken out of context that misinforms. The situation is exacerbated by the fact that the briefs filed by the attorneys are limited. They are limited in number of pages and scope, so they have to concentrate on the legal issues at hand. So all my hours, and I mean working everyday much like I did in graduate school working on research, it was all for nothing. My attorney could not use it. It is another case of the judges "can't handle the truth!" They would not read an expose´ of HSUS. They are only interested in First Amendment and constitutional legality. Moreover they would be turned off and tuned out by paragraphs to them wasted on exposing HSUS lies and propaganda. HSUS and PETA know this well. That was a stressful time and I am reminded by a 2010 statement by the basketball phenom LeBron, "It is like watching a move. Just when you think it can't get more stupid, it gets more stupid." However, I hope you keep this in mind when reading the epilogue and my daily prayer citing Psalm 35. The HSUS plotted my ruin with their craftiness, lies, and deceit, but it ended up they were turned back in dismay. Like chaff before the wind they were chased by an invisible but real angel of the Lord (I know this in my heart), and the trap they set entangled them. Read the story in the ensuing epilogue.

    The point here is that ACF has done so much in a pile of animal activist cases to expose this egregious behavior from animal rights groups and their attorneys. In 2006 ACF filed a federal lawsuit against Colorado for passing a breed specific ban and using manipulated data from Denver. So you see these are not passionate statements thrown out by a victimized author. They are real facts and you can check them all out. You can read how in the Tellings case they caught a prosecutor taking vital evidence from the file and failed to return it. The file proved Pit Bulls are *not* responsible for killing Ohioans and their bite statistics fall far below other breeds of dogs (Toledo, Ohio sought to ban the breed based on statistical data provided by prosecution that Pit Bulls are a killer breed and a threat to the nation). ACF exposed them. What amazes me is any time Pit Bulls harm someone it makes huge national news. Why is it that the pile of cases in which HSUS and PETA become exposed for their criminal activities none of that ever gets into the news media to any significant extent, or at least rarely does, and they never get sent to prison? The animal activists have to pay fines and some individuals go to prison, but the public rarely hears much about it and the organizations continue to operate and be accepted in the justice system as "experts" and "protectors of animals." How can this be? I am continually exasperated by our justice system and the attorneys so willing to listen to HSUS and other criminal activists, believing their nonsense yet ignoring clear evidence of their criminal activities. Even attorneys defending against animal activists close their eyes to evidence incriminating HSUs and the others. Why?

As mentioned, Glen Bui was acting Vice-President for ACF. He was also an expert on the Pit Bull breed, having owned them for thirty years. Glen has testified in innumerable canine issues in court, on a variety of canine issues including the American Pit Bull Terrier breed. He has a very effective track record lobbying and testifying as expert witness against breed specific legislation and animal cruelty issues. He is also an accredited expert of dog fighting, working undercover with the Dog Fighting Task Force in Pierce County Washington. What bewilders me is how the prosecution could get away with bombarding the jury with hours and hours of argument and testimony against dog fighting when the defendant is equally and has an even longer track record in disputing the same activity. I really don't understand this. My attorney repeatedly objected to this context and the objections were denied by the judge. This meant most of the trial consisted of unrelated sensational propaganda designed to make it appear I was some cruel dog fighter. The case was not even about dog fighting; it was about my documentaries, which were so diluted compared to the exact same documentaries put out by Animal Planet and Dateline etc. I still don't understand how they got away with all that foolishness.

Glen also worked for the FBI as an undercover agent investigating HSUS and other animal rights criminals. Included in his investigations was NARN a radical organization that filed an amicus brief for prosecution. NARN (Northwest Animal Rights Network) happened to be the F.B.I's top suspect for their criminal activities. And again I am flabbergasted they get away with convincing the courts and the public they are goody-goody animal welfare people.

NARN along with about a dozen other animal activist groups, were accepted as "friends of the court" and filed amicus briefs in support of the prosecution. Here is the statement NARN makes in its introduction to the Supreme Court: "Northwest Animal Rights Network is an all-volunteer Seattle-based animal protection organization. NARN has been dedicated to ending the exploitation of animals by raising awareness of animal suffering in the food, entertainment, experimentation, and fashion industries since 1986. NARN's efforts include outreach, demonstrations, litigation, and educational events. NARN's purpose in filing this brief amicus curiae is to supplement the arguments presented by the Solicitor General (Elena Kagen) in her brief on behalf of Petitioner (prosecution) by providing additional information on the compelling interest of government in regulating and prohibiting animal cruelty and on the de minimis value of depictions of animal cruelty as defined by 18 U.S.C. & 48."

What I do not understand is why is it HSUS can make this highly gruesome documentary showing bloody grizzly fabricated in terms of excessive unrealistic dog fights as a documentary, claiming that they do not promote dog fighting and asking for donations while I do the exact same documentary, not promoting, but educational, and my work has this "de minimis value?" And why is it the judges are touted to be interested in a dozen briefs filled with pure nonsense, but they would be offended if it was shown to them clearly and easily verifiable evidence, exposing the falsifications and fabrication. I still do not comprehend this. Well, NARN continued with page after page quoting the New York v. Ferber case.

The 1982 New York v. Ferber case was the core argument that the government used in my appeal and in Supreme Court. I warned my attorneys the government would use this argument, based on my study of law at my "law library;" the Barnes and Noble law books section! I am sure my warnings were not needed, they also probably expected this. If you look up the First Amendment in any law books that contain freedom of speech law you will find this case. Our first and most revered amendment that of free speech, originally contained only limited exceptions. It states that we have freedom of speech in America except we cannot excite the public that can result in harm, like holler "Fire!" in a building resulting in panic and people injured. We can also not make threats to people. It was not until the 1980's that an addition was made to the narrow, restricted exceptions to free speech. Child pornography was considered to have "de minimis" value. You would say, in court, for example, "the plaintiff suffered only de minimis damages or "the chilling effect on free speech is de minimis." The phrase actually comes from the Latin maxim de minimis non curst lex meaning the law does not concern itself with trifles. With child pornography they used the term to argue the value of my documentaries was so minimal that in the trade-off between free speech and depictions that can harm the nation, the depiction should be unprotected by free speech. The core argument proposed by the government was to analogize my documentaries with child pornography, which was, to me, such obvious, ridiculous baloney. The government (and

I posit under the direction of HSUS and I suggest this because all of this argument smacks of the same line of manure HSUS had used in courts since the 1970's, used this same line of argument, claiming that dog fighting is just as harmful to our nation as child pornography. This was the core substance of their whole case. They argued, that like child pornography, animal fighting venture had such minimal value that the any benefits to be derived from viewing such horrific depiction is far outweighed by the social interest in order and morality and that animal fighting venture is a social ill that must be countermanded. In making these allegations, all of the government testimony cited these same "studies" as I have seen the same cited from 1970's to present day reports of like ilk. So they go on for page after page citing both old and new studies that indicate that serial killers engaged in animal cruelty as children. And they cite a real study that indicated violent criminals engaged in activities such as pulling legs off insects, etc., as children. And that study exists. More recently, almost all modern serial killers have been shown to be cruel to animals as children enjoying torturing little animals. But again, they take the study out of context and provide misleading, inaccurate information. I pointed out to all of my attorneys hunting has been an intricate aspect of American culture since our founding. If ten percent, for example, of the young boys who engaged in the cruelties of hunting ended up violent criminals we would not have a nation. I think that is the best way to address ¾ of the argument the government put out, but again, I was ignored. Like fire alarm salesmen, NARN indulged in many pages of horrific animal cruelty stories. They included a story about a poor little donkey that some children tortured, strangled with a rope that had a hangman's noose on it. I begged my attorney to point out what does this have to do with my case? I never engaged in any horrific depiction like that. My documentaries were much milder than any hunting video, other dog fighting videos and TV documentaries on the same subject, especially the ones produced by HSUS that were far more bloody and gruesome. My work contained absolutely no blood and had a motive of educating not titillating like HSUS. I suggested all those pages heaped upon pages of nonsense were an insult to the intelligence of the highest level of attorneys in the land. Well again, she did not confront those issues and at the time it scared me. It turned out she was very correct. Just as in my Psalm 35 prayers they ended up insulting most of the judges and harming their own testimony with ridiculous overtures. My attorney concentrated on the reality of free speech and the lack of even minimal harm in my work.

In the trial Glen testified that my dog fighting documentaries were of significant educational value. He testified that my documentaries were much milder than current videos of the street dog fights his undercover operations prosecuted. He found them valuable historical documentaries about the foundation of our breed and no way harmful and they do not promote dog fighting at all.

As just one example of the significance of ACF and Glen Bui, I would like to share the following letter Glen received from Representative Debbie Stafford of the Colorado House of Representatives–House District 40. She writes:

Dear Mr. Bui, I want to thank you and the American Canine Foundation for your tireless assistance in providing data which helped me convince my colleagues in the Colorado Legislature to do the right thing and strengthen Colorado's dangerous dog laws and prohibit breed laws at the local level in Colorado.

In the past fifteen years in Denver, THOUSANDS of INNOCENT family pets have been taken from their responsible owners and massacred. Denver's own statistics indicate that in 2003, only 2.6% of the dog bites were from Pit Bulls. The FACTUAL data from the ACF assisted me in the challenge of bringing fairness and equity for all dog owners. We have now put the burden of responsibility where it belongs, on the dog owners, not on the breed of dog.

I hope that other states will utilize your valuable resources as they find occasion to re-evaluate their dangerous dog legislation. Thank you for helping Colorado do the right thing. (caps mine for emphasis).

Glen's testimony in the trial was an eye opening provision; evidence my documentaries are just as legal as could be. But since he was a witness, he also could not file an amicus brief. Meanwhile, when I won the appeal I received a threatening call from some coward who would not give me his name and present himself to me man-to-man. He spoke of wanting to cut me up. Well, different world today. If I did meet this foolish person and put him in the hospital they would just put me in jail for ten years aggravated assault. This is why I have amped up my study of aikido and Gracie Brazilian Jiu-Jitsu. I also received a threatening call from an animal activist right after I won in Supreme Court. This fellow said he was "sharpening his axe" for me. I am ready for a conversation. Or as one version of 1 Peter 4:11, puts it "Do you have the gift of speaking? Then speak as though God Himself were speaking through you." I truly speak and often without anger but a desire to sincerely (Phil 1:10) explain the Word of our Creator, and to do so not for my reputation one single bit, but for the glory of God (1 Cor. 10:13, and my email signature Col. 3: 12 -17).

Glen had worse. He not only received threatening calls, they put a dead cat at the top of his driveway along with the call. Of course this is the world's greatest protector of animals that the nation donates millions to. Also, I hope you will note they make all these accusations about my work not having value to the nation while their gruesome video depictions are supposed to protect animals. Yet they violate the most basic exception to freedom of speech by making death threats and killing cats to threaten. Just when you think the movie can't get more stupid, it gets more stupid! Glen, parenthetically, is also a martial artist and runs his own school. Glen, because he was a witness in the trial, also could not file an amicus, but he did send an email to the Solicitor General informing her of the phone threats, dead cat, and that he had filed police reports on them. He also informed the solicitor General and my attorney of his undercover work for the FBI investigating the criminal activities of HSUS and NARN. The FBI considers NARN one of the more dangerous. He informed the Solicitor General of the scathing comments depicted in the dogsbite.org site. You can Google DogsBite (at least at the time of this writing) you read it and it reads like they are these goody-goody people who protect animals. Fact: they are a terrorist outfit from what I have read and been informed. The radical, criminal organizations such as HSUS, NARN, PETA, etc. are all connected to this DogsBite. I cannot comment enough how truly amazed I am the courts accept these criminals as "expert" witnesses with "valuable information for court decisions regarding animal cruelty." DogsBite.org had a site that featured myself, Glen Bui, and Dr. Brisbin, and the book you are about to read. NARN and other radical groups like them engage in such activities as letting commercially bred minks loose, fighting Pit Bulls and videoing them getting torn up (generally big dogs not true bred pits), poisoning dogs at AKC shows, arson, and death threats. Animal protectors? In any event the picture they used of me was the picture you will read about in the Epilogue. It was taken when I left the courthouse after being sentenced to federal prison and told I had to get rid of our family pet Pit Bull. This is not the same as being told you have to get rid of your daughter of course, but the feeling is similar. I was so angry and the stress was beyond description. The picture does make me look like some serial killer (as they describe me). They describe all of us as cruel monsters that are a threat to the nation. This was pretty scary to Glen and ACF because the animal activists were being investigated as terrorists, not just loud mouths. One of the ACF staff was a retired Federal agent and she expressed grave concerns. Fortunately, to my knowledge nothing further happened. I do want you to get a feel for what we went through fighting for our freedom right here in America. And none of this is fabricated or one bit exaggerated.

None of the allegations made by me in this "Cast of Characters" and in the Epilogue as well as in your *Dogs of Velvet and Steel* book, originated with me. Unless otherwise noted, they do not represent my feelings, my prejudice, nor am I imposing my resentment or anger. They all come from primarily organizations with the funds to investigate, such as Consumer Freedom and National Rifle Associations, court transcripts, and news reports. I have boxes full of these facts. Like early 2010 all over the news, Ringling Brothers filed a lawsuit against HSUS charging them with bribery, tax evasion, and money laundering (HSUS has been charged and investigated multiple times for tax evasion), and racketeering. It was disclosed that HSUS illegally paid a former Ringling Brothers employee over $190,000 to give false testimony about the mistreatment of animals by the circus. For $190,000, the employee testified in court that the circus staff routinely beat elephants and chained them up for long periods of time, hitting them with sharp bull hooks, breaking down baby elephants with force to make them submissive, and removing baby elephants from their mothers before they are weaned. The rascal was caught and it was proved to be all fabrications and lies. The news report also disclosed that another funded organization, Humane Watch, exposed HSUS false claims, that the organization presents itself as saving animals when in fact only one dollar out of every $200 dollars they receive annually from donations goes to help animal shelters. Humane Watch exposed the fact that HSUS has accumulated over $113 million dollars in assets, while capitalizing on the misleading impression its name invokes. Humane Watch states that HSUS raises enough money from their campaigns to finance animal shelters in every single state, with money to spare, yet it doesn't operate a single one. Also it was disclosed that during Hurricane Katrina, HSUS hauled in 30 million dollars in donations. The Louisiana Attorney General called for a criminal investigation on HSUS to arrive at an explanation why the organization actually spent a very puny percentage helping animals and most of the donations ended up in HSUS expensive legal department and campaign expenses. Google Albert Rash (theaschoutdoorchronicles@msn.com). Read documents that prove the Federal Government knows HSUS and PETA are terror groups. Read the group's appeal to the public to communicate with local Senators and provide them with the documentation and ask your Senator why known terror groups are allowed to write legislation and allowed to testify in support of unconstitutional legislation.

HSUS is a huge international organization and they are split so many ways it is, so far, impossible for the government to catch them. In the Ringling Brothers situation, it turned out the $190,000 was allegedly funneled through an HSUS "wildlife advocacy," a non-profit group that the activist lawyers used as a pass-through. The section of HSUS that was responsible for the money laundering was run by a DC law firm that was named in a RICO suit. Two HSUS staff attorneys were named in the RICO lawsuit. HSUS has been compared to the Mafia and their high priced lawyers. HSUS leaders are very good at working the system. They make legal demands through certain legal loopholes and it can take five to forty years tied up in courts. One article stated that PETA is just a fringe group connected behind closed doors with HSUS, that HSUS is bigger, more funded, smarter, and more covert. HSUS is touted to be PETA with a Rolex watch and fewer naked interns.

I could continue for many more pages. I just want to make the point that the statements I make did not originate with me; they came from accurate *documentation*.

Dr. I. Lehr Brisbin

Dr. Brisbin has the highest of credentials. He is a Professor on the graduate faculty at the University of Georgia. In this capacity he teaches graduate students. His area of specialty is ecology and wildlife biology/animal behavior. He is also a Senior Ecologist at the Savannah River Ecology Laboratory. Dr. Brisbin has professionally studied pigs for over thirty-five years and has co-authored a book on wild pigs in the United States. His book is the definitive book about the history and ecology and status of wild pigs in the United States. The senior author of the book is his own graduate student who got his Ph.D. under him, Dr. Jack Meyer. Dr. Meyer is recognized as the foremost authority in the world on North American wild pigs. Dr. Brisbin also lectures, in addition to the University of Georgia, at other universities such as Clemson, South Carolina, and Colorado Universities, where he has adjunct appointments. As a nationally renowned scientist he enjoys many honors; too many to list here. For thirty-seven years, Dr. Brisbin has studied wildlife on the Savannah River Ecology site. He studied feral pigs, hybrids of feral pigs, and wild boar. He used, and testified to that fact, Pit Bulls as catch dogs in his many years research. He testified that catch dogs were a necessity as the hogs would not go into traps and could not be otherwise caught. He testified that using Pit Bulls as catch dogs result in the pigs not getting unnecessarily hurt.

Dr. Brisbin is also an expert in dog behavior and has testified as expert on Pit Bulls many times. In his necessary study of the genetic development and the selection and behavioral background of the breed, Dr. Brisbin also became a qualified expert on dog fighting. Dr. Brisbin was also the American Kennel Club's expert on Pit Bulls for about 18 years.

In the trial, my defense attorney initiated relevant questions for Dr. Brisbin to inform and testify. Dr. Brisbin was contracted by the Department of Forest Service to help clear the Savannah River Basin of wild hogs that damage the environment. In this capacity, Dr. Brisbin also conducted his scientific research. Dr. Brisbin testified that pigs are not native to America; they came into our country from Spanish explorations. Hogs seriously damage our native habitat. (In the news in 2010 this was verified. It has become a national threat and the government needs to weed out the damaging wild hogs; referred to as "invasive aliens"). Dr. Brisbin provided an educational lecture on the type of pigs found in the wild, a far more thorough and informational one than the government "expert." Over and over, the government insisted that I had lied; claiming I only hunted wild hogs. Why the jury would buy this I have absolutely no idea because I explicitly explained one catch depicting a farmer requesting the use of my catch dog for a free-ranging hog on his land that needed catching. I repeatedly announced the wild hogs were hybrid; local hogs gone wild and mated with local feral hogs. I don't know what all that foolish dialogue had to do with the case anyway. My take on it is the government never had a case so they just used a series of red herring for damaging innuendo. The part I do not understand is despite my pleading that the nonsense be exposed it was never challenged.

Dr. Brisbin testified that he used his own Pit Bull and found that the use of Pit Bulls for catch work is the least invasive means to catch wild hogs and he started doing this in the mid 1970's. Dr. Brisbin testified that in his opinion my Catch Dog video and the accompanying booklet was highly educational and unique. My work alone *teaches* how to train Pit Bulls to safely catch in a manner that minimizes harm to the hog and to the dog. My attorney asked him if using Pit Bulls for catch work was common in the southeast and Dr. Brisbin testified that it certainly is. He said there are small rural towns in Georgia where almost everyone owns a Pit Bull catch dog. Everyone knows the dogs by name and if you go to the local barber shop you'll hear their stories.

My attorney asked him if he had ever seen eclectic prods used. Perhaps this is because I had informed my attorney that catching a hog with a well-trained catch dog is far easier on the animal than the electric prods. I mentioned I have seen them repeatedly jab the hogs over and over, more often than naught when it is not even needed or to just plain make them hurry up, while the hogs squeal and jump. Dr. Brisbin's views in this respect were the same as mine and I had never discussed them with him.

Probably the area of my work that the government focused on more than any other was a scene I thought was quite educational. My hunting buddy, Mike Chellis, featured in the South Carolina hunts in my video and booklet, quit his occupation as a construction worker and became a Christian missionary. He moved to Mexico to build churches, met a Mexican girl, married, and had children. His Pit Bull catch dog was too old to hunt at the time so I gave him one of my Velvet/Panther bred pups. He named the pup Katie. Katie seemed like she might be another one of those natural catch dogs. The first time she saw a hog (with the old dog as a "teacher" for her to watch and emulate) she went right in, caught by the ear and held on. Perfect! Mike later said he needed to catch another free ranging farm hog for a big cookout planned. I was in the middle of putting together my educational Catch Dog video so I asked him if he could video it and let me use it for my film. He said he would be glad to. After the catch he called, but there was a hiccup, more like a belch I would say. He said she caught on the ear opposite the side from where he stood to video. So you can't see the damage done for most of that videoing, except for at the end when he saw the problem and that part I edited out. Evidently she switched to the jaw and nearly tore the whole jaw off (she was a beyond normal biting power dog, which was the plan for Catch and Schutzhund behind my breeding to this Panther dog!) Mike is not a sensitive man; he is a hunter. All his life he has hunted, but he doesn't believe in unnecessary harm or damage. So I know he did not mean for that to happen. He said he did not know until he set the camera down. By then the damage had been done. From his perspective it appeared she had a good hold on the sow and had her caught so he could tie her. I edited out the damage, but I explain what happened and I can use this to show the importance of training a Pit Bull on proper catch technique that will minimize harm. So I did not show the harm to the hog. In editing there is a split second splash of blood if you blink you will miss it where you see some blood on the other side of the hog at her mouth. Very brief, very small, but in the narration I explained that while this dog seemed to catch naturally she did not have the training to catch a hog by the ear. Hardly any hunters train their dogs to do this; they just put them in with experienced catch dogs and let them go. I did not invent my training techniques; they were taught to me by a couple hunters. Very few hunters know how to train this way. Since I edited out any bad stuff, except for a brief blink, I had no idea it would cause all this brouhaha. In fact it is really just another example of the government not wanting to admit they made a mistake attacking us in our home and confiscating my small business. They had no case so they had to fabricate a case. I did not depict any animal cruelty and the narration was designed to explain how to prevent this type of accident.

Let me at this juncture explain a bit how the justice system works. The government announced to the jury and I'm paraphrasing, "You watched a horrible example of a very gruesome bloody scene where a hog's jaw was torn off. This is the highest level of grizzly depiction." Well, in that little educational vignette, I didn't depict it, I explained it. But since that testimony went unchallenged subsequent defense briefs in my appeal and to the Supreme Court could not change it or at least this is what I was told. So even though I did not depict this jaw torn off that testimony by the prosecution could not be corrected and the judges and justices had to make decisions based on *being told* I had depicted a hog's jaw torn. I completely do not understand this, but hey, we won and the liars and deceivers who were so very cunning, lost.

With that background, my attorney asked Dr. Brisbin if he thought the scene with Katie was educational and the response was yes, definitely. He noted that my work is unique in that respect that it *teaches* how to avoid harm and the consequences of not following his training program, while no other hunting videos he is aware of teach this. He said when he teaches, or when anyone teaches for that matter, the *educational value* of the material you use is not predicated on the fact that material shows everything going right. Otherwise, I would say football coaches wouldn't review last week's game films. You don't want to watch the film to show the team they did everything perfect. They want to show who missed their coverage, which didn't block, and that's the *educational value* of showing how things didn't go right; what you shouldn't do.

As far as the dog fighting documentaries are concerned, my attorney asked him if he saw value in them. Dr. Brisbin said he planned on using them, and particularly the *Pick-A-Winna*. The booklet was a very thorough explanation of the true nature of dog fighting. Far more extensive, educational, true, objective, and pointed out that the inexperienced testimony given in the trial by the government witness, who had never attended a dog fight or knew any real dog fighters, didn't know what he was talking about. Parenthetically, I had begged my attorney to display my educational booklets to the jury and was promised it would be done; even minutes before we went into the courtroom. It never was. The jury was never informed of the totality of education in my work. In any event, Dr.

Brsibin testified He would use my videos and booklets as what he called required optional reading in his Canine Behavior and Dogs in Research teaching classes at Georgia and elsewhere. His students include science and non-science majors that are in nursing, education, law, or business disciplines. Required Optional Reading in education means they are required to pick a topic (such as bloodhounds – another aspect of Dr. Brisbin's canine study, or the Pit Bull and dog fighting) and the student must write a paper for a grade. The trial took four days and it's beyond the range of this little section or even this book to report the totality of the dialogue.

As a side note, Dr. Brisbin mentioned that he is engaged as an expert witness on behalf of the Pit Bull breed. He testified that he received a $200 fee to testify in my trial and that that every bit of witness money he receives he deposits into a special research foundation at the University of Georgia on dog behavior in a variety of fields, not just Pit Bull or bloodhounds.

To me, Dr. Brisbin resolved a case that should not have gone beyond the pre-trial hearing. He so effectively put to rest the sheer volume of malarkey set forth by the foolish government "experts" showing that even the infamous head of the Virginia pork industry, with all his educational and experiential certification, was either full of baloney or he didn't know what he was talking about.

When the government attorney engaged Dr. Brisbin in cross-examination, Dr. Brisbin was too much for him. Dr. Brisbin displayed a self-contained, experienced self-reliance that was intimidating to the government attorney, or to any prosecuting attorney trying to build a case on false allegations, in my opinion. The government attorney tried every trick imaginable. He asked Dr. Brisbin if he agreed the dog fighting documentaries I did, showed the destructive power of Pit Bulls. Dr. Brisbin said the dogs seemed virtually unharmed, even after 40 minutes of fighting. Tired, but unharmed. The government attorney persisted trying to discredit the witness before the jury. Dr. Brisbin, undaunted, calmly replied, "No. I saw two worn out dogs. I saw abrasions, but no gaping wounds." The attorney tried again, "Are you denying, sir, that any of these dogs were punctured in those fights?" Dr. Brisbin commented "I can't tell." In so doing he pointed to the fact that my documentaries were edited so you don't see any wounds. Fact is, I didn't have to edit all that much. Again, people want to get on the bandwagon calling horror at something they never really have watched live or engaged. They think huge teeth tearing and ripping away; believing the ridiculous sensationalism of the HSUS driven attorney allegations. The truth is, these dogs have genetic fighting ability so it is not that easy to inflict harm. Analogous to a professional boxing match you watch, after 12 rounds no perceivable damage. If the same boxing match was the professional boxer versus a nonathletic English teacher, the English teacher wouldn't last one round and he'd be in the hospital. Most of the fight the dogs vie for holds and there is a lot of skin holds that result in mere abrasions. I don't mean to Mickey Mouse it. Sometimes the dogs fight the muzzle and when they do scar tissue often (but not always) remains. Some dogs can also have ears that resemble a boxer's cauliflower ears. I would say about the same ratio as professional boxer or mixed martial artists. There are Mike Tyson types also; dogs like the old Zebo dog or the Art dog that would put serious wounds on a dog (or the infamous Tornado dog depicted without showing serious harm in the short snippet, in the *Pick-A-Winna* video). They are as rare with competing dogs as they are with competing boxers. Actually, you have to know your bloodlines. Many of those really hard biting bloodlines go back to blending in an outside breed, which, to make a very long genetics story short, breeds in a strong prey drive. The kill drive attenuates the game drive, which is a love for the "game," a soft biting drive that can overcome the hard biting but lower (recessive) game gene. And people watch professional football and hockey in which there are no teeth, but there is impact that causes permanent injury far exceeding that of almost all competing Pit Bull dog fight. The spectators holler and scream "kill 'em! Mow 'em down!" They don't see the retired athletes that are permanently harmed, many disabled. Actually, in the news October 2010 a college football player, permanently paralyzed from the neck down, documented a highly visible permanent injury from the "blood sport" of football (blood sport term mine; a joke). In Tim Tebow's autobiography he relates how in 2009 he received a concussion, but he still held on to the ball (so he is a national hero!). Are we going to put football coaches and sponsors in jail for half a life-time? When you see a retired athlete like Joe Namath that is so obviously permanently damaged, you think, "Oh, what a hero!" I have seen many retired football players that can hardly lift a coffee cup up to drink. But this is not cruelty. This line of observation I received from countless Pit Bull folks. A significant aspect of the American public, like the attorney general in David Tant's case, would respond, "Well, in football they don't drug the athletes and force them to fight to the death." To which the dogfighter responds, neither do they drug pit dogs and force them to fight to the death; the rules disallow this. It is ongoing and again a changed America; changed world for that matter. I chose to try and stay out of the debates as my forte´ is to respond by offering healthy challenges for the gladiator bred dogs: weight pulling,

Schutzhund, etc., and to allow them to do farm and ranch work that no other breed could do and to educate and teach how to train dogs to mitigate harm in the ranch and farm work. But the point in this context is I *did not depict serious harm*. I produced an artistic documentary. I want to add at this juncture that one cannot blame the public or the media or even prosecuting attorneys for views they derive from some idiotic Pit Bull people that have, in recent years, splashed all over the internet these dog fight challenges and comments like my dog has killed ten dogs and my dog will tear out any opponents. Then the Pit Bull community wonders why people think the breed is comprised of killer dogs. I think the Pit Bull community needs to monitor itself or not bemoan the perspective of the public.

I think this is the best spot to deposit a side note about what Pit Bull dog fighting really is. I believe you should be truthfully and objectively informed.

Animal activists love to build sensational stories for court rooms and the media. They love to fabricate reports of dogs trained for blood lust, call the competition blood sport, report the dogs ripping and tearing each other apart and made to fight. It is alleged they stage fights with large cross-bred pits that indeed tear each other up. The constant public allegations about blood lust and tearing limbs, is all animal activist malarkey is the point here. I don't condone dog fighting, but I don't condone using lies and malicious degradation of the APBT breed in courts to convict innocent people either.

Actually Pit Bull dog fighting is about volition; the ability to make choices. You cannot make a dog fight beyond a male domination or food dispute. You cannot make a dog stay in competition for a length of time. One of the educational aspects of my dog fighting documentaries is to educate the breed owner of the gladiatorial genetics of the breed. These dogs can be highly affectionate, tender-hearted, and playful, even to a degree submissive with other breeds, until one day challenged. This is not a breed you let run loose in your yard, and it is not a breed you have as a house pet with another dog. Beagles would rather put their nose to the ground and figure bunny trails than anything else. Coon hounds hunt coon. Bloodhounds figure out tracks. Sled dogs compete pulling sleds. Pit Bulls would rather compete than anything. I like to say compete because in my opinion the game is a deep seated desire to compete; not to kill.

As mentioned the really hard biting dogs are operating out of a kill prey drive. When a Neapolitan Mastiff/Pit bull cross is matched with a pure pit, the cross bred dog can often bite down the pure pit. Then he will (tend to) just stand over his "prey" uninterested in continuing. This is true. And it is behind the excessively hard biting (pure bred on paper) match dogs that when rolled to see what they have bite very hard, only to quit standing up when not even bit. I say this from a knowledge of genetics and from incidents I saw in the 1970's and 80's. The traditional foundation dogs I experienced in the 70's in the Carolinas were soft mouthed dogs that would stay in there until their handler picked them up, tails wagging away to beat the band even when competing for a prolonged period from the bottom. A dog that operates out of fear for his life bites the hardest. A killer dog bites next hardest. A dog biting out of kill prey drive bites next hardest. A dog playing bites soft, so a dog that is biting something, say a ball, for instance, that is wagging his tail, is mostly just mouthing the ball. Wagging tail equals a soft bite! All this makes the prolonged testimony of the government "expert" described in your book so laughable. Dog matches end when the dog no longer wants to compete. For that matter probably 90% of the matches end when the losing dog does not want to come out of his corner and cross the pit in ten seconds. The standard match rules mandate the handler can verbally encourage, but he cannot even gently push the dog out of his corner. If he does he forfeits the match. The other way a match is decided is when the handler sees his dog is taking too much, is outclassed, and he picks his dog up. If you were to list the top ten dog fighters in the history of the sport, one of them I have seen repeatedly pick up his dog and concede the match far sooner than most. He then has found a home for that losing dog in every instance that I am aware of.

And again, a government lawyer or HSUS or other animal activist can protest and exclaim, "Bob Stevens claims he doesn't promote dog fighting, but over and over he sides with dog fighters and the match dogs and the activity. He repeatedly claims it is not harmful." I didn't say it wasn't harmful. You will read in this book that although the sport is not at all like the animal activists describe it, it is still more than I want my dog to engage in. You will also read my "blanket statement" that is designed to still all the hoopla about Bob Stevens said this and Bob Stevens said that. The general gist of it is dog fighting is an anachronism, just as the western gunfighter is. It makes a good read; it is part of our history, but it does not fit in today's America. What I *do* promote is steering our breed away from its outlaw stigma and into mainstream America through such activities as The Schutzhund (the highest level companion dog – the PhD. of canine), weight pulling contest, the conformation show ring. A more thorough blanket statement appears in your epilogue. So no, I did not say the sport is not harmful. I say I am a journalist that believes in reporting truths, not fabrications, objectivity not sensational titillating dogma and exposing fraudulent, damaging dialogue. That is what I am doing here.

The government attorney tried everything he could to trap Dr. Brisbin with catchy questions regarding the primary thrust of their argument. There was a long list of tricks the attorney tried, beyond the scope of this context, but finally he tried to pull out his last trick. He asked if Glen Bui was a close friend and had he worked with him on other cases. That sounds innocent enough, but you see he successfully used the same tactic in my pre-trial hearing. My neighbors testified under oath that they *saw* the federal agents attack us at our home and noted the time was as we testified, 5:30 in the morning. An illegal and a criminal act. The federal agents, under oath gave conflicting times, while testifying that their watches were all calibrated to the same time at the home barracks. But anyway, under cross examination, the government attorney asked the neighbor husband if they were our friends (spoken in an accusatory voice and ambience designed to impress and make an unspoken statement). The neighbor caught the gist and rather sheepishly replied, "Yes." He should have left out the sheepish expression and he should have more correctly responded they are neighbors and acquainted with us, met us a few times and spoke, but not really close enough at that juncture to be referred to as friends. They had just recently moved in. You see the innuendo: the neighbors are friends of this criminal Stevens family and of course will lie for them. In my opinion, attorneys as a general group are the predators of the world. In this instance the government attorney was attempting to invoke the same statement, but he was dealing cards to an experienced witness who has already been through this trickery. Dr. Brisbin responded. He said he has worked with Glenn Bui in cases and mentioned the case referred to earlier – the Tellings case that exposed some of the criminal actions of HSUS. He mentioned his relationship with Glen Bui as an expert witness for cases where prosecutors attempted to victimize the breed and breed owners, had broadened. Exclaiming that it is not relevant to the case and so not to be lengthy, one example is that he was working with a much endangered breed called the New Guinea singing dog, one of the rarest dogs on earth, and entrusted Glen with several puppies. The attorney quickly bowed out at that juncture.

I feel that Dr. Brisbin diluted all of the outrageous and ridiculous allegations of the prosecution and their witnesses. My feeling is that while at one nexus in my trial experience it looked like I would not be allowed any witnesses, turned around and I couldn't get better, more informative witnesses. I was shocked to find that Dr. Brisbin was campaigning now for our breed and other animals victimized by animal activists and was so experienced at this. I was overwhelmed that he would be a witness in this trial. I am saying, in my heart, this has to be a provision of the Lord.

This is a good place to inject the following observation: I realize you may not be a Christian. If that is the case, it is my wish this is all a good read anyway. I am a journalist and I seek to give a thorough report of my feelings and my own perspective. That does not mean I think I should or could force my perspective on anyone else, nor is it innuendo to impress that I am cleaner or more moralistic than others. I am human and as weak and "dumb as a sheep" as any human. Yoga is Hindu. Christians engage in Yoga, but that does not mean they have to be Hindu. I practice Yoga, but I do not seek oneness with an unthinking unloving cosmos. I seek oneness with the *Creator* of the cosmos. My personal perspective is the same as my little grandson had when he was no taller than my belly button. You can't make something out of nothing, unless you're God. I have read Yale and Harvard professors/scientists that don't comprehend this; who believe our earth was formed when an atom split with a huge bang. Where did the atom come from and how do the electrons within the atom behave in a mathematical pattern? And how does life come about? A child has these questions. But that is my personal paradigm. I am well read in Buddhism, particularly Zen Buddhism and Taoism. Christianity is me. Some Hindu Yogis celebrate Christmas with a Christmas tree and presents, but that does not mean they have to be Christian. I look at it that way. Karate is an art based on the Shinto religion. I am ranked and teach karate. I don't believe or teach the Shinto religion myself. This is America, and so it's okay. Right? Please enjoy your read.

So Dr. Brisbin testified that all three videos in my case contained serious educational and/or scientific value. He stated that he will use some or all of them as teaching tools in his graduate and undergraduate courses in animal behavior. And one cannot help but wonder, did the jury not hear all this? And why then was I convicted. It took the jury a very short time to come back with a unanimous vote: guilty.

First, the justice system, in this case, gives the government the first closing argument. Then the defense is allowed to give his closing argument and rebuttal. And then, since the burden of proof is on the government to prove beyond a degree of reasonable doubt that the defendant is guilty, the government gets a last say. I comprehend the reason for the government having the last take, but it is still not fair. Defense cannot come back and object or complain about misinformation given in that ending closing argument. I am of the personal opinion that the government perhaps should have the last close, but not be allowed to make new convincing statements the defense cannot respond to. When a man's future life is on the line, the defense should not be limited in that manner, in my opinion. Well, again it is beyond the scope of this book to cover that whole travesty of a trial.

In his instructions to the jury, the judge informed them that the statute that accused me does not apply to any depiction that has serious religious, political, scientific, educational, historical, *or* artistic value. This is a significant aspect of that law. It means the depiction does not have to have *all* of those elements, only one. The judge instructed the jury that the defendant does not argue that the depiction in the videotapes at issue have serious religious, political, journalistic or artistic value, but *only argues* that they do possess serious educational and historical value. If I were sitting on the jury I would miss that little word "or." I would conclude, based on the defendants witness, there is no question the defendant's work is educational (how could anyone conclude otherwise). In fact, when my defense attorney argued this before the judge in the pre-instruction meeting, the judge responded that he would give the charge. On a personal note, I had begged for my attorney to point out I was a journalist for the breed by profession. I traveled to Japan and around the nation gathering data, I researched, interviewed and reported my findings; this is journalism by any definition, including Webster's and any stretch of any imagination. I pointed out that although not large, it has a political bent. The animal activist issue and that I refer to myself and my hunting buddies as "Christians" and make comments like God bless; this is a small, but still a religious testimony. But only *one* aspect is needed. I was not guilty under that law even as written. The judge, legally I suppose, did not misrepresent, but I personally feel the jury was given an inaccurate concept. The videos came with educational booklets as part of the package and that important concept was omitted. As mentioned, my work was and remains the only production in the world to do a dog fighting documentary with video and educational booklet.

So far as my *Catch Dog* video and attached booklet is concerned, the jury was totally uninformed of the degree of education included in the educational booklet as well as the artistic aspect. There was an artistic bent in the quality of the video and it taught how to catch in a manner that mitigates harm to the animals. Most hunting videos are about killing animals. Dr. Brisbin rendered impotent the foolish testimony put out by the governments' "pig man expert." In the "points for charge" from the defense attorney it was pointed out to the judge and to the government that it is perfectly legal in Virginia and Pennsylvania (my business came out of my residence in Virginia and the federal agents that closed down my business and charged me came from Pittsburgh, Pennsylvania) to hunt hog with dogs (as it is in every state in the union!), and that prosecution is prevented from making allegations otherwise. In addition to that, in side bar during the trial my defense attorney reminded the judge that it is legal in both states to hunt hogs with dogs. I have copies of the points for charge and the trial transcript shows this instruction to the judge. However, the judge in his instructions to the jury informed them that there is no provision under Virginia law permitting the hunting of a domestic pig. Virginia maintains a continuous season for (hunting) wild animals, which includes feral hogs. However, nothing in Virginia's hunting laws permits a person to torture or inflict inhumane injury or engage in or on in any way further any act of cruelty to any animals, including a feral hog. If you were sitting on the jury what impression would you get? What would you derive from those instructions? Would you consider the testimonial (and truthful) evidence that using Bulldogs for catch and farm work hunting is common and widespread in Virginia and it is not inhumane? I feel that the judge imposed his will and did so in a manner that is a shame for the legal profession, but I do not know law and so I may be incorrect. But if you want to know then, how could I be convicted given the exposure and truth my witnesses provided, now you have it. The judge added to those instructions regarding my catch dog work, by instructing the jury that the law does not apply to a normal agricultural operation. I instruct you (says the judge) as a matter of law, this exception is not applicable in this case. My attorney objected in side-bar and the judge overruled him and refused to retract that instruction. He had informed the jury that the rules concerning inhumane treatment of animals did not apply to normal farming practices (so for instance the use of electric prods is normal and part of an agricultural operation). Regardless of our feeling, when you sit on the jury you must abide by the judge's instructions in rendering your verdict. What would you conclude from those instructions? This section cannot hold the entire trial, but I must lastly note that the judge instructed the jury that the constitutional right of freedom of speech does not extend to a depiction of animal cruelty when the work taken as a whole lacks serious value. The government attorney (who was allowed, under procedure the first closing argument and then a final closing argument after defense closing) in his ending conclusion, reminded the jury that the judge in this case, Judge Bloch, has drawn a line where the First Amendment ends and a criminal offense can occur. In my view, the judge unprofessionally imposed his will on the jury. I don't know, what do you think?

All three of my witness provided the jury with cogent, concrete, factual evidence clearly showing the true social, serious social value. It wasn't sufficient because it was eclipsed by the sensationalism and fantasy fed to them by the government attorney and his witnesses and the instructions to them from the judge brushed the final layer of cement on the direction given to them. But, as I said, turns out better all the way around. Seven years is a good long wait to a simple human, but it was all for the best. The Breed became firmly protected by a Supreme Court decision that put a closing on the animal activists' attempt to end our first amendment rights, I became stronger in my spiritual wisdom, evil and cunning did not prevail, and the Lord was glorified. So I tack on an Amen to all that.

Jade M. Harris

Jade was not a witness in the trial, but she worked behind the scenes to provide help. She has fought many battles with animal activists and in so doing she has learned so much about animal litigation; in some measure she knows more than most trial attorneys. I will use the same analogy I have used many times. Very few surgeons can emulate the ability to stem the swelling and blood flow of a boxer between rounds like a professional corner man; most of whom lack any real formal education. I have watched many doctors treat their nurses like school children, when fact of the matter, outside of the doctor's specialty, the nurse often appears to know some things more than he does. I have watched this. It is like that with Jade. She has reviewed far more legal documentation, court transcripts, etc. dealing with HSUS than most trial attorneys. Many times when my attorney would say, "Bob, you can't do that," Jade would show and cite, "Yes, he can!" It was then my job to help my attorney feel it was her idea. Which is okay. Were I the attorney, I would be okay with that. My attitude is not that I know it all. I have been involved with Pit Bulls the better part of my life. But when Gary Hammonds speaks to me, I don't have this attitude I know it all, I listen! It was Jade who spent many, many, hours researching the big brouhaha about crush videos. She got online. She Googled. She surfed the net I guess they say these days. She researched the Library of Congress. And she *proved* the fact there never was any real crush video market. Not one single attorney in my case even considered that step and the attorneys ignored the results of clear evidence that crush videos were one big fabricated lie. That is just one example. One company produced this limited release (2,000) crush videos and on their own discontinued. I understood why my attorney could not be bothered with all that. But it is my nature that even when on the bottom over and over, I stay in holds. So I sent my defense attorney several email messages. I suggested that I fully understand she has to concentrate on constitutional law, not exposing the malarkey set forth by HSUS. But, I suggested, if you totally ignore it the prosecution's attorney will be prepped by these animal activists and believe me they are good at what they do. So said I tell you what, why don't you give all that Jade Harris sent you to one of the paralegals or law students interning, or even one of the firm's secretaries. Inform them I *challenge* them. I challenge them to use all the younger generation's expertise surfing the net or any other source and find any crush videos of live animals (the limited run was marketed on this website that almost all of the general public never heard of. I sure haven't. It features girls urinating on things and stomping stuffed animals and all kinds of "weird" is the only word I can come up with. Even that limited run of live animals was viewed only by those sick people anyway). I said suppose you assign that challenge to a few people that work in your firm. If they are unable to find anywhere, anytime, any crush videos apart from that small limited run that discontinued on its own, won't you then be prepared to honestly and confidently respond to any question from the justices regarding your opinion on those crush videos? Surely it will come up. Well sure enough Jade and I were ignored and again I can't find fault. We probably sounded a bit over the top to people not experienced with HSUS. And sure enough, one justice probed my attorney concerning the crush videos. He said she needs to get with the *real* world. In the real world the statute would not be used to take down hunting videos and documentaries. It has already successfully eliminated the heinous crush videos and that is what it is designed for. This justice, parenthetically, was the *only* dissention in the vote to give us free press. If he were informed of what the real world situation really is we would have won unanimously. She was not prepared for that and although she responded, she wasn't ready for that. To me, she should have said, well justice, in the *real* world, in fact the statute has already convicted one hunting video that is about catching hogs; a very common hunting and farming procedure. While most hunting videos are about killing this one is about catching and that video is the work of the Respondent (defendant) here. Moreover, in the *real* world, there never was any live crush video apart from a short run that discontinued itself. That statute didn't have anything to do with its discontinuance. And finally, the American citizenry is not interested in such horrific "entertainment" as watching sexy girls stomp live animals to death. No statute is needed to address that nonsense. In the *real* world, that crush video was nothing more than HSUS fabricated nonsense. That crush video malarkey, in the real world, is an insult to the intelligence of a common law student, never mind the Supreme Court of the land. Of course if I addressed the justice like that I sure would lose the case. So good thing

I had my more astute attorney. The shame of it is, we won that case by a landslide. Eight out of nine votes. But the shame is that one dissenter in his brief, made those same conclusions about the *real* world. In my opinion he should have been apprised of the real world situation. You know when I was younger, if I won a karate fight 5 to 1, but the one point against me was a technique I blocked and the referee just didn't see it (and that happened many times), it bothered me. Now that I'm older, it wouldn't bother me, but it did at the time. It is like that. We won, but it is just wrong that justice was allowed to believe the crush video ridiculous malarkey.

In addition, Jade sent a letter to the Supreme Court Justices. In my opinion that letter was more informative and spoke more on concrete legal issues than piles of amicus filed by the animal activist groups and by the Solicitor General herself. Oh, and the quote by Lyndon Johnson is my source for the quote I used elsewhere. Here it is:

"You should not examine legislation in the light of the benefits it will convey if properly administered, but in the light of the wrongs it would do and the harm it would cause if improperly administered." Lyndon Johnson.

Unbiased truth and the unfettered exchange of ideas are compelling societal interests. In 2008, the HSUS used graphic and exploitative depictions of dog fighting as part of a fraudulent Internet fundraising scam, ending abruptly with an FBI investigation. Under &48, tax exempt political organizations such as HSUS could effectively suppress any opposing political or moral viewpoint, while simultaneously using disturbing images of cruelty to create deceptive fundraising propaganda. The HSUS owns numerous for profit subsidiaries and generates "commercial gain" from the sale of "Off the Chain." In the footnote Jade shows their advertisement, along with their "forewarned, the DVD includes graphic scenes of animal cruelty and may not be appropriate for children." *(I want reiterate why is it so acceptable for them to profit in the millions and my work that edits out the rough scenes is such a felon? Other videos and print media depict animal cruelty far more graphic than that of mine.)* Also in 2008, the HSUS withheld publicizing videos of animal cruelty for four months, allowing unconscionable suffering, so as to release the carefully edited footage for maximum fundraising impact (and in footnotes she provides the public statement of two government agents to that effect, and a third notation that HSUS was being investigated in this situation for potential severe public damage and investigated for potential committed perjury). Animal rights groups on the FBI domestic terrorist watch list such as PETA have graphic depictions of animal cruelty to fundraise as a front for arsonists and other terrorist activities. In her footnote she cites FBI Documents: "PETA was formed as a cover for the Animal Liberation Front (ALF) and PETA and ALF were one and the same." In the same footnote she also cites the "Taking Action for Animals Conference"– cited by the nonprofit Center for Consumer Freedom as featuring at least one organization with direct ties to organized terrorism. The event was sponsored by HSUS and PETA. Nonprofit extremists believe that their (pernicious) activities have "serious" value and are often *contra bonos mores* (legal term meaning against good morals). It is used in the context of offensive to the conscience and to a sense of justice. Or specifically, "conduct of such character as to offend the average conscience, as involving injustice according to commonly accepted standards," in achieving their goals, yet are preferentially exempted from &48.

Unlike neglect, defining catch phrases such as animal "cruelty" or animal "kindness" have become increasingly objective. Defining them by animal rights terms is offensively over broad and encompasses activities that benefit virtually all law abiding citizens in some manner, such as food and clothing production, pet ownership, zoos and marine parks, or even lifestyle vaccine production. Friends of &48 openly target these legal activities while simultaneously striving to find new and better ways to kill animals (her footnote cites public stated HSUS Statement of Policy 2009).

Correlation is not causation. &48 has no provable influence on criminal potential. According to experts, animal fighting has continued to rise since the passage of &48, but statistics are easily manipulated (she cites as examples the many reported statistics of dog bites, manipulated data. *(And I would add that in graduate school statistics we learned there are lies, white lies, and statistics!)* Many children hunt, fish, and swat insects, yet mature to become productive members of society. According to HSUS, over half of convicted rapists and more than two thirds of convicted child molesters engaged in childhood acts of animal cruelty. Speculation has no place in suppressing the freedoms that our great nation was founded upon. We already have strong laws addressing actual acts of animal "cruelty," often having milder penalties than the speech criminalized by &48.

While there may be valid opposition for stepping on rodents while wearing high heeled shoes, the fewer than 2,000 people worldwide that theoretically enjoy watching it could hardly constitute enough of a "brisk business" to warrant the carving out of a new category of unprotected speech. At this juncture, Jade provides an extensive footnote providing the websites that were original but since taken down on crush videos provides "Search the Urban Legends Reference Pages" – and what to Google that unequivocally proves the crush video scare was a hoax. She cites several hoax sites and the fact that there had been an increase in these hoax sites, although distasteful, offensive and sick, not live animal crushing and all legal. Many of the sites alleged, didn't exist. In short, the HSUS introduced a crush video to Congress that nobody checked the credibility of, with the result that new legislation was enacted and a statute went all the way to Supreme Court, and it was all a hoax. Jade Harris provided concrete, very thorough, easily documented and verifiable evidence of this to my attorney and to the justices. Tragically, the language of &48 did not specifically target "crush videos" nor was its semantic construction ever really intended to. &48 mocks its legislative history to the extent that it constitutes a fraud of crisis marketing, perpetuated upon Congress and the American people. But "every collectivist revolution rides in on a Trojan horse of emergency." Jade cites Herbert Hoover who observed: Every collective revolution rides in on a Trojan horse of emergency. It was the tactic of Lenin, Hitler, and Mussolini. In the collective sweep over a dozen minor countries of Europe, it was the cry of men striving to get on horseback and 'emergency' became the justification of the subsequent steps. This technique of creating emergency is the greatest achievement that demagoguery attains. And now &48 is a source of legal ridicule. She cites a legal blog that indeed finds &48 a legal mockery.

Depictions of cruelty purely for commercial gain proliferate in mainstream media. Jade points out the *White Fang* movie that features an organized dog fight based on the famous Jack London book. Probably the most relevant here is a film documentary that I viewed back in the 1980's. I watched five minutes and then went into another room. It was disgusting; the most disgusting film I have ever in my life seen, and I only watched five minutes of it. The film was entitled *Faces of Death*. How in the world this film can be allowed (perhaps it has since been found illegal, I don't know), and the sick films of IISUS, and they make my work that edited out that gory stuff a felon, is way beyond my comprehension. Anyway so Jade cited *Faces of Death*. She also cited the 2007 TV documentary on dog fighting entitled *Real Sports* by Bryant Gumble. What Jade didn't know, and I was not allowed to introduce as evidence as proving social value to my work, Bryant Gumble wanted to feature me in his program on Pit Bulls and my work! He contacted my attorney for this. I had turned him down. History must be accurately documented and publicly available when unpopular speech or depiction might make society uncomfortable. All history is relevant, even the alleged "prurient interests of the depraved" cock fighters who framed our constitution, or that of former U.S. Presidents. Jade pointed out that Cockfighting was popular in the United States and was a big part of our culture. The government attorney for prosecution claimed bull fighting videos not subject to &48 because it is an integral part of the Spanish culture, and therefore art. I do not read that as any exception cited in the statute, but it impressed the jury and the testimony went unchallenged. To me it makes no common sense at all, and some of the most famous American presidents such as George Washington, Thomas Jefferson, and Abraham Lincoln were fans of the sport. Abraham Lincoln is also quoted "As long as the Almighty has permitted intelligent men, created in His likeness to fight in public while the whole the world looks on approvingly, it is not for me to deprive the chickens of the same privilege." (Cited in Journal of Popular Culture in Jade's footnote.) Also so cited, "the Happy periods with friends George William Fairfax and his wife Sally, who had left England never to return, as well as the days of foxhunting and cockfighting and evenings of dining and playing cards are all now behind him, replaced with the society of the officers' mess," *The George Washington Papers*. Jade also cites Jack London about President Roosevelt's comments on his book *Call of the Wild* that features a pit fight between a Pit and the wolf-dog. "President Roosevelt does not think a bulldog can lick a wolf-dog. I think a bulldog can lick a wolf-dog, and there we are. Difference of opinion may make, and does make, horse racing. I can understand that difference of opinion can make dog fighting. But what gets me is how difference of opinion regarding the relative fighting merits of a bulldog and a wolf-dog makes me a nature faker and President Roosevelt a vindicated and triumphant scientist." I would add to Jade's footnotes here by observing that in the 1970's I interviewed many old time dogfighters. To a man they announced that their daddy matched dogs and many of them their granddaddy and some for as back as they can remember. They all felt this is *America* and I have a free right to engage in my sport that doesn't do any more harm than human sports. All we want is to be left alone. And in those days, they all felt they would fight for that free right and the government would take and kill their dogs over their dead bodies. In those days, however, it was either legal in their state or where it wasn't it was minor and the police would confiscate their dogs and they paid a fine to get them back from the local shelter and a minor fine for the incident. That is the truth. They all felt that way back then. It was felt that matching dogs and chickens formed an integral part of American culture from our founding father's days. Before we get into Bob Stevens said this or that, I didn't say one way or the other.

    That was a long footnote; back to Jade's letter:

The seriousness of something's value should not be legally defined or dismissed solely by the perceptually distorted. *(Another footnote here – "Animal Rights Activists only see a certain segment of the population and assume they are representative of the entire population. It is called perceptual distortion, or cop syndrome."* Anger is sometimes displaced toward readily available targets rather than toward those who are actually responsible, who may be harder to deal with. Buyers of my documentaries were not injured, nor innocent. These documentaries were never intended to "seek a sexual response" and do not constitute a grave threat to human beings, nor were my materials disseminated to unwilling recipients. Attempting to modernize the definition of a word (obscene) does not change the legal context under which a statute was originally created.)

Obvious by the phrasing of their arguments, supporters of this statute desire to set a legal precedent, devaluating the legal status of humans by elevating the legal status of all animals to that of America's children. "The life of an ant and that of my child should be granted equal consideration," Michael W. Fox, former HSUS Vice President. *(I hope you can see how utterly ludicrous these HSUS people are and why I really do not comprehend why professionals that are supposed to have a degree of education and one would think common sense, such as judges and Supreme Court Justices, do not want to even consider clear evidence. These people are radical nutcases and as criminals who fund and support arsonists and other terrorist activities, a danger to our nation and why, oh why do they accept their really obvious nonsense?)*

As evidenced by numerous published statements, "animal rights" (as opposed to "animal welfare") has an end goal of using this legislative instrumentalism or "ratcheting up" as they call it to restrict America's diet (they try to restrict restaurants from serving meat dishes) and control the food supply. (This last sentence has a footnote that cites a list of published statements from "The Dynamics of Social Change" Get Political for Animals and Win the Laws, in the National Institute for Animal Advocacy with acknowledged contributions including those by convicted dog thief Tammy Grimes, The HSUS, The Animal Legal Defense Fund, National Center for Animal Law and Advocacy, etc.) It is a long list of radical statements and I am concerned I will bore you so I'll just share two excerpts. "Our laws don't require even remotely civilized care of cats, dogs, and horses, much less for animals used for food, fur, medical research, or entertainment. Our culture continues to allow animals to be hunted and trapped for recreation. Nearly everywhere, people can legally breed a dog or a cat repeatedly. Standard legal husbandry practices for animals used for human food are so cruel that the devil could not have invented them, and consumption of animal products has grown." "Change is incremental, ratcheting up the culture in fits and starts. At this stage, enacting laws is the most rapid means, far faster than public education. In the animal-rights world, 'compromise' is a dirty word. It should not be. Compromises can provide animals with far more protections than they have now. And so critical, they can ratchet up the cultural norms more quickly than public education and shorten, not lengthen the journey to much stronger laws." Jade then quotes the *public* statement made by HSUS President Wayne Pacelle (he was sitting in on my case at Supreme Court and made all the radical statements about me to the press, intimating I am this cruel animal person). "We have no ethical obligation to preserve the different breeds of livestock produced through selective breeding. One generation and out. We have no problem with the extinction of domestic animals. They are the creations of human selective breeding." The judges and all the courts want to accept these crazies as "friends of the court" and "experts" and "the largest protection of animals in the world organization." This makes absolutely no sense to me; how any professional with normal intelligence can accept these people for legal testimony. It is way beyond me.

The commerce of depictions currently for sale in the AKC Museum of the Dog gift shop, or books by respected authors such as Twain or Thurber, should not become subjectively criminal. Jade quotes both famous American authors: *"We went to a cock pit in New Orleans on a Saturday afternoon. I had never seen a cock-fight before. There were men and boys there of all ages and colors, and of many languages and nationalities. But I noticed one quite conspicuous and surprising absence: the traditional brutal faces. There were no brutal faces. With no cock-fighting going on, you could have played the gathering on a stranger for a prayer-meeting; and after it began, for a revival - provided you blindfolded your stranger - for the shouting was something prodigious . . . evidently there is abundant fascination about this 'sport' for such as have had a degree of familiarity with it. I never saw people enjoy anything more than this gathering enjoyed this fight. The case was the same with old gray-heads and with boys of ten. They lost themselves in frenzies of delight. The 'cocking-main' is an inhuman sort of entertainment, there is no question about that; still, it seems a much more respectable and far less cruel sport than fox-hunting – for the cocks like it; they experience, as well as confer enjoyment, which is not the fox's case."* This comes from *Life on the Mississippi*, by Mark Twain.

And then, *"His name was Rex (my two brothers and I named him when we were in our early teens) and he was a Bull Terrier. 'An American Bull Terrier' we used to say proudly; none of your English bulls . . .* (Rex once engaged in a dog fight that lasted most of the day. Thurber reminisces about this event with nostalgia, even fondness). *"Though Rex came of a family of fighters yet he never started a fight himself with any dog. But whenever some other dog started the fight he taught him a lesson. He always caught the ear of his opponent and never left it easily, once a fire brigade had to be called to separate him from another dog."* This one appeared in *A Snapshot of Rex* by James Thurber. Current "animal fighting" rhetoric has already created a reverse onus, destroying the livelihood and reputations of innocent Americans such as Mahon Patrick (known as Pat Patrick. I knew him. He was one of the top breeders of quality Pit Bulls in the world, and in the history of the breed) and Floyd Boudreaux (this gentleman also represents one of the top breeders of quality Pit Bulls in the world and in the history of the breed). A significant percentage of almost all Pit Bulls today have Boudreaux breeding in their foundation blood). These two gentlemen were to the Pit Bull breed what Babe Ruth and Ted Williams were to baseball. The government, with firepower just as they did with me, raided the homes of both these gentlemen and the HSUS saw to it that all their dogs were mass murdered before the men were proven to be just breeders and innocent of any crime. HSUS consistently, for decades, has murdered pets and stigmatized owners of disparaged dogs. In a footnote here, Jade cites a number of news articles such as "PETA and HSUS advocate murdering, not rehabilitating alleged fighting dogs, and acquittals can't revive dead pets..." Jade provides news reports of both Pat Patrick and Floyd Boudreaux having been acquitted of trumped up dog fighting charges and HSUS "fly-by evidence" leaves judges unimpressed. However HSUS saw to it that all his dogs were mass killed before he was acquitted. They started slaughtering Floyd Boudreaux's dogs (the result of a lifetime of devoted breeding) the night they arrested him and didn't stop killing until the next morning. The intake forms indicated all the dogs were normal and healthy. The horrific mass murder included 19 puppies and a pregnant bitch. Without evidence and without a trial they killed those dogs. This was an illegal act in violation of the 5th and 14th Amendment. The government is prohibited from depriving an American citizen of his life, liberty, or property without due process of law. Floyd Boudreaux was an old man, a renowned breeder for goodness sakes and I don't see why HSUS people responsible are not given jail time for this. The HSUS was quoted as observing that the puppies confiscated had to be protected from their mother because their mother's nature would be to kill them. Another HSUS spokesperson said the puppies were not big enough yet or they would be used as bait to get the blood lust going. What a bunch of malarkey! And the public and lawyers and government officials believe all this sick nonsense. And I again, fail to see how the courts can accept the HSUS as the largest protector of animals in the world when they mass murder more Pit Bulls in one day than the entire history of dog fighting.

They also mass killed Pat Patrick's dogs, publicly announcing that they are unsuitable for adoption. These are breeding dogs for crying out loud and even match dogs have been repeatedly proven to be rehabilitated and made into pets. This is another example of how huge and damaging to our nation HSUS lies are. They mass killed I forget how many, over a hundred I would say. Both Mr. Boudreaux and Mr. Patrick were famous breeders of quality Pit Bulls. So their dogs would win in the conformation show ring and all other acceptable endeavors including wonderful companion pets. They also were famous match dogs because again, high quality genetically superior breeding. The breeders cannot monitor what the owners of the dogs do with them. So the fact that their dogs are sought after and famous in the fighting arena is no reflection on the breeder. I don't want to bore you with all the public examples of innocent breeders that HSUS had law enforcement raid and then have their loved pet Pit Bulls mass killed. One other example was a Pima County woman whose property was raided. HSUS alleged she was part of a major multi-state dog fighting ring, parenthetically, almost every "dog bust" HSUS is involved in, they claim to be a major dog fighting ring. Actually, there is no such thing as any "dog fighting ring" and the police raided four separate properties. Before it was proven bogus and that she had nothing whatsoever to do with dog fighting, they mass killed *hundreds* of dogs. Actually I could fill this page and more with examples of not famous breeders, plain ordinary American citizens whose loved companion pets were killed by HSUS and PETA in the same manner.

Next Jade shows a picture that appeared in newspapers around the nation. It shows HSUS President Wayne Pacelle standing shoulder to shoulder with Dr. Steven Best. They are both smiling and showing a victory sign with their fingers. The caption underneath reads, "We will break the law and destroy property until we win," (Dr. Steven Best). Dr. Steven Best is the co-author (with other terrorist people) of books that advocate "direct action" and illegal terrorist actions. Dr. Best is a spokesperson for the Animal Liberation Front mentioned earlier that engages in arson, bombing etc. So, the President of HSUS has provided the perspective of HSUS to the public and really that tells the story and that tells the truth. Next to that picture Jade placed a picture that appeared in the news, of the HSUS CEO J. P. Goodwin (at the time). In the picture John Paul Goodwin is wearing an ALF tee-shirt (he was an active member of the ALF and HSUS recruited him from that terrorist underground organization). He made the public statement, "We have found that civil disobedience and direct action has been powerful in generating massive attention in our communities." Goodwin was and publicly announced his feelings about it, a distinctive member of the Animal Liberation Front. He was recruited by HSUS and became a noted legislative affairs HSUS staff member. Goodwin was a high-school dropout and he co-funded the Texas-based coalition to abolish the fur trade. He publicly stated "my goal is the abolition of all animal agriculture." He wrote that and other similar statements in an Internet activist listserv. Goodwin is a criminal who has been convicted of multiple crimes in several states. He was the leader of a gang that vandalized fur retailers in multiple states during the 1990's. The animal-rights watch dog newspaper *Animal People News* profiled Goodwin in 2000 and quoted him as "gleefully announcing a string of Animal Liberation Front mink releases and arsons against furriers and fur farms." Goodwin was a public spokesman for the terrorist groups. He made shocking public statements to the press such as referring to the 1997 arson at a farmer's feed co-op in Utah; a fire that caused almost $1 million in damage and could easily have killed a family sleeping on the premises. Goodwin told the news, "We're ecstatic." I have a news article dated May 17, 2005–Washington D.C. "As our nation continues to fight the international war on terror, eco-terrorism is steadily gaining prominence within the United States. Animal-rights extremists, including the ALF and the Earth Liberation Front (ELF), have claimed credit for more than 1,100 terrorist crimes and $110 million in damage. These have included arson, assault, vandalism, and other crimes against scores of American companies. The Department of Homeland Security recently added ALF and ELF to its list of terror groups. Also alarming are the relationships these domestic terrorist groups have with tax-exempt organizations like PETA, HSUS, and the Physicians Committee for Responsible Medicine." The article noted that Senator James Inhofe (R-OK), Senator James Jeffords (I-VT) and the Senate Committee on the Environment and Public Works will explore these domestic terror groups on Capitol Hill. Another article states that HSUS was exposed for financial contributions to an Internet website that was the main distribution site for the press releases of the terrorist ALF, between 1987 and 2002. When their relationship and financial support for terrorism was exposed, HSUS immediately severed ties with the web domain and ended funding it. The ALF then moved to another Internet. I would add here that my mention of HSUS and PETA and the other animal activist organizations as criminal is not me sounding off. I am a journalist and I am reporting the allegations and evidence provided by funded organizations, Senate investigations, FBI investigations and news reports. While HSUS convince courts and judges that they are "the nation's largest and most effective animal protection organization," I am appalled that the judges and justices do not appear to read the news. For example Peter Singer, who is the acknowledged founding father and chief guru of the Animal Rights movement (his disciple, Ingrid Newkirk co-founded PETA) makes the statement in the preface of the book *Animal Liberation: A New Ethic for Our Treatment of Animals*, "We are not especially interested in animals. Neither of us had ever been inordinately fond of dogs, cats, or horses in the way that many people are. We didn't 'love' animals." Here's more. It came with a Consumer Freedom write-up concerning the news report you will read in the epilogue about the RICO lawsuit by Ringling Brothers accusing HSUS of tax evasion, bribery, and falsifying records when they were caught illegally paying a former employee $190,000 to give false testimony claiming circus mistreatment of animals. I quote: "The Humane Society of the United States presents itself as an organization intent on saving animals, but in reality does almost nothing beyond increasing its wealth, which is about $100 million in tax-free donations annually. Only one dollar of every $200 HSUS receives actually goes to animal shelters. Meanwhile it put 2.5 million of the money donated into its personal pension plan last year. Yet its ads often say 'Join us in saving the lives of animals everywhere. Donate today!'" So what happens is that many people are duped into thinking they are donating to help animal shelters and other highly worthwhile endeavors. The majority of the donations HSUS takes in annually are used for hefty administrative salaries and benefits. It's also used for promoting and expanding its agendas via its large promotions and legal staffs. Additionally it's used to purchase advertising, buy mailing lists, lobby for a variety of animal rights agendas, including stopping all hunting, trapping, fishing, farming and ranching, medical research, and even pet breeding and ownership. HSUS is big, rich, and powerful, and a "humane society" in name only. While most local animal shelters are under-funded and unsung, HSUS has accumulated $113 million in assets and built a recognizable brand by capitalizing on the confusion its very name provokes. This misdirection results in an irony of which most animal lovers are unaware: HSUS raises enough money to finance animal shelters in every single state, with money to spare, yet it doesn't operate a single one anywhere. An example is what happened during Hurricane Katrina, when there was a second "storm" involving the backlash of grassroots activities complaining that HSUS had obstructed their animal rescue efforts, and then commandeered the lion's share of credit and by doing so hauled in $30 million dollars in donations. *$30 million dollars*! Whew! Subsequently, many activists groups and the Louisiana Attorney General called for a criminal investigation into HSUS fundraising. I recall seeing this splashed all over the news and I wonder if perhaps you did also. I am not fabricating all this, in other words. An explanation was demanded as to why this organization disregarded the clear intent of donors and spent such a puny percentage of money donated on helping victims of a catastrophe. Thanks to HSUS expansive and expensive legal department, the investigation was stonewalled. I want you to note – this is par - the shear power and influence of HSUS has made this type of cover up happen countless times. Instead of helping animals in need, HSUS spends millions on programs that seek to economically cripple meat and dairy producers; eliminate the use of animals in biomedical research labs; phase out pet breeding, zoos, circus animal acts, and demonize hunters and anglers as crazed lunatics. HSUS spends $2 million dollars each year on travel expenses alone, just keeping its multi-national agenda going. HSUS CEO Wayne Pacelle made a quarter million dollars in salary and benefits in 2009 and that amount is now probably over $300,000. It annually shells out over $30.9 million in salaries, wages, and other employee compensation. In contrast, it contributed only about $3.1 million of its $91.5 million operating budget to hands-on pet shelters. The article goes on to divulge the Ringling Brothers law suit for illegal payments, avoiding federal and state income taxes, and the attempts of HSUS to conceal the payments and evade taxes and the money laundering. In all of the blogs and public statements made by HSUS, I have not read one single denial of this in the last ten or so years, or since. It may be there, but I personally, have not read it at the time of this writing. I have read some blogs put out by HSUS trying to vilify Consumer Freedom and Humane Watch, but the allegations are fabricated groundless declarations.

Jade also wrote: "Statutes allegedly aimed at 'animal protection,' often yield the opposite result." I believe she means the constant legislation HSUS and PETA promote that gets turned into law. And Jade provides another footnote here. H.R. 857 (I don't know what new law that is, but another animal activist engendered one, I'm sure) is another first step into federal legislation restricting your rights as an animal owner. It has to do with equine slaughter and it does nothing for horses but everything for the political growth and bank account of the HSUS. It fails to provide any standard of humane care for horse rescue facilities now receiving federal funds. It fails to provide funding (minimum $1,800 annually for minimum care) for the huge numbers of sick and elderly horses that would be kept alive in order to promote their political agenda. It fails to provide care/facility funding for horses confiscated from violators or voluntarily turned in due to new slaughter restrictions, thus causing unnecessary suffering for the horses. It restricts euthanasia methods, hampering vets and forcing inhumane killing of horses. It fails to address the significant environmental issues resulting from the necessary disposal of thousands of carcasses presently being "recycled" through slaughter houses.

Jade then quotes Thedogpress.com.HSUS.Horse.Slaughter; "Like other such bills pushed by anti-animal agendas, it 'sounds' as though it would benefit horses when in fact, the exact opposite is the case. It is devious and deadly to animal owners." I don't know the bill title, but I do know I viewed a program that depicted a team from a shelter along with a bevy of HSUS officers with their law enforcement-type jackets raiding a rescue farm and containing this gaunt recently rescued horse and killing the poor horse in cold blood. The horse had just been rescued. It was still gaunt because there had not been time to properly feed and strengthen it. The owners had fallen in love with the horse, planned on keeping it as a pet. They were forced to stand aside and I saw the family openly weep and put their hands over their eyes while they watched their loved pet horse killed. The documentary said HSUS initiated this without getting the approval of a veterinarian, which makes it an illegal act - right there in full color on the TV documentary. That doesn't sound like the nation's largest protector of animals to this reporter. What say you?

Jade's letter continues: "Then, as if intentioned, non-profits sadistically traffic in the misery and exploit the suffering. The once dying sport of dog fighting experienced a dramatic revival soon after the passage of the Animal Welfare Act and has been a cash cow of epic proportions for the animal rights fund raising machine ever since." I would like to indicate another reason this aspect of Cast of Characters and Epilogue is relevant, is because you will note that back in 1980-83, I warned of this in my *Dogs of Velvet and Steel*. More laws never made fewer criminals. Historically, prohibition increases demand. Indeed, since my arrest, the resale price of this book has increased tenfold. The "drying up" fallacy is a legislative failure. I hope you will not misinterpret Jade's comment here or that animal activists will quote it out of context and make claims that show she is saying this book promotes dog fighting. She is responding to the claims made to the news media and in court, that since my documentaries and my book which they tagged a "dog fighter's manual," were closed down, dog fighting has been dramatically curtailed. It was another huge lie. Actually dog fighting apparently thrived and became more of an activity that could fit their description of a bloody sport, because some people started doing what did not previously exist. People read the wide-spread propaganda that dog fighters steal or buy little dogs and kittens from the pound and make their Pit Bulls kill them to feed their blood lust. People would donate thousands of dollars to HSUS to fight this; however, the problem didn't exist and the money was used for other purposes. Dog fighters made their Pit Bulls fight to the death and tear each other to pieces, tearing off limbs etc. and then donate to HSUS to fight this. So people would donate thousands of dollars and HSUS didn't have to spend any or much of it. They just show up when there is a dog fighting bust in their uniforms and take credit for eliminating some national dog-fighting ring. This gets splashed all over the news. So inner city people cross breed the pit to large aggressive breeds then back to pit. You get a huge dog that wants to kill and they put studded collars on them and walk them around the city, agitate them, and carve out an aggressive attitude toward humans so they can brag about their dog. Then they match them and video them tearing each other up. HSUS gets these videos and solicits millions. What did not exist they created. In addition, and speak of acute stress during the seven years we fought this tragic railroading, people started selling my book for anywhere from $300 all the way up to over $1,000! I was sick! I spent the better part of my adult life building this wholesome business to have our government close it down after raiding our home with assault rifles; meanwhile people are making huge profits on my work, the result of many years travel, research, and writing.

    Jade continues: "While our compassionate stewardship of animals is important, we do not need the over broad language of &48 to undermine the rights our forefathers fought and died for." Censorship is an affront to deeply rooted American values and here Jade produces her last footnote. She quotes Frederick Douglas, "I hold that every American has a right to form an opinion of the Constitution and to propagate that opinion and to use all honorable means to make his opinion the prevailing one." The Constitution exists not to repress but to "secure the blessings of liberty." "Federal courts were not created to adjudicate local crimes, no matter how sensational or heinous the crimes may be," – Chief Justice Rehnquist. "Serious" renders &48 void for vagueness, "intent" requires impermissible speculation. The failure of &48 to include non-commercial financial gain is a violation of the 14th Amendment. For all the foregoing reasons, and for the reasons set forth, &48 is constitutionally invalid in toto (legal term meaning considered in its totality).

    Respectfully submitted,

J. M. Harris, Executive Director of Legislative Affairs, All American Dog Registry, LLC

I'd like to add a few more comments to Jade's footnotes. I think they are relevant to the footnotes and to the other testimony provided in my Cast of Characters. In the news January 2010, a photo shoot involved in a feature story in Denver, Colorado, (Denver has a twenty year ban on owning Pit Bulls) showed photos of Pit Bulls compounded in a section of the municipal animal shelter known as Pit Bull row. The pictures displayed 3,487 Pit Bull carcasses that have been carted away from the shelter since the ban was enacted. In 2005 and 2006, 1,454 Pit Bulls were killed and the pictures show them piled up, including puppies. An updated picture dated October 12, 2009, shows even more. And they want to call dog fighters cruel? I wonder what the Pit Bulls have to say about this. Again, I am *not* defending dog fighting; I am just against the malicious killing HSUS and PETA are responsible for. I am against their lies and propaganda and I am against them using their influence to get innocent American citizens convicted and killing their family pets.

Early on and repeatedly in your Cast of Characters and the following Epilogue, I have asked you to Google Consumer Freedom, Activist Cash, and Humane Watch, etc. and find the sources for most of my exposure of HSUS and PETA and the other criminal organizations. As I started to wrap these introductory chapters, I decided to Google these sources myself to see if anything was new. I was thunder struck. But then, on reflection I understand it. It points to the *huge* funding and influence of the underground animal activists. The sites for Consumer Freedom are overshadowed by one site after another by HSUS. They go into great detail to discredit Consumer Freedom and Humane Watch. For years they never even had a comment concerning the criminal exposure they received from these funded organizations. However, it has gotten to the point of serious for them. These organizations, like Consumer Freedom, have testified in courts and in Congress exposing the criminal activities and the breach of the non-profit status of HSUS and PETA and provided clear evidence that HSUS and PETA have ties funding, legal assistance, and public statements of support to criminal terrorist affiliates like AFL and EFL. They point to the constant allegations and investigations of HSUS for tax evasion, bilking money from the public, and all kinds of rascal activity. So serious, HSUS was forced to respond. They have a huge panel of highly paid experts in animal law and debate and have had years to prepare. So you will find page after page of their argument and allegations about Consumer Freedom now. They have so much influence and power it blankets the exposure we got by Googling Consumer Freedom. And they try to mimic Consumer Freedom. They contend Consumer Freedom tries to misinform with flawed studies and op-ed pieces. They allege that Consumer Freedom infringes on the integrity of its non-profit status. They quote the president of Consumer Freedom, "We must shoot the messenger." It is an aphorism meaning expose the misinformation disseminated by animal activists' media statements. Give us a break! And it goes on and on and on. Folks, it is all malarkey as far as I can see. I have pages and pages of copies of news reports highlighting Wayne Pacelle defending charges against HSUS for outrageous and illegal lobbying, illegally obtaining tax-exempt status, etc. Consumer Freedom and the other funded organizations that investigate and expose the criminal activities of HSUS and PETA are not being investigated by the FBI or any law enforcement. They are not charged with illegal or even questionable activities at all. If any of the allegations of HSUS are true, I just do not know. However, I do ask you to notice HSUS does not even claim any of the exposure of HSUS testimony is not true that I can see. They sure do not provide any evidence the allegations are not true. Consumer Freedom and Humane Watch are not on the FBI or any other law enforcement list for investigation, nor is their non-profit status questioned by any apart from the allegations of HSUS in their blogs and Internet sites.

In Jade's letter, the picture of the President of HSUS with the Dr. Steven Best, together, smiling and holding up victory signs while they make the statement to the public, "We will break the law and destroy property until we win," should answer any questions regarding allegations Wayne Pacelle and HSUS made about Consumer Freedom. Consumer Freedom has not made any public statement about the need for terrorist acts and while they are in favor of the right of American citizens to eat Veal (a bit of contention with the animal activists and the core of their allegations), they don't commit arson or promote arson or make death threats or any other crimes in defending the right of folks to raise calves. I feel it is very cruel to raise a calf in a dark stall, unable to hardly move. I for one do not like it, but I leave all that to other people to write and argue about. You can Google all of this if you want to, I don't want to overly use up this book's space. My point here is how very cunning and clever the animal activists are. They have high salaries and are paid to study all this every day, all day. So I will present just one of HSUS published arguments against Consumer Freedom so you can get a taste of the forum as it exists at the time of this writing the year 2010. In the 1980's (as I recall), HSUS was exposed, despite all the expensive campaign solicitations, for not spending any of their funds to help animals by contributing to any local

Humane Society shelter. Their only response was to start giving a thousand dollars here and there; being very sure the news media knew of it. It was subsequently exposed that in fact they only spent less than 1% of their multi-million dollar budget to help animals. This was not much of a concern, until it became testimony in courts and in Congress in recent years. Here is just one example of their responses. It shows a great deal of planning and it is convincing. They say (dated February 2010, regarding the exposure of the fact they give less than 1% of their budget to help animals in local shelters): "Not donating enough to local shelters is like arguing the president is failing to stand up for the poor because he hasn't volunteered at the local kitchen. Donating to your local animal shelter is admirable; donating to your legislative advocacy group, one could argue, is also admirable. Arguing that a legislative group is wrong for not operating an animal shelter is as misguided as arguing that an animal shelter is wrong for not lobbying on a national scale for animal friendly reforms." And they reiterate their mission statement: "The nation's largest and most effective animal protection organization." Well, enough of all that, it is beyond the scope of this book to put the political scores at its core. This book is not intended to be an exposure of HSUS and PETA and related organizations. It turned out or evolved that way in sections of the "Epilogue" and this "Cast of Characters" because of my case and battle to protect our freedom from those rascals. But my motive is to journalize the history behind the book you now own and the federal case that it was a part of (I was not convicted for the book, but the book and my whole business promoting the show ring, weight pulling etc. was closed down) and to thoroughly inform you that I am no dog fighter and I am no promoter of dog fighting, but rather a journalist. I am a writer and a journalist for the breed and a promoter of those activities that put our breed into mainstream America. The book is about the American Bulldog, but the animal activists have made the book you hold a forum and that is why I want you to know the truth.

I hope you can see how very impressed I am with Jade Harris. And keep in mind please; Jade was not motivated by gaining accolades or a track record for winning a case or professional standing. She was motivated by exposing the truth. She did this with her own time and expense. She didn't charge or make a penny for it! At the time, she had never met me and didn't even know me! Rendering the charge that the best things in life are free a truism. At a time when America is suffering from a recession, when small businesses are going bankrupt in droves and we are plagued with terrorists (including the top of the FBI's list of eco-terrorism HSUS and their affiliates, AFL and EFL), the animal activists have rubbed raw this issue of animal cruelty. To me, in two short pages (along with five pages of footnotes that *documents* every piece of evidence and testimony – easily verified) she efficiently and very methodically, meticulously, in detail, disabused the whole argument by the HSUS and animal activist influenced government, in my case. In my opinion she cut through the chase and presented the entire case in a manner far superior than every one of my attorneys. I must diffuse that statement by acknowledging, that as mentioned redundantly, the highest judges in the land "can't handle the truth." It is not about justice, truth, or legality. It is about attorneys who know how to work the system the best. And therein is the rub.

Jade also answered legal questions for me that my attorneys just did not have time to answer or would ignore. She does not know more law than a professional attorney, of course, but she does know a lot about the law. She knows animal activists up one side and down the other and has been involved in numerous court cases. She knows animal activism and the legal tricks of attorneys. She was as helpful in my case as a boxer's corner man, as far as I am concerned. So I feel compelled to tack her onto the Cast of Characters in this historical account of the book you hold in your hands. When we won in Supreme Court, Tom Lundberg, President of the Lone Star Pit Bull Club, bought me a plane ticket to come to the Lone Star Annual ADBA sanctioned show. What a wonderful gesture. I was guest speaker. Jade was there and she had a table set up displaying her art. I was thunder struck. Her art was so creative and impressive.

I think the speech I gave that day is relevant so I would like to share it with you. Here it is:

AMERICA

Thank God we can still say thank God for America. I still have faith in America. We are not a Nazi, book-burning nation. We are not going silently into the night. America does have troubles. We have activists. Criminals even in the courtroom. Activists who want to make it illegal to say in God we trust. Activists who get all a-n-g-r-y and pass anti-tethering laws, mandatory breed specific insurance laws, all based on misinformation, which is a nice word for "lies."

Police violence is escalating exponentially, in America. I am, unfortunately by far, not the only victim of police violence. Police banging on our door, attacking our home in the dead of the night (which is illegal), and attacking us with assault rifles, clad all in black, including black ski masks and screaming at the top of their lungs, waving their assault rifles at my disabled wife Julie, in her bathrobe. And when I calmly told them we are cooperating and she has a weak heart, they just ignored me and kept up, their idiotic adrenalin screaming. They acted like school boys playing cops and robbers, but they played with deadly weapons; bullying a middle aged housewife in her bathrobe for goodness sake. When done, they went around, high fives. Yeah! Completed their mission. Idiotic kids!

The federal agents committed perjury in court, that is another nice word for "they lied" and the judge ignored it. You can read it in the court transcripts. The court recorder left my exposure of that segment of their testimony and mine out of the court transcript; again, illegal.

In America we used to be innocent until proven guilty. But in my trial, the jury was informed that my case was the United States Government vs. Criminal number 04-51 (that's me). The ironical thing is I did not lie, not even some little exaggeration or use legal tricks. The U.S. Government did nothing but break the law, lie, manipulate, deceive, and resort to cheap legal tricks. Just to build a case and win.

Well the story is long; I was more than railroaded down a long, long, winding road.

We don't have to lie down and give up. Stand up, get up, and fight. How? All I can do is share my way.

My way was the same as a warrior named David. He wrote it down for us in Psalm 35. Read it. Pray it. Psalm 35. I added only a few words to embellish the whole Psalm. I began, contend – o Lord, divine warrior, contend with those who contend with me. Fight against those who fight with me.

I have a question, and I am not being one bit melodramatic. Is the HSUS more powerful than our God; God who created the stars and calls them by name (Psalm 147)? The God who created the United States of America; and He created us?

I will tell you the truth. I was set up and I was going down. I prayed to our Living Creator God who hates crafty, deceiving, liars.

I didn't win the case. My attorneys didn't win the case. God did! God won and the glory is His.

Well, let me wrap this up with some words for Americans; for Texans. Will Durant was one of the most influential and renowned experts on the history of civilizations. He wrote: "Civilization begins with order, grows with liberty, and dies with chaos." And, he said: "A great civilization is not conquered without until it has destroyed itself within."

Do you know that one word, just one word, could change the entire destiny of the American Pit Bull Terrier? Yes, I said American. The legal destiny and therefore the right of the entire legal realm of the show ring and field trials for the American Pit Bull Terrier hinges on that one word. That one word is **honesty**!

And that one word won our case in the Supreme Court, and it changed the American government and special interest animal activist groups back to the SPIRIT of Thomas Jefferson, Patrick Henry, James Madison, and George Washington, which is government by the people. Freedom is not free.

Carl Sagen said, "Credulous acceptance of baloney can lose you money; that's what P. T. Barnum meant when he said, 'There's a sucker born every minute.' But it can be much more dangerous than that, and when governments and societies lose the capacity for critical thinking the results can be catastrophic." How true.

"Government is not reason. It is not eloquence. It is force. Like fire, it is a dangerous servant and a fearful master." Who said that? George Washington. Ladies and gentlemen, I rest my case.

That was my speech at the Lone Star Pit Bull Club in Texas, and it is still my speech today.

When I was in the ring and so many thought I was going down, the above characters stayed with me and they kept faith in me and faith in justice and faith in America. So I feel they play an integral role in you having a legal right to read the book you now hold in your hand and in its history.

Well that is a wrap for the Cast of Characters section. Except I believe this is the proper place to fulfill my vow to the Lord that I will glorify Him all the days of my life in this body with my pen. So I have this prayer, another one I want to share. It is Psalm 116. The Psalms were songs sung in the Holy Temple of God. I pulled the relevant-to-me sections out of the Psalm and embellish it just a tad here and there. Here it is:

Psalm 116

I LOVE YOU, O Lord. I love the Lord. He heard my voice and my cries. He inclined His ear to me. I will call upon Him as long as I live. I found trouble and deep sorrow. Then I called upon the Name of the Lord. The Lord delivered my soul from death and He delivered my eyes from tears. I will walk before the Lord in the land of the living. I believed, therefore I spoke, I am greatly afflicted. Well what then, how shall I repay the Lord for all His goodness to me?

I will honor the salvation He gave me and will call upon the Name of the Lord. I will fulfill my vows to the Lord in the presence of His people. I will glorify Him with my pen. I will sacrifice thanks offerings to Him and with thanksgiving, I'll be a living, sanctuary for His Living, Holy Spirit. I will fulfill my vows to the Lord before people and glorify Him with my pen. Praise the Lord! Enjoy your read.

DOGS OF VELVET AND STEEL
Pit Bulldogs: A Manual for Owners
Bob Stevens

Chapter 2: The Epilogue

I have questions. The American Pit Bull Terrier is and has been an all-American breed since the formation of our country. We all know the famous RCA's Nipper depicted while cocking his head to hear his master's voice and those who are my age remember Buster Brown's Tige and Petey who was a stalwart member of the *Little Rascals* gang in the Our Gang TV series. Some of the most decorated dogs in both World Wars were American Pit Bull Terriers. The most famous, of course, was Sergeant Stubby, the most decorated dog in American military history. He fought in the trenches in World War I, saved many soldier's lives and even captured a German spy. The American Pit Bull Terrier is as American as apple pie and the breed that played more a part of the American frontier than any other. My question is this: why did these dogs all of a sudden become "killer" dogs in the 1990's? How come they were never a problem until the animal activists spread all the media rumors? Why did we not have constant news propaganda featuring these terror dogs mauling people until the 1990's? Some of it began on a smaller scale in the 1980's with the Rolling Stones depicting Pit Bulls used in gang fights and the now famous *Sports Illustrated* cover depiction of a pit with open snarling mouth. Pits don't do that by the way. *Time* magazine compared Pit Bulls to "the vicious *Hounds of Baskerville*" and covered a "story" of a pit mauling children in a "frenzy of bloodletting." All of this is pure nonsense. Until our American public began donating millions of dollars to organizations like HSUS and PETA to help rid the nation of this horrible breed, there were no Pit Bulls in the news. If you think perhaps I am sour grapes over my conviction and exaggerating or fabricating, I invite you to Google Consumer Freedom or Humane Watch or Activist cash. I am saying none of my allegations in this epilogue or in your book are personal fabrication; it is all easily documented and well known facts on the part of a significant aspect of American citizenry, breeders, and show people of many breeds, not just Pit Bulls.

Yes, the sad fact is that today the American Pit Bull is illegal in some countries and near illegal in many. It is all based on lies, deception, and misinformation.

I hope your *Dogs of Velvet and Steel* book provides you with a more honest education about the breed. It remains the only book in the world that not only promotes, but instructs and fully educates, international participation in the conformation show ring, weight pulling competition, the elite companion dog – Schutzhund, the hunting dog, and a socially accepted pet. I suppose this is the reason the animal activists have wanted to incriminate me so badly. The animal activist organizations have disseminated the allegations that this book is a "dogfighter's manual." That is obvious blarney if you read the book in its entirety.

So please, if you feel my statements concerning animal activists are a bit out there and far-fetched, then please Google ConsumerFreedom.com and HumaneWatch.com, ConsumerActivist.com, and Goggle news articles where HSUS and PETA have been caught with their illegal mischief and exposed as a covert underground criminal organizations that fund and promote eco-terrorist affiliations such Animal Liberation League and Earth Liberation League (again documented in Consumer Freedom and others). Read the myriad news articles where HSUS and PETA have been caught killing hundreds of dogs (sometimes all in one day) and tossing them into dumpsters. I have many of these news articles. I could write a whole chapter on it, but this is not the subject matter here. I'll let you do your own research. Please do it. Actually, I pray for the HSUS and other criminal animal activist organizations. "Lay aside all malice, and all guile, and hypocrisies and partake as babes of the milk of sincerity." (I Peter 2:2)

Without guile. And I would like to state that in my opinion, not all of the members and certainly not most financial supporters of HSUS or PETA or other animal activist organizations, are criminal or hurt animals. As many members and supporters of the organizations in which the top CEO cipher high salaries and financial perks tax-free, genuinely believe the misinformation disseminated by the top echelon. So I hope they will engage in the suggested Googling and find out for themselves.

Someone, in my opinion, must witness to the upper echelon of HSUS and it could come from someone within the organization. "For so is the will of God that with well doing ye may put to silence the ignorance of foolish men." (1 Peter 2:15) Keeping in mind "Professing themselves to be wise, they became fools." (Romans 1:22) So I mean well, not harm by the negative commentary you will read in this epilogue concerning HSUS.

I pray that their criminal activities in which they have been caught and court cases and news exposure is evidence of that statement and becomes persistent and numerous enough so that finally they are investigated thoroughly. Many news articles attest thousands of people petition the IRS to investigate their illegal practices. The FBI has been investigating them for many years. Like the Mafia, Consumer Freedom reports they are good at covering up; to make a very long story short. I hope they are closed down, but not completely closed down. I pray their criminal activities be ended and they return to their original animal welfare paradigm (HSUS was originally an animal welfare organization that received tax-free credit for its humane work helping animals and indeed they did contribute to shelters and help animals until the criminal element gained control, according to Consumer Freedom). As a postscript and you can find veracity for this by Googling the above, HSUS has absolutely no connection with the local Humane Society that *does* help animals in need; no connection at all. The HSUS took on that name only for the innuendo; they don't help animals at all. Since being exposed, they have started and make sure it hits the news, that they spend, on a small scale relative to their budget, less than ten percent. This is minimal funds to help animals. Until exposed, by the NRA, if I recall, in the 1990s, they didn't contribute a single dollar to any animal shelters or Humane Society outlets; at least I have a plethora of reports that allege that. At the time of this writing, 2011, they solicit and receive millions of dollars, about 130 million annually, and contribute less than ten percent. I am being generous; published allegations say less than 2%, of their contributed income goes to helping animals. They pocket and pay huge salaries and perks to the top CEO's and the rest goes to funding terrorist organizations, and programs like making dog racing, rodeos, and circus' illegal. In the news, HSUS was caught financing illegal false statements concerning animal cruelty at Ringling Brothers. Google it, you can find it. I will report differing income flow and percent because it differs depending on which year the report exposed. They even want to make it illegal for restaurants to serve meat, and fund animal activist sections in premier law schools. Over 75% of received donations go to solicitation expense; the largest percentage solicitation expense in the world it is alleged. So if you hear about them spending five thousand dollars here and there, that is like you and I spending a dime. They have been caught numerous times soliciting donations for incidents like Katrina to help animals and then only spending about one percent of it to help animals. All of these allegations I garnered from more Pit Bull publications and blogs than I could list here. But again, my prayer is that the criminal activities end and they once again become an animal welfare organization and this aspect of my *Dogs of Velvet and Steel* book becomes an historical aspect rather than the situation we are in at this time in American history.

    To paraphrase Gordon Gekko in the second *Wall Street* movie, if they will stop telling lies about us, we will stop telling the truth about them.

    It was a different word in the 1970's when the book was written. The primary concept in writing this epilogue is to negate having to write the whole book over again. Rather than correct all the errata, I want to present the book as an historical aspect of the history of my work with the American Pit Bull Terrier breed. However, I must retract many of the statements I made in the book you are about to read, because the nation has changed these past years and I must stay in the vanguard. I don't want to go through line-by-line and take back everything I said in those days that does not apply today. Rather, I want to make a blanket statement.

Dog fighting is an anachronism. I liken it to the western gunfighter. An interesting read of heroism, but something that just does not fit in today's world. The book you are holding may give the impression that I am not against dog fighting. Again, it is a different nation now and we must deal with the cards we have in our hand. However, I want it to be clear that dog fighting has always been too strong for me personally. I do point out in this book that dog fighting is not anywhere near the horrific engagement the crazy activists like the public to think it is (so people will continue to donate literally millions of dollars they put in their pocket), but it is still pretty rough and not something I want my own dog to engage in. However, the breed has been developed over centuries to be the only dog in the world that can engage in the activities I have promoted and participated in as you will read below. I'm saying my book deals with truth and the reality of the breed not fantasy and fabricated sensationalism. Our frontier was developed by tough Americans whose paradigm would not fit in today's world and so it is with our breed. That is my blanket statement. But I must go deeper.

As I have mentioned, I was a journalist for decades. My journalism was not limited to any single aspect of the breed; I studied it all and reported it all. I was accepted as a trusted journalist by the dog fighters of the 1970's because I did not lie or make up exaggerated sensational stories. I told it as it was. Moreover, I told the stories about their dogs and they wanted that. So I attended a large number of dog fights and interviewed most of the then active participants. In those days, almost all of the matches I attended were in a state in which it was legal or in a state where it was such a minor misdemeanor, the penalty was a fine lower than a speeding ticket and the sheriff and deputy sheriff were often in attendance.

And if I am to go on record, I want to go on record with the statement that I believe dog fighting is an anachronism that does not belong in today's society. I say that for many reasons. From the inception of the breed in old England and Ireland, the dogs have been used and bred for competition in the pit-gladiators. From my very first introduction to the breed I recognized the fact that you cannot have generation after generation of stupid dogs survive that demanding test. You cannot have a weak strain of dog and the epitome of courage is a prerequisite. Athletic endurance, reflexes, and ability are all part of a grand package that produces a superlative creation of God and developed by His created humans in His image. Those evolved athletic attributes can be channeled and maintained in the modern world with the now readily available activities that I have avidly promoted since the 1970's; that being weight pulling contests, Catch Dog work and the elite PhD of the canine world, Schutzhund. As I will repeatedly emphasize, Schutzhund is only partially about controlled man protection. It is first, foremost, and primarily a test of temperament and stability. What better way to rescue our breed and end its outlaw stigma and still retain its qualities than to engage in these activities.

I, an objective journalist, do not side for or against the dog fighter. I report truth as near as I can and report what I'm told and what I read in the Pit Bull magazines, Googling Consumer Freedom, Activist Cash and Humane Watch, and copying news articles from my files. No allegation of criminal activity or bilking funds from the public are my own; they all come from copies I have kept in my files from the above named sources. My paradigm is not to present a lengthy diatribe about the actions of HSUS and PETA; I leave that genre to others. I do, however, mandated by objective journalism as a segment of the historical content, find it necessary to present some truths. And anytime a journalist exposes truths it can sow dragon's teeth. I do attempt to attenuate the stigmata associated with our breed these days.

The very first article I wrote contained a bit of background on where my perspective comes from. I wrote, "As a boy, I read and was so impressed with all of the Jack London dog heroes and Terhune and I was especially impressed with the book entitled *The Bar Sinister* by Richard Harding, a book based on the true story of a Bull Terrier that lived in Canada at the turn of the century. He was a fighting dog when young and ended up a show champion. The story impressed me, especially because it was true, and I vowed one day I'd get an honest Bull Terrier. All that is well and good, but then I wrote that "when I first became introduced to the breed, I felt that matching dogs in a pit was a very narrow and inhumane treatment. As I became more involved with the dogs, I learned the truth, which is that dogs are happiest when doing that for which they were bred. That regardless of how they appear at pit side (when reporters choose to take their pictures), 90% of them live long, happy, healthy lives." Now I followed that statement by observing that I am so much of an animal lover and influenced also as a boy by Bambi that I won't hunt deer. I don't want to kill a deer. However, I don't get on the bandwagon wanting to make hunting illegal. I love venison (and parenthetically wild meat is from two to ten times more nutritious than meat from domestic animals) and if my family was hungry that would be how I would need to provide and I would not hesitate. I don't like hunting raccoon. We don't eat raccoon. They have value for the pelt, but you don't need to kill thirty of them in one hunt. Again, this is nothing I am going to campaign against and I love to read stories about famous coon dogs. Nobody who wants to denigrate me and bad mouth me is going to include those statements I made about loving animals and not hunting deer. They will take the statement I made about the truth being dogs are happiest when they do what they were bred for and make me out to be a cruel inhumane person that promotes dog fighting. So that and all statements of like ilk must be retracted. Dear reader, I cannot go back and retract every statement I made that does not fit in today's world from my decades of journalism. So I must cover those statements as well as statements made in the book you now hold, with the blanket statement: Nevertheless, dog fighting is an anachronism and those gladiator genes must be channeled into healthier accepted activities such as weight pulling and Schutzhund. Hunting can and should remain. I do not and never have promoted actual dog fighting itself. That's it. Period, exclamation mark. That is my answer to all the Bob Stevens said this and Bob Stevens said that; in and out of context.

There is a story behind the book you have and I'd like to share it with you.

"They touched my very soul and I tumbled, but I did not crumble."
Paraphrased from Whitney Houston

In 1999, Congress passed Title 18 of Section 48 U.S. code that makes it a felony to sell images of what is loosely defined as "animal cruelty" across state lines. It provided an exception for depictions that have "serious religious, political, scientific, educational, journalistic, historical, or artistic value." In my case, the government said speech could not have such value unless it was "significant and of great import." The congressional hearing that culminated in that law was all about crush videos that depicted women stomping small animals to a perverted form of sexual interest. Subsequent to my trial, I found out, through much research and the help of a colleague, Mrs. Jade Harris, that there never was any market for these so-called "crush videos." One company made 2,000 videos that depicted sexily clad women stomping and killing small animals. They sold 2,000 videos and on their own stopped marketing them. That was the extent of it. The HSUS convinced congressman and attorneys and even one Supreme Court judge that these crush videos were disseminated around the world and spreading. All one big fabricated lie. It is endemic of the sheer power of this underground criminal organization, HSUS (again the allegation comes from piles and piles of magazine, news and organizational reports I have on file). Moreover, a fact my defense attorneys refused to point out to the justice system; animal fighting ventures were referred to in the legislative history that became Title 18, Section 48, as not proscribed in order to not chill the first amendment. Animal fighting venture was not intended to be part of the statute to begin with! No judge was apprised of that fact and I do not know why. That reference could have prevented the case even going to trial. I never did understand why we could not simply *inform* that it was written into it animal fighting venture is not included in the definition of animal cruelty depiction. I showed *all* of my attorneys that recorded statement and they all ignored it; repeatedly. What did the attorney on NYPD Blue say? "There is as much of a relationship between truth and justice as between a hot dog and a warm puppy."

The government indicated the breadth of its power, however, by convicting this professional journalist for his authorship and educational and historical work claiming it has no "serious value" because it was not "significant and of great import" to one jury hundreds of miles away from my business home. Lyndon Johnson once said, "You should not examine legislation in the light of the benefits it will convey if properly administered, but in the light of the wrongs it would do and the harm it would cause if improperly administered."

Lyndon Johnson's remark resonates because this situation was not about an individual; it was about a nation that values free expression even about controversial issues, and the right to build our own business with our own creative God-given talent and work ethic without fear from an overbearing government that tells us what we can see, read, and learn about. Benjamin Franklin understood freedom. He said we must respect the rights of creative property because it is best for the security of a nation. My documentaries provided historical data in an artistic manner while educating the public about the true nature of the Pit Bull breed and the political activities of the animal activists. I advocated for the betterment of the breed by guiding owners to healthy activities, while avoiding the violent scenes that those whom I oppose so crave. And yes, while my work is indeed creative, the case was not about Bob Stevens; it was about America and all the other journalists', educators', and historians' rights to be American citizens as envisioned when our country was formed.

April, 2003, federal agents representing the American government, attacked our home clad totally in black including terrifying black ski masks, screaming at the top of their lungs and brandishing deadly assault rifles at my disabled wife while she quivered in fear and cried. They refused to calm down and speak rationally even after I repeatedly and calmly informed them we were cooperating. My wife has a weak heart. These young men bent on playing cops and robbers then saluted each other with high fives; they had completed their imaginary mission! Here is the story:

The Government Attacks A Peaceful Law-Abiding, Little Country Retirement Home

BAM, BAM, BAM! The whole house reverberated with the shock waves of constant affright. It reminded me momentarily of my general quarters when I served on active duty with the U.S. Navy. My general quarters location was underneath the gun mounts on the U.S. Salamonie. But this was not the Salamonie; it was my home, affectionately named "Windfall" by my wife Julie, when we moved here in 1995. Nestled in between little hills and on the edge of Leesville Lake in South Central Virginia, Windfall acquired its name because of it's near total isolation on the edge of the lake and it has a soft breeze that flows from the lake and bathes us with the smells of cleansing pine and antiseptic cedar blended with the friendly aroma of maple and poplar and elm trees. Windfall is part of a wooded subdivision of about two hundred acres. Although we own a sparse two and a half acres, at the time, with the exception of our neighbors that lived in a cabin on a hill across the street, we were the only full-time residents in the sub-division. With that exception, our neighbors consisted of black bear, wild turkey, deer, red-tail hawk, chipmunks, squirrels, and the proverbial field mouse. You entered our sub-division on a gravel road from a narrow two-lane winding country road. We don't expect company at five o'clock in the morning especially in our secluded spot on this planet. This was a motorcycle gang. Bikers. We had been hearing about several armed, forced break-ins in our community, but no motorcycle gang!

BANG, BANG, BANG. That whole bucolic ambience is blasted as the whole house shook to its foundation with the inexorable banging on our front door. I awoke with a sudden start. Why would a biker gang try to force their way into our home? Probably on the run from the police and seeking temporary hiding quarters. I am a martial artist with 30 plus years' experience, ranked in GojuRyu Karate, Aikido and trained in a variety of other martial arts. I had a ministry – Christian Martial Arts, I called "Crusaders for Christ." I have also trained in small arms, so I consider myself quite responsible with weapons. I had a concealed weapons permit, and kept a .357 magnum revolver, loaded, under our bed. With company, if children were included, it was put up. I knew that door was coming down any time so I leaped from the bed slipped the bullet proof vest that I also kept under the bed over my shoulders, the black long sleeved karate shirt, slung the gun belt around my waist, and snapped the belt shut. The operation took less than a minute and I was dashing to our side door. This was a pre-planned paradigm. That is standard for a martial artist; pre-plan. I had noticed that if the UPS driver or a salesperson knocked on our front door, if I opened my other, side door quietly, they wouldn't notice me. I ran to our side door, softly turned the lock and slowly, carefully, eased the door open. I bent low and eased my revolver and just my right eye (the main door is to my left) around the door. There they were dressed in black leather, black leather pants and black boots and all heavily armed. I called out for them to not move or I will shoot. They whirled around and I fired, bam, bam, shooting out the legs of the biker in front and immediately leaped to the side toward the railing, fell to one knee, and fired at another biker as bullets splattered the door where I was originally, and shot out the legs of a second biker. I shot for the legs because even a center mass won't stop many, but legs, while not a killing shot will end the capability to continue. Immediately I leaped over the railing and dropped to the ground and scooted into the thick weeded trees and brush and dropped prone, firearm at ready. And then I would wake up. Unrealistic? Yes, of course. It was a recurring dream I had that started not long after we moved to our peaceful home. The dreams began around the year 2000. Oh, it varied somewhat. Sometimes I dreamed the bikers surrounded us so I fired from the front door then ducked back in and dashed to the rear door, out that door over that railing and into the woods at the rear of our home. There always ensued a running gun battle when I repeatedly shot down one biker after another, John Wayne style. Don't worry, it was just a dream. I don't have any illusions about the fantasy.

    I am a born-again Christian and not just a Sunday-go-to-meeting one either. I study the Word of God and I study it as deeply as I can. I try to learn from David Jeremiah, Chuck Swindoll, Billy Graham, John Hagee, T. D. Jakes, Paula White, Kenneth Copeland, Chip Ingram, Sprugeon; the list is long. In other words I take my limited experience and add the spiritual wisdom granted to these apostles of Christ. I share what I learn from these people, along with my own spiritual voices from my Lord, with the Bible class I taught at our local Baptist church and with my beloved Crusaders for Christ organization. As such, I am not supposed to believe in the Paranormal and I certainly keep away from it. Nevertheless, it is very true that those dreams were constant and vivid; until they came, to a degree, true in April, 2003. To this day, I do not know what the dreams were trying to tell me because I cannot think of anything I could do to change the situation. But who can figure God; and I attribute *everything* to God. God lives in a totally different time frame from us humans and I have found sometimes He waits *decades* before He explains things to me that just appear to make no sense whatsoever.

April 22, 2003, Julie and I went to bed looking forward to our morning coffee in our little alcove watching the little criminals vie for the birdseed she tosses out every morning. Word gets around and the golden finches swarm to the feeders like Boston's Filene's Basement in the 1950's. The proverbial Chickadee and Titmouse dart back and forth. The cute Nut Hatch backs down the tree to get his share. Golden and bluer-than-blue finches display God's wondrous colors. Julie has named many of these critters. King of the hill on the mound we call "café alfresco" is Cheerio, a beautiful stately Red Cardinal. He is boss of the hill as he struts in proud dominion overlooking the situation as Mrs. Cheerio feeds. Mr. Baltimore Oriole enters the scene and partakes gently of the feeder and the Chipmunks, Short Tail and Cleo, argue like school children over choice spots. After a bit, the Downey woodpecker, Big Bill, with his unbelievably bright red top knot, always comes to the poplar tree and backs down the tree and enters the foray for birdseed. Cheerio may be "boss" of the hill, but I tell you no one messes with Big Bill. He just is not aggressive unless pushed. I like him. If a squirrel or an aggressive dove tries to push him away, he has only to present that deadly weapon, his bill, and they decide to go the other way. Sometimes Chubby Checkers, our very fat woodchuck shows up. Meanwhile the hummingbirds flirt with the flowers and their feeder. The flowers they seem to have worked out but the feeder; they squabble continuously over that all day long. There is enough for all of them to have their fill and four of them could feed at once, but they are not satisfied with sharing one bit. They just are not smart like us humans.

Pristine white dogwood flower petals dot the ground as God seems to have tossed them there just for our pleasure. The crimson red dogwood berries splash around the flower petals. I am no artist, but I have not seen the most famous artists duplicate those lush colors created by God. The whole exhibition is emblazoned with extravagantly beautiful butterflies fluttering randomly about Julie's planted rose bushes and busy bees hum and pollinate Julie's polychromatic plants. The whole landscape scintillates with a profound, lively brilliance. As day time elevates higher and higher the rhythm goes to cicadas and the scurry of squirrels through the leaves. No sound of cars passing, only the silver silence of God's wonderful woodland. So placid and pacific a peaceful spot on God's created planet. In the evening we would have our coffee on the back deck and listen to the crickets and the katydids sing their squeaks. Nestled between wooded hills, the chuck-wills widow and whippoorwill symphony that no human can duplicate would echo. The hunting call of the horned owl and the screech of the screech owl would send their clarion call, that rapturous, lyrical resonance of God's harmony that said thrice-fold cannot be replicated by any human technology. We moved to this arcadia shortly after I retired as a Professor of Accounting and Management, ready to live out the rest of our days in peace on the income of a small retirement business I had built since the 1970's. We thought.

About 5:30 the next morning, it was pitch black outside and about ten minutes earlier, Julie had wakened me because through our skylight she saw bright flashing lights and then through our nearly all glass side bedroom windows, it looked like a caravan of cars or something coming down the hill. The gravel road leads to our home. We have a lot of shooting stars or something, which we see when we watch the planetarium sky through the skylight above our bed at night above our wooded home and I joke, telling her they are space aliens. I joked again, telling her the space people probably came to visit; don't worry they are friendly. Oh, Rob! She got up to go to the bathroom and saw the lights, briefly outside. Probably those neighbors up on the hill. I went back to sleep. Suddenly, my dreams materialized like a sudden thunder strike. BAM, BAM, BAM on our front door, the whole house shaking. I hear a bunch of hollering and screaming outside. Immediately I follow up on my plan. Except that door is coming in; I don't have time for the vest or even to click on my gun belt. I whisk my revolver from its holster, eared back the hammer, dashed to the aforementioned side door, and as planned very carefully ease it open and sight around it. So dark, I suddenly change my planned sighting on the legs and sighted in on center mass on the very dark figure in the lead facing my front door. Then I focused on the legs. They don't see me and all I see is a gang of fellows dressed completely in black. I start to sing out and one little fortuitous thing probably saved my life. Through the trees and brush I spotted, out of the corner of my eye, blue lights flashing, such as police vehicles have! Whoops! This might be the police! In a flash I ducked back into the house ease the hammer back down and set my revolver on the floor and very carefully stepped back out for a closer look. The lead person then sensed me and in a flash he whirled leveling an assault rifle dead center on my center mass. Too late! I propelled back inside. I had come within a *finger twitch* of shooting a federal agent, which would have resulted in my being riddled by a federal assault team. Very s-l-o-w-l-y, I stuck my hands outside and sang out, "I am coming out unarmed. I have a loaded revolver I set on the floor." Very slowly I stepped out. Immediately they charged me yelling and screaming. I ended up on my knees with my hands up and Julie in her bathrobe trembling in fright and crying while they leveled assault rifles at us. They were dressed entirely in black with black ski masks and black boots. They ordered us back into the house and we sat in the kitchen while they surrounded us screaming at the top of their lungs. So many yelling I could not tell what anyone was saying. I tried to be the calm and restless breeze that tames the violent sea as taught in karate. In a quiet but firm voice I asked them, "Gentlemen, my wife has asthma, emphysema, COPD, and a weak heart. We are co-operating. Would you please calm down and tell us what this is about? What you are doing is very dangerous to her." I nodded at Julie. They ignored me and continued screaming. Something about, "You will tell us where all the weapons are in the house – now!" I got that. Repeated my request and told them I will tell you where all my weapons are; and I did. They continued to keep their assault weapons leveled on us while Julie trembled. To say she was petrified is mild. I don't have the words. You would have to be there and smell the ambience of the terror.

 How can I describe my feelings without seeming to make statements about my bravery and "what I would do?" You see I was so torn. It is a male thing. We were created to have a natural inclination to protect our family. That is what makes young men be soldiers to defend their country and family. I knew if I defended my wife against their idiotic stares and assault rifle pointing, I would die. I would be literally riddled with bullets and given their mentality, Julie probably caught in crossfire. Yet, several times I slapped my thigh and sighed, starting to "get it on," as they would not stop their childish adrenalin attitude, frightening Julie so badly. Just when I thought of selecting the most prominent character, they would soften their eyes and slightly lower their firearms. I hope you will not get the impression I had some romantic idea of what I could do. I am a highly trained martial artist, but they surrounded me with assault rifles and they were too far away and they were hyped to fire at the slightest sign of aggression or even a "smile and approach with hands in view." Again, I am simply a family man who has a mindset that I am supposed to defend my family from unwarranted attack. Nor am I an idiot who thinks he could get away with a disarm under those circumstances. It is true that I am ADD (attention deficit disoriented), one syndrome of which is a lack of common sense fear. When younger, there was no question. I would have been thoroughly convinced I could probably take them all down and then I would have been killed. Now, I have learned to control those tendencies. One more time; I just didn't know what to do because I should be prepared to die for my wife if she is sobbing while they threaten her. It bothers me to this day.

At this point I thought (as I have seen happen repeatedly on court TV and read in the news), they had the wrong house and were looking for drug dealers. So I would ask them to "please tell us what is going on, I think you have the wrong residence." At that point they would raise their firearms and one would shout that I am to not talk and I will be informed when the house is cleared. More adrenalin. I kept thinking– I am supposed to defend my home with my life, yet this is not Nazi militants, not bikers; this is our own American government. What am I supposed to do? I have asked many, many church members, men who have been in the military and fought for our country, the same question. What would they have done? I found a unanimous response; each one said, "I guess I'd be dead now, as I would defend my wife against such an assault," or words to that effect.

After they had secured all of my "weapons," they informed the lead agent the house is secure. He nodded and they removed their black ski masks and lowered their weapons. The agents then approached each other and slapped hands in high fives, yelling, "Yeah! Yeah!" Their eyes held the wild-eyed adrenalin of wild horses. More like school children playing cowboys and Indians; only they played with assault rifles. I was astounded that representatives of our law enforcement had the mentality of little boys playing cops and robbers and I am not exaggerating, that is not hyperbole. Real brave men these cowboys. They completed their "mission impossible" terrorizing cooperative middle aged people. I may be a martial artist, but we are peaceful folk who tried to retire to a friendly quiet rural community with our small retirement business. I think it is a pathetic thing for the American government to do to us, and a pathetic thing to do to this little corner of God's planet.

The head agent at that time, standing in the middle pointedly looked at his watch and announced, "It is now 6-oh-three; ah, make that six-oh-two." This statement would subsequently indicate an aspect of perjury on the part of this agent when he lied in court. In court he stated that he was outside the house in his car at this time while another agent quoted a different time in court under oath. It means, as we will see, that they made an illegal search and seizure, committed blatant perjury in court and the court system not only ignored but allowed it. You will see that the court recorder even eliminated my testimony in part of this from the transcript of the court hearing; another illegal act that was ignored. We used to watch stuff like this in the movies. We found that indeed the government and law enforcement really does stuff like this. What a terrible thing to happen to America. Not to say America was ever perfect or were our founding fathers for that matter, but we have truly degraded what our country was founded for. Moreover, we are astonished to note that while this journalist never committed one illegal act or lied, the government, and even the judge in this author's abject opinion, repeatedly lied and committed illegal acts! While some of them continued the search of our home, a few were assigned to watch Julie and me. They talked about how close they came to shooting me and talked about how earlier in the year they had killed a retired police officer "by accident" while on the job. Evidently they attacked his home in similar fashion and he greeted them with a revolver. They would find later that the revolver was empty. I guess it was justified as they are still on the job. Part of the genre of this book, as explained in the prologue, is that America needs to wake up. I thought this type of atrocity was what we left England for.

While Julie and I were seated in the kitchen, I looked outside and noticed the spring dawn breaking. The sun rose from the rear of our home and bounced on the path down to the front of our house from the road, and with, at the time amusement, I watched the state trooper assigned to this event, walk down the path to our home from his patrol car on the road as a buttery yellow sun reflected around him like an painter's rendition of an angel's image, a halo. No angel here, though. He had his trooper's hat jauntily tilted to the side and the front brim pulled low. His head slightly down, one dauntless thumb hooked in his belt while the other hand hovered over the revolver on his side belt. He walked with careful measured steps. Oh my! How impressive! I recalled doing the exact same thing – when I was ten years old! In his mind he is Gary Cooper in "High Noon," for those of my generation, or Clint Eastwood in "Outlaw Josey Wales" for today's generation; Wyatt Earp marching to the gunfight at the O.K. Corral might be better said. And I thought, my God, we depend on these boys to defend us and protect us? If this is representative, and from what we see on Court TV it very often is – America is in trouble.

"Our Lives are defined by *moments*. Especially the ones we never see coming." - Russell Crowe from the movie "The Next Three Days."

My Julie still suffers from the sheer terror those black ninja police imposed screaming at her. And to this day I do not know if I should have fought to defend her. I guess I did the right thing.

This hilarious State Trooper did provide a moment of smile.
He was so serious as he strutted on his walk to the gunfight of all gunfights!

They proceeded to serve their illegal warrant; illegal because they served it in the dead of night at 5:30 in the morning, which is illegal federal (and State) procedure. Witnesses testified to this and their egregious behavior at the pre-sentence hearing, but it was all swept under the rug. The federal agents lied under oath, which is supposed to be perjury; you can actually read it in the transcripts. I pointed it out under examination, but it was ignored and the court recorder left that sentence of my testimony out of the trial transcript. I am told there is nothing I can do about it. In this free country of ours. What message are we giving the world about our "free" country? What is the message? They proceeded to seize my small business; one that I worked and bled to create for all of my adult years to prepare for my own retirement income. I believed in not depending on social security, but I believed, at the time, in the American dream one reads about; starting from scratch and from your own work ethic providing for your own family with your own created business. They confiscated my entire business and refused to return the legal aspect of it; the primary income producers such as an inventory of cases of books that would have taken us out of our debt ridden bankrupt state induced when they confiscated my legal business and ordered I could have no earned income apart from social security. This is illegal since they are by law only allowed to retain what I am convicted for. And I was told there was nothing I could do about it. It seems to me the government flies as above the law in America today as the government we fought to gain our freedom from; that my Minute Man ancestors fought to give us. In trial, I was convicted for a small portion of my business, but the true income producers that contributed very positively to the nation, they refused to return or allow me to market. We had only two sources of income. My wife receives a small disability each month. That gets used for her heavy medical expenses and generally it spills over into my income. I received a lower social security each month because I was forced to apply for early social security at age 63. That situation did not change for many, many years. The reason we were in this situation is not due to unwillingness on my part to work. All of my life I've been a work-a-holic and it is highly embarrassing, humiliating, and de-humanizing. But the government confiscated my business and took away my free right to travel or to have earned income for seven years until the Lord took over and I finally won my freedom by Supreme Court decision.

What business? Here is the story.

DOGS OF VELVET AND STEEL
Pit Bulldogs: A Manual for Owners
Bob Stevens

In the 1970's, I obtained a family pet I called Morochito (Sweetheart in Argentinean). He was pure bred, a breed the general public had not heard of, the American Pit Bull Terrier, simply called the Pit Bull today. The majority of people who owned them were mostly rural folk and relatively uneducated; not all, but for the most part. My personality is such that when I become seriously involved in anything I attempt to learn all I can about it. I was surprised to find only one modern day book about the breed; only one. That book was a small one authored by a Dick Stratton in California (now world renowned author of about six books on the breed). The book was totally historical and featured primarily old pictures of Pit Bulls in America and short stories. As a businessman I saw *an opportunity*. Bookshelves are filled with many volumes about specific breeds – German Shepherds, etc., but none about this then outlawed breed. But I was *amazed* and thoroughly struck with the sheer high intelligence, power, tenacity, and more adjectives than you want to hear at this point, that I found in this outstanding puppy. So I decided upon the encouragement of the many breeders I interviewed, to embark on a book. I traveled across the nation, interviewing Pit Bull people of all forms: famous dog fighters, famous dogs, conformation show winners, consistent winners in weight pulling contests, national level competitors in Schutzhund, the top breeders in the world, and researching periodicals and books. I reported my very thorough and deep research in all of the Pit Bull periodicals. In time breed magazines in other countries paid me for my articles. My journalism became in such demand that I was repeatedly asked to write a book about the breed. This galvanized my effort to spend five years writing the internationally acclaimed book *Dogs of Velvet and Steel,* now a worldwide best seller on the breed. The title of the book described my view of this singularly distinctive breed. This book contains chapters for the Pet Owner, the Conformation Show Dog, the Weight Pulling Competitor, the Catch Dog (to hunt and catch prey), the Schutzhund Dog, an historical chapter on the dog fighting, and a chapter on the care and upkeep of Pit Bulls. The chapter titles alone indicate it is not some dog fighter's manual and proves that is all nonsense. I typed it late at night on an old fashioned home typewriter. I found that book publishers make all the money and so I took a chance and embarked on to this day untested marketing ground. I did the layout all myself and provided the book completely camera ready to a publishing company. I, in effect, published it myself. I instructed them to await my orders to make either a minimum run of books, or a few books for myself and family for which I would pay the exorbitant fee. I wrote an article for the *American Pit Bull Gazette*, the periodical put out by the American Dog Breeders Association, the primary registering body of the breed. At the time they had only recently embarked on starting conformation shows for the breed and some previously dog fighter people were seeing the writing on the wall and that the old days of dog fighting was a fading thing. An anachronism. To be accepted in America, the breed must change its paradigm. I placed my first advertisement for the book you now have. My intention was that if, based on that one ad, I received sufficient response by the American Pit Bull public to finance the run, I would do it. I would keep all monies received in a bank account and if the break-even point was not received, I would apologize, return the money, and simply print out enough books for myself, family, and a few friends. *It was an immediate sellout.* I had to order another run on top of it. It was, as I had hoped, a matter of supply and demand. I had no competition. To this day the book remains, to my knowledge, the one and only book in the world that objectively covers and educates on all aspects of the breed. As a result I was invited to become a contributing author for the *Gazette* and remained so until the feds attacked our home. I also became the recipient of a prodigious quantity of fan mail that resulted in my becoming aquatinted with a staggering amount of remarkable minds around the world; some wonderful, some good, some bad, and some ugly. I was also motivated to enter the vanguard of the future with my own line of Pit Bull blood. I traveled to one of the top breeders in the world and obtained an inbred female puppy of the best blood available on this planet for the breed. I gave her to a breeder as I had no time for that, in return for my breeding my Morochito to her and keeping my pick of the litter. The result was my International Velvet. I entered her in every aspect of the breed, including the show ring. She shined in everything she did, including becoming a weight pulling, nearly undefeated, grand champion and was fully Schutzhund trained. I journalized everything she did so I could be a quality writer, I mean *quality*. That is the only way to address quality art. To me it is like growing grapes in a vine yard. It is like a vintager, cultivating grapes for a vintage wine. You have to love and cultivate and nourish so it will grow and flourish. The art of a quality author needs loving care, consideration, and constitution. That was way back in the 1980's and an integral part of my journaling. I reported my discoveries in many, many magazine articles. Velvet, and the plethora of articles written, was to be the subject of a third book I had in the oven, which included a chapter entitled the good, bad, and ugly of the Pit Bull breed. The book, a sequence to my *Dogs of Velvet and Steel* book, which represented many years of time sacrificed, and has nothing to do with dog fighting, was confiscated and retained by our government. It was not returned until after I won in Supreme Court and then I had to fight and threaten to go to the bar association, to get my work finally returned. That book will be the fourth in a series of books following this one. Along the way I became accepted, not as a dog fighter, but as a "safe" journalist by the now famous dog fighters of the day and interviewed and even got to know the more famous ones on a first name basis. I was one of a select few journalists in the world they trusted to write articles and report true events objectively and not harm them. Most of those people are now either very old or dead. They are now part of the history of the breed and I planned on writing about it. I had boxes and boxes of correspondence and notes, letters and interviews from dog fighting people, conformation show people, weight pulling competitors, the ones constantly in the winning circle, breeders and pet owners, Schutzhund people who were nationally acclaimed with German Shepherds; good people and sick people, from around the world. A collection of research data I doubt is available anywhere in the world. Confiscated by our government, including piles of data that have nothing whatsoever to do with dog fighting but rather the healthy alternatives such as notes I took when I visited some nationally rated Schutzhund trainers and videoed them. What the government had such a "compelling interest" in by confiscating and illegally retaining that extraordinary material I still do not comprehend. I know they reviewed it when it was finally returned after the Supreme Court set me free. I found a pile of notes they made tagged to all the good works and study I did for the breed. They knew it. I believe there is not one single person in the world as qualified to write and depict all aspects of this wonderful breed as myself. I do not mean to say that in a bragging manner. I mean to say I do not know anyone as versed in the dog fighting of the 1970's as I was, and also studied and participated – experienced- in catch hunting, Schutzhund, as well as show and weight pull – all of it! I do not say this to puff up my reputation; I say it to point out that I am certainly no dog fighting enthusiast, nor have I promoted dog fighting and my work attests to that fact. I have put in the hours of study that no one else has, into all these areas. I also planned to introduce the breed to Search and Rescue training and more.

At the same time, I found I made more income from this business than I did professionally; a strange thing indeed. I found that I kept my profit margin higher than probably any author, by until very recent years, not advertising or selling my book in any public bookstores; they all receive at least 40%. I found I received direct viewer interest and ultimate sales for advertising cost by simply advertising in Pit Bull periodicals. These days they call it targeted media. It was never intended to promote dog fighting. If it promoted anything it was to move this breed into modern activities, which indeed my work has proven to do more than any other with the exception of the American Dog Breeders Association, which I have supported all these years. These facts were never disclosed in the trial.

My International Velvet never failed to place
in the conformation show ring.

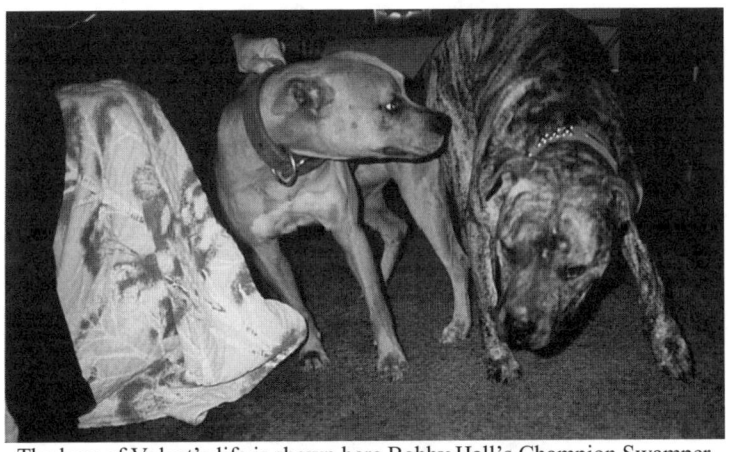

The love of Velvet's life is shown here Bobby Hall's Champion Swamper

The result of Velvet and Swamper was my International Victory;
the best Catch Dog I have ever seen or heard of.

But Velvet also loved McGee's iconoclastic Panther. She produced many
Panther/Velvet pups like these and they grew to be outstanding representations of the
breed.

This is Bobby Hall showing me his dog working his jenny. Velvet ran that thing all night
long. I checked her every two to three hours and she was still running/walking that jenny.

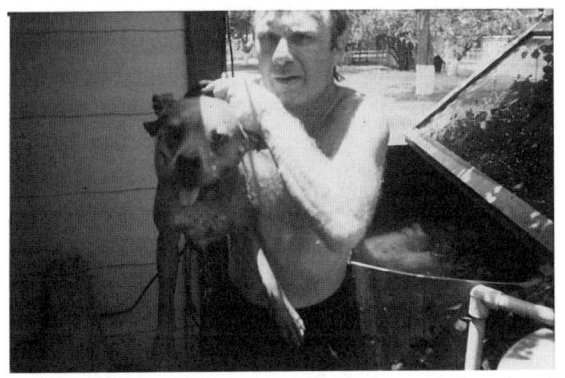

This is me pulling Velvet out of Bobby Hall's homemade swimming pool.

Me and Gene Smith of Greensboro North Carolina. When I knew Gene, he had the largest collection of inbred Honeybunch blood in the world. Gene's bloodline was central and made its statement with Ricky Jones his famous Rebel Kennels. We lost Gene to lung cancer.

This is Bobby and Swamper's father, Bobby's "keeper" Bullyson bred dog,
Jeanette's Robert. Scary dog, Robert. Same personality as Bullyson.
I learned a lot about conditioning from Bobby.

Here is me, Nick the Greek, and Bobby Hall.

As a Professor of Accounting and Management, I had numerous retirement annuities available, but I found more independence and pride of ownership in carving out my own small business that I could continue to work out of my home in old age. So I determined that rather than let an investment firm make the lion's share of funds, I would make current income work and let my retirement income be this business. Since I marketed and distributed the book myself, my profit margin was and remains far higher than most authors. My book rose in sales volume to the point where it generated more income than any other author in the United States on any one book except for a mere half a dozen; Stephen King, for instance, according to published statistics. Authors don't make money on published books, book publishers do. Authors make their income by continuously coming out with books until their sales volume provides high income. Since I received the total income on my book, rather than book publishers or book stores, I accomplished this with a far lower sales volume. However, as with any author, you can't coast on your laurels. It reached a point where except for newcomers to the breed, everyone had my book and sales declined. I had found a niche of untouched and fertile soil. The time *involved an overwhelming sacrifice on the part of myself and family for many years*, but was justified. Or so it seemed until our government attacked us in our home and confiscated my legal small business and closed it down.

But my next idea was to provide, market, and distribute a video that utilized the breed. It would be the very first video in the world ever made using Pit Bulls, to be marketed in volume on an international scale. To this day I remain the only author/producer in the world to do this, to my knowledge. This video was *Pit Pro,* the motive is using the Pit Bull for basic Schutzhund (a German word meaning "Protection Dog"). Actually aspects of the video are unique in the Schutzhund training to this day, for any breed, it is fair to say, as attorneys like to express. This was possible because when I decided to train Velvet for Schutzhund, I studied and traveled to learn from high profile trainers. I found even the elite Schutzhund trainers had a very limited, almost no, knowledge of canine conditioning and even their nutrition knowledge was limited. My *Pit Pro* video provided an education not found in any other Schutzhund training manual or video. Another immediate rise in sales of both book and video spiraled upward. I feel that my book and the video also opened up an exponential upsurge in the growth of the breed, not only in show activities etc., but in total breed ownership in general, until it received much public acclaim. Unfortunately, as I predicted in my book, mostly very sensational and negative, reminiscent of the "Doberman craze" the country suffered.

So I knew my retirement income was not only preserved, it was written in stone, with the plus that I would never grow old or bored. It motivated me to produce more videos; generally when sales volume declined. Events happened however that were defining moments. The government confiscated all that and wanted to put me in jail if I marketed this material that steers the dogs away from dog fighting and into field trials. Why? Because self-serving government officials want to *win* a case and get kudos for it. "Whoops we made a mistake" is not what they do.

Along the way I engaged in using Pit Bulls for catch work, which is hunting and catching (not killing, when it can be avoided) wild boar to bring back and put in a farmer's pen or for farm work. I did a video on that and prepared an educational booklet that went out with it. The educational booklet was not disclosed in the trial. There is a plethora of hunting videos readily available that depict more than double the number of dogs I used in my catch video, hunting down and tearing apart coons and foxhounds killing fox, even a pile of videos that depict more bay dogs and more catch dogs taking down hogs, but contain absolutely no *education* on how to train a dog to safely catch. My video and booklet remains the only one in the world to do this. Yet the jury found me guilty in part, because I "used too many bay dogs" in my video, and mostly because what I consider an illegal judge informed the jury that my work was illegal because it is illegal to hunt hogs with dogs; a lie. But the justice system did not allow me to bring this to the attention of the jury; that and the fact that hunting hogs with dogs is legal and common and that hunting videos are legal! You see, it was never about depiction, it was about the power of the government to do what it wishes to anyone.

In the book you are holding, I present my breeding program. I based it on the study of the famous King Ranch (founder of the modern day Quarter horse and beef cattle) as well as books written by the world's most famous and successful canine breeders. In my book I propose a breeding of my Morochito (based on his pedigree) to Jeep, based on the similarities as well as commonalities in their bloodline. I traveled to James Garrett who owned and retired the famous Jeep dog; a dog that subsequently became touted as the best producer of pits in the history of the breed, and his mother had an equal or better distinction. This points to the credibility of my breeding studies. From James Garrett I acquired a bitch that was inbred Jeep and double (inbred) Jeep's mother again in her third generation. That was the Born to Win (Winnie) dog mentioned along with her pedigree in my book. The result, not in your book, was my International Velvet referred to above, a dog that to my knowledge was the only dog and remains the only dog in the world or history to ever achieve all her accomplishments. I bred her to Bobby Hall's Champion Swamper to get International Victory, my third dog. I have always concentrated on one companion dog at a time. Victory was obedience trained and won first place in his puppy obedience beating a laundry list of high bred Golden Retrievers. But I never engaged him in any activities apart from catch work. But he was the best, way beyond best, catch dog I have ever seen or heard of. I guess I sound like the usual proud owner. But in my heart I tell you truth. Every hunter that saw him perform, and it was a lot, would say that is an understatement. His story will come in a future book. He was really something. I made several breedings of Velvet to a dog named Panther (who was very inbred Zebo, see Zebo in the book you have). My paradigm was to build my own bloodline that would shine supreme in the ultimate companion dog sport of Schutzhund as well as a superior bloodline of hunting catch dogs. Panther because this was and is the hardest biting bloodline in the world (in my opinion) and it would mean the protection phase, as well as catch work for the heavy holding qualities, would be preternatural. It worked. I did not keep any of those dogs since as I mentioned, I like to keep just one dog at a time as my ultimate companion. I farmed them all out to various individuals with partnership agreements for pups. And the pups I farmed out to others for my one day breed into. Well the government closed down all those partnerships and dogs faded and I have lost touch. Years of planned breeding went down the drain because of the nonsensical conduct of our government. I also bred the Victory dog to a Wildside Kennels bitch I named Beauty. Beauty was a final outcross that had related and the highest producing Jeep blood to get my current Pit Bull. Her name is Victory's Secret and we call her Vickie. Since the government closed me down I never got her bred and was not allowed to do anything with her, not even let her leave our property and now she is too old. More plans down the tubes because of the ridiculous actions on the part of our government. It really, really hurts because I so wanted my next generation to come from Vickie. This is where I am at the time of this writing. I don't give up. The final epilogue is yet to be written.

    For my next venture, I started on a video documentary on Japanese dog fighting in Japan where it is legal and conducted in tournament style much like karate. It had developed into a national sport and part of the culture. The travel and research was completed and it just needed to be put together, edited, and completed. I had no idea it was wrong in any way. I still don't. The video was an immediate success albeit not as significant as the others had been. Knowing that even the current dog fighting periodicals were not touched by the government, even when the editors served prison sentences for dog fighting. I assumed since the dog fighting magazines were protected by the First Amendment, as well as some pretty strong other stuff, surely a documentary on the historical, gladiatorial aspect of the breed would be safe and noteworthy for breed aficionados. I learned a bit more with each video and each one contained a slight degree of better quality. I finished my last documentary entitled *Pick-A-Winna*. To add to the educational content of these videos I prepared booklets that contained a great deal of educational material. I do not understand why this fact was not brought out in the trial, as the booklets point clearly to the educational aspect of my work. My work has clear historical impact, but I feel that is the weakest aspect of it, not the central. The central core of my work is *educational*. My position, and I believe it still, was that the public needs *education* concerning the genetic tendency of this breed to be the ultimate warrior. The gladiator. My position has been that you can't listen to what you have not heard and countless people are irresponsible to the harm of the nation because they are uninformed. Like a beagle will hunt and a retriever will retrieve, this breed will compete when challenged. They are soft and tender hearted, but in the competitive arena they will not quit. This martial artist can relate. I have been a martial artist for over fifty years. I have a very sensitive tender heart. I will meet *anyone* in the ring. Simpatico here. And that is another qualification I have to report the true inner nature of this breed. I believe it is fair to say I have been more responsible in steering people away from dog fighting and into healthy alternatives than any law or activist. Because I understand these gladiator dogs and my book was designed to find healthy avenues to channel that genetic tendency. Better the ring than the streets. Better the show and weight pulling ring than the pit. That has been my paradigm.

The Japanese proposed to complain to the American government concerning this atrocious denigration of freedom, but our justice system did not allow this for defense so it was squelched.

Authors live through very lean years to reap the rewards they seek. You need a great deal of faith in your abilities. I had that faith. From 1995 until the feds attacked our home instead of working for McDonald's or similar income producing activity, we sacrificed, living on as little as $500 a month so that I could secure our future. Concurrently, Julie's medical situation declined to a dangerous point and she became legally disabled. We had some very serious years indeed. We had finally come out of it, and I was in a position to complete the two books and two videos I had in the oven, and we would live comfortably and pay back the family that helped us and I could again become the patriarch of the family; until the government took our business. It left us with nothing, nothing at all.

Friends and family helped us survive while I applied and received early Social Security income, which robbed me of the higher income I would have received if I waited until age 65. That is where we were for seven years until my case finished at the Supreme Court level and my business restored. And that is why each month Julie received her small disability which always got used up and we lived on my low income social security and support from family. I became a convicted felon. My work may be considered a bit rough to many, but it wanes compared to Animal Planet and a host of more graphic yet accepted depiction. The Red Sox won the series, I am told, while the pitcher suffered a constant bleeding from his ankle. I was told the TV cameras constantly panned in on his bleeding ankle. That depicted more flowing blood than all three of the videos I was convicted for, put together. I edited out blood and rough scenes in my dog fighting documentaries because my motive was not to titillate with sensational footage (like Dateline, Animal Planet, and others who are free to depict bloody Pit Bull dog fighting with no educational aspect, with impunity) but rather to educate. Primarily it is a depiction of two dogs wrestling around vying for position, although one cannot completely edit out the harshness of the sport. My chiropractor informed me *all* sports are harsh, by the way. This is a report, not a trial, but I am, and for most of the rest of my life, will inform the public sector and anyone I can of this atrocity.

During all those years before the government confiscated my small business and vilified my work, I never received one single complaint or comment about my book or videos, publicly and internationally marketed, having anything to do with cruelty. I did receive piles of acclaim for the value of my work. For nearly thirty years my work did nothing but promote the healthy activities and positive growth of the breed, and I am internationally acclaimed in that respect. My work has never promoted dog fighting. I am no criminal and my family and I were in *shock* the American government can do this and we do not understand. Friends and family are also in shock and everyone cannot believe the actions of the government. We were all stifled and there was no one we could turn to. As Winston Churchill said in his "Notebook of Quotes," I felt like I was standing in a bucket trying to lift myself up by the handle.

We feel that since a simple 38 cent postage stamp would have been the total cost to inform this author he *might* be violating some vague and unknown law on depiction and all that would be necessary for him to remove his products from the market pending his own business generated legal counsel. The case was never really about depiction, it was about gutter politics and money. But again, there was no one we could turn to for help and we had no income.

You see it is not the American government that is at fault. It is an enclave of self-serving individuals within the government, controlled by a sick enclave of animal rights groups that operate like a cancer. Unchecked, they will spread.

That is my story. None of this was brought out in the trial and the jury never apprised. I don't know why, but I know nothing about legal proceedings. But there is the story as it happened, from the 1970's to April, 2003. That is my story and that is the history behind the book you have in your hand. The government took our business and source of income. What it did not take is the memories. And then there are the countless Pit Bull folks that have benefited and wrote me telling how much they have learned from my work, for three decades. I have had lines formed at my table when I went to dog shows and sold my products. People wanted my autograph and additional information. Please do not misunderstand. I do not mean to put myself on some foolish pedestal. I am not the only one or the primary one or ones who have helped this breed develop. I am just reporting that the contributions I did make were not recognized in all three court trials; only the innuendo that I promoted dog fighting which is completely false, a lie. A very damaging lie. Even the win in Supreme Court has the expressed connotation that although my work may be gruesome and cruel, I have a first amendment right to publish it. How wrong! Again, I edited out far more rough scenes in my videos than Dateline or Animal Planet or most hunting videos and a host of other sources have. My genre has been to educate not to titillate and yet I stand accused of cruel depiction with a first amendment right to that cruel depiction. It is wrong, wrong, wrong. My journalism involved reporting all aspects of the breed from famous historical dog fighters I met and interviewed, to those who win in the conformation show circle, winners on the weight pulling platform, and far more. I played an integral role in the development of the breed in America along positive avenues. None of that was pointed out to the jury in my trial, but it stands. The people I have helped along the way and the Pit Bulls whose lives I've made easier by educating folks that stands. And moreover, I stand.

This is me presenting the famous "Mountain Man" Lester Hughes with his Appreciation award for his years developing our breed award on his birthday

Me and Louis Colby at his home in Newburyport, Rhode Island

Me with John Colby on my right and Louis Colby on my left

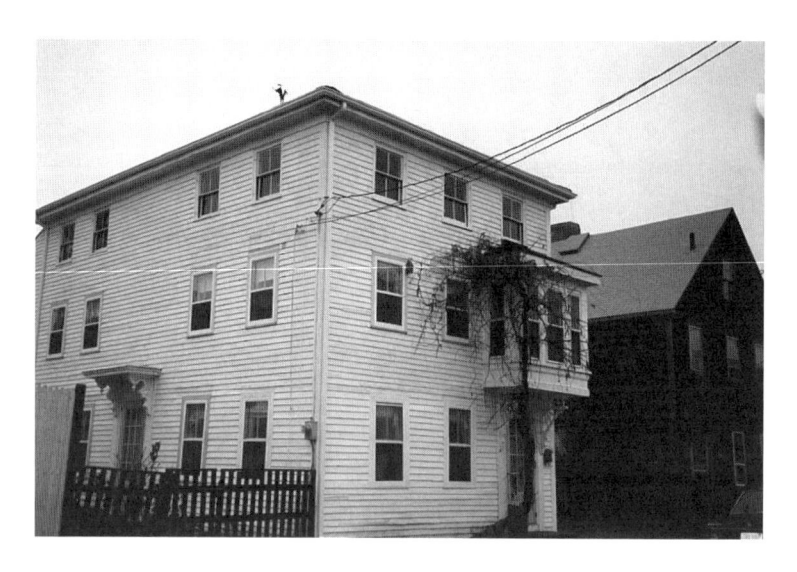

Went to see the original Colby home – it all started here.

Me and Pete Sparks (one of the original gamedog men).
He is over 90 years old here. This was Fat Bill's pig pickin'.
My belly is round from a pound of barbeque and barbecue beans!

This is me and Randy McCollum at the same pig pick.

Following Grand Jury indictment based on trumped up evidence, I went to trial. The transcripts and the instructions to the jury indicated this trial was the United States Government vs. Criminal 04-51, Robert John Stevens. Now I had been taught in high school that one of the unique aspect of America is that in our justice system a man is innocent until proven guilty. I was *no criminal*! I had not even committed a gray area criminal act at all. In fact, just the opposite. My business was all about steering the Pit Bull Terrier away from its outlaw heritage and into healthy, clean activities. Moreover, beginning with the built-case that went to Grand Jury, through the illegally served search warrant and all the lies and legal trickery in the courts on the part of the government, it is fair to say our government was the criminal. The whole case is under the umbrella of their legal tricks and deceitful maneuvers and illegal acts. And it is also the truth that I never told one single lie and did not resort to even standard legal tricks. Not one bit. So I ask who is the criminal here? Again, I am not a lawyer, but in fighting this case I examined many Pit Bull cases including those acquitted. I assume all cases are like that. Criminal so-and-so before proven guilty. That is wrong, sad and wrong. What message does that give the jury? More importantly, what can we do about it? If Bob Stevens complains, so what? I ask you does anyone know anything that can be done about this atrocity?

Me and Ken Newman, weight pulling champion breeder and handler. The '92 Nationals

Me and Jean Carpenter, breeder of top quality. Also the '92 Nationals.

Me and Katie Greenwood – '92 Nationals.

"The fight that I lost is the fight that I learned the most about myself." Enson Inoue, mixed martial arts fighter. Cited in the movie "Red Belt" commentary.

So I was convicted, following a Grand Jury indictment based on trumped up evidence and sentenced to federal prison. My attorney had informed me the judge was a full sentence judge and I had to "plead out;" that is plead guilty to a lesser sentence, which is one of the most foolish aspects of today's justice system I can imagine. It means hardened criminals serve shortened sentences and are released back out to damage our public, while perfectly innocent folks are literally forced to lie in court and say they are guilty of crimes they did not even begin to commit and are unjustly imprisoned. And I'm talking about thousands of innocent citizens. I was told that if I pleaded not guilty the judge would give me the full sentence proscribed by the law, fifteen years in federal prison. If I "plead out" he could probably get me off on 18 months in prison. *Fifteen years*! We were in shock and shock is not even close to the trauma we had to endure. My wife Julie literally broke down and begged me to take the plea. I almost did, more for her than for myself. If I didn't, it looked like she would lose her husband, possibly for the rest of my life as I would be about 85 by the time I finished prison – if I lived that long. For a disabled housewife that is terrifying. And I was accused of cruelty? I cannot think of much more illegal and cruel than what the sorry representatives of our government did to us, just so they could win a case. There is very little in humanity less cold-hearted I would think.

The fact that I had written the book you have in your hand with the obvious motive of promoting good things for the breed if one simply scans the chapter headings for goodness sake, and had produced the basic Schutzhund video and the conditioning video to enhance the show performance and that I had been a journalist by profession since the middle 1970's was not brought to the attention of any judge or jury. The fact that the dog fighting documentaries I produced had an educational motive and that I edited out all blood, unlike the titillating sensational genre produced by Animal Planet, was never brought to the justice system until we reached Supreme Court. Instead the jury and all subsequent judges (including Supreme Court) were informed by prosecution that my work was a bloody gruesome depiction and the allegations went totally unchallenged. I don't know why. We went to my sentencing having been informed I must be ready to put my affairs in order as I was going to prison. I would be given the option of being handcuffed and carted off to prison right then and there or to be able to return home and wrap up my affairs but to report to any prison they indicated. My public defender fought the judge and he fought hard. Finally, the government attorney agreed that since I was going to appeal the decision it would serve no purpose for me to do prison time pending the appeal. I went home under a "supervised release." I was charged by the court to not have any communication with any Pit Bull people. I could not write any journalistic articles to promote weight pulling or show participation (what did that have to do with eliminating dog fighting I do not understand to this day!), and initially told I would have to get rid of my pet Pit Bull; my loved fourth generation Vickie mentioned above. Again my public defender fought the judge and again prevailed and I was allowed to keep my pet. The public defender, Michael Novara, probably saved Vickie's life. The dog had been my constant companion since she was a new born I held her in my arms watching TV. She would not understand a new home where she would probably be ignored most days apart from feeding. The pictures that went in the newspapers were the ones taken when I left the courthouse being informed I would have to get rid of Vickie. I look like a Nazi killer. The animal activists went to town over that picture. They loved it and referred to it in blog after blog. I was so very angry! I had to ask God for forgiveness and help in my thoughts concerning that cruel supercilious judge. I am not joking. I really did. Well it turned out good and she has lived to old age with me.

I was fighting from the bottom, to be sure, and didn't have much of a prayer. But prayer I had; we *always* have prayer. So I didn't accept, his admonition to "plead guilty" to a crime I did not commit. I told my attorney I would not lie in court and say I committed some crime I did not and that I would fight it with the last of my breath. And fight I did. Every day, like working on a term paper in graduate school, I studied law and researched my enemies, my attorneys, and everyone involved. From breakfast to late at night I fought. Every time my attorneys said I could not do something, I pointed out from my own study of law that yes, I could. Over and over I did this. For seven years I fought like that. For seven years I fought and prayed, and I'm glad I did.

I had three expert witnesses testify on my behalf at the trial. For the legality (morally and legally) of my hunting video I had long-time friend T. Michael Riddle. Michael owns a 1,000 acre ranch stocked with imported Eurasian Wild Boar, Fallow deer, feral hogs, buffalo, black tail deer, quail, dove, and turkey. His occupation is that of guided hunts on his ranch. His business is called Native Hunt. You can find him at www.nativehunt.com to view his guided hunts. I also had I. Lehr Brisbin who you will find in this book in the "Catch Dog" chapter. Dr. Brisbin reminds me of the street lawyer in the book of the same name, by John Grisham. Dr. Brisbin doesn't like to fly. He hops in his car and travels around the country to appear as a witness in court trials where victims of HSUS and PETA and other criminal animal activist organizations are being railroading. Let me present you with just one example. HSUS used an "undercover agent" to bring a Pit Bull lover to trial. The undercover agent found the *Pit Bull Gazette,* a show dog magazine that has nothing whatsoever to do with dog fighting. Allegations otherwise are the epitome of ridiculous and skullduggery. The Pit Bull fellow was acquitted, of course, he didn't have anything to do with dog fighting, but not before HSUS had killed all six of his dogs they confiscated. When I say HSUS killed them, they didn't even spend the money to kill them. What happens is they get some poor breeder to trial and his dogs confiscated. While waiting for trial, HSUS informs that the dogs cannot be rehabilitated and need to be killed immediately. They kill the puppies and old brood bitches in the process. I ask you, does this make any kind of sense? What threat to the nation are puppies and old brood britches? How can courts accept this criminal organization to be a "friend of the court" and the "greatest protector of animals in the world?" Protect them by mass murdering them? I really and truly do not understand this evil foolishness. Neither can a significant aspect of American citizens. HSUS has killed 30, 40 up to 100 dogs and more in one single day, repeatedly for years in this manner. In this manner, HSUS has killed more dogs than the entire history of dog fighting in America, at least up to the 1980's. Incredibly crass. Incredibly cruel. Incredibly cold-blooded. Incredibly criminal. HSUS gets accepted by courts all across the nation touting themselves to be "the world's largest protector of animals" while they systematically every month kill hundreds of animals and not just Pit Bulls. I have never understood how this is supposed to be humane and protecting animals. I wonder what all the animals they kill have to say about it. There was a blog up by an organization called Friends; they rescued the fighting Pit Bulls when Michael Vick was convicted and rehabilitated them. When a dog breeder was convicted by an HSUS undercover agent and 43 of his dogs confiscated, HSUS was pushing very hard to get them killed. Friends could not afford to rescue all those dogs so they had a blog up appealing to the public to not let HSUS kill those dogs (meaning make the shelter kill them). Before the public could even begin to respond, the dogs were all killed. All of them including old, harmless brood bitches. In the news, HSUS has killed fifty Pit Bulls in one day, more than once.

The third witness I had was Glen Bui, who at the time was the leader of an organization called the American Canine Foundation, a non–profit organization dedicating to defending people who are victimized by animal activist organizations. They depended on public funding and didn't have much. Mr. Bui worked five years as an undercover agent for the FBI investigating the underground criminal organization HSUS. His organization had been responsible for a great deal of exposure of HSUS criminal activities and even had a judge sanctioned for inappropriate judging. As of the year 2010, you may be able to find the details of this and a pile of court cases where HSUS and PETA are exposed for their criminal activities. The American Canine Foundation had financial difficulties (depends of the donations of animal lovers – but they have trouble meeting the huge legal expenses) and seems about to disband at the time of this writing.

The government used HSUS affiliated "expert" witnesses in my trial, and they used the trooper who assisted in getting my conviction. My witnesses were self-contained, honest-to-goodness experts. They felt no need for a prolonged speech about their expertise. Simply stated, they got on with proving my work had educational value. It is not sour grapes or histrionics when I say the government "experts" and the trooper were really and truly on the other side of the world experts. They were very foolish animal activist individuals. And I really and truly am not saying this because I was a defendant and felt wronged. I mean by anybody's book, by all standards of morality and common sense, the trooper and the so-called experts dealt such an overwhelming pile of horse manure that it is beyond concise description. The trooper goes on and on and on about all the work he has done in law enforcement. The innuendo being he convicted a criminal and he is a nationwide expert in all this. He explained he is a certified instructor for the HSUS and instructs training in "blood sports" (a term fabricated by the animal activists that garners them millions of dollars in donations not promoting dog fighting or saying dog fighting is some good). The trooper is allowed as an expert because he has talked with four or five individuals that engaged in dog fighting and has helped in fifteen Pit Bull dog fighting busts. I had provided my attorney with a list of questions that could easily discredit all of these individuals, including the trooper, as "experts" and showed him this is because I happen to be the expert and these individuals have no idea what they are talking about apart from sensational malarkey fed to them by their HSUS associates. But again, for some reason attorneys all seem to be very afraid of contradicting HSUS in any manner and judges are all pre-disposed to use HSUS testimony as expertise. This has resulted in countless victims being criminalized when they are totally innocent of any wrongdoing. My attorney didn't think my list of questions to put before them in cross-examination could be used. The stress and fight I went through was out of bounds. So the trooper spent hours instructing the jury all about dog fighting and the horrific cruelties full of sensationalism and designed to shock. My attorney objected and objected and objected. But the justice system has no rules that govern when a judge has to accept an objection, or so it appears. The judge simply overruled. My attorney pointed out that we do not argue dog fighting is not cruel, we do not argue dog fighting should be legitimized. That is not the issue in this case whatsoever. Essentially, based on my reading and understanding of the law, it was illegal for the judge to allow this, but I could be inaccurate there. The defense and the prosecution are on equal ground on the subject of dog fighting as a sport so it is not an issue whatsoever in this case. The jury's time was wasted and they were dramatically misinformed with no objections to that fact allowed. The issue is, does the defendant have a first amendment right to provide the public with quality documentaries and is it legal to convict an individual for the exact same documentary a TV show markets and the TV show is not convicted. But, the judge overruled all objections. The trooper wasted hours of jury time describing dog fighting. The entire description of dog fighting was not even close to the level of information, however truthful and accurate some of the trooper's descriptive sensational dialogue may have been that was provided in the video and booklet I was convicted for. We could have (and I begged my attorney to do it) put up on a projector screen showing the booklet that accompanied my *Pick-A-Winna* video and show *me* as the expert and the educational impact of my work. But my attorney wouldn't do it. I always felt that if we had done this the case would have not gone beyond that trial. Well, one never knows what the Lord does. I couldn't see it. Turns out it was better, even through intense suffering, to go ahead and win in Supreme Court. It then turned from just an individual being victimized to putting a huge dent in animal activists being able to victimize American citizens. The government used a veterinarian as expert witness, and he also wasted jury time with this long boring dialogue about all he has done as a veterinarian. I must observe courts always assume that if a man has an advanced degree and is professionally certified, such as veterinarian, his word is truthful evidence. No amount of degrees or certification guarantees a person cannot be a liar. This expert witness wasted hours of jury time with sensational, foolish, silly gibberish. It was absurd testimony. But of course the jury bought it all. Soaked it all in. The judge overruled all objections. The most farcical of his testimony was when he wasted over an hour of jury time with this ridiculous dog skull which he proposed as a model to use for his "expertise" to indicate the tremendous damaging power of a Pit Bull bite when competing. The skull was placed on a table purposely close to the jury so this expert veterinarian could explain all the different types of teeth a dog has and how the biting strength of Pit Bull can wreak havoc. Again my attorney objected as to the relevance of all this nonsense, but it was of course overruled. My witness, Dr. Brisbin, who happens to be one of the foremost experts in the nation on this subject, his face was red as a beet, and he was holding his sides, laughing so hard I thought he was going to fall out of his chair! And every nonsensical statement made by this expert veterinarian threw him into further fits of laughter. I don't want to waste your time in this epilogue with full details, but you cannot measure the strength of a dog's bite based on a skull formation. A dog's bite has to be measured, among many other variables, by his attitude. A dog that is playing will hardly do more than mouth a toy. As a postscript, many dog matches go for over half an hour with both dogs hardly more than mouthing because for them, battle is play. But I must be careful lest I again accused of making up stuff to side with dog fighting. For sure not all dog fights are that "gentle." I just want to print the truth here. I am reporting facts! A dog that is bringing down prey bites harder. A dog that is angry bites harder still and a dog that is scared bites second only to a dog that is very scared, which is why dogs competing in the pit do not really bite as hard as animal activists claim. If they bite out of fear they will very quickly quit when bit back! Again, I'm not promoting or even suggesting dog fighting is okay or mild, I'm just reporting the facts devoid of sensational malarkey here. I could go on, but this expert veterinarian was feeding the jury information that a third year student of animal medicine, in my opinion, would know is highly inaccurate, useless, misleading, and well, a lie, is better said. The judge kept disallowing my attorney's objections so that a whole day was spent engaging in nonsense that was not relevant to the case and misinforming the jury. However whenever the government attorney objected to even picayune comments the judge would sustain. Then they played my Japan Pit Fights documentary. Again, I edited out all blood and primarily you just viewed two dogs wrestling around vying for a hold. However you can't edit out everything and there are, of necessity, scenes where a dog has a hold and shaking it out. I tried to keep most of the scenes mere skin holds that do very little real damage; far less damage than a boxer sustains on pay-for-view TV. The judge kept sending messages to the jury by putting his head down and shielding his eyes. Before the time was up, the judge got up with a disgusted expression, slammed the podium and loudly announced we will continue in the morning. All designed to impress the jury. It did. Of course the judge can always respond that he was truly shocked by what he thought he was viewing and I guess he never watches Animal Planet that depicts many times more vivid bloody scenarios every week. I don't know. I do know it made a pretty good impression with the jury.

Here I am on Alan Wolfe's mountain with Boston Blackie. Alan grew up in Boston, same ward as I, and attended the same high school. He was much younger so I didn't know him then. He owned a whole mountain at the time called Wolfe Mountain. He also raised pure bred wolves. This is me with Grand Champion Bronson.

Here I'm working Velvet on Blackie's springpole

Velvet loved Blackie's jenny.

122

Velvet could really burn up Blackie's jenny

"As sands through the hourglass, so are the days of our lives."
1970's soap opera, Days of Our Lives

Oyez, Oyez, and now comes the infamous pig man to the stand. The next "expert" witness the government used was indeed an expert in the area of hogs. This one really was an expert. He was the head of the Virginia pork industry. Of them all this fellow was the biggest rascal. We came to call him the pig man. He began his testimony from a special podium the government set up just for him, which my witnesses did not have. He faced the jury and he had special TV monitor in front of his podium as he faced the jury. He began his testimony with this long, and I mean real long, dissertation on his credentials going back to when he was a child raised on a small pig farm. Long and very boring. His story was equally ridiculous. But the jury bought it. He had this down country good old home boy dialect and used comments like "land's sake, yes," etc. All designed to impress the jury that he has the very highest in expert credentials, but at the same time he is a good old clean cut country boy who would never harm any animal. But then he grew up hunting he said – rabbit, squirrel. I wanted to ask him if he cooked and ate the squirrel or did he hunt for "sport," but I couldn't. He wasted jury time with this real long dialog of how he was a member of the 4H club as a child, Future Farmers of America, and a show judge of hogs – to impress the jury he is this real nice clean cut feller. He was just a rascal. He went into a long dissertation about different types of domestic and feral hogs. He did this because he kept saying that the hogs in my video were not wild hogs as I claimed (the prior "expert" made the same observation repeatedly). The thing is, I never claimed I caught only wild hogs in that video. One scene is where a Virginia farmer hired me to catch his *huge* domestic hog he let run wild (and I noted that in the video plain as could be.) Some farmers do that so they don't have to feed them, then they catch them for market. Some of the hogs we caught were domestic hogs that got loose or somehow ended up wild in the swamp. But it was a huge lie that I claimed I only hunted wild feral hog. Huge lie and complete waste of jury time, if I was allowed to object, which I wasn't. In fact, in the video as well in the attached booklet I was very clear the hogs we hunted were a mixture of local feral hog, imported Russian hog, and largely local domestic hogs that ran wild in the swamp. The government witness spent hours showing the hogs in my video were not feral hog (although some were). It was a huge waste of time. But my public defender refused to make one single objection; I surmise because he knows nothing about hogs and perhaps he didn't believe me. But the prosecution's piles upon piles of lies stayed with the jury without one single objection. The "pig man" stated that what he viewed was domestic hogs turned loose and wild dogs sicked on them and it is a slaughter. That is a bunch of obvious malarkey, but it again went without one single objection. He said he just saw dogs sicked on hogs turned loose. He said in a true hunt you have dogs you are proud of and they pick up a cold trail and you follow the dog to the hog and then shoot the hog. He said you follow your hound dog and then quickly shoot the hog. What he said he saw on the video was disgusting. This fellow could not be serious. We had very high quality Plott and Catohoolie hounds; the best. I was not allowed to inform this "expert" that hogs you cannot trail, even deer are easier to trail in a South Carolina swamp. We *often* came across hot, never mind cold trail, and couldn't find the hog. By the time the bay hounds found the hog they could be a mile (or more) away. You cannot walk up and shoot them! That is why you must have a good bay dog so you can find them and that can take an hour. You go through thick briars and wade muddy slew. It is rough country. The hogs don't herd. They will run, but if the dogs get close, they go after the dogs – to kill the dogs. So you need a catch dog to catch and hold them until you get there. This fellow was unbelievably stupid, or fantasizing, regardless of his long list of credentials and growing up in rural North Carolina on a pig farm; or one big liar. This expert said that in all the years he has been associated with the swine business (which he spent a good hour impressing the jury about), he has never heard of Bulldogs being used to catch hog. He has only known collie dogs to herd swine. I wanted my public defender to challenge that. In all my years hunting I know that it is *impossible* for any collie dog to herd wild hogs in a swamp and have never heard of this. None of the hog farmers in Virginia ever heard of such nonsense either. They use catch dogs when they have free ranging hog. Using bulldogs as catch dogs is quite common in Virginia and all over our nation. I mean even hunting catalogs sell catch dog protective vests and depict Pit Bulls and bay dogs wearing the vests they sell, proving it is a very common agricultural and hunting endeavor. Regardless of his long list of credentials, this expert either fantasizes, is a foolish clown, or a liar, or all of that. But you see, my experience indicates that committing perjury is punishable in today's courts generally, only for innocent defendants, certainly not by the government or their witnesses. The expert went on to say that when I indicate we sometimes have a good meal after catching the hog, it is impossible to do that. He said the stress of the catch spoils the meat and it can't be eaten. Either another complete lie or the "expert" did not know better. The expert should interview hundreds, make that thousands of people who live in the rural areas and eat pork like that every year, all year long, for many generations since the founding of America. What he means, and thinks he knows, is that the stress of being caught will make the male boar hog secrete stress hormones and that can spoil the meat. But what the hunters do is disembowel the hog immediately and the meat is not only good it is fresh and far tastier than the hogs brought to market and stressed with electric prods far more than hogs caught by catch dogs. The expert either had no idea about what he was talking about despite a lifetime with hogs and being head of the pork industry or he was a liar. I would need several more pages to list all the trickery this fellow came up with in that trial. I'll save the biggest one for last. As I mentioned, the government placed this witness in front of the jury with his own special TV monitor to watch my Catch Dog film which was on a big screen for the jury. None of my witnesses were given this special seating. This should have been challenged, but it wasn't. It was another legal trick. The expert pig man throughout the filming kept shaking his head, placing his hands over his eyes and his dramatic eloquence with expressed sorrow would earn him an academy award if it were in a movie. The judge did the same thing for the movie. The judge imposed his personal will on the jury and that is supposed to be a breach of the ethics of the legal profession and according to my law reading. But again the law only applies to American citizens. It often doesn't apply to the government or to judges.

"Criminal" number 04-51 had a small business and was a journalist and author that did nothing criminal whatsoever and all his work geared toward the betterment of the breed and steering them *away* from the dog fighting stigmata. The government and HSUS did nothing but fabricate a case.

I lost that trial. I was allowed to go home pending sentencing date. Before I returned for sentencing, I was informed I would be going to prison and needed to get my affairs in order. They said I would be given a choice. They can cuff me and process me and send me to prison right after sentencing or they would allow me to go home to finish getting my affairs in order until they assigned me to a prison. I would then have to travel at my own expense to whatever federal prison I would be sent to. I was told that I would have to go to a half-way house where all criminals, including hard core criminals were sent, until assigned my permanent prison. I was very afraid of going to that place because I knew that if any of those criminals tried any of that homosexual stuff on me – and I do look like the tender hearted little guy – I would put them all in the hospital and get into deep trouble in the doing and probably have my prison term extended. I was very afraid of this. It turned out that I was sentenced to three years in federal prison (followed by three more years of supervised release) and had to get my loved family pet Bulldog away from her home. I was so very angry over what that judge wanted to do to her. She would not understand. But my public defender fought that judge over and over. Three times he went back and showed the judge that he was not following federal guidelines in his sentencing. The short story is the judge responded that he is a federal judge and can do what he wanted. As a postscript, I later found he had been sanctioned three times in the past by the third circuit for his rascal sentencing. Anyway, my public defender also went back again and again for my pet Bulldog Vickie and finally the judge allowed her to stay home. My public defender also informed the judge that it would be wrong to send me to prison while I appealed, since I might win the appeal and the prison term would be an injustice. The judge wanted to put me in prison anyway, but the government attorney agreed and said he saw no reason for me to go to prison pending appeal. So I went back home on supervised release. Before I went home, however, I had to be processed. I got a real close up look/feel for the prison ambience. I had to go through these big doors that slam shut in back of you leaving you with this strange lonely abandoned feeling. I was finger printed and humiliated. But folks I stood tall when that judge sentenced me I looked him right straight in his cold grey eyes and I never flinched. When the law folks processed me I just slightly smiled and showed them no down whatsoever. I had to go to this room where they assigned me to a parole lady. She had my record of supervised release pending the trial. During that time I had to stay in my area and if I traveled anywhere, I had to inform them of where I was going, a telephone number I could be reached at, etc. I used to go down to the town Julie and I spent most of our adult years, Greensboro NC just a hundred miles south of our Virginia mountain home. We went down there to visit friends and family and I used to hop on my Honda Shadow motorcycle and go down and train at my karate school. From time to time I traveled to visit my son in Philadelphia and my daughter in Colorado Springs, Colorado. Now, after losing the case and sentenced, the parole lady gave me this evil cruel smile and said, "Well, Stevens, I guess you won't be going to visit your kids anymore." And they accused *me* of being cruel. She didn't let me go visit my daughter on her fortieth birthday. And that hurt. They illegally took away my free right to travel and visit my children. I later got reassigned to a local parole fellow and he allowed me to travel. But those were very hard years. My sand was slowly falling out of my glass bubble. Given time, my life would be over. If I went to prison, I would, by the law of our government, lose my social security. We would then not be able to pay the property taxes on our home. Actually, we were not able to pay property taxes much for the seven years we went through this and the Lord pulled me out just in time before the government would take our home. Julie's medical bills had piled up and my family tapped out helping us. It was close, real, real close.

    On July 18, 2008, I won the appeal. God set me free and gave me hope. The description of the trial and the justice system enumerated above only touches the extent of the railroading attempted and I point that out only to again proclaim it was God Himself who finally prevailed. I could do nothing. I know this in my heart. The third circuit designated Title 18 of Section 48, U. S. Code unconstitutional and hence my sentence vacated. I was set free, the Bulldog breed was set free and the Lord gave me hope. While preparing for the appeal, I studied the law at my "law library" – Barnes and Noble law section. I purchased books and read the law and communicated over and over with my attorney. While communicating with my attorney, collecting protest letters from the Pit Bull fraternity around the country, researching and stressing, and all the filing of briefs, through those stressful and stultifying years, I developed a prayer. It was this prayer that won the case. A bit of background is needed in order to comprehend the prayer. First it was inspired by an incredible book I suggest can bless and says a lot to Christians searching for answers. The book is entitled *Praying the Names of God* by Ann Spangler. Do not let the title give you a meager impression of the content. It goes way beyond merely teaching the attributes and variety of names our God assumes. I was inspired by the chapter El Chay (the title is found in 2 Kings 19:15-16). El Chay is the title of God that in Hebrew means the Living and Eternal God. It is the attribute we can pray to for deliverance from evil enemies. Also I have the news article where a leading spokesperson for HSUS informed the press that the Judeo-Christian and the Christian community were the enemies of the HSUS. So HSUS proclaimed both God's chosen people, the Jewish population and those who spread His gospel, the Christian community, their enemy. I have the news article. With that this was my prayer through all those years and I now read that prayer from time to time and give thanks to Him who answered and granted.

Listen, O Lord, El Chay, and hear; open your eyes and see. The HSUS has proclaimed You their enemy and seeks to make me your servant a felon and destroy Dogs of Velvet and Steel Productions, using the American Government. The American Government and the HSUS are very, very, powerful, very influential. But YOU created the heavens and the earth and the United States of America and us. You are the Living Eternal God. El Chay. Protect me from the intrigues of these enemies of God, these liars and deceivers. Deliver me from evil and speedily bring Glory to Your Name, for I will testify to it. They came to your property, Windfall, and took your business, Dogs of Velvet and Steel, which seeks good, and they seek to make your servant a felon with their lies and deceit. Will you allow lies and deceit to prevail, Lord? You are El Chay, the Living God, who loves me, the One who sees, hears, and acts to save me – my Refuge. Amen, Lord.

Over and over again, I had begged my public defender to inform the Third Circuit (appellant court for my case) that even as the law is written concerning depiction, I have done nothing criminal as I am a journalist for the breed by profession. I had traveled to Japan and I had interviewed, taken notes, researched the organizations and the dogs and the dog fighters, was provided with film footage by the Japanese and was paid for my journalism. That is journalism by any definition; Webster's, legal, and moral. That meets the first exception allowing the depictions. Only one exception is needed to make my work legal. I met all of the exceptions except scientific or religious; and perhaps religious as I often make testimony to the Lord and perhaps somewhat scientific in my education. My work was educational and far more thorough, pointed, detailed, quality education than Animal Planet or other depictions of the exact same product. Moreover, my work was historical and artistic; it is right there you read it and you view it. It is also political; it is a forum which is supposed to enjoy an even higher freedom of speech. All this makes my work very legal by the law that convicted me! Well, again, I studied the law, but the law is not about justice. As I quoted above from a lawyer characterized on the TV series, NYPD Blue, there is as much a correlation between truth and justice as between a hot dog and a warm puppy. My work may have been legal, in other words, but your attorney knows the political machinations and has to deal with it for you. So my public defender refused to inform the third circuit that I was not guilty of any crime. I had fought long and hard daily, trying to communicate with her and show her I am not guilty and it is an easy argument to show I am not guilty. The government's arguments that my work was as sick as child porn is easy to show not holding any water since one can see I didn't even depict any blood and my work is far milder than a plethora of hunting videos and TV documentaries of the same genre. I had predicted every single one of the legal arguments the government would make in regard to the first amendment; from my study of law. It turned out I was as accurate as a Rolex on every single one of their legal case arguments. Every one I fed to her before she filed her briefs. I showed her how their interpretations were inaccurate and misleading. Actually she either used most of what I fed her or I was just plain correct and we were on the same page. But that legal argument was pretty attenuated on either side. The core of the government argument was blanketed in sensational blarney they obtained from HSUS. The sheer volume of lies and manipulated data would fill over a hundred pages. Just one example to illustrate, they make the *old* announcement that children exposed to animal cruelty grow up to be serial killers. Based on recent research that indicates most serial killers did things as children such as pulling legs off bugs etc. They made the same proclamation when they solicited donations decades ago. They cite an actual psychological study when they do this. But they cite out of context and turn it into misleading manipulated baloney to make a long explanation short, I pointed out to the attorney if she wants to be thorough she will investigate every one of their claims. They were all either false or based on partial information or in many, many cases fabricated. I showed the fabrications to her. And I gave her the citations paragraph and verse. And regarding the children exposed to animal cruelty I pointed out that in the history of American hunting has been a core aspect of American Culture from our founding. The majority of rural American fathers take their children and teach them to hunt beginning age ten or earlier (and have since the founding of our country). I have observed this; including bow hunting. I pointed out how cruel is it to shoot a deer with a bow and arrow and can a young person be guaranteed to make an instant kill with one shot? Actually very few adult experienced and trained bow hunters can for that matter. Young people get exposed to animal cruelty during their formative years hunting that makes dog fighting a game of dominos by comparison. If the government attorney's argument has any credibility then the majority of American citizenry would be serial killers. I could fill this section with 200 pages of further legal information I fed my attorney. The point being the sheer volume of stress I endured. Because it fell on deaf ears. Probably for many reasons. She would have to spend as many hours as I did and they ended up being the lion's share of most hours of most days to document the credibility of my information. I did point out that her opposition was spending the time with data fed them by animal activists and begged her to respond in kind. I asked her to listen to me because while she knows the law and the ins and outs of the justice system, I am the Pit Bull expert and in that capacity also an expert on the manipulations of the animal activists. I think she probably just didn't believe me and I can understand that. But I also pointed out that while I begged her make her core argument my work is journalistic and educational, historical and artistic, she still needs to touch on the umbrella of first amendment right that should cover my work. I warned her to be careful in her argument because most of the government attorney's argument about child exposure to animal cruelty, the horrific cruelties and danger to our society of dog fighting would be a red herring designed to engage her in a spitting contest over the atrocities of dog fighting and the case is not about that. I pointed out if they go there she should respond defense, and that means her client is in agreement with dog fighting being harmful, so why waste time on it, it is not relevant to the case. All of my work made proclamations against dog fighting and indicated healthy alternative venues for the breed. In other words I didn't just *say* I do not promote dog fighting I showed/proved it by emphasizing and educating activities that draw interest away from dog fighting. The government argued anyone can *say* they don't promote dog fighting and my public defenders refused to respond that. In addition I *showed and educated* alternative activities. I suggested to her that if she let the prosecution draw her into their ball game she will lose. Stay away from that argument or it would mean she would not have room for serious, pointed, evident informational argument. All things considered I felt it would be best to go with *truth* and show the judges I had done nothing criminal even as the law is written; and the law as written is unconstitutional because it allows situation like mine where I was railroaded and convicted of a crime I did not commit over an allegation that there is a million dollar industry of alleged "crush videos" that does not even exist. Instead she chose to argue that the law that convicted me was unconstitutional. Period. But I wanted the argument about the unconstitutionality of the statute to be a secondary argument while her core argument should be that even as written, her client violated no law. She did not agree. She knows the justice system and the appetites of the judges. Truth won't work. So I was sure I was going down into the swill. Every day I prayed the El Chay prayer. But week after week into month after month, it looked worse with no gleam of hope.

I felt like Jeremiah (see Jeremiah Chapter 20). Jeremiah felt deserted by God so much that he said he would make no more mention of God. And yet he could not keep his heart away from the Lord. He said *His* Word was like a burning fire shut up in his bones. And so it was with me. I wondered if the Lord had overlooked me, or was not interested in helping. Jeremiah said he was weary of holding back (telling the people the TRUTH) and all he heard was mocking on every side and everyone watched for him to fall. I felt much the same. But like Jeremiah, I just kept pleading with the Lord to look at my cause and not let evil prevail against me.

I read and related with David in Psalm 39. David testified that he was mute with silence (such was his fear and discouragement) and that he held his peace and his sorrow was so stirred up that his heart was hot within him. And yet like David I prayed He would deliver me. Often I felt too weak to get out of bed. My legs were like rubber and my heart ached so much I felt I had to force my way into each daily martial arts training. Often I would just lay in bed eyes closed too weak to function so great was my trepidation. I would *not* give up. I pressed on, each day fighting with my attorney. Yet from the Lord I heard no answer and hope seemed to fade. Emily Dickinson said, "There comes a time when the begging stops; when the long interceding lips perceive their prayer in vain." It was like that.

And then, earlier, in the spring of 2008, a little chickadee flew in through our living room door that opened out to our deck. Terrified, she flew around banging into windows. She didn't understand. She hadn't done anything wrong on purpose. She was terrified and the angst was overwhelming. Trapped she couldn't get out. Her grief overwhelmed her until she finally collapsed on the floor. Still she hung on to hope. We rescued the little chickadee and set her free. It wasn't easy. Her little legs were so tiny and thin. Her wee talons were as thin and flimsy as thread and she clung to the rug. We were so afraid we'd break her legs or feet as we slowly and gently pried her loose. She just lay limp in Julie's hand with her eyes closed. We put her outside on the deck in one of Julie's plants and left her. But we watched. She didn't know we watched. I guess she felt deserted. We were so concerned we said a prayer for her. Poor little bird meant no harm, she was just a bird. Finally we looked out the window and saw that she was up and her eyes open. We felt excited, gleeful, and warm. We didn't disturb her and the next time we looked she was gone – free. Flew away to her home. We had set her free. I cannot portray the glorious feeling; the warmth in our hearts. I just don't have the superlatives to describe how it felt to release that helpless, frightened bird from her terror. And I thought - I wonder if God feels like that in His surreal *love* when He rescues us. I prayed. I prayed that He would rescue me in like manner and set me free. I asked *Him* wouldn't He have that same ambience?

And what else did Emily Dickinson say on this subject of hope? She said, "Hope is the thing with feathers that perches in the soul and sings the tune without the words and never stops." An evangelist (and although he has no idea he has helped me through many storms on behalf of the Lord) Chip Ingram said, "The clearer you see your eternal hope, the more anchored you are to sustain temporal storms."

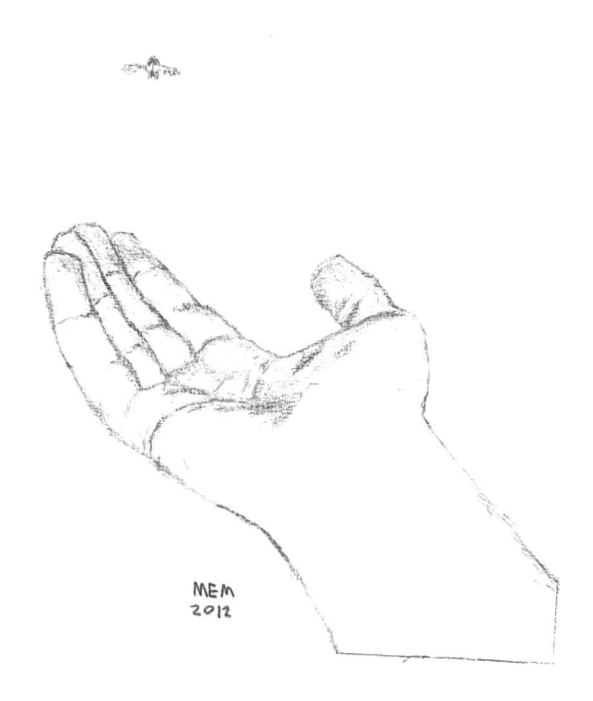

What a warm, tender sensation – an emotion God created –when we set that little bird free.

We would see her from time to time perched on a limb outside our window. How to portray this? We became her friend.

We are defined by what we believe. I believe in the Word of God. Psalm 91 is a constant. The Lord *is* my refuge; the Most High *is* my shelter.

Well the third Circuit agreed and I was set free and the Lord gave me hope. But I want to state that going into the appeal I had no chance. The "justice" system had not been provided with any argument or evidence of my being innocent of any crime and my case went before them by in effect, agreeing my work is highly egregious, but that I had a first amendment right to it. I knew, again from much daily research and study, that it is very rare that an appellant court will overturn a federal statute. Recent court decisions have all upheld what sometimes appears to be damaging to the public laws engineered by legislation. It is currently very unpopular in the justice system to overturn a statute formulated by Congress. My case is a long story filled with political intrigue and legal maneuvers so juicy that it can make a John Grisham book boring by comparison and therefore subject for another book. But I was blatantly railroaded and many would say I did not have a prayer. I view the situation from an entirely different perspective. I say all I had was prayer. I had no earthly chance of winning that case on appeal and every chance in the world of going to prison. Prayer worked where humankind didn't. As a postscript, it is taught to us in the very center of the Bible (Psalm 118:8) that "it is better to trust in the Lord than to put confidence in man." And I believe this in my heart because God has shown me it is so. That is my personal testimony. And sometimes it makes me tremble. Tremble.

Oh! By the way, the first century celebration of Passover ended with the singing of Psalms 116 and 118. These are known as the Hallel songs. The Gospel of Mathew records that when Jesus and His disciples finished the Passover meal they left the upper city of Jerusalem singing these Psalms as they went to the Garden of Gethsemane. I'd say that is pretty good gospel. In His most difficult moment the Son of God, our Savior, sang these songs. In case it is of interest to you, dear reader.

I won my appeal and the Lord gave me hope. Hope is a wonderful God-created word. It refreshes the human soul. And I could not help but notice that the afore-described Psalm 39 was followed, in Psalm 40 by David's epilogue. He had waited patiently for the Lord and the Lord finally inclined to him and brought him out of the horrible pit and out of the mire and set his feet upon rock and established his steps. It evoked a new song in David's heart. Praise to God and many will see it and fear and learn to trust in the Lord.

But I knew it was not ended. Because unlike my attorneys, I had decades of experience with the animal activists. I had begged my attorney to simply show the appellant judges that I had not done anything illegal even as this Title 18 Statute is written. I had, again, traveled, researched, reviewed books and periodicals, and reported the results of all this research in the videos and booklets I was convicted for and the work was educational; far more educational and far deeper more thorough research devoid of sensational malarkey than TV documentaries produced of the *exact* same genre. My work had obvious historical bent and was artistic and I showed how it is artistic. From my Barnes and Nobles law library; I had also informed her that if she simply informed the judges that my work unequivocally fit those exemptions, the court would have no choice but to find me not guilty. In that case, the law states that in order to protect the American citizen from an overbearing government, the government would be prevented from appealing the case any further and it would be ended. However, if she insisted in making her core argument that however cruel my work might be, I had a first amendment right to it and we won the case. The government *can* appeal a constitutional first amendment case. And they were more than overbearing and they *did* appeal. It was a huge waste of American taxpayer's money. As mentioned, she insisted on not going with showing that I was not guilty but that the statute that convicted me was unconstitutional. She was not comfortable arguing my being not guilty of any wrongdoing because of all the manipulated data submitted to the courts that cannot be retrieved and exposed. That is just how the justice system is set up. This exemplifies the reason you need an attorney that is versed in all the intricacies of a justice system and the term justice is an oxymoron. It appears that just as in the movie *A Few Good Men*, starring Tom Cruise and Jack Nicholson, Nicholson exclaims, "You can't handle the truth!" Judges can't handle the truth; and that is the truth! Bottom line – the judges would buy the lies and deceit fed to the government attorneys by the animal activists. I believe she misjudged the power of the animal activists. She didn't think the Supreme Court would accept the case. It is a fact that the Supreme Court only accepts (about) a hundred out of a thousand or more cases that petition for acceptance. I told her I had no question they would accept because Pit Bulls are a vox populi in today's society and the animal activists would know how to push their hot button. She didn't appear to believe me. But the Supreme Court accepted. I was going down. None of the trial or appeal court transcripts contained any affective argument in my favor. There was no way I could achieve justice. But I prayed anyway. I found another Psalm of David. Psalm 35. It is an appeal to the heavenly King, as Divine Warrior to come to the defense of "His servant" who is being maliciously slandered. David does not refer to himself as "one of the righteous;" he appeals to the Lord rather as an innocent victim of an unmotivated attack. David appeals to the Lord as Divine Judge, as Divine Warrior, and the petition is followed by an elaboration of David's vow to praise Him for it. That fit. And so I set about again praying this prayer most every day and usually often each day while I reiterated the "El Chay" prayer described above. Here then is the prayer from Psalm 35:

Contend, O Lord, Divine Warrior, with those who contend with me. Fight against those who fight with me. Come to my defense. Chase them away. Say to my soul, my life, I am your salvation. Make those who seek to incriminate me with their craftiness and lies and deceit be disgraced and put to shame. Make those who plot my ruin and Dogs of Velvet and Steel, *and the attendant American Pit Bull Terrier and Bully Breed, be turned back in dismay. Like chaff before the wind, with the angel of the Lord pursuing them, driving them away. Make their path be dark and slippery with the angel of the Lord pursuing them. Since they sought to trap me in their deceitful net without proper cause and without cause dug a pit for me. May ruin overtake them by surprise and the trap they set entangle them. May they fall into the pit of their own ruin. I will testify the Kingdom of God prevailed. I will testify and bring glory to Your name. And my whole being will exclaim Ruwa (Hebrew shout for joy Revelation 5:12) – who is like You O Lord. You rescue the poor from those too strong for them. To the nations, to America and all who read my testimony, I will thank You and praise You. They do not speak peaceably but devise false accusations. O Lord, You have seen this; be not silent. Do not be far from me, O Lord. Rise to my defense. Contend for me, my God and Lord.*

That is Psalm 35 almost verbatim. Read it and see.

In the midst of my sinking ship suddenly I received a phone call. One of the most proficient and effective constitutional attorneys in the nation was interested in my case and wanted to take it on pro bono. Her name is Patricia Millett. She represents the prestigious Washington D.C. law firm of Akin Gump. This attorney was first class. However she also had her hands tied by the justice system. Statements made by prosecution that were misleading information, false allegations and in some cases downright lies, cannot be retracted, or so I was told. You have to stand with the trial and appeal court transcripts you cannot expose falsehoods. That is the way the justice system is set up and it seems so often to protect the criminals and persecute innocent American citizens. I hope one day we can overcome this. I still feel America is the best place in the world to live and has the best chance of living justifiably in this world, but I hope a lot of damaging aspects will one day be overturned. So I went around Robin Hood's barn with Ms. Millett in much the same manner that I did with the public defender. I found there was nothing I could tell this attorney about the law, but she also had, of course, no concept of who or what HSUS is and what they are about or had any experience with the Bully breed world. I did find, however, that this attorney had one of those rare-among-attorneys attributes; she would listen and respond.

In the meantime, HSUS posted numerous blogs with ad hominem attacks such as found in their "Who Is Bob Stevens?" in which they named me as the defendant in my case in which I had produced horrific dog fighting videos depicting gory scenes. Meanwhile, HSUS sold for donations and for profit, a video that is chock full of horrific, bloody, gory scenes depicted in fabricated non-typical dog fights they manufactured to shock and solicit funds; videos they titled educational and quality documentaries. HSUS cites the question is not Bob Stevens just a Pit Bull enthusiast who has documented the dog fighting industry? To which they responded, no, although Stevens claims to have no interest in promoting dog fighting, his own videos for which he was convicted demonstrates the contrary (so it is okay for them to produce utterly ridiculous bloody to extreme videos but I promote dog fighting with my sensible educational – come on!). They point out that in my *Pick-A-Winna* documentary I narrate and explain "match after bloody match" Again only two scenes were in America, decades prior and one in a state where it was legal at the time and the other in a state where it was a very minor misdemeanor at the time.

The others took place in countries where the sport is perfectly legal and the matches are public. The two American snippets were about five minutes long and depict two dogs wrestling around; no blood at all. HSUS mentions that I was convicted not only because I was distributing these videos, but because I was distributing them for profit. They didn't mention the fact that they distributed and still do, videos full of dog fighting blood and gore and for donations with profits far exceeding mine. And their videos are loaded with sensational malarkey and mine is devoid of blood and were educational. Within that same question/answer section the question was asked, "Has the law been successful at deterring crush videos?" They responded by saying, "Yes." After the passage of the law that convicted me, the market for such videos all but disappeared since the Court of Appeals declared the statute unconstitutional in 2008, there has been a lot of crush videos available for purchase on the Internet. I don't know why, but nobody seems to check to see if this is true (and I *begged* them to test the veracity of that lie). It was one big huge whopper. Again there never were any real crush videos to speak of. *One* very small company ran 2,000 videos that were brought to the attention of Congress by congressmen who seek a platform and kudos, and were influenced by HSUS who presented them with *one* beyond description hideous video. That is accurate. A whole statute and a subsequent law that went all the way to Supreme Court was based on *one* video some sick company made a very limited run of. This shows the tremendous extent of the influence of these animal activists. Those videos sold themselves out and were never marketed again. On the Internet under crush videos you can find all kinds of really sick stuff, I am informed by those who did research for me (I have never viewed this). The Statute, title 18 didn't end anything! I have no idea why my attorneys would not believe me. I gave them Library of Congress and websites and Google, along with a challenge: to find one single crush video apart from that initial little run. And publicly HSUS was also challenged to show any crush videos. They couldn't because there were none. But even the Supreme Court judges were not apprised of this. Why not? Because of the way the justice system is set up and the overwhelming number of court cases in America. Today you cannot simply iron out differences with your neighbor, even if his dog is eliminating on your front lawn you have to go to court and you have to pay large legal fees. The courts are beyond overwhelmed and the jails are full. So the attorney who files a brief with Supreme Court judges (or appellate judges) must be concise and deliberate. They cannot afford to get on tangents and my attorney could not let go of pointed legal argument concerning the constitutional aspects of the statute and spend time exposing HSUS, which could lose the case as the judges would probably not believe her even if she provided them with a whole book of HSUS criminal convictions or arguing over crush videos. And HSUS knows this well, very well! So, the crush video nonsense went unchallenged. HSUS again wins on that level.

Of course all of these blogs come with a solicitation to donate to HSUS. And it has been they obtain over a hundred million dollars annually in this manner. They show themselves to be protectors of animals with a posted $5,000 reward if you report dog fighting. To them that is like a dime and they don't tell us how many $5,000 rewards they actually pay. I have no way of knowing, but I suspect very few.

I learned and my life became so very enriched by my experience of seven years to finally reap justice. I experienced the dejected depression of Jeremiah and the terrified cries of David in Psalm 39 and 40. But I learned.

With the Word of God at your center, at the very core of your being, you can be completely alive in the present, without clinging to the past, caring for the future or holding to the fleeting present. I became rooted in faith and *anyone* can find happiness there. Anyone. Faith does come from reading the Word and it also begins with a little seed of hope. Hope is a step on the staircase to faith.

I re-learned a lesson with this case, a lesson taught to me many times by my Rabbi, Jesus. The Lord controls all and what so often seems a tunnel of despair down to destruction, turns out to be another trust in the Lord lesson. Wait on Him. Turned out, it was better for me and even better for Bulldogs that it became a matter of freedom of speech, the Constitution, and went all the way to Supreme Court. God showed the world that greed does *not* work.

Before we wrap, I have some dialogue I would like to share regarding the content of the book you hold in your hands.

As mentioned, many times, I am and was a journalist. Any misinformation you find in this book came from interviews I made with renowned pit dogmen. I put into print what I garnered by interviewing experienced and respected dogmen. However, some of the information I gathered I now know was just plain inaccurate. Much of it is pretty inconsequential. I made the statement that the bite of the American Pit Bull Terrier is twice the biting power of a German Shepherd. That was what I was told and that was the belief in those days. It is just plain not true. Many of my comments throughout the book were taken from the then very legal fighting dog periodical, the *Sporting Dog Journal*. But that was then and now we live in a different America and the *Sporting Dog Journal* has been taken down. That is not a criticism, just a fact. In the very beginning of the "Medicine and Miscellaneous" chapter, I make the statement that, "The fact of the matter is that many people will fight their dogs, law or no law, and if the dog is going to be fought anyway, anything we can do to help him is good." Further on I go into some medical advice on treating wounded dogs when they can't be delivered immediately to a veterinarian. This can be, as I note, a fighting dog, but it also applies to a hunting dog. Dog fighters are very well versed in caring for their dogs after the match and do not need this book to instruct them. My point is not that dog fighters should have the responsibility of performing veterinarian work, which is illegal; it is that I don't promote dog fighting by providing very basic medical care for these dogs before they go to the vet. I do not refer to dog fighting; I refer to the hunting dog or the dog that just plain gets into trouble. We humans are told, for instance, we can save a human's life by providing immediate CPR, but we leave the wrap to the medical profession also. I suggest the same concept for dogs. The statement was well intended and actually it came from a veterinarian I spoke with back then who said he hated dog fighting and if he found any he would turn them in to the police, nevertheless he would do what he could to help the dog. My statement was like that and was not meant to promote the illegal activity. This was in a day and age when dog fighting was such a misdemeanor that the penalty was lower than a speeding ticket and the sheriff and his deputy often at pit side. Different America now. My comment would not engender any hue and cry back then. In other words, that and any statements like it no longer apply. I will say it again; dog fighters in those days were very experienced in caring for a match dog after a match. I have seen veterinarians, for example, give dogs an IV with far too fast a drip, which shocks the dog. I have also watched dog fighters do a much more professional job even though they never attended any medical school. Lest I be quoted out of context, I have also viewed the opposite, one good reason for the law. It is illegal for a nonprofessional to medically treat like that. I have visited dog fighters and been there as they stayed up all night long with their fighting dog in their lap petting them with a very slow IV drip. A veterinarian may give a dog a slow IV, but they are of course not going to stay up all night petting the dog. And please do not take me out of context and make a big thing out of that statement either. I don't mean all vets are like that, or all dog fighters are that good at it; it is just something I have observed. Perhaps it is like very few doctors can stop the bleeding of an eyebrow gash on a boxer like a boxer's corner man who has never been to medical school; some have not even graduated from high school. What I am saying here is that the statement I made was actually ill founded. Dog fighters can't use simply the basics on a wounded animal although many hunters and pet owners possibly could. But I had no idea back then that America would evolve to where it is today. I did not mean to promote dog fighting or create any ballyhoo over that small sentence. So I hope to present the book to you without a lot of noise over sentences like the above. They were never meant to encourage dog fighting and none of it teaches a dog fighter anything. I can't go over every comment made in the book that animal activists make a big deal over. I'd have to re-write the whole book. My motive here is to provide you with an historical account. There is however, one special ingredient in your book I would like to address and explain. If you look in the index and find packed cell volume you will find some writing you will find nowhere else. I now know it is inaccurate. And I think it deserves an epilogue read because in explaining it, I also demonstrate how I did my journalism; how I wrote the book.

    When I began interviewing dog fighters I wanted to know it all. It wasn't that I wanted to participate in dog fighting. You know what? We love to watch the romanticized western gunfighter in the movies, but how many of you would want to actually shoot and kill someone? It was like that. I figured there *had* to be something special about these gladiator dogs and I wanted to find out everything about them. For them to engage in the pit contests I had read about meant they had to have something special that no other canine on earth had. I didn't interview just a few; I interviewed all the famous ones who would let me. I put in hours and hours visiting these old time dogfighters. I sacrificed time I wanted to spend with my children. I was building my retirement business and it started by putting in the time to learn all about these dogs. I explain this to perhaps help you feel the shock we experienced when our government attacked us in our home and confiscated my business that I spent most of my adult years building. I read the old Armitiage and Colby books. I figured these people have got to be the elite in conditioning canines. I figured that you could change the show ring much like Arnold Swarzenegger did body building, or perhaps more specifically, the way Joe Weider changed body building. In those days I saw dogs entering the show ring fat as a hog and lazy as librarian. I didn't know anything at all at the time, about dog training, but I figured a dog is going to be a whole lot sharper in obedience if he is highly conditioned. I later found out I was correct. I joined a dog training club with my Morochito when he was young. We met in a park for training. After about half an hour of on-leash training, the instructor would call a break and tell us to put the dogs in sit and rest them. It was summer and all the dogs were fat and panting to beat the band, tails drooping. Except my Morochito. From the time he was a puppy I conditioned him. I used methodology I knew from my years as a boxer and in karate and I tried techniques I learned from dog fighters to see what worked. Morochito was lean with no fat. While the fat dogs in that training class panted and seemed affected by the heat Morochito was jumping around and looking for mischief. I don't share this to brag about my dog or my conditioning methods. I share it to give you the history and my canine concepts. My dog was far healthier and alert. Although he constantly irritated me looking to get into mischief while I was new at this, he learned very quickly. He was very alert and this taught me a lot early on. Anyway, I wanted to learn how these dog fighters got their dogs into condition to compete in what is the single most demanding sport I know of for dogs. I studied the old methods presented in the Armitage and Colby books and said nothing when I interviewed the then known professional dog fighters. They all said the same thing; you don't give a fighting dog too much fluid before a match. If you do he will run hot. The last week you gradually decrease his food and water. The last food and water is given twelve hours before his match. As a boxer and a karate athlete this made absolutely no sense to me. In effect they said to have your dog in a mild dehydrated state. All of them said this and I never mentioned to any of them what others had said. It is my persona, my modus operandi, to be so very thorough when I get involved in something. Two years after I began karate I knew more (from reading) than almost all known black belts of the day. So I searched and I studied and I investigated every source I could find as to why this semi-dehydrated state could possibly help pit dogs stay in battle longer. The only conclusion I could find that could possibly explain it was the then reasonably new practice of blood doping. That is what you will read in this book concerning packed cell volume. Now, let me add this. The reason that no part of this could possibly be construed to be a dog fighters manual is because I am a journalist and I documented as thoroughly as to my knowledge to this day any book on the market what the Pit Bull is all about, including the whole match dog scenario, from known dog fighters who already know far beyond anything in this book. I include those fighting styles that I considered most effective, the intricacies of feeding, and preparation for the match as it existed in those days. But it is journalism only. Calling it a manual for dog fighters is like getting a basic text on boxing for YMCA youngsters from the library and calling it a manual for professional boxers. Or the book about Rocky Marciano or Archie Moore or Mohammed Ali or Holyfield and many more as a manual for professional boxers. And that is absolutely no exaggeration, not even a little. And the practice of not giving a match dog water for 12 hours before match time is as old and as wrong as the training methods that old time boxers received back in the 1920's as opposed to today. And that is why I took up space here to explain the section on packed cell volume in your book.

  Now, I can add to it. As a martial artist I have some training methods you will find nowhere else. One I learned from those old dog fighters. The withdrawal of fluids and putting the body into the ultimate exertion does have an effect on the blood circulatory system that emulates blood doping; somewhat akin to training at high altitudes if you can't afford to travel and train high in the mountains. But, here is what I discovered. You should never enter athletic competition semi-dehydrated. In 1984 I had to train and earn a black belt in a system called Tai-atari-do. For this examination, only a very select few qualified. I had to ride my motorcycle all the way from Winston-Salem, North Carolina to the Dos Cabezas desert, part of the Anza Borega Desert State Park in Southern California. This is said to be the southernmost and hottest arid section of the country. We had to drive straight there with no sleep and then walk five miles into the wild desert carrying our karate weapons we would test with. Prior to going out we had pre-contests. We were each given directions to some place in the North Carolina mountains and we would travel to the designated place and meet our opponent. We would not know who it was and with no words spoken, engage in combat. The only rule was we go until one person announces he cannot continue or is unable to continue. I won every single one. My last contest, I won with a dislocated elbow I incurred in training. My opponent didn't know this and announced he wished he had when afterwards he saw my arm swollen up larger than my leg and we went to a convenience store to get a bag of ice to wrap it in. He said if he had known he would have endured a few more minutes, but it would not have mattered. To train for this, much of my "secret" training methods are commonplace with today's mixed martial artists, but in those days nobody trained like that. Plus every routine I tried with my Pit Bull I experimented with myself to get the feel and the effect on my body. For example, I used to load up tires with weights and pull them up the street and up the hill in my yard as I did with my dog. I experimented to see the effect in conditioning my dog by having him pull me on a bike (I learned that from a dog fighter). I had to live it. I soaked it in and *felt* it, because whenever I did my roadwork I had my bulldog pulling me. So when I'm exhausted and can't make my legs turn over fast enough, my dog helped propel me; the same effect as bike and dog. And when distance and heat made my Bulldog lag, I pulled my dog. We became very close warrior/mates doing all that. I don't know many journalists that have experimented with all this stuff on their dog and on themselves as well. I also trained in the heat of the summer at noon, every day, on the street barefoot, to toughen my feet for the hot desert. And I did my road work barefoot. Now to the central point. That area of California at the time had these large water tanks about every thirty miles out on the interstate because it was so hot and dry cars tended to overheat and radiators burst. Hitchhikers were often found dead by the roadside from dehydration. We had to train for this and sign disclaimers as our test could easily kill any one of us. Perhaps you can see why I love our breed so much and feel highly qualified to provide quality objective journalism for the breed. Simpatico. I am so like them. Tender hearted and affectionate beyond most males and yet I love battle. I despise ill feelings and can't handle arguments. But fighting competition is me. I only feel alive when training and engaging. The point is I used to teach (accounting and management) in those days and I had my mid-day free and no classes in the summer. I trained every day at noon. I would train not having had any fluids since the prior evening. Dehydrated. Now I insist you get this straight; in my case perhaps it is genetics, *but anyone who tries to train this way does at their own risk; it could kill you*. My high degree of conditioning was responsible along with probably my genetics, but although I loaded up with fluids for my contests in effect I engaged in my own form of blood doping up until three days prior to contest. I am telling you I was – whoa! Fire! At the end of our test in the desert, as a sort of ritual, we all engaged in a race around the perimeter of the desert basin. I think it was 120 degrees during our three mile run, I forget. There were these large chemical barrels, similar to what a lot of folks use as dog houses for our breed, all around the perimeter. People camp out there and use them for bon fires I think. I was twenty years older than the next youngest of the competitors (I was 44 years old). I was in the lead by I'd say twenty lengths when we were ¾ of the way around. When I didn't see one of the barrels and went on the inside for about ten yards. The person in back of me, Mike, called out, "Bob, you missed the barrel." I ran back, around the barrel and finished the race in first place; still about twenty lengths ahead of the person who came in second. On the way out, one of the competitors went into shock. He was cold and his eyes were in shock. We went in (as part of the requirements) with no water. I half carried him out; five miles, and he made it. As a memorial to me he put a saying I gave him in front of his school in Kinston, North Carolina. Now all that is not to brag about my martial ability. It is to indicate I tried the packed cell volume training on myself and I say it worked like you would not believe, but in training, not at contest time. I also engaged my Victory dog in this training. But again – in training. Before we went into the humid South Carolina swamp to hunt, I loaded him up with fluids. If I tell you how he could run through that swamp, swim across slew, through thick briar and then engage a tough boar hog, you would think I am romanticizing. You couldn't handle the truth! As I mention this I can't help but truly belly laugh at that foolish government "expert" pig man that said you need collie dogs to herd the wild hog. Unbelievable!

Okay, I hoped to accomplish a lot with that dissertation on packed cell volume you read in your book. It was old time dog fighter stuff. That was really dated at the time I wrote the book, but I did not realize it. That chapter, that is the result of countless hours of interviews on the dog fighting aspect of our breed, has nothing whatsoever to help any dog fighter match dogs. But there is something to that packed cell volume as far as I am concerned because what it did for my body competing was incredible and it worked for my hunting dog. But it was so antiquated. It would not work for modern day dog matching. I described how it worked for me and for Victory, but don't try it yourself. It is only for those who are highly, very highly conditioned and only needed when you are going to engage in highly demanding situations like a desert at 120 degrees and zero humidity or sweltering hot humid swamp with very thick briars and swamp. It is only for those human and canine athletes who happen to have the genetics for it in my opinion.

To this day I still train in the heat of the day, semi-dehydrated at times. And I still go with my head swimming and weak and all the symptoms that say this could kill you. I go with what Conan the Barbarian said, "That which does not kill you will make you stronger." But I say again, don't do this yourself. I have been doing this for a third of a century, actually longer. I know my body and I know when to stop at the danger point. I practice relaxing and fast recovery. In fact the relax, don't panic, recover fast is not only as important as driving the body to the brink. It is the most important aspect of it. A dog, by the way, will also learn this, but you have to teach him and you have to know your dog. You have to be part of your dog to know what he can take and where to make him recover. I don't know one single animal activist that knows or has ever come close to experiencing this. But knowing when and how to quickly recover is the secret. The axiomatic statement "adapt or die" applies here. I do not want to be responsible for anyone or any dog being harmed. This is not something I can teach in a book. I have been doing this for over fifty years. It started when as a little boy. I used to pretend I was an Indian warrior and I'd play intense in the hot sun without drinking any water and pretend like I have been hunting for three days with no food or water and now the enemy is attacking me. It has to do with knowing how to relax and not panic. You learn to accept and embrace the heat. Instead of Arrrrgh – it is mmmmm. It is about embracing the heat and thinking warrior, with a calm and happy heart, much like a boy playing cowboy and Indian. And blood flow has a lot to do with it. I stretch far more than modern mixed martial artist and I practice Yoga. For dogs it is about massage. Plus you have to be skinny. There is a lot to it that cannot be described in a book. That is as close as I can describe it. And it takes years, not months to cultivate. When I am not engaging in this dehydration training I sip water all day long as well as pomegranate and cranberry juice. This is not something I do all the time. Same with dogs. I started my Victory dog as a pup, taking him with me for roadwork in the hot sun. Half way through I would tie him up do my karate kata then unhook him to finish the run. He smelled the sweat and warrior mode on me as I would be psyched. The same warning for humans is doubled for dogs. I messed up a few times and had to carry him on my shoulders back home where I slowly poured small gulps of cool water from his water bottle in his mouth and poured a bucket of cool water over him and sponged his groin and under his neck and belly with cool water and revived him. You have to learn your dog and his points. In the swamp when we hunted, he could burst all out and run like a cheetah with a relaxed grace through thick jungle-like swamp and wrestled wild hog. At rest times, when the bay dogs would lay down panting and exhausted, he would just lay there hardly panting (and bay dogs have a much higher endurance threshold than Bulldogs). I used to carry his water bottles in a back pack when we hunted. I was the only hunter that did that. A couple times I had to carry him as he had slow leaking wounds, to a creek to revive him. He would come around and finish his hunt and catch again. How much of that was his genetics, and how much to my packed cell volume training, I do not know. I did the same with his mother Velvet when she competed in weight pulling (she was a grand champion who won in her weight division, light weight as well as in middle weight and heavy weight). I took off my shirt when she competed and she smelled the excitement warrior on me as I called her on. I do not know of anyone else who did that. I must admit I have always, for myself and for my dogs, engaged in some unusual stuff. Also I want to say that to this day when I go to a karate or Balintawak or kickboxing seminar and they call for the usual water break, and all the young twenty-year-olds scramble for water or Gator Aide. I calmly stand by feeling no effect. Sometimes I go and sip my Endurox or Accelorade (much better quality and it won't give you belly situations). Gator aide will make those youngsters blanch when they receive belly shots. Accelorade, if sipped, won't. Sometimes I don't consume any fluids. But that is a follow up on the packed cell volume you will read about in your book.

On the dehydration. In the year 2006 I received permission from my parole officer to travel to Richmond, Virginia and compete in the WKKO Annual Kickboxing Challenge III. I was not up front about my age and stated I was 45 years old. I was 66. For many not relevant reasons, I did not engage in that packed cell volume training mentioned above, but I did enter my full contact competition fully dehydrated, and that is why I share this battle with you. I *know* what a pit dog feels like that goes into competition trained in the old timer's manner. My training went great and I did great in my pre-contest sparring sessions. In the warm up area before my match I had the usual butterflies, but I had been to that arena so many, many times, I was used to it and it energized me rather than controlled me. My kickboxer instructor led me down that path to the ring and my fellow school kickboxers walked down hands on each other's shoulders. I went up to the ring under those bright lights with the audience clapping. This is one of the most exciting experiences an athlete can experience. I can taste, this my last, to this day. I felt good. But, I was badly dehydrated. Not because I planned it. You see, I was and am in great physical condition for any age, however there are certain aspects of old age one cannot bury with quality nutrition or high tech training. I have a highly swollen prostate. It is in my genetics. The prostate is a muscle much like any other muscle. Given time, testosterone makes it grow larger. My father came very close to dying from prostate cancer and would have if it were not for modern technology and his tough game blood. My grandfather and great grandfather all died of prostate cancer. Anyway, when the prostate grows large, it cuts off the flow of urine so you feel like you have to pee and you can't. Then, all of a sudden you have to pee badly and if you don't make it to the bathroom, you pee in your pants. Old codger I am, training or nay. I know where every restroom is in every town we visit. I often have to had pull over and pee by the side of the road, unable to make it to the next service station. So I was so afraid that even after I had emptied as much as I could, right up to warming up before I am announced, I would get to the ring and have to pee uncontrollably. The day before I was to compete, I consumed very little fluid. My last fluid was about ten o'clock p.m. and the next day I had no fluid or food. On the way to the match we stopped for breakfast. All the fighters had pancakes. Pancakes and syrup: my kickboxer's pre-contest meal. It is high carb, quickly and easily absorbed by trained muscles and the carbs go right to those trained muscles and carries you for your bout. But I didn't even have my beloved coffee. By the time I was warming up in the dressing room, I was weak as a kitten. One thing that helped and one reason my packed cell volume training works for me but can damage most is that I had done this so many times my body was used to it. Still, I cannot describe how weak I was. My legs were like rubber and I hadn't even heard the bell for the first round. When we got in the ring my instructor told me to "get used to the ring," which meant I cruise the whole ring like this ring belongs to me. I own it. I danced around the ring jumping laterally and looked at my opponent. My instructor had taught me to look at my opponent as he warmed up. He was in his early twenties and he could hit his instructor's focus mitt head high with slow controlled kicks, but I said inwardly, "Oh, good! He likes roundhouse kicks. Please throw high roundhouse kicks at me. I eat them. Because my opponent is on one leg and being ready even if a powerful Muay Thai kicker, I am ready and I fight inside like a boxer." So I felt good about this. My weakness forgotten the thrill was infusing my whole body and I felt so very alive.

    When the bell rang for the first round, I exploded across the ring into my opponent. He was game. It was a war from the beginning, non-stop. I didn't give him time or space for his kicks, but he punched back; fast. The audience was screaming. I started out feeling weak, almost faint. But after about 30 seconds, with the battle raging, I felt strong. I didn't breathe hard once. When the round ended I walked back to my corner. I generally jogged mostly to show my opponent how strong I was, but this time I almost wobbled back to my corner. No standing in the corner this time. *My* instructor did corner work and his instructor, a former world champion kickboxer, asked me how I felt. "Weak. Real, real weak," I replied. Second round, I again exploded into my opponent. I always do no matter what. Scratch hard, always. For 30 seconds I thought I was going to pass out dizzy and weak, but then something kicked in and instead I felt like I had more endurance than I ever had. It was still a war. My opponent knocked me through the ropes only my feet remained in the ring. I came back in and exploded again. I drove him all the way to the other side of the ring to the ropes. He fired a roundhouse kick and I came in with a straight right that broke his nose. My stable mate later told me he overheard the man talking to his girl friend in the dressing room after the fight and told her he could not believe he lost his fight to a 66 year old man. When the bell rang my inner voice said doggone it! I cannot recall any fight I have ever been in that when the bell rang or the referee called *Time*, I have not been disappointed and wished I had another minute. But again, walking back to my corner I felt like I was going to pass out, but my heart still sang as the audience was standing up clapping. The third round was still a war, but I won decisively. This time I began strong and I ended strong and felt like I could fight another fight and another after that if they would let me. I raised my hands in victory and my instructor put his arms around my legs and lifted me up while I kept my hands raised. I got a standing ovation. Then when the referee announced me winner and raised my gloved hand, I got another standing ovation. Then the referee came over to my corner and asked, "Excuse me, sir, if you don't mind my asking, how old are you?" I apologized and confessed I was not up front when I contracted for my match. I informed him I was 66 years old. He was aghast and asked if I minded if he announced that. I said okay and he did and I got another standing ovation. I cannot help but wonder, does a pit dog have that feeling when he wins a match because there is this electricity in the air. I cannot describe it. It is like the best pie you ever consumed with Dunkin' Donuts coffee quadrupled. It is not just inside you; it floats in the air like fragrance after a spring rain. I wonder if that is what made a pit dog's tail raise and curl up over his back and the corners of his mouth grin as he is patted after his match? I wonder? The point is, I think those old time Bulldogs won when the old handlers matched them starting out in a semi-dehydrated condition because at least they didn't have fluid sloshing in their belly like the inexperienced handlers did, but also because the dogs were tough enough to win anyway. I think I know how they felt. I also know this: I will never, ever, forget it. I had a wonderful time and I thank my instructor Kent Eanes from the depth of my foolish missing link heart. That night my kickboxing buddy bought my dinner. I had blueberry pancakes.

And, I feel, rookie or nay, very qualified to be a journalist for the history of our breed.

Lastly, I shared all that with you to dish up a spoonful of my writing style; how I construct and carve out my journaling. I research everything and sometimes what seems wrong, may not be. If you read the breeding chapter in your book know that a great deal of study went into it. And the scientific breeding concepts in that chapter are not dated; they apply today. Read how the King's Ranch used inbreeding and line breeding, outcross for highbred vigor and then bred back into to the original inbreeding, which brings the original many generations ago foundation right back up front without the attenuating and weakening aspects of over inbreeding. It works to this day.

At this juncture, I would like to address the comments the HSUS made concerning my book.

In a blog www.hsus.org/acf/news.bob_stevens_quotations_book.html, written August 3, 2009, and still up at the time of this writing, you can find "Excerpts for Bob Stevens' *Dogs of Velvet and Steel*." I want to share this as it epitomizes what I must put up with from HSUS. They took out of context actual ingredients from my book and inform you what section of the book.

Introduction: "Generations and generations of pit fighting (sic) have resulted in a very tough animal. These dogs will continue fighting even though most of their ear or a section of their mouth has been chewed off or a leg rendered inoperable." As usual it is taken out of context. I did not say all dog fights result in ears or sections of mouth chewed off. It happens as often as cauliflower ears or permanently damaged fascia in human boxers or the bulbous broken nose that is revered in the human athlete, but the ultimate in cruelty for the canine athlete. Leg rendered inoperable is from biting pressure, very much like wrestlers and Brazilian Jiu-Jutsu fighters apply in their contests. I was journalizing. I told the truth. What in the world is wrong with that true historical paragraph?

Chapter 1, "History:" "Friend of mine put a young, inexperienced Pit Bull against a huge German Shepherd. The Shepherd was literally (sic) more than twice the Pit Bull's weight and size. Early in the fight the Shepherd had the little Pit Bull's head in his jaws. The Pit Bull (named Snapper) was a little black dog with white chest. My friend said that the Pit Bull actually turned white all over. Said that he'd not seen that happen before and he thought he'd lost his dog. But as it happened, the Pit Bull shook out of the hold and proceeded to tear that German Shepherd to pieces." Again, I was journalizing. By "friend of mine" I meant a Pit Bull fellow who bred but didn't match pits. He was an acquaintance, not really a friend and it was wrong for him to do that with the German Shepherd, but in those days nothing was thought of this. Prior to that story I related how another person put his Pit Bull with an Akita. The point of this journalizing was that the little Pit Bull prevails with much larger dogs because of the genetic quality called gameness and inherited fighting ability. I should not have used graphic terms like "tear to pieces," but it was true. A pit can do far more damage to dogs not bred for battle than they can with each other. An analogy would be; suppose an English school teacher (with no martial training) did something so terrible to a professional boxer that they got into a real fight. Let us suppose you viewed that boxer fight five professional fights went 12 rounds and neither boxer had any marks at all. The contest was won on points. That same boxer would put the teacher in the hospital a bloody mess. The ability makes the difference. It is like that. The Pit Bull is not only a very tough breed (from centuries of breeding gladiators), but the *ability* is there. So the same pit that might engage in a pit contest and neither dog receive more than surface skin wounds that heal to barely noticeable if noticeable at all, against another breed the damage the pit might do could be described in words you does not want. But, point is, I was a journalist and not promoting anything.

Also in the History chapter, "The Mating of Black Widow to Spike also produced Don Maloney's Toot. In the middle 60's Toot was considered one of the best ever by many. He was a 54 pound Bulldog who, in his two contract matches, killed both his opponents in less than 20 minutes." Dear Reader, that is pure history. It is true and it is an historical account. HSUS uses it to give the impression this is how pit dog fights go and that my book is about cruelty. Dogs that were killed in the pit have, historically, happened about as often as human boxers killed in the ring. This Toot dog was a famous dog, historically, and hence his story is in the history chapter. But HSUS is just full of manure. You can find far more graphic animal description in more books than you or I could count.

Also in the History chapter: "Anyway, the other thing reporters like to do is show blood pictures of the dogs all chewed up. Well, as far as I know those are true pictures. As I said the Pit Bull is capable of taking a lot. It's not cruel to them; it's fun." Yes, I said that. It is true. I am reporting what these dogs are about. And, I am not taking up for dog fighting when I report that news reporters like to jack up the sensationalism. I have pictures of Mickey Ward in his Ward/Gatti fight where you cannot distinguish his features he is so covered in blood. After the fight, cleaned up he is clean and healthy. For that matter, in many of my karate battles, I have been covered with blood (with contests I won!) and it looks horrific. Cleaned up I am fine and dandy; it just looks bad. And so it generally is with dog fights. Cleaned up after their match, most of the time they are fine and dandy, albeit exhausted. Read the book *Becoming Holyfield* for a lot of his fight and post fight descriptive narrative. It emulates almost any dog fight I ever viewed. I do not say this in order to promote or indicate I encourage dog fighting. I am saying my book is devoid of sensational hyperbole and unrealistic malarkey. The dog fighters I interviewed all liked to mention this comparison between their sport and boxing. That is to say, they saw more blood and body damage in the boxing ring than they did with their dogs. For that matter many Pit Bull folks who never matched dogs but were spectators at many matches would make the same observation. I do know that I have read that it has been reported there are an average of ten deaths a year in boxing matches world wide and that the American Medical Association reports about nine hundred deaths in the boxing ring since 1920. How the dog fighting situation is today I do not know. I have had some Pit Bull folks inform me the dogs bite a lot harder today and that many of the modern dog fighters leave their dogs in too long and do not pick them up as soon as they should to concede a match when their dog is obviously, game or nay, not going to win. He is just going to be bit down. But I don't know. I want to go on record that I do not support dog fighting and when I mention that I read about boxers (as in the Holyfield book) or when I relate my own marital experiences as being related to and no more severe than the pit contests I interviewed when I was a journalist for this aspect, I am merely reporting what I have observed and experienced and I am being truthful. I have also observed dogs like Grand Champion Luther and what they can do to a dog I don't want to describe. Dogs like that happen as often as Mike Tyson (and usually quit when they find a dog that is equal to them as quick as Mr. Tyson). I am saying I do not mean to imply matching dogs is like playing ping pong. I also report that real damage does happen in some of those matches. In the same breath, while I may enjoy competition in the ring for myself, dog fighting happens to be too much for me as far as my own dog and that has always been the case. I believe the gladiator genes are better channeled into Schutzhund. Better the ring than the street. Better the field trial than the pit. That is my take on this and I hope my statements are not taken out of context. If you quote me, quote all of it please.

Lastly in the History chapter: "Our standard of conformation cannot be based on what someone who never saw a dogfight thinks a fighting dog should look like, but should be based on those physical attributes displayed on winning pit dogs." HSUS is trying to make implications and innuendo. That statement was not mine. It is in the conformation standard designed by the show conformation organization for our breed. It is the same thing you can find in the show standard for let us say a wolf hound or any other canine that originated as a performance breed. It means that the American Pit Bull Terrier, in the show ring must display the structure of what makes the breed what it is. In that respect it is no different from any breed conformation standard. Again – HSUS is just full of baloney.

Chapter 2, "The Pit Bull Pet:" "I attended many pit fights and saw some real hard, deep biters and I saw some who were very hard (for Pit Bulls) biters." HSUS is trying to find things to make innuendo. It is true; I attended those many matches and I did observe these things. I was a journalist and I did nothing illegal and I was not promoting a doggone thing. I reported.

And then, "If a Pit Bull is not given proper people socialization, if he spends his life either on a chain in his keep (training for a fight) and receives very little socialization with strange people, he can be a people biter." I can't find that statement in my book. If I made it, it would be in the context where I strongly encourage obedience training and proper people socialization. But, yeah I was still a rookie then. The statement is not accurate. Even for Pit Bulls that do not receive people socialization the breed is by nature very people affectionate and it is as difficult to get them to bite people as it is to get a beagle to bite people. What about the current 21st century reports of Pit Bulls mauling people? I contend again, since the breed has just started coming up with these people biters it comes from breeding pits to other breeds and registering them as pure bred. I document that contention again, with the observation that these people biting pits didn't exist in the history of America until the 1990's (began on a small scale in the 1970's, more in the 80's and escalated as the HSUS became bigger and more powerful). Where were they in America from 1800 to 1990? HSUS took that statement and wanted to make it their statement that the breed is a people killer breed; sheer malarkey.

Chapter 7, "Scientific Conditioning:" "After a couple minutes let the puppy catch the rope and play with it. Every time he shakes it, excitedly say, 'Shake it, Boy (or girl).' When the puppy matures, upon hearing the command 'shake it,' he will shake hard whatever he's holding onto." Well – yeah! These scoundrels again take my statements out of context. Read it - you will notice before that education, I suggest that hemp rope is the best because that is the material used in Schutzhund sleeves and you get the puppy used to it and loving it as a toy. Then after that statement, I explain that is how you prepare the puppy for Schutzhund trials as an adult. Schutzhund is the ultimate companion dog and I am promoting this activity. Schutzhund is probably as healthy an activity as you can find for your dog. Take the dogs away from dog fighting and into Schutzhund. I was very clearly promoting Schutzhund not dog fighting. It is so obvious; you can read that they knew it! Those rascals are just full of misinformation and trying to damage my book. They are again, liars and deceivers.

Also in the scientific conditioning chapter. "I put bones under the category of conditioning because they are probably the best way to exercise a Pit Bull pup's jaw muscles and teach how to use his mouth correctly for the hardest bite." Well again – yeah! I guess I should have said for *any* dog, not just a Pit Bull. It is like pushups are great for human boxers. But pushups are great for anyone not just athletes. Should I be put in jail for this? I had no idea these rogues would pick apart everything I said. Bones are very healthy for any dog. It especially prepares the pup for adult Schutzhund.

Chapter 10, "The Combat Dog:" "Immediately after the match the dogs will, of course, be pretty bloody and cut up if it is any kind of a fight." I couldn't find that statement. I think it is included in one of the interviews I included in this chapter with an old-timer dog fighter. But this chapter is historical and educational. I do not agree (as you find in many places throughout the book) myself as I have viewed countless matches with world class pit dogs in which there was no blood seen at all.

And then, "In my personal opinion the best style (if there is such a thing) would be the rough, boring-in style of the chest dog. This dog tends to be stronger for his weight class and has more leverage. Wherever his opponent grabs him, doesn't matter, he bores in and buries his snout in that dog's chest or underbelly whenever he can. This type of dog also tends to be a hard biter." Well I am a journalist and I was reporting the results of years of research. Okay, so it was okay for the "expert" in my trial to explain about fighting dogs and he didn't know what he was talking about. He was just trying to impress with his false sense of expertise, but for me as an educator for the history of the breed it is a felon? This is just more trumped up allegation.

Another one in the Combat chapter; "The Rose dog won her match, stopping her opponent in 58 minutes, and she looked like she could go for another hour. Her opponent was a good dog too, but you know that Pit Bull had puppies that night after the match. The word I got was that evidently her owners didn't know she had bred and was pregnant." Again I was an historian. The situation was true. The dog fighter was not cruel. It was a true mistake as she showed absolutely no sign of having pups in her belly. This can happen and it indicates how very tough this breed is. I just shared one of many, many stories I experienced. You can find stories about mafia gangsters in many books. Should those writers be put in prison for telling the gangster stories? It is just more trumped up blarney on the part of HSUS.

Here was another one they quoted. "The dehydrated dog has thicker blood, so the wounds do not bleed as freely." I was a journalist and at the time this was what many old-time dog fighters told me. It was wrong. That subject has already been addressed. HSUS is again trying to toot their horn. Actually, the dogs were not matched dehydrated, I later found out.

Lastly in the Combat chapter: "That Jocko is one hard-biting Pit Bull. I tell you he'll finish a fight very quickly. You may recall the incident related in the medicine chapter, when a dog nearly died at pit side. His pulse was so low they had to cut open his leg to find a vein to put fluid in. The dog survived and became a four time winner. He was a good pit dog. Well the dog that nearly killed him was Jocko." Again, very few people in the world are qualified to write about this breed in all aspects as I, since I have studied it all. And I wrote about it all. Jocko is historically, one of the best and most effective pit dogs in the history of the breed in America. That pit fight (I was there) is by no means illustrative of pit fights. These were among the best in the world. The dog that lost to Jocko that night went on to become a four time winner and then retired a very healthy dog with barely discernible scar tissue, to live a long healthy life being bred and fed the best. Now I am not I say *not* promoting dog fighting with that observation! I am saying it is just not what these tricksters play it up to be and I am reporting true incidents. And again it is historical. Jocko appears in the pedigree of a huge number of current Bulldogs who are not fought at all. Jocko, I have seen, in the pedigree of current day show dogs a lot. And these people should have a free right, especially in America, to read about the historical stories of famous dogs in their pet's pedigree.

Chapter 11, "Conclusion:" "Under controlled circumstances, particularly where no money is on the line, I don't see how the Pit Bull would get seriously hurt. I don't feel that rolling a Pit Bull for 20 minutes is a sufficient game test unless a second more demanding test is planned later on. I feel that the Pit Bull should be allowed to go for a good long time or well two-dogged to determine the strength of the inherited gameness. The Pit Bull will heal up just fine afterwards." Again, this was in a day when dog matches were legal in the state I went to view and interview, or a very minor misdemeanor in North Carolina. Modern boxers and kickboxers train this way. My national champion instructor trained like this at our head school. He would spar two or three rounds and then spar two more rounds with a new fresh sparring partner with a different style, and then a couple more with another. This training is commonplace. I was rendering my opinion based on years of observations of dogs being schooled (getting experience and testing their gameness for a match) and finding them very healthy and leading long healthy lives afterwards. Plus my conclusion summation; please note HSUS left out my statement that followed their out-of-context quote, "a large majority Pit Bull owners ought to become involved in the legal activities described in this book; obedience, tracking, weight-pulling, and the ultimate challenge, Schutzhund." I warned that if the dog fighting situation becomes a "big thing" it can lead to widespread abuses and cruelty. Well, this has happened. Yes, it is a different world and my conclusions must now blend with our current situation in America. Hence the conclusion chapter in my book must be re-stated. My blanket statement: Nevertheless, dog fighting is an anachronism and those gladiator genes must be channeled into healthier accepted activities such as weight pulling and Schutzhund. Hunting can and should remain. I do not and never have promoted actual dog fighting itself. And that blanket statement applies to almost the whole Conclusion chapter.

Like John Denver, I've seen desert storms. I drove through them on the California and Arizona desert on my Nighthawk motorcycle. I've been in the Colorado Mountains in the springtime with my daughter. Did my roadwork thorough the origins of our nation at Valley Forge where my son resides. In the Navy, I've been on the high seas in the eye of a hurricane and relaxed under a sleepy blue sky. I've smelled the sweat, blood, and testosterone of countless boxing and karate gyms and I have known the most tender, sweetest affection in all of human nature with my wife Julie. It has been a good life. But still, the fat lady has yet to begin singing "God Bless America."

I am of the personal opinion that every man before he flies to the starry heaven, needs to have a beautiful wife that loves him and treats him right. I got that with my Julie. Perhaps it is because there is seven years between myself and my little sister, but there has never been any sibling rivalry with us. We have always loved and cared and helped each other out. Perhaps it is because our parents were kind, tender, unselfish, hard, old fashioned, New England work ethic parents as were our relatives. A blessing all the more valuable; far more valuable than gold and sliver. Every man should own and travel across and around the back roads of America in a midnight blue Dodge van with his Bulldog in the back seat. And know the feeling of freedom in the wind slamming your hair by owning and breezing across our nation on his own motorcycle; or as Kris Kristofferson sang in "Leaving Her Was Easier;" "aching with the feeling of the freedom of an eagle when she flies." He should own at least one unique Bulldog and feel the fire. He should live the warrior and feel the high of kata (karate forms). Solidify all that by raising children that turn out to be good folks the world is better because of, and be an educator and impact and inspire young people to make a positive place in the world. To see yourself in your grandson and watch him grow to be a tender hearted but great (Krav Maga) warrior (his name is Jubal Smith and the lion and the lamb dwell together within him). This will fill your soul to the brim, almost. Almost because who can describe the birth of a granddaughter, Rachael Emme, twenty years after your grandson's birth? But second that emotion. How can a man put it into words? I can't. I call her Rosebud and she taught me important lessons about our God because I prayed fervently and feverishly for her for twenty years and she came when I thought the prayers were denied. And finally to fulfill the ultimate reason for being: teach the Kingdom of God. I have been blessed that all of the above has been my life through the time of this writing, seventy years old. So, what is left? He who lives by the sword shall die by the sword. My pen is my sword.

Well readers, therein is the epilogue, which is actually a sort of epilogue to the book you hold in your hands. The true epilogue is yet to be written. My good friend Tony Robbins provided the closing epilogue. In his Breakthrough program in July 2010, he said "Your story is not where you start; it is where you take it to." Mr. Robbins has never met me and wouldn't know me if we met on the street. I say "good friend" because I have read all of his books, I have his motivational audio tapes and booklets and I *did* everything he taught. My son has attended his training seminars and I have his notes. Good friend because of how Mr. Robbins has impacted my life. The Lord used Tony Robbins to teach me many things. It is fair to say you have the *Dogs of Velvet and Steel* book because of the inspiration and instruction I soaked into my core from Tony Robbins.

Chapter 3: Bibliography

My bibliography is a tad different than most. It comes with some narrative about mostly books. The Ed Faron book comes with a story. Some of the narrative may be inaccurate because of the length of time, my age, and the stress of my case has rendered me a bit forgetful. I do not know if any of these books are in print or available and don't want to take the time to find them. I know the authors, but that case has left scars. Some I have not communicated with since. Please do not correspond and ask how you can obtain the books as you can probably find them easier than I can. I live a very isolated life. I train in my martial arts 24/7 and have my own Bulldog stuff and I hate phone calls and shooting the breeze. Same goes for emails. That said here is your bibliography. Much, if not most of this bibliography is about the historical gladiators of the pit that form the backbone of the American Pit Bull Terrier. To make a lot of noise about it is like taking people to court and writing long nasty blogs whenever one reads of the Mastiff breed as war dogs, proclaiming the historian promotes fighting the Mastiff at American shopping malls. Or getting red-faced angry at western historical novels that popularize Jesse James or Josey Wales, proclaiming the historian is promoting bank robbery or violently shooting people. Please!

American Dog Breeders Association Inc. Box 1771, Salt Lake City, Utah 84110-1771.

This organization (ADBA) is the primary registry for the American Pit Bull Terrier (APBT) and sanctions the breed's conformation show and weight pulling competition. The organization also publishes the *American Pit Bull Terrier Gazette*. This is the APBT equivalent of the American Kennel Club (AKC). As mentioned, I've been a journalist for the breed for decades. As such I have been privy to the gossip. Two enterprises you cannot engage without being bombarded with criticism and gossip. The pastor of a church and a dog registry (and for the APBT – quadruple that observation). Pit Bull folks either love ADBA, or they don't. Like, unfortunately, pastors and leaders in a church, if ADBA did what one group of critics wanted, everyone else would complain. I often observe how these animal activists get away with all their obvious malarkey! Why are they so successful in their mission to eradicate the Pit Bull breed in courts, legislation, and public media? Why? Because the Pit Bull fraternity operates very similar to the Native American Indian when we started on the Atlantic coast and campaigned across the continent to the Pacific taking their land and their homes. Eventually, advanced technology, including firearms and sheer numbers would have accomplished this anyway, but the Indians lost from the get-go because they would not band together. The very few times they momentarily did, they prevailed. But the band together never lasted more than a battle or two. Not only were the tribes constantly bickering and at war, they constantly bickered within their own tribe. People, support the ADBA or don't wonder why the animal activists prevail, misleading the public about the APBT breed painting them as a criminal threat to America. How support? To make a long story short, rather than gossip about how bad a job they do or how they are doing it wrong, spend that time exposing the enemy. And participate in the healthy activities like the conformation show ring. It is fun. Don't get all bent out of shape if you don't like the judging etc. Hey, it is a *fun* match, not a measure of your ego. When I went to my first ADBA show after released from the case, I was so very pleased at the sportsmanship and the high quality of the dogs. It is always the minority that ruins it for everyone else. Anyway, the ADBA has my total support and is at the top of your bibliography.

Crenshaw, James. *My Life and Times with the American Pit Bull Terrier.* Charlotte, N.C.: Walsworth Publishing Co 1999.
    Can't say enough on this one. Real dogs, real dogmen by a real famous dogman. It is his autobiography.

Dayan, Colin. *The Law is a White Dog.* New Jersey: Princeton University Press. 2011.
    Colin Dayan is the Robert Penn Warren Professor of Humanities at Vanderbilt University. She's written other books of similar genre and is a regular contributor to the *Boston Review* and the *London Review.* She reports very shocking news concerning the worldwide slaughter of Pit Bulls; outrageous, hideous, sick slaughter. *The Law is a White Dog* is a shocking expose´ of America's justice system today. Very pointed; part and parcel of her revealing, rolling back the covers that blanket our justice system dialogue, is a constant reference thread to legal ambiguities and legal abuse of dogs. Anyone victimized by an activist and preparing for trial, in my opinion, should ask the defense attorney to read this book. Our new generation law students could improve America if the law professors read this book, took it to heart, and made it required reading. I know this one is definitely available.

Faron, Ed and Chris. *The Complete Gamedog.* Charlotte, N.C.: Walsworth Publishing Co., 1995.

I knew (about) Ed. We corresponded because my book. He had a good bit of personal suffering in his life and Bulldogs were the only things on this planet that were loyal to him, loved him without question, and would never betray him. He was a breeder. He always called his dogs his "babies." For Ed his dogs were his family and there is not a shred of exaggeration there. He loved his dogs every bit as much as most parents love their children. He called me one day, from Cleveland if I recall, and said it was a hot bed in that area. Animal activists were getting police to raid innocent breeders, fabricating cases, confiscating their dogs, and getting court orders to kill them by the hundreds. It was at a point where he was very scared. I told him he should move to North Carolina; even dog fighting was a misdemeanor and that fine was lower than a speeding ticket. Even match dogs when confiscated in a bust were returned the next day if they paid a fifty dollar fine. Innocent people, like breeders, show dogs, and Pit Bull clubs were left totally alone. I offered help. He surprised me and came to NC. He ended up living in Lonzo Pratt's old cabin. In Cleveland, Ed had worked in a pet shop and became experienced enough to become manager, if I recall. After getting firmly settled in Greensboro, N.C. and beginning to develop his yard, he landed a job at a pet store in a small town about 20 miles north of Greensboro and moved, along with his beloved dogs, there. His love for his dogs had no boundaries. His whole life was those dogs. He had no wife and little communication with family. He studied the breed with a passion. He knew every breeder in the country. He built his yard from a few ho-hum to a potpourri of as good mixes as you can find. To my knowledge, in those days he was a breeder only. It takes a lot of time and dedication to match dogs; as much time as a full time boxing coach does. From what I saw there is no money to be made in it. In later years he did match a very few dogs, I think.

In any event, Ed's many years of experience in animal training and retail management in the pet industry was responsible for him going right up the ladder in the pet store he worked with that managed a chain of stores in North Carolina. I recall it was mentioned he would be promoted to management level back in a Greensboro branch. There was an employee there who resented Ed getting recognized above him when Ed had only been with the company a couple months. He found out Ed raised Pit Bulls because, like a child with new toys, Ed constantly, excitedly, talked about his "babies." This said he had acquired a Pit Bull from the Guilford County Humane Society, but had to return the dog as it was a people biter. Anyway, this fellow listened to Ed constantly talk about his dogs and he kept telling him he wished he had a real true bred pit. What he didn't tell Ed, it turned out, was when he returned the people biting so-called Pit Bull he had noticed a huge poster that offered a thousand dollar reward, per conviction, for any information leading to the arrest of dog fighter. When he approached Ed, he seemed like a real nice fellow, all friendly and excited about the breed and sincere about wanting a family pet that would have a nice home. So Ed offered to give him a real old bitch who was crippled up with arthritis, but she had very high quality breeding and could still have pups. If Mr. Moore would provide her a good home, Ed would let him have her in return for a puppy from her in the future. Her name was Tootsie and the plan was she would have a nice home as a family pet to finish her days. Sounded good. So Mr. Moore and his wife came to visit and look at Tootsie. Ed's place is very country and hard to find so he arranged to meet them at a nearby store to follow him. Mr. Moore later testified in court that he met there to go to a dog fight. I am amazed how much scoundrels get away with telling lies in court. Well they had a nice visit and said they would love to give Tootsie a loving home. Moore came over to visit a lot after that and he first showed up with two fifty pound bags of dog food. It later turned out each time he came to visit he first went to the Humane Society and made up stories about dog fights where he was going. I know they were lies because at least in those days, I knew Ed didn't match dogs. He was a breeder. One story he told in court was that Ed took Tootsie off her chain and told him, look she may be old but watch what she can do and he set her down with a fifty pound young male and she cut the dog to pieces. Ed fed the corpse to the other dogs to feed their blood lust. What a sheer pile of manure! Tootsie was eleven years old had only one tooth and was crippled up with arthritis and had trouble walking. I was standing in the back of the courtroom and with this story I kind of loudly coughed, bull hockey! Moore's visits increased and he began to act more and more weird. They had given him a puppy in addition and he told Ed he thought Ed was stringing him along about this quality breeding because the puppy would not fight but would play with stray dogs. Ed patiently explained this is not what the breed is and was beginning to have doubts about how good a home his dogs were getting. The fellow acted increasingly strange. One day he showed up with a big Doberman Pinscher and wanted Ed to let one of his Pit Bulls kill it. Turned out the Humane Society put him up to this one. He told Ed he was going to push the Doberman's head out his car window and let him get clipped by a semi; what a weirdo. Ed was sorry he trusted this fellow. The fellow told the Humane Society and the police that Ed was armed, dangerous and a big cocaine dealer as well as a dog fighter. This happens all the time, all across America. It was a circus Ed later related. They came in with a full S.W.A.T. team, even had air support, early one Sunday morning. They came storming in with assault weapons screaming and threw Ed and his friend on the ground. He had a really great bred out of Ch.Chinaman female chained up near the back door. She had puppies. She was barking like crazy and these police with assault guns were afraid of her. They kept yelling they were going to shoot her if she didn't shut up. Ed tried explaining she was just protecting her puppies. But these bad dude policemen were scared to death of her. The police stormed into Ed's home after dragging him over to a police car and shoving him in. They tore the place apart, dumping out dresser drawers and just trashed his home. No this is not old-time Communist Russia; this is 1989 America. Ed told them as they were carting the dogs off not to put them in the same cage. They did anyway and then the dogs began fighting. They didn't pay any attention. Ed frantically beat his head on the window of the police car trying to get their attention. Finally it was noticed and so they yanked the dogs out by their back lags pulling apart the legs and doing more damage to the dogs than they did to each other all in the name of humanity! In the shelter, they put the dogs together – or said they got loose – and they got all cut up. They had to call in a vet to suture and medicate them. Foolish, so foolish. They shot the poor mother that had the puppies with tranquilizers. Wild Cherry was her name. I knew her. She was affectionate to an extreme with people; old and harmless to people! They dragged her from her home with puppies hanging off her. In the animal shelter kennel she caught an infection that partially blinded one eye. The world's largest protector of animals. There was just one incident that gave some humor, bright light on a dark day and a bit of "serves you right!" Mean Jolene gave them a run for their money. She kept six armed and so-called experienced animal control officers at bay for quite some time. She kept snatching their catch poles away from them and shaking them around. Finally they shot her with a tranquilizer gun. Mean Jolene was abused as a pup before Ed got her and it took months for him to win her trust and affection, but she never trusted strangers; not one bit. I loved Mean Jolene. Her story is in Ed's book. She was true bred Nigerino. She was line bred Nigerino through Cates Cujo on her top side and Townsend's Black Widow on the bottom. True bred because she looked and acted like Nigerino. I thought enough of her that she was in my breeding; my Victory's daughter Vickie. The mother, Wildside's Beauty, was double bred on Jolene and the best producing son of Jeep, Werdo. In another book I'll explain the breeding. Nigerino has a reason for breeding the same as Jeep; gene clusters that have a higher mathematical probability of reproducing and of course Jeep was heavy in my bloodline.

Anyway, the trial was a complete sham. A misdemeanor trial, at the time, the courtroom was filled with an angry crowd all there to watch the wonderful HSUS take down this "dogfighting ring." Packed with reporters and sensationalism. The trial went on for two days. All evidence that Ed and his friends had done nothing illegal whatsoever was ignored. The witness continually made contradicting statements on the stand. These real large glossy photos were shown of Ed's dogs; dogs that were supposed to have been involved in long bloody, gory dogfights. The dogs were healthy with no scar tissue. This big piece of wood a foot long and two inches in diameter was indicated as the breaking stick Ed used to part the dogs when he fought them. There were supposed teeth marks on the end. Ed posits Mr. Moore himself chewed on the end of the wood as it would be impossible to be used as a breaking stick. I could go on, but Ed was convicted and received a year and a half in jail (suspended) and a $1,000 dollar fine. How about the dogs? Well they assured Ed that old Tootsie was in a "safe place" during the trial. Turned out she died. Mr. Moore testified that he and his wife came home from a dinner date to find someone had come onto their yard and split Tootsie's head open with an axe. The prosecution returned some of the dogs and some they kept and murdered, including a young eleven month old dog with no marks on him and a female Ed had rescued that had a deformed leg; deformed from a birth defect. The D.A., who was loud and frantic in testimony, was convinced Ed was this cruel dog fighter who fed dogs blood to stimulate blood lust. She was convinced the old female was injured dog fighting, which of course that type of injury would be impossible to be the result of fighting.

Ed and all his friends were shocked he was convicted on such obvious trumped up evidence. His lawyer informed him the State Bureau of Investigation and the district attorney would never admit, "Oh, we made a mistake." His lawyer said he believed they ended up realizing Ed was totally innocent, but if they admitted that they would be open to a civil lawsuit for their violations. They had no choice but to be sure he was found guilty. Ed's lawyer informed him he could appeal and that if he did he would most likely win. Ed started to do that, but the cost was at least two or three thousand dollars just to begin. The SBI and the District Attorney contacted Ed's attorney and said if Ed would agree not to pursue an appeal, they would return the dogs Mr. Moore had been given, except of course poor Tootsie whose head had been split open with an axe. Ed could not even afford the bill he already owed his attorney and he wanted to at least save the lives of those dogs as the judge had already ordered the dogs in the shelter be killed, so he agreed not to pursue. Subsequently the

SBI and the District Attorney stated (off the record of course) that they had believed the original brouhaha and had to run with that ball and could not turn back. That is just the way the system works. Ed's comment, "Some system."

That trial was very expensive. A whole lot of Pit Bull people chipped in and tried to help Ed from being railroaded. Hard to fight the government. Tom Garner paid *a lot* and worked very hard. When the trial ended I went to the shelter where they held the dogs they planned to kill. None of them were fighting dogs, except for a retired dog whose dog fighting days were ended and he was retired to Ed's yard for breeding not for dog fighting, because he proved he has genetically superior intelligence and performance of the highest caliber. That dog I did not know. And another retired fighting dog (actually two matches as I recall) – he was deep game but a soft biting dog in competition, named Stabber. Stabber was a big black dog that was a canine Arnold Schwarzenegger, which again illustrates the big dog with the big head and large healthy teeth, does not necessarily bite hard in performance. Strength of bite is more a matter of attitude and intention. In the pit Stabber won not because of any damage he inflicted, but rather he could not be put down and he would not quit. So one would think such a dog would be too aggressive to be allowed to be around other dogs. Well again I proved the animal rights people base their beliefs on stuff they read about. Stabber was a half-brother to my Victory dog. The shelter would not let me release him; they were determined to kill him. But I persisted, and I fought those rascals tooth and more tooth let us say. I didn't quit. I called, and asked and searched and searched. Finally I found a retired Humane Society woman who listened. To me it is only the upper echelon that are criminals based on what I read. Many, I find, are real animal welfare caring folk, unaware of the animal activists and terrorist activities of the HSUS. She was very sympathetic and she didn't like what that local Humane Society was doing, not one bit. So she fought them with me. And she had some juice. Over and over she argued with them. She let them know the news media, the mayor, the governor of the state, all the king's horses and men, would be informed of their refusal to find a home for Stabber. They finally relented with the stipulation I had to get Stabber completely out of the state within 12 hours and he could never re-appear on Ed's yard. If he did I would be liable for criminal prosecution, I was told. So she went with me when I got Stabber out. I noticed the other dogs were in pens that were not cleaned; days of excrement and filth and they all looked sick and pathetic. Stabber's release made the TV news and a number of animal activists and people at the shelter were all so very angered. They called me a leader of underground dog fighting activity and showed pictures of me and my "dog fighters manual."

Stabber was released from death row and on the plane to Arkansas within 8 hours. They killed the other dogs. Stabber went to a friend I had who was a chicken farmer. The chicken farmer said when he got Stabber he was full of fleas and lice and had kennel cough (that is humane you see). But Stabber became a very healthy and loved pet and would not harm the farm animals (giving, again, lie to the sensationalism – lies – that the breed cannot be rehabilitated). However, the chicken farmer decided to go to law school and become an attorney. The farmer, whose name is Kurt, was another interesting, inimitable, character I met through Bulldogs. I took him on a couple wild boar hunts and he had, he said, some of the best adventures he ever experienced; and he had a lot! Kurt ran away from home as a teenager, skipped out as a kid on a merchant marine, went to work mining diamonds. He found a large diamond and smuggled it out and when back in the States, sold it, and paid cash for a brand new pink Cadillac convertible. He became a bronco rider for a rodeo and a big game hunter. Then he found a doctor, older than he, married her, and she purchased a chicken farm which he ran while she was a round-the-clock-in-demand surgeon. Again, long time ago so I may have some details inaccurate, but this is the gist of it. Kurt was so excited to get Stabber and the dog had a wonderful home. But he couldn't keep Stabber at law school. My hunting buddy/mentor N. W. Hayes in South Carolina took Stabber. He got along fine with N. W.'s dogs as they were used to the social aspect of hunting together and never challenged Stabber. Stabber died years later of the ubiquitous South Carolina heartworms (when hunting in that swamp you often become the subject of a feast by these huge pre-historic, dinosaur mosquitoes!). Some years later, Kurt, now over half completed law school with all A's, called. He was home on break and found his wife addicted to hard drugs. I've forgotten the details, but it went something like – to pay for her addiction, she sold the drugs on a small scale sort of Amway style. I think this is fairly common. When I went home to visit the street kids I grew up with in Boston, that's what one did. Anyway, Kurt said she was going out to return some drugs to some dealer she owed a great deal to and never returned. Few years later I saw the case on TV, the Unsolved Mysteries show. When I was convicted, and it was clear that with my public defender defense, I was going to spend, perhaps the rest of my life span in federal prison, I tried to find him. I searched everywhere, including law.com list of attorneys in America, couldn't find him.

Anyway, back to Ed. During all these years he was so lonely. His world, from sunrise to bedtime evolved around his dogs. I think he matched a few dogs then, but I know he never did on a large scale. He didn't have the time and I think I would have known if he did. Anyway, I had been corresponding with a woman in Canada who also had no mate. Long story, I played cupid, and they got together and married and completed the *Complete Game Dog* book together. Many years later they split up. And then – Ed's next chapter. This happened after my conviction, before I finally achieved Supreme Court justice. An HSUS undercover man, seeking the HSUS reward went to Ed's home. He said he was interested in a quality Pit Bull, not mediocre, a true bred pit. Ed responded with his archetypical (Ed is not the only breeder that gets enthusiastic about the gladiatorial history behind his loved breed). "I breed the best fighting dogs in the world." (Or words similar, I forget). I have to inject, the top breeders of Pit Bulls in America, because their bloodlines are pure and are based on historical pit champions, are of course in demand by dog fighters. But dog fighters are still, so far as I know, by far the minority of owners of the breed. I'm saying those who breed the best blood in the world cannot necessarily control where his pups go. They can research everyone who buys of course, but most don't have time or inclination to mess with all that. They feel the government should not dictate their right to breed with love and care either. But I knew Ed's dogs and they were all very high quality bred. Ed studied (and Chris was an expert) genetics and he even engaged in the pedigree study called inbreeding coefficients. This is a statistical study of a dog's pedigree useful for planned breeding. It accomplishes a lot and it would take several pages to detail it, but among many things, it indicates the (approximate) percentage of identical genes in a dog. The more gene pairs are identical, the more uniform the dog's offspring will (tend to) be. Breeding and genetics is a dice throw, but you ever notice some gamblers consistently win? Why? Because they know statistics and the percentages favor them. It is like that. I'm saying Ed devoted every day of his entire adult life to building up this yard and these foolish activists killed them in one ridiculous slaughter all in the name of humanity. Well Ed's excited statement resulted in Ed going to prison and they destroyed him. Yes, they confiscated his dogs and HSUS, as usual, got a court order to *kill* every one of them, including brood bitches, some old, and pups if I recall (that may be inaccurate – but it is very common – happens every month across the nation). Dear readers, the organization that rescued Michael Vick's dogs from death row and proved the animal activists lie by finding secure homes for them and showed they make great pets if people understand what they are getting, put out a national plea for donations as they could not afford the exorbitant fees asked for the release of Ed's dogs. I saw this national plea by the Friends organization, by the way and they did mention please donate before HSUS has the poor dogs killed. Well, HSUS expedited, and before the money could be raised, all of the dogs were mass slaughtered. It was the humane thing to do. This story goes way beyond the normal bibliographic listing, but the read is educational as well as historical.

Hall, Bobby. *Bullyson and His Sons Vol. I & II*. Privately published.
   The author's name says it all. Chock full of entertaining stories and history. Real dogmen and famous dogs.

Hammonds, Gary. *A Half Century with the American Pit Bull Terrier*. Texas: IN-CO. 2003
   This book is mentioned and described in the "Cast of Characters" chapter. It is still available and you can get one by ordering it from Gary through his website www.catchdogenterprises.com or call him at 817-473-9092. He gets a lot of calls so patience might be needed. You can get a DVD of his breeding at the time of this writing also. The book sells for $50. Or you can write Gary at 6520 Newt Patterson Rd., Mansfield, Texas 76063.

Kelly, Jack. *Conditioning the Pit Dog*. Self-published booklet.
   In this booklet, Jack shows the keep of old-timers like Armitage, 1935, J. P. Colby, 1936, Hanna, 1935, Earl Tudor, 1973, and more. It is interesting historical documentation. Outdated of course, but then those dogs also went the distance. An interesting aspect of history. Jack grew up in New York City. He served in the U.S. Marine Corps and fought with the 3rd Marine Division in the Pacific campaign. He was there when the flag was raised on Iwo Jima (read about it in the Crenshaw book). He also boxed for the Marine Corps. When he retired from the Marines, he worked as a policeman in New York City, if I recall. He was part of America when America was the healthiest nation in the world and represented freedom and Christianity to the nations. A time when professional sports players were not forced to take drugs; that is not foolish exaggeration. I happen to know someone "on the inside" of professional sports who informed me for no reason just conversation, that there is (almost) no such thing as a professional football or hockey player that doesn't take steroids in order to play through the injuries. Movies, of course always exaggerate, but most are based on true situations. The NYPD series, for example, every episode was based on actual police files. Take the movie *The Last Boy Scout* with

Bruce Willis. Of course no football player has committed suicide and shot fellow players, but the forced drugs aspect is real. Jack never thought of himself as a criminal. He felt he was a patriotic American a true blue post-World War II American. He felt he had a right to be an avid fan for his sport that he felt was as American as the New York Yankees. I grew up in a similar world. Dogfighting was never my cup of tea apart from a study of the breed to learn and make a living as a journalist, but I grew up in an America where we had prayer in school, we trusted in God and the dollar bill was world secure. I served the U. S. Navy from 1960 to 1970, Navy Reserves, two years active. It was a time when communism was a threat to dominate the world, called the domino effect. Historians say we lost wars. Not the military folk and not me. I ask those historians, where is the in-effect dictatorship, militaristic, imperious communism today? Hmmmm? (I refer to the militaristic communism that did seek to dominate the world – not the non–militaristic communistic government).

In any event, Jack is most noted for his publication, the *Sporting Dog Journal* in which dog fighters reported their matches and he issued championship and grand championship certificates and listed those dogs in the journal. He knew all of the dog fighters, big ones and small scale ones for many decades. He knew the dogs and he is an integral aspect of the breed's history in America. I've been informed his *Sporting Dog Journal* magazine had a longer and more successful run than any other Pit Bull periodical up until the government closed him down, but please, activists – don't take this out of context, and make statements about this is endemic of the breed. I say again, to my knowledge dog fighting has always been and remains the minority of the breed. I also know for a fact, because I interview countless dog people, probably the majority of subscribers to his magazine were not dog fighters, but rather folk who were interested in what the dogs were doing. The magazine also contained historical and educational content. For over twenty years, all law enforcement agencies including the federal government were well aware of Jack's magazine. Even when he did jail time for matching dogs, his magazine stayed published. But when HSUS got the 21st century powerful, they shut down his magazine and put the man in jail. As post script here, a Pit Bull person mentioned to me that a Chris Norton won the 2011 "Courage in Sports" award. Evidently he is a professional football player who broke his neck in competition. He was given a 3% chance of recovering. He didn't quit. He worked and worked rehabilitation. Now, he is back on the playing field. He made the public statement, "There is *nothing* I love more than competition." It was mentioned to me that if Chris Norton were a dog, the public would be shocked, all in an uproar; they would kill Mr. Norton and put his coach in jail for life. This is the dog world of the 2000 first decade in America.

Koener, John A. *The Pit Bull Bible*. Infinity. 2003.
   I never met John Koener, known as California Jack. I have, of course read him in various periodicals. Here is another outstanding book about the dogs by a real dogman that has been there. I think this fellow is highly intelligent (because he thinks like I do – ha, ha!) He came in a generation after me so I don't know him. But I have his book. It was a present and the book tells you a lot. One of the significant aspects I read is that he mentions the modern dog fighter is not the same as the old-time dogmen I interviewed. He says too many (not all by any means) of the new breed do not understand the sport and they expect too much from the dogs, do not love the dogs like the older sportsmen. They cull them too quickly and leave them in the box too long, etc. In any event the book is a modern education on nutrition, conditioning, breeding and dog care. It also contains a chapter on the evils of HSUS and PETA. He exposes that these organizations are not existing as humane societies but rather as giant propaganda, lobbying and fund-raising organizations. He provides website material for the Center for Consumer Freedom, cites PETA kills animals (www.petakillsanimals) and a couple more organizations that expose the criminal activities of HSUS and PETA and other activist organizations. He cites U.S. Sportsman Alliance and National Animal Interest.

Lemm, Robert F. *Seen Through the Eyes of the Millmaker*. Privately Published. 1995.
   The author shares forty years' experience in the dog fighting world. I would like to reiterate, *not* promoting dog fighting as so commonly alleged. I promote healthy alternatives. I think it is very wrong to accept outrageous and ridiculous testimony by people, regardless of credentials, who blatantly lie or just plain don't know what they are talking about. Like experts who are experts because they participated in half a dozen dog fighting busts initiated by HSUS. If you want the true history of the breed and the sport of matching dogs in the pit the history behind the dogs in your pedigree then I think it is more accurate to read the stories by real dog fighters who were there and raised combat dogs and participated in the sport. Actually I don't consider myself an expert on their level, but I see enough commonality in all my years of journalizing to say I have not found much exaggeration or prevarication. Although I have viewed TV documentaries of so-called leaders of the dog fighting ring (which does not exist), they are men I never heard of. They uphold dog fighting, these men

that got caught, but their testimonies seem shrouded in the purview of the beginner. Plus, the ones I saw were country boys with the overalls and ball cap and uneducated speech. Then the undercover HSUS fellow comes on to testify about all the blood and gore that is "reality." The HSUS fellow speaks like a history professor, clean shaven, and expensive silk suit. He indicates credibility. Anyway, my personal view is again, that dog fighting is an anachronism, but if you want the education and true history then I suggest you read reality education and reality history. I don't know Mr. Lemm personally, but I met him several times and often spoke to him, although I doubt he remembers me. Mr. Lemm made treadmills, world famous high quality treadmills. Making a quality, balanced mill that can handle hours of hard abuse is not as easy as one might think and it takes a lot of experience. There exists a plethora of "little" things that make a big difference. A set of directions including exact lengths, etc. (I found through correspondence with people who are experienced welders and steel works) is usually insufficient. The booklet is about conditioning a pit dog for match competition, but just as exercising a dog on a treadmill does not a fighting dog make, the conditioning concepts are not a narrow bridge to conditioning the match dog. The concepts represent the experience of the highest expertise of half a century experience in canine conditioning for arguably the most demanding physical sport in the world. To me, this means we can use this to shape the epitome of a healthy, alert, sharp dog and that can't be anything but good. The Dog Whisperer owns, uses, and recommends strongly to his clients, lots of treadmill work. I still cannot comprehend why it is in countless court cases the last decade, the jury gets informed a treadmill means dog fighter. It is okay for the Dog Whisperer but illegal for the pet owner or show breeder who wants a lean healthy dog? It really and truly has become so unbelievably ridiculous and sad for America. In any event, my point is you sure don't need to be a dog fighter to reap benefits from this book. Kind of like the Wall Street executive who goes to a boxing gym to train three times week. Pretty good for you.

Miller, Lemuel D. *American Bulldog.* Privately Published. 1998.

Now this book is not about the APBT. It's about the related American Bulldog (AB). Big white dogs that look and act much like the original English Bulldog. They are original pits brought to America with other breeds bred in and the establishment of a breed, mostly pit but much bigger. I love these dogs. I've hunted them. If you ask an AB man he'll tell you they are as deep game as a pit. This is because you have about the same percentage of AB's that will stay with a hog even when repeatedly gutted, taking far more damage, and I do mean far more, than a pit dog, and stay to his death if not pulled out. Hogs fight to protect themselves and their herd. They also fight to kill. A wild boar is the king of his habitat and acts accordingly.

The poor piggy the "expert" pig man in my trial tried to convey is pure fantasy fabrication (analogous to mentioning the poor helpless grizzly bear). A wild boar will kill anything in the swamp and that includes you if you don't have a high powered firearm. A .357 mag. won't even make a hog snort even if hit multiple times in the head. I've seen this many times. Deep game is as difficult to find with AB's as it is with pits. The average is game. You have about the same percentage that are not worth spit for performance. Those who are not "in" the breed do not comprehend this gameness. Since it involves the ultimate performance it doesn't happen by studying pedigrees and breeding for structure. It happens only, and I do mean only, by breeding experienced proven game dogs. You can lose this trait of game in about three generations. It is difficult to get in the first litter. It is almost impossible to find a litter with every pup turning out game. Game for the AB is not the same as game for a match pit. An AB is very big; a war dog descended from the gladiator dogs used in Greece and Rome, the Mastiff. So is the pit, but they went different directions. The AB does not have the endurance for the pit. In the swamp with wild hog, he is more useful than a pure pit on the catch. Think of a professional power lifter. He couldn't go one round in the boxing ring. He'd regurgitate, in most cases, five miles into a marathon, especially a desert country or humid or high mountain marathon. If he did finish it would be at the pace of a turtle. But power – oh my gosh! The boxer would look foolish trying to budge what the power lifter can easily toss around with one hand. It is like that. Here is a bit of an excerpt from a chapter entitled "Makin' Memories."

"There has never been anything to compare with the commitment made by a Bulldog when asked to catch and hold. The warrior mentality, the willingness to place his life on the line, the power involved, the tenacity that's called for, and sheer desire to seize. It is an awesome spectacle of God-given ability." He describes a hunt and it makes my heart do funny things reading his experiences that mirror mine. He describes this boss boar hog they found in a thick palmetto patch on the edge of a slough. The bay dogs went in, but the hog would pin them and cut them to pieces. He had tough bay dogs that would get just a tad too close to the poor helpless piggy. It was thick and it got dark. He found the hog and to make a long story short (get the book – it is chock full of stories that will grip you) they spent 40 minutes with that hog. The hog went after them! This has happened to me many times. The author got sick from the heat and exhaustion. He passed out in a fire ant bed and got bitten all over. His AB catch dog was named Bull. 'Ol Bull stayed with the hog and when his sons found them Bull still had that hog. Bull saved his life. They told Bull to out and he did and went over and lay down beside Mr. Miller. The author finishes that story by exclaiming: "Most hog hunts are fun, this one wasn't but let me tell you – I've got me a dog!!!" I include this book in the bibliography, even though it is about AB's not pits for several reasons. It is a *great read* is one reason. Also, it shows how much the "pig expert" in my trial lied. The book explains the need (and how common it is) for catch dogs to catch hogs that some rural farmers raise by letting them run wild (so the feed cost is – zero), but then they need to be caught to go on the dinner table and/or go to market. Read the book you have evidence it is a very common agricultural endeavor (indicating the judge, federal or nay, lied to the jury in my opinion). Lastly, again it is full of adventure stories. I can report that they are not exaggerated hyperbole because I have lived the same adventures many times with my Velvet and her son Victory. You can get this book by writing Joshua Kennels, 530 W. River Road, Jacksonville, Georgia 31544. Also go to http:www.joshuakennels.com. I don't know the cost. The book was a present from my friend John Gerard when I was real down; no income when the government closed down my legal business and would not allow me to have earned income.

Mullins, E. L. *The Evolution of Rule for Canine Combat.* Privately Pulblished, 2007.

This little book is a treat. It has great historical value in that it presents the history of the rules for the match dog sport from circa late 1700's England to modern day.

Reid, Ed. *Memories of Staffordshire Bull Terriers and American (Pit) Bull Terriers.* London: Srockquest Ltd. 1977

This is a great little hard back book that relates the Old English Bulldog and Terriers, the Staffordshire, and Irish dogs whose ancestors came to America, New Zealand, Australia, Germany, and Finland. Cockney Charlie Lloyd is in it, a story of Stubblefield's Buddy 4X match winner is there. It is worth mention here as it represents the old-time American dogfighter's position regarding the dog fighting sport. The dog is described as a dogfighter's naturally gifted (game dog bred) ideal. Buddy was Kingfish bred; very popular at the time, and representative of what quality match dogs were about. In his testing rolls he easily outclassed experienced dogs and handled a much bigger dog. His fourth match is described in detail and it took place March 30, 1974. The match description has detail you don't get in the standard match reports and it is endemic of the old-time foundation characteristics of the American Pit Bull Terrier. Buddy's opponent was named Tuffy. Tuffy had a reputation that harmonized his name; a rough, tough competitor. At "release your dogs" the Buddy dog was slammed to the floor. Tuffy was the bigger dog; same weight, rules mandate equal weight. Tuffy was fast but buddy escaped being in one place too long. This went on for ten minutes with Buddy taking no particular holds, just rolling and putting constant pressure on Tuffy, making him exert all he had. At ten minutes, Buddy flipped Tuffy (I have often seen, in the 1970's, match dogs perform a canine equivalent to a Judo throw). In any event, at the ten minute mark, the Tuffy dog had blown his energy with his fast pace and getting no significant hold. As he began to weaken, Buddy began exerting himself, getting good holds and shaking them. Tuffy went to the bottom and was unable to find the strength to defend himself. At 34 minutes his handler conceded the match and picked up Tuffy. You may think because we read of these hour-long matches the dog quit at 30 minutes! I will bet you won't find a mixed martial artist finding fault. *If* you ever grapple or double that fight grappling as well with crippling Muay Thai, you know that most sports karate competitors can't last two minutes, period. In one minute the insufficiently conditioned competitor can feel as weak as a child with rubbery legs hardly able to stand and dizzy. That these dogs can go at the pace they do for ten minutes indicates this sport is the highest demand on the system of any sport in the world or history of the world. Buddy retired and lived to old age. He was bred some but not a lot. The point behind his story is that it seems to me to be endemic of what the true pit is as far as the real dog fighters of the 1970s were concerned. You see a hard biting dog was not in the vogue. Hard biting dogs quit when they burned themselves out when competing against a talented high ability game dog. That match was concluded with no serious damage done to either dog. If that Tuffy dog "got into it" with a dog of another breed, it would be true cruelty as more than likely if there was no one there to break him off he would kill the dog. He had already shown he could do serious damage to other match pits, but when he competed with a talented game dog, he couldn't do any damage. If a news reporter or someone not inured to the match sport viewed the match they would not see two dogs wrestling around trying to get a hold, and only getting ineffective skin holds when they did get something. The pace is fast and they would see a dog get a skin hold and shake hard. To them it would be a bloody gory sport tearing each other's limbs off. This is the position of the old time dog fighters. But again, I am no big-time expert; I just report what I have experienced in my research.

I know that in the dog fighting documentary I did entitled *Japan Pit Fights,* it is legal in Japan. They had a dog named Kane who was a Panther/Raleigh dog. I viewed his match. I didn't do any videoing; the Japanese did and sent the footage to me as they wanted me to do a quality documentary. I used his match in the documentary and a did a two minute snippet of it in my Catch Dog video to illustrate my position that a Pit Bull should be trained to catch by the ear and swing to the side (and I show how) because this mitigates harm to both the dog and the hog and since the tougher-than-rawhide ear with no pain/nerve ending in the hog's ear means the hog feels just about nothing, it is more humane than electric prods. In any event, my point was that a pit will tend to naturally fight a hog straight up. The smart ones learn to catch; the not-so-smart are quickly killed by the hog wild and domestic. Happens a lot. If the dog is trained as I taught in my educational video it becomes a rare incident. Those facts are mentioned here because as a side note, Kane was open to the world and was one of the few double grand champions (ten contract matches with no losses) in the history of dog fighting. In all those matches, I don't think he ever drew any blood. He just made his opponents over exert and they couldn't get a hold on him and they would get so weak they could not defend themselves, even very, very hard biting dogs. I used Kane in my documentaries because there is absolutely no blood depicted (court testimony was one hundred percent lie) in his match. And again, I am not promoting dog fighting; I am not saying dog fighting is free of harm to the dogs. There are match dogs that can do some serious harm. The Raleigh dog mentioned; I saw him when he was retired to breeding. He had some serious permanent damage to his mouth and jaw. The fact he survived his last match is a testimony of how tough the breed is as I cannot imagine how it is he survived. Miraculous! No, I do not claim dog fighting is free of injury and I do not want to be taken out of context for damaging remarks. I am reporting truths. So the point is, as a journalist and historian for the breed, I think I have indicated and educated what the 1970 and 1980's dogfighter posit, that like human boxers, in the match dog sport you have your destroyer type, you have slick defensive type and average and in between. All things considered the true representative of the breed seems to be the quality, game, defensive dog who loves his competition and for him it is a game. Perhaps that is how the term game came about. Still, though the betting odds may be on the aforementioned game dog you'd lose big time against Zebo, Art, or Tornado.

Another interesting aspect of this little book; way back in the 1970's he cites Ralph Greenwood and his new standard for the breed in the conformation show ring he established and established an acceptable place in America for our breed. The breed standard and reasons for it was first published in the third issue of the *Pit Bull Gazette*, in 1977. It is also cited in your *Dogs of Velvet and Steel*; the book the government tried to claim (incited by HSUS) is a dog fighting manual. How ridiculous!

Ed Reid used to buy my books by the case and I corresponded often. I don't know what is wrong between my ears, but I completely forget what ever happened to Ed.

The following books by Frank Rocca are out of print. I have seen them for sale, used, through Amazon, etc. Google around you can find them. They are very worth the search. It's a series of books by a real dogman, about real dogs and real dogmen. Frank is one of the top half dozen most respected dogmen I ever met. I've never seen his dogs, but I have met Frank often and talked dogs and the dog world and I know the reputation of him and his dogs. If he didn't live so far away, he would have been my primary Pit Bull mentor. As it was I never had one man I could say was my primary Pit Bull "sensei," but if I had a choice Frank would have been the one.

Rocca, Frank C. *A Living American Legend*. Rocca Enterprises, 1986.

This was Frank's first book written at a time when animal activists were not as powerful or influential as they would become in the 1990s. He reports how pit dogs were evaluated, schooled, fed, conditioned, matched, and bred. The book is replete with stories of real dogs and real dogmen that carved out what is now called the Pit Bull. Frank's education is real because Frank is as real as it gets. Pictures and pedigrees of famous dogs are included and a very interesting and pointed novella is included. Frank like so many of the smart old timers – gosh, Frank, are you okay with being called old-timer? Where did the years go? - has gone with the vanguard and has been for many years a registered ADBA show judge. He is a world renown recognized expert on the breed and in demand at large conformation shows and promotes the healthy alternatives for the breed.

Rocca, Frank C. *American Bull Terriers, a Legacy in Gameness*. Rocca Enterprises, 1992.

This book contains the same unique literary style and engaging stories as well as bristling with a Bulldog education I promise you can find nowhere else. He explains foundation and early American dogs and dogmen. He explains the breeding concepts behind most of the great pit dogs in American history and describes historically famous pit dogmen. The book contains large and strikingly clear pictures of famous pit dogs and dogmen and some pedigrees. As in *American Legend*, the book contains an entertaining Bulldog novella.

This is Frank with his Spice bitch. She was the true concept of what a real pit dog is. You can see how Frank loves her. She was something else. She appears on the cover of Frank's first book noted above, A Living American Legend.

The Assistant Producer snapped this photo of Frank for his role during the filming of the Chuck Norris movie "Invasion U.S.A." Fort Pierce Beach, Florida. The weapon is a Colt A.R. 15 automatic machine gun.

Rocca, Frank C. *Fighting for Life, the American Bull Terrier, An Endangered Species*. Rocca Enterprises, 1997.

This book contains as great a treatise on the trait that makes the APBT (and cousins like the American Bulldog, Staff, Argentina Dogo, etc.) the rarity of creatures they are; the trait called "game." The subject is not addressed over a few pages, but is a book in itself, and includes stories and match description of famous pit dogs that appear in the pedigree of most modern day APBT. It includes descriptive narrative of the longest pit matches in American history, probably world history. I do not know of anyone more qualified to describe these dogs and do so with an incomparable style of writing that is unparalleled by any writer, of any genre. There is an excellent chapter abut Ch. Jeep and the history of the dogs in his pedigree, including the famous Irish Jerry. The famous Canadian Andre Giroux and the dogs from his breeding carve out another historically important and informative chapter. His chapter titled "Some Existential Reflections on Gamedogs" is genius in my opinion. He has a chapter, "A Quarter of a Century" that cannot be duplicated in its historical value or its education into the essence of America's foundation of American Pit Bull Terriers.

Frank also wrote a novel entitled *I'm Jack & I Want More* published by Frank 2011. Not about dogs at all, it is a novel about the streets; it's realism. This book is in print.

Sheridan, Sam. *A Fighter's Heart*. New York: Atlantic Monthly Press. 2007.
This is an incredible book. Sam Sheridan graduated from Harvard, a New England nerd (or almost so). Before settling down to what he didn't know, he traveled the world. Along the way he became infatuated with the fighting world. His journalism is top notch because he is one who experienced what he wrote. He trained with the Mixed Martial Arts people, Muay Thai, American Boxing, Tai Chi, which is way beyond what the general public perceives, and even many American teachers. It is a very effective martial style such that true masters have the ability to disable and kill. It is founded in combat and it is not slow; it is quicker! Slow is smooth and precise and slow and precise develops ultimate speed and ultimate power in back of it. He fought in the Muay Thai pits and the boxing ring. So you read his thoughts as he personally felt all this, and you read his description of personalities, fighters and coaches. He met pit dog fighters in Thailand. To help understand the gladiator paradigm, he spent some time in the pit fight world. He devotes a whole chapter to the American Pit Bull Terrier as a gladiator. The chapter is entitled "Gameness." You can get this hard back book in bookstores like Barnes

and Noble. I'll share a few excerpts as they are relevant to our context. He describes how they don't get much water before match time. He describes the wash and weigh-in. Incredibly he met an old geezer who he said fancied himself, even though he was neither, what Mr. Sheridan didn't know is it was Captain Ben; one of the wisest most experienced dog men in the world. He is unassuming and normal and his self-effacement can be misleading if you don't know him. Sam didn't. Actually, while Mr. Sheridan's journalism about the fight world is mostly right on, he makes some errors in his accounting of the pit dog world. This is probably because he spent little time with it and relied on the interviews of a select few. But his errors are insignificant and what can I say; as a journalist I have made more than my share of errors. His guide made it clear that he was an expert. His dogs were truly game-bred and everyone else's dogs were worthless curs. What Mr. Sheridan should have journalized was this is endemic of the pit dogman. Ironically, it is almost equally endemic of the human fight world Mr. Sheridan experienced. I've spent half a century in that world and it is full of yak, yak, yak. Sheridan reports that the dog fighting world adheres to a strict code of honor. Well, this is what they told him. I found a lot do, but also a lot do not. He said the true pit sportsmen look down on dogmen who are just in it for the money and building a name for themselves, fabricating stuff so they can sell pups. That part is true. He describes a match. He describes damage done and the dogs wrestling around vying for holds. He reports they feel no pain or any pain they feel is overwhelmed by the desire to get the other dog. "I know the feeling," he reports. In the match he reports, he says neither dog had a "hard mouth" and the outcome would come down to conditioning (and gameness). He reports that his guide's dog is the better wrestler, but his opponent does well from the bottom and he shares how much it is like UFC-type competition. He reports how the dogs become exhausted and just lay on each other breathing hard. He describes a true scratch and turn match. He correctly observes that what is important in the competition is not the battle itself; it is the scratch. The well the dog searches into that gives him the will to continue even when totally wasted, sheer exhaustion. The match ended when one dog was just too exhausted to continue. It isn't the bite; it is the weakness. Any human who has ever wrestled knows this feeling. The general public can never understand this. Then Mr. Sheridan interviewed some other dogmen. One informed him that he much prefers a true game dog, a dog that "bites as hard as tissue paper" but will not quit. This is his kind of dog. I mention this because even though Mr. Sheridan is relying on a limited exposure his journalism is objective and true description for the most part. I could not help but notice he at times described damage he thought he saw not realizing, it was no more pronounced than what he received in his own human competition. For those not used to it, it is generally far less than it appears to the neophyte. But his journalism is true reporting of what the sport is about. Mr. Sheridan also records how impressive the dogfighters love for their sport is; how they can rattle of pedigrees and bloodlines and statistical information about dogs that equals that of a Red Sox baseball fan. There is a lot more and that is why I strongly recommend this book. The reading will tell you more about the game heart and the similitude between the human fighter and the canine fighter than any other source I know of at the time of this writing. Tells you stuff you won't read in many Pit Bull books because this man fully understands the fighter's heart.

Stratton, Richard. *This is The American Pit Bull Terrier*. New Jersey: T.H.F. Inc. 1976.

This was the first book internationally distributed about the American Pit Bull Terrier breed (except, of course, for the old time match dog books of the 1930s, like the Armitage and Colby books listed above). In the 1970s, I was ready to fulfill a childhood dream to own a dog with true gladiator genes; an honest Bull Terrier (the white show dog). But I always study and research very thoroughly moves like that. I read volumes about the breed and I went around to every single breeder within reasonable driving range. I found one beauty I liked on a show breeder's yard. She invited me to go with her to a show and I agreed. I had never been to one before. The day of the show I went to her home and watched her prep her dog. She kept telling me he was the area's next regional champion and all the experts thought him the best representative of the breed. She said this dog will lay down his life for me. He acted like a spoiled lap dog to me, but again I said nothing. She put him on this table and commenced to rub chalk all over every little blemish and that made no sense to me at all. She started cutting off his whiskers as I guess that was also needed for the show and I don't understand this; to each his own I suppose. Every time the dog would move she'd say, Naughty doggie, you must stay still!" I'm thinking, this is not what I expected and dreamed of all these years. So we went to the show and again she kept telling me what a great specimen of the breed this dog is. At the show, to me they all dressed funny and they walked weird. As a postscript, they walked weird in Schutzhund also, the reason is to keep an excited attitude and keep the dog's attention on you. This is one aspect of Schutzhund I dislike. Doggone if I'm going to act like that. With my dog, with no leash and no excitement, I used to walk with Velvet perfectly heeled, most of the time tail up and attention on me.

I just walked casually and normally. If I walked briskly, it was like I normally walk if hurrying. You are supposed to change pace. It is like, in the 70's when I used to do my roadwork, and all the local church people used to laugh at me and called me crazy (the jogging fad had not yet come into vogue). Years later, I looked out the window of my house and see them walking by. They looked like Nazi soldiers marching stiff leg and swinging their arms because the doctor told them to do this. And I was weird? The Bull Terrier did look beautiful in the show, but he did some performance faults I didn't understand. He moved when he shouldn't, didn't look pretty when he should. I was flabbergasted. I never forgot how that lady treated this "great" dog after the show. Disgusted she called him a piece of trash and yelled "get in there!" and tossed him into his crate. I decided after all these years, "This ain't the dog I thought. Surely not the people." Then I came across Dick's book and like countless across the nation, found out the APBT existed and what they were (in those days, nobody ever heard of Pit Bulls and, for some reson, from the founding of our nation, until then, they never bit anything.) I guess I read that book a hundred times. Dick went on to publish the *Book of the American Pit Bull Terrier*, *The World of the American Pit Bull Terrier,* and many more. I've got them all. I finally went to visit him in 1984. Anyway just Google Richard Stratton APBT and you'll find his books all over, including Amazon. Dick sent a letter to the government on my behalf during my case, by the way.

Williams, T. L. *Pit Dogs, A Profile in Portraits*. Y F7 M Press. 1974.
    The cover depicts Earl Tudor with his Ch. Fighting Peter, 1924. This is a wonderfully clear photo album of excellent examples of the breed. Many of Ed Faron's dogs are in there. Part and parcel of the dogs depicted have Boudreaux bred dogs depicted, and Patrick's dogs are in there also.

It is a dangerous thing for humans to engage in lies and deceit. It is not always apparent in the body on earth, but what did the Lord say to the Assyrians, a long time before it came to pass (documented now by dated Dead Sea Scrolls)? "When you are done destroying, you will be destroyed. When you are done betraying, you will be betrayed" (Isaiah 33:1). Doesn't seem like it, I know. Truly no offense, but it is something to think about.

The Whole Dog Journal.
    I tack this little periodical on the end because of the totality of suggested reading; this is, in my opinion the highest. And to my

knowledge, at this time, very few Pit Bull aficionados have even heard of it. Google it or go to their website (www.wholedogjournal.com). This is to the canine what Consumers Reports is to appliances, TVs and computers. They are completely independent of any organization or supplier. They go to great lengths to assure you of their complete independence and objectivity. They accept no advertising, and have no sponsors. Their product reviews are 100% objective and unsolicited. They analyze popular dog foods and report their findings. They analyze home-prepared diets, and report the considerations. They study animal behavior, puppy selection, dog training and behavior, massage techniques, care of the senior dog. More complete and compact subject matter than I can list here.

It is a Cracklin' world we live in now. In so many ways America seems to have devolved as though from slow cooked, strong foundation oatmeal with substance, to Rice Crispies. Tastes good, goes down easy, full of hot air and snap, crackle, and pop. What did Thomas Jefferson say? "Yes, we did produce a perfect Republic, but will we keep it? Or will they in their enjoyment of plenty lose the memory of freedom? Material abundance without character is the surest way to destruction. Indeed, I tremble for my country when I reflect that God is just." (cited in Donald Trump and Robert Kiyosaki's eye-opening book *Why We Want You To Be Rich*.) When I was a kid, every morning in school we pledged allegiance to the American flag; and to the Republic for which it stands. Do you know we are no longer a Republic? If we were, the government could not tax us to where they confiscate our homes and take our land. No we are now a democracy and there is a difference. Still it is a great place to live and it is still free. And the American Pit Bull Terrier is still standing. You know there is an aspect of the breed that goes beyond the gladiator genes I have tried to depict in this Epilogue. In all my years of interviewing Pit Bull folk, so many times I hear, "These dogs have taught me a lot about life." That is so difficult to explain. Like explaining the world of the fighter; you have to live it. You can't begin to comprehend unless you have owned several generations of the breed. In decades you never quite fully understand all about them. But they teach you things you'll never get from any other breed; things that no doggie activist could ever understand. I learned a great deal for my mixed martial arts by watching the Henley Big Boy/Molly Bea bred Grand Champion Mickey perform, as well as Morochito's half-brother Butch, Jocko and Tornado. That is not hyperbole; not romanticizing. I mean I really and truly have stuff that works for real. When I reached points in my life like when it would be impossible to win my case and for sure I am going to prison and I should plead out, I could not. Not only would I remember - I'd feel the attitude of that crazy Velvet Bulldog of mine. Can't; she never could understand; just plain not there. I have seen her over and over do things that just plain cannot be explained; like bumble bees flying. How in the world she did some things that just plain cannot be done by a 42 pound dog. She would *never plead out.* Yeah, these dogs teach you a whole lot, but I can't really explain it you have to find out for yourself.

    I hope you are lifted and buoyed up by the read; liberated and given some depth into the nature of our gladiator breed. I have tried to present my writing in a conversational tonality to connect with a penetrating intimacy with my readers and share my thirty plus years' experiences side-by-side with the American Pit Bull Terrier to you so that the footsteps of the past might inspire legacies for tomorrow. I want it to be like a sit-on-the-front-porch chat. Like a friend talkin' dogs. I feel that I have the game dog persona within myself. I am happy-go-lucky, friendly, and very, very affectionate, but I do love battle, with a deep passion; it defines me. I feel this puts me under the skin and into the heart of the game dog and I feel thus qualified to describe the breed. We humans have been created in the express image of the Creator God, right? So what is there about humans that attracts God and makes us worth the aggravation? Something to think on. It reminds me of the tale about the origin of the Arabian horse. It is said that way back yonder, the Sheik, owner of the largest and most formidable herd of quality horses in all of Arabia, decided to thin out his herd and select the finest for future breeding. He took the herd on a very long trek in the desert; no water for days on seeming end. When they approached a water hole in the distance, he waited until the herd smelled the water and began the stampede. In that era horses were trained to come to the master's horn, like a bugle. When they were close to the water hole he let out the bugle blast they were supposed to respond to. Only a select number came to him. Those he retained and that is said to be the foundation of the modern Arabian horse. Does God love about us similar traits? Like the soldier that puts his life on the line for family and country. The love of the mother/housewife who sacrifices for her family; the true heroes of humanity. I think God is infatuated with blind faith and loyalty love. With those people who think they can when they can't and then they do. Everyone knows an ant can't knock over a rubber tree plant. Whoops! There goes another rubber tree plant (old-time Frank Sinatra song). Is that what God loves? I wish for you the heart of the Bulldog.

    And now, turn the page and go back to the 1970's era of the American Pit Bull Terrier. I hope you garner a deeper insight into the world of the quintessential gladiator and modus operandi of the American Pit Bull Terrier. I hope you enjoy your original *Dogs of Velvet and Steel* read.

Thank you and good night.

DOGS OF VELVET AND STEEL
Pit Bulldogs: A Manual for Owners
Bob Stevens

PUBLISHED

BY

HERB EATON HISTORICAL PUBLICATIONS
CHARLOTTE, NORTH CAROLINA

AND

WALSWORTH PUBLISHING COMPANY
MARCELINE, MISSOURI

LIBRARY OF CONGRESS CATALOG CARD NO. 82-061977

COPYRIGHT 1983

BY

BOB STEVENS
GREENSBORO, N.C.

Front Cover by Henry W. Stevens, my father
Illustrations by Chris Gallagher, Greensboro, N.C.
Edited by Bill Jo Stevens, my wife

Dedication

I give the glory to the Lord, and the dedication to my daughter Lisa Anne and my son Michael; my sister Judy who has always believed in me and to my mother and father who have provided encouragement and helped me become what I am.

Finally this book is dedicated to Old Smuggler, a Pit Bull that lived at the turn of the century. Smuggler, who fought from 1915 to 1918, is not a well-known, famous dog, but to me he represents what the breed is all about. He was pure Colby and was owned by several people and even twice by the same person. He fought all over the country, as far north as Medicine Hat, Alberta, Canada, and down to the Mexico line. Smuggler was at death's door several times, but he was always willing to go across the pit. He didn't win every match, but the times he lost, he was picked up – he never, never quit. He fought several times with dogs that outweighed him – his pit weight was 40 pounds. One time he was matched to a Pit Bull that nearly killed him and his owner had to pick him up. A week later, still sore from his wounds, he was rolled for ten minutes with a dog that out weighted him by twelve pounds. Smuggler was an old dog then and the bigger dog shook him all over the pit – that old Smuggler was willing to go to the end and his tail stayed up. He finally retired to stud and sired some game Bulldogs. He was a loveable old boy, well-liked by all his owners. He was an average Pit Bull – average weight, slightly above average ability, and bite, won more than he lost, not an outstanding dog, but one thing you could say about Smuggler – he was game, game as could be, and to me, that's what these dogs are all about. I'd like to have known that dog! His poem appears on the next page. It comes from an early 1900's book, author unknown.

It is my desire that this book be like a banquet to the reader in that every part be considered in the light of its individual flavor – some of it perhaps discarded, some of it rekindling pleasure with its familiarity, and some of it savored for its uniqueness. So warm your hands around your cup of coffee, let the outside world go on its own journeys and come with me to the somewhat different world of Pit Bulldogs. When you finish, add this book to your library and refer to it from time to time. I hope you have half as much fun reading it as I have had writing it.

Farewell To The Game From Old Smuggler

I have grown old

In this game of life

I will retire to the kennel

For I have fought my last fight

But I have fought from Canada

To the Mexico line

And no dog has ever

Heard me whine

When the fight

Was against me

It can never be said

That Smuggler backed off

And hung his head

Yes, I'm proud

Of my record

I'm proud of my name

And those who have knowledge

Will say I was game

But now I am old

I am feeble and grey

My fighting days are over

I have changed my way.

I will take a long rest

That I so badly need

And in the comforts of the kennel

I will sow my seed.

So my sons may carry on

The name which I bear

For no dog can say

But what I fought fair.

But I have fought my last fight

I have heard my last gong

I have done some good

I've done some wrong

So now I bid you

A kind good-night

From your friend Smuggler

The bull that would fight.

(Cited in <u>Pit Bull Sheet</u>, Sept./Oct., 1978. Illustration by Chris Gallagher.)

Acknowledgements

I'd like to thank all the people who shared with me a great deal of invaluable information but wish to remain anonymous. In addition I'd like to thank the following people for their support:
  Bill Ashford – North Carolina
  Dr. I. L. Brisbin, Jr. – Aiken, South Carolina
  Marilyn Brubaker – Miami, Florida
  Mary Carnahan – Sunnymead, California
  Dr. James R. Dohner, D.C.
  Joan Gilman, former editor of Pit Bull Sheet – Yulan, N. Y.
  Ralph Greenwood, President of the American Dog Breeders Association and Editor of the Pit Bull Gazette
  Gary J. Hammonds – Mansfield, Texas
  Sam Haynes – Riverside, California
  Ray Heather – London, England
  Jan kuiper, Editor of the Holland magazine, The Game Dog
  Don Livingston – South Carolina
  Boyd McCormick – Hillsboro, Tennessee
  Tom Needam – Riverton, Utah
  Russ Norman – North Carolina
  Cher Petersen – Cerritos, California
  Eddie Pickard – North Carolina
  Joe Placer – Ontario, Canada
  John B. Reid – Dallas, Texas
  Dr. Jerry Stubblefield, D.V.M.
  Mark Susanka – Orange, California
  Jack Swinson – North Carolina
  Jim Uselton – Iowa Park, Texas
  Pam Willet – for the drawing of the Pit Bull "catching" a bull

I would also like to thank the following dog food companies for their contributions to the nutrition chapter:
  Eukanuba Division of IAMS
  A.N.F.
  Nutra-Vet Research Corp.
  Science Diet

Howell Book House allowed me to use in my History chapter a substantial portion of a book published by them – The New Complete Bulldog by Col. Bailey C. Hanes.

The following friends' encouragement provided an immeasurable constant resource:
My childhood friend Charlie Colburn and Lawrence McSwain, my karate instructor.

A special thanks goes to Chris Gallagher for her excellent illustrations.

Also to my Dad for his work on the front cover and my Mom for her support as well as my children for their assistance in various sections and my sister for her support. Finally, to my very special Pit Bull, Morochito, who has endured his master's constant experimentations.

Cover of the original *Dogs of Velvet and Steel*

DOGS OF VELVET AND STEEL

PIT BULLDOGS; A MANUAL FOR OWNERS

BY
BOB STEVENS

The drawing is by my Dad, Henry Wheeler Stevens

Table of Contents

Dedication 185

Acknowledgements 186

Preface 191

Introduction 193

Chapter 1: History 207

Chapter 2: The Pit Bull Pet 272

Chapter 3: The Catch Dog 310

Chapter 4: The Schutzhund Dog 340

Chapter 5: The Competitive Weight-Pulling Dog 366

Chapter 6: Scientific Nutrition 380

Chapter 7: Scientific Conditioning..423

Chapter 8: Scientific Breeding..476

Chapter 9: Medicine Chest And Miscellaneous.......................532

Chapter 10: The Combat Dog 556

Chapter 11: Conclusion..627

Index 639

Preface

The subtitle to this book is "Pit Bulldogs: A Manual for Owners," and that is exactly what the book is primarily designed to be. The first chapter, on the history of the breed, helps gain perspective on the breed we are dealing with and provides insight into many of the popular bloodlines. Throughout the book personal experiences and stories related by other Pit Bull fanciers are injected for interest and to gain perspective on the type of breed we're studying. The main thrust of the book, however, is concerned with instructing Pit Bull owners how to breed, condition, and train this unique animal.

As the acknowledgements section discloses, I have had considerable support from the Pit Bull fraternity. In my correspondence and conversations with various Pit Bull fanciers, I have found dichotomous (and strongly expressed) opinions as to the pit fighting aspects of the breed. Many of those who belong to the group of owners of Pit Bull pets or obedience trained dogs feel that the book should denounce the use of the breed for fighting purposes. The pit fighting group, however, does not want a "Mickey-Mouse" book that presents fairy tale accounts of unrealistic exploits of a breed of dog that is bred for the pit and nothing else. In other words, they feel that trying to present the Pit Bull as some kind of super dog capable of outperforming the fictitious "Lassie" is unrealistic. The Pit Bull is just a dog that is especially good at what it has been bred for - pit fighting. There is also a considerable amount of concern these days with the outrageous legislation that has been passed that might endanger the breed because it comes close to making it illegal even to own a Pit Bull. These are topics well worth discussion by Pit Bull fanciers. Although I touch on them, this book is primarily concerned with helping Pit Bull owners understand and raise their Pit Bulls better. I do not care to get into arguments over pit fighting. It is just about impossible to avoid the subject with this breed, however, and so, throughout the book, I repeatedly announce that I am not suggesting or promoting pit fighting. I leave my personal opinion on the matter to the conclusion. I would hope, however, that the reader will read and enjoy the book before reading the conclusion. The content of parts of the book do provide a basis for my opinion.

Some of the information in this book may seem a bit farfetched to some, for example, my suggestion that ionized well water might increase a Pit Bull's endurance or at least be very good for him. Ionized water can be thought of as a ridiculous amount of unnecessary trouble to go to in order to provide a dog with drinking water and the fact that I recommend it may provide doubt about my credibility. All I can say is that, as an athlete (it's actually good for everyone, not just athletes), I drink it myself and am personally convinced that while it is no "miracle drink" it is in fact very good for you. I share this and many other "unusual" tidbits with my readers because many people do enjoy "trying out" health foods, etc. I am aware, of course, that a dog is primarily what his or her genes dictate, and all the health foods and conditioning methods in the world won't make a good dog out of a genetically poor Pit Bull.

I'd also like to mention that throughout the book I refer to dog owners, handlers, conditioners, etc. in the masculine tense. I do this to avoid having to say "him or her" every time, which seems awkward, and "person" doesn't fit into the context of the sentence. You may notice that I also refer to Pit Bulls as "him," and this is for the same reason. I do not attach any importance to male pit Bulls over females - in fact, if I have a preference, it would be for females.

I have a tendency to be long-winded and often digress from the subject. I do this because I have many experiences to share and it's difficult to find a relevant place to insert them. My general approach is to discuss Pit Bulls as though the reader and I were sitting around a campfire having a chat. Sometimes over-explain a point, but in those instances I feel the verbiage is either necessary to emphasize a point or that it is colorful.

Writing this book has been an exciting adventure for me and I hope it brings hours of pleasure to my readers and is informative to many experienced Pit Bull owners as well as to newcomers to the breed.

Introduction

I chose the title for this book - *Dogs of Velvet and Steel* - because it represents a most accurate description of the Pit Bulldog. These dogs are probably more misunderstood, usually by people who have not owned or lived near one, than any other breed. If you mention Pit Bulldogs to most folks, the immediate comment is "Oh, you are talking about those mean dogs they train to fight." It's not uncommon for these people to then relate some story about a Pit Bull that mauled an adult or child. Well, for one thing the Pit Bull does not have to be trained to fight – it's in his blood, just as strongly, if not more so, than hunting is in a hound dog's blood. He doesn't fight because he's mean - he fights because he loves it, just as a coon hound loves to hunt coon. Not only does the Pit Bull love to fight, but he's very, very good at it and has unbelievable courage. Many of them will fight to the death; even though they are extremely weakened from loss of blood, in a state of shock and dehydration (loss of body fluid) and heat exhaustion, they will just keep going. They also have a high threshold of pain, meaning they can withstand considerably more pain than other animals. To illustrate this point, I'd like to introduce my Pit Bull, Morochito - Tuffy Morochito to be exact. He's named after an Argentinian boxer back in the '60's who was a real scrapper and was nicknamed "Morochito," meaning "Sweetheart." He added the "Tuffy" because of our puppy's rough-and-tumble nature. When Morochito first came home, we kept our two house cats away from him for about a week until he had become adjusted to his new surroundings. He first caught sight of one cat when he was nine weeks old. Immediately he charged into the cat, who happened to be bigger than he was then. He was just a baby and wasn't at all well-coordinated yet, often stumbling and falling while playing at that age, but when he tackled that cat, he became so coordinated that I just couldn't believe the difference. Of course, he was just playing with the cat, but my cats do not appreciate strangers, especially the cat he decided to pick on. So she was pretty angry and tried to scratch his eyes out. I shouldn't have let him near her that early. The thing is, though, she couldn't touch that little puppy - he was just too fast for her and she wasn't able to scratch him. However, he could get inside her paws and nip her. pretty soon he was chasing her around the yard! Sure was a funny sight. (I have a home movie of the incident.) Well, as soon as the cats found out he was part of the family, they accepted him okay and we kept him from playing too rough.

Morochito – "the brave cat fighter"

One of his favorite games, however, was to stand over one of the cats and hold her neck in his jaws. If she scratched him, he just wagged his tail and bit a little firmer - not hard enough to hurt, though. One time I saw a cat get her claw stuck in the skin on his forehead and there he was just wagging his tail - showing no discomfort whatsoever! They get along pretty well now, but we have to speak to him every once in a while when he "forgets" and plays too rough. The point is that these dogs don't hurt easy. Don't ever put a puppy to the test, though: you can ruin him. I just used this example because I wanted to tell a story about my pup. Not all pups can do that and whether they do or don't has no relationship to how good a dog they are, as we will see. The above characteristics show the "steel" part of the Pit Bull.

In striking contrast to this bravery and love for battle is their attitude toward people. These dogs can be as much a lap dog as any other breed. They just seem to expect people to love them and they'll never get tired of being petted. They particularly love children and will frolic as long as the children want - they will never tire of it.

Morochito - three months olds
He was a beautiful puppy

In striking contrast to many other working breeds, particularly those who have been bred for guard, a Pit Bull can be trusted with children - he won't turn on them. The children can pull his ears, accidentally step on his paws, pull his tail – it's fun to him. Of course there are exceptions to every breed type and occasionally you'll find a Pit Bull that's unfriendly to strangers, including children, without cause - just naturally has always been that way; but most of these exceptions are due to some frightening experience in early puppyhood, and/or the fact that they haven't been around people very much, or have had negative experiences with people. These factors will produce "mean" dogs in any breed. As a general breed type, however, the Pit Bull is friendlier and more stable and trustworthy around people, than any other breed I know of. That's the "velvet."

ADBA show champion Haynes' Red Ike displaying the Pit Bull "smile." This dog was shown seven times and was best in show four of those. He won six first places and one second place.

In the home they can act like babies at times. They are extremely intelligent and are very clownish by nature. My dog has a funny way of wrinkling up hisbulldoggish forehead and cocking his head to the side when he can't understand something. He is very expressive with his eyes. When he gets scolded he looks so sorrowful. Pit Bulls are very flexible - loose jointed like cats. Morochito has a cute habit of sleeping in all kinds of awkward positions. Sometimes he sleeps on a big chair in our living room with the upper part of his body twisted around and hanging over the edge of the chair so that his head is pointed up toward the ceiling. He does the same thing in the summer in his dog house - sleeps with part of his body hanging out and twisted around. Sometimes he sleeps in the yard on his back with his paws drawn up and looks as if he were dead. The first time my wife saw him do that when he was a puppy she was scared to death - went rushing out to the backyard - thought he was dead. (She still feels uneasy when he assumes this position and sometimes calls his name just to see if he's okay.)

Cook's Taffy Two from Hammond's Willie and DC - an escape attempt

You should have seen him the first time he saw me take a bath. Boy, was he surprised and curious to see me get into that tub. He sure looked funny. When I got in and saw his curiosity, I held my breath and dipped my head down under the water just to see what he would do. He must have come over to the tub and looked down at me because when I popped my head up, he snorted and jumped back into a fighting stance, ready for whatever. I thought I'd die laughing. One thing a Pit Bull owner must be prepared for is the fact that his dog can be quite mischievous. To do our roadwork Morochito and I used to drive to a cemetery where there are no dogs running loose. Once when we were returning home Morochito started his ritual of rolling around on the car seat, presumably to scratch his back. Suddenly he got his collar stuck on the emergency brake! He immediately began squirming, twirling, and going into all sorts of antics to free himself. The emergency brake started up and I caught it. I had to push down with all my might because he was pulling and tugging to beat the band. I braked and slowed the car down as quickly as I could. I spoke calmly to him, telling him to go easy and he paused a minute and I slipped his collar off the brake. I'd hate to think what would have happened if I hadn't been able to hold that brake down. We'd probably have gone through the windshield.

Like many dogs, he has never liked machines like lawnmowers or vacuum cleaners. One time when we were doing our roadwork, I had him on a leash and we stopped to talk to a boy on a motorcycle. Morochito was still a pup at the time. The boy was sitting on his motorcycle, but it wasn't running. He was interested in my pup and listened intently while I bragged about all the famous pit veterans that are in his blood. (His bloodlines are shown in the chapter on breeding.) This was by no means an uncommon incident. It happens quite frequently. People are really interested in these dogs when they see them and I'm continuously asked, "Hey, what kind of dog is that? Man, he looks like he can do something." Or by those who have seen them before, "Hey, is that a Pit Bull? Wow!"

Anyway, when the boy decided to be on his way, he jumped up and started his motorcycle. Morochito immediately lunged at the cycle and grabbed the fender. He let go when I scolded him. (He obeyed me better when he was young.)

Mark Susanka's pits (darker color) and Ma Barker

Heather's Zak from Reid's Al Capone and Reid's Lucy

    I have an electric lawnmower. (I hate to mess with starting a gas mower, gas mixture, and all the problems involved with gas engines. I'm even willing to put up with the electric cord rather than mess with the gas engines.) Morochito never did like that lawnmower and the third time I mowed with it when he was a pup, he attacked it! My lawnmower was not grounded properly I guess and for some reason gave a pretty good jolt if you touched certain places on it. Morochito chose one of those places to attack and got zapped! Dogs are much, much more sensitive to electric shock than a human being because of their higher metabolism. A dog can be made neurotic with continuous electric shock. He kept away from that lawnmower after that - well, almost, anyway. The next mowing time he started after it again but all it took was a sharp word from me and he quit.

Rose's Red Cole

Here's a story from *Bloodlines* entitled "One of the Family" submitted by Cleo James.

"I have never written to *Bloodlines* before. But I sure love reading all about these beautiful American Pit Bull Terriers. We have an American pit she is a U.K.C. registered female. We love her like she was one of the family. When she was small she was almost red, but she is getting lighter it seems. She is like brown velvet to touch.

She really loves children, and it is pretty dangerous to try to spank one when she is around. She is quite a dog and is jealous of our little Pekingese dog.

When I ask her do you love me Tasha, she will shake her head up and down. When I tell her you mustn't do that she will shake her head from side to side.

Her name is Peanut Butter Tasha James, she is 'PR,' they are the most loyal dog I ever saw. She can tell when one of us is sick and she really worries about us. We just wouldn't part with her at all.

I look forward to receiving our *Bloodlines*. I read it through and through.

Her biggest pleasure is chasing the cats off from our house and chasing her tail and playing with our grandchildren.

Tasha loves apples and bananas, especially apples, she will just beg for one."

These dogs can be so friendly that I have seen many people play with a little Pit Bull and remark that they just couldn't believe that friendly, affectionate little dog would bite another dog, which brings to mind another question. Since these dogs are friendly, can they be used for guard work? Many folks become concerned because their Pit Bull, despite his obvious abilities, is so friendly with strangers that they wonder if the dog would protect if the need should arise. My answer to that question is that time and again I have heard stories of a Pit Bull that had always been very friendly toward strangers, seemed to sense true danger and rose to the occasion when needed. Their instincts seem much more developed in this area than the dogs bred for guard. It is not at all uncommon for one to hear of a guard-dog breed biting someone's friend or children. Pit Bulls seem better able to distinguish true danger. The Pit Bull's cousins, the Staff and the Bull Terrier also have this ability.

In *The New Complete Bull Terrier* [2] the main book for the white show variety cousin to the Pit Bull, there is a story about a little white Bull Terrier bitch. Seems that Mr. Eberhard, the writer of the book, had this dog with a real sweet disposition and who was friendly with everyone. He had a guy who worked for him, cleaning up the house. The Bull Terrier had known the guy all her life and was quite friendly with him. One day, however, she turned on him when he was in this room supposedly cleaning up. After that, every time he went into that room she would go into a rage and the owner had to shut her up. However, after he shut her up, he found that his liquor was disappearing at an alarming rate from the liquor cabinet in that room! When he locked the cabinet, he had no more trouble and the Bull Terrier never bothered the clean-up man again. Now that's what I call smart!

How'd she know that it was okay for him to handle other items which he cleaned, but not the liquor which was her master's property?

Not all Bull Terriers are going to be that smart, of course, but they do seem to have an above average ability to distinguish between friendly and unfriendly strangers. In addition, most Pit Bulls have an unafraid, direct stare that can be quite disconcerting. Their muscular build and wide confident stance can also be scary.

They are also very hard to kill. Generations and generations of pit fighting have resulted in a very tough animal. These dogs will continue fighting even though most of their ear or a section of their mouth has been chewed off - or a leg rendered inoperable.

My Pit Bull was run over by a car when he was only four months old. It was my fault I let him play in the front yard while I trimmed the hedges.

When I was looking the other way, he crossed the street to investigate the neighbor's yard. I called him to come and he didn't respond. I had just started training him to come on call and knew that it was wrong to keep calling him if he didn't come right away. He just learns that he doesn't have to obey right away. So I let him play a little longer while I worked. Then I turned and called to him. I forgot to look for cars and he came running - right in front of an orange Datsun driven by a teenage girl. As the car came to a sliding stop, I thought I would die of fright. I couldn't see Morochito so I ran around to the other side of the car and there he was pinned under the front wheel, kicking. He had never made a sound.

    I had to run back around to the driver's side and yell to the girl to back off. She was in such shock that she just gave me a blank look. I had to yell three times before she put the car into reverse and backed off. Morochito crawled over to our yard and turned around. He tried to get up but fell down. His whole side was caved in. He raised himself up part way, looked at that car and told it off proper with a "ruff!" When he did, blood poured out of his mouth and he collapsed. (That's what I call game!)

    I picked him up and carried him to the emergency clinic where they had to aspirate his lungs but didn't think he would live through the night. I was heartbroken, but one week later he was ready for a run and was completely healed (no broken bones). Praise the Lord! Another week after that I took him to some woods near us that belong to the grammar school. In those days I let him run loose, didn't have to worry about dogs too much. He was so glad to get back and run I thought he'd go crazy! In about a minute he ran up a hill and disappeared on the other side. I hollered and hollered for him. but he was gone out of sight. Scared me to death. thought I'd lost him. Fortunately he went to some house to get petted and they found our telephone number on his I.D. tag and called up. That pesky Pit Bull has given me plenty of scares.

Morochito resting after a hard workout.

Morochito's sister Brandy

203

Here's a story that was given to me by Cher Petersen in California. It's about one of her dogs, a bitch named Fonseca's Ginger.

"One day my two children, ages 2 & 3 years old, were playing in the back yard of my home on the swing set. Suddenly two rattle snakes came underneath the fence just a couple feet away from the kids. One of my dogs, Fonseca's Ginger, was out back with the kids and spotted the snakes. She immediately dived into the middle of these snakes & the fight was on. This gave me time to get the kids into the house. I rushed back out to see one snake take off into the hills and Ginger still had a hold on the other. I got a shovel & chopped the snake's head off and took Ginger inside the house to see if she'd been bit. She acted real groggy and her face started to swell. I could see the snake's puncture on her muzzle. I cut the bite so she bled freely and I immediately called Howard Heinzl. The 'Rev.' told me not to worry, that not even a rattler could kill one of his dogs.

Ginger slept quietly all night. The next morning the swelling was gone, except around the actual bite, and she was up and bouncing around like her old self. She wanted to go out back real bad so I let her out. She ran over to the spot where the snakes had been & was sniffing the area like crazy. I had put the one snake that I killed up on top of the swing set and she started jumping up at it. So I took it down and threw it at her. She jumped right on it and started shaking it around.

Howard had told me on the phone that once these dogs tangle with a snake, they'll go hunt 'em down after that - - - one more time the 'Rev.' was right."

Pit Bulls are also very strong for their size. You can find stronger dogs, the big Husky is generally stronger, for instance, but pound for pound I don't believe there are many breeds, if any, that are as strong as a Pit Bull. I know one story of a Pit Bull bitch that entered a weight-pulling contest when she was eleven months old and weighed only 41 pounds. She won first place against three Siberian Huskies and one Samoyed. She won first place in the lightweight division, beating a Siberian who outweighed her by twelve pounds. When she matured her best pull was 485 pounds, but the winner of the super heavyweight division (125 pounds and over) pulled 725 pounds. No way she could pull that. Still, I'd like to see what a solid 60-pound (semi-conditioned) Pit Bull could pull. I think he'd compete well with a super heavyweight!

Here's another story that was submitted by Cher Petersen of California.

"My husband and I go to the Colorado River quite often with our boat. We always take our dog Tuff. He loves the water. He can swim all day& never tire. One weekend we were up there, we were camped out on a real sandy beach. Every time Don and I would take off in the boat, Tuff would jump in the water and try to follow us. I got a little worried because he wouldn't just swim out a few feet and quit, he'd go 100 yards off shore and tread water till we came back. I was just sure he'd drown or get run over by a boat.

So next time we decided to take off, I took Tuff over to this boulder alongside the cove and tied him up to it. This boulder was about the size of a console T.V. and had to weigh 200 lbs. So Don and I took off in the boat with no worries of Tuff. We were gone a couple of hours and when we returned, it looked like a giant snail had been thru the camp. That crazy Tuff had drug that boulder thru the sand, down to the water, into the water, and there he was swimming around about six feet off shore still tied to the rock which was now under the water."

Petersen's Tuff, five months old - Heinzl and Colby bred.
Littermate to "Beast" who beat an opponent fourteen pounds heavier.

I don't want to try and say these Pit Bulls are some super dog, something more than they are. I don't want this to be some fairy tale, unrealistic book. They were bred for the pit and that's what they're best at, but I'm saying they also make excellent pets, loyal companions, and good all-purpose type dogs.

We'll look at some practical uses to which a pit Bull can be put, but first let's see what makes a Pit Bull the way he is, by studying his historical background.

Hammond's Troubles - pure Heinzl and all heart

Haynes' Red Ike

Chapter 1: History

"The seeds of our destiny are sown in the past" – an ancient proverb from Chinese Taoism.

The history of Pit Bulldogs is especially difficult because they have never been considered a show dog and therefore their history is not well documented. They are beginning to be shown now and at first I really didn't see why. I was concerned that we would lose that deep gameness so hard to obtain in breeding. These dogs are just not supposed to be bred for being pretty and we will rue the day we begin to. However, the Pit Bull shows are sponsored by top Pit Dog men who are very much aware of this and participating breeders are still breeding primarily proven dogs. The pit shows sponsored, for example, by the American Dog Breeders Association are promoted by some of the best dog men around and they are fighting to keep our breed. I respect them very much for this. I know that it entails a tremendous amount of time on their part and they are faced with a most difficult task because of the bad name the Pit Bull has in show circles.

Actually, the ADBA has developed what I consider the best standards you can find because it is more directly related to a particular performance than other standards I'm aware of developed by people who know (experienced) far more in the area of performance than developers of other standards. That, of course, is merely my opinion.

Take a look at the ADBA standards provided at the end of this chapter and see what you think. Notice that conformation does play a part in modern breeding - the theory being that given two equally game (brave) dogs - equally unwilling to quit - the dog with the best ability is more likely to win. The dog that is built so that he has more leverage, etc. is likely to have the deciding factor in this case. In other words, if he's built correctly, he has an advantage; but conformation should take second place to gameness, which is a very elusive trait. By gameness, I mean deep gameness. Just about every well-bred Pit Bull has a degree of gameness not found in other breeds of dogs, but to have better than average Pit Bull gameness - that's hard to get.

Let me take a moment at this point and explain what is meant in Pit Bull circles by this term "gameness." Gameness might be translated courageous, or unwilling to quit - but should never be interpreted as aggressive. Let me put it this way, in the animal kingdom there are very few fights to the death. The human being is probably the most bloodthirsty creature in existence in that so many humans will kill for reasons other than food. In the animal world, fights are usually over territory or mates. Generally it is a matter of survival of the fittest. When two males fight, as soon as the stronger one dominates, the other one will give up and run away. The fights usually begin with a great deal of threatening display (bared teeth, growls, raised hackles, etc.) to get the point across – "I'm bad news; don't mess with me." Often the point is made and fight ends before it really begins, because one animal is often able to out bluff another with the display of strength and "meanness," so that the potential opponent runs away.

This type of behavior is fairly standard in the animal world with few exceptions. The gamecock (fighting rooster) is one of those. When two male cocks meet, they just naturally fight to see who's king of the roost - and they'll fight until one is dead or incapable of fighting further - at least most of them will. Weasels are somewhat the same way, I understand. In any event, the Pit Bulldog does not resort to growling, barking. or other means of bluff or threatening display. He will immediately attack an opponent and make no sound whatsoever. A Pit Bull is not a barky dog which makes him a pleasant pet, by the way. A Pit Bull that is playing in the backyard will bark like most dogs, but he won't go on and on like many other breeds. If he is on a chain or leash, he'll bark at another dog or other animal; but take him off the chain and he'll go straight into another dog without a sound except snorting noises or breathing heavily if it is a long match. In fact, when Pit Bulls are matched and one starts growling - even just a little, you can be pretty safe in betting on the other dog if you can get a bet, that is. The dog that growls will quit soon.

There are exceptions to every rule, of course. I know of one match in which this little Pit Bull whined and howled for about an hour and I'm sure a lot of people lost their betting money that night. Anyway, he went nearly two hours and beat his opponent when his opponent couldn't make his scratch. He scratched hard every time and then acted like he wasn't too happy. Maybe he was growling because he was feeling the pain. I don't know.

As I said, Pit Bulls have a very high pain threshold when they are fighting. It may be that their system produces more adrenal or some other substance that helps them; I don't know. Pit Bulls have happy-go-lucky personalities, but just as a hound dog is happiest on the trail, so a Pit Bull is never more content than when gets in the pit.

A spectator observing a pit fight for the first time might be really surprised to see two Pit Bulls chewing on each other - each one chewing the other's leg for all he's worth (and believe me. there is tremendous power in a Pit Bull's bite), and both of them wagging their tails to beat the band. Many folks have difficulty understanding this. An athlete has less trouble comprehending. I am 42 years old and have been taking karate for 11 years. As a youngster I boxed in Y.M.C.A. clubs. I have always enjoyed fighting - for fun. I don't like a fight for real, a grudge. I don't enjoy hitting other people in a sadistic or bully-type manner, but like a man who loves to play football, my best workouts are when my sparring partner and I go home black and blue. Why? I really don't know, but I've seen some people who think I'm crazy for enjoying that, work for a whole week getting about 20 hours sleep in five days, cry, sweat, etc. working for a play or recital that their children are participating in. Why? Because they love it. That's their bag and I don't criticize them for it. I say don't criticize me for getting in a ring and banging around with another guy who likes to box - and don't look down your nose at an old Pit Bull who loves to get in a pit and try to be a champion.

Hammonds' Onedia - pure Alligator

Hammonds' Taffy - double Musty bred Heinzl bitch - dam to Hillie Boy, Hack, Haggie Nae, pinky, Judo, and Massey's Bridget

I'd like to point out one other thing about this concept of gameness. Folks who do not know much about Pit Bulls are inclined to consider aggressiveness to be gameness. As I mentioned earlier, there is no correlation between the two. Many dogs of other breeds will aggressively snarl, attack, and bite. The game dog will stay and fight no matter how hard he is bitten or tossed around. The dog that is not game (called a "cur" in Pit Bulldog circles) will give up when bitten hard enough or after fighting a relatively short time without winning. The point is this - the dog who is aggressive is not necessarily game - and the dog who is passive may be the gamest one in ten counties. Well, I can't make the point nearly as well as a gentleman referred to as "The Farmer." He is Ralph Greenwood, Editor of the *Pit Bull Gazette*.

The following section by "The Farmer" is taken with permission from two articles in the November, 1977 and February, 1976 issues of the *Pit Bull Gazette*.

The Way it Was – Part 1

Recently an old friend asked me, "Why do you have such an interest in fighting dogs?" If you've ever asked yourself that question you know that when you truly have the answer you know a lot more about yourself. In trying to explain it to my friend. I realized that for me it all comes down to gameness.

I think gameness is the attraction. For that small hardcore element that has been known to set them down for money even today. True, some people call them gamblers, but there are plenty of ways to gamble that offer faster action than bulldogs.

I also don't think you have to be a dogfighter to appreciate that gameness: as evidenced by a new breed of fancier who keeps the dogs for show and companionship. Of course, every Pit Bull fancier has admired the power, agility, stamina, and biting ability of a well-bred bulldog, but these qualities are also present in other breeds. I've heard knowledgeable people say an Airedale bites harder than a bulldog and it's probably true. It would be awfully hard to beat a Walker or Bluetick hound for stamina: and just watch a German Shorthair quartering a field if you want to see a beautiful exhibition of fluid motion. But when it comes to single minded drive and persistence, and indomitable will to be master, nothing on earth compares with our American Pit Bull Terrier.

When a dog fighter had a dog "open to match," he only specified the weight not the breed. Now, if a man could have won the money with any other breed of dog you know he would have used it. But in many years, as a fancier, I've never even heard of another breed of dog being used in a fight. That's because regardless of their physical attributes, they can't compete with the Bulldog's will to win. True, over the years, we have developed a dog with some pretty impressive physical equipment, but without the gameness, he's just another pretty face.

I realize in talking to my non-violent lady friend that trying to describe gameness to some people is next to impossible. It's like describing how something tastes. If you haven't experienced something just like it, words can't convey the thought.

My friend however, has an advantage over most people because of her work. She is a psychologist who counsels people who have terminal illnesses. We talked about her experiences with
the way different people handle their adversity. She spoke with pity of those who, having learned of their fate, break down completely, becoming incapable of continuing their day to day lives; crying and sobbing; a burden to themselves and their families. Invariably, she said, the end comes sooner for these people.

She spoke admiringly of some of her "favorites." They were persons who, although they knew the prognosis, either wouldn't accept it, or they wouldn't allow it to change their outlook on living. They went about their daily lives, sometimes with more vigor than before, not giving up, even though the handwriting was on the wall. My friends. THAT'S gameness!

Harking back to the days when dogs were fought in the pit. When an owner had conceded a long hard battle in order to save his dog, he frequently asked to be given a courtesy scratch to prove the gameness of his dog, even though he had lost the fight. He may have made a good scratch, but if at the end he had been lying "out of holds," not trying to win, then in my opinion he wasn't as game as some, regardless of how many scratches he made.

Gameness is not the willingness to fight. It's not the courage to be killed by a better opponent. It's the will win!

Nothing tests that will to win more than the instinct for self-preservation. In the Pit Bull, we have one of the few examples of an animal whose will to live is consistently suppressed by his will to dominate; to rule whatever ground he's standing on.

Sociologists have told us for years that the primary instincts are for sex and survival. Well, take a look at man. How many men have died for their women compared to the number who have died for their country? As for survival; there are a lot of bodies lying in the fields, ditches, and forests of the world that belonged to men who wouldn't run. Of course we're not always that brave. There was a time in our culture when we were taught to aspire to be, but I guess even that's fading.

In spite of that, I believe that every human being who walks the earth admires gameness when he recognizes it. Some of us even seek it out. We look for it in sports that test man's courage. We find traces of it in race horses, wild animals, and to a great degree, in gamecocks. It has nothing to do with being a tough guy who will "fight at the drop of a hat." It's when you're getting whipped that you find out how game you are.

The same is true of a pit dog. You don't know how game he is until you've seen him in trouble. It doesn't matter how he bristles when you walk another dog by his chain, or how quick he was to take hold of the neighbor's Cock-a-poo. As a matter of fact, I don't believe that the overt aggressiveness of a dog is at all relevant to how game he is. For example, I had the honor to own a dog that came from the bottom to win a big fight in over two hours with no turns. The loser died and the winner was only saved by timely shock therapy. I would say he was reasonably game, yet, it was not uncommon to see him romping with cur dogs that strayed through the yard. Many game, game dogs would not fight a cur dog. On the other hand, many very game dogs were like kegs of dynamite. They would explode when they saw anything with hair on it. Some rank curs that would turn and run the minute they were topped, were the same way, and still others couldn't look a good bulldog in the eye. Initial aggressiveness just doesn't seem to relate positively or negatively to gameness.

Now aggressiveness in battle is something else, again. A game dog will keep his hold and what's more important, he'll always have a hold. When called on to scratch, whether he runs across or walks, he'll be leaning into your hands when you turn to face his opponent. He'll keep his eye on the dog and scratch straight into him without turning his head. He'll aggressively take advantage of every opportunity to hurt his opponent.

But when it comes to dogs, why partner, there's only one. He's not backed into a corner, fighting to save his life. He can't be ordered to do battle. His tail is up, there's joy in his heart. He's going to whip you because you're standing where he wants to stand. He fights because he IS.

"The Way It Was" - Part 2

"Gamest dog that ever looked through a collar,"... "Front running cur," ... "Dead game" ... "couldn't take what he handed out." How many times have you heard Bulldog people use those terms? Especially those who go back to the days when dogs were commonly fought in the pit? And isn't it the truth that one man's "dead game" was another man's "cur?"

"Game" and "Cur" have dominated the conservation of American Pit Bull fancier since the breed began, because it is a natural fact that without gameness, you don't have a fighting dog.

Most people who are fanciers of any breed of dog are fascinated by what Bulldog people call "gameness." Many's the time I've been to a dog show and listened to owners of everything from Irish Wolfhounds to Lhasa Apsos talk about their particular favorite's "courage," "loyalty," "persistence," etc. Those are just other words for what we refer to as gameness. It's pretty hard to lie about a shallow rib cage, straight stifle or other conformation point because they're right out there for all to see. But talk about courage, and man, watch the imaginations go wild. Every handler's dog has a heart like a lion.

That's not a problem as long as there's no way to find out, but the Pit Bull fancier was frequently faced with a "Put up or shut up" situation. For that reason we have become much more definitive about those general terms used to describe gameness in other breeds; and also more polarized in our opinions. Many a valued friendship has been destroyed by the injudicious use of the words "game" and "cur."

So when is a dog "game" and when is he a "cur?" And what distinguishes him from "dead game" and "rank curl?"

If we use the commonly held opinion that a game dog was a dog that wouldn't quit and a cur was one that would quit we're going to be in trouble, because it was the contention of some of the most successful dog fighters and breeders of the past that "they'll all quit." True, some of them took their death and didn't quit, but that doesn't mean they wouldn't have quit under different conditions.

In a previous column we discussed gameness and defined it as the "will to win." If we can accept that definition, we can also accept that anything that has to do with "will" is relative to other values that also have a "will." For example, the will to survive.

As soon as we inject the possibility of relative values into the discussion, we take a giant step toward understanding the driving force that makes the ideal of the American Pit Bull Terrier different from the ideal of all other breeds. We ask him to have the will to win (or dominate) that is greater than his will to survive. If we had the opportunity to watch hundreds of dogs in pit contests (as many old-timers did), we would realize that there are two huge variables in these two competing value systems.

1) That the will to dominate varies within the individual. For example, some bitches did not fight the same when they were in heat. Some male dogs did not fight bitches as hard as other males. A sick or undernourished dog would not be as game as when healthy. The list could be much longer.

2) That the threat to survival varies with the opponent, conditions of the contest, and the dogs assessment of the threat at the time.

I believe that a Bulldog somehow equates his ability to dominate his opponent with his ability to survive. You very rarely saw a dog quit if he dominated the fight completely, even if he was very badly injured. However, when he lost the initiative, started to go down, was unable to take his favorite holds, his will to dominate began to be tested. For that reason, dogs that fought the ear or the nose were enormously successful even if they couldn't bite hard because they frustrated their opponent by holding him off and were able to dominate the action even if they weren't punishing.

It also seems obvious that when a dog becomes fatigued, he will be less able to dominate a fresher opponent, and as fatigue becomes severe, he will recognize some threat to his survival which will be computed against how badly he wants to win. There have been many cases where both dogs were going into fatigue-induced shock, but one dog quit before the other .Obviously, some combination of factors gave one dog's will to win precedence over the other dog's will to survive.

When a well-conditioned pit dog goes into shock and stands in his corner, does that make him a cur? I don't think so: just not "dead game."

On the other hand, if Bowser screams, turns and jumps the pit the first time he goes down, I would say he's gone a long way in the direction of being labeled a cur. Somewhere within these two extremes lay the vast majority of the ancestors of our present-day American Pit Bull Terriers. Hopefully, the dogs on our pedigrees represent the higher end of the scale.

How did the really successful dog fighters select their prospects? Many a conversation between Bulldog men reflected the importance of selection. For example, one well known fancier frequently says, "A match well-made is a match half won." Another time a beginning dog fighter asked a more experienced man (who should have known because he lost more than he won), "What is the most common mistake made in conditioning?" The response was, "Conditioning the wrong dog." So how do you determine how game a dog is? (Note that we are not asking if he is game or not game.)

The opinion of some present-day breeders notwithstanding, I submit that you can't tell by the look in his eye. You have to bring into play the conflicting forces of the will to survive and the will to dominate. You have to "roll" them to see what you've got. Serious practioners of the sport, (that is, those who put their money on the line) rolled their young dogs for three reasons: to school the dogs, to determine the dogs' ability, and to determine the dogs' degree of gameness. I never knew a serious dog man who rolled his dogs for any other reason. Sadism is a waste of time, a waste of valuable animals, and is an abuse of the purpose for which the dog has been bred. Sadists have been scorned and ridiculed by serious fanciers and should continue to be ostracized with every means at our disposal. However, if the dogs had not been rolled and fought, there wouldn't be an American Pit Bull Terrier today.

How did the dedicated fancier conduct his rolls? Obviously in looking for gameness, he tried to simulate pit conditions that induced a dog to quit. The degree to which the dog resisted the temptation to save his hide had a lot to do with deciding whether he could win. We already have recognized that fatigue and dominance are the major factors that influence the will to win (pain probably enters into it but I believe a Bulldog's threshold of resistance to pain is so high in the heat of battle, that it's not significant.) To insure that some semblance of the fatigue would be felt without burning the dog up, dogs were usually rolled when they were a little fat. Thus, they didn't have to stand and watch them for two hours. The dog they wanted to know about was usually rolled with a bigger opponent. The smaller dog would tire more quickly from pushing the heavier weight and would also have considerable less ability to dominate a bigger, stronger opponent. The idea was to attempt to discourage your prospect as quickly as possible (after of course, he had developed his confidence in schooling rolls) and make your judgment of whether to match him or not without leaving his best fight in the gym.

It was a truism that the more a man knew about fighting dogs, the less he needed to roll them. His experience (and lack of subjective involvement) led him to rely on signs. These signs were never absolute, but were very subtle and were widely open to interpretation. Thus when a successful dog fighter brought a dog to the pit and said laconically that the dog, "had never made a bad sign," he spoke volumes with that phrase, much more than some beginner who bought the dog because he was the color of his wife's hair.

The surest "sign" is to look for a holding dog. A dog that takes his hold and keeps it. Old timers liked a dog that would only swap one hold for a better one. Beware the dog who had a good hold on the nose, ear, or chest and when he went down, released it to grasp frantically for everything in sight. A game dog would keep his good hold and try to wrestle his way up with it. A really game dog would work the hold from the bottom and not put any great priority in being on top. He might also get killed doing this.

The more game in the fighter, the more pressure he would put on his opponent. Even if he could not get a good hold, he'd always have a nip somewhere, trying to get a better one. Many dogs that were not so game would keep a good hold if they were up, but never kept a hold when they were down. They could win a fight against a dog they could outwrestle but look out when they got tired and started to go down.

Of course a "turn" was always a telltale sign. If a dog turned his head and shoulders away from the other dog, it was a sure sign he was thinking about getting out. If he fuzzed up at the base of the tail when he lost the advantage, or if he howled and cried when bit, chances were that he was not a pit prospect. These were not the only signs. Dogs were judged and evaluated for gameness by the way they scratched, the way they looked at their opponent (or more importantly, if they looked away from their opponent) and how they felt in the corner.

Occasionally, you would hear someone brag about his dog's gameness by saying he had been "two dogged." In other words, a fresh dog had been put on him after he had gone long enough to stop his first opponent. The only thing that tells is that the handler couldn't see what he should have seen with one opponent. It meant nothing as a qualitative assessment. The first, and for that matter the second, dog could have been a totally inept bum and you simply were looking at the best of three bums; or they could have indeed been long, hard rolls and your game dog had left 20% of his ability behind him. It was the task of the handler to select the opponents in the roll to make the best possible judgment with the least possible trauma.

In an attempt to put a handle on this very nebulous subject, I think we can state with assurance that the best dog men couldn't tell much about a dog's gameness in less than twenty minutes. They might roll him for less time and decide to match him based on his ability, but they were betting on his gameness. For in the final analyses, the test was going to the pit for money: one man's conditioning, breeding and judgment against the other man's. When the men who created this breed looked at a dog, they didn't ask, "Is he game or cur?" They asked, "Is he game enough to win?"

A few examples may illustrate the point further. One of the best and most respected dog men in Pit Bull circles is Gary Hammonds of Mansfield, Texas. He seems to be a straight shooter as far as I can see, and I surely respect his knowledge and his yard of Pit Bulls. His article is in the "Catch Dog" chapter. Anyway, he told me that "Some dogs (Pit Bulls) fight only when called on to do so. The Heinzl dogs (tend) to be like this to some degree. For example, my old Taffy bitch would follow me around while I fed the dogs and just stay out of the other dogs' way. On the other hand, put her in the square (pit) and she'd do her thing as good as any bitch I've ever owned. Won three before she was thirty months old and was mother of several good ones. Cactus Jack was like this also." Mr. Hammonds does not match dogs but his yard has excellent blood.

The best example I can think of, however, is the dog who is probably the most well-known dog of them all and is in the pedigree of probably more dogs (since his time in the 1950's) than any other dog. His name was Dibo (pronounced Die-ba). Dibo was one of those lucky accidents that just happen. His bloodlines are excellent (highly line-bred, by the way). His breeding was primarily Con Feely. Can Feely was one of the old time greats. He lived in the early 1900's along with George Armitage, J.P. Colby, and others. He was highly thought of and respected by his peers, especially by the critical Armitage in his book, *Thirty Years with Fighting Dogs*, a book that you must get. It's the best, in my opinion, of the old era books available. Armitage describes his experiences with Pit Bulls and with other dog men. He describes more than thirty battles, some of them famous ones. He provides a program for selecting a combat puppy, feeding, training, and conditioning him. Most of it is still good today. The feeding is a bit antiquated, but, again, his knowledge of these dogs was second to none. A whole lot of his dogs stayed in there beyond the hour mark when called upon, so his methods couldn't be too old fashioned. Anyway, old Con Feely was a breeder (He imported some game dogs from Ireland) and a dog fighter – a respected fighter, too. Armitage said he was one of the best handlers he had ever seen with a Pit Bull. He was shrewd, never lost his cool, and was able to intimidate other handlers so that they would make mistakes. Consequently, pit men didn't like to pit their dogs against a dog he was handling. He also loved to bet on the dogs. Well, Dibo (named "Dumbo" at that time) was a Feely-and-Colby-bred dog, bred by an amateur named Smith who sold him as a pet to a man named Jensen. Jensen traded "Dumbo" to Howard Heinzl for a Collie, which Heinzl had gotten out of the city dog pound for around $10. Jensen wanted a Collie for his son because Lassie was popular then. Two-year-old Dibo, still a dedicated pacifist, ran loose in the yard and didn't try to fight the other dogs on the lot - he even followed Howard around when he fed the dogs. Well, Dibo might have spent the rest of his life right there in Howard's yard as a pet and might not have ever been bred, but it just so happened that one of Mr. Heinzl's friends, Earl Tudor, one of the greatest pit men in U.S. history, visited one day and was offered Dibo because he seemed to like the dog. Dibo turned out to be an excellent pit dog and became a three-time winner. His real value, however, was not in his fighting ability, but in his ability to pass on hard bite, wrestling skill, and the rare quality of deep gameness. (The ability to pass on characteristics is called prepotency. Tudor bred Dibo to a bitch named Red Lady because she came into heat and he just happened to breed her. He really wasn't very excited about the breeding, and Red Lady was sold to a man named Gordon with the understanding that they would split the litter. Red Lady had six pups. When Tudor's three died, Gordon gave him the remaining three. Well, two of these dogs happened to be the famous dogs: Tudor's Spike and Tudor's Jeff. Both dogs were also fabulous producers. Tudor's Spike sired Carver's Miss Spike, said by many to be the best producing bitch ever. When Earl Tudor died in 1977, he had been totally involved with Pit Bulls for nearly sixty years, remaining active with them until a few years before his death. There are not many pedigrees that do not have Tudor blood. So you see, a dog definitely does not have to be aggressive to be game.

Little Plumber Soko - a littermate to Champion Alligator and known to take 2nd place to none

Hammonds' Willie Boy - sire, Bruno; dam, Taffy

Now that "gameness" has been explained, let's continue with the history. The Pit Bull is not registered with A.K.C. (American Kennel Club), the largest registration body in the U.S., because they are not recognized as a pure breed. This is the case even though, as I am about to demonstrate, they are probably one of the least tainted, most pure of all breeds. The real reason they are not admitted to A.K.C. registration (not that many, if any, of their owners would want them to be) is because of their bad name for fighting in the pit.

Many of the early breeders of Pit Bulls didn't register their dogs at all - they had no need to. They wanted to keep their strain to themselves and constantly strove to breed only the gamest - in their own yard. The breed was kept pure by performance. If the dog didn't perform, he wasn't bred. The performance trial, that is the pit, is far more demanding than a field trial or other popular endurance tests. This performance test has resulted in the development of a superior breed, not a mean, vicious breed of dog, but a dog that, when considered in the light of an all-purpose dog, is superior. I do not want to conjure up fairy tales so as to make exaggerated claims about these dogs. I do contend, however, that selective breeding and high performance standards set in terms of endurance, stamina, courage, and intelligence, has resulted in the development of a far above-average breed of dog.

I'm told that in England crossbreeds can be registered, and in four generations they are classed as purebreds. The breeding of the Pit Bull is ancient; yet they are considered by show-dog people, to be a breed of inferior quality.

If you go back far enough in dog history, you'll find that present-day breeds evolved from four basic types: those bred for speed and used for running down prey, the scent hounds used for locating and tracking game, the herding dogs used to contain and protect the domestic animals, and the fighting dogs. The fighting dogs ran with the scent hounds and were used to finish off the prey when it was caught. They were sometimes called "tie dogs" - dogs that were kept tied up in the yard and let loose only to run with the pack when hunting game or at night to guard property, that is to protect against thieves, wolves, or other predators. They were also used as war dogs. The fighting and war dogs were called Mastiffs and Alaunts. These dogs had to be strong and agile, but above all. they had to be courageous. If they showed fear, they were not bred. In Chaucer's "Knights' Tales" there is mention made of Mastiff-type dogs that were used to hunt deer and lion. Some were white and some were piebald (covered with patches of two colors. especially black and white) colored. The time - about 1400 A.D. As early as 3,000 B.C., we find archaeological paintings resembling the modern-day Pit Bull in early Egyptian drawings depicting bull-like dogs fighting large prey.

Most of the known history of these dogs takes place in England. Many historians say that the dogs came to Britain from Phoenician traders in the 6th century A.D. These dogs were known as Mastiffs and were supposed to be very large and mean. They are believed by many to be the original foundation for our modern Pit Bull. There are some historians who feel that the Bulldog resulted from a mixture of the large Mastiff and the pug dog - the Pug which originated in Holland and Germany. No one really knows. Personally, I doubt it. I think they are going by appearances and that actually that pug was merely a very distant relative. There is agreement that the Bulldog and the Mastiff probably had a common origin in the Alaunt. The Alaunt was defined in a dictionary published in 1632 as being like a Mastiff and serving butchers to bring in fierce oxen and keep them in their stalls. Actually, early writings (in the 1600's and 1700's) refer to Mastiffs and Bulldogs interchangeably. Another word for these dogs was Bandog, meaning a dog that is kept chained up or kept in bonds. These dogs were used for sport, engaging them in combat against bulls, bears, horses, donkeys, lions, badgers, etc.

In any event, the Britons used them as war dogs when fighting Caesar, and Caesar was so impressed with them that he brought many home with him where they were used for sport in the pit, which may be the earliest use of the dogs in pit contests. The Roman Claudian (A.D. 395-404) talks about a British dog that "brings the bull's forehead to the ground" and describes the dog as courageous and enthusiastic.

We do not have much written account of these activities because there were no newspapers and very few books in the early British history. In the 1600's, however, we do have some accounts. There is a reference to an old Bear Garden on the south bank of the Thames that collapsed in 1583, indicating that it must have already been old then. During its heyday, between 1550 and 1680, few sports in England have enjoyed more popularity than bear-baiting. It was an expensive sport sponsored primarily by the courts. The general consensus is that Edward III (Edward the Confessor), King of the Anglo-Saxons (1004- 1006), was the first to introduce the Roman sport of bear-baiting to England. In the "Merry Wives of Windsor," there is mention made of a bear named "Sackerson" which evidently had a high reputation. During the days of James II, there was a very popular bear called "Young Blackface" who was owned by an Irishman named O'Sullivan. This bear fought twenty-two matches in one day against the best dogs in the country, but was finally killed when they matched him, muzzled, against three dogs at once, without his "protector," which was his protective iron collar he normally wore.

An old picture depicting bear-baiting in England during the 19th century.

Bear-baiting died down during the plague and never became popular with the court after that. It didn't completely die out, however, and was still going on at the end of the eighteenth century even though it was banned in 1835. By that time, however, this once favored pastime of kings and queens and nobles was exclusively patronized by the working classes. In addition to being illegal, it was expensive to obtain and maintain bears, so the sport eventually died out completely.

Another use to which the Bulldogs were put was bull-running and bull-baiting. Bull-running was very popular for many generations at Stamford, Lincolnshire, on St. Brice's Day, November 13. It is said that bull-running began because of an accidental incident in 1209 during the reign of King John. It seems two bulls were fighting in a field owned by some butchers and when the butchers tried to break them up, they infuriated the bulls so that they began running down the public highway. The butchers chased after them trying to catch them and they let their Bulldogs loose to help because they were afraid their bulls would be a danger to the public. The bulls ran all the way into town and of course the townspeople panicked and there was a general uproar. The Earl of Warren, who happened to be on horseback at the time, saw the commotion so joined in the pursuit of the animals. It was a very exciting chase and great sport to the Earl, so much so that he wanted to do it some more. So he offered the town, as a gift, the meadow where the fight took place, on condition that a bull be provided each year for the purpose of being run on St. Brice's Day. It got to be a kind of gross affair because the lower classes, horse-jobbers, hostlers, butchers, and the like from neighboring villages joined in and a great riot always resulted. The bulls were goaded with sticks and knives. Bull-running was also popular at Tetbury in Gloucestershire and Tutbury in Staffordshire.

Bull-Baiting in Old England

Bull-baiting was common all over the country, and its history~ seems to be as old as England. With bull-baiting, a bull was tied to a stake with a thick rope, four or five yards long, fastened to a hook or swivel so that it would turn around. If a dog was successful in pinning a bull, the owner received a prize, such as five shillings, or a gold laced hat, or an ornate dog collar. The betting was generally pretty heavy. Some bulls were more "game" than others and of course were preferred. A good experienced bull learned to circle, keeping his eye on the Bulldog and would stamp and scrape a shallow trench in the ground so he could get his horns down real low and protect his nose, knowing from experience that this most tender part of his body would be his enemy's primary target. He also positioned himself near the center of the ring so he could charge into the Bulldog. The

Bulldog, if he was well bred, invariably attacked the bull in front, charging straight forward, trying to latch onto the bull's nose or lip. The experienced Bulldog ran real close to the ground (called "playing low") in order to avoid the bull's horns. If he failed, he might be trampled or tossed by the bull. Records of the bull fights indicate that the dogs were sometimes tossed 30 to 50 feet high and when possible the men in the crowd would catch them on their shoulders to break their fall. The dog would then rush in again for another try. Sand was usually laid about the area to help break the dog's fall. Quite often the dog was momentarily stunned when he fell (called lying "doggo"), but when he recovered he would charge in again. (It is a curious fact that a bull will seldom attack a dog or man who is lying prone on the ground.) When a dog was tossed high into the air, he survived his fall only if he was very sturdily built. There is one account of a dog that broke his leg when he fell from a toss. The leg was spliced and the dog proceeded to run again at the bull, with unabated fury. In other words, it was a very rough sport and only those with raw courage and those exceptionally hard to kill survived. If the bull was unsuccessful and found he couldn't trample his opponent or toss him, he tended to then go on the defensive. When this happened, he usually lifted his head and turned to the side, trying to get out of reach of the dog. The well-bred Bulldog would instantly spring into the air and with amazing speed and agility latch onto the bull's nose or lip. It is this background that accounts for the amazing jumping ability of Pit Bulls. Many of them have a clownish habit of jumping straight up in the air when excited. It's all in their blood.

    I'd like to add at this point the observation, of the disastrous, and I do mean disastrous effects of show breeding. The show variety Bulldog, that is the short, fat, funny looking dog with the pushed-in mug, sourpuss look, and highly undershot jaw (called the brachycephalic Bulldog) is the original Bulldog - but its fighting days ended in the middle 1800's when it became a show dog. The ones who continued fighting became the American pit Bull Terrier. Can you imagine the show variety Bulldog performing in the manner just described? He'd be lucky to jump as high as a bull's knees, never mind leap up in the air and latch onto his nose before the bull can turn his head away! Let's look at the opinion of a fellow Pit Bull fancier Gary Hammonds[6].

A Thought

    A great deal of time and forethought undoubtedly went into the recent "Standard" put forth by the American Dog Breeders Association in the *Pit*

Bull Gazette. Their motives were more than justified as it is quite possible that the game dog of today will, in fact, become a relic of the past. If nothing else, the American "Pit" Bull Terrier deserves to at least look like the gladiator he once was.

In the past, many of the show breeds have become virtually useless in their given roles among the dog world. This has come about in most cases due to the breeders' attempt to improve on an already near perfect animal. Now we know that all deterioration among the American breeds have not been due to the show breeder. I am sure many among their ranks would be quick to point the accusing finger at the amateur breeder or puppy peddler. While they may be responsible for some genetic defects, I doubt very seriously that the amateur breeder is to blame for the over-selection and exaggeration found in anyone of the super weak K-9 breeds of today. Could it be the "style of the day" along with the show ribbon that has left the general public with a beautiful yet worthless animal?

For example, the Basset Hound's sad expression. The Boxer, Boston or English Bull's extra "pug" nose. The short legs, long legs, bowed legs, pig eyes, wrinkled faces and miniatures of the various breeds are all examples of the factors that have weakened so many breeds. All these and many more exaggerations were brought about by the breeders who were seeking an animal with some unique characteristic deemed standard or more appealing to the eye by some individual or group of people.

Consider, if you will, some of the show breeds degeneration in usefulness. The Collie (like Lassie) with absolutely no herding instincts or ability. The beautiful bird dog with neither the stamina to work the fields nor instinct to point, if he could. What ever happened to the "pack bred" Airedale that could run the big cats for days? Granted, he would hardly pass for the second cousin to a show dog, but then his show counterpart, beautiful as he might be, would not chase a rabbit a mile and have a rough time with ole Bugs Bunny if he happened to catch him.

Surely our breed will not go the paths set by others! If sight of the goals set forth by the American Dog Breeders Association are ever put aside for a more perfect or beautiful animal, that the American Pit Bull Terrier could easily become a "hull of an animal" much like the Airedale. If this is to be his fate, then let this noble beast become extinct along with all those who admired and loved both his ability and gameness.

Take a look at the show standard for Bulldogs sometime. They can't have a wrong colored nose, their ears have to be a certain way, they have to be short and fat, etc. Compare that standard with the ADBA standard you find at the end of this chapter. Notice this standard doesn't give a hoot about color or any other characteristic that doesn't affect performance.

Central to the ADBA standard is performance, and you had better believe that is a high standard and I'll bet it took many hours to develop it. I've got nothing against a good old English Bull (show variety); he's an excellent pet and very lovable. I just wanted to point out that in my opinion, pitting Bulldogs is not nearly so cruel as breeding them so as to develop dogs with hip dysplasia, nervous temperament, and all the ills of nearly all modern breeds, that have occurred as a result of breeding for good looks. My Pit Bull has a little "broke" tail that would disqualify him in any show ring, but you had better believe there's not a darn thing wrong with his hips or his strength of character.

Back to the days when bull-baiting was practiced. Once the Bulldog had latched onto that nose, he had to hang on for dear life. If he couldn't and the bull was able to shake him loose, he often fell between the bull's hoofs and was trampled to death. The dog had to be able to breathe through his nostrils through the bull's blood and swollen nose tissue, which the modern Pit Bull would also be able to do. (The show Bulldog variety. however, has trouble breathing period, never mind latched onto a bull.) After a while the bull would weaken from pain, fatigue, and loss of fluid. And, though still resisting, would slowly lower his head to the ground. He'd still stamp that dog's guts out, though, if he could get him. A well-bred Bulldog had strong neck and shoulder muscles and was agile so he merely backed out of reach of the hooves while continuing to shake the bull until finally with a thunderous roar, the bull would totally collapse and refuse to resist while the victorious Bulldog dragged him around the ring amid clamorous applause.

It was not uncommon for a breeder (butchers being the people that bred Bulldogs the most) to bring a Bulldog bitch with her puppies to a bull-bait. He would then proceed to bait the bitch to prove her gameness. A few were known to chop off extremities of the Bulldog while she held fast to the bull. If she died holding onto the bull, the puppies sold for a small fortune. Fireworks were also used at the baits bear and bull to add to the excitement. Sometimes a rope would be lowered through a pulley device to a Pit Bull in a pit surrounded by fireworks. The dog would latch onto a piece of sponge attached to the rope and hold fast while he was raised to safety above the flames and explosions.

Badger-baiting was also quite popular as an old English sport. There were two types of this sport, one of which was called a draw. This method involved putting a badger in a box. A dog was then set down in front of the box opening and had to drag the badger out. The dog's owner would then pry him loose from the badger and the badger was flipped back into the box. A badger is an extremely ornery character and a very effective fighter. He is fast and mean and has sharp, ripping claws. Another variation was called a "turn loose." In this case, the badger has his tail fastened to a short rope that is attached to the floor. In this contest the badger has no protection like he did in his box.

There were a few contests between lions and Bulldogs, but I guess lions were pretty scarce so there weren't many fights. In this case the Bulldog usually suffered the loss. Generally three or four dogs were run at the lion at one time. The lion usually killed them or their owners pulled them off when they found them losing: but they died game. The Pit Bulls didn't always lose though. James the First once selected one of his fiercest lions in the tower and turned him loose on a couple of Bulldogs. To everyone's astonishment, the dogs overcame the lion and threw him on his back. It was said by some that it took four Bulldogs to lick a lion and three to take a bear. How true all this is we can't say. It does seem obvious that these dogs did impress and even astonish people in Old England.

Monkeys were popular between 1799 and 1822 and provided some exciting fights with Bulldogs. The most famous one occurred about 1822 between a famous "Bull and Terrier" bitch named Puss owned by Tom Cribb (the champion boxer) and a famous monkey named Jacko Maccacco, who bad killed fifteen dogs in previous contests. Jacko was an inbred monkey from another famous fighting monkey (more poof of the potential of selective inbreeding from a century past!) The wager was ten pounds to one that Puss, at twenty pounds, would stay with Jacko for five minutes or kill him. This was longer than any dog had ever stayed with the monkey. After several minutes, the contestants were bathed in a ring of blood and the crowd demanded the contest be called a draw, which it was.

In 1835 under Queen Victoria, bull-baiting was officially banned in England, but it did continue on a very small scale until the end of the century. Now for the great debate. At some point in the early 1800's the "bull" dog seems to have been crossbred with some terriers. There is considerable disagreement, however, as to what kind of terrier, when the crossbreeding took place, and even whether they crossbred. I mention this now because one opinion is that when bullbaiting was banned, dog fighting became popular, and Bulldogs were crossed with terriers to make them more agile and courageous for fighting other dogs. There are several problems with this theory, however. For one, dog fighting had become very popular long before the ban. We have several pictures and sample posters showing pit dogs fighting in the 1700's and earlier. In addition, as far as the theory of crossing the Bulldogs with the terriers is concerned, the Bulldogs must have had to be agile and courageous to fight bulls and bears to begin with. The terriers may have been spunky, but I don't see how they proved any deep gameness killing rats. (Another popular sport of the time was to put terriers - later small Bull Terriers - one at a time - in a pit with a number of rats and see who could kill the most rats in a given amount of time.) For this reason, and the fact that the modern-day American Pit Bull Terrier looks just like the 18th and 19th century drawings and paintings of "Bulldogs," Richard Stratton (one of the foremost authorities on Pit Bulls and author of *This Is the American Pit Bull Terrier* and *The Book of the American Pit Bull Terrier*) contends, "there was no reason to outcross and lose the gameness and ability that many centuries of selective breeding had achieved. I would agree with him, except that in those days (1800's) the dogs were called "Bull and Terriers" and did tend to be smaller than the older breed of Bulldog. The name had to come from somewhere.

In reading an account of an 1821 pit contest in England (Westminster Pit), I noted the contenders to be a Staffordshire pit dog and a Black and Tan. A Black and Tan Terrier (came to be known as a Manchester Terrier) was supposed to be a fairly game dog in those days. The fact that it had engaged in pit contests suggests that it must have had some gameness. Some modern Pit Bulls are black and tan and at least one well-known breeder prefers them. Other terriers that some historians (and I use that term "historian" rather loosely) claim were crossbred with Bulldogs were the old English White Terrier and the Fox Terrier. After considering all the arguments, my feeling is this and that's all it is (my opinion) - no one really knows. I think that in some cases these pit dogs were highly linebred back in those days, just as they are today. When a fellow had a good thing going he tried to keep it, but on the other hand, many of the people back then did not know as much about breeding as they do today.

If they got a good, mean fighting dog. they would breed him regardless of whether he was a Bulldog or not. So, a proven terrier might easily have been bred to a good fighting Bulldog. And here's another point; in those days a pit dog was considered by many to be a street or gutter dog, he was just not in the class of aristocracies fine English show dogs.

Many a "swell" (young rich gentleman) owned one and pitted him, but still the dog was considered a low-class type dog. What I'm trying to say is that the Bulldogs were not purposefully crossed with the terriers, but that they just got bred a few times because they were both "low-class" type dogs and both good fighters. I would suggest that their blood "nicked" and the result was a dog that retained the Bulldogs deep gameness and tended to be smaller. The smaller dogs were not only as game, they tended to be gamer. They were more convenient in that you could carry them around easier and bring them into taverns to show off. They were a lot cheaper to feed (Most were owned by the poverty-stricken lower class) and were easier and hide under a man's coat when the sport became illegal. I think the thing that really made them most popular was being cheaper to feed. I bet those big Mastiff-type Bulldogs could really eat!

Hammonds' Queenie - If you could see her color, you'd agree she's a true black and tan.

Early Fighting Dog - circa 1820

Another point - even today the experienced dog men prefer smaller dogs. You ask them why and they'll tell you that they are easier to handle and, most importantly, they tend to be gamer. These dogs are fought by weight and that weight makes a big difference. Just one pound difference gives a most significant advantage to the heavier dog. So the big dog will (usually) beat the small dog: but the fights with the smaller dogs can be longer and they will tend to show more gameness and put on a better show. Another point - some of these dogs come out more "Bulldoggish," that is heavier set, shorter legs, heavier boned, etc. Others are more rangy, longer legged, smaller head, etc. Others are in between. I have seen some Pit Bulls with excellent (full blooded) pedigrees, and they look like a small terrier - just like the old English Terriers. Others can be very "Bulldoggish."

One last point: the eyes of some Pit Bulls are round and hazel or brown like the old Bulldogs, while some are squinty and coal black (like the Bull Terrier or old English Terrier). Larger Pit Bulls have a deep-throated bark and smaller ones have the higher pitched yap of a terrier. Some, like mine, vary their bark from deep-throated to a higher pitched yap, depending on the situation and reason for their barking.

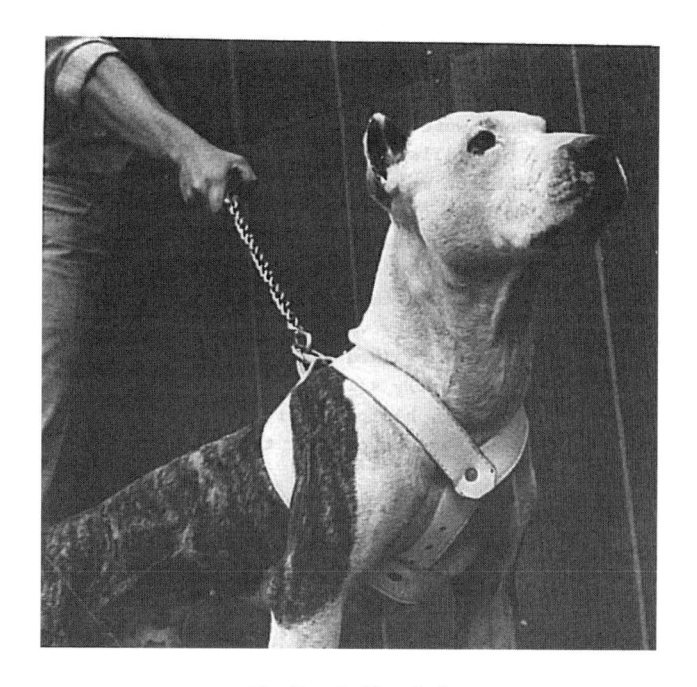

Needham's Hannibal

Another dog which is believed to be part of the Pit Bull's heritage is a now extinct dog called the Blue Paul. This dog was used exclusively for fighting in the mid 1800's in Scotland. He was a bigger dog than the Bull and Terrier, weighing around 60 pounds in hard condition and measuring 20 inches at the shoulder. He was a bluish or blue/brindle colored dog with hazel eyes. Legend has it that the dog was imported to Scotland by the pirate Paul Jones, hence the name Blue Paul. Another story has it that the Blue Paul was of the old Bulldog stock in a mining area in England and that one of the fighting Bulldogs was a bitch whose name was "Poll," a very popular name in those days. Soon, a number of people began calling their dogs Poll. (This sounds reasonable - even today in America, many of the names of pit dogs have become popular because of old pit champions - such as Spike, Mike, Jeff, Bull, etc.) The name Poll came to be called Paul. A number of those dogs are said to have been brought to Scotland where they became popular and that later they were fought against and became instrumental in the breeding of the Staffordshire Terriers (to be mentioned shortly). Some of the Scottish fighting dogs were red or red/brindle and these dogs were called Red Smuts in England. Some say the Red dogs tended to be smaller than the Blue ones.

In any event, pit fighting maintained its popularity in England, Whales, Scotland, and Ireland. It was in England, however, in the Black Country area near Birmingham that pit fighting was really big at the turn of the 18th century. These people pitted their dogs against the best in the world. This was coal mining and iron workers' country and the people were rough and they valued courage. They bred the best fighting dogs and gameness was valued above any other trait. If a dog quit in a fight, he was instantly killed. If he fought to the death after an extremely long fight, his pups were bred again. The dogs in the Staffordshire district were so popular that they became known as Staffordshire Terriers. In any event, at this point in time, the best fighting dogs were the Bull and Terriers in England. Shortly before the Civil War, sailors, merchants, and English and Irish immigrants brought the fighting dogs to America. Some writers say that a type of Bulldog or Bull and Terrier existed in America prior to the middle 1800's, possibly Spanish Bulldogs brought over by conquistadors, and that they were crossbred with the English imports. This may be true: I don't know. The pit fighting dogs in early American days did tend to be on the small side, the average male weighing around 38 pounds in hard condition. These dogs actually have not changed much at all, however, and there was a wide variety of sizes in the early 1900's just as there is today. In the western states a larger breed of Pit Bull developed. They were used as cattle dogs or "catch dogs." These dogs tended to be larger because they had to handle larger animals (bulls and hogs).

Many of these dogs were all around cattle dogs, that is they would round up, herd, and, if ordered, would "catch" a bull. All the owner needed to do was point to a bull and order the Pit Bull to get him and he would catch him by jumping up and latching onto his jowls. He would hang there and shake himself until the bull turned his head. Finally the Pit Bull would throw the bull on the ground by vigorous shaking. (He doesn't loosen his grip and his jaws are very powerful.) Once on the ground the Pit Bull would maintain his grip (or he might let go and take hold of the bull's throat) until his master ordered him off. He would hold and control the bull without killing him if properly trained. Some catch dogs are used to weed out wild boars when they become too plentiful and become a problem. These dogs run down the boar and kill them. In the early 1900's there were not very many Pit Bulls out west (or anywhere in America for that matter), but as farm owners learned of the breed, they became more and more popular. Today they are still used as cattle dogs and catch dogs. (see "The Catch Dog" chapter.)

It has been claimed that the pit dogs of the early 1900's were much gamer and fought longer than pit dogs of today, or of the middle 1900's for that matter; but this is really not true. Ask some of the old timers who saw the dogs fight in past eras. Most will tell you that the dogs of the past wouldn't hold a candle to the dogs of today. Maurice Carver has said it's true. I'll tell you why I think this is the case. For one thing, every additional generation of selective breeding has got to eventually produce a better animal (in the area for which it is bred). Today's thoroughbred race horses, for example, are faster than they were ten or twenty years ago. Secondly, the new breed of Pit Bulldog fanciers breed for ability as well as gameness. It has been found that the Pit Bull who can dominate a fight will tend to keep his gameness and he'll beat the dead game dog that lacks ability. I think many of today's Bulldogs have the gameness of the Pit Bulls of the past but also have more ability.

Probably the reason that some people feel that the Pit Bulls of past generations were better is because there were a lot fewer pit dogs around and of course we hear only about the good ones. We don't hear about the curs; they get forgotten. Read Armitage's book. He mentions some real good dogs, but he also tells about the many cur dogs he met.

In early American times some people thought (just like they did in England) that you could increase the gameness of a breed by crossbreeding a pit with another breed that proved game. People just like to experiment. We are always searching for something better. Some of the early American Pit Bulldogs were crossbred with Bull Terriers, English Bulldogs, etc. As an example, Armitage mentions in his book, that the very first fight he attended was between a Pit Bull from J.P. Colby's yard and a cross between a Pit Bull and a large Boston Terrier named Deafy, who was deaf. Deafy won in 36 minutes and Armitage's brother bred him. This type of breeding does not, however, produce game fighting dogs. A crossbred dog (Pit Bull to another breed) may, in rare instances, prove to be game and have ability, but there are too many non-fighting genes in the dog's blood for consistent success. Even if the crossbred dog is bred to a pure Pit Bull, the litter will tend to be curs. Pit Bull fanciers call any dog that is not a Pit Bulldog a "cur." This sounds sort of deprecating, but it is a traditional word stemming from the origin of its usage. A dog that quits in battle (including a Pit Bulldog) is called a cur, or said to have curred out. All breeds outside the Pit Bull breed will quit fighting when subjected to a Pit Bull's punishment. Some crossbreeding has involved an attempt to increase size while keeping the gameness, by breeding to large related breeds like Boxers, Mastiffs, etc. This hasn't worked either. The tiny Pit Bull will tear the larger crossbred dog to pieces.

These are generalities of course, and there are exceptions to every rule. Not all Pit Bulls are game just as not all hound dogs can Hunt, but most hound dogs just naturally hunt and most Pit Bulls just naturally fight.

A friend of mine brought his experienced Pit Bull (around 40 pounds conditioned) to meet a man who owned an Akita which is a large Mastiff-type dog that has been used as a fighting dog in Japan. This Akita was supposed to have killed several dogs (not Pit Bulls). My friend and the owner of the Akita wanted to see what would happen if their two dogs got together. My friend said that his dog was feeling sick that day and he wouldn't have fought him for money. For the first ten minutes of fighting, the little Pit Bull suffered extreme punishment from the huge Akita. Soon, however, the Pit Bull seemed to get warmed up and learned the big dog's fighting style - then he poured it on. Well, you know there's just something terribly disheartening about an opponent that you hit with everything you've got for an extended period of time and the dude comes back at you stronger than ever. That'll tend to make you want to give up. So it was with that big old Akita. Soon the little pit Bull had him in his terrible punishing jaws, shaking the life out of him and the owners had to break him off. Then my friend put his Pit Bull on his leash and said, "Now let me show you something." He let go of the Pit Bull and he lunged out to the end of his leash toward the Akita. The big Akita put his tail between his legs and cringed. The Pit Bull would have killed him if allowed to. This incident was observed by several people.

Another story. Friend of mine put a young, inexperienced Pit Bull against a huge German Shepherd. The Shepherd was literally more than twice the Pit Bull's weight and size. Early in the fight the Shepherd got the little Pit Bull's head in his jaws. The Pit Bull (named Snapper) was a little black dog, with white chest. My friend said that Pit Bull actually turned white allover. Said he'd never seen that happen before and he thought he'd lost his dog. But as it happened, the Pit Bull shook out of the hold and proceeded to tear that German Shepherd to pieces. They had to break him loose.

In any event, the point is, that to obtain gameness, you must breed pure Pit Bull, which is the result of centuries of breeding exclusively for gameness.

In any event, the American Pit Bull Terrier originated primarily from the Irish and English imported dogs. Of course we don't know much about many of the original dogs; however, just as almost all of the modern thoroughbred racehorses, most poodles, prize bulls, and any other animal that are bred for a special purpose, originated from a few "super animals" (which were linebred), there are a few dogs that formed the foundation of the better strains of American Pit Bulls. The modern strains of Dibo, Lightner, Colby, and other successful strains trace their ancestry to a number of imported dogs, which were high-quality bred dogs, the result of many generations of fighting dogs in England and Ireland. Not too much is known about the Irish dogs. They were primarily from Cork, Kerry, Waterford, Kilkinney, and Galt, and were called Old Family. Most of the dogs were exported to Boston, which was where most of the Irish immigrants lived. The Irish dogs resembled the "Bull and Terriers" from England so either they went through the same historical process as England (Their "bulldogs" mated their "terriers") or they originally got their fighting dogs from England - I don't know. In America many of these "Old Family" dogs were crossed with Pit Bulls from England, but they called them "Old Family" because of the reputation Old Family dogs had. Most of the Old Family Irish dogs were brindle or buckskin. As was mentioned earlier, most of the professional dog men did not write down pedigrees, but kept them in their heads because they wanted the breeding to be secret. They put their earnings (usually hard earned in those days) down on these dogs and some earned their living with pit dogs. Most of them inbred their strains, breeding best to best. Because pedigrees were not kept, it is extremely difficult to trace our dog's ancestry. There were, however, some very famous dogs who were also very prepotent. They were quite popular of course and you can't keep the big money fights secret and people bred to these dogs. James Boutelle of Boston kept a stud book that helps us today. Some of the early Old Family branches were Gas House and McGough's Bob, better known as Bob the Fool, who was descended from a very game producer called the Bob Tail Bitch. Bob the Fool was a foundation dog for many of the good Old Family dogs in the U.S. He was a foundation for the Gas House Line, which produced some of the gamest dogs in the country in the 1870's, the most famous being McDonald's Grip, called the Gas House Pup. He was considered by many to be the best in the world at that time. He once fought a three-hour match that ended in a draw. They were called Gas House dogs because their owner. Johnnie McDonald of the Boston Gas Light Company kept his dogs in Boston Gas Light Company's stables. Out of this line came Galvin's Pup, said to be one of the best ever. He won ten matches and in his first nine killed his opponent, and there wasn't a single turn in any of the matches.

 Con Feeley of Chicago, mentioned earlier, based his strain on these imported Old Family dogs, as did Jim Cocoran. The most famous one Cocoran had was called Waterford Jack. These dogs were also the foundation of the William Shipley line to follow.

Of equal importance is the influence of a few key dogs from England (primarily Staffordshire's). These dogs came from London and the Midlands primarily around Birmingham and the Black Country. These dogs were famous all over the world for their gameness and fighting ability. Probably the most influential have been the ones imported by Cockney Charles Lloyd in the middle 1800's, whose dogs seem to be the most well-known; Lloyd's Paddy and Lloyd's Pilot, especially Pilot. He is considered to be another foundation of our modern strains and is most famous for the very popular match between him and Harry Krieger's Crib, another dog imported from England. They were small dogs (28 pounds). It was a big money match (for these days) and attended by most of the known fanciers at the time. The match had been highly advertised in the *Police Gazette*, the magazine that was popular at the time. It was owned and published by Mr. Richard K. Fox. It had standard rules for pit contests and published records of fights, advertised dogs for sale, recognized winners, and was used to issue challenges. The *Gazette* also printed training and conditioning articles at times. In any event, it was a very fast paced fight. At one point it seemed as if Crib would win but Pilot came back strong and showed that he was a real finisher and won at one hour and twenty-five minutes, beating a dog with fantastic ability and of course becoming very popular in the process.

A key figure in the history of the American Pit Bull Terrier was an Irishman named John P. Colby from Newburyport, Massachusetts. He was one of the first to advertise and sell quality bred Pit Bulldogs beginning in the early 1900's. The professional dog men at the time didn't like it and he was at times referred to as a "peddler," which was very degrading in those days. His dogs were good, however, and many of our present day quality strains are Colby. In fact, many people outside the fancy are under the impression that the Pit Bull breed is a breed of "Colby" dogs. Actually I know a few old timers who have said they feel Colby and Lightner blood are the only pure strains. Colby's dogs were bred from Bob the Fool, Lloyd's Pilot. Rafferty (an imported dog), Rock, Rye (Old Family), the Gas House Pup, and Connors' Bismark, another famous dog. He sold, it is said, over 1,000 dogs. Naturally, he had his share of bad dogs, as you will find in any strain, and with as many as he sold, there were bound to be some bad ones. On the other hand, some of the best dogs in the world, right down to the present day, have developed from this strain. Although Mr. Colby sold his dogs to the public, he was very careful to keep his own strain, and he linebred his dogs and had only one outcross in the 30 odd years he bred dogs. We'll look at that outcross later. The pride he had in the quality of his dogs and the faith he had in his strain are responsible for many of the quality dogs we have today. As you will see in the chapter on breeding, it is this kind of selective linebreeding that maintains high quality characteristics.

Mr. William J. Lightner, mentioned above, is another gentleman who was very instrumental in the development of the Pit Bull breed. He came from a family of breeders. His father and his grandfather before him bred pits. It is said that they never sold a dog, though. By the early 1900's, Mr. Lightner had developed a very successful strain, many of them descended from Bob the Fool and the Gas House Pup. Many of the Lightner dogs were Colby and a significant number were Old Family red nose, a fighting train of Old Family dogs from around Cork, Ireland. They are unique in that they generally have a copper-colored nose, red lips and toenails, and amber eyes. They usually have a red or brown brindle coat. They have been intermingled with other Old Family and other strains in America, so that they seem to show up in some litters from time to time whether they are bred that way or not. Mr. Lightner had a considerable number of red nose dogs although he didn't breed for them and in fact didn't like them for a long time even though they were of high quality. I don't know why he was so much against red nose dogs because although they have their share of bad dogs like any strain, they also have some of the best, particularly the Lightner ones. I think the reason he didn't like them was because they tended to be larger and large dogs were not so popular in those days. It is sometimes difficult to match large dogs because they are in the minority. In any event, Mr. Lightner developed a new strain of smaller dogs with black noses and dark eyes. No one knows where they came from. Some say they were from the ones in his original strain which didn't have red nose characteristics. They were of at least equal quality.

Sometime around 1917-18, Mr. Lightner moved from Louisiana to Colorado and when he did, he let most all of his dogs go, especially the red nose ones. Joe Peace got some of the dogs Mr. Lightner left behind, bred them to some other Old Family dogs and started his own line. In the 1920's Bob Hemphill of south Carolina was extremely interested in those old red noses and went all over the countryside getting all the pure Lightner red nose dogs he could find and inbred them. Some excellent matings resulted, particularly Red Devil, Centipede, and Goldust. These dogs trace their lineage back to Bob the Fool and the Gas House line. Dan McCoy and Bob Wallace were also instrumental in the development of the red nose pit Bulls. There are no pure red nose strains to my knowledge, although some breed for them and some people get a preponderance of red nose dogs even though they don't breed exclusively for them.

To show the importance of bloodlines, let's look some more at the Colby strain. His line began with Teddy, a male belonging to Jack White from Salem, Massachusetts. Teddy, grandson of Lloyd's Pilot, won a 2-hour 15-minute match. He also won some other battles in the 1890's. I don't know how many in the Boston area. Colby's Pansy was a three-time winner. She was a vicious nose fighter and beat some of the best dogs of her time. She had tremendous punishing ability. From the breeding of these two, he got Colby's Pincher and Colby's Major, a good dog, but not nearly as famous as his brother. Pincher was a huge Pit Bull, whelped around 1910. He was around 76 pounds (I've seen it recorded as 72 and 75 also) (56 pounds pit weight). He was fought 40 times including rolls and is said to have stopped or killed 24 dogs. He was never defeated and he never met the dog who could stay with him more than 40 minutes. He is in the blood of many of the Colby dogs and therefore many of our dogs today. Pincher was a throat and chest fighter with an amazing ability to punish. He was the most famous fighting dog in the country at the time. In addition, and more importantly, he was a producer. His progeny have proven to be game, punishing dogs. One of his sons was a 44-pound dog named Colby's Bunch who was extremely powerful. His mother's grandfather was Galvin's Pup. Bunch, also, was a fantastic producer and sired many game dogs, like Jim Curry's Man-O-War who fought Armitage's Bob in a 3-hour 50-minute match in 1918. The fight, described in the Armitage book, is a picturesque event. Total money involved was around $14,000, a small fortune in those days. Of course, it was attended by most of the active dog men of the day. The fight took place one evening in December in Lexington, Kentucky in an open field with a bitter cold north wind blowing, and nothing but an old farmer's oil lantern for light. It was a fast, hard-fought fight for an hour and a half; a long time to fight with no scratches for either dog. There was a man attending the match that was convinced that Armitage's Bob would quit; so convinced that at the one-hour mark he began betting $100 that Bob would quit and he increased his bet each 30 minutes, $100 a throw. That's one heck of a lot of money (equivalent to about $800-$900 in the current money market). The fight went, as mentioned, for three hours and fifty minutes. Both dogs were so game they were still trying to fight each other when they were both so tired they could barely move. They were just lying on the ground in skin holds (A skin hold refers to ineffective-with-Pit-Bulls holds where the dog has clamped down on his opponent, but he's just biting loose skin), so they decided to call it a draw. Armitage scratched his dog to see if he would go and he did. Armitage's dog had an interesting history, by the way. His pedigree was questionable. Harry Clark thought he came from his yard but wasn't sure. Bob was just a street dog running in the streets of Cincinnati and was never aggressive with other dogs in the city and usually merely passed them by in his travels, ignoring them. If they tried to pick on him, though, he'd kill them. Armitage eventually bought him for $15 and fought him in a battle that would determine which side collected $14,000. Same thing happens today. To get consistently good dogs you need to inbreed and linebreed selectively; best to best. But every now and then a scatter bred or questionably bred dog shows up who is a real beauty.

Another dog sired by Colby's Bunch was also owned by Jim Curry, a dog named King, who fought to win for four hours and twelve minutes against a Redicon dog named Captain. It was a long fight, but after the one-hour mark, the Redicon dog was so badly whipped the fight consisted of King standing over a submissive dog and biting or dragging him around the pit until he tired. The match should have been conceded long before it was.

The most famous of Bunch's progeny, however, was Armitage's Kager, often shown in pedigrees as Clarke's Tramp, whelped in 1914. His mother was Colby's Goldy who traces her blood back to Galvin's Pup twice. So Galvin's pup is in both his father's and his mother's blood. Kager was at one time a whiskey and beer wagon driver's pet and rode on the wagon with his master all day long while deliveries were made. In any event, Kager's story is a very interesting one. In Colby's yard Whiskey was a very docile dog and seemed afraid of his own shadow. He refused to fight or even take a hold. In those days, Boston was in its heyday for pit dog men, and whenever a man had a bulldog he wanted to school or tryout, Colby's was one place they went because he had such a large yard of good dogs. Well, one day this guy who was a well-known gambler and also a dog man dropped in with a big catch-weight dog. Whiskey, who was three years old at the time, was the biggest dog in the lot, but Mr. Colby informed the man that Whiskey was just a pet, and no good as a pit dog, that he wouldn't take a hold. The man persisted in his requests to roll his dog with Whiskey, so Mr. Colby set Whiskey in the pit with the man's dog. As Colby predicted, Whiskey wanted no part of the battle and just tried to get away: and he would have, except the other dog grabbed his hind leg before he could escape and pulled him back into the pit. Well, that hurt Whiskey and it made him mad, and that, my friends, was the beginning of the end. Whiskey poured it on and in ten minutes he stopped the dog cold. And so began the illustrious career of one of the best pit dogs in history. He won four contract fights at 47-58 pounds and did most of his fighting with George Armitage who got him from John Colby and changed his name to Kager. Harry Clark was the referee with Kager's last battle for

Armitage and later purchased him. When he was seven years old, he won a match for Harry Clark, who changed the dog's name to Tramp. Tramp died when he was eight years old in an unfortunate kennel fight. He got loose in the yard and ran over to one of Clark's promising young dogs named Mustard. They fought for more than two hours before some neighbors separated them by turning the hose on them. Mustard died that night. He had been cut to ribbons, and Tramp died four days later. He had only one tusk at the time. Both Armitage and Clark said he was the best dog they'd ever seen, and many said he was the greatest pit dog that ever lived. He was a real finisher. He seemed to get stronger and stronger as he fought and as soon as his opponent let up, he would pour it on. It is my personal opinion that a pit dog with this instinct, providing he has the basic qualities of gameness, bite, etc. is the best. In other words, in watching a young dog being schooled or tried out, I would look for the dog's instinctive reaction to turn on when his opponent slacks up a bit, rather than just retain a hold.

This story should be particularly interesting because of one important point. Kager could easily have been ruined if he had been pushed too early, and we never would have heard of him. Even worse, he wouldn't have been bred, and we'd not have had a slew of good dogs that followed. Kager is by no means the only example of a Pit Bull that was not ready to fight until he was three years old. I believe that the most important virtue needed by a dog man is patience.

This is just one line of the Colby dogs. You can see that Kager, although he didn't seem to be much of a pit fighter at first, traces his blood, through many fantastic pit dogs, right back to that of Lloyd's Pilot and Galvin's pup. It's all in the blood, my friends. Kager appears in Dibo's pedigree eleven times, although he's fairly well back in the pedigree. Some of his sons that are in Dibo's
pedigree include Tramp's Boy, Clark's Sport, and Clark's Spider, all good dogs.

It was mentioned earlier that in 30 years of breeding, John Colby made only one outcross. This outcross was a dog named Galtie (named after the place in Ireland where his father came from). Galtie was a very game dog with deep bite. He was severely tested against three dogs consecutively (a very severe test of gameness - how would you like to fight someone for five or ten minutes, then fight a stranger who was fresh, and then another? If you've ever boxed in a ring, you know what I mean.) John Colby said he was the best he'd ever seen. He must have been very impressed because, as mentioned, he was so confident of his strain that Galtie was his only outcross.

Today, probably the best producing Colby blood is Colby Dime and Colby Rifle, Dime's grandfather. Both dogs are linebred from Galtie and have Colby's Tiger several times in their pedigrees. Colby's Tiger was Galvin's Pup's grandson and was the best 35-pound dog of his day. He fought one battle for three hours and twenty- seven minutes.

Howard Heinzl, who most people would agree is one of the most knowledgeable Pit Bull men today and one of the best breeders, told *Pit Bull Sheet* that Colby Dime was the best producing dog he had ever owned - said his father, Tweedy, was a red and white dog that reminded him of pictures of Galtie. All that pleased me greatly because my dog, Morochito, is pretty much linebred (about 3/4 Colby Dime on his mother's side).

This book is not an historical one, and it is far beyond its realm to discuss every dog and every strain of Pit Bull dog. The Colby strain is one of the biggest, however, and I tried to pick the ones that were most influential in the Colby strain. I think it is interesting to note that the great ones had great blood in them.

Let's examine how blood lines work by looking at the pedigree of probably the most well-known producing Pit Bull in America today Dibo. Colby plays an important part so it should be interesting. As was mentioned earlier, Dibo was one of those lucky accidents. He was a devoted pacifist until Howard Heinzl gave him to Earl Tudor. While Mr. Heinzl has been one of the best breeders in modern Pit Bull history. Earl Tudor has been one of the most influential in the development of the breed. It has been said that Earl Tudor has fought more dogs in one season than George Armitage did in his entire life time. If Howard hadn't given Dibo to Earl Tudor, he'd have never been a famous dog. Tudor was not a breeder, he was a performer. I've been told that he generally randomly bred his dogs (Of course, they all had good blood). Such a breeding was Dibo bred to Gordon's Red Lady. She was not really as well-bred as Dibo. Out of that breeding came three famous dogs – Crenshaw's Buck, Tudor's Spike, and Tudor's Jeff.

Spike was the most famous fighting dog. He was also a prepotent producer, as was Jeff. Jeff didn't have Spike's pit record but was every bit as prepotent. One time Jeff was rolled with Spike because there was always a controversy over which was the better dog. Jeff was much bigger and so he got the better of Spike, but Spike didn't show any signs of quitting. In any event. Dibo and other Tudor blood appears in the pedigree of a significant number of today's pedigrees. Dibo being considered some of the best. Dibo's blood is formed by Corvino, Feeley, Shipley, and a dog named Black Jack. Dibo was a Colby cross. A great deal of the Colby blood was from Kager as mentioned, and came from Joe Corvino, who was a blacksmith in Chicago in the early 1900's. Old Corvino blood is considered the best by many of the experienced dog men today. He was very instrumental not only in dogs in Dibo's pedigree, but in the development of the Dibo strain. Corvino's early dogs were of Feeley and Colby origin. As mentioned, Kager played a big role. Con Feeley has already been mentioned. His dogs originated from that same Lloyd's Pilot we talked about earlier. So you can see the influence that little dog had on the American Pit Bull Terrier. Feeley, also, resided in Chicago and some other Chicago top dog men bred to his dogs, two of which were W. T. Delihant and E. E. Swineford. Feeley, Delihant, and Swineford often owned the same dogs at one time or another. Feeley had a dog, Jim, who was a son of Lloyd's Pilot. This is the dog that fought a controversial fight, described in Armitage's book, against Farmer's (Galvin's) Turk who was a son of Galvin's pup's brother. This was the fight that went for 4 hours and 58 minutes. Who's to say both dogs were not fantastic? In any event, Jim was a key dog in the Feeley strain.

You study a dog's pedigree from right to left - that is, from the earliest ancestor to the grandparents. Many beginners start studying a pedigree with grandparents, but you must remember that old adage about a house being only as good as its foundation. Looking at the top side of Dibo (his father's line), we begin with Lloyd's Pilot - who else? His son was Feeley's Jim that we talked about, the foundation dog for the Feeley line and great grandfather (through selective inbreeding, all Feeley) of Bruce's Turk, who was owned by Earl Tudor. Turk was bred by Jack Williams of Colorado who was an old friend of Con Feeley and ended up with Feeley's dogs. Williams developed one of the better strains in the country, keeping his strain pretty pure. He has had his share of bad dogs like anyone else, but he had faith and patience in his strain, so he also bred some aces. His son, Jim carried on the strain, by the way. Jim William's son-in-law, Darwin D. Weidenmaier, who lives in Norman, Oklahoma, has them at the time of this writing.

In any event, a man named Bruce, also a friend of Feeley, had Turk, and Earl Tudor ended up with him. Turk was a champion and he won a fight when he was seven years old. All the male dogs from Turk down to Dibo and Dibo's sons were prepotent, even when outcrossed to another line. I suspect Earl Tudor knew that: I don't know. In any event, Dibo probably got his ability to produce top quality Pit Bulls from Turk. Joe Corvino, as we said, was responsible for our best strains. His dogs were linebred off Turk and other Feeley dogs and Williams and Kager. He had a dog named Bounce who was Dibo's father. Bounce's father was Hubbard's Gimp, son of Corvino's Gimp. Corvino's Gimp was a grandson of Bruce's Turk and another Feeley dog. His mother, Fly of Panama, was linebred Kager. Hubbard's Gimps mother was Corvino's (and also Tudor's) Goldie. Goldie was one of Tudor's favorites. Her breeding was Shipley (which is really the same as Feeley) and Turk and Black Jack, Jr., whom we will look at later. Goldie died dead game in the hands of Joe Corvino. He linebred off her and produced some beauties. Twenty-five years later he got another bitch that looked just like her and named her Corvino's Goldie. This Goldie died dead game in the hands of Indian Sonny.

Corvino's Bounce was also the father of a dog named Rascal (Trahan's Rascal). Rascal was Dibo's half-brother. Rascal was a fantastic producer. One of his very famous sons was a dog named Country Boy, who lost his first fight, by the way, which shows that patience and proper training, conditioning, etc. has a lot to do with a pit dog's career. It also shows that blood, not a dog's initial performance, is the most important factor. In other words, in the long run bloodlines account for success. Rascal's mother was Corvino's Make-up and her bloodlines also trace back to Turk, the inbred Kager bitch, Fly of Panama, some Williams' dogs, and to Goldie. Bounce's mother was Hubbard's Lena, and guess what? Lena's father was Corvino's Gimp's brother (which is Bruce's Turk on his top side and inbred Kager on his bottom side). Lena's mother had two important dogs in her blood – Tudor's Black Jack, II (We'll look at this dog in a little bit) and Fighting Peter, who was a brindle red nose. He was a champion and fought for Earl Tudor. His father was Colby's Galtie, the Irish dog that was Colby's only outcross. I don't know if Peter was a red nose from Galtie or from his mother. Peter was influential in the Lightner blood.

Dibo's mother, Heinzl's Bambi, was no fighter. She was a mouse, but what a producer! Bambi was very linebred from the Turk dog, and Hubbard's Gimp is her great grandfather twice (so then Goldie, being Gimp's mother, appears twice also). Bambi's grandmother was Bounce's litter sister. Naturally Bambi's blood would nick with Bounce.

Another dog that was very influential in Dibo's blood was Black Jack. If you remember, we mentioned the bitch Lena who was Bounce's mother. Since Bambi's grandmother was Bounce's litter sister, Lena is in Bambi's blood, too. Lena was fairly linebred Black Jack. Earl Tudor felt that Black Jack was the best dog he ever saw. In order to study Black Jack blood, we go back again to Con Feeley blood. Feeley also had another dog from Lloyd's Pilot whose name was Jesse. The mother was a bitch named Peggy (also out of Pilot) who was also the mother of Colby's Thistle by a son of Galvin's Turk. Thistle played a part in Colby's Dime's breeding.

Thistle was a nine time winner. Some say he was undershot: some say he wasn't. Delihant had a bitch that was inbred Lloyd's Pilot (a bitch bred to Pilot to produce a bitch which was bred to another son of Lloyd's Pilot, called the pig to produce a bitch that was bred to her brother to produce a bitch who was bred to another dog who was son of Pilot). This bitch was called Delihant's Crazy Kate. She was the foundation of Swineherd's famous strain of fighting dogs. Kate was bred back to Jesse in 1900 to get Delihant's Paddy, who is the great grandfather of Tudor's Black Jack. A gambler named Henry had some Delihant dogs and an imported English dog named Richmond who was supposed to be a great dog. Henry also had the Colby bitch called Thistle mentioned before, who was out of Peggy who was from Lloyd's Pilot. Henry's dogs were also in Black Jack's blood. Black Jack was a fantastic dog and he began a famous strain of dogs through his even more famous son, Black Jack, Jr. The Black Jack line bred by Al Brown was famous for its potency. It produced game dogs of fair size (50 to 52 pounds), that were very hard biters. The Black Jack dogs were also noted for their lack of psychological problems, no sullen dispositions, people biters, or other neurotic problems that can sometimes appear with linebreeding. Al Brown kept most of his dogs to himself and didn't use them much for stud. Brown grew up in Texas and eventually settled in Arizona where he still lives today at the age of almost 90. In addition to the Black Jack dogs, he had Dibo's brother Arizona Pete and other Feeley dogs. Black Jack was originally owned by Earl Tudor and fought at 56 pounds. He was said to have won 16 pit fights, which is an incredible record. Black Jack's blood was Delihant and Swineford, as mentioned, which was inbred Lloyd's Pilot, and Colby Pincher, whom we've talked about.[12] Black Jack, Jr., known as Peterson's Black Jack Jr., or as Tudor's Black Jack, Jr., was original owned by a man named George Peterson. He was a seven time winner, not as many wins as his father. One reason he didn't have as many fights, however, was that he was so game and such a terrible punisher that it was hard to get him matched. He fought at a pit weight of between 48 and 51 pounds, which is quite a range, and was often matched with dogs that dramatically outweighed him. He even won one contract match in which his opponent was ten pounds heavier than he was. This is really incredible because a few pounds are very significant if the dog weighs only 40 or 50 pounds. In most pit contests, if the dog is over the pit weight as much as even half a pound, the opponent wins by forfeit. Seven wins is a formidable record for any dog and there are very few dogs that have ever really won that many (although you do see quite a few claims to it). A pit fight takes a lot out of most of the dogs and they are generally matched in a contract fight only one or two times. A champion must win three consecutive matches and there are not many champions. Al Brown ended up with Black Jack, Jr. and the dog lived a long life on his lot.

Al Brown also had two dogs named Tacoma Jack and Jack Dempsey. Jack Dempsey, a son of the original Black Jack out of a bitch that was half imported Irish (from an Irish dog named Jack), was Al Brown's favorite, claiming him to be the best dog he had ever owned. Tacoma Jack had a bigger reputation, but in those days there was a big controversy over which was the better dog. They were both the same weight and awful punishers. Tacoma Jack won nine pit fights and was so terrible a punisher and destroyed his opponents in such short order that many people said he was not game. This is often the case. It is rare that you have a real hard biting dog with wrestling ability that is also dead game. When you do, you have an ace (winner of five consecutive fights - a rare thing). Tacoma Jack had gone well over that, but no one saw him prove his gameness because no dog ever stayed with him 30 minutes and lived. Al Brown knew he was dead game though. There are two ways to determine if a dog is dead game. One is to let him fight a dog that's bigger than him until he's dead. That, of course, is undesirable. The other way gives you just about the same assurance - that is to have the dog fight for an hour against three dogs. He must fight twenty minutes with one dog, then twenty minutes with a new, fresh dog, and then compete against a third, fresh dog. Changing opponents is extremely demoralizing to a Pit Bull and tends to challenge his gameness. A Pit Bull may fight to the hour mark against another Pit Bull that's beating him, but change dogs on him after fifteen or twenty minutes and he might quit. If you pit him against a new dog, he might quit even if he's winning. This is a method pit fighters often use for purchasing a pit dog when they want to test gameness without having the dog hurt too much or depleting his inner energy. Al brown sent Tacoma Jack over an hour against three dogs and Jack was still ready for more. Black Jack, Jr. and Tacoma Jack never met. It would have been one heck of a fight. These two dogs had very similar breeding and even looked a lot alike. Tacoma Jack was so aggressive that it was practically impossible to breed him.

Mr. Brown did breed a dog named Tacoma Jacks Replica who was son of Tacoma Jack and a bitch who was a daughter of Jack Dempsey, son of Tudor's Black Jack. Replica was never the dog Jack was, though. It is rare that a superlative dog will produce an equally good dog in one generation. I think you've got to be patient and keep selectively breeding and you'll end up with an even better dog, if you're lucky. Notice I injected the luck part. I'm sorry, but I've come to the conclusion that there are no guarantees, and Old Lady Luck plays a big part. I say help her out as much as you can, though, with selective breeding.

Another dog Al Brown had was Tudor's Black Jack II. He was a big dog who became a champion. He also had a hard time getting matches. That Al Brown sure had some good dogs. I mentioned that he didn't let many of them go. He finally retired from the game because of his health (Although he has a few dogs now, he is not active and doesn't sell to the public). You might, understandably, wonder what ever happened to those awesome old Black Jack dogs. Well, a good part of Dibo is Black Jack, but the purest Black Jack breeding today is found in AKC show dogs. Pit Bulls registered with AKC are called Staffordshire Terriers. Many owners of Stafs do not like to have their dogs referred to as Pit Bulls and I don't mean to anger anyone. The Ruffian line of Stafs, considered to be among the best as I understand (I really don't know much about Stafs and the AKC shows), is primarily Black Jack breeding. Knight Crusader was the top winning Staf for a long time, I'm told. Well, he was Black Jack and Feeley breeding (including the Turk dog we'll take a look at in a minute). In a way you might say his breeding was similar to Dibo. Seems a good Pit Bull is a good Pit Bull no matter how he competes! I saw a picture of Crusader and he looked awfully fat to me, but no doubt about it, he's a pretty dog.

Hammonds' Happy - inbred Bruno-Heinzl

Well, this is the history of the pedigree behind the great Dibo. As you can see, he was linebred off great dogs that were proven producers. Like the Colby dogs (actually he was part Colby himself), traced his lineage back to that good old imported Pit Bull, Lloyd's Pilot. In the long run, good dogs beget good dogs. As mentioned, Dibo's main contribution was his ability to produce. He was bred to a bitch named Gordon's Red Lady and produced three dogs that became famous. One, Tudor's Jeff, was an excellent producer, also. He was the largest and looked more like his father except he was more reddish while Dibo was a buckskin. Pound for pound, Spike was supposed to be the best fighter. He was also a producer and fathered Miss Spike who is considered by many the best producing bitch of modern times, and several of the best dog men have based their strain on her. Buck was also a good dog, although I don't know much about him. All three dogs were champions. It is very, very rare to have three champions in a litter. It's hard enough to get three good dogs. Gordon's Red Lady was not really that well-bred I don't think. She had some good Old Family red nose on her bottom side (mother's), Ferguson's Centipede is there twice, and so is Corvino's Goldie. On her top side there is some Armitage and I think Billy Sunday is there but I don't see anything really exceptional. Dibo was also bred by Howard Heinzl and produced a dog named White Rock who was said to be the hardest biting dog ever. He became a champion in the hands of Earl Tudor in less than a year I'm told. He was such a hard biter, his matches were no contest.

Well, I tried to cover fairly briefly the development of our Pit Bull Terrier by looking at Colby and Dibo blood. There are so many strains I'd never be able to cover them all. Lightner blood is also excellent. (I've already discussed Lightner.) His dogs were really bred the same as Colby in the beginning, if you remember. Don Mayfield of Texas has carried on the Lightner strain as well as Dibo and has some excellent dogs. Buckshot Sorrells of Arizona has an excellent strain of selectively bred Pit Bulls. They are Lightner, Colby, and Dibo. One of his foundation bitches is Fitzwater's Goldie an exceptionally well bred Pit Bull whose blood nicks well with that of Dibo. Howard Heinzl is still breeding. Many feel that his are the best. His dogs are mostly Colby Dime, Dibo, and original Heinzl blood. He had the last living grandson of Dibo, a dog named Gringo, whose blood is very popular. Some of the tightest bred Dibo blood was the Boudreaux line. Boudreaux had Dibo bred dogs such as Blind Billy, Eli, Boze and others. Blind Billy was the foundation dog for the Boudreaux line. He was a son of Dibo and his mother was a daughter of Al Brown's Arizona Pete (Dibo's brother). Thus Billy was the most inbred Dibo dog we have had, as far as I know. Billy was known as Blind Billy because he lost a match one time when he scratched to the wrong corner. The pit rules state that the dog whose turn it is to scratch must cross the pit and mouth his opponent within a given amount of time. When Billy scratched to the wrong corner, he was counted out. (I don't agree at all with that rule.) Probably the most important Boudreaux dogs were brothers: Clayton's Eli, Jr. and Wallings' Bullyson. Bullyson was made famous in the hands of one of today's top dog men, Bobby Hall, of Texas , and his blood is very popular. These dogs were linebred Blind Billy (and therefore linebred Dibo). Their father was Boudreaux Boze, who was linebred Blind Billy and had the Rascal dog in his blood (Trahan's Rascal, Dibo's half-brother) and their mother, also was linebred Blind Billy. Both Eli, Jr. and Bullyson were terrible punishers. Bullyson lost one fight, to his son, Benny Bob. Bullyson also produced Midnight Cowboy who won three and best of show in all three (a champion). Eli, Jr. produced Stinson's Art (called Art the Dog with a Heart). Art was a terrible punisher, with fantastic ability and is considered by many to the best of all time. He became a seven-time time he was three years old. Art was stolen in 1977, I think.

Hammonds' Bull Dozer – three quarter Bruno dog that was one of the best 30-pounders ever.

Swinson's Boss - Sire, Hoods' Bart: Dam, Garrett's Judy. This dog is linebred Carver's Ironhead and looks very much like Ironhead.

Well, I can't cover all the Dibo strains in the county, but I have to mention one other popular strain, that of Maurice Carver of San Antonio, Texas. He has had a really large yard of dogs that were primarily Dibo bred. Mr. Carver passed away in October, 1979. To list all the champions that came from his yard would take up a whole page. In fact, if I listed the dog men who used Carver dogs extensively in their breeding, it would probably take nearly a whole page. Carver bred a bitch to Blind Billy and got Blondie, the father of Carver's Ironhead, one of the best producers of modern times. There is a memorial statue of Ironhead in Texas on Mr. Carver's land. Ironhead's mother was a daughter of Dibo and Carver's Black Widow, who was a daughter of Cannon's Black Shine (son of Dibo) and Hanson's Amber Girl (daughter of Williams' Sarge). All of those Pit Bulls are proven producers of some of the best and appear in many pedigrees. Williams' Sarge was owned by Jim Williams in the 1950's. He was pure Williams bred (Old Family red nose mentioned earlier). Carver's Black Widow, considered excellent breeding, was bred to Dibo: and a daughter of this litter. Carver's Black Girl is the mother of Ironhead mentioned above. Carver's Black Widow was mated to Tudor's Spike to get the mother of Mayfield's Nigger. Nigger was a champion and also considered good breeding. His father was Dibo's son, Jeff. The mating of Black Widow to Spike also produced Don Maloney's Toot. In the middle '60's Toot was considered one of the best ever by many. He was a 54-

pound Bulldog who, in his two contract matches, killed both of his opponents in less than 20 minutes. He never met the dog that could stand up to him. He is the foundation of Maloney's strain.

Hammonds' Dempsy - pure Heinzl

    Some people consider Carver's Pistol to be some of the best breeding. His mother is the daughter of Dibo and Black Widow. His father is Rascal and Boudreaux breeding. As mentioned previously, Miss Spike (daughter of Dibo's son Spike) is considered some of the best producing blood and is very popular. Her mother is Womack's Mert, who is the daughter of Fitzwater's Goldie, a beautiful producer and one of the foundation bitches for one of the top dog men in the country, Buckshot Sorrells. She is Heinzl and Colby bred. Mert's mother is a daughter of a Dibo and Black Widow mating. She also has Amber Girl (daughter of Williams' Sarge and Cannon's Black Shine) in her blood.
    Carver's Pistol and Miss Spike bred to each other produced Boomerang, who was a grand champion and won best of show at three of the matches. One heck of a dog. He just blew right through his opponents. Some say that Dibo's and Rascal's prepotency was passed down to him. He is the father of Miss Pool Hall Red, another grand champion and producer of game, hard-biting dogs. One guy said he saw a match between two of her sons and that they were both the hardest biting dogs he had ever seen in his ten years' affiliation with pit dogs. Miss Pool Hall Red's mother was a daughter of carver's Ironhead and Carver's Miss Spike. She

is, therefore, inbred Miss Spike. Boomerang also produced the Gator dog, who won his championship before he was two years old. Actually Gator is inbred Boomerang.

Ironhead mated to Miss Spike also produced the snake dog. He died game. Snake bred to Art's Missy (daughter of Carver's Pistol and Miss Spike and an excellent producer) resulted in the Snooty dog that was popular. He won two and lost one. (That loss was to Morochito's half-brother, Butch.) Snooty was a good pit dog, but an even better producer. He and Pool Hall Red blood is very popular these days. He (along with his pedigree) appears as the centerfold in Pit Bull Gazette, February, 1982.

A son of Black Widow and Dibo was mated to a daughter of Trahan's Rascal (Dibo's half-brother) and Black Widow to get Carver's Amber, who was mated by Maurice Carver to Bullyson (mentioned above) to get a bitch named Honey Bunch. A good dog man in Georgia, Irish Jerry, bought her and made her a champion. She was probably one of the best on the East Coast. James Crenshaw, also of Georgia, had her the last I knew. (Crenshaw, also, has excellent Pit Bulls.) Honey Bunch has produced a number of champions, one of the best of which is, in my opinion, her son, Garrett's Jeep. In my opinion this dog is the best Pit Bull of today. He is now retired to stud.

A very distinct example of Dibo breeding is found in Plumber's Champion Alligator, who was one of those few big dogs that was game. In his day (the late 60's I think), he was probably the best at his weight. Alligator is the father of Gary Hammonds' Rufus (pictured in "The Catch Dog" chapter). (You will find several articles by Mr. Hammonds in this book.) Rufus' pedigree illustrates a perfect example of planned breeding. Study it carefully and you'll see why the mother, Williams' Satin Lady should produce excellent pups from a mating with Alligator. The blood should nick because of the common high-caliber Pit Bulls in both pedigrees. I am not going to state that this is the best Pit Bull blood you can find. There is no such thing. It is a matter of personal preference. I use it because it is an example of excellent selective breeding by a known, reputable breeder who takes pride in his strain. These Pit Bulls are, of course, relatively expensive. I find that, as a breed, however, Pit Bulls are less expensive than more popular show breeds. You can buy some of the best bred Pit Bull puppies in the country for much less than a show bred pup. (An adult Pit Bull that's been proven is a different thing - they come pretty expensive.)

Plumber's Champion Alligator - one of the best big ones to ever wear a collar

```
                        Tudor's Dibo
          Tudor's Jeff
                        Gordon's Red Lady
     Mayfield's Nigger
                              Tudor's Dibo
                        Tudor's Spike
                              Gordon's Red Lady
          Tudor's Baby
                              Cannon's Black Shine
                        Carver's Black Widow
                              Hanson's Amber Girl
Plumber's Alligator
                              Boudreaux' Blind Billy
                        Carver's Blondie
                              Carver's Blondy
          Carver's Ironhead
                              Tudor's Dibo
                        Carver's Black Girl
                              Carver's Black Widow
     Wms.' Satin Lady
                              Crenshaw's Sad Sack
                        Crenshaw's Reno
                              Crenshaw's Polly
          Carver's Black Beautee
                              Tudor's Spike
                        Carver's Miss Spike
                              Womack's Mert
```

(Hammonds' Rufus' Pedigree)

```
                        Boudreaux' Blind Billy
          Carver's Blondie
                        Carver's Blondy
     Carver's Ironhead
                        Tudor's Dibo
                                              Tudor's Dibo
          Carver's Black Girl    Cannon's Black Shine
                                              Wms.' Shine
                        Carver's Black Widow
                                              Wms.' Sarge
                              Hanson's Amber Girl
     Williams' Satin Lady          Cotton's Bullet   Wms.' Bucky Mac
                        Crenshaw's Sad Sack
                              Spark's Haley's Comet
          Crenshaw's Reno
                        Crenshaw's Polly
     Carver's Black Beautee
                        Tudor's Spike
          Carver's Miss Spike
                        Womack's Mert
```

62   253

Hammonds' Kybo – pure Alligator and plenty big

You'll notice Cottons Bullet several times in Rufus' pedigree. Some say Bullet blood is the best in the East Coast. I don't agree, but it is good blood (Cottons Bullet is in my Pit Bull's pedigree).

There are hundreds of Pit Bulls that really should be mentioned, but we just don't have room here. I traced the two most widely known strains - Colby and Dibo and tried to show that both had commonalities in Lloyd's Pilot and other foundation dogs. I noted Kager and others that were common to both Colby and Dibo blood and underscored the influence of inbreeding and linebreeding in the development of the American Pit Bull Terrier. I discussed some of the key dogs that were used in linebreeding. Before we conclude the historical chapter, let's look at the development of the two organizations that have probably been the most influential in the propagation of the American Pit Bull Terrier.

One of those organizations is the United Kennel Club (UKC), started in 1898 by Mr. C.B. Bennett. He established UKC as a registering office for Pit Bulls and established their official name as the American Pit Bull Terrier (A.P.B.T.). The Pit Bull fanciers now had a way of formally keeping track of pedigrees and tracing their dogs' ancestry. In addition, Mr. Bennett established standard rules governing the pit fights and made it possible for a dog to gain recognition for performance in the pit by becoming a champion. A champion had to win three consecutive contract matches with witnesses including a U.K.C. registered referee. Mr. Bennett's goal was to promote more pit contests and to establish fair rules that had a degree of standardization. He wanted to cut down on the feuds and foul play that often existed with pit contests and to increase the quality of the contests. He also wanted to increase the quality of Pit Bulldogs, establish their bloodlines, and popularize the breed. U.K.C. didn't work out as well as Mr. Bennett planned, however. It seemed like a good idea, but the Pit Bull fanciers didn't help out like he had hoped.

Many continued to keep their dogs' strains secret, wanting to stick to the traditional feeling that the only true way of keeping the breed pure was to breed only dogs who proved their gameness in the pit, pedigree or no pedigree. A sufficient number of good dog men did stick with U.K.C., however, and it eventually grew to be the second oldest and second largest registration office (stud book) of all breeds of purebred dogs in the United states. There weren't just Pit Bulls included, though. U.K.C. began to grow by registering other breeds that were not interested in show trials but were more into field trials and other performance activities. They started by registering coon hounds and now they also have Eskimo dogs, Fox Terriers, Beagles, and others. The official publication of U.K.C. is a magazine called *Bloodlines*. Originally it served as a forum for issuing challenges (indicating dogs open to match and their weights), articles about Pit Bulls, advertising pups and adult dogs, selling equipment such as treadmills, reporting results of matches, and informing the public when a dog made champion. In the early 40's the U.K.C. began to be pressured by the American Kennel Club and other organizations for promoting fighting dogs, and they felt compelled to change their image, which they did very gradually, trying to satisfy groups that continuously pressured them about the fighting aspects while also keeping the Pit Bull people happy. They began by refusing to print challenges or report on pit matches. Now they must go to extremes to convince the public that they are in no way connected with pit fighting. U.K.C. periodically reaffirms its position in *Bloodlines*, stating that they are "against the pitting of a dog against another, in a fight to determine the winner, whether it be for fun, money, or as sport." In addition, having to be especially careful of their image, they refuse advertisements for breaking sticks and even treadmills. Treadmills are an excellent conditioning device used by many breed owners, including A.K.C. show dogs. The treadmill is particularly valuable when time does not permit a long run or walk or where the dog doesn't have a place to run.

U.K.C. has also had problems with Pit Bull owners complaining because they purchased a pup that was supposed to be quality bred, but had some psychological problem (such as hypertension or aggression, or the reverse - extremely shy and cowering) or physical problem (extremely cow-hocked, infertile, lack of strength) that they attributed to inbreeding or linebreeding. It is true that if both parents carry a defective gene, even a recessive one, it will theoretically show up in at least 25 percent of the litter. For this reason, the following statement appears on every U.K.C. litter application: "Please do not Inbreed, Linebreed, or Familybreed, as it weakens the bloodline. Always select a non-related mate when breeding purebred U.K.C. registered stock." I do not entirely agree with this position, but feel that it is incorrect or uninformed inbreeding, not inbreeding itself, that causes the problems. (See the chapter on breeding for a full discussion of the subject.) In any event, the point is mentioned here because it is significant to the historical development of the Pit Bull Terrier. The result of these positions on the part of U.K.C. (no connection in any manner with the fighting aspect and being totally against inbreeding) has led to U.K.C.'s being a registering body primarily for Pit Bull pet owners, while those who want to maintain the traditional type of Pit Bull (preserve the gameness with less emphasis on appearance) have tended to register with the American Dog Breeders Association (A.D.B.A.) the registering body to be discussed next. This is merely a generality, however, because U.K.C. and A.D.B. A. register both types. It has recently become very popular to register with both agencies (dual registration). For some time now U.K.C. has sponsored dog shows very similar, I think, to the A.K.C. shows, and the Pit Bull as a pet and not as a fighting dog is becoming a growing concept for the breed. This book hopes to assist in the enhancement of this group of fanciers by letting folks become aware of the many roads open to Pit Bull fanciers, like Schutzhund training and catch dogs.

The American Dog Breeders Association has always existed for Pit Bulls only and has never registered any other breed. The organization has always been an advocate of maintaining the Pit Bull's original characteristics of gameness and personality. Since pit fighting is illegal and stronger measures to combat it have been taken in recent years, this organization has had to tone down somewhat, but it has grown by leaps and bounds under the direction of one of the most knowledgeable Pit Bull fanciers in the world, Ralph Greenwood. This man knows his dogs and he knows the dog men. As far as Pit Bulls are concerned, he's seen and done it all, and he's a worker, a very hard worker. In August, 1976 he began the official publication of the A. D.B.A., the *Pit Bull Gazette*, a magazine you'll find referred to often in this book, and one that does allow advertisements of treadmills and breaking sticks. It does not formally denounce pit fighting and has articles of historical nature telling about some of the great ones (dogs and people). It does make the following statement in every magazine: "This magazine will not knowingly publish any material conflicting with the animal welfare act of 1976," and it doesn't. The A.D.B.A. has also started dog shows and developed a breed standard that I think is excellent. The first A.D.B.A. sanctioned point shows began, I think, in 1977. They were very successful and were attended by many quality dog men. In the initial shows there were some wise guys who would face their dogs to other Pit Bulls and offer challenges, but this practice was quickly squelched. They were promptly told to leave and that if they wanted to bait their dogs, they should go elsewhere to do it (good advice for more than one reason. If they wanted to, most of the men there would probably have dogs that would beat them!) Anyway, the shows are strictly fun matches and that stuff is not allowed. The goal is to promote the breed while maintaining gameness. The shows allow the dog men to get together at a legal function and "shoot the bull" (Who can outperform a Pit Bull fancier at "shooting the bull?"), share knowledge, discuss breedings, etc. The point is that with this organization Pit Bulls are still not bred exclusively for and do not gain recognition for appearance only, but are bred based on performance. A breed standard is recognized, however, and an open public awareness of the breed is encouraged. In the August, 1979 issue of *Pit Bull Gazette*, Mr. Greenwood wrote the following article explaining the development of this breed: [13]

"The ADBA was started in September, 1909 as an exclusive association of Pit Bull Terrier breeders. The president, Mr. Guy McCord, was an avid fancier and breeder of the dogs, and was a close friend of Mr. John P. Colby. Mr. Colby was the mainstay of the ADBA which prompts our boast of being the "home" registration office of the Colby dogs. All members in good standing could register their dogs and litters with the registration office upon the yearly payment of $2.50 dues. It seems that the club idea soon fizzled, and the association opened its doors to all owners and breeders of purebred American Pit Bull Terriers to register their dogs. The registration papers in those days consisted of one paper which was the registration certificate and the pedigree of the dog to the third generation. We thought it interesting to note that on the reverse side of this pedigree paper it read, in part:

"The Pit Bull Terrier is now recognized as a standard breed, where a few years ago, the name Pit Bull Terrier was unrecognized as a breed and the majority of the American public carried the impression that the Pit Bull was synonymous with dogs used for fighting purposes only. This idea has been dispelled by persistent efforts of the breeders who compose this association. Now classes for Pit Bull Terriers can be found at almost every local dog show. By concerted effort, our faithful friend will in time be classed as the leading American dog, who will give his life if necessary in defense of his master or mistress, we trust that you will unite with us in our efforts to bring this dog to the place where he belongs. The STANDARD DOG of the American public.[1]"

The ADBA passed from Mr. McCord to Mr. Frank Ferris in 1951. He, along with his wife, Florence Colby, the late wife of John P. Colby, continued to run the ADBA on a limited scale, but with ever increasing emphasis on the registration of the ADBA exclusively. In 1973, through the aid of Howard Heinzl the Greenwood family received the reins of the ADBA from Mr. Ferris. Mr. Ferris' retirement was due to his advancing age. Mr. Heinzl was a good friend of Frank Ferris and a staunch supporter of the ADBA by registering his dogs exclusively with the ADBA. I often wish Frank would have lived to see the growth of the present association. He would have been pleased. In 1973, the registration of the dogs took two hours a day, and we could offer "same day service." We now have an office of six full-time workers, and so we continue to grow by leaps and bounds.

In 1976, the ADBA was petitioned by the owners of the breed who possessed a very competitive spirit, to develop a standard on the breed by which pointed dog shows could be held. They did not want a standard that copied those of the UKC or AKC, but a standard for those dogs that they owned and continued to breed for the traits of character, loyalty, and athletic prowess, and the traits that the breed was originally bred for hundreds of years ago. Thereby they could continue to compete, in a legal endeavor. Thus, the formation of the ADBA standard. We have just held our 17th point show, with five more scheduled before the end of October. We started the publication of the Gazette about this same time, and the first issue was mailed out in August, 1976. Our aim is to enlighten the public to the truth about the Pit Bull Terrier, and to counteract the propaganda of the animal lovers' societies who are dedicated to the extinction of our breed. The *Gazette* is the official publication of the ADBA and it offers articles of history, pedigrees, ads on dogs for sale and at stud, books on the breed, a bit of humor, dog care and training, a place for a sounding board, and all around anything that is concerned with the Pit Bull. We try to bring the past and the present to our readers, in all aspects of what the dog was and is now. And we will continue to do so!

I mentioned the breed standard developed by ADBA (as did Mr. Greenwood). It was developed with the help of many experienced dogmen. Let's take a look at it as found in the *Pit Bull Gazette* Volume I, Issue 3, 1977[14]

Experience with dogs, horses, human athletes, cattle, hogs, and chickens indicates that for everything that lives and breathes, there is an army of experts to tell you how that particular thing should look.

A lot of these experts seem to lack the ability to quantitatively distinguish one physical attribute from another. Most start with an animal they love and build a standard to fit, but some few are really awesome in their knowledge of which physical dimensions work best.

Those persons whose opinions on conformation have borne the test of years have, without exception, come from the ranks of the professionals who use the animals to make money. There are cattlemen who can look at two hundred calves and pick the ten best gainers by looking at their conformation. A year later those same calves bring more profit than their less well conformed brothers. Race horse men are the most knowledgeable conformation people you will meet. They all like the same basic things in a horse; although they claim to differ greatly, their differences are minute. As evidence, look at the bidding at a yearling sale when a foal of good conformation is brought in and compare it with the prices offered for an equally well bred foal with conformation faults. Good cattlemen and good horsemen judge conformation by what the animal is supposed to do. Cattlemen know from experience that they will lose money feeding narrow shouldered, hollow backed, longlegged calves. Horsemen know that shallow girthed, crooked legged horses with straight hocks seldom cross the finish line first, and that's where the money is.

Now, money doesn't give you good judgment, but it takes good judgment to hang on to it. You can bet that anyone dealing with cattle, horses, or Pit Bulls for a long period of time professionally has been excercising good judgment.

Professionals look for an animal that can get the job done. Amateurs, because they have no way to test their theories, wind up feeding their imaginations.

So let's get to the point of establishing a conformation standard for the American Pit Bull Terrier. If we are going to be forced by the laws and today's social standards into breeding a dog for looks rather than performance, in the interest of preserving the most extraordinary animal that man has ever created, let's take a good look at what the American Pit Bull Terrier is supposed to do.

His existence today was not because he was bred only for gameness. He was not bred only for power. He sure as hell was not bred only for his intelligence, loyality, boldness, round eye, rose ear, red nose or his inclination for dragging children from the paths of speeding trains. He was bred to win. That's right folks, he was developed for competition.

The professional dogfighters have made him what he is, the professional dogfighters are improving him and when the professional dogfighters are gone, the real Pit Bull Terrier will gradually fade away. What we will have is something the amateurs have preserved that reminds us of the gladiators of old.

Thank God for the amateurs: professional dogfighting is a dying occupation. Preservation of this grand athlete that was bred to go to war is inevitably going to be in the hands of the amateurs. So, let's look to the profession of the dog in establishing our standard so that our grandchildren will at least see an authentic physical reproduction of a fighting dog.

If we start with the premise that conformation should reflect the ideal for the dogs usage and that this particular animal is supposed to win a dogfight, we come naturally to the question, what does it take to win?

Most of those who have backed their judgment with hard-earned money would agree on the following to some degree or another.

1. Sameness
2. Aggressiveness
3. Stamina
4. Wrestling ability
5. Biting ability

Note that only one of these qualities, wrestling ability, is directly related to conformation. One other, stamina, may be partly due to conformation, but is probably as much reliant on inherited efficiency of the heart and circulatory system. Some people seem to feel that the shape of the head determines hard bite, but in practice, it seems there are a lot of other factors involved. Earl Tudor said that the great "Black Jack," who killed 4 opponents in 7 wins in big money fights, bit hard "because he wanted to bite hard." That about sums it up. Good biters seem to be where you find them regardless of the shapes of their heads.

When we talk of conformation we really only mean one thing—wrestling ability. This is the reason the American Pit Bull Terrier varies so much in conformation. His wrestling by itself is not nearly as important as the sum total of gameness, aggressiveness, bite, and natural stamina; none of which are directly related to conformation.

Any dogfighter will tell you, "If you've got a game dog with good air, he's worth a bet." I might add, "If he can also bite, put a second mortgage on the house and take him to a convention." In other words, never mind what he looks like.

However, wiser men than I have said, "The only game dogs are dead ones." Also, "under certain conditions most dogs will quit." I believe there's a lot of truth to that, and to reinforce the fact that conformation is important, remember that conformation and wrestling ability are very closely related and it's usually the <u>bottom</u> dog in the fight that quits. It's hard to stop even the rankest cur if he can stay on top. The dog whose muscle and bone structure don't permit him to wrestle on even terms needs more of everything else to win. He's always coming from behind. He frequently dies after the fight, win or lose. His career is short because each go takes so much out of him. So I believe that wrestling ability (and therefore conformation) is a very important ingredient in a fighting dog.

Our standard of conformation can not be based on what someone who never saw a dogfight <u>thinks</u> a fighting dog should look like, but should be based on those physical attributes displayed on <u>winning pit</u> dogs.

AMERICAN PIT BULL TERRIER CONFORMATION

Look first at the overall profile of the dog. Ideally, he should be be "square" when viewed from the side. That is, about as long from the shoulder to the point of his hip as he is tall from the top of the shoulder to the ground. Such a dog will stand high and have maximum leverage for his weight. This means that standing normally with the hock slightly back of the hip, the dog's base, (where his feet are) will be slightly longer than his height. Using the hip and shoulder as guides will keep the viewer from being fooled by the way the dog is standing.

Height to weight ratio is critical. Since dogs are fought at nearly identical weights, the bigger the dog you have at the weight, the better your chances. Hence, stocky dogs with long bodies, heavy shoulders and thick legs usually lose to taller, rangier opponents.

Nature usually blesses a tall rangy dog with a fairly long neck which is a tremendous advantage in that it enables him to reach a stifle when his opponent may have his front leg, take an ear to hold off a shorter necked opponent, or to reach the chest himself when the other dog is trying to hold him off. The neck should be heavily muscled right up to the base of the skull.

Secondly, look at his back end. That's the drive train of any four legged animal. A Bulldog does 80% of his work off his hips and back legs.

A long sloping hip is most important. By its very length, it gives leverage to the femur or thigh bone. A long hip will give the dog a slightly reached backed appearance. Hence the "low set" tail so often spoke of.

The hip should be broad. A broad hip will carry with it a broad loin and permits a large surface for the attachment of the gluteal and the biceps femoris muscles, the biggest drivers in the power train.

The femur or thigh bone should be shorter than the tibia, or lower leg bone. This means that the stifle joint will be in the upper one third of the hind leg. It is not uncommon to see dogs with a low stifle. They are usually impressively muscled because of the bigger biceps femoris, but are surprisingly weak and slow on the back legs because of leverage lost by the long thigh. A short femur and long tibia usually means a well bent stifle, which in turn leads to a well bent hock. This last is a really critical aspect of wrestling ability. When a dog finds himself being driven backward, he must rely on the natural springiness of the well bent hock and stifle to control his movement. Dogs with straight or the frequently seen double jointed hock of many of the Dibo bred dogs, will wrestle well as long as muscle power can sustain them, but if pushed, will tire in the back end more quickly and soon lose their wrestling ability.

Thirdly, look at the front end. He should have a deep rib cage, well sprung at the top, but tapering to the bottom. Deep and eliptical, almost narrow is prefered to the round and barrel chested. The rib cage houses the lungs which are not storage tanks, but pumps. The ribs are like a bellows. Their efficiency is related to the difference in volume between contraction and expansion. A barrel chested dog, in addition to carrying more weight for his height, has a air pump with a short stroke. He must take more breaths to get the same volume of air. Depth of rib cage gives more room for large lungs.

Shoulders should be a little wider than the rib cage at the eighth rib. Too narrow a shoulder does not support adequate musculature, but too wide a shoulder makes a dog slow and adds unnecessary weight. The scapula (shoulder blade) should be at a 45 degree or less slope to the ground and broad and flat. The humerus should be at an equal angle in the opposite direction and long enough that the elbow comes below the bottom of the rib cage. The elbows should lie flat, the humerus running almost parallel to the spine; not out at elbows which gives a wide "English Bulldog" stance. This type of shoulder is more easily dislocated or broken.

The forearm should be only slightly longer than the humerus and heavy and solid—nearly twice the thickness of the metatarsal bones at the hack. The front legs and shoulders must be capable of sustaining tremendous punishment and heaviness can be an asset here.

The relationship between front legs and back should be, at first appearance, of a heavy front and a delicate back. This is because in an athletic dog, the metatarsal bones, hock and lower part of the tibia will be light, fine and springy. The front legs will be heavy and solid looking. The experienced Bulldog man however, will note the wide hip, loin, and powerful thigh which make the back end the most muscular.

The head varies more in the present day Pit Bull more than any other part of the body, probably because its conformation has the least to do with whether he wins or loses. However, there are certain attributes which appear to be of advantage. First, it's overall size. Too big a head simply carries more weight and increases the chances of having to fight a bigger dog. Too small a head is easily punished by a nose fighter and is especially easy for an ear fighter to shake. In an otherwise well proportioned dog, the head will appear to be about two thirds the width of the shoulders and about 25% wider at the cheeks than the neck at the base of the skull. Back of the head to the stop should be about the same distance as from the stop to the tip of the nose. The bridge of nose should be well developed which will make the area directly under the eyes considerably wider than the head at the base of the ears. Depth from the top of the head to the bottom of the jaw is important. The jaw is closed by the Temporar Fossa muscle exerting pressure on the Coronoid process. The deeper the head at this point, (that is, between the zygomatic arch and the angular process of the bottom of the jaw) the more likely the dog is to have leverage advantage both in closing the jaw and in keeping it closed. A straight, box-like muzzle and well developed mandible will not have much to do with biting power but will endure more punishment. "Lippy" dogs are continually fanging themselves in a fight which works greatly to their disadvantage. Teeth should meet in the front, but more importantly, the canines or fangs should slip tightly together, the upper behind the lower when the mouth is closed. The eye eliptical when viewed from the front, triangular when viewed from the side, small and deep set.

In general, such a head will be wedge shaped when viewed either from the top or side, round when viewed from the front.

Skin should be thick and loose, but not in folds. It should appear to fit the dog tightly except around the neck and chest. Here the skin should be loose enough to show vertical folds even in a well conditioned dog.

The set of the tail is most important. It should be low. The length should come just above the point of the hock, thick at the base and tapering to a point at the end and should hang down like a pump handle when relaxed.

The feet should be small and set high on the pasterns. The gait of the dog should be light and springy.

Most of the above relates to skeletal features of the dog. When we look at muscles, from the breeders standpoint, it is much more important to look at the genetic features of musculature than those features due to conditioning. A genetically powerful dog can be a winner in the hands of even an inept trainer, but a genetically weak dog needs a good matchmaker to win. Conditioning won't do much for him.

CONFORMATION STANDARD FOR AMERICAN PIT BULL TERRIER

Think of bones as levers with the joints as the fulcrum and the muscles being the power source. The power being applied to the lever is more effective the farther away from the fulcrum it is applied. Muscles should be long, with attachments deep down the bone, well past the joint. Short muscled dogs are impressive looking but not athletic. A muscle's power value lies in its ability to contract. The greater the difference between its relaxed state and its contracted state, the greater the power.

The coat of the dog can be any color or any combination of colors. It should be short and bristled. The gloss of the coat usually reflects the health of the dog and is important to an athletic Pit Bulldog.

Above all the American Pit Bull Terrier is an all around athlete. His body is called on for speed, power, agility, and stamina. He must be balanced in all directions. Too much of one thing robs him of another. He is not a model formed according to human specialists. In his winning form he is a fighting machine—a thing of beauty.

In judging the American Pit Bull Terrier 100 points will be possible for for the ideal dog. The break down is as follows:

Overall appearance - 20 points
Attitude of dog - 10 points
Head and neck - 15 points
Front end of dog - 20 points
Back end of dog - 30 points
Tail and coat – 5 points

Disqualifications: Any dog that has been sexually altered, that is spay or neutered.

There are some other magazines that have made a contribution to the development of the Pit Bull - *Your Friend and Mine*, which is no longer around, and *Sporting Dog Journal*, still distributed. They report pit fights, acknowledge champions, and have a few articles about training or other Pit Bull interest articles. Most of the magazine is fight reporting. Many people subscribe so they can follow winning dogs and winning bloodlines. One thing I notice -when you get a hot performer, all of a sudden the magazines are packed with sales of puppies out of that dog. There are a lot of puppy peddlers around, I'm sorry to say, and you have to be careful who you buy from. It is not an easy matter to tell whether or not a breeder is reputable. If you know him, that helps. Reading all the material you can find about Pit Bulls also helps. Most of the well known active dog men are proud of their strain and breed best to best because they are constantly striving for that ace dog.

Many of the dog fights reported are short articles like the following one taken from the January, 1977 issue *of Pit Dog Report* (another fight magazine, not as widely distributed as *Sporting Dog Journal)*.

J. LEWIS vs COLD TACO
REF: BIG LOU
FEMALES: 37 3/4 lbs.

Lewis, using a one time winner "Penny" conditioned and handled by Lewis. Cold Taco using a one time winner called "Rosie" conditioned and handled by Cold Taco. Dogs meet in the center both fighting fast and exchanging holds. Both dogs seem to be fighting even at the 16 min. mark. A turn is called on "Penny." She scratches hard. At about the 35 min. mark "Penny" seems to be biting harder and on top. At the 50 min. Cold Taco concedes making "Penny" and Lewis the winners. Reported by: Locally.

Notice the weights. The majority of the fighting Pit Bulls are small. Of course, they've been conditioned so that their fighting weight is considerably lower than their chain (unexercised) weight –I'd say about ten pounds lighter, but that's just a generality of course - depends on whether it's a big dog or a little dog. Notice the owner picked up his dog when he saw him losing. I didn't pick that example for that reason, but I would like to point out that that is very common. The point is that most dog men do care about their dogs and are not the bloodthirsty, narrow-minded people reported by newspaper and magazine reporters. These reporters are just trying to make money with a flamboyant story. Take, for example, a dog fight article in the magazine *GEO*. November, 1979, entitled "The Savage Pit." I'm not saying the reporter is lying, but I do have a few comments. For one thing, he portrays those he met as narrow-minded people who take dope, gamble, and have prison records. No doubt that's true and there are quite a few pit dog men like that. On the other hand, there are quite a few who are not at all like that, but are really quite normal, everyday people, except they like to fight their dogs. It's like everything else in life - you have your good guys and your bad guys. I will say that probably the majority of the pit dog men are rural folk. If that reporter had approached one of the top dog men, he might never have seen the fight - the dog man would have probably been too smart for him. Experienced men who match their dogs have established procedures for avoiding infiltration. The procedures have been handed down for generations. The inexperienced men are not so cautious, however, and as pit fighting becomes more widespread (primarily through media coverage) infiltration becomes easier.

The reporter has a picture of a Pit Bull on a cat mill (a conditioning device described in the chapter on conditioning). The picture shows the Pit Bull chasing a dead cat tied to the mill to motivate him to run. Well, there are some guys who do this - but nowhere near the majority. You can find kooky guys such as this who own other breeds like Dobermans and German Shepherds and will indulge in animal cruelty. Any good dog man knows that a cat or chicken is not needed to get the dog to run and not worth the effort of tying the animal up. Sometimes, a dog will not run, and so to give him the idea, a dog man might use a chicken or something - but you can put the animal in a cage and not harm it. It's certainly not as cruel to the chicken as the commercial chicken nurseries where chickens are raised three to a cage - and there isn't enough room for them to move around. Once the dog has gotten the idea, he'll run on his own. He'll usually run just as hard after a water bucket, by the way. The reporter describes the fights pretty well - except in one instance when a man's dog quit in 50 minutes and the guy screamed out, "I'm gonna go and shoot the @#*@***!" Well, maybe that happened; as I have stated, you have your good guys and your bad guys everywhere; but it's not a representative incident, as it implies. This sort of thing does happen. Pit Bull people cull their dogs in about the same manner as show dog people. In other words, most Pit Bull people keep their best ones and sell (or give away) those that aren't so good. If a dog doesn't work out, they give him away if they can't sell him; but some cull their dogs by killing them (not puppies because you just can't tell at that age). Same thing with show people – except they will cull puppies. They generally sell or find homes for puppies with conformation faults (ones that don't look right), but some will kill them - this I know. Notice in both cases, I said most people are humane. Personally I want nothing to do with someone who'll kill an animal just because it doesn't look right or doesn't want to fight. I can see keeping the best for yourself - but to kill because you feel it is for the betterment of the breed is not my cup of tea.

    Most of the reporters like to describe the fights they see with flowery language - like an audience that "gives vent with lusty screams and laughter as blood splashes around the pit." "The smoke-filled room" - they love that one – "the smoke-filled room" - supposed to add to the immorality of the atmosphere. Heck, I've been in smoke-filled rooms when company executives have meetings - really stinks with Havana cigars; boy, the liquor would flow, too. But, we were working, not attending a pit fight, so that's okay - oh yeah, and there was often plenty of "lusty laughter," too. Let me tell you (if you haven't attended a pit fight or two), the people watching the fights don't laugh or holler for blood - they are encouraging or excited about their favorite dog - like in a race. You'll hear them call out "Bite 'em, Butch," "Shake it out, Boy," etc., but it's not the blood – it's the ability and the gameness, and their dog they root for. Harry Crews wrote a short story about pit fighting for *Esquire* magazine (February 27, 1979). He was defending the pit fighting issue, but I don't like his position. I've read some of his books and he's kind of a bloodthirsty character. In his story in *Esquire,* "A Day at the Dog Fights," he describes his enjoyment of the blood and gore and makes the following statement:

Why can't we tell the truth about blood sports? We are a violent culture and always have been. We like to see players break each other's heads, or a racing driver fried alive, trapped in his car.

My gosh, I don't want to talk about people, but this writer is reflecting the point of view, in my opinion, of a small segment of our society. I surely don't know any people who enjoy watching a race driver fried alive in his car or who watch auto racing with that in mind. It's statements like that that bring a bad name to Pit Bulls. (By the way, the picture of the Pit Bull at the beginning of the article is not really a Pit Bull – he's a Bull Terrier, the white show dog cousin to the Pit Bull.) But people are different - we can observe an event and perceive it differently from each other. One person can watch a deep-game, truly crave Pit Bull crawl across a pit to make his scratch and *say* to himself, "How gross, how cruel and inhumane - sickening!" Another person, watching the same event will feel goose bumps go up his spine and a lump in his throat - I swear it can almost make you cry - to see such bravery, such courage and determination. In that *GEO* article, the guy said, "fights often last two hours." They don't. That's rare and those are two game, game dogs that can go two hours. Of course you have to consider the pace of the fight, too. By the way, in the same article he said the dogs are trained for an upcoming fight by running eight hours a day." Hog wash! If you did that you'd wear your dog out - any dog - and he'd be too weak for his match. Conditioning a dog is an art. (See the chapter on the combat dog.) Anyway, the other thing reporters like to do is show blood pictures of the dogs all chewed up. Well, as far as I know, those are true pictures. The ones in the *GEO* magazine are. As I said, the Pit Bull is capable of taking a lot. It's not cruel to them; it's fun. Let me point out a few other things. They are nowhere near as bad off as they appear. I can recall being hit in the head one time, left a pool of blood in the street. After I was washed up, however, the gash was only about 1/2 inch long and not really that deep. Let me put it this way - all the pictures show the dog during the fight or immediately after - never all cleaned up. Usually three weeks later they look and act as good as new except for perhaps some missing fur where they've been bitten (only noticeable if you look closely). Sometimes they might have part of their ear chewed off and even perhaps part of their lip or something, but those are veterans of some long, game battles. A whole lot of Pit Bulls come out of their matches really not that badly marked up (after they've been cleaned up). The majority of the Pit Bull pictures in this book are dogs that have fought - many are champions. Do they look maimed or unhealthy or like they have received cruel treatment? Let me be a reporter and give you some before/after pictures. Coming up youll find a picture of Morochito after he's been in a battle with a Pit Bull. As I mentioned, I don't fight my dog, but he had an accidental meeting with another Pit Bull in a ball field one time. (Both myself and the other dog's owner happened to have chosen the same field that day to exercise our dogs.) The other dog was much bigger than mine, but Morochito made a mess out of him before we were able to break them apart - but not before he did a pretty good number on Morochito, too. As you can see, he doesn't feel too good. His throat was chewed up pretty badly. His leg swelled up and he limped badly for two days and his ear was chewed pretty good. Next to that picture is one of how Morochito looked three weeks later. I think he looks pretty fit, don't you? Neither dog was really harmed. In any event, I injected those comments not to defend or make judgements about pit fighting, but in order to disclose facts as I see them.

Morochito after accidental battle

Morochito looking fit three weeks after battle

Well, that's about it on the history; hope you've enjoyed it. Let me wrap it up with a story. It goes back to the beginnings of the breed, in old England, and concerns a bull-bait in Bristol, England -the time - March, 1822.

An old and crippled bitch had been standing calmly at the side of a butcher watching the flight of the numerous dogs through the air as the bull cleverly and effectively disposed of his adversaries. At the command of the butcher, the bitch slowly hobbled into the ring. She was covered with scars, blind in one eye, and altogether deprived of the use of one of her hind legs. Unlike many good dogs, she did not run directly up to the bull's front, but sneaked cautiously around him, with her remaining eye vigilantly bent upon the bull's every motion, apparently watching for an opportunity to bolt in and grab the bull. This was rather un-Bulldog-like behavior, but considering the infirmity of the old bitch and the little chance of success she would have had if she had gone in like a strong, fleet, and unmaimed dog, it may have been in some measure excusable. She had pinned this same formidable bull about a dozen times, and she and the bull had slept many a night in the same stall. In the stable the two were as amicable as doves, but on the turf the situation was different. The bull's fiery and bloodshot eyes were fixed upon her the moment she made her appearance. He seemed to be perfectly aware of her capabilities and steadily kept his front toward her, turning as she turned and, disregarding all other objects, keeping his keen eyes fixed on her alone. Another dog unexpectedly burst into the ring while the two thus steadily eyed each other, but the bull sent him curvetting and gamboling over the heads of the spectators, without deigning to honor him with so much as a momentary glance.

It was some time before the bitch had an opportunity to get in close to the bull. At length she suddenly darted forward with a velocity of which she seemed incapable, and at one bound reached the bull's nose. Despite repeated attempts, she was unable to hold fast. Although her sturdy old friend tossed her off several times, disaster only tended to prove her invincible courage and she repeatedly went in to the old bull; at one time she managed to evade his horns so cleverly and grapple with him so stoutly, that it seemed she would eventually pin him. But he trod her off by main force, and running over her maimed body, left her to be picked up by her fond old master.

Although this account (along with some others I have included) indicates the barbarianism of earlier times, I think the story is an excellent illustration of the origin of our breed. This female was the type of Bulldog that would have been bred several times and those of her puppies that proved themselves would have been bred and so on until you have the modern American Pit Bull Terrier. Our breed has retained much from those Bulldogs of old England and have become even better, because they've been selectively bred for performance ever since.

Early 1800's Bulldogs – their names were Wasp, Child, and Billy

Chapter 2: The Pit Bull Pet

> Unto the end the humblest dog I ever knew was to the man that loved him true.   - Author Anonymous

In the introduction and history chapters, I went to great lengths to communicate the idea that although the American Pit Bull Terrier is very, very courageous and he is an awesome fighting animal, he makes an excellent pet, loves people (especially children), and has a very steady disposition. No one really knows why the Pit Bull is so friendly; traditionally, they haven't been bred that way. Many dog men today feel that there is somehow a correlation between gameness (in the pit) and a friendly, stable disposition - that is, that the genes that produce deep gameness also produce an even temperament; but there are many examples of mean (people biters) Pit Bulls who were also very game in the pit. Cotton's Bullet was one of them. My dog's granddaddy, Trouble, was another. (Although neither was dead game.) These dogs are, however, in the minority. Some say the breed is so friendly because they are such terrible fighters with so much jaw strength that Pit Bulls who were vicious had to be put to death - they were simply too dangerous - so not many of that type were bred. Many experienced dog men feel that the even temperament developed in the better strains because a nervous, easily agitated dog won't last long in the pit. The survivors were those dogs who were high in self-confidence, not easily intimidated, and were able to keep a cool head. A dog who fights out of fear will soon burn himself out, hence a breed with an even disposition. Also, many of the good ones, the very game dogs (game because they kept going though extremely exhausted), kept going because they were fighting to please their masters. That is to say, they responded to the encouraging words of their masters when the going got rough. All this is conjecture, but the fact remains that as a breed, the Pit Bull has one of the best dispositions. This is a very popular fact that Pit Bull fanciers are quick to point out when the breed gets attacked by the public as being a "vicious breed" because of its fighting. The point can be exaggerated, however, and often is. The even disposition of Pit Bulls is, for one thing, merely a tendency, a generality. If a Pit Bull is not given proper people socialization, if he spends his life either on a chain or in his keep (training for fight) and receives very little contact with strange people, he can become a people biter. I've seen quite a few Pit Bulls that'll bite a stranger and I think there are really more of them than many Pit Bull fanciers want to admit. There are some (not very many) yahoos who think their dogs will be rougher if they "don't baby them" but treat them pretty rough. This can result in a dog that can't be trusted with people. If a Pit Bull gets harmed by a child when he's a puppy, he can grow up to be vicious around children.

What I'm trying to say is that the same environmental conditions that produce vicious dogs in other breeds can also produce a vicious Pit Bull. Most Pit Bulls can take more inhumane treatment than other breeds so a lot of them will live in the conditions I mentioned and still have a mild disposition - but Pit Bulls are by no means immune to psychological problems due to an improper environment. As with any breed, moreover, you can have a genetic throwback that is neurotic -just as you can with people.

On January 16, 1980, the following story appeared in newspapers all across the country - you may recall reading it:[16]

WOMAN ATTACKED BY 2 PET TERRIERS

MIAMI (AP) - Fletcher Tiggs says he bought Elton and Snook, a pair of bull terriers, because "I understood they were good dogs to have around the house."

On Tuesday the dogs turned on Tiggs' 71-year-old wife, ripped one of her ears in half, scored her body with bites and tore off her clothes before police bullets brought them down.

Ethel Tiggs was in satisfactory condition early today at Anne Bates Leach Eye Hospital. Officials there refused to disclose her injuries, but police said she was bitten on the face, head, arms, back, buttocks and legs. Police officer Richard Wagner said he and his partner found Mrs. Tiggs in her back yard, screaming "Get them off of me!" as the dogs snarled and bit her.

As Elton backed away, Wagner shot and killed him.

"That one was biting the back of her left leg," he said. "Then the other one, which was biting her on the head, leaped at me. I leaned back with my arm up and (Officer Michael) Dannelly shot the dog as it was in the air." Snook, wounded in the stomach, was taken away by animal control officers for quarantine. Officials said the dog would be destroyed unless Tiggs wanted it back.

The incident came less than two months after a youngster in Hollywood, Fla., was injured by a bull terrier - a compact, muscular breed often used in illegal dog fights.

Seven-year-old Frankie Scarbrough lost an ear and large sections of scalp in the Dec. 1 attack. Doctors say he faces years of reconstructive surgery.

Mrs. Tiggs told police she stepped into her yard to find that both dogs had escaped from a pen. She said Elton and Snook chased her until she fell, then pounced on her.

Neither police nor Tiggs could explain the attack. Tiggs said he bought the dogs as puppies in October 1978 "to take with me for company when I go fishing at night."

Tiggs said he played with both dogs morning and night, and that his wife sometimes played with them.

"Sometimes she seemed afraid of them," he said. "But she never said she was."

The earlier incident referred to in the story - about the seven-year-old boy in Hollywood, Florida - resulted in the City Commissioner planning an ordinance requiring that owners of Pit Bull Terriers carry $25,000 liability insurance and register their dogs with the city, providing proof of such insurance. I have no idea why those Pit Bulls attacked the lady. The article said that the owner, Mr. Tiggs, played with the dogs every morning and every night so they were apparently not socially ostracized. The behavior of these dogs is more characteristic of breeds that are close to the wild, such as Shepherds or sled dogs. They will have more pack instinct and are more likely to team up and attack a human that they perceive as subservient (in the "pack") to themselves. Pit Bulls are further away from the pack instinct. By the way, the people at the animal control said (in another article) that the dog seemed very friendly.

As I said, you can have a neurotic dog show up from time to time due to a heredity throwback, just like with humans. That couldn't be the case in this instance, though, because two Pit Bulls were involved and you can't really say they were both neurotic because of heredity factors - that, of course, would be too much of a coincidence. I would say that the dogs had received no obedience training whatsoever, that they probably had been spoiled and encouraged to "play" rough, and then left alone most of the time in the back yard. The lady probably inadvertently agitated them and they became too excited and she couldn't control them.

A friend of mine has a Pit Bull named "Boss," heavy Ironhead breeding. Boss is a very friendly Pit Bull, but also very strong, 60 pounds chain weight, and thinks he's a puppy and loves to play. When I brought him back from his roadwork one evening and started to put him back on his chain, well, he just didn't want to go back on the chain - he wanted to play, so he played. He bit me on the arm a couple times, breaking the skin. He'd let go when I hollered, then "nip" again. This dog's "nips" were pretty hard. His owner came over and helped me get him on the chain. It took us about ten minutes and when we finished, the owner was covered with dog bites - his lip, arms, legs. Boss was not being "mean." His tail was wagging and he was playing. If he were biting for real, he'd have broken bones and taken chunks out of us. That dog could bite hard. Boss has never received any obedience training, lives his life on a running chain, and has played rough like that with humans since he was a puppy. The bites he gave us would probably send an elderly person or child to the hospital.

This story and discussion are brought out here because I feel an important point needs to be made. Neglected animals of any breed can lead to trouble. I used the newspaper example of an extreme case to drive home the fact that a Pit Bull can be a very dangerous animal. True, the incident is very rare and happens much more frequently with other breeds; but when it happens with a Pit Bull, there's more publicity because of the many misconceptions that exist about the breed. Also, I have read somewhere - I don't know how reliable the source - that a Pit Bull has more than double the biting power of a German Shepherd, so when they do get vicious they can do more damage. So if you want a Pit Bull for a pet, although they make ideal pets and the Florida incident is an aberration, there are some important considerations to be made:

1. A Pit Bull has a hereditarily developed proclivity to fight other animals.

2. Along with the Pit Bull's friendly disposition is a lively, rambunctious, playful nature.

3. A playful, energetic Pit Bull pup grows up to be an extremely strong, agile adult, with a very, very hard bite.

Put these three considerations together and you can see that a Pit Bull raised in an unrestrained environment can be at the very least one big pain in the neck when he's not tied to his chain in the back yard. A rambunctious Pit Bull can wreak havoc in a house (not on purpose, just being himself). Pit Bulls love to exercise their jaws so they'll want to chew on everything. They like to shake toys and tear things up. In addition, many of them, but not all, will instinctively attack the first animal they see. These traits are also true for the American Staffordshire although perhaps to a lesser extent. All this can be easily avoided - well, it may not be really all that easy, but if you buy a Pit Bull puppy for a pet, I suggest you plan on either spending some time with him or not buy the pup.

There are those who believe Pit Bulls cannot be trained to be non-aggressive. This is far from true. As mentioned in the introductory chapter, Pit Bulls are not really more aggressive than many other breeds, particularly when they are young. All it takes is plenty of early supervised socialization and your Pit Bull will grow to be a dog who never starts a fight - but you better believe he'll still be more than willing and capable of finishing any fight that another breed insists on. In many instances you'll find that because of their even disposition and high threshold of pain, they will tolerate up to a certain point, quite a bit of aggressive behavior from another breed. I recall one instance when Morochito was about nine months old. He was pretty aggressive at the time, sort of feeling his oats you might say - like a young boy. We were doing our roadwork together when suddenly this yappy Terrier came charging out of his yard and lit into Morochito. He jumped up and latched onto Morochito's lip. Morochito seemed quite interested and curious about the little dog - because he could have easily avoided the bite –Morochito's very fast. The little Terrier hung on, feet dangling. I was afraid to do anything for fear Morochito would get excited and kill the dog with one crunch. However, he just wagged his tail and looked down with a real curious expression. Finally I think it bothered him because he suddenly shook the little dog loose and pinned him on the ground with his paw. He just stared at the dog, but he looked a little to me like he was thinking about that crunch. Guess the Terrier got the same impression because he let out with a squeal and took off lickety-split. A lot of Pit Bulls won't bother any other breed but will instinctively go crazy at the sight of another Pit Bull. I understand that other breeds are the same way. In any case, in choosing a Pit Bull pet, you'll want to study pedigrees (See the chapter on breeding) and find out as much as you can about the parents and grandparents. Try to determine if any have been aggressive toward humans, and any other personality traits (positive or negative) in which you are interested. This is probably the most important step. I think that the traits of the grandparents are very important. After studying pedigrees (and the breeder's reputation), select the litter you want to get your puppy from. You may feel compelled to send away for your puppy because the particular bloodlines you want may not be available locally. Obviously, your preference should be to get your puppy locally because you can choose from the available puppies in the litter rather than rely on the breeder's choice and, of course, you don't have to pay the shipping charges. I feel that there are some other important reasons for selecting a local breeder. Although a dog's personality and physical structure are largely shaped by heredity, environment can play a large role in enhancing the dog's strong points and de-emphasizing the dog's weak points if you know what to do. You begin with the very small puppy. In fact, you can actually help out quite a bit with the mother before birth. If you are willing to pay extra for pick, of the litter and get in an early deposit before anyone else, so much the better. I suggest you find out what the breeder feeds the mother and how much exercise she gets. Chances are she doesn't get the best of either. Not too much you can do about the exercise, but I do think that if a bitch is conditioned before she conceives, her circulation is better and the pups will get more from their mother than if she were sluggish. You may be able to convince the breeder of this. I know that in the karate classes I have attended, several women have had babies and had to momentarily drop out of the program. They returned to work out as soon as possible. They reported that they felt like they had an easier time, felt healthier, and were stronger after having the baby because of their karate conditioning - not exactly what you might call documented research, but a good many women have reported these feelings. As far as nutrition is concerned, see the chapter on nutrition for suggestions. If the breeder does not want to pay for the extra nutritional program for the mother (which I think should begin before conception), he may be willing to let you provide the food as part of the agreement for letting you get pick of the litter. None of this is absolutely necessary, of course; I'm just sharing as much knowledge and as many ideas with you as I can. You pick out what you want to believe in and can afford. Some of it may seem far fetched to you - not to others. Few can afford all the suggestions I'll be providing, either in terms of money or time.

Let me share something unique with you. Many will poo-hoo this, but then many felt that accupuncture was blarney not very long ago. We still have many new horizons to reach in medicine. Biomagnetics is not really new – we've known about it since, I believe, the 1930's. We are just beginning to discover some very important uses for it, however, in the field of medicine and other areas, let me say that the subject is being researched in many major universities. We are just beginning to touch on it but I want to be among the first to use it with Pit Bulls. I first became aware of it through my chiropractor. In his office he had a beautiful magnolia in full bloom on the front desk. He said he was experimenting with biomagnetics. One flower, placed on a south pole magnet for only three hours a day produced a much larger, healthier plant that lived longer. Another flower from the same bunch, but not placed on the magnet at all, developed nowhere nearly as well.

Biomagnetism has been successfully used on humans in treating cancer, joint problems, and blood problems - although not so successfully yet as had been hoped. Let me explain what biomagnetism is and how it can be applied to Pit Bulls. My information comes from a medical report entitled "The Anatomy of Biomagnetism" by Albert Roy Davis (H)DS, 1974. It's a bit old, but the basic principles should suffice. The prefix bio means living tissue, so the word biomagnetics means the application of magnetic energy to living tissue. Biomagnetics is the study of the effects of a magnet's energies - north pole energy and south pole energy. With atomic dating we have been able to measure the amount of magnetism that was on earth millions of years ago, and we know that during the time periods of the large animals, the earth's magnetic fields were higher than today. If you were to take a sample of animal or human blood and spin off the fluids, the plasma, and leave only red blood cells, and place the red blood cells on a slide with a magnet under the slide and view them through a microscope, you'd see some interesting phenomena. The red blood cells would all spin around and point in one direction. This process is called polorization. You have aligned the iron and the ions in the red blood cells. What previously was a separated, random source of energy has now been changed to a unified gathering of energy. In early research with biomagnetics, it was found that the horseshoe-type magnet did not produce any effect on organisms because the two poles are located too close together to allow either pole to act as a separate source of energy. It was found that a rectangular bar was best. You must isolate the poles. A presentation to the American Medical Association by Kathy Solis, after four years of exposing many animals to magnetic fields, disclosed some interesting information. Animals having transplanted cancer and leukemia were exposed to 3,000 gauss magnets (standard measure of magnetic energy is in units called gauss - 3,000 gauss is roughly eguivalent to a magnet having a lifting power of 40 pounds). The erythrortes (red blood cells) in peripheral blood were greatly increased, while the number of leukocytes (white blood cells) was reduced. However, when she removed the animals from the magnetic field of both poles, the condition grew worse. One reason was over exposure to the cancerous conditions, and the other was that she used both poles of the magnet at the same time.

    Some of the earliest research with isolated magnetic poles was with vegetable seeds. It was found that when seeds were placed on the south pole of a magnet (for as little as six hours and up to 200 hours), then planted, they grew to be a hardier plant and had a significantly better yield. When seeds were placed on a north pole and then planted, they produced tall, thin plants that yeilded inferior vegetables (inferior to the same seeds planted without magnetic treatment). Untreated seeds and plants served as controls. It was found that the protein , sugars, and oils were higher in the leaves and stems of seed plants treated with the south pole magnet than the untreated (control) plants. South pole treatment of sugar beets resulted in a greater production of natural sugar and peanuts treated likewise had more natural peanut oil and higher protein content. Another area of research was with earthworms. It was found that when worms were treated with south pole energy, their baby worms grew larger and stronger than untreated worms. Earthworms are something like 90% protein. In university research, it has been found that when female rats sit on a south pole magnet for short periods every day, they produce larger, healthier baby rats that are more aggressive and curious and have almost a complete absence of psychological problems. The same thing has been found to be true with rabbits, but, to my knowledge, no one has tried it with dogs; however, I feel that the same positive results can be obtained.

North pole energies consistently produced the opposite effect in that it arrested life and slowed the development and maturity of all life systems. It was also found that south pole magnetism had a positive effect on all life forms - including bacteria, germs, and cultures - so that south pole treatment tended to make infections, for example, worse, while north pole treatment tended to arrest infection. South pole treatment also seemed to help animals that were stiff or lame.

One other application of magnetic energy is with water. When you place water on a north pole magnet, the water becomes ionized. Drinking this water tends to make you feel "up," energetic. It has absolutely no relation to exposing the body to the magnet. The effect is similar to the air just after a rain - you tend to feel good. I drink my north pole ionized water before a workout and it works. It's nothing really dramatic, but I do feel more energetic. Water exposed to a south pole magnet has just the opposite effect - you feel sluggish. You feel similar to the way you feel just before a rain storm. Water plants with south pole magnetized water, however, and your plants will grow like nobody's business. I suggest you begin your pup (and yourself) on north pole ionized water. It helps with mid-morning letdown and uplifts your physical senses. Eight ounces given to puppies when they are in a listless mood (providing they are not sick) will tend to make them curious, playful, and more active.

Well, as I said, this is relatively new, and I haven't tried it with dogs (nor do I know anyone who has), but I fully intend to try it one day. If you are interested, you can write to the Maryland Magnet Co., 8825 East Allenswood Road, Randallstown, Maryland 21133 for information. What you want is solid state, ceramic, flat magnets. These are the modern ones that are non-metalic and hence do not have to be recharged. At the time of this writing, the magnets cost about $25 per pair. Just thought I'd share this tidbit with you.

One last little suggestion on the mating step. It was reported recently in Medical World News, by Dr. Joseph Barkay, that the caffeine in coffee can arouse sperm that have been stored in a deepfreeze for artificial insemination. (By the way, see the chapter on breeding for information on how you can achieve artificial insemination with dogs.) Dr. Barkay and other researchers reported that they noticed peppier performances by the spermatozoa when caffeine was injected into their solutions. I guess I'm a little like those folks who like to raise chickens - if there doesn't appear to be any harm, I like to experiment. I might try giving the male a caffeine pill a few hours before mating. Of course I'd have no way of knowing if the results were better or worse than if I had not given a pill. I've been told that the caffeine would have to be injected directly into the sperm, that taking it as a pill would have no effect on reproductivity - still, no harm trying it.

Once you have decided on your litter and the mating has been completed, your next task is to select the puppy from the litter. If you wanted a combat dog, one you wanted to pit, this would be a nearly impossible task (See the chapter on the combat dog.) because traits like gameness generally do not mature until a Pit Bull is older.

There are, however, adult brain waves present in the brain of a three-week-old puppy, and basic personality traits that are present at that time are generally the ones they will have as adults. Thus a significantly aggressive or shy pup will tend to be aggressive or shy as an adult. Either can make an excellent pit dog - but for a pet, you want the middle of the road. The shy Pit Bull may not be very trustworthy with children or humans in general. The aggressive Pit Bull is likely to be much more difficult to train and can be a real pain in the neck. Select the puppy that is average, neither shy nor aggressive. Remember, as mentioned in the introduction, the aggressive Pit Bull is not necessarily the braver one. He smarter one. There are some personality, temperament, and intelligence tests that you can use. You can find some in the book *Understanding Your Dog* by Dr. Michael Fox and in *The New Knowledge of Dog Behavior* by Clarence Pfaffenberger. The main principle in temperament tests is, again, middle of the road. Many, many people choose the cute puppy that breaks away from the litter and prances up to them, saying "The puppy chose us!" This sounds good, but that puppy is likely to be more dominant and therefore much more difficult to handle. Then again, it could be mere coincidence that the puppy happened to notice you before the others. Try not to rely on your emotions in choosing your puppy.

Most of the following temperament tests appear in Fox's book and in several others, while some are my own. Begin by observing the litter every day (or every day you can) for the first three weeks. Bring a notebook and keep a record of your observations for each pup. Use the breeder's names or if he has none yet, make up names. Record every identifying characteristic you can for each pup - color of coat, spots, runt of litter, largest, first one born if you know - everything. This sounds very time consuming - it is. You may not be able to do it. If not, fine; it's not crucial, of course.

Like just about every endeavor in life, you get out of it what you put into it. The following observations should be made:

1. Record which are the most vigorous and competitive when nursing, and which ones are passive. Also note which ones are most often attached to the more productive posterior teats.

2. Record which ones are first to crawl out of their nest and which ones stay as long as they can.

3. Which ones are consistently outside the pile?

4. Which ones cry more than others?

5. Which ones remain still and give contented grunts when handled and which ones squirm and cry?

6. Which of the pups cry sooner (Record the time) and which act more distressed when placed on a cold surface?

7. Pinch the tender web of skin between the puppy's f oretoes or pinch his ear. Note how long the puppy stays distressed and how quickly he responds to petting (Record the time).

At first it will be difficult to distinguish the pups, but with constant interaction, you'll know them all. When you test them on cold surfaces or response to leaving their nest area, test each puppy individually. Many puppies will react differently when alone than when with their "pack." You'll need a stop watch so you can record exact time. The time difference is not much. When I mention a cold surface, I don't mean real cold. During the first two weeks (called the neonatal period) of a puppy's life, he is not capable of maintaining a proper body temperature. Puppies at this age are wholly dependent on mother and littermates for warmth. A puppy less than two weeks old is very underdeveloped and even depends on the mother for elimination (The mother's licking stimulates the needed response). Removing a puppy from its nest at this age, and placing him on a linoleum floor in the house is extreme stress. If you overstress the puppy at any stage, you can ruin him. Be careful.

This puppy's daily stress test can be very important if you have the time and access to the litter. If you select a puppy that does not have the temperament or intelligence you are looking for, more compensatory training will be required. In addition, it has been found that you can begin "training" from birth. In the early 40's it was found that orphaned babies had a very low resistance to disease and suffered from more psychologically related problems than children raised in normal home environments. When institutions began a policy of daily fondling and playing with the babies, the response was overwhelming. They were healthier with far fewer illnesses and, most significantly, they grew up to be better socially and emotionally adjusted. Being aware of these findings,

Dr. Fox and others have tested many, many puppy litters for their responses to socialization. They have found that early puppy socialization is just as important with dogs as with humans. An interesting research project is found in Dr. Fox's book. Chapter Six, entitled "Superdogs." It was found that if rats were removed from their nest and kept at room temperature for three minutes a day for the first ten days of their life (Remember a rat's life span is much shorter than a dog's), their body temperature falls significantly. This mild stress effects part of the hormonal system of the developing animal - the adrenal, pituitary system. When the mice matured they were super animals (much better able to withstand stress). In experiments with the adult mice, litter-mates that were not subjected to the early mild stress developed several ulcers when tied down so that they couldn't move for twenty-four hours. The littermates that did receive early mild stress treatment, did not ulcerate when tied down and were more resistant to disease and other types of stress. Both male and female mice that received the early stress treatment, were more resistant to disease, attained sexual maturity earlier, and - watch this now - WERE SIGNIFICANTLY BETTER AT PROBLEM SOLVING (i.e. solving mazes). Wow! To me that is very impressive when you think of the ramifications of similar treatment with our Pit Bulls that are already more resistant to disease than other breeds, tend to be more stable in temperament, and appear to be already high on the intelligence scale (in there area of performance). Dr. Fox experimented with Beagles and found that although they tend to be a docile breed (probably because it is necessary in order for them to cooperate in a pack as they hunt), he was able to consistently develop Beagles that were of more even temperament, more aggressive, more outgoing and eager, more resistant to disease, etc., and more curious and explorative. In summary, subjecting Beagle puppies to early mild stress treatment consistently produced tougher Beagles than littermates that did not receive the treatment. Dr. Fox applied mild stress daily from birth to five weeks of age. The mild stress consisted of brief cold exposure, cutaneous stimulation by stroking (Cutaneous means of the skin - he patted and rubbed the pups every day), stimulation of the visual and auditory systems by electronic flashes and clicking noises, stimulation of the balancing organs of the nervous system by gently tilting and rotating the pup. (The balancing organs are the semicircular canals, that is inner ear structures that serve to maintain balance. Note: In the Navy we were taught that if you lie on your back while in the high seas you won't get sea sick because getting sea sick results from imbalance in the inner ear which doesn't happen if you are prone. We also learned that a more emotional person is much more likely to get sea sick.)

Dr. Pfaffenberger stressed his Bloodhound pups (another breed that is very low on aggression) by banging pots and pans on the roof of their house. He obtained the same results as Dr. Fox, who was quick to point out, and I think this is terribly important, especially for those of us who have a proclivity for getting carried away, trying to do things better, that any stress more severe than what he applied can cause adrenal exhaustion and increased susceptibility to disease (in other words the opposite of the results of mild stress).

Handling puppies is very important. Dr. Fox, Dr. Pfaffenberger, and many others have found that, within a litter, handled pups are far more active and exploratory, and are always dominant in competitive situations, than nonhandled littermates. Dr. Fox found that handled pups were better able to solve puppy I.Q. tests such as detour problems (a wire fence that the puppy can see through and can't climb over is placed between him and his owner. The length varies with the age of the puppy). He states that "The nonhandled pups were extremely aroused, yelped a good deal, and made many errors. They were clearly more emotionally disturbed in the test situation than the handled pups. The latter kept their cool, making fewer errors, and solving problems very quickly and with less distress vocalization."[17] My suggestion is that you perform the stress tests at the same time every day until most of the puppies seem to be adapting better. Then vary the time of the day you perform the tests; also vary the place.

Dog psychologists now agree that there are certain defineable stages of development in the early life of every puppy during which dramatic and relatively permanent changes occur. The puppy's environmental exposure during each of these stages can profoundly influence later behavior. The amount and type of stimulation the puppy should receive depends on the degree of maturity of the animal because the puppy is not affected by a stimulus unless a particular part of the nervous system is sufficiently developed to be receptive to the stimulus. The "experts" do not seem to agree exactly on the length of each period, but the following is representative. There is not much difference in any of them. These stages of development are as follows:

1. First two weeks - the neonatal period. As mentioned above, the puppy is practically helpless and about the only stimulus that he can respond to is temperature and odor.

2. Third week - the transitional period. The third week is separate from others because dramatic changes occur in this week that mark a transition from the helpless neonatoal stage to the social stage. At the beginning of the third week, the eyes begin to open and in one short week motor and sensory capacities develop that will

determine the pup's ability to grow socially in the following weeks. The puppy usually begins to walk instead of crawl? There is a dramatic increase in exploratory behavior, and the puppy begins to develop a sense-of-fear response. This is a very critical week in which the puppies can develop a fear response because of any small emotionally upsetting incident that can have a lasting effect on the puppies' future temperament. This is important information because many a good pup has been unknowingly ruined during this short period of time when his emotions develop. He should receive plenty of gentle handling and petting with a reduction in the stress stimulation.

    3. Fourth to twelfth week - the socialization period. Here is another important period in the development of a dog. By the age of seven or eight weeks, the dog's E.E.G. has reached the adult pattern. This is pretty rapid growth. It is during this period that temperament differneces become apparent and the puppy learns scent differentiation, becomes interested in the visual environment, and, most importantly, forms its social behavior. Puppies taken from the litter too early (prior to seven weeks old) may never learn to interact with other dogs. Play fighting with littermates is extremely important to the development of the puppy. On the other hand, if the puppy receives too much dog socialization and little human socialization, he will tend to grow up to be a dog that is hard to train and does not relate well to humans. The puppy's memory is better at this age, while his emotional development continues to be formed. From eight to twelve weeks old, the puppy is especially sensitive to disturbances and can develop permanent fears for such things as children (if hurt by a child during this stage), objects, or situations. If the puppy's experiences are positive, he grows up to be a more resilient dog.

    The American Pit Bull Terrier is a relatively tough breed and can survive adverse conditions and still come out with a strong personality. He is quite resilient, as has been brought out before. If all these socialization and stress tests can work so well with other breeds I'll bet you can do a lot with Pit Bulls, too. In selecting German Shepherd puppies for seeing-eye training schools, only about ten percent used make it through and pass the strict standards of the school. With mild stress treatment and selective temperament tests such as we are about to look at, ninety percent passed. I feel that the quality of Pit Bulls can also be enhanced. So let's get back to the temperament tests. Most of them originate with Dr. Fox, but they can be found in most dog psychology books. They can be applied to puppies eight weeks old.

    1. One of the tests you will have already observed as you administered the mild stress treatment. That is which of the pups are more

distressed when isolated and which appear more stable? Which ones, if any, begin exploratory behavior and for how long? All should be recorded.

2. Remove the mother from the puppies' pen and put in some novel item like a ball. Notice which ones are first to show interest and go over to investigate it. After their interest is aroused, which ones win the battle for the item and which ones persist even when they don't have the item?

3. Remove the mother and all the puppies from the pen. (Do this on a different day from test.) Put each puppy individually in the pen and on the other end of the pen put a wind-up toy. Record the puppy's response to the toy and how long it takes him to investigate the toy if he does.

4. Get two puppies and put them alone in the pen with a juicy beef bone. Let them compete one on one for the bone. Match aggressive puppies first. If they both share the bone, they are equal in their "pecking order." (Pecking order is a term that originated, I think, with chickens. In a barnyard, young chickens (roosters) establish early an order of dominance, that is, which young rooster is most dominant, which is second, etc. down to the weakest, most docile. This socialization is common to most of the animal kingdom. Cows, for example, horses, dogs, they all go through the same procedure. Ironically enough, there is absolutely no correlation between peckeing order and which Pit Bull pup will grow up to be the gamest pit dog or the most skilled. You may find it hard to believe, but the shyest, most docile pup may turn out to be the best pit dog in the litter. That is absolutely true. There is no way you can determine gameness or pit ability in a pup. The same is true with roosters. Basic personality, however, has pretty much developed by eight weeks. Those pups who are aggressive at this age will usually be aggressive when they grow up. Those who are shy will tend to be shy when they grow up.

5. Play with each pup individually with an old rag (or a squirrel skin would be better). Record how long each pup plays with the rag and the ones that shake it most vigorously. Keep hold of it and tug easily on it – don't be too rough; you can permanently damage the puppy, especially his teeth because they're easy to loosen.

6. On a different day repeat the above test, but suddenly shout (not too loud) and slap the ground. Record each pup's response. Some may persist and become even more vigorous in their play with the rag.

7. Put each puppy on a low box, low enough that he can jump off if he will. Record each puppy's response. Does he cringe and wimper or cry or does he sniff and explore around? When he gets to the edge does he immediately jump off; does he think about it for a bit, obviously unsure and finally jump; or does he cry? I like the puppy that thinks about it for a bit

and then jumps – he's both smart and courageous. The pup that immediately jumps might be braver but stupid. I don't know; that's just how I feel. The point is you look for the pup whose personality suits you. After all you'll be living with the Pit Bull for a good long time.

8. Put each pup invidually in an empty room and stand silently in an opposite corner and see how long it takes the puppy to come to you . Quietly walk around the edge of the room. A good pet will want to follow you around. Again, record the puppies' responses.

9. Do the same test as above, but this time suddenly turn and squat down and vigorously clap your hands and maybe give a little yell.Record the degree to which the puppy is intimidated. Remember the puppy that is not intimidated at all may be a good Schutzhund dog (although more training time will be needed), but may not be the best pet. Actually, the better Schutzhund potential is probably the one who seems a little intimidated at first, but quickly recovers. For Schutzhund work, you want a smart dog, very responsive to people. (See the Schutzhund chapter for a description of exactly what Schutzhund entails.)

10. There are other tests you can find in the books mentioned and also in the <u>Schutzhund</u> book by Susan Earwig. The tests I listed give you a general idea of what you are trying to do. You can fabricate tests of your own - just remember to be very, very careful not to harm the pups; they are just babies. Better to be overly cautious than sorry. I mentioned keeping a notebook. The design of your notebook is a matter of individual preference, but I have a few suggestions. List the puppies' names across the top and traits you are testing down the side. Put each day's test and each week on separate pages. A primary principle to remember is that paper is relatively inexpensive. Spread out your notes and write large. Don't squeeze your notes in small spaces. You want to be able to easily review your notes and compare the puppies' performance over a period of weeks. You could set up a numbering system for traits observed, such as 1-excellent, 2-very good, 3-good, 4-poor, 5-bad, or you could be more specific. For example, if recording the puppies' reactions to sudden loud noise, you could write out a concise description of their reaction similar to the following:

>shows interest and scampers toward noise; picks up ears, curious expression
>stays still, ignores noise
>cringes, tail down, stays still
>cringes, tail down, runs away to you for protection
>cringes, tail down, runs away to solitary place to hide

You may or may not want to be that specific. You may want the full description combined with a numerical rating. Notice, by the way, the category ignores noise." This may, on the surface, appear to be a desireable response in that the pup is not at all intimidated by the noise. In Susan Earwig's book, *Schutzhund,* this reaction is said to be undesireable. The observation is based on the research of a Dr. Joseph Bodingbauer, who seems to be a pretty knowledgeable guy. He was a professor of veterinary medicine in Vienna and has done extensive research, both on his own and in conjunction with other noteables. Dr. Bodingbauer has found a distinct difference between courage and fearlessness. The fearless dog is not afraid and so will have an indifferent reaction to danger because he does not recognize the danger. This reaction, Dr. Bodingbauer postulates, is due to an insufficiently developed self-preservation instinct or inadequate response development. The elusive trait of courage is indicated when a puppy is willing to confront a perceived menace or at least a novel situation and faces the threat even though he is aware of the possibility of retreat.

Well, I hope you have benefited from all this information. It's the "in" thing with people who are into obedience training. I think that Pit Bull folks can benefit from this knowledge, too. As I mentioned, you can find this information in many of the current, popular dog books and magazines. Few people take the time to use it, though. I know a lot of Pit Bull fanciers that spend the better part of their lives dealing with Pit Bulls, however, and I feel they can truly benefit from the early stress treatment and temperament testing. It takes a lot of time and work, but you will get out of it exactly what you put into it. If you invest a year of your life in your Pit Bull pup, you will be greatly rewarded. I think that if you build that strong foundation by working on the Pit Bull's character in his first year of life, it's downhill from there.

After picking your pup, the socialization and character training continue when you bring him home. The ideal time is between seven and eight weeks - earlier than that and the pup does not get enough dog socialization and will have trouble as an adult getting along with other dogs - later than that and the dog tends to be too dog-oriented and has trouble adjusting to humans. The puppy is like an infant and forms his first impressions of you and his environment during the initial months in his new home. Patience is probably the most important quality an owner needs to be successful. If you are firm, fair, consistent, and confident in raising your pup, he will instinctively respond and will be more stable. It is also very important that your puppy be socialized as much as possible with both people and other dogs. You'll find in the bibliography, under "general," the book by the Monks of New Skeet, excellent material for any dog owner. The writers are a group of Monks that live in relative seclusion in their village in New York state. One of their major sources of income is breeding champion (show and obedience) German Shepherds. They also take in problem (behavioral) dogs for special training. The Monks have researched quite a lot of studies of wolves in their wild habitat and applied their observations of how wolves (so closely related to the domesticated dog) behave in the pack. The Monks feel that dogs are happier, will have a more stable personality, and will be more trainable and predictable, if they live with the family as though they are "pack" members - subservient pack members, not leaders. They accomplish this by having their dogs live with them all day long, from the time they are puppies. Their dogs sleep with them in their rooms and follow them around all day. Of course it isn't practical for most of us to go to the same extremes, and not everyone wants to. Their observations resulting from their rapport with the dogs, however, can benefit any dog owner. For example, they have observed how pack leaders control other members and mothers control their young. Young wolves must learn the rules of nature in order to survive and they learn very quickly from their mother and older wolves in the pack. The monks never swat their puppies with a newspaper or use other conventional methods of discipline. A mother wolf conveys the idea to her pups that they shouldn't engage in certain behavior by grabbing them by the back of the neck, growling, and shaking them. When a young wolf gets out of order, the leader controls him, usually with a low growl and eye contact. The leader stares directly into the young wolf's eyes. Before reading the Monks' book, I had always heard that you should never stare into a dog's eyes - that it can make them shy or even neurotic: but, according to the Monks, eye contact can be effectively used, if correctly used. You simply smile and look happily into their eyes and use positive voice tones when the puppy pleases you (for example, coming to you when you call him), so that he associates that type of eye contact with positive, happy moments. Scowl and stare daggers at him when he misbehaves. In other words, in many ways you are handling your puppy very similarly to the way you instinctively handle a human child. If you spend enough time with your pup, you can have this type of understanding with him.

  An adult Pit Bull is often quite stubborn in addition to being very hard to teach. I'm not saying, by the way, that all Pit Bulls are that way - not by a long shot. Many of them just naturally fit into a home environment with very little training – it's just that when a Pit Bull is the frolicky type and stubborn, he is exceptionally hard to live with in a home. My Pit Bull's mother is very quiet and docile in her owner's home and spends most of the time laying in the corner or at her master's feet. Morochito's brother is the same way, but Morochito has never been. He's always been rambunctious and he's stubborn to boot. I spent some time with him but not enough. I don't want others to make the same mistake. Start early with your pup and take no chances. For minor infringes I merely grab the pup by the nap of the neck and shake (not too hard) and say, "No" in a low gutural tone. If your Pit Bull does something you consider particularly wrong, add to the discipline by rolling the pup over on his back, pin him down and stare sternly into his eyes and firmly (doesn't have to be too loud) announce, "No!" (I think you should make a <u>short</u> list of what you think should be very definite no-no's. For example I would suggest that a serious crime would be chewing on household items, like the corner of the couch or - probably the most tempting of all to a Pit Bull pup - one of the children's furry stuffed animals or dolls. Another bad habit is running around and jumping in the house. You had better curtail this early with your pup because, believe you me, when he's an adult he can literally tear a house to pieces in a short time just playing. The discipline for serious crimes is very similar to the manner in which control is established over a young wolf who's overstepped his bounds. You will get better results with this type of discipline and you'll establish mind dominance (but not the fear dominance that harsher discipline can instill). Establishing mind dominance will not make your Pit Bull shy or less game. To the contrary, just as a child that is reared in a home where they receive firm, but fair, consistent discipline will tend to be actually more secure and hence tend to be more confident in his interactions with his environment, so too will a dog. Let me share with you my own mistakes. I do not fight my Pit Bull, as I said; he is a pet. As a puppy, he had plenty of people socialization, not much with other dogs, though. I spent more time conditioning the pup than I did in obedience training, even though I had no intention of fighting him I took him with me when I did my roadwork - both running and bicycling. I believe that unconsciously I spoiled him a bit because I didn't want to ruin his confidence (a mistaken notion on my part). I was wrong. I've paid for it by owning a Pit Bull that I love dearly but is often hard to live with. <u>Proper obedience training would not have had a negative effect on his confidence - to the contrary, it would have been positive. This book will not deal extensively with obedience techniques, but the biblioaraphy lists the books that are currently</u> more popular. My suggestion is that, for whatever pupose you want your Pit Bull, you read as much as you can about obedience, as soon as possible, if you haven't already. I think that, rather than confine yourself to the opinions of one author, you need to read at least two books and subscribe to *Off-Lead* magazine.

Morochito giving his master a kiss - Pit Bull style

Some Pit Bulls were practically born fighting; they are ready to fight any animal that moves from the time they are eight or nine weeks old - Morochito was like that; but most Pit Bulls are not. Contrary to the belief of most people unfamiliar with Pit Bulls, they usually will not fight until around a year old, some two years or even older. If they are allowed to play and frolic with other breeds very often as pups, most of them will grow up to be a perfect dog pet (defined as a dog that never starts a fight with another dog, in fact is quite tolerant of an aggressive dog trying to pick a fight if he doesn't go too far, never intimidated by any dog, but will finish off any real threat from a dog of any other breed). You can also socialize Pit Bulls with others of their own breed, if you know them. You can't just put together two aggressive or competitive Pit Bulls, even pups. A lot of them will play together and never fight – I've seen it, plenty of it. In fact, I've been truly in awe of how non-aggressive most Pit Bulls are. You can't tell, though - I know of one three-month-old bitch who killed her litter sister in their pen - tore her to pieces. You can tell by observing a litter, though - using the methods I outlined earlier. If you want a pet, you simply don't bring home the little fighter. Let me put it this way. I know a

Pit Bull fancier, who has some very well-bred pit dogs - some of the best. He has one that is a real big catch-weight dog - big head and powerful jaws, and if you put him in a pit and match him, he'll go until he drops; but you can put a puppy or a little dog of another breed in his pen and he'll just play with the dog. He's just as friendly as could be - seems like a big baby. He's got another Pit Bull - a little black bitch that's a killer. She'll attack anything and she'll fight it until she kills it, whether a puppy or whatever. She's also a game fighter. The owner has been around Pit Bulls for 20 years and made this statement to me: "You can never figure Pit Bulls; every time I think I've got the perfect breeding program, I get disappointed - every time I start to give up, I come up with a beauty. They're all different, they're smart, and any man who tells you he knows all about Pit Bulls is a liar." The point I'm trying to emphasize is that a Pit Bull can be a dangerous animal, but careful selection, depending on what you want, can give you all you want in a pet and not sacrifice any gameness.

I recommend you take your Pit Bull with you wherever you go, as much as possible, beginning as soon as you bring him home. Take him with you when you go to the store - purposefully stop at a laundromat where there are generally a lot of people - anything to expose him to as varied an environment as possible. I believe it adds significantly to their intelligence. It is an established fact that a human who lives in a restricted environment will not perform as well on intelligence tests (a generality of course). I believe you'll have a more open, inquisitive Pit Bull if you give him more socialization and in addition you'll have a dog that will be better able to solve problems on a canine level. We learn primarily by observation (with our eyes) but a dog learns primarily with his nose. I think that when you take your puppy out for his walks (See the chapter on Conditioning), you should take him to different places. I used to take Morochito to the park one day, to the woods in back of the kids' school another, over to the high school football field, all kinds of different places, and let him sniff around. Get him used to his leash as early as you can, and take him to crowded places like shopping centers, malls, etc. - places where there are crowds of people, noisy cars, and mass confusion. With your calm attitude and example, he'll soon learn to be composed and not lose his head, especially if you selected correctly. The Pit Bull is a breed that is particularly adaptable to this type of "stress" treatment. Many of them will not get excited at all. They are not very easily intimidated, but be very careful. Pay attention to everything that's going on around you and make <u>sure</u> the pup doesn't get in trouble and get harmed. That can make the Pit Bull permanently shy. In any event, there will be an increase in their intelligence level. You may have trouble believing that all this varied environment exposure will actually improve intelligence -probably merely adjustment to the conditions you say. Dr. Michael Fox has done some research that may interest you - read about it in his book in the chapter, "How Your Dog's Brain and Behavior Develop." He found that when either rats or dogs receive "superstimulation" when young, their brains mature faster and tend to be larger than normal, contain more and larger nerve cells with longer and more elaborate connecting processes. He shows pictures of young Beagles' brains. When animals are deprived of experiences, their brains are smaller and their nerve cells are smaller, fewer in number, and have less connecting processes than normal.

My daughter Lisa and my son Michael with Morochito – 5/82

A little more insight into the Pit Bull's personality. I had quite a problem with my Pit Bull when he was a pup, with chewing. I was unaware, at the time, of the disciplinary measures I outlined in this chapter. Something that helped a lot and has nearly completely solved the problem (He "forgets" every once in a while) was giving him a box of toys that I keep behind my easy chair in the den.

I have an old leather shoe, leather belts, leather strips, a tennis ball inside a sock (that toy doesn't last lon.), pieces of balls (large and small) that he has already chewed up - all kinds of things. This gives him an alternative to chewing on the kids' toys and other household items. In addition, I had a box when he was a puppy that I kept in the backyard while we were away at work. I rotated the toys in it about every other day because he's always been quick to grow tired of a toy. In fact, it seems to me that I have seen a lot of dogs of other breeds that have a "favorite" toy that they prefer and play with all the time. Most Pit Bulls that I have seen that have toys of any kind, seem to tire of them pretty quickly. Two exceptions - most Pit Bulls dearly love an automobile tire. They love to grab the inside rim of the tire and chew it up, shake it around, and pick up the tire and carry it. The other toy is a rubber tire tube (auto, or better still, a truck tube) hanging from a tree limb. They like to jump up in the air so that they have to hang off the ground. Pit Bulls love it. As I have mentioned before, however, you just can't figure them out - they all have their own personalities; they're all different. Morochito, for example, won't have a thing to do with these types of toys by themselves. If you play with him he will tug on the innertube. I don't know why it used to worry me that he didn't seem typical in that respect. I shouldn't have worried; he has since demonstrated that he's all Pit Bull.

Now there are three things in life that dog loves: fighting, road-work, and affection. He just dearly loves to fight, but unfortunately (in his opinion) he doesn't get to do that too much. There are on occasion unavoidable instances. For example, he has found the front door to be not very securely closed (Oh, the joy!) and dashed out to confront a cur- dog (non Pit Bull) on the street, but in most cases like that, the other dog isn't at all interested and won't even fight back - and usually screams bloody murder even though Morochito hasn't even taken hold - and then Morochito has to endure the wrath of his embarrassed master (His mistress is even worse!). I can't bear to see a Pit Bull pick on a cur dog, personally. It has no meaning and is cruel in my opinion. Morochito has his moments though. One day he and I were on the tail end of our roadwork (four miles running with me, followed by three miles on leash - with me on bike, him occasionally pulling me). It was early in the evening, but pitch dark. Suddenly, out of nowhere, some mongrel (looked like part St. Bernard to me) charged right into him, fighting. I'll bet it'll be a long, long time before that dog picks another fight, though. He surely made a mistake this time, although he was bigger than Morochito. Morochito was a living blur and before you could literally blink an eye, he threw the dog on the street and clamped down on his stifle and shook it like there was no tomorrow. You'd think the dog was a little rat. Well, the dog screamed - and I mean <u>screamed.</u> He finally grabbed Morochito's leg and bit. Morochito's tail then commenced to wag and although I was trying to get my breaking stick (which goes with us at all times) into his mouth, he began to shake again more vigorously and the dog kept hollering. This is a good time to inject some "words of wisdom." When you find yourself in a similar situation, you <u>must</u> keep your cool and be patient. If the dog is not too small, your Pit Bull isn't going to kill him very quickly - a dog is a very hardy animal, and you'd be surprised - it takes a lot to do one in. My vet has told me I would be surprised at the dogs he's seen brought in all battered up from automobile accidents - so bashed in a human would never survive, yet the dog will. Anyway, you'll have to wait a few minutes for the Pit Bull to pause a second. At the very first opportunity, straddle him and grab the thick folds of skin on his neck, or his collar, with your left hand (if you are right handed) and then with your right hand, push your breaking stick between his lips right in the corner of his mouth where his crunching teeth are, and pry his mouth open. You may have difficulty - be patient, keep prying, working the stick up and down - eventually you'll pry him loose. You must be quick or he'll immediately grab hold again. At that point, pull back and up with your hold on his neck while simultaneously dropping your right arm under his belly, and pick him up and turn away. Do this as quickly as you can. At all times keep your eyes on the other dog, as a cur dog is normally in an extreme case of panic. Quite often, out of fear and panic, he will bite you. (They can snap pretty quickly so be prepared to flick your hand back out of the way.) When you pull your Pit Bull off, the other dog will high-tail it. Just remember, you won't save the cur dog by panicking, hollering, and carrying on, nor will you accomplish anything by kicking or hitting your dog (unless you kick him so hard you break a rib or something -but he still won't let go) or pulling his tail, or lifting his back legs - that won't work with a Pit Bull. If he has hold of a little dog, you may not have much time because he may kill the dog, so act very quickly. You stand a chance of saving him if you have a breaking stick.(Which I think all Pit Bull owners should have no matter how docile they think their particular dog is, because you never know when you may be faced with an instance like what I'm describing. There are a whole lot of people who let their dogs run loose in the neighborhood and some of them think they are "king of the county"). Grab the Pit Bull from wherever and pull him between your legs, ignoring the little dog because he is not really a threat to you. Grab the Pit Bull by both sides of his head, by his jowls, and try to stop his shaking physically and with verbal commands. You may succeed in slowing him down momentarily. At that point, quickly insert the breaking stick and work away. If you should encounter a fight situation and do not have a breaking stick, there again be patient; circle around as the Pit Bull shakes and throws the dog around and at the first opportunity straddle him and grab him as I instructed for the larger dog as victim, and verbally command him to let go or "out." Sooner or later, most dogs will very momentarily let go in order to bite again, deeper or for a better hold. You must be alert and watch for that moment and pull him out immediately. The time you wait may seem like a real long time to you under the circumstances, when actually it may be only two or three minutes.

Needham's bitch Sunshine

Anyway, I broke Morochito loose and the big dog took off. By that time the people in the surrounding houses had all come running out thinking a dog had been run over and there was all kinds of excitement. So Morochito had a very good day, much to the expense of his poor master. I didn't say anything to him about it, though; I don't think I should try to ask him to stand there and let the other dog bite him!

Another thing Morochito loves is his roadwork. I take him around our neighborhood or to the cemetary (which is heavily wooded). At the cemetary I ride on my bike three or four miles while he runs free. It's all fenced in, no dogs. He runs all out most of the time, of his own volition. When we're getting ready to go for a run, he gets all excited and then stands very still to be fastened into his harness.

His third greatest pleasure is affection. He dearly loves to get a toy to chew on and sit at my feet while I study. (I should say on my feet - he literally lays down on my feet, rubbing against my legs. Seems he can't get close enough.) At 56 pounds he still tries to lay on my lap sometimes like he's a big baby.

Continuing with miscellaneous tips, here is something that may be of benefit to some of you. I have mentioned before, many times, that aggression has no correlation with gameness. I bring it up again here so that I can share some of the mistakes I made so that others might be spared some unhappy experiences. I assume that people who want a Pit Bull for a pet, although they don't want to fight them, enjoy the courage and game potential of their dog. There is a tendency in the novice owner, to be concerned - does my Pit Bull live up to the breed character? Can he really do it? As I have mentioned, my Morochito was a particularly aggressive pup. I did not allow him any socialization with other dogs because I had been informed that Pit Bulls must be kept away from other dogs because they will fight. When we went for our runs in the park, however, I let him run off lead because I figured that as a pup he couldn't do much damage to an adult dog, which he couldn't. On occasion, however, he would spot a dog and would charge into him like a bolt of lightning. I figured it was just puppy play, which it was; he never took hold or even bit the dog. He loved to wrestle the dog to the ground and grab him by the throat and growl at him, daring him to move - at which point I would catch up with him and pull him off. I must admit, however, that I was very pleased with his ability to wrestle adult dogs, much larger than he, to the ground - Dobermans, Shepherds, a Collie, a Schnauzer. The occasions were relatively rare and fun to me when they happened since neither of the dogs really got hurt. I figured that when he grew older I'd have to keep him away from other dogs anyway, so no need to discourage this puppy play. When he was 15 to 18 months old, the age at which most Pit Bulls begin to become interested in fighting (although I mentioned that many wait until two or three years old), he still would not take hold of a cur dog, but would only play. His idea of play, however, is very rough. I knew he was playing because he was growling and carrying on and I knew that if he meant business, he'd make no sound whatsoever except for an occasional snort or grunt. I also knew he was playing because he didn't usually take hold unless the other dog bit him and made him mad.(Of course you can't blame the other dog for biting such a terrifying barnstormer.) But the owner of the dog he chose to play with would understandably be very irate - I would be, too, if it were my Collie or whatever. In addition, Morochito sounded like a herd of Tasmanian devils and really appeared to be pretty awful. So, beginning with his last embarrassing incident in the park at about six months old, I kept him on a leash. Oh, there was one occasion I'd like to relate to you. Down the street from our house there is a Shepherd that's a real bully in the neighborhood. He'll bite any dog or pup that's scared of him. I didn't think much of that dog because several years ago he used to love to pick on my wife's little mongrel dog, Sandy. She was about the size of a Dachshund and scared of her own shadow. That Shepherd would chase after her and bite her on the rear end continuously. Well, one day when Morochito was about nine months old, and we were doing our road-work, Morochito on leash, the Shepherd and his buddy, a smaller dog about the size of Morochito but not nearly so sturdy), went after Morochito. Well, I let go of Morochito's leash. Now I hope that those of my readers who are totally opposed to the fighting aspect of Pit Bulls will be patient with me and realize that I know better now, **and that I'm sharing this experience in order to point out the fallacy** of my thinking and help others who will have similar feelings - I feel there are many of them. The Shepherd thought he was picking on a puppy. Wow, did he make a mistake! He attacked from the front and the other dog circled around and charged Morochito's rear. Morochito was a blur. He hit that Shepherd so hard he knocked him down and grabbed his leg and shook - the Shepherd hollering to beat the band - at which time the other dog got there. Morochito immediately spun around and went after him. The Shepherd took off for the high hills and the other dog turned tail and took off after him. I had grabbed Morochito's leash as he lunged toward the other dog so he wouldn't get away.

However, as Morochito got older, I began to get concerned. Although I didn't want him to hurt a dog, I was worried that because he didn't have the awesome bite Pit Bulls are supposed to have, he wasn't a good example of a Pit Bull, didn't live up to the heritage of his grandparents and great grandparents. At this stage of his life, however, I kept him on a leash whenever we went for our roadwork, not wanting to get into trouble. I attended many pit fights and saw some real hard, deep biters - and I saw some who were not very hard (for Pit Bulls) biters. I began to worry that Morochito was like the latter. Then when he was about nineteen months old I made another mistake. Boy, I hate to tell this one, but it might help someone who finds themselves in a similar situation. One day I brought Morochito with me when I went to visit a man I had met who seemed to know quite a bit about pit fighting. I was going around talking to every pit man I could find in order to gather as much information as possible for this book. This man had retired from pit fighting although he would roll his dogs and game test them. He gave me quite a bit of information and helped me out a lot. Of course I had to bring my Pit Bull in the house and show him off and show off his pedigree. When our visit was over, we went over to look at his prize dog, a 45-pound, white Pit. The dog was a retired fighter who the man claimed had been a good one in his day - said he was a hard biter (showed me where he had put holes in his galvanized steel water bucket). When he saw my dog he casually walked up to the edge of his pen (knowing he was restricted). Morochito immediately lunged on his leash and got away from me and ran up to the fence, trying to get at that Pit Bull. I didn't hurry to get him because I didn't see how either one could get into any trouble since a chain link fence separated them. My friend hollered at me to get my Bulldog quick because they can still fight through the fence. I still didn't hurry, though, because I just didn't see any danger. He was right, however, and I was dreadfully wrong. Morochito made the mistake of sticking his paw through the fence. That Pit Bull immediately moved - very quickly - and latched onto Morochito's paw, and wouldn't let go. For a few moments, I didn't realize what had happened, and I ambled over to pull Morochito away because he was lunging against the fence hard. Then I saw that the other dog had hold of his paw. I reached through the fence and tried to pry him off, but of course couldn't do it. The guy looked around for a stick but couldn't find one; he finally remembered he had a breaking stick in his barn, went and got it, climbed over the fence, and pryed his dog off. I did find out, rather painfully, that Morochito is game. I was told by the vet that a dog's paw, especially his pad, is one of his more sensitive areas. There are more nerve endings there and he feels pain more there. His pad was torn off and he had been fanged deep into his paw - a real spike hole. Well, Morochito didn't holler or even whine once the whole time. He kept chewing the fence and even got a small piece of the other Pit Bull's lip. When we got him loose, he was raring to go and it was all I could do to pull him away and get him back to the car. He wanted to go after that Bulldog bad. Well, that was the second time his dumb master messed him up. He lost his toe as a result of infection but has no problems from it now. I was worried that he wouldn't enjoy his runs like he used to - turned out okay, though: he can run just as well and his foot doesn't get tired on long runs, but one hard lesson learned. (He could have lost more than a toe.) Don't let Pit Bulls who are strangers get too close to each other even if they are separated by a chain-link fence.

 I also inadvertnetly found out that Morochito also has strength and ability. One day when he was about 26 months old, we went for an early morning run at our local high school's running track. The track adjoins the football field and a practice field. (This is the incident I referred to earlier). The whole area is enclosed in a high chain-link fence and there are usually no dogs there, especially in the morning. This was very early on a Sunday morning. Well, it so happened that while Morochito and I were on the other end of the field, this guy came in the gate with his Pit Bull. (He was visiting a friend in Greensboro.) Morochito took one look and away he went. He charged into that Pit Bull. Well, that was as big a Pit Bull as I've seen. His owner said he was 70 pounds (chain weight) and he was line-bred Lonzo's Mike (a very well-bred Dibo dog who was a very game pit fighter and, more importantly, an excellent producer – he's local). I thought Morochito was done for. That Pit Bull immediately shook off the little skin hold Morochito had and rooted deep into Morochito's throat- fortunately, he wasn't as hard a biter as some – but he was hard enough. He bulled Morochito around and it seemed Morochito couldn't get out. They were going too hard for us to get them apart. Neither of us had a breaking stick. After a little bit, Morochito got mad, though, and that was the beginning of a different story. He shook loose of the hold, then he came in low using his leverage and pushed that Pit Bull about ten feet back and over the edge of a slight hill into some brambles. We couldn't get to them there, but Morochito was going to beat the band - had that Pit Bull by the nose shaking him, but the dog was too big for him and he couldn't barnstorm him. Finally they got out of the brambles and again Morochito tried to barnstorm; still couldn't reach them to separate them. Morochito found that he couldn't wrestle this dog down, and that when this dog bit, he didn't let go and it was hard to get loose. The dog made a mess of Morochito's front leg, shaking it good. Morochito had the idea now, though, and he got loose. They both vied for position with head holds - and everytime we'd grab them, they'd twist out of our hands. Morochito's tail was up and he was really enjoying himself. Instinct is a funny thing. At first Morochito made quite a few mistakes and had primarily skin holds. He was also thrown all over the place by a Pit Bull that outweighed him by 14 pounds. (He was in fair condition - he and I were running/bicycling around eight miles a day.) But now it was a different story. Morochito had discovered how to use his legs and was pushing the bigger dog all around. He had learned right much in just a few minutes. Now, whenever that dog dived for his legs, he'd tuck them in so that he couldn't get them and then he'd go after the dog's nose, or general head area if he couldn't get the nose. He found that if he went after the other dog's legs too slowly, the dog would also tuck his legs in. But he found that if he dived at his head hard then suddenly dived for his front legs, he could grab the leg up high near the shoulder and shake hard and throw that big old Pit Bull down hard. Soon he was slamming the dog very hard to the ground and shaking good so that the other dog couldn't get to his nose. He also had learned by now to bite hard and buried his fangs into the muscle. In the meantime the other guy had run over to the woods to try to find a breaking stick we could use because it looked like it'd be a good while before we'd get them out of holds. When he got back with the stick, the dogs had mouth holds - Morochito had a good hunk of the other dog's mouth. We had a heck of a time prying him off, but we finally got them loose. I had found that Morochito is basically a leg dog, shakes hard, bites hard, but doesn't keep consistently going for the legs - he waits for his opportunity and he protects his nose when he does go for the legs. He made a mess of that bigger Pit Bull, but he was okay in a couple weeks. Morochito's mistress wasn't too happy with either one of us. We were both in hot water (again)! Morochito's throat bothered me. He looked like a buffalo at first, the folds of skin hung down low, flapping around, but in three or four days it was back to normal. His leg was swollen and he limped badly. I restricted him from all roadwork and just walked him around the front yard to empty out his first couple days, then forced him to walk the rest of the week when we went to the park. He didn't like that much. He kept his bad leg up in the air - but he lunged, pulled, and did his level best to run with his other three legs.

Folks, I probably shouldn't disclose some of the dumb things I've done, but I'll sacrifice any image I might have created of myself in order to help others. I've been lucky in all these incidents because (in my admittedly biased, egotistical opinion) Morochito has an exceptionally strong constitution and so he was not permanently damaged, but the auto accident (in the introduction chapter) when he was a puppy could have ruined him, made him shy for life. I've seen it happen with well-bred Pit Bulls. The other incidents could have had negative effects on his personality if they had happened when he was younger (and they sure weren't planned, so they could have). The point is, never let your Pit Bull off lead unless you have trained him to recall (come when you call him) at any time under any circumstances. When I run Morochito now, he's on leash and he does his windsprints on leash with me on my bike. The other point is that I was foolish to worry about Morochito's abilities or gameness or whether he'd bite hard. Rather than keeping him away from other dogs when he was a puppy, I should have given him plenty of supervised socialization. If I didn't teach him anything else, I should have taught him to come on recall. The trick is to begin as a puppy and give him plenty of positive repetition. Never call him to you to punish him - he won't make the correlation that you are punishing him for what he was doing. He'll get the idea that when you call him and he responds, he gets punished. If he does something wrong, go to him if possible, but whatever you do, don't call him to you and punish him. That point is so very, very important, let me repeat it – DON'T EVER CALL YOUR PIT BULL TO YOU AND THEN PUNISH HIM. One of the best ways to expedite learning to come on recall is to have your family or friends gather around in a circle and squat down (You don't appear overbearing to a puppy then) and take turns calling the puppy by name. He will soon get the idea and will love it. You also are beginning his conditioning. You can also use treats. Now I know you've probably heard to never train a dog with treats because they'll depend on the treat for performance. Take away the treat and they won't perform. But dog training techniques have really progressed in recent years and continue to progress at a rapid pace. Those who have had some problems when using treats in the past (such as developing an animal that learns quickly but is inconsistent in responding after having learned, or responds only for a treat) can obviate these problems by using differential reinforcement. This is a term that is used by a branch of psychology called behavioral analysis. Many modern dog trainers have picked it up. It is based on the fact that an animal learns much quicker when he's motivated with treats. In the wild, much of an animal's behavior involves survival which includes getting food. So commands become more meaningful when the animal is rewarded for correct response with a treat - couple it with praise and you magnify the learning. With differential reinforcement, however, as the animal learns the correct response and it becomes habitual (imprinted) (Animals do not rationalize nearly as much as humans, they respond more instinctivel.), you gradually reduce the treat. For example, begin giving praise but no treat every third response. Do not routinely withhold the treat every third time, however, or the animal will learn that.You vary treat reinforcement, withholding it, sometimes several times consecutively, sometimes not. The animal is never sure whether he'll get a treat or not. Gradually, over a period of time, the treat is completely phased out and no longer needed or used. You can, on very rare occasions, give a treat. This type of training tends to produce much more enthusiastic responses with less hesitation or balking. The "untrainable" animals like domestic house cats have been successfully trained with this technique. A man who is recognized as one of the best trainers of big cats (lions, tigers, etc.) is Gunther Gabel-williams, the master wild animal trainer with Ringling Brothers Barnum and Bailey Circus. He has been very successful in training lions, tigers, and elephants to perform using food rewards. Even birds can be taught to perform with food rewards.

Carnahan's Red Cole

As a manual for owners of Pit Bull dogs, this book suggests various tips for raising a Pit Bull to be a pet. Without proper obedience training, you must keep your Pit Bull chained at all times. I'm not suggesting you cannot enjoy your Pit Bull under those conditions. I purely love my Pit Bull and we have a heck of a time together. He stays chained to a running cable in the backyard but comes in the house almost every day. We run almost every day also and sometimes go for long-distance runs. But realize that if your Pit Bull doesn't receive the socialization and obedience training (and it will have to be more extensive, I believe, than with other breeds), you'll have to keep him chained. In any event, it is beyond the scope of this book to go into a detailed obedience program, so consult several sources, make notes and references, and make out a program of your own.

Anyway, let me continue with miscellaneous suggestions. I also suggest that even if you do not plan to compete in obedience trials, pulling contests, or Schutzhund, you ought to keep your dog conditioned (See chapter one) and provide proper nutrition (Also see chapter one). As I mentioned in each of these chapters, there is no question about it - proper exercise has proven to have a significant, positive effect on the mental attitude of humans as well as on physical well-being. More ancl more Americans are finding out that exercise and proper nutrition eliminate sluggish feelings and actually make you feel happier. Well, animals are the same. If you have a nice plump Pit Bull, to me you are being cruel. Mr. Gary Hammonds wrote a short article on the subject entitled: "Is Fat Beautiful?" quoted as follows:

> Since the evolution of the "big dog" fad, among the American "Pit" Bull Terrier fanciers I have seen more and more dogs that look like a cross between the Goodyear Blimp and a male walrus. While the over-sized, over-stuffed bull dogs may look good to some, generally speaking, they are not the physically fit, healthy animals some might think.
> The fat bull dog is more succeptible to everything than his lean counterpart. There are some instances when cold temperatures dictate more weight, but I dare say, not to the extent that I have seen. The dog's fatty tissue gives him a head start on respiratory, heart and kidney problems, not to mention a much better chance for heat stroke.
> Overweight dogs do not just happen, but are made that way by over-feeding, reinforced by lack of exercise. Generally speaking, if the American "Pit" Bull Terrier is in good health and free of parasites, his ribs will show slightly, covered by a moderate layer of fatty tissue.
> A lean stud dog will perform his duties better, with a higher reproductive rate, than his overweight cousin. Likewise, the brood bitch that is overweight will come nearer having trouble whelping her consistently smaller litters than the lean dog. Most significant of all, your lean pet will outlive the fat dog, usually by five to six years. Even the moderately fat dog will be subject to more problems and be shorter lived than the lean to underweight dog.
> Do yourself and your dog a favor - cut down on their feed and exercise them more. If not now, start next spring - they will do better next summer for it and will conceivably be around longer for your enjoyment. --------------
> Gary J. Hammonds, November 11, 1977

Most Pit Bull fanciers who own combat dogs don't have to be told this - they know the value of proper health and conditioning, and they also know that a thin Pit Bull lives longer. That's why you read these newspaper stories about "half-starved dogs being fought in the pit." Actually, what you have is a superbly conditioned, healthy, happy animal. But pet owners inevitably feed their dogs too much. When I took Morochito to obedience school, everyone was constantly onto me about how thin he was. They kept asking me what was wrong him. Their dogs were, to me, unbelievably fat. The lesson was just an hour long; yet we had to take a break half way through, usually, "to rest the dogs." This was especially true when we had them going over jumps. Morochito always sat alertly, looking around, waiting for something interesting to happen while most of the others laid on the ground panting. One time, when I was playing with him during break time, a lady mentioned to me that I ought to let him rest. When I told her that we came to the lesson after we had finished an eight-mile run, the last half of which was all-out, me on a bicycle, she was astounded! But I remember one summer, when I took him for a run after we had returned from vacation. He had stayed chained up in the backyard for about two weeks and my friend had fed him much too much because she thought he was too skinny. He wasn't real fat, but was heavier than usual. It was a hot day and after five miles he was hyperventilating badly. I had to walk him back and was scared he was sick or something. He was okay though. I soon had him lean and conditioned again.

I know that the last time we went on vacation, I left strict instructions for my friend not to feed in excess of three cups a day -two in the morning, one in the evening. (Morochito weighed about 56 pounds.) She followed my instructions, but when I returned she said to me, "Bob, I love you dearly and all that, but if you don't feed that poor dog, I'm calling the humane society!" (She had the same notion another friend of mine did.) She was kidding, of course, about calling the humane society, but actually felt I was being eccentric because my Pit Bull's ribs show. But since I work out with him, I can tell the difference. I think you can have fun conditioning your dog. Pretend you're conditioning him for a match and see if you can get him in peak condition just for the fun of it.

Well, friends, that's about it on the pet chapter. If you follow the advice in this chapter, your life will be made richer. You can develop a champion at whatever your Pit Bull endeavors, I do believe. The next three chapters will show you some aspects of utilizing Pit Bulls that you might consider if you have the time and you <u>really</u> want to enjoy your dog. I began this chapter, rather dramatically, with a pretty negative picture of the Pit Bull. Let me end it with what appears to be a true story of another Pit Bull. It's a short story that appears in a book by James Thurber entitled *Carnival*, and is about a Pit Bull he owned as a child. The name of the story is "A Snapshot of a Dog."

    I ran across a dim photograph of him the other day, going through some old things. He's been dead twenty-five years. His name was Rex (my two brothers and I named him when we were in our early teens), and he was a bull terrier. "AN AMERICAN BULL TERRIER," we used to say, proudly, none of your English bulls. He had one brindle eye that sometimes made him look like a clown and sometimes reminded you of a politician with derby hat and cigar. The rest of him was white except for a brindle saddle that always seemed to be slipping off and a brindle stocking on a hind leg. Nevertheless, there was a nobility about him. He was big and muscular and beautifully made. He never lost his dignity even when trying to accomplish the extravagant tasks my brothers and myself used to set for him. One of these was the bringing of a ten-foot wooden rail into the yard through the back gate. We would throw it out into the assey and tell him to go get it. Rex was as powerful as a wrestler, and there were not many things that he couldn't manage somehow to get hold of with his great jaws and lift or drag to wherever he wanted to put them, or wherever we wanted them put. He could catch the rail at the balance and lift it clear off the ground and trot with great confidence toward the gate. Of course, since the gate was only four feet wide or so, he couldn't bring the rail in broadside. He found that out when he got a few terrific jolts, but he wouldn't give up. He finally figured out how to do it, by dragging the rail, holding onto one end, growling. He got a great, wagging satisfaction out of his work. We used to bet kids who had never seen Rex in action that he could catch a baseball thrown as high as they could throw it. He almost never let us down. Rex could hold a baseball with ease in his mouth in one cheek, as if it were a chew of tobacco.

 He was a tremendous fighter, but he never started fights. I don't believe he liked to get into them, despite the fact that he came from a line of fighters. He never went for another dog's throat but for one of its ears (that teached a dog a lesson), and he would get his grip, close his eyes, and hold on. He could hold on for hours. His longest fight lasted from dusk until almost pitch-dark, one Sunday. It was fought in East Main Street in Columbus with a large snarly nondescript that belonged to a big colored man. When Rex finally got his ear grip, the brief whirlwind of snarling turned to screeching. It was frightening to listen to and to watch. The Negro boldly picked the dogs up somehow and began swinging them around his head, and finally let them fly like a hammer in a hammer throw, but although they landed ten feet away with a great plump. Rex still held on.

The two dogs eventually worked their way to the middle of the tracks, and after a while one or three streetcars were held up by the fight. A motorman tried to pry Rex's jaws open with a switch rod; somebody lighted a fire and made a torch of a stick and held that to Rex's tail, but he paid no attention. In the end, all the residents and storekeepers in the neighborhood were on hand, shouting this, suggesting that. Rex's joy of battle, when battle was joined, was almost tranquil. He had a kind of pleasant expression during fights, not a vicious one, his eyes closed in what would have seemed to be sleep had it not been for the turmoil of the struggle. The Oak Street Fire Department finally had to be sent for - I don't know why nobody thought of it sooner. Five or six pieces of apparatus arrived, followed by a battalion chief. A hose was attached and a powerful stream of water was turned on the dogs. Rex held on for several moments more while the torrent buffeted him about like a log in a freshet. He was a hundred yards away from where the fight started when he finally let go.

The story of that Homeric fight got all around town, and some of our relatives looked upon the incident as a blot on the family name. They insisted that we get rid of Rex, but we were very happy with him, and nobody could have made us give him up. We would have left town with him first, along any road there was to go. It would have been different, perhaps, if he'd ever started fights, or looked for trouble, but he had a gentle disposition. He never bit a person in the ten strenuous years that he lived, nor ever growled at anyone except prowlers. He killed cats, that is true, but quickly and neatly and without especial malice, the way men kill certain animals. It was the only thing he did that we could never cure him of doing. He never killed, or even chased, a squirrel. I don't know why. He had his own philosophy about such things. He never ran barking after wagons or automobiles. He didn't seem to see the idea in pursuing something you couldn't catch, or something you couldn't do anything with, even if you did catch it. A wagon was one of the things he couldn't tug along with his mighty jaws, and he knew it. Wagons, therefore, were not a part of his world.

Swimming was his favorite recreation. The first time he ever saw a body of water (Alum Creek), he trotted nervously along the steep bank for awhile, fell to barking wildly, and finally plunged in from a height of eight feet or more. I shall always remember that shining, virgin dive. Then he swam upstream and back just for the pleasure of it, like a man. It was fun to see him battle upstream against a stiff current, struggling and growling every foot of the way. He had as much fun in the water as any person I have known. You didn't have to throw a stick in the water to get him to go in. Of course, he would bring back a stick to you if you did throw one in. He would even have brought back a piano if you had thrown one in.

That reminds me of the night, way after midnight, when he when a-roving in the light of the moon and brought back a small chest of drawers that he found somewhere - how far from the house nobody ever knew; since it was Rex, it could easily have been half a mile. There were no drawers in the chest when he got it home, and it wasn't a good one - he hadn't taken it out of anybody's house; it was just an old cheap piece that somebody had abandoned on a trash heap. Still, it was something he wanted, probably because it presented a nice problem in transportation. It tested his mettle. We first knew about his achievement when, deep in the night, we heard him trying to get the chest up onto the porch. It sounded as if two or three people were trying to tear the house down. We came downstairs and turned on the porch light. Rex was on the top step trying to pull the thing up, but it had caught somehow and he was just holding his own. I suppose he would have held his own till dawn if we hadn't helped him. The next day we carted the chest miles away and threw it out. If we had thrown it out in a nearby alley, he would have brought it home again, as a small token of his intenigty in such matters. After all, he had been taught to carry heavy wooden objects about, and he was proud of his prowess.

I am glad Rex never saw a trained police dog jump. He was just an amateur jumper himself, but the most daring and tenacious I have ever seen. He would take on any fence we pointed out to him. Six feet was easy for him, and he could do eight by making a tremendous leap and hauling himself over finally by his paws, grunting and straining; but he lived and died without knowing that twelve-and sixteen-foot walls were too much for him. Frequently, after letting him try to go over one for awhile, we would have to carry him home. He would never have given up trying.

There was in his world no such thing as the impossible. Even death couldn't beat him down. He died, it is true, but only as one of his admirers said, after "straight-arming the death angel" for more than an hour. Late one afternoon he wandered home, too slowly and too uncertainly to be the Rex that had trotted briskly homeward up our avenue for ten years. I think we all knew when he came through the gate that he was dying. He had apparently taken a terrible beating, probably from the owner of some dog he had got into a fight with. His head and body were scarred. His heavy collar with the teeth marks of many a battle on it was awry; some of the big brass studs in it were sprung loose from the leather. He licked at our hands and, staggering, fell, but got up again. We could see that he was looking for someone. One of his three masters was not home. He did not get home for an hour. During that hour the bull terrier fought against death as he had fought against the cold, strong current of Alum Creek, as he had fought to climb twelve-foot walls. When the person he was waiting for did come through the gate, whistling, ceasing to whistle, Rex walked a few wobbly paces toward him, touched his hand with his muzzle and fell down again. This time he didn't get up.

Haynes' Bloody Mary

My daughter Lisa handling Morochito

Catching a bull

Chapter 3: The Catch Dog

"Catch'em and Fetch'em - We catch and haul anything!" -Don Livingston

As an introduction to the Pit Bulldog as the epitome of the working dog, Mr. Gary Hammonds of Mansfield, Texas, has provided us with the following article entitled "The Catch Dog."

In today's automated, complicated world, what on earth would anyone do with a dog that's bred to catch cattle or hogs? Regardless of what the general concensus is, there is a great deal of demand for dogs to be used with livestock and the American "Pit" Bull Terrier is one of the best in the field.

During the 40's and 50's, nearly every farm or ranch in Texas had an American "Pit" Bull Terrier or at least a Pit Bull crossbred dog or two for over-all ranch use. His ability with livestock, varmits and stray dogs made him a priceless possession. During the late 60's there was a surge of popularity and many of the Leopard, Catahoula and Pit Bull crosses were replaced by the pure American "Pit" Bull Terrier. Then came the "big dog" fad, where everyone wanted 80 and 90 pounders. Today, most people who use the dogs know that biggest isn't necessarily best and generally agree that the 40 to 50 pound dog can catch anything his 90 pound cousin can and usually do it with more finesse, much quicker and with less chance of doing permanent injury to the animal being caught.

Let us consider the "Catch Dog" and exactly what constitutes this highly specialized animal. Among the cattle dogs, there are basically two types. The heeler is one which moves the cattle by basically working the hind quarters, while the "Catch" type dog will also work the animal in this or any way necessary for the end result, but will go primarily for the nose when called upon to "catch." The American "Pit" Bull Terrier is unsurpassed by any member of the dog world in his ability to catch and hold cattle. This would even include his ancestor of old, the original Bulldog.

Another field for the "Catch Dog" is hogs, both wild and domestic. The "Catch Dog" is the ultimate animal in this field and makes this task look easy by taking hold of the hog's jowl, lip or ear and bringing "the bacon home." Many good dogs have been killed by an enraged boar, but most learn quickly and are hurt more by the terrain than the animal they are called upon to catch. Very often, the places where a hog will hold up are inaccessible to man and a dog will often take a beating in the underbrush before he gets full control of the hog, but as tough and wirey as he's bound to be, he is rarely bested by the hog and his environment.

While the American "Pit" Bull Terrier is often praised for his many abilities, I think none more impressive than a 40 pound dog catching a 1500 pound steer or 500 pound boar. One of the most amazing factors of their ability with cattle is a psycological one. For example, if you use an electrical cattle prod on a bull once a year, he will generally mind you as long as you have the prod or something like it. On the other hand, if the "Catch" dog ever brings him in or catches and holds him, then you can very well bet that he will mind that dog as long as he lives.

Many of the best "Catch" dogs have come from Texas and a few I'm personally familiar with would include Flory's Susan Renee, one of the best female cattle dogs ever. She is a full sister to the Plumber's Champion "Alligator" and had to be retired as she became overly aggressive as she got older. When we bred her to the "Macho" dog, it produced a very good litter, among which were several good "Catch" dogs, along with such great dogs as Anderson's Champion "Spade" and Skip McMichael's "Mesquite Sam." "Bruno," bred to Ackel's Katy Ann also produced some good "Catch" quality dogs, used for both hogs and cattle.

The American "Pit" Bull Terrier for use as a "Catch" dog is not for everyone. Only the top notch dog-man needs to obtain an untrained individual to use as a "Catch" dog. The owner must have tireless patience and a good deal of determination to acquire the much sought after end-product, which many feel to be well worth the effort.

Terry Flory and his Susan Renee, full sister to Ch. Alligator and dam to Ch. Spade, Mesquite Sam, Kizzie, Oilman's Diamond, and Gill's Thor

Hammonds' Kizzie from Macho and Susan Renee

Hammonds' Bruno – the cornerstone of the Hammond's line

Remember, the "Catch" dog must have all the trademarks of a battle dog. He must be game, with a high tolerance to pain and stress, have plenty of stamina and ability, but above all, he must be the cream of the I.Q. crop. Without a great deal of intelligence and trainability, the owner is fighting a lost cause because an animal with uncontrollable aggressiveness very well may cost his owner more than his worth.

In closing, I contend that regardless of this noble animal's fate, he will have to go down in history as one of the most successful breeding attempts ever made by man.

Hammonds' Rufus - an excellent catch dog

Hammonds' Bejoba from Rufus and Kizzie

To me, this activity, more than any other, brings out the Pit Bull's breeding. As we saw in the historical chapter, the dogs were originally bull-baiters. In my excitement to find out more about this catch dog business, I searched all over the country. I was fortunate to find, in South Carolina, a gentleman who has done a considerable amount of research on the subject. This man is Dr. I. Lehr Brisbin, a wildlife ecologist with the University of Georgia. As such, he works quite a bit in the Georgia swamps. Part of his research involves the study of the wild feral hogs. This man seems to lead an extremely interesting life. He is a great lover of dogs and does quite a bit of work with animals, some of which is fairly unique. He is active in the Staffordshire Terrier Club of America and has spoken in defense of our breed before the American Kennel Club.

Dr. Brisbin has a Bloodhound named Blue who is both a tracking and a conformation (show) champion. Blue also holds an all-time weight-pulling record for Bloodhounds which he obtained in 1975, pulling a weight of 500 pounds, quite a bit for any dog. Blue has been available to the police for search and find work. Dr. Brisbin also has a Laborador Retriever named Goose who helps him in the swamps researching ducks. Goose can be in the swamp mud one day and the next day he may win a ribbon at a conformation show. His work keeps him looking fine, I think. Lastly, Dr. Brisbin has an American Staffordshire Terrier, Pete, who helps him with his work with feral hogs, which is, of course, to the point. Here is the article Dr. Brisbin has provided for us:

The Use of the Pit Bull Terrier as a "Catch Dog" in the Hunting of Big Game and Control of Domestic Livestock

When the early settlers of the New World first brought the Pit Bull Terrier to North America, they suddenly found themselves in the harsh and inhospitable environment of the frontier, which offered little time or opportunity to indulge in the luxury of leisure-time sport such as gaming or pit fighting. While such sport undoubtedly did exist to some degree on the early American frontier the majority of pit fighting dogs which arrived in this country undoubtedly found themselves quickly thrust into a new role and form of service to their owners and their families.

Because of the selective breeding for stability of temperament (a "cool head"), in combination with strength, agility, stamina, and courage, these dogs soon became recognized as the ideal breed for the role of "varmit" and predator control on the early American farm or frontier homestead. An excellent example of the use of this breed in such a role is presented in the book, *The Yearling,* by Marjorie Kennan Rawlings. The "bulldog" in that story, "Rip," was indeed almost certainly a dog of pure Pit Bull ancestry; and in the later movie adaptation of the same book, an obviously purebred individual is used in all sequences on the screen. As depicted in this book, the role of such dogs, which were left free to roam the family homestead and barnyard, was to provide complete protection for the younger children and property from potentially dangerous wild predators and various intruding "varmits" - ranging from rats to raccoons and even including wolves and bears! A particularly striking sequence in the film adaptation of *The Yearling,* for example, shows the family's Pit Bull in full confrontation with an adult black bear! Moreover, the dog is successful in protecting his family by driving this bear away, and the film leaves little doubt that the conflict was not staged and that the dog did indeed prevail!

The fact that such "varmit-control" dogs of the early American frontier were apparently able to roam freely amongst the barnyard chickens, cats, and other domestic animals, however, indicates that some modification of temperament had already taken place in the breed, from that of the pure pit-fighter ancestors of the earlier gaming pits in Europe. Such fighting dogs were usually kept chained and thus maintained a radius of territory within which few of the smaller animals mentioned above were generally safe. The more peaceful early American frontier temperament of the breed, however, indicates that Pit Bulls are apparently capable of being so raised and socialized by careful training, discipline, and introduction into proper social environment, such that individual dogs may indeed be trusted loose around small children, cats, poultry, and other domestic livestock with being "turned on" into an attack syndrome unless circumstances so warrant. Unfortunately today, however, such an early frontier type of temperament in the breed is becoming all too rare - particularly in the case of certain show-breed lines of the American Staffordshire Terrier, where reports of serious attacks on small children are now becoming all too frequent. Perhaps efforts designed to retrain, breed, and develop the Pit Bull Terrier for such purposes as it originally served on the early American frontier may help select individuals with better temperaments and a higher degree of trustworthiness.

Besides changes in temperament and disposition, the selection and use of the Pit Bull Terrier as a "varmit-control" dog on the early American frontier undoubtedly also demanded a certain change in selective criteria of breeding for body size. In the pit-fighting game, matches were set and agreed to at specific weights. Dogs which exceeded these agreed-upon weights at match time were disqualified and forfeited the match. There was thus a strong selection pressure for breeding and producing dogs for the pits which were of a very specific and limited size, since dogs which exceeded certain body sizes were frequently unable to obtain matches at their higher weight levels. As a livestock and "varmit-control" dog on the frontier, however, bigger was undoubtedly better! As long as agility kept pace with size, the larger dogs were certainly better equipped to attack and stop marauding predators such as bears or wolves or even domestic bulls or boar hogs that may have threatened them. As will be discussed later, larger dogs with heavier body weights are also today invariably more desirable for use as "catch dogs" in hunts of wild or feral hogs, since their heavier body weights give them greater power and leverage to stop and maneuver their adversary once they have seized it. Such factors as these need careful consideration in the development of breed standards which may specify certain size or weight limits; and fanciers who would like to exhibit a dog in the conformation show ring as well as use him for the hunting and livestock control purposes for which his ancestors were earlier adapted, should not be penalized because their dog may exceed some specified limit of desirable size or weight which originally was established in the breed as part of its pit-fighting heritage. It is also interesting to note, in this regard, that the Staffordshire Bull Terrier which originated from similar, if not the same, pit-fighting stock of Europe as the Pit Bull or Staffordshire Terrier, has not undergone any such shift to increased body size. It is indeed likely that the fact that this latter breed was never used as a "varmit" or stock-control dog on the American frontier may have contributed to the tendency of the modern Staffordshire Bull Terrier to still show the smaller body size of its original ancestral pit-fighting stock. In many ways the past development and history of use of the Pit Bull and/or Staffordshire Terrier, including changes in temperament, working ability, and body size, would seem to dictate that the American Staffordshire Terrier of today, as it is currently registered by the American Kennel Club, probably more properly belongs, at least on historical grounds, in the working group, rather than in the terrier group. This has indeed already been suggested by a number of fanciers of the breed. Almost certainly, there are more Pit Bull Terriers working livestock today in this country than is true for most other pure breeds currently classed in the working division by the AKC.

As most livestock control and big game hunting with "catch dogs" is practiced in this country today, crossbred dogs are by far the most common form used. In almost every case of such crossbreds, however, the Pit Bull Terrier is almost always one of the parental breeds used in making such crosses for "catch dog" work and most such animals have a purebred Pit Bull ancestor somewhere in the past two generations of their pedigree. In appearance, the majority of the crossbred "catch dogs" look more like Pit Bull Terriers than any other single identifiable breed. Other breeds frequently used in making crosses for such work include German Shepherds, Doberman Pinschers, smaller terrier breeds, or, even more commonly, some breed of trailing hound such as one of the foxhound or coonhound strains. Conversations with experienced hunters of wild and feral hogs in the Southeast have indicated that most such persons actually prefer dogs with some crossbred ancestry as opposed to a purebred Pit Bull Terrier. In their opinion, the pure Pit Bull is frequently too reckless a dog and becomes difficult to control in the all-out frenzy of the pursuit and capture of dangerous quarry such as feral hogs or wild boar. Under such circumstances, an overzealous dog which is not under proper control can often be injured or killed and frequently others may also be injured as a result. Proponents of the crossbred "catch dogs" also cite the improvement in scenting ability and tendency of most hound-Pit Bull crosses to bring their quarry to bay and thereby aid the hunters in locating their quarry by their voice. As will be explained in detail later, however, it is the contention of this article that purebred Pit Bull Terriers can, if properly trained and socialized, be used effectively as "catch dogs" in their own right. Moreover, as will also be explained later, radio transmitter collars placed on the dog can be used to help locate the dog and his quarry, thus obviating the need for baying. Finally, it is also the contention here, that the scenting and tracking ability of the Pit Bull may also be more acute than the breed has often been given credit for.

Although most fanciers of purebred Pit Bull and American Staffordshire Terriers have had little direct experience with the actual use of dogs in such activities as livestock control and big game hunting, recent correspondence received by the author in response to an article in a national all-breed dog magazine, suggests that there may be a surprisingly large number of fanciers throughout the country who would like to learn more about this activity - particularly in a form in which it may be later adapted to serve as a means of competitive testing of temperament, courage, strength, agility, and speed, in a breed in which the initial selection for such traits by pit fighting is no longer either legal or morally defensible. It is indeed the purpose of this article, therefore, to provide some framework of background information about this activity so that those who may be interested in the purebred and even showbred Pit Bull or American Staffordshire Terrier might then also begin to develop their thinking along the lines of working with their dogs in such a form of sport and possibly in competition.

In the United States today one of the most frequent uses of trained "catch dogs" is in the hunting and live capture of either wild or introduced feral hogs in the southeastern Appalachian Mountains and Coastal Plains regions. Such hunters frequently particularly seek to use such dogs to catch and restrain their quarry so that they can be taken alive and then kept in a pen and fattened prior to being killed and butchered for meat. The hogs which are generally hunted may be grouped into two main categories: wild European boar and feral domestic hogs. The wild boar of Europe has been imported to this country on several occasions and either accidental or intentional releases of these boar and/or their progeny have occurred in the Appalachian region of the Southeast where such released animals may have subsequently interbred with escaped feral domestic hogs of the area. These European wild hogs and their crossbred progeny have frequently become important agents of ecological destruction and may pose a threat to many plant species in the Great Smoky Mountains National Park. Park authorities have thus instituted a program of trapping and control to reduce the numbers of these hogs. Outside park lands, however, these same wild boar are highly valued as prize game animals, both for trophy heads with long, curving tusks and as a source of prime game meat. A quick reading of the classified advertisements of any popular hunting and fishing magazine will indicate that a sizeable hunting, guiding, and equipping trade has grown up around this sport. Generally these hogs are hunted with a breed known locally as a "Plott" hound or with crossbred dogs as described above. However, because these wild hogs are generally considered to be more agile and dangerous to dogs than the feral domestic hogs, there is little actual catching of them, and hunting in this case is largely confined to bringing the boar to bay and then shooting it from a safe distance. To the author's knowledge, there are no purebred Pit Bull Terriers currently engaged in the hunting of these wild European hogs although further inquiry may well prove this not to be true.

Unlike its wild counterpart, the feral hog of the Southeastern Coastal Plain of the United States, was originally brought to this country by early explorers and settlers of the New World. These people brought domestic hogs with them which were either intentionally stocked on coastal islands to breed and increase in number or subsequently escaped from landing parties or farming operations. Environmental conditions for these animals were ideal in the lowland hardwood swamps where an abundant food resource was available in the form of annual fall acorn crops. In fact, as late as the 1940's in certain parts of the South, it was still a common practice for backwoods farmers to release their domestic hogs and let them run free in the woods in the fall and then try to shoot or recapture them for butchering in the winter. These escaped feral domestic hogs grow considerably larger than the wild European hog, frequently reaching weights in excess of 400 pounds in the case of large boars. While not as agile as their wild counterparts, hogs such as these, with tusks that frequently exceed three to four inches in length, represent a formidable and very dangerous adversary to dogs which may hunt them, as well as the human hunters who may accompany the dogs.

At the Savannah River Ecology Laboratory, under the sponsorship of the United States Department of Energy and the University of Georgia's Institute of Ecology, ecological studies of these Southeastern free-ranging feral swine have been undertaken for a number of years. As part of these studies, it is frequently necessary to capture hogs in their swamp habitat, collect weights and measures, blood samples, etc., ear-tag the hogs for future identification, and then release them. Subsequent recaptures of the same hogs can then provide information on growth rates and movement patterns. Later refinements of these procedures involve capturing hogs and outfitting them with locational radio transmitter collars which can then be used to follow the movements of the animals in greater detail. In those portions of this research in which the author has been involved, the use of trained "catch dogs" has been an invaluable aid in conducting these studies, being of particular value in the case of work which requires the multiple recapture of the same animal which may have become trap-shy and difficult to recapture with baited corral traps. While the majority of the dogs used in this work have been the Pit Bull-crossbred variety, as described previously, the author has also been successful in training one of his own dogs, a dual-registered AKC/UKC, Pit Bull/American Staffordshire Terrier, for this work. This dog, Ch. Sertoma's Genesis C.D. , holds an AKC conformation championship and a C.D. degree in obedience, with some qualifying scores in advanced C.D.X. obedience competition. This four-year-old male dog weighs 69 pounds and was bred by the Sertoma Kennels of Theo S. and Eulie Raborn of Aiken, South Carolina. Much of the following discussion of training dogs for "catch dog" work is based on the author's experiences with this particular dog and with the other crossbred dogs that have also been used in the program from time to time.

It has been the author's experience that the majority of hog hunters in the Southeast who use "catch dogs," provide them with very little if any formal training for their work - relying mainly on instincts and the dogs' innate tendencies to attack and hold such quarry. While there is little doubt that most of these dogs with any substantial amount of Pit Bull Terrier breeding in their background do indeed have well-developed instincts along these lines, it is also true that without training, control, and discipline, such dogs usually have a very short life span in the hunting "catch dog" game since their proverbial courage frequently may become their undoing when they recklessly attack too large or dangerous a quarry without the proper support of back-up firearms, or under field conditions (e.g., bamboo or switch-cane thickets) where their adversary has a decided advantage over them. A dog which will not return to its handler when recalled, for example, may well run off and attack a large and dangerous boar hog in an inaccessible area of a swamp where the hunters cannot readily get in to help him in his struggles. Untrained dogs of this kind are therefore often viewed by their owners as an expendable commodity and are treated much like so much replaceable livestock, with relatively little time and energy being spent in the training and development of the hunting and catching skills of any one particular dog.

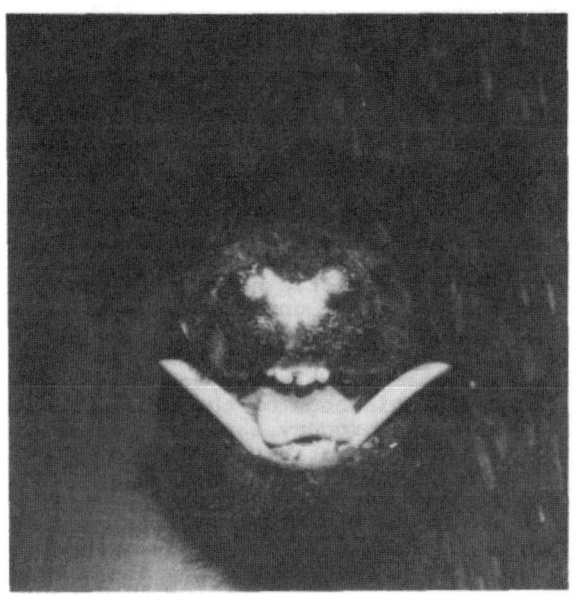

Here is Don Livingston's mounted boar (caught using Pit Bulls). Look at those tusks

Quite naturally, however, fanciers of the Pit Bull Terrier who have worked closely with their dogs as a family pet, companion, and/or show dog, will not find this "expendable livestock" approach to "catch dog" training acceptable. Moreover, it is now becoming clear that there are indeed ways in which a purebred Pit Bull Terrier can be trained and carefully introduced to "catch dog" work with big game and domestic livestock, in such a way that the risk of physical injury to both dog and handler can be greatly minimized, if not in some cases completely eliminated, provided that proper judgement is used in selecting the size of the quarry to be taken and the particular time and situation under which the attack is to be made. It is the purpose of the remainder of this article, therefore, to outline some of the basic aspects of such training as it is practiced by some hunters in the Southeast today and as has also been successfully employed recently by the author with his own dog.

Basic to any program of training a working "catch dog" for use on big game or domestic livestock, is the establishment of a high degree of control so that the dog can be manipulated off-lead by voice and/or hand signals from the handler at a distance. The basics for gaining this kind of control can be obtained in any good training class for obedience instruction. Examples of the kind of hand and voice control as should be sought with a "catch dog" are the drop-on-recall, hand signals, and directed jumping exercises of advanced obedience routines leading to the C.D.X. and U.D. degrees. However, even the amount of control needed to execute a simple recall, as in C.D. obedience work, would be invaluable for working with a dog in the field and may on occasion even save the dog's life! It should be remembered, however, that the ability to exercise such signal and/or voice control in the back yard or even under the distraction of show-ring conditions, will not guarantee that such a dog will also be obedient and steady to control under the excitement of the chase, with game in signt, under field conditions. This is a most critical and difficult problem which has not yet been fully mastered by the author in the training of his own dog. There is probably no more acid test of obedience control, for example, than to give an order to halt and drop to a down position, when an eager "catch dog" is in full-flight pursuit of a fleeing quarry. The author was actually successful on one occasion, however, in recalling his dog with voice alone while it was in full chase of a hog. At this time the dog was only 22 months of age and was still quite inexperienced in the field. The recall was used effectively to stop him from attacking a hog that was much too large and dangerous for him to handle. As this dog grew older and logged more successful catches to his credit, however, he became much too eager and intent on the hunt to be stopped any longer verbally and recalled from a distance in the field. At the present time further training and other methods, including the use of a long line, are being considered as means of reinstituting the desired control over this dog. In the mean time, the inability to stop this dog's attack by voice at a distance now dictates that he can be used only in situations where the quarry is assured to be of the proper size and under proper conditions for a capture, before the dog can be released from the lead.

    The use of a long line has always been an effective means of training and developing control over a dog at a distance in obedience work, such as recall and drop on recall. Those few hog hunters whom the author has known to practice some degree of prior training with their "catch dogs," have also used this tool, not only to institute and enforce verbal control over an inexperienced dog at a distance, but also to, as they claim, teach an inexperienced dog how to catch a hog safely so that the dog will not be injured. Because of the short, stocky conformation of a hog's neck, these animals are physically unable to turn and bite a dog which is holding them by the cheek, ear, or immediately posterior to the head - on the neck or throat. These locations are thus the prime "catch sites" to which the dog must be trained. Since the author's dog has never shown a tendency to catch a hog by any part of the body other than those described above, there is reason to believe that the tendency to catch in this way may be somewhat innate. Other hog hunters, however, have told the author that they have frequently had to teach inexperienced dogs how to catch a hog safely, and to do this they have used a domestic pig without tusks, so that the dog could not be hurt if it should mistakenly attack in such a way as to be bitten by the pig, at a location such as forward on the snout or on the lower part of the forelegs. Using these domestic pigs in a corral, these hunters claim to use the long line to pull the dog off his quarry and verbally reprimand him whenever he catches incorrectly and then reward and encourage him when he catches in a proper location.

Of critical importance after a hog has been caught and is under the control of the hunters, is the rapid and effective removal of the attacking dog. Long a topic of fables and tall tales, the proverbial "gameness" of the Pit Bull has been cited as the need for such methods as spatula-shaped "breaking sticks" inserted between the teeth, suffocation of the dog by covering the nostrils, and even severing veins in the dog's legs to weaken his grip from lack of blood! Undoubtedly, a determined Pit Bull may be somewhat difficult to convince when it comes time to release its prey, particularly in the heat of battle. Generally, however, an obedience-trained dog which has been taught to retrieve and then release a dumbbell, can easily be adapted to commands to release his hog catch-hold also. The author, for example, has had no trouble in removing his Pit Bull from a hog - simply by taking the dog by the collar and giving the verbal command to "leave it." Nowhere is this trained ability to release on command better demonstrated, however, than in the sport of Schutzhund competition, where an important aspect of the work demands an immediate release of the agitator's sleeve at one word of command from the handler. The fact that many well-bred Pit Bull Terriers are now excelling in this sport, is conclusive proof that these dogs are sufficiently trainable to develop this kind of immediate response to command.

Many other aspects of Schutzhund competition are also excellent training for producing a working "catch dog." This includes learning to track scent on command and finding and "baying" quarry on command (the so-called "revierre" exercise). With very little additional work, a trained Schutzhund dog should also make an excellent working "catch dog."

Once the dog has been properly trained and sufficient verbal control is established, he should be introduced to quarry in the field under conditions where the dog will be assured of an easy success with little threat of a serious fight or injury, until he has gained more experience. This requires two factors: (1) the quarry on which he is introduced should be relatively small or no tusks, and (2) the inexperienced dog must be introduced only on quarry in a situation where there is no possibility that unexpected encounters with unseen quarry might occur. In the case of feral hogs, for example, an inexperienced dog must never be released from the leash until it has been determined that the small hog who will be his quarry is not traveling as part of a band of several other hogs which may be out of sight in the cover of the habitat. Such an inexperienced dog may find himself in serious danger, for example, if he pursues one small immature sow into a palmetto thicket from which may suddenly emerge several large adult boars! If there is any doubt about the possibility of other hogs being in the area, the dog should not be released on quarry until he has gained more experience in dealing with such situations.

Many hog hunters claim that a significant degree of experience and training may be obtained by the procedure of releasing an inexperienced dog with an older, more experienced one. However, this procedure probably will have only limited use in the case of purebred Pit Bull Terriers, where it has been the author's experience that most such dogs which possess the courage and aggressiveness of spirit needed for this kind of work, will also, in the heat of the struggle, have a tendency to start fights with the other dogs with whom they are working! Thus, while many hog hunters will use crossbred dogs in groups of up to three, four, or more at a time, these same hunters will seldom, if ever, use a purebred Pit Bull Terrier with other dogs. The author, for example, has always used his dog alone in hunting or "catch work" and this work has therefore been limited to quarry and situations which this dog was capable of handling alone.

The selection of the proper size of quarry and location for attack is of great importance to the success of any "catch dog" hunt and also to the safety of the dogs involved. Too large a pig and too inexperienced a dog, for example, would place an undue risk of injury on the dog as explained earlier. Too large a dog matched to too small a quarry, on the other hand, could easily result in serious injury to the animal being caught and this is not only unnecessarily inhumane, but also often results in the capture of an animal whose injuries demand attention and treatment before it can be successfully kept in captivity for either fattening or research. It has been the author's experience that his 69-pound male Pit Bull is most ideally suited to catching feral hogs in the 75-100-pound size class. At this ratio of size of dog to size of quarry, little or no serious injury generally occurs to the hog and the dog seems to be able to catch with perfect safety.

Don Livingston's Spike - the best catch dog he's ever met

Finally, a word should be said concerning equipment which may be used to help "catch dogs" in their work. A locational radio transmitter collar was mentioned earlier as being of necessity in helping to insure that the hunter will always be able to find his dog and assist him in his struggles if he should find and attack a quarry out of sight of the hunters in the party. If the hog is being hunted with "bay dogs," the use of such a collar is less critical. However, as mentioned earlier, purebred Pit Bull Terriers are frequently not well suited to hunting free with other such dogs. Moreover, purebred Pit Bulls almost never bark or give tongue while attacking their quarry, but usually just take their hold and hang on in silence! A heavy leather collar with a small radio transmitter package and self-contained antenna can generally be purchased from suppliers who can be contacted by either state or university wildlife biologists. County farm agents or foresters may also be helpful in locating suppliers of such equipment which may well cost several hundred dollars but could very likely result in saving many a dog's life! Special heavy, wide leather collars equipped with metal studs and/or connected Y-shaped, leather, yoked breastplates may also be helpful in providing some degree of protection for the dog from the hogs. Care should be taken, however, to insure that such equipment does not fit either too loosely or restrict the dog's freedom of movement in any way. It is the author's general feeling, in fact, that such equipment is really not necessary as long as sows or young boars are the only quarry being pursued, providing the size and experience of the dog is being matched properly to the size of the quarry.

There are undoubtedly many other aspects of the use of "catch dogs" in sport such as hog hunting, that could be mentioned here. The author would, in fact, be most pleased if this article could serve as a focal point to generate correspondence, discussion, and a further exchange of information concerning other aspects of this work. Details concerning the training and use of Pit Bulls on quarry other than wild or feral hogs, for example, would be of particular interest. No matter what the prey, however, the hunting and pursuit of big game animals by a working team of man and dog is probably a close re-enactment of one of the most basic aspects of the relationship between human and canine in its most ancient and intimate form. At no time does a man depend more on the courage, stamina, strength, intelligence, and training of his dog as critically as he does when such a dog is holding and controlling a large and dangerous game animal such as a wild boar, where a mistake or miscalculation by either dog or handler could result in the very real possibility of death or serious injury for either one. As practiced today, the author has found this form of sport to be one of the most exciting and rewarding means of both testing and putting to a positive use, those many desirable attributes which so well characterize the strength, character, and abilities of the Pit Bull Terrier.

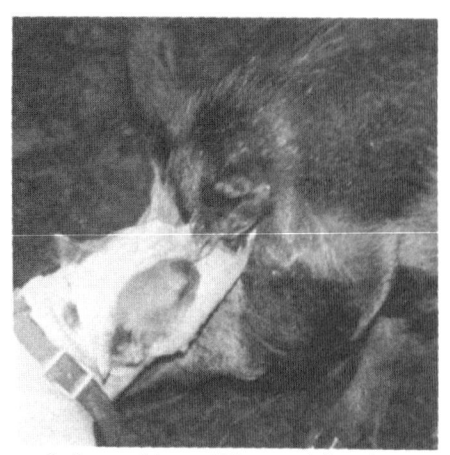

Spike catching a 525- pound farm hog

Spike catching a smaller farm hog

    In addition to the two excellent articles on the previous pages, I wanted to also locate somebody that actually works with farmers in training Pit Bulls (both purebred and crossbred) as well as a variety of other breeds for use as catch dogs. I found that in Mr. Don Livingston of South Carolina. South Carolina and Georgia have the best areas, at least in the eastern part of the country, for wild boar. The swamplands provide ample vegetation, and the underbrush, etc. is so thick and the terrain so rough, that they are difficult to hunt and clean out - so they multiply relatively undisturbed. The south Georgia area around Brunswick is probably the best.

These wild boar are really something else. They are much smaller than a farm hog, but they are one heck of a lot meaner, gamer, quicker, and more agile. A 135-to-140-pound wild boar is much more deadly than a 500-pound farm hog. That's why catch dogs begin their training with a farm sow and later advance to catching a hog. Actually, there are very few full-blooded Pit Bulls that are used as catch dogs. Most of the catch dogs are mixed blood with a predominance of Pit Bull. They are bigger dogs, 70 to 90 pounds, like Mastiffs. They look like large Pit Bulls, and, according to Don Livingston, many of them in his area are called English Bulldogs or English Terriers. They are large, white Bulldogs. They are more prevalent because in that region there are not many purebred Pit Bulls and, you see, not all Pit Bulls are good catch dogs. Don has a Pit Bull - a large 75-pound Red Nose whose brother is a successful combat dog that fights in the pit at 38 pounds (in hard condition); but the Red Nose is no good as a catch dog. He's very aggressive, but he's not catch smart. One time he took off about 200 yards across a pasture and hit a 225-pound hog like a locomotive. He mauled the hog, inflicting serious injuries; but, you see, a wild boar would have killed him because of his eagerness and lack of technique. The best catch dog is an ear dog who hangs on, won't let go, and will turn with the boar, not letting himself get stamped or gored. A nose dog can be more easily overpowered by a boar who can push him down to the ground and gut him with those tusks. When you see a boar with about two-inch tusks showing, he's probably got three or four inches total. A leg dog is really vulnerable. The ear is the safest place to latch on. The big mixed-breed dogs are game, just about as game as the Pit Bull, and, because of their weight, are better finishers. They don't have the enthusiasm and careless lack of fear that the Pit Bull has and are less likely to get themselves killed therefore. All things considered, however, there's not a breed or mixed breed that can hold a candle to a Pit Bull who is experienced in catching. Don has hunted many times with these mixed breeds, but the best catch dog he's ever met is his full-blooded Pit Bull, Spike, who weighs 65 pounds and is a natural. When Spike was just three months old, he "caught" a young sow, going directly to the ear. Don lost Spike in the swamps one time when his dog was less than a year old. Spike was gone a week and came home with a mouthful of boar bristle and gristle in his teeth. Spike will go all day hunting boar and not lose his enthusiasm. He has caught as many as 30 in one day. Don had a heck of a time with him. That dog still didn't want to go home. He's been gutted, dragged through swamps and brush, and just goes back for more. He doesn't have the weight of the 70-90-pound white "English Terriers" but he's quicker and smarter. Well, Spike is a natural. Catch dogs, just like combat dogs, or Schutzhund dogs, or show dogs, or whatever, have inherited characteristics. In other words, some (but not very many) are ready to catch even when they are very young. Others are no good until they mature (two or three years old). Still others are no good at all. In fact, a real good catch dog is fairly rare. A Pit Bull can be a good combat dog if he's a leg or stifle dog, but catch dogs, as far as hogs go, really need to be head dogs. So you have to be quite a bit more restrictive in selecting a catch dog. A hog, and especially a boar, is a pretty game animal himself. Don had to pry a boar off a Pit Bull's leg one time with a breaking stick. That boar had latched on and wasn't about to let go.

Don never tires of telling about the roughest boar he's ever come across. Spike had that old boar by the ear, his favorite hold, but this boar was a rough one and Don could see Spike needed help. He shot the boar seven times with .22 hollow-point bullets as it ran through the brush with Spike on it. He was unable to shoot the boar in a vulnerable spot because Spike was on its ear. The boar kept fighting. Don then shot him with his 12-gauge shotgun, but the boar turned and ran Don up a tree with Spike still on it. Don shot it again with the shotgun and the boar ran into the brush. Don tracked him down and had to use a breaking stick to pry Spike off the dead boar! Spike hadn't let up the whole time.

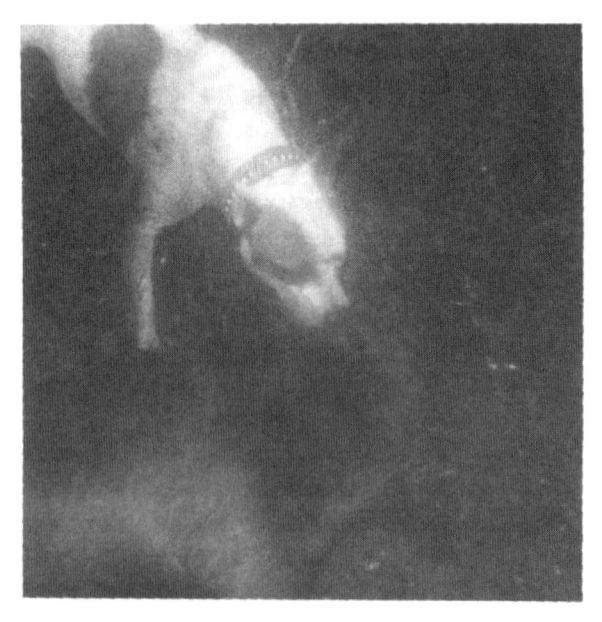

You can't see the boar very well in this picture, but it is the one that chased Don up a tree after it had been shot seven times in the head with 22 cal. bullets and two 12-gauge loads of double (00) buckshot. The boar is dead but Spike is still fighting.

Spike after the hunt, displaying his battle wounds. His left shoulder is pretty badly messed up, but he'll heal quickly

    I am a city boy raised in Boston, Massachusetts, and know very little about farm life (although I did work on a farm for about a month one summer), so I don't know how true this next story is. This farmer told me that once when he went to shoot a hog for meat, he shot it in the head and it just snorted and looked at him! He shot it again and it busted out of the pen. He had to shoot it several more times before it keeled over.

    Cattle are not nearly so game. Some Pit Bulls that work cattle will control a bull by clamping down on his leg, which is enough for Mr. Bull and he'll then behave and obey the dog. A farmer told me that when he wants a bull to go into a pen and the bull is being obstinate, he zaps him with a cattle prod, which is an electrically charged stick (as stated by Gary Hammonds). Usually, after one zap, all the farmer has to do is walk toward the bull with the prod and he will be obedient. But, he usually has to be "reminded" each spring. Well, if a bull is handled once by a Pit Bull, he'll obey that dog for the rest of his life and won't need reminding. A good Pit Bull can be invaluable to a farmer who works cattle. Some will both herd and catch. If the farmer needs a bull, all he does is point at it and the Pit Bull will go get him. If the bull won't come, the dog grabs him by the ear or jowls and shakes as the bull lowers his head. The dog will instinctively turn with him and won't let go. The bull will eventually quit and lay down in subjection. Most Pit Bulls then have to be pulled off but some will let go when called off.

Dog Catching Bull illustrated by Pat Willett

    Now for the training of a catch dog. Most farmers will begin by letting a pup "catch" an old farm sow. Some pups need somebody to get them started; others will just naturally go in and grab the sow by the ear. If a pup doesn't catch on, you let him go after a sow with an experienced Pit Bull and he will tend to copy the adult dog. This is probably the best training method, especially if the experienced dog is a good ear dog. The pup will then tend to go for the ear also. Another training method is to get an old sow and push a puppy up to her ear and the pup will tend to grab it. Do this with a litter or with three or four pups. If you get one on an ear, the others will compete for it. All this helps train them to go for the ear. It doesn't bother the sow much. She doesn't get harmed. When the dog gets older, you put him on a bigger farm hog and see if he can handle it by himself. You don't let him catch too many farm hogs, though, if you plan to use him to hunt boar. He'll develop bad habits (not being careful enough) and might get killed by a boar. It's easy for a Pit Bull to be too reckless. This situation is analogous to that of the combat dog -you don't let him get near a "cur" dog or he might develop careless habits that will cause him to be harmed if he subsequently goes against another Pit Bull. This won't necessarily be the case, but it can happen. I will say that I have seen several Pit Bulls "rolled" that had had several scraps with "cur" dogs prior to their roll with a Pit Bull - and they didn't seem to have any trouble catching on.

Pups out of Castelli's Savage Captain Bob, on a Florida wild hog

Anyway, you choose the pup that seems to pick up the catching techniques best and then let him go on a hunt with an experienced dog. Another obvious prerequisite is that the Pit Bull be one that will cooperate and hunt with other dogs without fighting, particularly in the excitement of the catch. Fighting amongst themselves is not as unusual as you may think. Pit Bulls, when raised with other dogs (Pit Bulls or other breed) will generally establish a "pecking order" (explained in the "Pet" chapter), and socialize quite well.

That's about it for the training. There's really not much more you can do. Most of it is a matter of genes. The dog either has it or he doesn't. I agree wholeheartedly with Dr. Brisbin, however, that an extremely well-trained Pit Bull, say of Schutzhund caliber, can perhaps be controlled by voice. We don't know yet, because, to my knowledge, no one has attempted it. I guess I like to challenge new horizons because I'd like to try it myself some day.

1 believe you can <u>train</u> a dog to be smarter. I believe that with animals as well as people, environmental exposure plays a large role in the development of

demonstrated intelligence. I think that a youngster that receives plenty of peer socialization in school, is active in sports, and is scholastically inclined, will, as an adult, react with much more confidence and assertiveness to novel situations than the youngster would who led a more restricted life. Moreover I think that such an individual will, as a generality, perform better in life situations than a genetically highly-gifted person who has led a restricted life. Catch dog activities and the activities we look at in the next two chapters are a means for enhancing a dog's potential to an immeasurable degree.

Don Livingston has shared with me his hints on training as well as his experiences in the field. When he goes on a hunt, he usually has two dogs - could be two Pit Bulls, or could be his Pit Bull Spike and a mixed-blood, part Pit Bull. He also takes a black Laborador dog as a trail and bay dog, which is used to trail the boar and then give voice, thereby being a valuable asset to the owners, enabling them to find the dogs and the boar. Pit Bulls won't bay and they can be a mile into the swamp on a bad boar (or a pack of boars) and might get themselves killed. With a good baying dog, the owners can catch up and shoot the boar if the dogs are in trouble. When a hunter gets reasonably close, he doesn't have too much trouble, though, if it's a male boar, because he gives off an odor that stinks like nobody's business, especially when he's excited. When the hunters get to the boar with the dogs (or one Pit Bull, if he's a good one) on him, one guy will grab the boar's hind legs, lift up, throw the boar, and whip a strong rope around them. At the same time the other guy will try to hold the boar by leaning down and pressing his knee on the back of the boar's neck. When the boar's legs are securely wrapped, the guy who is pressing on the boar's neck can pry the dog(s) loose with his breaking stick and his partner can bind the front legs of the boar. This operation should be performed as fast as possible because the longer it takes, the more the dog(s) get(s) cut up. As I mentioned, these boars are pretty tough customers. Don said that when a boar gets mad, his eyes get firey red and the hair stands up on His back and he looks awful! (I wish I could have presented these boar pictures in color - you could have seen their bright red eyes.) These boars are lightning fast - not sluggish like a farm hog. It's when the Pit Bull goes in that he is in the most danger. If he is too reckless or if he's not quick enough or evasive enough, the boar will rip open his throat or stomach with one quick swipe. If the Pit Bull doesn't get a good hold or doesn't move and turn with the boar, the boar will use his far superior strength and push the dog down on the ground and gore him; or if the dog is not agile enough to get out of the way, the boar will stamp him with very sharp hoofs; however, if the Pit Bull gets in and grabs the ear, he's boss, and that is the beginning of the end of the fight for Mr. Boar.

Anyway, once the boar is "hog-tied," they will tie up his snout good because if he gets loose, even with his legs tied he can whirl around and cut you quick as a blink. Then they cut down a small tree about as thick as a man's leg and pass it through the boar's legs and carry him on their shoulders. Don can sell them alive for up to $150 each (depending on the size of the teeth).The buyer in turn sells them for around $200 each to hunting clubs that advertise in *Field and Stream.* One in particular is located in Tennessee. They charge $500 for you to go there and hunt wild boars in their natural habitat.

Well, that's it. A good deal of this catch dog information came from notes I took during telephone conversations with Don so there may be some slight inaccuracies, but nothing significant. I feel we can all be quite thankful for Gary Hammonds, Dr. I. L. Brisbin, and Don Livingston for the time and effort they spent in providing us with the information on the Pit Bull as catch dog.

Spike and the brindle Pit Bull in holds. Notice Spike digs in deep.

A breaking stick is needed to get the dogs off the boar. Grabbing the boar's rear legs and lifting up helps immobilize him.

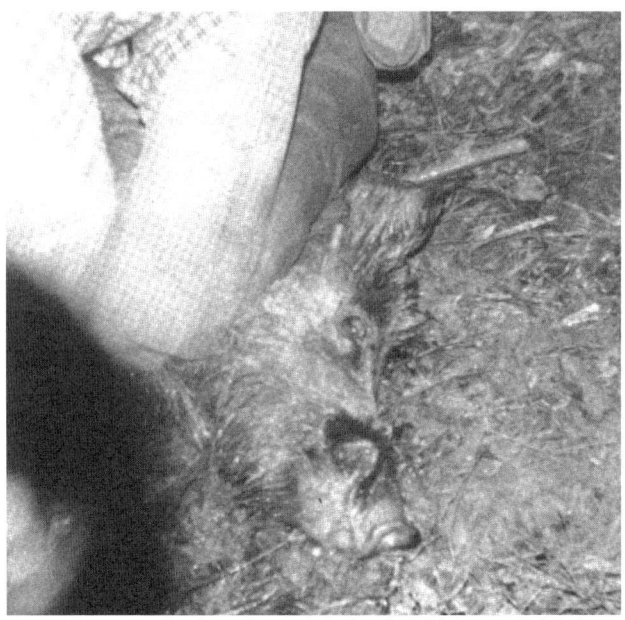

Pressing your knee on the boar's neck helps hold him until his legs are tied

Spike and the brindle resting between catches. Just minutes after this picture, the trail hound bayed another hog – this time it was a sow

Don's two hunting buddies field dressing a sow in the swamp - this one went in the freezer.

Beginning the trip back with their boar, Don (in rear) and his friend take a live boar back to sell

Heading back to civilization with a truckload of dogs and hogs. The dog in the middle is the trail hound.

This is Don's oldest dog, Patch. The vet believes he is a Bull Mastiff/Pit Bull cross. He weighs 90 pounds.

Patch (front) and another catch dog in what is called "cane grass." This is very dangerous hunting because there are no trees to climb and the grass is often higher than your head. You have to be very careful. A wild hog can charge from this tall grass and be right on top of you before you realize it. This picture shows the boar already tied, being dragged to the boat. Patch is waiting for the slightest movement from the boar so he can "catch" him again.

This is Patch by himself demonstrating his catching technique. After he takes initial hold, he pulls straight down very low to the ground and holds successfully. He's a good catch dog. (The boar is solid black and can't be seen very well.)

This is Joe, a young, mixed Pit Bull - most likely Pit and White English mixture. Joe weight 85 pounds, is strong as an ox, and is very good on cattle.

Kid's Panda Bear, U.D.T., SchH III, A.D., F.H. July 28, 1974 - May 19, 1980

Achievements

First Female	To Obtain SchH I	May, 1977
First	To Obtain SchH II	May, 1978
First	To Obtain SchH III	March, 1979
First	To Obtain A.D.	May, 1978
First (in 30 years)	To Obtain U.D.T.	November, 1978
First (in 30 years)	To Obtain Tracking Degree	December, 1977
First	To Obtain F.H.	November, 1979
First Female	To Obtain U.C.D. Legs	May & November 1979

Chapter 4: The Schutzhund Dog

> "I like the Pit Bull Terrier because he can do anything any other dog can do and then whip him." Harry F. Clark

To me, this is the most important chapter in the book, because it explains the highest of all aspirations for the Pit Bull. I believe this breed can and will perform above average in this sport. Please understand, I realize Pit Bulls have not been bred for protection and I am aware that gameness in the pit does not necessarily mean courage when faced with a human threat. Anyone that is familiar with Pit Bulls knows that a good many, if not most, outstanding pit generals are either very shy or excessively friendly with people. In this respect I believe that the American Staffordshire Terrier actually has a temperament more suited to Schutzhund than the Pit Bull. Selective breeding, however, can very quickly develop the desired traits while maintaining any gameness that exists in the foundation dog. This can be accomplished by testing the dogs for both. Breed first for gameness, second for temperament – you'll get both. I would also like to point out that one can definitely be misled by the excessively friendly Pit Bull. Many of the owners of Stafs and the white Bull Terriers are aware of their breed's uncanny (and unique to the breed) ability to discern the difference between a friend and a real intruder or threat. The Pit Bull has that same unique instinct. As with any breed of dog, they need training to be effective and controlled.

The Pit Bull/Staf has for years proven its tenacity and it is felt in South Florida that Schutzhund is an excellent way to prove the courage and fighting instinct in an <u>accepted</u> world-wide event. This feeling that Pit Bulls are not good for anything else, or not truly happy doing anything other than fighting, is erroneous, regardless of their breeding. I want to suggest that not only does Schutzhund training provide a natural outlet for their energy and drive, an outlet that they will love, but that the Pit Bull is a breed that can be an exceptional performer. Their gameness, intelligence, ability, and power can be channeled into a legal activity that will not only be extremely rewarding for both dog and master, but can actually upgrade the quality of the breed. It is important to note that to qualify for any Schutzhund degree, all dogs must pass the temperament test and be of sound body.

I feel like there is a tremendous future for Pit Bulls in this area so I wrote a chapter on the subject for my book. I have read a great deal about it but having no experience or working knowledge of Schutzhund, I felt my information should be reviewed by an experienced handler of Schutzhund trained Stafs/Pit Bulls.

Marilyn Brubaker, of Miami, Florida, is probably the most well known person in the United States in this field, so I sent my chapter to her for criticism. She found that I, being a neophyte, had made a number of errors in detail, so she and Phil Hoelcher (a man very knowledgeable in the field of dog training and one of the people responsible for Marilyn's proficiency in training) spent quite a bit of time rewriting my chapter. Their contribution to this book is therefore very important.

Both Phil and Marilyn are active members of the South Florida Schutzhund Club. Among Phil's numerous credentials are the following: He has been Vice President and a founding member of the United Schutzhund Clubs of America; President of the South Florida Schutzhund Club; U.K.C. Approved Obedience Judge; is a professional dog trainer and owner of the largest kennel (Landmark) in the state of Florida. He has given seminars all over the United States and Canada on the sport of Schutzhund as well as seminars on A.K.C. Obedience; and has given seminars to owners of the Pit Bull/Staf through the Everglades Pit Bull Club. Phil has also titled many different breeds of dogs through A.K.C.'s U.D.T. and SchH I, II, III, and F.H. In 1980 Phil and his two German Shepherds won the D.V.G. U.S.A. Championship in SchH II and III, and also won the Canadian Schutzhund III Championships. He is also a founding member and the training director for the D.V.G. Schutzhund Verband - Florida.

Marilyn is the owner/handler of the world famous Pit Bull/Staf Kid's Panda Bear, who achieved her titles under the guidance and teachings of Phil Hoelcher and the South Florida Schutzhund Club. In 1976 Marilyn began to seriously train her Pit Bull for obedience. It was the South Florida Schutzhund Club's first experience in working with a Pit Bull in Schutzhund. Panda Bear had a good temperament but she had grown up and was no longer the helpless puppy Marilyn had brought home. She was beginning to be hard to handle. (We've already discussed the problems that can arise with Pit Bull pets when they do not receive adequate obedience training.) The exceptional thing, to me, about Panda Bear was that she was two years old when serious obedience training was begun. Because of her age and the fact her owner was a novice, some bad habits had to be corrected. (The Club has since worked with younger Pit Bulls and found them to be very trainable.) Panda Bear's subsequent adventures in Schutzhund and the A.K.C. obedience ring have made her the most obedience titled Pit Bull/Staf in the history of the breed – Kid's Panda Bear, U.D.T., SchH III, A.D., F.H. (OFA). She has obtained every A.K.C. Obedience title and also a tracking degree. It is interesting to note that she was shown in A.K.C. at the same time she was competing in Schutzhund. A Schutzhund trained Pit Bull/Staf, as you can see, <u>can</u> be shown safely in A.K.C. or U.K.C. or wherever.

Almost all of Panda Bear's progeny have performed in an outstanding manner in obedience work. In fact they have so impressed German judges (who have always dogmatically felt - because of their experiences - that the German Shepherd is the only breed that can consistently measure up to Schutzhund standards), that some of the top judges have taken some of Panda Bear's offspring back with them to Germany. Marilyn informed me that Panda Bear is, therefore, the foundation of the American Pit Bull Terrier in Germany. Panda Bear was a very unique animal and achieved many firsts, as the previous list indicates; and several other Pit Bulls and Stafs have since performed in an outstanding manner on Schutzhund tracking, and general obedience tests, thus demonstrating that a Pit Bull can more than adequately perform.

I dedicate this chapter with love to Panda Bear, a Pit Bull I never met but wish I had. Here, then, is the Schutzhund dog.

>Each step we take is a step on an endless ladder,
>and each step depends on the rung before.

What is Schutzhund? Schutzhund is a sport. The application of this sport is two-fold: (1) the sport itself; and (2) it was originally a test to determine which dogs were quality dogs for breeding purposes. Being very interested in Schutzhund, I am following the advice I give my readers - that is to read everything you can find on a subject before engaging in the activity. (By the way, there is an <u>excellent</u> article on beginning Schutzhund training with a younger dog in the September, 1980 issue of *Off-Lead* magazine. See Bibliography.) What we will attempt to do in this chapter is to interest you enough to the point that perhaps you may want to learn more about the sport of Schutzhund. I strongly recommend the book *Schutzhund* by Susan Barwig. To my knowledge, the Barwig book is the most informative source on Schutzhund available at the time of this writing. Another "must" is to obtain the English Translation of the Schutzhund V.D.H. Trial Rules (the <u>only</u> rule book approved by Germany) by Dr. Robert Egolf, Rt. 2, Box 2769, Land O'Lakes, Florida 33532. This book translates the Rules for SchH A, I, *II, III,* FH. WH (Watch Dog), VB (Traffic Proof), RH (Rescue Dog), and also gives general information about the degrees, eligibility, points and ratings, conduct of participants, duties of the judges and trial chairman along with translations of D.V.G. forms and documents and tracking diagrams.

The word Schutzhund means "protection dog." It originated in Germany about one-hundred years ago to test the breed of the German Shepherd dog, for breeding purposes. The Schutzhund movement in the United States is growing rapidly all over the country, becoming very popular with various other breeds such as the Doberman, Rottweiler, etc., because breeders have a way to judge the breeding potential of their dogs regarding correct temperament and working ability. Correct conformation is extremely important in a breeding animal but is reduced to nothing if the dog is unwilling or unable to perform. With the breed of the Pit/Staf, more dog owners are realizing that besides participating in a "fun sport," the dog becomes functional and is a loveable member of the family. The dog competing in Schutzhund must prove himself to have a reliable temperament and show courage without viciousness. The end result is trustworthiness.

Schutzhund training involves three phases: tracking, obedience (including retrieving), and protection. In addition, there are three levels a dog can obtain: Schutzhund I, the most elementary title; Schutzhund II, intermediary level; and Schutzhund III, the master level. We like to think of Schutzhund III as the Ph.D. of dogdom. As we will soon see, a Schutzhund title is not at all easy to obtain. It is an undertaking that requires "dedication to the sport." The way I look at it - even if you fail, you're still a winner, because you will have a much better trained (and therefore easier to live with and happier) pet.

First we will discuss the tracking phase. Tracking is basically development of a dog's natural abilities and instincts and encourages confidence in himself. Tracking is and should be enjoyable for the dog and handler and helps to develop a happy, relaxed bond between them. In Schutzhund competition, dogs are judged on their accuracy and must track with their nose to the ground. There are many different ways to start a young dog. It would be impossible to discuss them all, so again I will refer to Earwig's book. There are also many other books on tracking; one of the most popular is by Mr. Glen Johnson.

The Schutzhund I tracking test involves locating two articles on a track approximately 500 paces long. The handler uses his own articles (usually gloves) and lays the track himself. The track is aged no less than 20 minutes with two ninety degree turns. The handler follows behind the dog at about 30 feet with a line attached to its harness (or collar).

For Schutzhund II, the track is longer (approximately 700 paces long), and is laid by a stranger, using his own articles (two - about the size of a wallet), with two ninety degree turns. The handler does not watch the track being laid. Again, the handler follows behind the dog at about 30 feet.

In Schutzhund III, there is a tremendous jump as to what is expected of the dog's tracking ability. The track is about 1200 to 1400 paces long, at least 50 minutes old, laid by a stranger, with three articles, usually smaller than a wallet, with four ninety degree turns.

In all Schutzhund tracking, you have the option of tracking your dog with or without a lead. If you track without a lead, you must still stay 30 feet behind the dog. You also have the option of tracking with a collar or a harness; point wise, it does not matter. In all Schutzhund tracking, there is only one starting flag. (In

A.K.C. - there are two flags, one at the beginning and another about 30 paces out, so you at least know which direction to start.) In the Schutzhund II and III track, when you bring your dog up to the <u>one and only</u> flag, that dog better know what he's doing, because you as the handler, have no idea which direction it may go. Many people have failed right there on the start, because they didn't trust their dog! On the other hand, it is also important to know your dog well enough as to be able to tell when he is having trouble. You are allowed to talk quietly to your dog and if you know him well enough, with just the right encouraging word (such as: "Good Boy. . . Find it. . ."), you can help him over a rough spot, by giving him that little bit of confidence he needs to make it. This is where the bond between you and the dog comes into play. A dog who tracks out of confidence, love, and enjoyment will be far more reliable, than a dog who tracks out of fear.

While on the subject of tracking, I will describe the most difficult Schutzhund tracking degree - the FH (a German word, "Fahrtenhund," which translated means "Master in Tracking.") In order to compete in the FH, a dog must have at least a SchH I or a V.B. title. The track is at least three hours old laid by a stranger, with six ninety degree turns and a cross track over three of the legs, laid by a secondstranger. There are four articles usually very small (Panda Bear's were two inches square), of neutral color. Most judges will require at least three different terrain changes. For instance/ grass to dirt, to tall grass to paved road, and so on. The scoring of the FH is concerned only with the dog's performance in tracking. Practically all dogs that track in the Schutzhund manner, indicate finding an article by downing with it being in front of his chest and between his front paws.

Obedience, the second phase for Schutzhund I, II, and III, makes a dog a more enjoyable house companion, develops his character and confidence, and adds to the personal pride in man and dog. Schutzhund obedience looks at the handler and dog as a team and puts much more emphasis on a stable working relationship than absolute perfection. Thus it makes the dog much more reliable in everyday situations. In the sport of Schutzhund, the rules and regulations are very clear. The judge rates every dog giving a clear explanation to the audience as to how each exercise was rated, be it good or bad. The rule book explains the point value of each exercise.

South Florida Schutzhund Club's 9th Sanctioned Trial in Miami, March 25, 1979. – Earn-Schutzhund III and receiving 3rd place in the competition was Kid's Panda Bear. She also won Highest Trackign Dog in Trial and "V" rated in the protection phase with a score of 96. The Judge is Herr Reinhard Lindner from West Germany. The man on the far right is Mr. John Joslin, President of the club.

Panda Bear and a few of her pups doing "sit-stays." Left to Right are Panda's Gallane Bruiser, Panda's Gallant Ruffian, C.D., Kid's Panda Bear, OFA, U.D.T, SchH III, A.D.

Tracking: Just starting; Marilyn is letting a 30-foot line slide through her hands and will follow at that distance. Panda Bear indicates the article toy downing on it. Notice the very "deep nose."

Tracking: This photo shows the tension of the lead on the harness. A good tracking dog will "pull." Panda Bear is right-on the track with good concentration & a good "deep nose."

Schutzhund I obedience consists of the following: (1) Heeling On Leash - The dog and handler are judged as a team at a normal pace, fast, slow, 40 paces up and back (the length of the field), with two right turns, two left turns, and two halts with automatic sits. Then you heel into a group of moving people, circling one person to the right and another person to the left, haulting twice while in the group. As you move out of the group, you remove your leash and repeat the whole heeling procedure as described above again off leash. While heeling out of the group, about 15 paces away, off leash, two gunshots are fired. The dog must not exhibit gunshyness, or undue aggression. The rule book states that the dog must be indifferent to the gunshots. Should the dog be gunshy, he is immediately excused from the trial. If the judge is not sure, he can test the dog with further gunshots. (2) Sitting from Motion - Dog will be told to sit stay until the handler returns. (3) Down in Motion with Recall - Dog will be commanded to down while handler continues walking away, then handler will call his dog to "come." (4) Retrieve on the Flat – 1 ½ -lb. dumbbell (or an article belonging to the handler) will be thrown and the dog must retrieve it promptly. (5) Retrieve over the 39" Jump -1 ½ -pound dumbbell thrown over the jump and upon command from the handler will retrieve promptly, jumping the hurdle in both directions. (6) Go Ahead and Down - After heeling 10 paces, the dog is commanded to go out ahead of the handler (at least 40 paces) and down when told do so. (7) Long Down under Distraction - During another dog's performance of obedience, the dog must remain down, with his handler about 40 paces away, his back to the dog. The Schutzhund long down lasts the entire time another dog/handler team is doing the obedience routine. This routine can take as long as 20 minutes.

The Schutzhund II obedience pattern consists of everything a SchH I dog does with the addition of retrieving a 2-pound dumbbell on the flat and retrieving a dumbbell over a 6-foot wall. In all levels of Schutzhund obedience, the handler must know the pattern by heart. The judge does not tell you what to do (like in the A.K.C. ring). So it is very important for the handler to practice his routine, get it down pat to make it as smooth as possible. This is very important, because only then can you get the maximum points, along with being able to transmit to your dog (and to the judge) the look of confidence as a team.

With Schutzhund III obedience, much more is added, of course, because the SchH III dog/handler team will be the masters (if they make it!). Again you must Know rue pattern and. run it yourself.

LONG DOWN under distraction. While another dog is working the obedience procedure. A gun is fired 2 times. Marilyn is standing approximately 50 paces away with her back to Panda Bear.

Panda Bear with her dumbbells.

Retrieving the dumbbell over 6-foot wall. (This is the new type wall called an "A-Frame" which Germany now uses.)

There are several variations you can do which is permissable. The main thing is knowing exactly how many paces to take and where on the field you will make your maneuvers. All Schutzhund III obedience is done off leash. The basic heeling pattern is similar to SchH II with the exception of the following: the heeling pattern is 50 paces up and back; the down in motion is done at a run where the handler runs out of sight for one minute, reappears and calls his dog to him; there is a walking stand-stay with a recall. The dog must now retrieve a 4-pound dumbbell on the flat; and of course retrieve over the 39" hurdle and the 6-foot wall. The long down under distraction while another dog/handler team is working is done with the handler out of sight.

In all phases of Schutzhund competition, there is a certain protocol one must follow. Before and after each phase, you must introduce yourself and give your dog's name to the judge, telling him you are to begin, or you have just completed the phase (in tracking, obedience, or protection). The judge will acknowledge and tell you to begin, or that you are permitted to leave upon completion. Also, after each phase, the judge critiques you and your dog and your score is announced immediately so you know exactly where you stand. This procedure is considered by some to be much better than keeping you in suspense until the very end. But even though you may have failed a particular phase, you may continue on to the next (unless your dog has disqualified for unsoundness or bad temperament). Almost all Schutzhund judges are brought over from Germany and they know their business. In all instances the judge, through his critiques, tries to help the handler by pointing out errors and many times offers suggestions to correct problems. It is a learning experience not only for the handler, but also for the audience.

Well, that is the obedience aspect of Schutzhund. As you can see, a great deal of control is required. It sounds really great, and it is. If you can ask your dog to do the things required in these tests, I am sure your imagination can dream up a hundred practical applications for individual situations. At the very least, you'd really have a relationship with your dog that few people have. Schutzhund does require a great deal of time and dedication. The first two years (the formative period of the dog's life) are where most of the work is involved. By this time your dog should be able to live in your home and be a regular family member, and you'll be spending plenty of time witn him because it will be convenient to do so. If you want a Schutzhund, you'll still have to train, but you will have established communication patterns so that training will be easier, more mutually enjoyable, and less time consuming.

Even though protection is what Schutzhund is all about, it is the most <u>misunderstood</u> activity in this sport. Persons not familiar with the Schutzhund protection procedure erroneously compare a Schutzhund trained dog to a police attack trained dog. In police procedure, the dog's function is to apprehend and hold by biting. The police officer then takes over. Protection training for Schutzhund competition is more intricate and advanced than average protection training. The dog who is competing in advanced Schutzhund work must make his own decisions and use his own judgement. He works completely off lead and at a distance from his handler. He is trained to alert and bark at the suspect unless there is aggression or an escape attempt. At such time he must bite and hold, and release automatically when the suspect ceases fighting. This provides a safety factor against overdone aggression with little control.

The Pit Bull has the natural instinct to protect, which a good Schutzhund dog must have; but the abilities of this breed have been hidden or obscured to a great extent because of the many falsehoods spread about it. In the past there have been strong feelings by many that a Pit Bull could not be trained to stop once he attacked. However, with Schutzhund training, the dog is not only more capable of protecting his master - he will be more consistent and reliable in doing so, and only to the degree his master wishes. A Schutzhund dog is a controlled dog - perfectly controlled to protect only when instructed and where instructed and to stop <u>immediately</u> when instructed. With the proper handling and the right (and fair) obedience training, the Pit Bull can be taught control as easily as any other breed of dog, especially if started at an early age. With the combination of their courage, spirit, loyalty, and extreme intelligence, they are beginning to be recognized as the "companion par excellent" and protection and working dog. This last phase of Schutzhund training is, for most folks, the most exciting.

When relating the protection phase of Schutzhund to the Pit Bull/ Staf, we must emphasize that Schutzhund is a "fun sport" for this breed and they thoroughly enjoy participating in it. It is also extremely important to mention that in starting a Pit Bull in the protection phase of Schutzhund, it should be kept a fun game. In other breeds it may be necessary to tease or agitate the dog, to "bring him out," but as Mr. Phil Hoelcher (who according to Marilyn BrufcaKer has worked with more Pit Bulls than anyone else in the sport of Schutzhund) explains it, the toughness of the Pit Bull is there in almost every case and therefore it is not necessary to harrass them. It is better to teach them to like to bite the sleeve and not to dislike the man. As you would play with your puppy with a towel or rope, they enjoy the bite and are not mad at the man. With this concept in mind, as the Pit Bull progresses in the sport of Schutzhund, he will always be a <u>totally safe</u> Schutzhund dog. As the puppy matures his master will notice that along with the Pit Bull's natural protective instinct, he is also maturing with the intelligence of knowing the difference between a threatening gesture and the friendly approach of a man. The owner of a Pit Bull must above all, when working his dog in protection, be sure that the dog has the correct stable temperament and that he has absolute control of the animal! Not every Pit Bull, just as in other breeds, has all the ingredients to become a Schutzhund because Schutzhund is just not for all dogs! That is why I believe that when a person has obtained even the SchH I title with his dog, he has proven his dog to be of high quality and should be justly proud.

The Schutzhund I protection procedure is for the novice dog. He is required to search one or two blinds, as commanded by his handler. (A blind is about 7 feet high, usually shaped like a teepee, where the "agitator" hides. It is to simulate the dog searching areas for "the bad guy"). When the dog finds the agitator, he must hold him at bay and bark. The agitator is standing still in the blind, therefore not threatening. The dog should stay with the agitator but not bite. In SchH I, this is called the "Revier." The judge then instructs the handler to approach the dog and agitator. (The handler is standing approximately 40 or 50 paces away.) The dog stays fixed on guarding the agitator. The next exercise is Attack on Handler. The handler is walking with the dog heeling on leash. Half way to the next blind, he unsnaps the leash, having his dog heel off leash until they come upon the next blind, whereupon an agitator leaps out of the blind threatening and waving a stick. The dog must immediately attack and hold fast. The dog is now given two blows with a flexible stick (such as bamboo) in the area of the withers and hindquarters. (Use of the stick in the sport of Schutzhund is a part of trial procedure. The dog is not hurt. The bamboo reed simulates a weapon that an offender may use. It is necessary that the dog be exposed to this type of weapon in training.) At the direction of the judge, the agitator stops his attack and the dog lets go at the command to "out." The next exercise is the courage test. After the Attack, the handler holds his dog by the collar and the agitator runs straight away, making threatening gestures. After he has gone about 50 paces, the handler sends his dog. At this point the agitator turns and runs back toward the dog making strong threatening gestures and shouting. The dog must hit head on, and bite and hold: and upon command from his handler - who is 50 paces away - release when told to "out." The handler then walks to them as the dog is watching the agitator with full intent. The handler then disarms the agitator and escorts him to the judge with the dog at heel.

The Revier: The dog must search 6 blinds, find the agitator, bark, and hold him at bay. (not to bite)

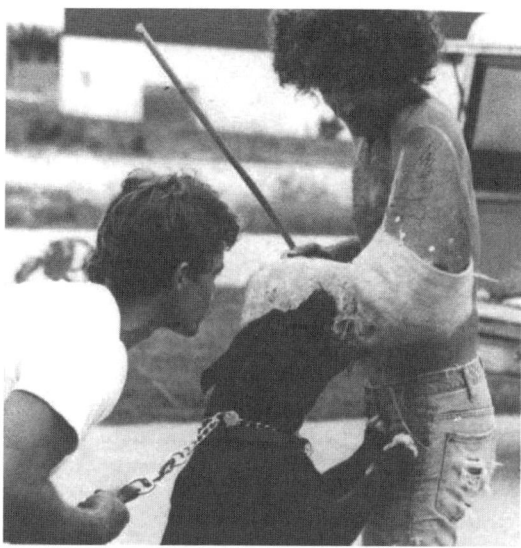

Owner Gary Gschwind working Panda's Gallant Bruiser in "Bite Work." Agitator is Kirk Thomas.

Courage Test: Agitator is Gary Gschwind. Notice Panda Bear hit head on & her hind feet are off the ground. Her bite is good & in middle of sleeve. Remember, Schutzhund is a sport. Panda Bear is geared to the sleeve & not the man! When the protection work is over, Gary Can drop the sleeve & pet & play with Panda Bear

In Schutzhund II the dog is required to do much more, showing more control and thinking on his part. He works completely off lead and must run a pattern of 6 blinds under the direction of his handler. Upon finding the agitator he must hold him at bay (The Revier) until the handler calls him to heel. The handler then searches the agitator. The next exercise is called Escape and Defense - The agitator tries to escape from the dog. The dog must immediately prevent this by biting hard and holding as the agitator is running. The agitator stops and ceases fighting. The dog releases when commanded to "out." Then again the agitator re-attacks and again the dog must hold fast while the dog is hit twice with the stick. He freezes; the dog "outs." The handler searches the agitator then tells him to turn around and move out. Then you and your dog do a heeling pattern (off lead) with the agitator about 5 paces in front of you. (This is a real test as to how much control you have over your dog!) The heeling pattern is about 40 paces with several turns: then, at the judge's direction, the agitator turns to attack and the dog must bite and hold while the agitator drives into the dog. The agitator ceases the fight; the dog is commanded to "out." Last is the courage test which is basically the same as in SchH I.

Courage Test: Agitator is Gary Gschwind. Panda Bear being hit with stick. Her attitude is "hit me again, I'll bite even harder." In no way has she ever been intimidated. She does not back off from pain. (Even in her training, techniques had to be changed to compensate for her extreme hardness and tenacity.

Panda Bear has been told to "out." She has released and must "watch," her total attention on the agitator (Gary Gschwind) in case he tries to escape. Points are deducted if the dog looks away. A dog can fail if it returns to the handler (Marilyn Brubaker, on right)

Lady Rattlesnake (trainer, Joe Placer) and Ed Wagner in action. Lady Rattlesnake (Stompanato – Art's Missy – 4x Kingfish)

Jacob Ben Satan (Actitator: Joe Placer)

The Schutzhund III protection is similar to the SchH II with more attacks and reattacks and "outs" and two transports to the judge. The Schutzhund III performance should be with more control and accuracy than I or II and is judged accordingly. The judge observes the fighting instinct of the dog throughout the whole protection phase, and only dogs who demonstrate exceptional courage and hardness receive full points. It's important for the dog to show independence and spirit; but should a dog, even if he has passed the temperament test before the trial, show any defects in temperament during the course of the trial, he can be dismissed by the judge. Also, a dog that does not "out" when commanded will fail. If the judge feels the dog is working out of viciousness or if he is too afraid to hold his bite, he will fail. The dog must show courage, coupled with correct temperament.

Marilyn feels that people who believe it is important to preserve the "gameness" in the American Pit Bull Terrier should try to find a "test" for our breed which is updated to these times, that is accepted, and that is legal. The Schutzhund Courage Test in her opinion is a gameness test. You see, a dog will instinctively chase after something that's running away, but when something comes at him, that's a different story. It takes an extremely courageous dog to attack a human that is running at him.

Marilyn informed me that the first Pit Bull/Staf in the world to receive the Schutzhund I title was CH. Gallant Titan, U.D., SchH I, owned by Mr. Ralph Davis of Dallas, Texas. Below you can see Titan's picture along with his pedigree. Notice he received a score of 98 (out of 100) in protection - the highest score that particular judge ever awarded for protection, a "V" rating. Also notice his pedigree is predominantly Knight Crusader and Ruffian. This line traces back to the very famous Black Jack Dog and his progeny that we mentioned in the history chapter if you recoil, carl Tudor said Black Jack was the best dog he'd ever met.

Ch. Gallant Titan, U.D., SchH. I, achieved Schutzhund I title on August 23, 1975, in Los Angeles, California. The match was officiated by internationally accredited judge, Kurt Marti. I think Titan looks very much like his famous great grandfather Knight Crusader.

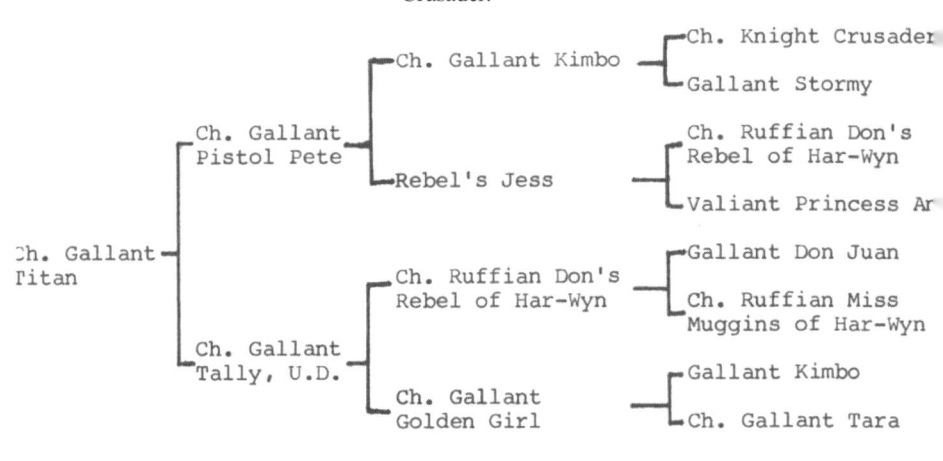

```
                                            ┌─Ch. Knight Crusader
                          ┌─Ch. Gallant Kimbo─┤
                          │                  └─Gallant Stormy
            ┌─Ch. Gallant─┤
            │  Pistol Pete│                  ┌─Ch. Ruffian Don's
            │             │                  │  Rebel of Har-Wyn
            │             └─Rebel's Jess─────┤
            │                                └─Valiant Princess Ar
Ch. Gallant─┤
Titan       │                                ┌─Gallant Don Juan
            │             ┌─Ch. Ruffian Don's┤
            │             │  Rebel of Har-Wyn└─Ch. Ruffian Miss
            │             │                     Muggins of Har-Wyn
            └─Ch. Gallant─┤
               Tally, U.D.│                  ┌─Gallant Kimbo
                          └─Ch. Gallant──────┤
                             Golden Girl     └─Ch. Gallant Tara
```

The Ruffian line also traces back to the famous Tacoma dog. In any event, Titan's accomplishment marked the beginning of a new era for the Pit Bull/Staf breed. Many dogs (of all breeds) fail the Schutzhund trials, not for lack of training time or quality, but because the dog just plain doesn't have the aptitude. Titan demonstrated quite dramatically that the Pit Bull/Staf can perform successfully in the sport of Schutzhund. There were plenty of obedience Pit Bull/Stafs before Ralph Davis' Titan, but Titan was the first to prove that it could be done on such a high level.

Panda's Gallant Spartagus Owner/Handler: Cindy Herron, Miami, Florida
Bred by: Roy and Marilyn Brubaker

*Youngest and fourth in the history of the breed to earn a Tracking Degree

*Obtained "Companion Dog" title in three consecutive trials with an average score of 192 out of a possible 200 points, with such honors as:
Highest Scoring Dog With Tracking Title
Highest Scoring Dog With Ip Number
Highest Scoring Dog Of This Breed (APBT)
First Place Novice "B"

*First male APBT to receive leg towards U-CD title (Second Place -Score: 193)

* Eight Conformation Best of Breed Wins (All Breed Fun Matches)
Six Terrier Group Wins   "   "   "   "
Two Terrier Group II Wins   "   "   "   "

*BEST IN MATCH - Everglades Pit Bull Club, August, 1978 (Taken from the Puppy Class)

*BEST IN SHOW WINNER - Everglades Pit Bull Club, May, 1979 - Plus BEST MALE IN SHOW and FIRST PLACE JUNIOR MALE - 30 UKC Points

*First male APBT to be obedience titled and UKC Pointed
All of the above was accomplished owner/handled prior to the age of two years!

Al Perez and his female, Wicca's High Priestess, whose father is Titan and whose mother is Panda Bear.

Panda Bear was bred to Champion Gallant Titan and produced some outstanding sons and daughters. Two of their sons have gone on to break even more world records for the breed of the Pit Bull/Staf, the first being Ch. Panda's Gallant Spartagus, CD, TD, SchH I, U-CD, VB, AD; and the other littermate MWP-Ch. Panda's Gallant Ruffian, CD, SchH I, U-CD, VB, AD. These young dogs are only the beginning of a new and historic lineage, focusing on a new direction for our breed.

More and more people are beginning to realize the potential of the Pit Bull. If given half a chance by their owners, raised in the correct environment the Pit Bull puppy will respond and perform at least as good and probably better than any other dog can, in any task that is asked of him. This sport of Schutzhund represents a unique relationship between man and animal. It is obtained only after many hours of work, and even then there is no guarantee of success if the dog does not have the innate abilities. However, if you and your Pit Bull do not attain the Schutzhund level, the worn you have put into it is not lost. At the very least, you have a much more enjoyable pet than if you did not undertake such an adventure. I say, if you are buying a Pit Bull pup, why not try it? Nothing to lose, much to gain. It is hoped that people reading this chapter will become inspired and meet the challenge afforded to you in the exciting sport of Schutzhund.

I am sure that most of my readers are wondering what all those initials following the dog's name stand for. Marilyn has given us a brief explanation of each, as presented on the following pages. By now you should know the abbreviations for the various levels of Schutzhund, (SchH I, SchH II, SchH III), and also the initials "F.H." which stands for "Master Tracking Dog."

There are various other Schutzhund titles that you can obtain with your dog. You will notice that Panda Bear and Titan's sons, Ruffian and Spartagus, have the initials of "V.B." under the D.V.G. which stands for (in English) The German Alliance of Utility Dog Sports Clubs, you and your dog have the opportunity to be judged by all-breed orientated judges instead of just S.V. judges. (S.V. stands for the German Shepherd Dog Club of Germany). The D.V.G. now has "Landesgruppens" (Regions) throughout the United States broken into Southeast, Northeast, Midwest, and West Coast. If you would like to know where there is a D.V.G. Schutzhund Club in your area, Dr. Egolf, the publisher of the Schutzhund Rule Book will probably be able to direct you.

Now back to the obedience and Schutzhund initials. I hope these will be plain to you. It can become very confusing to someone who is not familiar with showing a dog, but nevertheless, here goes. As I started to explain in the paragraph above, the "V.B." - another Schutzhund degree - translated into English means "Traffic Secure Companion Dog." The dog does not have to track or do protection work. All breeds and sizes are eligible. Minimum age is 12 months. The dog either passes or fails. He does the basic SchH I heeling pattern on and off leash with gunfire, but does not have to retrieve. Then your dog is taken downtown and must work in traffic. He must show that cars, bicycles, trains, and loud crowds of people do not affect him. You may be even taken to an amusement park (which was the case with Spartagus and Ruffian) and watch the roller coaster and other fun, noisy rides. Further in the test, you will tie your dog outside a store and go inside, leaving him alone. Perhaps someone will walk by and drop a book by your dog and have to pick it up. Also someone will walk by with another dog. All this tests the behavior of your dog in <u>all</u> situations. It is what I would call a "Super Temperament" test.

You will also go to an open field or park and turn him loose to relieve himself, allow him to wander around for awhile and upon the judge's direction, three different times you call your dog to you. Cindy Herron's Ch. Panda's Gallant Spartagus, CD, TD, SchH I, U-CD, AD, VB, and Marilyn Brubaker's

MWP-Ch. Panda's Gallant Ruffian, CD, SchH I, U-CD, AD, VB are the first Pit Bulls in the history of the breed to receive the VB, and one which they are most proud of. All eyes were on those Pit Bulls to see their reactions, especially the part where the dog walks past them. This proves that a Pit Bull (although dog aggressive by nature) can be taught tolerancei

The "A.D." - A Schutzhund "Endurance Test" - was originally devised for the size and gait of the German Shepherd. The dog must gait at 6 miles an hour for about 12 miles, with two rest periods in between. At each rest point, the judge examines each dog's condition. Unsound-ness, sore or bleeding pads, and so on will disqualify them. At the end of 12 miles, the dog must do a simple heeling pattern and jump back and forth over the 39" hurdle. Panda Bear was the first in the history of the breed to obtain the "A.D." and the 2nd, 3rd, and 4th were her sons: Panda's Blue Tiger and Spartagus and Ruffian.

The "W.H." - A Schutzhund "Watch Dog" title. All breeds are eligible. No points given. You either pass or fail. The dog is required to do a SchH I heeling pattern and retrieve an article on the ground. No hurdle and no tracking. The main portion of the W.H. is to guard - first an article, then property, like a home or a car. He is then attached to a running line with an agitator coming at him from either direction and he must show watchfulness. Another exercise the dog must do is to show his attachment to his master. This in my opinion is of great importance because it shows his true love and loyalty for his handler. The dog is given to a second person. The handler then goes into a group of people standing about 80 paces away. Without any signal or sound from his handler the dog is turned loose and he must want to find his master. The behavior of the dog, especially the use of his nose, is closely observed by the judge. If the dog does not find his handler, he will fail.

The SchH A - the exact same thing as SchH I, but with no tracking. The dog does only obedience and protection work.

As you see, Schutzhund - D.V.G. offers so many tests that are truly challenging and worthwhile for the Pit Bull. A Schutzhund is well-rounded indeed.

The other initials you see attached to some of the dog's names are from showing in A.K.C. approved obedience trials or U.K.C. approved
obedience trials with the exception of the initials "Ch." which stand for Champion - in the breed ring (AKC/UKC).

A.K.C. and U.K.C. obedience titles are very similar as far as the qualifications go, but each Club has their own variation of the exact pattern used. There are three levels: in A.K.C. it's called "C.D." -Companion dog, which is the novice dog. With U.K.C. It's the same except the initials are different – "U-C.D." and so on. The next level is for the Companion Dog Excellent – "C.D.X." and "U-C.D.X.," and the highest level being Utility Dog –

"U.D.", "U-U.D." As each dog progresses up the ladder of obedience (and in Schutzhund), he will drop the lesser degree initials and use the higher ones. When a dog has obtained a "T.D." which is the A.K.C. Tracking Dog title and gotten the highest obedience A.K.C. title of "U.D." they are combined to be "U.D.T." "U.D.T." behind a dog's name tells you that he has received all lower levels, too. To describe each and every A.K.C. and U.K.C. obedience title would require another chapter all to its own. I would suggest that if you are interested in showing your Pit Bull or Staf in approved obedience trials that you write to the appropriate organization requesting their rules and regulations. If you own a Pit Bull and you would like to compete in A.K.C., you must request a special registration form called an I.L.P. form. These initials stand for Indefinite Listing Privilege. This registry will allow you to compete in obedience and tracking trials only. You cannot show your Pit Bull in A.K.C. Breed shows, and you cannot register puppies. When you request this "I.L.P." form, you must register your dog in the name of American Staffordshire Terrier, because A.K.C. does not recognize the name of American Pit Bull Terrier anymore.

Well, we are down to just a few more initials. You will notice that among the titles listed behind Panda Bear's name are the initials "O.F.A.," which is not a Schutzhund degree nor is it an AKC or UKC obedience title, but is still something to be very proud of. It means that she is free of any hip dysplasia, a physical defect that can be a very cripling and painful problem for any dog. In a working or breeding dog it can be disastrous because it will affect his working abilities and is considered also to be heritable. Hip dysplasia is a deformation of the hip joints. O.F.A. stands for the organization "Orthopedic Foundation for Animals, Inc." which examines X-rays sent to them by veterinarians. The X-rays are reviewed by three separate doctors and they determine the status of the dog's hips if your dog passes, you are sent a certificate stating that he is free of hip dysplasia. This is a very common practice in the breed of the German Shepherd dog. A conscientious German Shepherd breeder will insist that both the sire and dam are O.F.A. certified before even considering breeding.

With the breed of the Pit Bull, O.F.A. is practically unheard of; whereas at this point in time, breeders of the American Staffordshire Terrier are becoming more aware and are just now beginning to X-ray their show stock, but still not very many. Each O.F.A.'s dog is assigned a number, and to give you an example as to how few of our breed have been X-rayed, Kid's Panda Bear's number was 46 as of November, 1978. Hip displasia has been showing up in the breed of the Pit Bull and Staf. In extreme cases of bad hips, it is easy for anyone to spot. The dog has a weak hind end, has trouble getting up and lying down, and may even wimper from the pain. The dog just can't seem to perform any task which requires power from his hips. In these extreme cases, the kindest thing to do is to have him put to sleep.

And now for the last set of initials! Have I lost you or have you been able to keep up with me? I told you it wouldn't be easy. What does "MWP-Ch." mean in the front of Panda's Gallant Ruffian's name? Although weight-pulling is relatively new to the breed of the Pit Bull/Staf, there have been several organized pulls. It is hoped that some day it will become a very popular sport for our breed because it, too, is truly an excellent "test" and should be recognized. At the Annual American Staffordshire Breed Specialty there was a weight-pulling contest. The Pit Bull/Stafs pulled in three different categories, depending on the weight of the dog: lightweight, middleweight, and heavyweight. There were dogs there from all parts of the United States, vying to break the previous known record - 400 pounds, pulled by a dog in New York according to Dr. I. Lehr Brisbin who was there in Louisville, Kentucky, September of 1980 to help officiate. All the dogs were weighed in, and there was a timekeeper and an appointed judge. Ruffian weighed in a 57 pounds and was classified as a middleweight. The first dog to break the previous known record was Ruffian. In fact he went on to pull a total of 550 pounds to be declared the "Middle-Weight-Pulling Champion." Since then, in Atlanta, Georgia in December of 1980, Ruffian topped the pull of the heavyweight pulling champion by pulling a total of 615 pounds at one pull! That's amazing when you consider the relationship between body weight and pounds pulled. Ruffian's new co-owner, Marty Harper says that she believes that this little Pit Bulldog is capable of pulling 1000 pounds, because of one very important ingredient – "He has the Heart!" Isn't this also an important asset that the Pit Bull was bred for when one refers to gameness. ... Heart. ...

Panda's Gallant Ruffian, C.D. - Breeder/Owner/Handler: Marilyn Brubaker; Sire, Ch. Gallant Titan, U.D., SchH I; Dam, Kid's Panda Bear, O.F.A., U.D.T., SchH III, A.D. Male - Whelped 9/20/77   Weight: 64 pounds Mahogany Brindle w White Height: 20 inches
*Won Highest Scoring Dog First Time Shown   *Won Highest Scoring Terrier
*Tied for High In Trial with a Score of 197

Chapter 5: The Competitive Weight-Pulling Dog

Outside show is a poor substitute for inner worth. - Aesop

In the previous chapter, we introduced a sport relatively new to America. Here is a really new sport. Well, it's not so new as far as Eskimo and Husky sled dogs are concerned, but it <u>is</u> a new thing for other breeds. It's weight-pulling. Pound for pound, at least according to articles I've read (by Pit Bull/Staf folks) most Pit Bulls can outpull most sled dogs. Of course most sled dogs are twice or more the weight of a Pit Bull, but a Pit Bull can win in his weight class (lightweight) and I think that many, if well trained, can even compete well with the heavyweight dogs. (*Pit Bull Gazette,* February, 1979 has an excellent story of a Pit Bull that won a contest when she was just 11 months old.)

The training can be a heck of a lot of fun for you and your dog, and I think it is as good an exercise for him as you can find. It will strengthen muscles, heart, and lungs, and improve endurance. In 1974 George Attla, a world champion sled-dog racer, wrote an excellent book on training sled dogs for competition. (See bibliography.) I think it's interesting to note that in his training schedule he works the dogs up to twenty-mile runs, pulling a sled, three or four times a week – that's running wide open the whole way. Of course these are sled dogs bred for this type of work, but I feel that a Pit Bull can be conditioned to emulate this performance. The Alaskan sled dog doesn't begin training until around October, after snow is on the ground. They, of course pull sleds, whereas the Pit Bull would pull a cart. As you will see in the chapter on conditioning, I consider cart-pulling to be one of the best techniques for conditioning. It can also be pretty convenient. There are two articles in *Off-Lead* magazine, December, 1977, and April, 1980, about a lady who uses her Newfoundland competition weight-puller to go shopping. She loads up the cart with groceries and he pulls them home. Her articles detail training methods (basic and advanced) maneuvering exercises, etc. and provide addresses for you to order carts and harnesses if you want. You really ought to order these articles, *Off-Lead* keeps back issues and will send them to you for little more than the regular price.

The February, 1978 issue of *Off-Lead* has an article that I believe best illustrates just how beneficial a conditioner weight-pulling is.

Hammonds' Reginald from Rufus bred to Trussell's Midget and littermate to Ch. Goose Anderson's Smiley and Cook's Effie

Written by Catherine Eastep, it is about Dr. Lehr Brisbin's Bloodhound Smokey Blue, who is a U.D.T. (Utility Dog Tracking). At the time the article was written, Smokey Blue was the only Bloodhound that had ever attained that title, the primary reason being the many structural faults inherent in the breed, which has been selectively bred to trail and for conformation, thereby developing the breed to the point where they have an unbalanced center of gravity over the neck and shoulders and are very weak in their hind quarters so that they cannot get the proper propulsion necessary for them to come even close to making the required jumps in earning the degree. In other words, the Bloodhound is generally physically incapable of passing the requirements for U.D.T. Smokey Blue was able to perform under the tutorage of Dr. Brisbin who acquired him from Mr. Roy Modler of Iowa. Blue was obedience trained and had earned his C.D. with the highest score ever recorded for a Bloodhound. Mr. Modler also had conditioned Blue physically and Dr. Brisbin attributes Blue's later success to that early training. His strength training consisted of a regular program of progressive weight-pulling, using a tracking harness Blue was hitched to a cart that he pulled, weights being progressively added as his competence increased. As a result of this training, not only was Blue able to earn his C.D.X. in three straight shows and then his U.D. (In training for utility jumps, Blue often cleared 44-inch jumps and 7-foot broad jumps), a more direct benefit was gained when Dr. Brisbin entered Blue in the Mason-Dixon Sled Dog "Mint Julep Classic" in 1975. Blue won the contest with a pull of 500 pounds dead weight, beating strong draft breeds bred for pulling, such as a St. Bernard, Huskies, and Malamutes! This is truly a fantastic feat to me, because Bloodhounds seem so floppy, disjointed, and weak in the hind legs. Well, now, if that training can benefit a Bloodhound so much, think what it can do for a Pit Bull! Dr. Brisbin's successes led him to become quite enthusiastic with this training and he has become an active proponent of weight-pulling contests. He has been good enough to provide us with the following article dealing with the sport:

Competitive Height-Pulling as a Means of Developing and Evaluating the Structural and Functional Capabilities of the American Staffordshire Terrier

Introduction

The past development of many breeds of pure-bred dogs has been shaped by artificial selection and breeding programs designed to produce animals which were particularly well-suited to the performance of specific tasks (e.g. hunting, racing, herding, etc.). Such programs of selection have often produced breed characteristics which have been subsequently valued in their own right, independently of the role that such characteristics may have played in the original development of the breed. In the case of the American Staffordshire terrier for example, past selective breeding designed to produce a winning competitor in pit fights, produced a breed whose individuals were characterized by their strength, agility, stamina, courage, and persistence to a task in the face of adversity. These characteristics have since been valued by fanciers of the breed completely independent of their original function in producing a more effective and successful fighting dog.

In the course of development of many of the current dog breeds now registered, by the AKC, however, direct selection for the original purposes for which the breed was developed has frequently been either abandoned completely or greatly diminished in importance relative to new selective regimes now aimed at producing animals which conform as closely as possible to a typologically-conceived breed standard. Thus, for example, many Labrador retrievers are now being selectively bred for a strong, rounded otter-like tail, even though little or no selection is being simultaneously maintained to assure that the dog with such a tail will still be an eager enough swimmer to really use his tail as a rudder - its original purpose in the development of the breed, as a water dog. This separation of the selective forces now directed towards the typological conformation to a breed standard, from the original selection directed towards the original purposes for which the breed was developed, is now frequently becoming a matter of concern to breeders and fanciers of those breeds which are no longer being used and hence tested in those functions and roles for which they had been originally developed.

Of all the modern dog breeds currently registered by the AKC, probably none other will ever have to face problems such as those described above to the same degree as will the American Staffordshire terrier. The reasons for this are primarily twofold: (1) In the case of the Staffordshire, the use of the breed in the original purpose for which it was developed (pit fighting) is now not only unpopular, it is actually illegal and has been formally renounced by the membership of the breed's parent club, and (2) Many of those characteristics which made the Staffordshire such a successful pit fighter (e.g. strength, courage, stamina, etc.) are nevertheless among those still most highly valued by fanciers of the breed today. The effects of this dilemma are unfortunately already becoming all to obvious. Commentary and correspondence published in Staffordshire club literature are now, more and more, beginning to document the occurrence of unstable and unpredictable temperaments in the breed, cowardice, lack of physical stamina, and above all, the appearance of heritable physical defects such as hip dysplasia - all being predictable consequences of a breed development program which has become overly directed towards a typologically conceived breed standard alone, with little or no consideration being given to the selective testing of potential breeding stock for those valued characteristics named above, which had originally been developed and maintained in the breed by selective breeding for pit-fighting ability.

To be sure, obedience competition, tracking, and above all Schutzhund work, all test to some degree, the temperament, character, and even courage of their participants. In none of these cases, however, is the physical strength and stamina of the dug really tested by truly Staffordshire standards; being a compact and generally well-muscled breed, even a dysplastic Staff can generally still clear the jump heights required in the obedience ring, and while a courage test forms a part of Schutzhund training, none of these activities ever serve to truly evaluate on a competitive scale, the true measure of an individual dog's physical strength, stamina, and determination in the face of physical adversity (i.e. the proverbial "gameness").

It is obvious therefore, that if those particular characteristics which are extolled and valued in the Staffordshire terrier are to be preserved, some new procedures must be developed to allow both the development and continuing evaluation of both the structural and physical capabilities of those individuals which will be targeted as prominent sires and dams, who will then pass their characteristics on to succeeding generations of dogs. It is the purpose of this report to suggest that competitive weight-pulling can be one such means of accomplishing these ends, while at the same time providing enjoyable and recreational experiences for both dogs and their owners. This report should in no way be construed as advocating weight-pulling competition as the only means of attaining such desired ends. Rather, weight-pulling competition should ideally be integrated with and considered as supplementary to, programs of breeding and training for bench conformation, obedience tracking, and/or Schutzhund work, in order to best realize the potential of such a program for producing structural and functional breed improvements.

Weight-Pulling - A Suggested Solution

The ways in which competitive weight-pulling offers criteria by which both the structural and functional soundness of a dog may be judged are generally obvious. Dogs which win such competitions have proven not only their physical strength and structural soundness, but they have also demonstrated a stable temperament characterized by a willingness to work for the gain of the favor of their handlers/trainers, despite physical adversity (i.e. a heavy weight to pull). Often, for example, the strongest dogs in a competition may be defeated by individuals which although physically smaller, emerge victorious as a result of determination and character (i.e. "gameness") alone. Weight-pulling competition, however, also offers a number of other advantages to both dogs and their owners/trainers. Some of these side benefits which are particularly attractive to the Staffordshire fancier include the following:

1) An opportunity to establish and demonstrate for all to see. the strength, stamina, "gameness," and general capabilities of the American Staffordshire terrier, in direct comparison with other breeds, within equal weight categories. This is possible since organized weight-pulling events are open to all breeds, even though they are currently dominated by working breeds such as Saint Bernards, huskies, and malamutes. There is thus, already in existence, a series of accepted rules and procedures which have seen the test of time and experience, in use by other breed clubs, and governing bodies are in existence in the form of the national and regional organizations sponsoring and regulating sled-dog racing competition.

2) Competitive weight-pulling may be undertaken by owners/trainers who have at their disposal only a single dog and a limited amount of land (A small backyard will suffice.) and the cost of training equipment is minimal - seldom exceeding twenty dollars.

3) In general, the show wins, level of obedience training, or similar past accomplishments of the dog to be used for weight-pulling are not of great importance to its potential for success. The only requirements for success in this endeavor are the willingness and patience of the owner/trainer to work regularly with his dog. This is no area in which wealthy individuals may buy "guaranteed success" through the employment of highly paid professional handlers.

4) Undertaken in the proper manner as discussed below, competitive weight-pulling can, and indeed to be successful must, be an enjoyable experience for both the dog and the owner/trainer. If the dog does not eagerly look forward to weight-pulling sessions, then the training regime has not been carried out properly and little or no success can be expected.

5) Particularly in the case of dogs which must spend extended periods of time during the day confined to a house or apartment, weight-pulling offers an opportunity to constructively focus and dissipate excess energy - requiring only access to a small piece of sidewalk, driveway, or lawn in a nearby park or backyard, which may be visited regularly as a 10-15-minute supplement to a regular evening walk.

The Equipment
The equipment required for competitive weight-pulling is generally simple and consists of the following:

1) Harness; A strong non-restrictive harness should be purchased from a source which is able to custom fit the harness to the measurements of the individual dog, or, alternatively, provide a harness which is capable of being later adjusted to the dog. Patterns and sources for such non-restrictive harnesses are generally best found through contacts with a local dog obedience club which provides tracking dog training. The same harness used in tracking work is generally acceptable for weight-pulling, providing it is non-restrictive and constructed of sufficiently strong material. Generally, sewn leather or nylon web belting is used. Rivetted leather harnesses are generally not of sufficient strength for heavier loads. If there is a sled-dog racing club in the area, they can generally supply information as to where pulling harnesses can be obtained. Finally, various dog-training publications (*Off Lead, Front and Finish,* etc.) also frequently carry advertisements for such harnesses.

2) Weight Cart; In actual competition, the weight-carrying device which is pulled is generally a four-wheeled, flat-bed cart, having bed dimensions of approximately two feet in width by four feet in length and a bed height of approximately twenty inches above the ground. The cart itself generally weighs between 50 and 75 pounds. Cart construction and wheels may be of any type that will allow the flat-bed of the cart to carry weights in excess of two tons. (The currently claimed world record for a single-dog pull is in excess of three tons)! The cart whould be equipped with a large ring or snap at either end of the undercarriage of the wheel base, allowing the cart to be pulled in either direction. When actually being pulled by a dog, a small brick tied to a rope is snapped to the ring at the rear end of the wheel base. Allowing this brick to drag on the ground acts as a passive brake, thus preventing the cart from rolling forward and striking the dog, if his pull

should suddenly slacken. When there is snow on the ground, weight-pulling rules call for the use of a dog sled which is used in a similar manner to the cart, with the exception that the runners may first be broken free of the ice before the dog is required to pull.

3) Practice Drag; Because most trainers would not want to go to the trouble and/or expense of building their own weight cart, such carts are frequently owned collectively by regional clubs which then provide them for use in competitions. For weight-pulling practice at home, however, a practice weight drag may be easily constructed from a discarded automobile tire casing. A hole is punctured in the face of the tire that would normally contact the road, and a nylon rope is then tied through this hole so that when the empty tire is laying flat on its side (like a doughnut) the tire can be pulled over the ground on its side, by the rope. A plywood board placed on top of the tire and secured with ropes, is used to hold the weights on this tire drag. It must be remembered that excessive friction with the ground on the part of the tire drag would mean that a dog pulling twenty pounds of total weight on such a drag is actually pulling the equivalent of several hundreds of pounds on a wheeled cart or sled on snow. An in-line strain guage, if available, can be used to verify and calculate the differences in pull required between the two, thus allowing a continuing assessment of the dog's progress.

4) Weights: A variety of types of objects may be used to provide weight. Full bags of dog food are generally useful and have the added advantage of being of known weight (25 pounds, 50 pounds, etc), although they are often bulky to use in the larger sizes. Cement blocks are more compact, but they must first be weighed and weights recorded for individual blocks if they differ by more than ½ pound. If necessary, young children, weighing between 40-60 pounds, may be allowed to ride on the weight cart after first having their weight recorded by the contest officials.

Rules and Regulations

The rules and regulations for competitive weight-pulling are set by the regional and national governing bodies regulating sled-dog racing competition. One such organization is the North American Sled Dog Racing Association (NASDRA). Rules are established which may change from time to time as these governing bodies may wish to modify the regulations under which such competitions are held. An up-to-date copy of the currently accepted rules for all-breed weight-pulling competition, as determined by these organizations, can usually be obtained by contacting local clubs invloved with the breeding, training, and/or racing of sled dogs. The rules suggested here are in general agreement with the rules for weight-pulling competition as they have been set forth by NASDRA, with certain modifications being made in weight classes, for particular application to the American Staffordshire terrier breed.

It is suggested here that the following rules be used to govern weight-pulling competition at one or more trial matches to be held at regional and/or national specialty shows, with a final set of rules for competition to be drawn up by the Obedience/Working-Dog Committee of the Staffordshire Terrier Club of America, and presented to the Board of Directors of the parent club for approval. by January 1, 1981.

Competition Format

Weight-pulling competition is usually held according to the following general format: dogs are entered into competitive classes according to weight, with dogs and bitches of equal weight pulling against each other in direct competition. NASDRA rules provide only for an "under 65 pound" class and a "heavyweight" class for all dogs exceeding 65 pounds in weight. Entered dogs draw for pulling order. Each dog must then, in turn, pull a qualifying weight in order to be allowed to enter the remainder of the competition. NASDRA rules establish a qualifying weight of 100 pounds for the under-65-pound class and 200 pounds for the over-65-pound class. All weights to be pulled are determined by first weighing the cart or sled at the beginning of the competition and then calculating total weight by adding together the weights of all the blocks or other objects subsequently placed on the cart.

In pulling the qualifying weight and all subsequent pulls, each dog is required to pull the loaded cart forward in a straight line for a total of fifteen feet on level or slightly rising ground. The dog must move the front wheels of the cart fifteen feet forward within a period of 90 seconds. Generally limed lines are used as on a football field, to mark the 15-foot distance across which the cart must be moved. The manner of actual pulling and the patterns of rest periods, if any, that may be taken by the dog during the 90 seconds allowed for the pull, are at the discretion of the handler with the following exceptions: (1) the handler may not touch the dog, cart, or harness, except in cases where the dog becomes entangled in its equipment and then only on the direction of the judge, (2) the handler must remain at all times, level with or slightly behind the shoulder of the dog, and (3) no baiting or the use of any devices creating noise or threats are permitted.

A dog is allowed three opportunities to pull the qualifying weight and all subsequent weight increments, 15 feet in 90 seconds. If a dog should fail in its first or second attempt to pull, it is retired until all other dogs have pulled in a round-robin fashion. Failure on the third attmept results in elimination. In the case of ties, winners are determined by the lowest number of tries required for the heaviest weight which was successfully pulled. In the event of an equal number of tries, the time required to pull the last heaviest weight determines the winner.

After the qualifying weight has been pulled, weight increments of a specified amount are agreed to by all competing handlers and are added to the cart. Weight increments may be determined by convenience (e.g. the weight of one added cement block), but all added objects must be officially weighed and the total weight added and announced by the judge before the first dog attempts to pull. At their discretion, handlers may choose to pass a given weight increment after having once pulled the qualifying weight. However, if the dog is unable to pull the specified weight at the time he elects to re-enter the competition, he is eliminated.

Morochito showing his "best" side

Weight Classes for Staffordshire Terriers

In order to provide greater opportunity for competition among Staffordshire terriers, it is suggested that weight-pulling competition in this breed be held in the following weight classifications:

Dog Weight	Qualifying Pull Weight
Less than 35 Pounds (Bantamweight)	50 pounds, (or the weight of the empty cart - whichever heavier)
35-50 Pounds (Lightweight)	75 pounds
50-65 Pounds (Middleweight)	100 pounds
Over 65 Pounds (Heavyweight)	200 pounds

Morochito resting after a hard workout

But not too tired to play with his master

Training Procedures

The exact training procedures by which an inexperienced dog may be brought into condition for weight-pulling competition are as many and as varied as are the philosophies by which coaches may train their charges for various athletic endeavors particularly competition in track and field, gymnastics and, of course, weightlifting competition. It is not the purpose of this report to develop detailed thinking concerning the relative merits of the various strategies that may be employed (e.g. the number of days per week to train, the exact weight levels with which the dog should be exercised, or what schedule to work prior to competition). This is indeed where the "art" as well as "science" of weight-pulling competition is developed and the interested owner/trainer contemplating such a program is urged to read what literature might be available from the area of human athletic training and/or contact those track and field or weightlifiing coaches who might be available locally, to better learn their procedures.

What will be presented here is simply an outline of how weight-pulling training should be initiated and from that point on, the individual owner/trainer will be more or less on his own. Letters and published comments describing experiences encountered in weight-pulling training, however, would be of great benefit to others who may also be engaged in similar activities. The Staffordshire Terrier Newsletter, for example, would be an excellent place to publish and exchange such information on a regular basis.

Basically, the introduction of the dog to weight-pulling is best initiated with the tire drag, as described above. Such a drag can be pulled around and sideways more easily than a cart, without the possibility of tangling the harness lines or being upset. The tire, with no weight on it, is placed on the lawn and the dog brought to it on a leash and chain training collar. The dog should be allowed to inspect the tire if curious, while being given verbal encouragement. The dog is then positioned in front of the tire and the harness is put on. Since the harness itself soon becomes something of an extra command to pull, it should only be put on when the dog is in position and actually ready to pull. It should then be quickly removed as soon as the pull is completed. Before long, the very act of putting on the harness will become an exciting event to the dog and this plus enthusiastic chatter during the harnessing process should greatly help to "psyche up" both dog and handler immediately before the pull.

In the case of the inexperienced dog, however, calming and reassuring words should be generously intermingled with enthusiastic exhortation during the harnessing process. Once the harness is on, the snap from the line attached to the tire should be attached to the harness' top-most "D" ring, or alternatively, the double lines from traces should be attached to side rings of the harness, if the latter style is preferred. The sound of the snap of the line onto the harness rings should eventually act as a signal, along with the handler's cheers, to start the dog pulling forward into the harness.

In starting an inexperienced dog, the handler should stand quietly and pet and calm the dog, with the dog standing in the heel position. The handler should then move forward slowly with a gentle tug on the leash which should still remain attached to the dog's training collar. The command "heel" may also be given if the dog has had any obedience training. If the dog acts frightened and jumps sideways when he feels and/or sees the tire begin to move behind him, the pace of the handler should be quickened in a <u>forward</u> direction, and more encouragement and praise given.

Once the tire has moved forward twenty to twenty-five feet (Always train to pull further than the fifteen feet required in competition), the harness should be quickly removed and <u>lavish</u> praise given. These procedures should be repeated until the dog is cheerfully and enthusiastically pulling the empty tire distances of 30 to 40 yards, always directly forward and always in a straight line, with the harness always being removed immediately after each pull. As weight is gradually added to the tire according to the dog's ability, the distances pulled should be gradually shortened to the twenty to twenty-five foot lengths described above.

At no time should the handler ever allow himself to be forward of the dog's shoulder as he moves forward in the pull. The temptation to move out in front of the dog, which is especially hard to resist when the dog is struggling with a heavy load, will only create a bad habit in terms of creating an expectation on the part of the dog that the handler will move out in front of him and coax him to come along and follow. Rather, the dog must be exhorted (not begged) to go forward <u>on his</u> own, taking the pull ahead of the handler.

After several weeks of pulling low weights on leash as described above, the leash can be removed and the procedures repeated using a weighted tire. Some trainers prefer to retain the symbolic control embodied in the leash and collar in nearly all but a few exceptional circumstances during training sessions. Others strive to have the dog pulling off-lead as soon as possible. While this may be partly a matter of taste, it is most important to realize that to whatever extent the training collar and leash are used to correct or pull on the dog in anything other than a symbolic manner, the dog's training progress will be impeded. That is to say, a reluctant puller cannot be threatened or dragged with a leash and then later be expected to pull in competition off leash. The correction for a dog reluctant to pull is an immediate lightening of the load to a level where the dog can and will once again pull it willingly off-lead even if that means going back once again to the empty tire drag!

As stated earlier, exact training philosophies will differ greatly in detail and will be left largely to the individual owner/trainer's skills and discretion. It is important to realize however, that in all phases of preparing for weight-pulling competition, a balance must be reached between two basic kinds of activities: (1) training sessions in which maximum possible weights are pulled in order to determine and test the progress that the dog is making, and (2) training sessions in which sub-maximum weights are pulled with greater frequency (i.e. "calisthenics" weight-pulling) through which the strength and confidence of the dog are gradually increased through repetitive successes and lavish praise. It is obvious, however, that the sessions must be relatively few and far between, in which maximum weights are pulled until the limit of the dog is reached. No dog will remain enthusiastic about weight-pulling for long if he begins to believe that most of the time that he pulls into his harness, the weight behind him will not move! Whenever in the course of a training session the dog's limit is so exceeded, one more pull of a much lighter weight should always be made to end the session, so that the dog leaves the training period with a positive feeling of success. Needless to say, all interactions between the trainer and the dog must be encouraging, enthusiastic and positive. Threats or abusive talk directed at the dog can only serve to make the dog less willing to give his best. Only in the most exceptional circumstances should the word "no" be used in weight-pulling training. If a dog should for some reason suddenly stop acting enthusiastic and/or refuse to pull, he should immediately be put back on leash and returned to the heeling forward exercise using the empty tire drag, as described earlier.

MWP-Ch Panda's Gallant Ruffian, CD, SchH I, VB, AD, U-CD, with new co-owner, Marty Harper, in Louisville, Kentucky, setting a new world record in weight-pulling!

A puppy from Morochito's litter sister Brandy bred to their litter brother Jake. Future weight-pulling champion???

Haynes' JJ

Chapter 6: Scientific Nutrition

>Tell me what you eat, and I will tell you what you are.
>- Anthelme Brillat-Savavin

How true that caption is! For a human, actually, the caption should say, "You are what you ate seven years ago." I attended a seminar given by a nutrition expert - has studied it virtually all of his life. He said, as I recollect, that the human cell replaces itself every seven years, so that it may take pretty close to seven years to correct a nutritionally-based problem. The idea is, of course, to begin eating correctly as early in your life as possible. Same thing is true with an animal. Actually animals in America generally eat better than people. Research is continually discovering new aspects of nutrition and I believe nutrition plays an important -perhaps the most critical - role in helping an animal reach its maximum potential. Diet is so very important. So many people "poo-hoo" it because they are able to exist in what appears to them to be excellent health. Their standard of what excellent health is, is measured by looking around at others in their environment within their culture. In a 1979 research study,[18] Dr. Peter Hill, an expert in cancer research, with a grant from the United States American Health Foundation, measured hormone levels in groups of black women from an area in South Africa where cancer is practically non-existent. Their diet is sparse, nearly pure vegetarian, and very low in fat. He compared their hormone levels with those of American white women whose eating habits were "normal" American diets. The black women had significantly lower levels of a number of hormones, including prolactin (associated with cancer). The black women excreted considerably less androgens and astrogens than the American women. He then switched their diets for three weeks and found that even in this short time, the hormone levels reversed. The conclusion can then be made that the difference in hormones was not ethnically or genetically determined -it was diet.

Of course, dietary needs are different for a dog than for a human, but there are some commonalities in principle. I'm by no means an expert in this field, but I've been interested in it for quite awhile, and I've read quite a bit on the subject. Let me share with you then, a little background on nutrition. We'll take a look at how a dog's body functions if it is properly nourished. In a well balanced diet energy needs are primarily supplied by quality carbohydrates. This is not a well known fact, because so many people who condition dogs put so much emphasis on protein (believing it provides energy). When a Pit Bull is in his keep (training period six to eight weeks prior to a fight), most conditioners put him on a total protein diet (generally lean meat and/or liver), with vitamin supplements, etc., most don't provide any carbohydrates. This is fairly necessary in this instance because the dog must be trimmed of all fat so that he goes in as lean as possible and at his lowest weight. But many pit fighting people feed their dogs a similar diet all the time (but give them more quantity and perhaps cut back on the extra vitamins) believing that the high-protein diet is best for their dogs. Actually this type of feeding is harmful to the dog. (You can't see the harm done; that's the problem with nutrition.) Many dog owners who don't fight their dogs feed them high-protein diets in the belief that the dog will grow bigger and stronger and have more energy. The popularity of the "high-protein" dog foods attests to this fact. As we will see, protein does contribute to growth, but it does very little for energy. In addition, providing more protein in terms of quantity (rather than quality) will not make the dog grow bigger or stronger. We will take a closer look at the misunderstood protein in awhile, but first let's see how carbohydrates work.

Starch from the carbohydrates is converted into glucose in the intestinal tract and then absorbed into the blood stream. The blood conveys it to all tissues of the body where it is oxidized (combined with oxygen) to form carbon dioxide and water. It is the oxidation process that provides the energy. Glucose is often thought of as a fuel, and in a way it is. But it acts as a fuel only when it is oxidized by a complex process that requires the active participation of fatty acids (primarily linoleic and linolenic), protein, minerals, and vitamins (mostly the B-complex vitamins), in order for the cells to extract energy from the glucose. Unused carbohydrates are stored in the muscles and liver as glycogen which the body can draw upon for energy when needed. Unused protein is also converted to glucose, but the process is slower than with carbohydrates. Moreover, protein cannot be digested and assimilated unless there is a proper balance of carbohydrates and fat. The point I'm trying to make is that vitamins, minerals, protein, carbohydrates, etc. are synergetic (They work together), so that a food must be balanced. Excess protein doesn't build extra muscle; it's passed through the system. In fact excess protein can be harmful if consumed over a long period of time. Excess carbohydrates are turned into fat. Too many vitamins or vitamins provided in the wrong proportion can be toxic and the same is true of minerals. It is a widely-held belief that bone deformities and conformation problems are caused by not feeding enough good food. Modern university research has proven that these problems are actually often caused by over nutrition. Pit Bulls who are inherently on the "bull-doggish" side put on weight awfully quickly during their formative years, which can place considerable stress on the development of their bone structure. They must have a proper balance of the nutrients that are essential to the development of sturdy bones. For one thing, the ratio of calcium to phosphorus must be in the proper proportion.

You might feel that these problems are taken care of today because modern research has solved them and most of the commercial brands provide all the nutrients a dog needs and then some. Not necessarily so. We have come a long way, and feeding the top-of-the-line commercial dog food is much better than the old-fashioned (and more expensive) diet of raw meat (or canned horsemeat if you couldn't afford the raw meat). The feeling used to be that because dogs are classed as carnivorous animals, they should eat nothing but meat. Some people still feed their dogs a diet that is primarily lean meat, thinking they are giving them the best. In the wild, however, flesh is only a small part of the canine diet. The wild animal consumes primarily blood, liver, tripe (stomach) and viscera (internal organs) containing partially digested grains and vegetable matter, and also intestinal bacteria (the good kind). Modern commercial dog foods tend to approximate the biologically balanced diet that nature provides and actually does a better job of it. Like any other commercial activity, however, the pet food industry is profit motivated and competitive. Actually it's a pretty lucrative industry. An article in our local newspaper, *The Greensboro Record,* January 31, 1980, dealing with the subject of pet foods, claimed that supermarkets allocate more space to pet foods than to any other product. Local grocers said pet foods are among their top five money-makers, perhaps the top one. Dr. Mark L. Morris, D.V.M., Ph.D., who developed the Science Diet formula (to be discussed later), considered by many veterinarians to be a top authority on the feeding of dogs, was interviewed in the article. He stated that pet foods are "a little bit like life. You get what you pay for." The less expensive brands usually have more cereal which acts as a filler and less animal protein or inferior protein that is not well assimilated. It is difficult, perhaps, to chose from the wide variety of products available and you aren't really informed of much by the guaranteed analysis or listing of ingredients.

By far the largest dog food manufacturer in the world is Ralston-Purina. Because of their size, they can afford to spend large amounts on research and they do; they spend millions. In fact, they spend more on research than the total sales of some other known brands. For this reason, I personally would select Purina for my dog if I were limited to the commercial dog foods available in the grocery stores. In fact, Morochito was started on Purina Puppy Chow and Puppy Chuck-wagon (also made by Purina). Since he was about a year old, however, I have found some dog foods that I personally feel are better than the dog food you buy in the stores. My vet clued me in on my first discovery, which is Wayne's dog food. You can't buy it in grocery stores but can often find it at places like a Farmers' Exchange or feed store; that's where I get mine. My vet said that he got better results with Wayne's in raising his Beagles. It is more expensive per pound but not necessarily per feeding. It is a higher quality food so the dog will assimilate more of it and so you don't have to feed him nearly so much of it as with the more popular brands. It's not a local brand because I notice that Walter Patton, a Texas breeder of Pit Bulls and Stafs, has noted on his brochure advertising his dogs, that he "recommends and feeds" Wayne's dog food.

I have also found that many people who have dogs that are subjected to stress like sled dog pulling contests, field trials, etc. feed extremely high quality foods and supplements such as I am about to recommend. I have written each of these companies asking them to explain why their products are superlative. They responded, providing me with the literature and permission to share it with you in my book. I must say that I have no connection whatsoever with any of these companies and they have not paid me anything nor have they provided me any products or discounts. Naturally they feel that their products are superlative and their brochures advertise their products, but I do feel like the information they provide is noteworthy. If you ask your vet, I believe you'll find that he'll advise you that their products are in fact higher quality although perhaps overpriced. My position is that perhaps they are overpriced, but if they have developed superlative products as a result of considerable research, they are entitled to healthy profits. I'll buy them. Actually, as we will see, they are not so expensive as they appear to be, the reason being that you will feed a considerably <u>smaller quantity</u> to obtain equal or better nutrition than the commercial dog foods sold in grocery stores. You feed less quantity because the higher <u>quality</u> means more of it is assimilated by the system. Therefore you can keep your dog leaner (and therefore healthier) while providing superb nutrition with more complete utilization. You will also notice (because of better assimilation) a healthier stool and coat. The stool will be relatively dark and hard and much easier to pick up than real soft stools, caused when food is not completely absorbed by the body. Some companies add tomato pomace or beet pulp to provide firm stools, but the better ones listed here do not; the firm stools are because of more thorough digestibility. When I put Morochito on Wayne's dog food. I noticed a decided improvement in his stool, and his coat took on more luster. A dog's coat is said to be (at least in part) a mirror of his health because the dog's coat receives nutrition only after the body has received all it needs.

With this background, let's look at some of the literature I received from the companies I wrote. (Write them at the addresses provided and you can probably receive more information and detail and prices, if you are interested.) You will find some duplication of information between that supplied by the companies and the information I give. I think this can be justified, however, because these points need to be underscored.

The company that supplied us with the most information was the Nutra-Vet Research Corporation, makers of the ABADY FORMULA dog food and MAGNUM and PROVIM supplements.[19] The following pages are copied from their brochure.

New Concepts in Animal Supplementation

Over the years the name Nutra-Vet Research Corporation has become associated with products that work extremely well, with high performance. We designed our products to work that way; it is the people who use them who have created our reputation. For us to define this reputation is difficult indeed, for our products enjoy a reputation of such excellence that a mystique seems to surround them.

For many years now, people have been telling us how Nutra-Vet nutritional supplements have benefited their animals. We have been told of dramatic improvements in coat condition and shedding, of improved quality of growth in fast growing puppies, of bitches finishing their championships in heavy competition a few weeks after weaning a large litter of puppies and testimonial after testimonial to the generally improved condition of animals receiving Nutra-Vet supplementation. These are undoubtedly some of the factors that have created this mystique about our products.

At Nutra-Vet we perceive nutrition as an art; an art which rests heavily on the unfolding body of scientific knowledge. It is our business at Nutra-Vet to create highly relevant nutritional supplements that may be of benefit to animals. We work with animals 24 hours a day, every day of the year. We care about animals, all animals, and our supplements reflect our profound concern. We are always happy to hear that an animal may have become fitter, healthier, or more beautiful as a response to a Nutra-Vet formulation.

At this point, we will discuss with more precision the ideas and concepts that underlie Nutra-Vet formulations and some of the philosophical implications of these concepts.

Our supplements are not drugs, nor do they have limited objectives. Animals have been known to show improvements in coat, intestinal function, weight, and endurance, all at the same time. The fact that our supplements work so well, so much of the time, on so many animals may well indicate that there are widespread deficiencies or plenty of room for improvement in contemporary feeding practices. Obviously if all feeds and all feeding were universally perfect for every animal under all circumstances, there would not be a place for Nutra-Vet formulations.

Nutra-Vet nutritional supplements are made from the highest quality source materials on the market. Our vitamins and minerals carry U.S.P. or N.F. ratings. Our protein constituents are among the very best that money can buy. High grade non-instant dried milk and milk solids from Holland and Scandinavia, the finest casein from Ireland and Australia, defatted liver powder from Argentina, quality dried yeast and whole dried eggs from the United States; all government approved for human consumption, to mention a few. We do not choose our materials in terms of their cost, but in terms of their ability to do the job, regardless of cost. The supplements are first designed, then they are priced. At no point from the drawing boards to the finished product are quality and integrity compromised. You are assured that every Nutra-Vet product was designed to work, not priced to sell. Our products do sell, to demanding animal owners, but they sell only because they work.

Nutra-Vet supplements are synergistic. They provide vitamins, minerals and protein at the same time. In most metabolic processes groups of elements must enter the digestive process simultaneously for proper assimilation and utilization. Amino acids (protein) and their accompanying vitamins, minerals, fats and carbohydrates work best when supplied at the same time and in the proper proportions. Should the total complement of elements be incomplete or deficient in some way, synthesis may fall far short of the optimum. Our formulations provide vitamins, minerals and protein in the ratios and at the levels which we consider optimal to do the job for which they were designed.

<u>Nutra-Vet Formulations Were Designed To Help Complement Commercial Rations.</u>

Commercial rations are the result of much research and painstaking effort by manufacturers. Many of the gross, obvious deficiencies that at one time plagued Dog and Catdom have been drastically reduced since the advent of the commercial feed as the principal mode of feeding. However, as with any system, along with the advantages have come disadvantages, and other less obvious but potentially serious deficiencies can arise, due to some of the inevitable rigidity of the concept. Our position on this matter is to take the best of the system and try to improve on the weaknesses. Here is how it works:

Dog and cat foods in general get their protein principally from cereals, such as ground yellow corn, wheat midlings, ground oats, wheat gluten, soybean meal, with small amounts of meat and bone meal. Cereal proteins are notably low in lysine, methionine, leucine, isoleucine, and tryptophan. These *elements are further reduced by the extensive processing; also vitamin potencies are affected. Although some companies try to complement one source of protein with another to help improve the total protein picture, it is often done in a manner which does not yield the optimum results. It would be pertinent at this point to discuss protein and its metabolism and the role that Nutra-Vet supplements play in helping to improve the protein picture of standardized rations.*

The nutritive value of the protein in any feedstuff depends on its digestibility, its amino acid distribution and content. For the dog and the cat both of these factors are better met by first class protein, as derived from meat, eggs, etc. Plant protein is considered as second class protein. The essential amino acids for the dog are arginine, histidine, isoleucine, leucine, phenylalanine, methionine, threonine, tryptophan, valine and lysine.

They must be present in the food and are needed in differing amounts, which must follow one basic pattern. In most food proteins all the essential amino acids are present but in disproportionately small amounts, thus deviating from the one utilizable pattern. Because each essential amino acid must be present in a given proportion at the same time, if a dog or cat were to eat protein containing enough tryptophan to satisfy 100% of the utilizable pattern's requirements, 100% of the leucine level and so forth, but only 50% of the necessary lysine level, then as far as the animal is concerned it is as if the animal had eaten only 50% of all the essential amino acids. The protein "assembling center" in the cell uses the essential amino acids at the level of the "limiting amino acid" and releases the rest of the amino acids to be used by the body for energy.

Although ingredient panels are provided on every bag of dog food, it is virtually impossible to make a meaningful assessment of the role that each ingredient plays. Moreover, when actual amounts are known, one cannot add the proportionate values of the different ingredients and obtain an average figure which reflects the nutritive value of the food as a whole. Because of the intimate relationships among the different nutrients, the summation may be much greater or much less than indicated by simple addition. For example wheat gluten is a very poor source of protein for the dog, because it is deficient in lysine, and has a biological value of only 40. Adding equal amounts of casein which has a biological value of 75, to wheat gluten will not provide a protein with a biological value of 58 (the average of 40 and 75 is 58), but one of 80 or more, because each has amino acids which complement the other. What it ultimately comes down to is that the biological value of a food, the digestibility of its nutrients or its ability to supply energy can only be measured by the dog. Even if biological testing were available to veterinarians, it would be of limited value for many dog foods, because they are prepared from open formulae and major ingredients are interchanged depending on their cost and supply. Thus even the same brand may vary drastically both analytically and nutritionally, from one batch to the other. The only control that is met is the "Guaranteed Analysis." Different brands having the same "Guaranteed Analysis" may have markedly different nutritional characteristics. The "Guaranteed Analysis" which is required by law merely lists tolerances (some maximum, some minimum) allowable for the nutrients in the food. A guarantee of "Maximum Ash 8%" for instance purely denotes that there are no more than 8 CMS of ash per 100 CMS of food. If the food contained less ash, it might cause severe problems for the growing puppy or for a bitch during gestation and lactation; and the food would have still met its legal requirements.

Deficiencies of essential amino acids can result in some serious problems. When the diet lacks tryptophan, methionine, or isoleucine, the liver cannot produce antibodies and susceptibility to disease and infection may result. The lack of tryptophan or methionine may result in hair falling out and toxemia in pregnancy. A lack of histidine and phenylalanine causes the eyes to become bloodshot. An under supply of arginine causes animals to become sterile and a reaction in the reduction in the motility of the sperm. Too little tryptophan can also cause atrophy of the testicles and females to lose their young (abortion). A deficiency of methionine allows fat to be retained in the liver. It is important to note that it is unlikely that any food is totally lacking in any one essential amino acid, whereas it is far from impossible that certain levels of deficiencies or availability could exist. It is also relevant to mention that a given set of symptoms may have totally different causes, and the advice of a veterinarian should always be sought to assist in making a proper determination.

Keeping in mind the above information, we will now describe how Nutra-Vet formulations may be of benefit to your animals and the reasons for it.

The vitamin and mineral constituents of the supplements have been designed to provide elements in relation to metabolic essentials and in relation to their occurence and availability in normal rations. The adage that "if a little is good, a lot is better" does not hold true. Because an element is necessary or beneficial within certain tolerances does not imply that massive quantities are better. In some instances they can be dangerous, or destructive in some way. Additionally elements in any compound must be in reasonable balance, as excesses of one element may produce deficiencies of another. Excesses of one element may produce the opposite reaction that one may be trying to achieve. The following *examples will serve to describe these points. When calcium and phosphorous are not supplied in proper ratio, the mineral present in the greatest amount will reduce the amount of the other that can be used by the body. If vitamin D is present in excess, while calcium and phosphorous are in proper amounts and ratios, calcium is reabsorbed from the bones because there is too much vitamin D in the blood. Excess calcium tends to exaggerate the need for zinc, especially if the calcium is given by itself. Given as calcium-phosphate it does not appear to create this problem. Thiamine must be increased along with increases in carbohydrates, because thiamine is intimately related to carbohydrate metabolism, pyridoxine must also increase with increases in protein. The list of these interrelationships is endless. Nutra-Vet formulations have, to as large a measure as possible, taken these situations into consideration. If average rations contain enough manganese for normal maintenance but not enough calcium, for instance, the elements in our formulations would be presented within appropriate parameters for safety and efficiency. If most rations contain near ample vitamins A & D, for instance, it would be senseless to provide additional large doses of these elements, as there would be a potential hazard in so doing. It is practically impossible to provide one supplement to complement exactly each feed from every batch. But researchers at Nutra-Vet have created formulae that generally complement the types of rations most normally produced. These formulae have proven, in the field, to be well appreciated for their sound theoretical and scientific bases and for the excellent performance characteristics.*

Nutra-Vet formulations have tried to also take into account some of the changing requirements of animals at different stages of life. We know for instance that more vitamins A & D are needed during growth, we also know that high levels of vitamin A during gestation can cause birth defects, we also know that more minerals are needed during growth, gestation and lactation, than for general maintenance. Protein quality must be superior during growth, gestation, lactation and stress, and protein must be well characterized by its lysine, valine, methionine, and tryptophan levels. Greater requirements for the B-Complex and vitamin E are particularly needed during the reproductive process and stress. We have tried to incorporate, to the best of our ability, these elements in relation to the concepts described above. Nutra-Vet has approached the question of protein in the following manner. It would be impractical and deceptive to provide large quantities of cheap protein to improve feeds that are already abundant in these materials. We have consequently provided small amounts of extremely high quality protein, structured to provide significant amounts of the essential amino acids, particularly those known to be undersupplied in cheap protein. The protein constituents are balanced and structured to help raise the limiting amino acids in commercial feeds. The high quality of the source materials, with their high digestibility coeficients have the ability to exert a salutory effect on the less well digested components of the ration. Our product Nutra-Plus, for instance, recommends one teaspoon for a thirty-pound adult dog. This dosage provides the following percentages of the following essential amino acids in relation to the Minimum Daily Requirements as established by The National Research Council: lysine 13.5%, methionine 14.756, tryptophan 16.4%, valine 9.9%, threonine 12.356, phenylalanine 12.5%, leucine 9.9%, isoleucine 9.4%, arginine 8.25%, histidine 11.67%. The obvious benefits to either a deficient ration, or the ability of this protein pattern and density to improve a standardized ration, precludes going into further detail. Further potential benefits are achieved by all the supporting elements of the protein constituents, the vitamins and minerals that are supplied at the same time.

The Importance of Relevant Supplementation

Although some people may not feel that supplementation is necessary, it is our position that it is beneficial in most cases and absolutely essential in many for a well rounded feeding program. Also there are clear distinctions on what type of supplementation that is being offered. Nutra-Vet supplements have little in common with most supplements on the market. And the results speak for themselves.

Despite aggressive campaigns by dog food manufacturers proclaiming the completeness and perfection of their products, these claims must be relegated, by thinking individuals, more to the realm of advertising and publicity than to the realm of reality. Although it is possible to make a good product, the very concept or claim that "perfection" has been attained is repulsive to the scientific mind. There is always room for improvement, for growth, for new insights and new knowledge. Elements that were not considered essential a few years ago have now been found, not only to be essential, but to be critical for survival. Even the National Research Council has changed the levels of some elements that are necessary for normal physiological function over the years; it has also placed elements on the essential list that they deemed unnecessary previously. Additionally, the pressures of competition in the marketplace, the structures of supply, demand, cost, and profits all play a role, and a limiting role on the quality of the ingredients that go into every bag of dog food. It has been stated by prominent researchers that it is practically impossible to make one dog food that can meet all the requirements of animals under all conditions. There are too many variations in individual requirements, age, sex, activity levels, temperament, genetic strains, stress, diseases, drug use, parasite loads, in addition to the changing requirements during the different stages of life to make the concept of one food for all, for all times, even remotely possible.

The requirements for normal maintenance for instance are far different from those of gestation and lactation. Protein content and quality and associated nutrient requirements may be needed at a level 300 times greater than at other times. It is often impossible for an animal to consume such great quantities of a bulky diet. One prominent manufacturer used to recommend 32 cups of his dry dog food for a 100 pound bitch during lactation. This manufacturer was being more honest than many. The simple truth however decries that no matter how good the food, it must be within the capacity of the organism to ingest!

Some manufacturers have recently introduced premium brands of dog foods, claiming that they are manufactured from better quality ingredients; they also sell for considerably more. There is justification in the adage "you get what you pay for." Also keeping this in mind, (that there are better quality dog foods) how can the others claim to be "ideal?"

<u>*Now Let Us Discuss the Canine Digestive System and Metabolism*</u>

The canine system is better designed to cope with small quantities of highly nutritious, concentrated foods, such as meat, organs, intestines and bones than bulky carbohydrates. Also the quality of health and the quality of condition are to a very large measure determined by the kind of food that is eaten. The statement that "one is what one eats" has great justification. With any complete feed, designed by man, the level of condition and health that can be produced will always fall within the parameters of the designer. Different foods will produce different results, and all of them can be improved on, by definition.

It is important to understand that animals partially regulate their food intake by the energy (calories) provided by that food. For a dog or cat to receive its full complement of vitamins, minerals, fats, and protein, he must consume the full measure that the manufacturer recommends. Commercial feeds have been balanced to provide nutrients and energy in relation to each other. There are conditions where an animal may consume less than the optimum of recommended amounts. In effect this is what would be happening: take, as an example, a 100-pound dog who consumes the amount of dog food that the manufacturer recommends, then let us take another 100-pound dog who for various reasons, be they breed differences, slower metabolism or what have you, will consume 9 cups of the food to the 12 cups that his control ate. The second dog may be getting enough calories to meet his energy requirements but will in effect be getting 25% less of all his other nutrients, including protein, vitamins, minerals, linoleic acid, etc., that he may require for his size and weight. There are many reasons that can cause a low food intake: lower requirements for total energy, vitamin, mineral and protein deficiencies, illness, inadequate food density, too much bulk, etc.

Our supplements may be helpful in many of these situations. In the case of the dog who consumed less food because his caloric needs were being met, the Nutra-Vet supplements may have been helpful in improving the quality of the protein in the ration, thereby allowing the lowered volume to more closely meet his needs for protein. For it follows that it takes a little more than half a gram of egg white protein per pound of body weight to keep a normal dog under "normal" conditions in nitrogen equilibrium, whereas it takes 2 times as much wheat gluten protein to do the same job. In other words, the higher the quality of the protein and the better the digestibility, the less is required. Also because of the small volume that is required for a Nutra-Vet supplement with very few corresponding calories, the dog is not obliged to increase his gross food intake. Had the supplements provided a large number of calories, that dog might then have decreased his total food intake, thereby defeating the purpose of the supplement. Consistently low vitamin and mineral levels can be deleterious to health. Some of the conditions associated with vitamin and mineral deficiencies are the following: Skin infections, flaky dermatitis, upper respiratory infections, constipation, diarrhea, gastrointestinal problems, susceptibility to disease, weight loss and unthriftyness, muscle weakness, conjunctivitis, nervousness, loss of stamina, bradycardia, enlargement of the heart, retarded growth, poor growth, gingivitis, foul breath, infertility, abortion, lack of milk, anemia, degeneration of nerves and loss of conditioned reflex, weakness of the hindquarters. Birth defects are also associated with vitamin deficiencies at times, such as cleft palate, harelip, structural abnormalities of the esophagus, hernia of the diaphram, deformed eyes, missing eyes, jaw malformations, to name a few. One thing that should be stressed is that in view of the many differing causes that any one set of symptoms may have, it is always essential to consult a licensed veterinarian for a diagnosis. Additionally the vitamin and mineral constituents of the Nutra-Vet formulations will help protect animals from deficiencies of these elements.

The importance of using balanced supplementation, cannot be over-emphasized. It is also extremely important to understand the distinctions among the different supplements on the market which do not all fall into one category.

The fact that there are poorly designed supplements on the market does not mean that the concept of supplementation is wrong.

Manufacturers of commercial dog food (this certainly applies to the best ones) have gone to some effort to ensure that certain nutrients are incorporated into their rations in specific ratios to each other. They strongly warn their customers that additions can unfavorably affect the balance of nutrients. These points are well taken but are entirely too general. Some types of additions could upset the balance of nutrients; it depends entirely on what is being added and for what purpose. Here is an example of what we mean. The scientifically accepted ratio for calcium and phosphorous is 1 part of phosphorous to 1.2 to 1.4 parts of calcium. The addition of large amounts of muscle meat, which is substantially higher in phosphorous than calcium could upset the ratio in the food. So can the addition of calcium by itself, or the addition of vitamin, mineral supplements that have a substantially higher proportion of calcium than phosphorous. Nutra-Vet supplements present no such problem as the calcium-phosphorous ratios in all our formulae are within the accepted range. Nutritional supplements do exist on the market, many are well known brands, that have exaggerated levels of vitamins A & D and unusual calcium to phosphorous ratios. These supplements could perhaps, in our opinion, be justified on a therapeutic level; but this type of supplementation would be better handled by a veterinarian familiar with animal dietetics, than by the layman.

Nutra-Vet nutritional supplements are designed to maintain the integrity of the essential ratios in commercial feeds. They are also designed to help improve the quality of these feeds. They can be added to any diet without fear of unbalancing the existing nutrient patterns.

In closing, we should mention that if you feel your animal is in optimum health and condition, then these supplements may not be for you. However, if you are dissatisfied with your dog or cat's condition, or if you feel that they are not reaching their full potential, and that your veterinarian believes that they are free of disease, despite using an accepted feeding program or should you wish to improve the plan of nutrition that your animal is getting, then perhaps Nutra-Vet Research Corporation has some of the answers.

I am really pleased to be able to pass this information from Nutra-Vet on to my readers and hope that you will gain much from it.

I notice that these supplements can be given without upsetting the balance of the nutrients and I like that.

Nutra-Vet describes the Abady formula as a dog food that blends two, often opposed philosophies - the strongly scientific (where nutrient patterns, levels, and utilization are determined by the Scientific Method - and the Traditional-Empirical approach which emphasizes the carnivorous character of the ration, the freshness of the ingredients, and the relative absence of artificial non-nutritive elements such as preservatives, dyes, humectants, bacteriostats, or flavoring agents. The supplements that Nutra-Vet provides are as follows:

1. Magnum. It was the Magnum product that motivated me to write the company. In my correspondence with various breeders and owners of athletic dogs across the country, I kept hearing about this supplement Magnum that they give their puppies and how pleased they were with the results. These are owners of Pit Bulls and they said they had no connection with this company, but they used the products and got excellent results. Magnum is a complex product that took seven years to develop. It is a concentrated supplement that collects the elements that promote the growth process. It is for puppies only. Part of the growth stimulus is added directly and part is achieved by creating special, complex synergisms with already existing elements in the regular feed. Additionally, Magnum contains those elements that nourish in the right proportions all of the vital metabolic systems so that growth is balanced and overall health and condition are markedly upgraded. It is designed to allow the puppy to grow to a bigger, stronger, better muscled dog with more stamina, who has grown much closer to his genetic potential than if the supplement were not administered. Forty-seven nutrients are included in the product. Maximization of size and weight with strong, well muscled straight limbs, true gait, good nerves, and proper skeletal development do not happen by accident; they are attainable only when all aspects of essential elements are supplied. I think this product is especially good for those highly inbred Pit Bulls, bred for true gameness, but perhaps lacking in proper structure or having inherently weak teeth. The food supplement cannot correct hereditarily derived problems, but it can strengthen weak areas, so that, for example, weak teeth will not be so weak as they would otherwise be. The Magnum supplement is for larger breeds (dogs maturing at over 60 pounds). Actually, they have another product called Minum for growth. It is for puppies of the small and medium sized breeds (dogs maturing at under 60 pounds). This is the same formula as Magnum calibrated for the smaller dog. Most Pit Bulls, of course, are much smaller than 60 pounds. The folks I talked to used Magnum instead of Minum even though their puppies grow up to be smaller than 60 pounds. I guess that's because they figure they are giving them more. Evidently it's working well, but I would

caution you that too much can be toxic. Pit Bulls tend to be a very active breed and those breeders who are giving Magnum to their puppies are exercising them pretty heavily (or at least they should be), so they can take the extra nutrients. I'm saying that it's probably okay to give Magnum to the smaller Pit Bull pups if they are heavily exercised, but if they aren't, I think you should use the products the way they are designed.

2. Provim. This is a vitamin-mineral-protein supplement designed to build condition in dogs and for dogs under stress. When an animal is stressed, as with heavy conditioning, the need for nutrients is greatly accelerated, so that a vitamin-mineral-protein food that would be highly toxic under normal conditions becomes necessary because of the demands placed on the body. Provim is recommended during illness and convalescence. It's used by owners of racing dogs and hunting dogs. It's designed to increase alertness, stamina, and endurance.

3. Forlac. A premium grade vitamin-mineral-protein supplement designed for bitches during gestation and lactation. A puppy's nutrition really begins with his mother so I consider this super important. To me the mother should have the best – the sky's the limit as far as I'm concerned. Puppies that have mothers that had specially formulated quality supplements, not only develop better during gestation, they will also have better resistance.

4. Natural Vitamin E Powder. The natural vitamin E (d-Alpha Tocopherol Acetate), not the synthetic dl form used by many dog foods, has approximately 62.5 i.u.'s per teaspoon. The product is almost nine times as potent in natural vitamin E as the best wheat germ oil. It is calibrated for easy dosing.

5. Calcium Trace Mineral Complex. Helps to correct the imbalances in calcium and phosphorous that occur when meat and eggs are added to a balanced ration.

6. Dibasic Calcium Phosphate. Extra calcium and phosphorous in the proper ratio - valuable during growth, gestation, and lactation.

7. Bone Meal Replacer. A product that offers a similar chemical analysis as bone meal but offers the following advantages that bone meal doesn't:
    a. not as subject to decomposition
    b. all ingredients premium grade
    c. consistent potencies (Bone meal potencies vary.)

8. Scorbucin Vitamin C. Scorbucin is a vitamin C powder with normally occurring associated elements. Each teaspoon contains 430 mgs. of vitamin C plus small amounts of the bioflavanoid and hesperi-dine complexes and rutin.

9. <u>Nutra-Plus.</u> This is the maintenance supplement. It adds a margin of safety to many feeds, assuring the dog receives all necessary nutrients.

Another product I recommend is Hill's Science Diet. My veterinarian informed me that Hill's enjoyed a good reputation with him and other vets for their integrity (not being so profit oriented that quality is sacrificed). It is supposed to be one of the highest quality foods. It is also thought of as one of the highest in cost. It also has one of the highest caloric densities per pound. Commercial foods average 800-1200 digestible calories per pound, while Science Diet averages 1860-2360 digestible calories per pound. On a per feeding basis, however, it is only slightly higher in price than commercial brands – I've already explained the reasons. Science Diet averages 90% digestible compared to 70% digestibility with commercial foods, and the dogs will have less stool.

Science Diet has a fixed formulation whereas commercial foods change base ingredients from batch to batch as they compete for price and use the least cost formulation. Like Nutra-Vet, they don't sell through the grocery stores so they avoid the middle man (retailing) costs. The Science Diet products that are relevant to us are as follows:

1. <u>Canine Growth.</u> This product is for growing puppies. The vitamins, minerals, and raw nutrients are in proper proportion so that the puppy can reach full genetic potential. It is much more than a few extra supplements. The puppies get the extra calcium and protein necessary for bone development and tissue construction. They also get the extra vitamins and minerals they need. The Science Diet formula provides the puppies with twice the caloric intake of adult dogs. The "grocery store" brands cannot provide this because the puppy would have to eat twice as much as the adult dog which of course he can't. Many of the commercial brands do provide extra calories in puppy foods, but their food is not concentrated or of the quality found in Science Diet so the puppy still has to eat too much in order to get all the calories he can utilize.

2. <u>Maximum Stress Diet</u>. Stress is not just physical; it is also emotional. (This is true for humans as well as dogs.) This means that a dog that is receiving heavy obedience protection or Schutzhund training is subjected to stress even if he's not being exercised. Maximum Stress Diet was originally designed for feeding sentry dogs. Over the past ten years its use has been expanded to feed the majority of all the Armed Forces sentry dogs. The primary requirement for feeding a stressed dog is to provide increased energy (calories). This necessitates a diet with maximum caloric density (more useable calories per pound of food). Also, nutrients must be balanced to this higher energy level. To reduce food

intake, the ration must be highly digestible. One cup of Maximum Stress Diet provides more useable energy than 3-4 cups of ordinary dry dog food.

    3. <u>Canine Lactation.</u> A highly concentrated and palatable diet especially formulated to provide the additional demands of pregnancy and nursing. You should start the diet during the last two to three weeks of gestation so that there won't be an abrupt feeding change to meet nutritive requirements which exist immediately before and after whelping. This will prevent digestive upsets.

    4. <u>Canine Maintenance - Dry</u>. This is their regular dog food formulated for the adult dog being maintained under normal activity.

There are a couple more dog foods that you might consider, which are also not available in retail stores, but must be ordered direct (or from dog training schools where they order in bulk quantity). One such product is Eucanuba which is produced by IAMS Food Company.[21] Eucanuba is their stress diet for sled dogs and hunting dogs. Their maintenance food is called IAMS Chunks. Eucanuba was initially developed as a food for the commercial mink farms. It produces an especially glossy coat and has the attributes of the other quality products; healthy stool, digestibility, and less quantity needs to be fed in order to provide adequate nutrition. At one time this company had the most expensive dog food processing equipment in the world, I am told. The unique aspect of their equipment was the heat processing. Corn gluten is one of the central ingredients in almost all dog foods. As I have mentioned, digestibility (assimilation) is the key to nutrition. Maximum assimilation of corn gluten is obtained only when it is cooked to exactly the right temperature, which is very high. IAMS Food Company was the only company that had equipment capable of reaching that temperature. When the food is cooked below that temperature, less is assimilated and is simply passed through the body. I was informed that their factory burned down and their equipment ruined, however. In any event, they have changed their procedure and ingredients and have declined in popularity with those people I have talked to. One of the changes they made was to use beef based animal protein instead of poultry based protein. One company, A.N.F. (Advanced Nutrition Formula) used to prepare the dog food for the IAMS Company and use the old process, I am told. They use the poultry based protein which they say has far superior digestibility and has a lower melting factor. I do know that chicken and turkey provide more digestible protein than beef; at least that's what I have read in a number of nutrition books and have been told by Dr. James Dohner, my nutrition expert.

    That completes the list of superior dog foods of which I am aware. To summarize, they are higher quality and therefore more expensive. You do save some costs, however, in that they are not retailed through the normal channels of distribution (supermarkets). You also save money in that you feed as little as one half the amount you'd need to feed of the brands found in supermarkets. What is fed provides a higher quality protein and the nutrients are more balanced and more thoroughly assimilated by the body - so the stool is firmer, healthier, and also easier to pick up, by the way. Most of the dog foods found in retail stores use soybean meal for protein, and it has the tendency to swell in the dog's stomach and has a tendency to ferment rather than digest. The high quality foods use a preponderance of animal protein that is much more digestible and doesn't irritate the intestine. The good ones (such as I have recommended) use the expensive egg protein also. It has been found that dogs fed the higher quality foods have less trouble with worms and other parasites. Because they are concentrated, more calories can be provided and yet the dog can be lean and healthy. This means the dog will have more energy, too. I must make this comment, however. There is a tendency to feel like you are providing your dog with the very best if you feed the high potency formulas (designed for dogs under stress). This is particularly true for those who show their dogs because they want to maximize the texture of the dog's coat. I believe this to be a mistake, however, and can result in an unnecessarily fat dog. I don't like fat dogs, perhaps because I'm athletic and have an appreciation for a lean, conditioned animal that other people may not have. In any case, the fat dog is not going to be as healthy as the lean dog. My recommendation is that if you are not exercising your dog (Actually I should say conditioning - a daily short walk for ten or fifteen minutes may be good for both dog and master, but it is definitely not providing physical stress to the dog), then feed the maintenance diet - more than that not only is more than needed, it is, in my opinion, unhealthy if continued for a long period of time.

    I have mentioned these dog foods because many, if not most, Pit Bull fanciers are either unaware of their existence (I didn't know about them myself until Morochito was over a year old) or are under the impression that they are overpriced foods that are designed primarily for show dogs to give them a pretty coat. These people feel that a good quality meat diet supplemented with vitamins is superior.

    There are some additional nutritional concepts I'd like to share with you at this point. I think scientific and veterinary medicine can be enlarged upon with good old tried and true home concoctions. Let me put it this way. Very few practicing doctors can treat cuts as quickly and efficiently as a boxer's "cut man," who may have never attended a formal school, but has learned how to treat cuts from the trial and error methods that have been proven for generations through countless boxing matches. On the other hand, you cannot completely trust homemade foods either. To me the best approach is a healthy combination and understanding of both. The supplementary foods I am going to recommend are designed for specific purposes and are nutritionally sound. I believe the same rule that I have suggested for the high quality foods should be kept in mind - too much of a good thing is bad and moderation is best in the long run.

As I said, to me a dog's nutrition begins with his mother. The mother's nutritional needs should in my opinion be considered even long before conception. If I found a female I wanted to breed Morochito to and she didn't live close to me, I would ask the potential breeder to agree to the following proposition (for puppies and money of course): Let me bring the female to a local yard (Morochito won't allow any dog, male or female near him) and put her in a comfortable pen about a month before she will be in heat. This would allow her plenty of time to get adjusted to her new environment and give me time to work with her nutrition and exercise. I want to prepare the bitch as early as possible for the reproduction cycle by building up tissue reserves. This may sound like a bit much, but I believe in going all the way. I'd also want to go and play with the puppies daily because that would develop more confident, aggressive, curious puppies with more stable temperaments. I would take the female for a daily run, about four miles (running at my pace on a lead). This would constitute daily exercise, not conditioning. I believe the mother that gets a chance to leave her pen and go for a daily fun run, investigating trees and flowers along the way, will be emotionally better prepared for motherhood. I also feel that she will assimilate her food better if her blood is circulating by exercising.

The following foods have been successfully used by breeders. Breeders have written articles in *Dog World* and in *Pit Bull* magazines like *Pit Bull Sheet* and *Bloodlines*. Some of the breeders of dog breeds that are highly line- and inbred for show purposes have stated that adding these foods to their program eliminated "fading" (puppies that don't survive). These are large kennels that move a lot of puppies and are in a pragmatic position to judge whether or not a food is working. One of the best is desiccated liver. We will take a closer look at this amazing food later, but I must mention it now because it is excellent for helping the mother nourish the rapidly developing embryos. Breeders report that puppies born of mothers fed desiccated liver every day, or every other day in some reports, are stronger and healthier. In addition, the mother is stronger. Another excellent food for the mother is egg yolks. Some people call egg yolks the "golden vitamin pill." I have read that the white part of the egg is difficult for a dog to digest, so that only the yolk should be fed. I have also read that if the egg is coagulated (made firm by cooking), the entire egg can be digested. My vet says that if you just simply scramble the egg, the dog should be able to digest it. The yolk contains everything to support life including nucleic acid and selenium, which is another substance we will look at in more detail later, but is relevant here because it works with vitamin E to produce antibodies (so the mother and her puppies will be more disease resistant). Iodine is also excellent for mothers. It is good for nerves and provides drive, endurance, and intelligence. As with all nutritional needs, too much is toxic, but you have to give really high dosages in order to reach a toxic level. I have read that it is better to give 10 to 50 times too much iodine than not enough. In one animal experiment (I lost my reference, so I can't footnote it.), cows were given 10,000 times the human minimal amount and showed tremendous improvement in health and milk production, and their calves were stronger and healthier than ones previously produced. You can buy iodine supplements at health food stores. Sardines and cod liver oil are rich in iodine. Sardines also supply selenium and other important nutrients. They are expensive, but you can afford to feed one sardine a day for a short period of time to the mother while she is carrying and feeding puppies, and then to the puppies until they are around say four months old. I'd give one on top of the dog food, Science Diet, for example, and pour about a teaspoon of cod liver oil over it. Get the cod liver oil from a health food store and get the kind that comes from northern, cold region areas like Norwegian cod liver oil. Here again, quality means better absorption by the body. Kelp also supplies iodine and stimulates the hormones that govern reproduction and keeps them in balance. Kelp also strengthens the thyroid. I had a weak thyroid at one time and kelp strengthened it in about six weeks. The thyroid governs, among other things, endurance and ability to handle stress. I feel like it should be given to all females from puppyhood into old age. I buy a brand of kelp called "Kelp Plus," which contains high grade kelp harvested off the Pacific Coast and Nova Scotia, with added minerals from Irish moss, alfalfa, and watercress. It's not expensive. I pay $2 for a bottle of 100; I take one pill a day. I suggest you give the female two or three a day as she approaches conception. By the way, the iodine in kelp is also an excellent metabolizer that helps a dog burn up fuel and trim off fat at a fast rate, too. You need a lot of kelp for that though.

 One supplement that I would add is not as well documented as the others - guess it comes under the category of folk medicine. This is rasberry leaf tea. Most veterinarians will tell you that there is no evidence that it works but that at least it won't do any harm. Host breeders swear by it and report positive results, both in the performance of a previously sluggish stud and with bitches that have had a history of problems whelping. The tea is supposed to have a strong tonic effect on the reproductive organs. Give it to both stud and bitch for a couple weeks before conception and continue with the bitch until whelping. (It is supposed to be especially beneficial at the whelping stage.) Because of the bitch's increased need for premium grade vitamins, minerals, and protein (in balanced proportions), I would give her a food supplement, either vitamin pills or preferably Nutra-Vet's Forlac. Wheat germ is also good for reproduction, although I don't consider it as important as liver. We will look at wheat germ later also. I would suggest something like adding a tablespoon of wheat germ one day, and a tablespoon of desiccated liver (use the powdered form) two days, the wheat germ one day, etc. Give her super yeast (a superior form of brewer's yeast - discussed later) for the B-complex vitamins and important calcium (in correct proportions) needed for the mother's milk and puppies' bone development. It also provides some of the highest quality protein that you can buy in concentrated form.

The lactating mother needs plenty of calcium for milk. <u>High fat and high protein foods tend to reduce calcium absorption.</u> Now pay attention to this - bone meal is an excellent source of calcium and combines well with the amino acid lysine found in super yeast (so that calcium absorption can increase as much as 50%). I would suggest four tablets of bone meal (acquired from a health food store) a day for the lactating bitch. If you are giving her a lactating formula from one of the companies I have suggested, then you won't need the bone meal. By the way, the first hour after a puppy is born is when the mother's colostrum (fluid secreted by the mammary glands for several days just before and after giving birth) is at its peak in antibodies. Watch the newborn pups and make sure they all get their fill. Give the mother a warm bran mash shortly after whelping. This aids in cleaning out her system.

Finally, after giving your girl all that good stuff, you need to give her alphalpha and mustard greens as a body cleanser during gestation. They provide chlorophyll, nature's body cleanser, and fiber to help elimination. Mustard greens are also high in calcium. An inexpensive way of obtaining these two greens is to grow your own - they don't take much, if any, maintenance. I suppose that seems like a lot of junk to feed a dog, but many people feed their dogs the things I'm recommending and get excellent results. If they didn't notice improvements, they wouldn't go to the trouble and expense. You must keep in mind that you don't need large quantities of the items listed - small quantities provided consistently (daily) is the key.

If you are interested in obtaining the magnets mentioned in the "Pet" chapter, you can give her ionized well water. If you live in the city, you may consider it worth the time and expense to drive out to a local farmer that has well water - I do. I fill up one gallon apple cider jugs with well water. I think glass keeps the water cleaner and tastier. You ever taste the water left in a plastic container all day? It tastes awful. Water left in a glass jug, however, tastes fresh for several days, even a week. Also, store it in a cool, <u>dark</u> place to aid in fresh taste. The well water contains absolutely no additives nor does it pass through the junk (corrosion) contained in the city water pipes. Some pit fighters add apple cider vinegar to their dogs' water. It is said that some hound breeders do the same because it is supposed to increase a dog's endurance tremendously. It is also supposed to be a home remedy to cure fleas - that is, a dog that drinks diluted apple cider vinegar should have less trouble with fleas. Personally I have never given it to Morochito because it is very bad for teeth. (It is a very powerful acid.)

Needham's Tigger

```
                                                   ┌─ Greenwood's Oakie
                         ┌─ Greenwood's Mountain Boy ─┤
                         │                         └─ Holliday
Needham's Tigger ─┤
                         │                         ┌─ Needham's Hannibal
                         └─ Needham's Winnifred ───┤
                                                   └─ Needham's Trudy
```

Let me give you a tip or two about watering your Pit Bull. Most people water their dog at feeding time. The dog gets excited when you are around and so may drink at that time. It's not natural for an animal to drink at feeding time, however, and, moreoever, it's not good for him. When water is taken in at the same time as food, it dilutes the digestive acids and the body will not adequately assimilate the nutrients in the food - a lot of the food will pass through undigested. (This is true with humans as well as animals. In some countries, people do not drink with their meals.) I dont believe in filling the water bucket once a day every morning (or evening) and considering it fresh water. The dog may not drink at this time or for several hours. I water Morochito when he's thirsty - right after our roadwork. That way he is sure to be getting fresh water. If we have a grueling workout, I wait half an hour before giving him water. (A dog can get sick if he drinks too much water immediately after a workout - if it's a strenuous workout or a hot day.)

In any event, as described in the "Pet" chapter, I believe in providing the Pit Bull with negatively ionized water. I would especially recommend it when a dog is being conditioned for field trials, weight-pulling, or other physical contests, as well as when the dog is competing in mentally demanding events such as Schutzhund or obedience training. The negatively ionized water has a positive effect on the mind, tending to promote an attitude of alertness and emotional well-being.

Negatively ionized air is also very healthy, and is the subject of considerable research in recent years. The following information is contained in a pamphlet, The Herbalist, April, 1980, in an article by Dr. Robert Massy, Chairman of the Physics Department at the University of the Trees and Director of the Ion Research Center. Dr. Massy states that we live in an atmosphere that is starved of negative ions. The negative ion count in the average American home (and especially in a large office building) that is air conditioned or heated is between 0 and a few hundred per cubic centimeter. Forests and pasture land far removed from "civilization" have a negative ion count of around 4,000 per cubic centimeter. This is not to say that every natural environment in the world has a high negative ion count. Some areas, for example parts of southern California, have high positive ions created by certain winds. Some areas that have historically been high in negative count have been noted for people with high mental achievements. Delphi was a center of wisdom for the ancient Greeks, and the ancient Rishis lived high in the Himalayas - both areas contained high negative ion counts.

Positively ionized air increases the serotonin levels in urine. Serotonin causes nervous tension and irritability. People who live in areas where positive ions are occasionally present (from winds - most places never have positively ionized air all the time) report irritability.

You can buy negative ion generators and install them in your home and in your car. They are supposed to make the air fresher, cleaner, alive - like the air in the forest just after a thunderstorm. They remove dust, smoke, pollen, smog, and harmful bacteria from the air. They are relatively expensive, about $100 each. I mention them here because I feel that it would be an excellent idea, if you are well off and can afford such a luxury, to have one in your car or van when you drive your Pit Bull to a competitive athletic activity. Of course it's a very expensive commodity to buy just for that - but I mean if you want one for yourself, it'll also benefit your Pit Bull. For further information about ion generators and how to purchase them, write the Ion Research Center, P.O. Box 905, Boulder Creek, California 95006.

The nutrition of the puppies is next. As soon as they are weaned, I suggest you start them on a high-quality, dry, chunky dog food-dry because it's better for their teeth and gums - cleans and strengthens them as they gnaw on the chunks. I also recommend the Magnum supplement that I described. Another excellent source of nutrition is goats' milk, which is cleaner, more nutritious, and, more importantly, much easier to digest than cows' milk which is designed to feed a much bigger animal with a much more sophisticated digestive system than a human, to say nothing of a puppy. Cows' milk is seen as one of the most beneficial health foods in America when actually it's not as good for you as most think. For one thing, it's highly processed -homogenized and pasteurized, which destroys many of the nutrients. In addition, although it is a high-quality protein, much of it is passed through and not absorbed by the body because it is so hard to digest. Goats' milk, however, is much more similar to human milk or to dogs' milk also. Goats' milk is therefore much easier to digest. You may live in the city and feel that goats' milk is not accessible to you, but you should check around; you may be very surprised to find how many people drink it. It's not as expensive as you would think if you buy it from a farmer or breeder that may be located not far from the city. Here in Greensboro, although it is the second largest city in North Carolina, there are several breeders within short driving distance that sell goats' milk. I was totally unaware of this, however, until I found that my chiropractor breeds and raises dairy goats and sells their milk. If you live in the county and have the space, you might consider raising dairy goats yourself. Let me share some information on dairy goats and their milk with you, taken primarily from a pamphlet distributed by the American Dairy Goat Association.

Dairy goats are small, easy to handle, and can be kept on small parcels of land. They are alert, intelligent, socially inclined, and affectionate. Many people who have had little interaction with goats are under the impression that they are dumb animals, but this is not at all the case. They make loveable pets and return the cost of their feed in the form of a valuable and healthful food product. It is a delicious, wholesome, nutritious milk. There is not much perceptible difference between the flavor of properly handled goats' milk and cows' milk. I like it better. It is whiter than whole cows' milk. Butter and cheese made from goats' milk is white and all goats' milk products (hard cheese, cottage cheese, butter, ice cream, yogurt, etc.) are smoother and more cream-like than cows' milk products. The fat globules are smaller than those of cows' milk and the curd is softer and smaller which is one reason it is easier to digest. Goats' milk is naturally emulsified. The cream does not rise readily, but it can be obtained with a mechanical separator. Goats are much cleaner than cows. Many people think goats are dirty animals and most are familiar with the cartoons that depict goats in a garbage dump eating tin cans. This is a fallacy. If a goat is starving, he'll eat garbage just like you would if you had no other source of food, but dairy goats have fastidious eating habits and are particular about the cleanliness of their food. Their natural curiosity may lead them to investigate newly found items by sniffing and nibbling, but they quickly refuse anything that is dirty or distasteful. Dairy goats are hardy, healthy animals that can be kept successfully in all climates. They do not need elaborate housing. They have a strong herding instinct and prefer brushlands and a varied selection of pasture plants including non-noxious weeds. They need a year-round supply of roughage. Goats seldom thrive when tethered and need to graze. They are curious and agile so they need well built fences. Dairy goats can average 3-4 quarts of milk daily during a ten-month lactation, giving more soon after freshening and gradually dropping in production toward the end of their lactation. Goat milk is not a miracle food but it does have distinct characteristics that make it beneficial.

These goats can be bred for show as well as milk production. In show, they are judged on conformation standards that have a relationship to goats' strength, stamina, and performance as a dairy animal. By the way, they are generally highly line- and inbred. There are different strains of dairy goats, two of the more popular ones being Alpine and Nubian. Alpine goats (from the French Alpines) are the most productive. Nubian (developed in England by crossing Indian and Egyptian goats with native British goats) are the highest quality -higher butterfat, better taste, etc. They have long, floppy ears. If you desire more information about goats, or the availability of goats' milk in your area, you can write The American Dairy Goat Association, P. O. Box 865, Springdale, NC 28160. They will provide you with a more local address upon request.

Back to nutrition for our dogs. The items I suggested you give the mother can also be given to the puppy. Remember if you give him a raw egg, you should scramble it, or you could give him a poached egg. YOU might add some plain yogurt (YOU don't want to give him any sugar), which provides acedophilis - friendly bacteria - which keeps the puppies' intestines healthy. Make sure you get high-quality yogurt that says "contains active cultures" on the package.

If you recall, one of the items I mentioned was super yeast, a special type of brewer's yeast, which is one of the "wonder foods" of the world. Most "health nuts" are very familiar with it. It is full of B-complex vitamins, and these are very popular now and you can find a great deal written about them in sports magazines and health magazines as well as medical and physical research reports - such as Research Quarterly. Many of the articles deal with the benefits derived from B-complex vitamins by describing the symptoms that exist when your food is deficient in B-complex. With most any modern commercial dog food, however, the dog receives an ample dose of B vitamins. I would like to point out, however, the benefits available from extra supplementation. In other words, I want to look at the positive benefits of extra supplementation rather than the negative symptoms of deficiencies. We call the B vitamins B-"complex" because there are several of them - 15 known and more than 15 unknown (not studied) B vitamins. One of the B vitamins is thiamin (vitamin B1). It helps the body to distribute and burn up sugar to produce energy. Puppy dog food contains extra carbohydrates to meet the extra energy demands of the active puppy. (The high stress formulas like Science Diet also contain extra carbohydrates.) Thiamin requirements increase in proportion to carbohydrate intake so active puppies and heavily conditioned dogs need more carbohydrates, and more vitamin B1. It is possible to increase tremendously the capacity for work without undue tiring, by increasing carbohydrate consumption together with increased B1. European swimmers consume half a gram of B1 daily when training. Niacin (vitamin B3) is also used to produce energy. Niacin is an enzyme that metabolizes carbohydrates, fats, and protein, breaking them down into glucose to meet energy needs. Niacin also promotes brain metabolism and increases the oxygen-carrying abilities of the blood. It is believed that Niacin will prolong the life of an animal. If your Pit Bull is being heavily exercised, he can require two or three times the normal needs, and that may not be enough. Two other vitamins associated with energy are folic acid and PABA (para-amino benzoic acid). They work together. PABA creates favorable bacteria flora in the intestine, enabling the dog to better utilize folic acid, which helps produce antibodies. PABA provides an extra "kick" for super energy and is instrumental in reducing fatigue. It helps the dog "go the extra mile." The newest discovery (at the date of this writing) in B vitamins is vitamin B15 (also called pangamate). It's very big with professional athletes and is considered a super energizer. Muhammed Ali's training diet included megadoses of vitamin B15. It is supposed to really enhance your blood's oxygen-carrying ability, so it makes your heart much more efficient and resistant (to stress). It also promotes the building of muscle and improves reflex time. It will help your Pit Bull through more aggressive training routines and increase his tolerance for hard work. It also enhances biochemical restitution during rest periods. The B vitamin called pantothenic acid is the antistress vitamin and can extend the life span of animals. It also develops the adrenal function. It is contained in muscle. Milk/eggs, and liver are excellent sources.

Vitamin B2, Riboflavin, helps body cells to use oxygen and develops muscular strength. Vitamin B12, Cobalamin, works in conjunction with folic acid and iron to build blood cells. It stimulates growth. Vitamin B6, Pyridoxine, promotes healthy teeth, strengthens gums, blood vessels, and the nervous system, and builds red blood cells. It conserves protein and helps cut fat. It also aids in the production of antibodies.

The B vitamins work best when they are taken together as a complex instead of, i.e., a bottle of B15 pills. In other words, you should use a food like super yeast. I had thought I would list all of the B vitamins and the benefits of each, but for the sake of brevity, I listed only the ones that are important to the athletic dog. To summarize, the B complex provides strength, improves reaction time, helps break down food into energy and keeps a clean supply of oxygen available to the muscles for strength. The B vitamins also make the dog's coat glossy and healthy. It is said that brewer's yeast, when added to a dog's food as a supplement, helps control fleas. It doesn't prevent them but the dog will be less bothered by them. In other words, fleas evidently do not particularly like healthy skin and hair.

The B vitamins are water soluble, which means that the dog doesn't store them in his body but passes out what the body doesn't immediately need. When a dog is stressed (for example, heavily exercised), the B vitamins are rapidly used up. The B vitamins must be re-supplied daily. Super yeast is a highly concentrated high-potency formula containing a blend of primary grown torula and brewer's yeasts. Calcium and magnesium are added to the formula to balance yeast's naturally high phosphorus content. The primary grown yeasts in the formula are not by-products, but are grown specifically for food use. No sugar, fillers, preservatives, artificial colors, or flavors are included in the formula. Super yeast contains iron, for the blood, 18 minerals, and a rich supply of the amino acids (protein). Brewer's yeast contains factor 3, a complex containing chromium and selenium, which, as we will see later, augments the action of vitamin B. Yeast, it should be remembered, is a <u>live</u> food, a raw protein. It is also rich in the anti-aging nucleic acids. For a given quantity, say a tablespoon, super yeast contains more than twice as much high-quality protein, B vitamins, and other nutrients, than brewer's yeast alone -and brewer's yeast is a very nutrient-rich food. We get our super yeast from our local health food store - the manufacturer is Plus Products. I would begin giving a puppy a teaspoon a day working up to a tablespoon a day for the adult Pit Bull (depending on the size of your dog).

I wouldn't give more than that because too much will give a dog gas and can make him fat.

It is said that feeding a puppy raw lean meat will make him more aggressive. I think this is not at all true and have not seen any evidence of it. Some people feed raw beef while others who cannot afford the beef feed raw hamburg. I wouldn't consistently feed hamburg, however - too much fat. If you feed raw meat, also feed raw cheese or cottage cheese because the high calcium contained in cheese balances the high phosphorus of the meat. I would feed the pup raw chicken livers instead, as a matter of fact. I don't think there's much, if any, fat in raw chicken livers. The animal in the wild does not, contrary to popular opinion, live on lean meat. Telescopic movies of carnivorous animals disclose that they prefer herbivorous animals (animals that feed on plants and grass) and that they eat the stomach (which contains partially digested grains and grass) first. Secondly they eat the organs - liver, heart, and lungs. They eat muscle meat last or, quite often, not at all. When we look at desiccated liver in a little while you will see another reason for feeding chicken livers.

A growing pup needs vitamin D^{22}. Vitamin D intake is most critical in puppies when growth and bone development are maximum. Adult requirements may, in fact, be rather low. Vitamin D stimulates the body's absorption of calcium and phosphorus, which are important in the development of bones and teeth. It also functions to maintain calcium homeostasis. Calcium demand is high when bone mineralization occurs during the growth stage. Vitamin D is the catalyst that regulates the process. It forms a steroid hormone complex that makes this possible. It has been found that vitamin D metabolism is quite pronounced when an animal is exposed to sunlight. An experiment showed that when adequate calcium and phosphorus was provided in the diet, ponies raised outdoors and exposed to sunlight, did not need vitamin D supplementation in order to acquire normal bone development. Ponies reared indoors and not exposed daily to sunlight, did not develop properly unless vitamin D was added to their normal diet. The results substantiated the knowledge gained from many years of practical experience - that animals tend to grow and develop better if exposed to sunlight. The conclusion - place the Pit Bull's dog house near some shade so he won't be over exposed in the summer, but be sure his chain reaches to a sunny spot every day. In addition, in order to attain maximum growth and development, supplement with a teaspoon a day of cod liver oil, which is probably the best source of vitamin D, and good for his coat, develops flexible joints, and contains many valuable nutrients. Natural sources of vitamin D are limited, and while too much can be toxic, the dog can handle quite a large dose of it.

Studies show that 10,000 IU per kg of body weight over a ten-month period was required in order for the symptoms of hypervitaminosis (toxic effects of vitamin overdose) to occur. These symptoms are retarded growth, deformed jaws and teeth, and calcification of soft tissue. A basic principle of nutrition is that overdosing of vitamins or minerals often results in the same symptoms as a vitamin deficiency. In other words, in the case of vitamin D, a lack of it in the diet generally retards growth and results in weak teeth. The same symptoms appear when you provide too much vitamin D. This same principle applies to other vitamins (more so with the fat soluble than with the water soluble ones) and with minerals also. Some people feed their pups a calcium pill as a supplement. You can obtain the ones from your veterinarian that contain vitamin D to assure proper absorption. It is a mistake, however, in my opinion, to feed these to your dog. My opinion is based upon a pamphlet I obtained from my vet, entitled <u>Calcium Metabolism,</u> by R. D. Kealy, M.D., for the Pet Nutrition and Care Research, Ralston Purina Company, Checkerboard Square, St. Louis, MO 63188, 1977. The study was conducted to "determine adequate levels of calcium and phosphorous and the proper balance of calcium and phosphorous to provide optimum growth in pups." In 1972, they conducted a growth test with two eight-week-old Springer Spaniel female pups who were littermates. The pups were placed on a diet that depleted their reserves of calcium and phosphorous. Then one pup was fed a diet that contained 2.3% calcium and 2.0% phosphorous and the other was fed a diet containing 4.3% calcium and 3.9% phosphorous. The one that was fed the higher level of calcium resulted in a marked depression in growth and radiological examinations detected bone immaturity. The pamphlet contained a picture of both pups side by side. The pup fed the lower level calcium/phosphorous diet appeared much sturdier. The lower level diet was still much higher than that found in regular adult dog food. The article also noted that calcium deficiencies are found when the calcium/phosphorous ratio is such that there is more phosphorous than calcium - regardless of the amount of calcium given. I wouldn't give plain brewer's yeast to a puppy because it is much higher in phosphorous than calcium. The article impressed upon me the fact that it is easy to over-supplement calcium. There really wasn't a whole lot of difference between the lower level and the higher level diet in the experiment. I feel that the high-quality dog food I have mentioned provides the puppy the exact amount of calcium/phosphorous and we shouldn't try to change it. (I don't believe the calcium/phosphorous in a teaspoon of super yeast is enough to throw off that balance.) If you feel you need extra calcium supplementation, I suggest a good natural source of calcium - bone meal -

purchased from a health food store. So long as calcium supplementation is not overdone, it aids in blood clotting, muscle contraction, intestinal absorption of B12, and in the activation of many enzymes needed to provide energy from carbohydrates, protein, and fat.[25]

Let me say that all these additional supplements that I'm recommending assume that whether your Pit Bull is involved in some form of athletic competition or is merely a pet, he is exercised fairly strenuously and regularly. If this is not the case, you would probably create more harm than good by providing extra supplements. I would recommend feeding one of the high-quality dog foods I have listed in this chapter and no extras - these dog foods provide all the nutrition needed and then some. Let me also say this about extra supplementation - even when a dog is being very heavily exercised you don't want to feed these supplements with every meal I I feed Morochito twice a day, providing the extra "goodies" in the first meal only - every other day usually, and I've come to the conclusion that twice-a-week supplementation would be even better, the reason being (as I have tried to emphasize) these extra goodies unbalance the dog's digestive system and when not properly digested they assault the body with noxious toxins, gases, and poisons. I emphasize this point because it is a little known fact even with experienced dogmen. I know one who fed his dog all kinds of "special" foods during the dog's keep. When matched, the dog gave off a bunch of gas (Boy, did he stink!) and although well conditioned, he also ran out of energy during the match.

Also, even if the Pit Bull is heavily exercised, I think you should give his system a rest periodically - by fasting. You may feel that fasting would be detrimental to a pup's growth or that it will weaken him. The opposite is true. Fasting is natural to animals. A wolf or wild dog lives with a frequent feast then famine. A few days fasting is not only harmless, it is highly beneficial - not only to dogs, but to humans as well. I fast periodically, and although I may feel uncomfortable, especially in the early stages, I always feel very healthy and active when I come off the fast. I gain strength and energy from my fasts. At the same time, fasting cleans out your body, getting rid of toxic build-up and gives your internal organs a rest. When a pup is given health foods and supplements after a fast, his body is very responsive and in the long run will grow better.

There is another benefit that was mentioned in the "Pet" chapter -fasting can increase tremendously the rate of learning if you are teaching your Pit Bull obedience, protection, training, etc. and Dr. Whitney, D.V.M., highly recommends it in his book. He suggests (based on his own experience in obedience and trailing training his own Bloodhounds - a good many of them - the following routine for those who train in the evening:

Monday - feed early in the morning

Tuesday - no food - train Tuesday night, then feed double ration
Wednesday - feed early in the morning
(Repeat the three-day cycle.)
If you prefer to train in the morning, he suggests the following:
Monday - feed in evening
Tuesday - no food
Wednesday - train in the morning, then feed double ration
(Repeat three-day cycle.)

These schedules are for adult dogs that are fed once a day. I assume that he means that you would follow the routine when you are teaching your dog some new technique, but not as a regular feeding schedule. I would suggest that in the regular feeding schedule you feed the adult Pit Bull twice a day rather than once like most do, the reason being that I believe he will have more strength between meals, and that you can keep him leaner with two half-ration meals than with one full-ration meal. When a dog, or a human for that matter, eats several meals a day, he does not put on anywhere near as much weight as a dog that eats once a day (or people who eat twice a day rather than three times). Bodybuilders who want to get "cut up" for a contest, and yet need carbohydrates for energy for their workouts, eat six times a day.

In addition, more nutrients are absorbed when more meals are eaten per day. The body assimilates only its needs at a particular meal; whatever is not needed passes through. When a dog is stressed (exercise, obedience training, etc.) between meals, more nutrients are absorbed by the more frequent, smaller meals.

When semifasting during an intensive training schedule, however, I would follow the schedule Dr. Whitney has outlined. Since the Pit Bull has been used to being fed twice a day, he will be that much more motivated with the changed feeding schedule. The following comments are also indicated by Dr. Whitney, based upon his experience.[27]

Excellent results have also been achieved by underfeeding for awhile until the dog drops to three quarters its normal weight. At this point, the dog is fed a maintenance diet that fulfills his needs but does not allow gain. The dog is then constantly motivated by food. This method allows you to train every day with the same motivation on the part of the dog. Dr. Whitney informs us that a short fast is all that is needed. The concept that the hungrier a dog is the harder he will work is true only up to a point. That point has been found to be 36 hours. After that time, the dog becomes less and less motivated by food. If you fast yourself, you will find the same to be true for a human. Your body becomes accustomed to being without food and the hunger response leaves you. It has also been demonstrated that a dog does not work better for a large meal than for a small one, but in fact may become disinterested in continuing to work if rewarded with too much food. Dr. Whitney states that "small reinforcements keep him working and attentive." You may be surprised to learn that Dr. Whitney has found that a dog will work more enthusiastically for small amounts that he is familiar with than for special savory treats. Finally, since thirst is also a strong need, a dog will work hard for water when he's sufficiently thirsty. When a dog is both hungry and thirsty, he will learn even quicker. All this makes sense to me. It means that we can understand the way an animal learns by studying the animal's natural habitat. In the wild, most of the learning process is centered around survival - the need to obtain food and water. I would suggest that obedience lessons ought to be conducted after the dog's daily conditioning. After a vigorous spring-pole, treadmill, long run, conditioning program. The dog should rest for about half an hour - with no water available. At this time, run through the obedience lesson, particularly the techniques that he's had trouble learning (except, perhaps, endurance lessons like jumping hurdles). Reward with small amounts of food and water and I think you'll find he'll learn quicker. At one time it was thought that food rewarding is a poor method of training because the dog learns to respond for the food treat - take away the treat and the dog won't respond - or will be reluctant to. This can happen if the dog is given the food reward for every response. But modern training techniques utilize discriminative reinforcement, which means that the dog is rewarded say every second, third, fourth, or fifth time. (You vary the reward pattern so the dog never knows whether he'll receive a reward or not.) You do this only in order to teach the dog what he's supposed to do. When he learns how to do it, you gradually eliminate the food reward (gradually increase the number of correct responses he makes before receiving a food reward) and retain only your verbal praise and physical pat.

Needham's bitch Winifred

Dr. Whitney is not the only veterinarian that recommends fasting. Dr. Pitcairn, a graduate of the University of California (Davis Veterinary School) and holder of a Ph.D. from Washington State University, has worked in most phases of veterinary practice, teaching, and research. In an article written for *Prevention* magazine (May, 1980), Dr. Pitcairn states that "when allowed to rest from the function of digestion, the body is better able to direct its energies to elimination of stored wastes, a natural process that all wild carnivores experience periodically. Most pets, however, do not get such rests, and indeed are often overfed as well." Dr. Pitcairn goes on to mention, in the article, that when feeding, the dog should be given nutritional yeast, kelp, cod liver oil, fresh garlic, vitamin C, and other supplements that I have mentioned.

You may feel that you don't want to run your dog for long distances while he's on a reduced feeding diet, thinking he will be weaker. This is not the case. For one thing, he'll have less weight to carry around. If a 50-pound dog loses five pounds, that's the same as 15 pounds (1056) to a 150-

pound human. Try running five miles with a 15-pound weight belt around your waist. Naturally running is considerably easier without the 15 pound-weight. When you skip a meal, of course, you do <u>feel</u> weaker. This is primarily because your blood sugar level is low. Exercise makes your body draw on your glucose reserves and gives you the needed strength. Let me put it this way. When I go on a short fast, the first couple days I do not <u>feel</u> like working out. I make myself work out anyway, however, and I have found that although I don't feel very good for the first five minutes of, say my run, after I have warmed up I feel very strong - and I find that feeling persists for several hours after the workout. You may not want to work your dog on the heavy pulling conditioning methods, but I think you can run him all you want.

When the puppy becomes old enough for serious conditioning, there are some additional nutritional needs. The items I am about to mention, however, are for the extremely heavily conditioned dog only, which can be fed one of the high stress formulations, which provides the carbohydrates needed to supply the required fuel. For overall endurance, however, there is no food, at the time of this writing, that can give your dog more than desiccated liver. There are a myriad of articles in sports literature on the benefits of desiccated liver. *Runner's World* magazine gave me permission to reprint the following article from their March, 1975 issue.

"Endurance in Capsule Form"
by Terry Howell

Some months ago, my runs were leaving me dead. Feeling as if my workouts had been run in a pool of honey, I turned to strength literature for suggestions. Comments by two writers especially interested me.

Vince Gironda, a weight training authority, wrote in Iron Man (March '74) that "athletic experiments have found liver to produce up to 300% (gains in) endurance."

Bob Hoffman, strength expert cited as instrumental in the development of Percy Cerutty's training philosophy in Cerutty's Athletics; How to Become a Champion, likewise endorsed liver for endurance in many of his articles and books. Hoffman, several times Olympic weight lifting coach, was running marathons in his early teens and later became a world canoe racing champion. Today, in his mid-70's, he still lifts weights regularly and runs several miles a week.

Intrigued, I began to uncover interesting and, at times, astonishing claims for "desiccated" liver. Desiccated liver is whole beef liver vacuum dried at low temperatures (about 140 degrees F) into a concentrate which retains practically all of the nutrients. It is then powdered for use as a food supplement, a product the equivalent ounce-per-ounce to four times as much whole liver.

In the journal Proceedings of the Society of Experimental Biology (July 15, 1951), Benjamin H. Ershoff, M.D., Ph.D., describes an experiment he performed with rats to test an anti-fatigue diet.

Three groups of rats were fed as much as they wanted of a basic diet for 12 weeks. Each group ate the same foods, with only supplements differing. The first group was fed nine synthetic and two natural vitamins. The second group ate the same diet and vitamins, plus a plentiful supply of B-complex vitamins in the form of brewer's yeast. The third group had 10% desiccated liver added to its ration in place of the B-vitamins (while retaining the other vitamins).

The first group of rats, fed only the basic diet, showed the least amount of growth after 12 weeks, while the second group, receiving the brewer's yeast, grew only slightly more. However, the group fed the desiccated liver grew about 15% more than group one.

Dr. Ershoff then tested the rats for endurance. He placed them one by one into a drum of water from which they could not escape. They either swam or drowned.

The rats in the original diet fortified with vitamins swam for an average of 13.3 minutes before giving up. The second group, which had the additional B-complex from yeast, averaged 13.4 minutes, before sinking. From the third group of rats, three swam for 63, 83 and 87 minutes before exhaustion. The other nine rats of the group, the ones fed desiccated liver, were still swimming vigorously at the end of two hours when the experiment was ended. In other words, the rats of this group fortified with desiccated liver were able to swim almost 10 times longer than those in the other two groups!

Runners should, as I did, find the implications staggering.

For 20 years, researchers were at a loss to explain what it was about liver that was so special. It contains first-class proteins and is rich in B-vitamins, especially B-12, as well as vitamins A, C, D, iron, calcium, phosphorous and copper. This had been known for some time. But these proteins, vitamins and minerals were never found to duplicate the power of whole liver.

The missing link was discovered in 1971 by Dr. Minor J. Coon, of the University of Michigan Medical Center. Dr. Coon, heading a team of five biochemists, succeeded in isolating and testing a red protein pigment named Cytochrome P-450. This pigment, tested repeatedly, proved to perform all the mysterious functions of liver that had been previously tested on vitamins but not found attributable to them.

Since Dr. Coon also discovered that P-450 is water soluble, desiccating liver does not destroy this pigment but instead concentrates it.

Most runners (at least regular readers of Runner's World) know that the production of energy is a process of oxidation of glucose within the cell. This in turn produces toxins which gradually slow down and eventually stop the production of energy. Dr. Coon believes that P-450 is a catalyst which speeds up oxidation in the energy production process and also improves the ability of the body to detoxify the fatigue toxins. Hence, the rats fed the desiccated liver were able to continue swimming when all the others had given up to drown.

Individual claims for liver's benefits abound. But little formal human athletic research involving liver seems to be available. That which is, though encouraging, is less than precise.

For instance, an article in Prevention (July '72) states that in England in 1960, trials were made on athletes performing exhaustive work. A long distance runner was fed a diet supplement of liver, vitamin E and wheat germ.

"Prior to taking the diet supplement," the study states, "his pulse on return from a seven-mile run was 120 per minute. After 2½ minutes rest, it was 109. After five minutes rest, it was 98. After 15 minutes, it was 95. And it took usually 40 minutes for the pulse rate to return to the athlete's normal rate of 70 beats per minute.

"After taking the diet supplement for one month, the normal pulse rate of the athlete at rest was 58, and corresponding readings after the seven-mile run were as follows: 2 ½ minutes, 105; five minutes, 75, and after 15 minutes it was at the rest rate of 58. This definitely showed that the heart was assisted in its function, and the recovery of the heart from this exercise was much improved. This test also proved that the circulo-respiratory system was much improved. The fatigue stage was actually delayed because of the easier functioning of the circulation."

Marked improvement, but the study fails to answer what percentage can be directly attributed to liver.

In another test, an athlete with a curling strength of 90 pounds was fed desiccated liver tablets. Another weight lifter was fed the same food without the supplements. Weights were gradually increased over a number of days. The first lifter reached a limit of 176 pounds, while the non-supplement athlete was only capable of 140 pounds, and then after long delays at certain weights - a difference in strength of over 20%. And runners know, strength aids speed and endurance.

Again, however, this is only one case. We cannot be sure whether the difference in strength was the result of the desiccated liver or rather natural potential.

A few years after Ershoff's rat experiment, Dr. John Yudkin, a British nutritionist, repeated the test with children. The growth results were confirmed in every respect, but no endurance trials were mentioned.

Experiments also indicate that liver has the ability to detoxify cortisone, many pharmaceutical drugs, nicotine, alcohol, marijuana, petroleum hydrocarbons and other poisons we breathe and eat. I'm certainly not suggesting Winstons and whiskey as a training diet. However, even the most careful of us consume many potentially dangerous chemicals every day. Road running in city traffic and around industrial areas especially increases our intake of pollutants. Desiccated liver may be the key in combatting many of these poisons.

Dr. Albert Szent Gyorgyi, M.D. - biochemist, a Nobel prize winner and one of the most productive researchers ever — is now convinced that certain liver components play a vital health role and even hold the secret of cancer prevention. That a man of Dr. Szent-Gyorgyi's reputation is excited with the potential of liver's effect on body functions is not to be taken lightly.

Aroused by the information, I was eager to do my own testing. As a vegetarian, though, I was at the same time reluctant to add liver to my diet, having learned years ago that meat cut my endurance tremendously. Finally, feeling beat so much of the time and dreading a layoff, I bought a bottle of 7 ½ -gram tablets.

I felt no difference the next day but reminded myself that Dr. Ershoff's results were not obtained after a single feeding. Nutritional results are never gained that quickly.

During the next eight weeks, however, my strength gradually returned and increased. Workouts were run faster and became longer (from 65-90 miles per week), and the nagging daily fatigue disappeared. There was no other significant change in my diet or training.

If you can tolerate liver a few times a week, fine. This would probably be the cheapest form of experimentation. If, however, you are a vegetarian (a number have accepted desiccated liver as a supplement - e.g., George Bernard Shaw), dislike its texture or taste or just don't want to be bothered with the inconvenience of preparing it, supplementation is your best bet.

Desiccated liver is available in three forms - tablets, capsules and powder. The tablets are relatively inexpensive and convenient. Capsules cost more but slide down easier for some. Powder is the most economical but least convenient form. Its taste, which can only be described as horrible, may be hidden somewhat in juices.

As for the amount of liver to be taken, there are varying opinions, ranging from whole liver twice a week to 30 or more tablets a day. As with all foods, you must determine your own minimum intake for maximum body efficiency.

I average eight tablets per day at a cost of less than four cents. I will undoubtedly experiment with larger doses in the future, but for the moment am happy to again be running easily and feeling so good.

If my own experience is typical, if stamina and strength can be increased so significantly at so little cost as indicated by Dr. Ershoff's rat experiment, if Dr. Szent-Gyorgyi's theories are true, then desiccated liver will no doubt become an integral part of all athletic diets and health programs.

Notice that the article mentions three ways to provide desiccated liver - tablets, capsules, and powder. As also mentioned, the powder is considerably cheaper. Many people are not aware that the powder is assimilated by the body much easier than either the tablets or capsules. It takes 12 to 15 pills to provide the same nutrition as one tablespoon of powder. You can get desiccated liver tablets that have B12 Activity (Cobalamin concentrated) supplemented to act as an enzyme. (You recall we have discussed B12.) Notice the findings that the experimental rats fed liver grew 15% more than the other rats. For this reason, I also recommend that puppies be fed the desiccated liver.

Another excellent conditioner is the oriental herb, ginseng. Modern sports literature abounds with articles demonstrating the benefits of ginseng in strengthening the heart, improving stamina, and increasing resistance to stress. Switzerland's Consultox Laboratories researched the effect of gingeng on mice and found that if fed very minute amounts of ginseng and subjected to swimming tests of stamina and endurance, the mice increased the length of time they were able to swim by 34 to 60 percent. They also demonstrated significant increases in speed and endurance when they performed rope-climbing tests.[28] Another example - one of Russia's leading scientists, Dr. Brekham of the Department of Physiology and Pharmacology of Adaptation, Institute of Marine Biology in Russia, states, "Daily doses of ginseng for 15 to 45 days increase physical endurance and mental capacity for work. The increase in efficiency was noted not only during the treatment itself, but also for over a month after the end of the treatment. Numerous experiments have shown that ginseng preparations increase physical efficiency and prevent over-fatigue." Ginseng is good for the blood, and is said to increase muscle tone. It is a staple in the diets of Russian Olympic athletes.[29] Ginseng is also supposed to be good for the heart and circulation and improves mental concentration in athletic events. It is claimed to be an aphrodisiac, increasing sexual prowess. It may be a good idea to feed it prior to breeding. It also regulates your metabolism so that you burn up fat more efficiently. I have read several times that Siberian Ginseng is the best for metabolism and endurance.

Another oriental herb that provides energy as well as having fabulous rejuvenating properties is fo-ti-teng (I find there are a variety of ways of spelling it.) tea. Sounds weird, I know. It is a Chinese herb - very powerful positive tonic effect on the body. You don't need much of it. I have read that taking a little fo-ti-teng with ginseng enhances the benefits of the ginseng.

Cayenne (red pepper) in capsule form is said to speed up blood circulation.

Wheat germ, of course, is also recognized as an athlete's food. One of its primary ingredients - vitamin E - provides stamina. Wheat germ became very popular in 1960 when the Australian Olympic swim team that in previous years had performed nominally in Olympic events, took every event, winning all the medals. They hadn't changed their training program that year, we are told, except they consumed large quantities of wheat germ. In *Nutritional Aids*, Fall, 1979, by Ken-L Ration (pamphlet already mentioned), the role of vitamin E as an antioxidant is explained. (An antioxidant inhibits the oxidative drain reaction which damages or destroys tissue by helping the blood supply fresh oxygen to the tissues. This function enables the body to conserve and better utilize oxygen and aids the oxygen exchange process in the lungs.) Vitamin E is probably the best anitoxidant we know of. As such, it can increase an animal's life span while at the same time increasing stamina. Vitamin E also aids in the release of energy from fatty acids and glucose and keeps the oxygen in the blood pure. Well oxygenated cells work harder and endure more stress. Consequently, vitamin E promotes vitality. It is excellent for the reproduction system, and this is why the wheat germ was recommended for mothers.

Antioxidants at low dosage levels are effective in preventing the onset of disease, but are ineffective, even at high dosage levels, as a treatment for disease once it has set in. Fats, especially polyun-saturated fatty acids (needed for energy) are prone to the oxidation process. The antioxidant role of vitamin E in controlling this process has been studied extensively in animals. Vitamin E protects cell membranes from the toxic effects of polyunsaturated fatty acids. The more polyunsaturated fat consumed, the greater the need for increased intake of vitamin E. The pamphlet stated that "myocardial hyaline" (whatever that is) degeneration was especially high in cod liver oil - but that the addition of vitamin E prevented the degeneration. The interrelationships of vitamin E with selenium, methionine, and cysteine (all contained in super yeast) was also mentioned. The fact that vitamin E and selenium are synergistic (that is they work together, so that, for example, the ability of vitamin E to increase stamina is magnified when selenium is also provided) is a relatively new discovery and many athletes take vitamin E/selenium pills. I discovered something in this pamphlet that perhaps many athletes are unaware of, however. At low levels, vitamin E and selenium are synergistic - but at high levels they may be antagonistic. Excessive intake of selenium is toxic, and the symptoms of toxicity appear to be the same as those for deficiency. To me, this means that a dog should be given vitamin E pills - but not the ones with added selenium – he'll get selenium in the super yeast and in the cod liver oil. Selenium is also contained in garlic which is also supposed to be good for the dogs - and, they love it. I get my vitamin E from the health food store - the natural E, not synthetic and I get the vitamin E with mixed tocopherols. The most concentrated sources of vitamin E are found in the oils extracted from grains such as wheat germ. These oils contain chemically related compounds with varying levels of vitamin E activity. The most biologically active of these forms is alpha-tocopherol. For this reason, most of the vitamin E you purchase is aipha-tocopnerol separated from the oil by processing in order to get a concentrated source of vitamin E. Many health nuts (like myself) feel that most anytime you process a food, something is lost in nutrition. Mixed tocopherols means that the alpha-tocopherol is not separated so that you receive the vitamin E in its natural state. No significant nutritional value has been found (to my knowledge) to exist in the rest of the oil outside of the alpha-tocopherol - but mark my words - in time we will find that there is indeed a nutritional value to the rest of the oil or it acts synergistically with alpha-tocopherol. The bottle that contains the vitamin E oil in the natural state will say "mixed tocopherols" on the label. I get 400 i.u. capsules. I wouldn't use anything stronger than that.

    Another important nutrient for the athletic dog is iron, which provides healthy red corpuscles in the blood and allows the blood to carry fresh oxygen through the body more efficiently. Some people give their dogs iron pills or iron shots - a waste of money in my opinion. You see, copper is essential before iron can be utilized by the body. You will provide a better source of iron if you supplement with quality foods that contain iron and copper. Molasses and liver are the best sources - particularly the molasses. Add a tablespoon of molasses per day to your athletic dog's diet and you will find his ability to perform will definitely increase. It is given to thoroughbred race horses, as I mention in the conditioning chapter. Some of the pit fighting people give their dogs a tablespoonful about an hour or two before a match. (I think it takes a dog a longer time to assimilate food than a human because of his slower digestive process. So, I think they should give the dog two or three tablespoonsful four hours before the match and another tablespoonful an hour before the match). I eat molasses myself. I like the unsulphured kind, which is much sweeter. I used to think blackstrap (sulphured) molasses was more nutritious, but actually it is more processed - usually a byproduct of the sugar making process. The sulphur taste is due to the sulphur dioxide residue introduced during this processing. Unsulphured molasses, as it states on the label of Grandma's Molasses (the brand I like), refers to molasses refined from the concentrated juice of sun-ripened sugar cane primarily for the purpose of making molasses - it is not a by-product. Honey is another energy provider. Many pit fighters feed their dogs honey before a match in the same manner described for molasses. The sugar provided by honey is natural sugar and it's predigested - so it's very good for your dog.

Finally, I recommend some supplementation of vitamin C, some of the benefits of which were enumerated in the description of Nutra-Vet's product Scorbucin. As pointed out in the pamphlet, the primary function of vitamin C is to help form and maintain the strong cement-like protein material known as collagen, which has the job of holding together all the cells in your body. It is sometimes called connective tissue, and is concentrated in ligaments, tendons, blood vessels, bones, and teeth. It is responsible for the strength and elasticity of these structures. In addition, when a dog is wounded, vitamin C (natural) is the best healer. When a dog is wounded, the collagen in the tissue will excite the platelets (little purple clotting factors that swim around in the blood) which will then stick together and form a mesh, a sort of screen like a spider web. When this happens, the mesh traps the red blood cells so that a clot is formed which will begin the healing process. This is not a very sophisticated explanation and I'm not a doctor or vet, but it is a basic description of the process. Anyway, vitamin C is instrumental in promoting this whole process. Vitamin C also conducts calcium to the heart, strengthening it. In addition, if you are training your Pit Bull with heavy resistances, such as weight-pulling, then vitamin C can be important in protecting the connective tissue. Probably the greatest value of this vitamin, however, is its ability to fight stress. It is said to be an even stronger factor in combatting stress than the B-complex vitamins (which would be the second best stress vitamin) because of its effects on the adrenal glands and the hormones these glands produce. The adrenal hormones are the major stress handlers in the dog's body. Their action is dependent on the presence of vitamin C. When a dog encounters any stress, vitamin C helps maintain cellular function, but vitamin C is quickly depleted under these conditions, and research studies have shown that adrenal exhaustion quickly follows. Reflexes and tissue development are then adversely affected. Current competitive strength-building and body-building magazines are talking about some new forms of ascorbic acid that may be more effective for athletes than the current form. They are sodium ascorbate, calcium ascorbate, and potassium ascorbate. These mineral-bound forms of the vitamin are new on the market and I haven't been able to find out how to obtain them nor do I know much about them at this time. Nutrition is an evolutionary process and we still have much to learn. I can tell you the general principle behind them is that they are forms of vitamin C that have been separated so they are easier for the body to assimilate - similar to chelated vitamins. I personally believe you are better off with vitamin C in its natural state complete with bioflavanoids, etc. We'll have to wait to see what the research findings are.

Vitamin C is a very controversial vitamin. Unlike humans, animals manufacture their own supply, so it is claimed that they don't need any extra supplementation. This is usually the case; but as this vitamin is very quickly used up when the body is stressed (I have read that experiments with animals under stress indicate that vitamin C requirements can rise by 100 times their normal amount) or when the animal must have any medicine, particularly any antibiotics. Today, in most sections of the United States, especially in the warmer regions, dogs must take a heartworm pill every day, as heartworms have been responsible for killing countless well-bred Pit Bulls in recent years - and it could have been prevented if only the owner would have provided the proper care. I feel, however, that administering a daily dose of heartworm medicine means that extra vitamin C is called for. I don't think you need to give the vitamin C every day, however, or in very large doses. I believe quality rather than quantity is important for the dog. Give him a pill two or three times a week. Give only _natural_ vitamin C that contains the associated bioflavanoids (called vitamin P, found in the pulp of fruit) and hesperidine complexes as well as rutin. Among other things, bioflavanoids protect and build the capillaries that carry blood from the arteries to the muscle cells and then to the veins. Bioflavanoids in sufficient quantities help provide the tissues with fresh oxygenated blood and nutrients. When you buy a bottle of, say 500 mg. vitamin C, you are buying man-made ascorbic acid. I say this because it's impossible to make a natural vitamin C pill of that much potency that would be small enough to swallow. You can buy some pure natural vitamin C that is only 30 mg. or some 100 mg. C that is natural with ascorbic acid added for potency. Ascorbic acid is effective in preventing (to a degree) colds with human beings and in eliminating colds if a human catches one. In other words, as stated in Nutra-Vet's pamphlet on vitamin C, "the number of bacteria that each white blood cell digests is directly related to the ascorbic acid content of the blood."

It should be noted, however, that this is true up to a certain limit - that limit being the saturation point beyond which the blood can absorb no more ascorbic acid. The excess is merely passed out of the system. With humans, this means that vitamin C is needed every two to four hours when a person is sick, because excess vitamin C is passed out, but the body can produce no more later when it is needed. With an animal this is not so true, because, as stated, the animal can produce the vitamin himself. Under stress, however, the animal will deplete his reserves and needs replinishment. In any event, I wanted to point out a little known fact - that while man-made ascorbic acid is effective in combatting virus bacteria, it will not function as well as natural C for all necessary circumstances. For example, man-made ascorbic acid, even in high level doses, will not cure common scurvey, whereas one small citrus fruit like a lemon a day (containing less than 30 mg. of natural C), will. It is for these reasons that I recommend feeding your conditioned Pit Bull low levels of natural C with bioflavanoids, etc. intact. I would buy either the natural C from a health foods store or get Nutra-Vet's product, Scorbucin.

Needham's Archibald

Well, that just about wraps up nutrition. Actually, the statement that we are what we eat should be modified a bit. We are what we are, primarily through genetics. If you want to be a superstar, choose your parents well! However, I believe we can come close to maximizing our genetic potential by providing our bodies with quality nutrition beginning at as early an age as possible. When I say as early as possible, I mean not just the child, but the parents and as far back as you can go. As stated, I believe the same principle holds true with animals. The sooner we begin, the better.

Chapter 7: Scientific Conditioning

That which does not kill us makes us stronger. -Conan the Barbarian

I define canine conditioning as a three-dimensional development.
1. Cardiovascular endurance. This is the strength of the cardiovascular system which includes the heart, lungs, andbblood vessels. Having cardiovascular endurance means you can sustain vigorous exercise over an extended period of time.
2. Muscular strength. This is the amount of weight a dog can pull.
3. Muscular endurance. This is the distance a dog can pull a given weight (an unspecified, relatively low weight that varies according to the size, weight, age, and pulling experience of the dog).

To me, proper conditioning begins with your puppy. I know a great many Pit Bull fanciers who wait until their dogs are around 15 months old before they begin conditioning them. I believe proper exercise is important to the health and well-being of a pet, and I feel that it gives a definite edge to the Pit Bull in conformation shows, field trials, and particularly in Schutzhund trials. For the combat dog, it makes all the difference in the world. My Pit Bull, Morochito, has been exercised, although not as well as I would have liked, since he was eight weeks old. I have experimented with several other Pit Bulls who did not receive early puppy conditioning but were raised on a chain or running chain. I took several Pit Bulls that were 15 months to two years of age and had never been run, with me for three miles of roadwork. (They were on harness.) All of the tested Pit Bulls were much less coordinated than Morochito and none of them knew how to pull in their harness like he does.

As I mentioned, conditioned should begin with the puppy. In fact, it is my opinion that the most important conditioning stage is between the ages of eight weeks and two years, because this is when they establish habit patterns that last them a lifetime; an enjoyment or pure love for exercise is developed that's hard to develop if you begin late, and a coordination is developed that's very difficult to obtain if you begin late. Therefore, let's start our discussion with the eight-week-old pup. A puppy of this age cannot be conditioned very strenuously, but can develop an enjoyment for exercise that he might not otherwise have. You can, of course, ruin a puppy's development by demanding too much. Really, conditioning a little puppy consists of strenuous play. We find an analogous situation with humans. A child that receives plenty of exercise will tend to grow up to be a healthier, better looking, stronger adult, better able to handle the stresses of life. If too much demand is placed upon the child, however, he can develop problems.

Conditioning a dog is a time consuming process and you'll get out of it what you put into it. I'll be enumerating some extensive conditioning programs that would entail a considerable amount of time to implement. Most people do not have the time or do not want to become that involved in conditioning. I am going to present sufficient material for you to have as finely conditioned a Pit Bull as possible so that he can perform at maximum physical level at any endeavor. You can pick out what to use and discard what you find impractical, given your needs and time constraints.

You should conduct your training and conditioning with your dog at the same time every day. A dog, especially a pup or young dog feels much more secure in his life when there is a lot of routine, just like human babies do. If a pup lives according to reasonably consistent time schedules, he'll tend to maintain a more stable temperament. It is better to split conditioning (and also training for obedience, tracking, or whatever) into two sessions rather than one long session. This is true for humans as well as dogs. A human athlete will benefit much more from a one-hour morning and a one-hour evening training session than one two-hour session, during which time he would become tired or even exhausted during the second hour, and mental concentration would lower so that performance and learnability are lowered also. The same principle is true with studying. You'll study much more effectively when you split study time into two one-hour sessions than if you study two hours straight. I suggest you get up an hour early in the morning and enjoy your Pit Bull. I think you'll find that you'll go to work with a high-spirited attitude. With your puppy, you'll want to begin with a piece of hemp rope for the following exercise. (Hemp rope is is very good for strengthening the teeth and gums - better than leather.) Roll up one end of the rope into a ball, like a ball of twine, about the size of a fist, and tie it tight, leaving about eight inches free to hold on to - whatever length seems comfortable to you. Dangle the ball tantalizingly in front of the pup, or drag it swiftly along the ground, then spin the rope around in circles so that the puppy keeps spinning as though he were chasing his tail. Keep changing directions and also do rapid figure-eights. Keep the circles small so that the puppy has to twist and turn a lot which will develop his flexibility. Pass the rope around and between both your legs, changing hands and forming figure-eights. After a couple minutes let him catch the rope and play with it. Every time he shakes it, excitedly say, "Shake it, Boy (or Girl)." When the puppy matures, upon hearing the command, "Shake it," he will shake hard whatever he's holding onto. This will be useful in Schutzhund work, as the dog will put on an exciting performance when "working the sleeve" (holding onto the antagonist's protected arm). The puppy will also want to play tug-of-war, an excellent game that develops jaw muscles, teeth, and overall strength. You must be very careful because the puppy can easily lose teeth with this game. You should always let the puppy win. On alternate days, use a different toy - a hide, or piece of leather if you can get it; or an old rag will do. This will keep the puppy's interest and enthusiasm higher. Shake it enticingly and let the puppy try to get it. Repeat the circles and figure-eights and tugging exercises you do with the rope. Again be very careful not to let the puppy yank out a tooth.

I have an idea that I've never tried but think it might be a good one. Animals respond to scent and I think if you give the puppy's hemp rope or rag to another dog to play with for a bit before giving it to the puppy, it may make the puppy more energetic in the play. There are some who might think that this will make him aggressive toward other dogs but this is not at all true. Dogs aren't the smartest creatures in the world, but they do know the difference between a real animal and a rag. In any event, it will not make the puppy at all aggressive toward other dogs.

Morochito is always very enthusiastic about his conditioning.

If you start a Pit Bull as a puppy, he will be enthusiastic about this game as an adult. I like to use a bicycle tire tube because he likes the flapping noise it makes when he shakes it, and he'll shake it longer.

Stop before the puppy gets tired, and begin a training session on fetching. You will be training your Pit Bull to respond to commands in a positive, natural manner, while at the same time providing exercise for him. The puppy will learn quickly because the exercise appeals to his natural instincts to chase a moving object and it will be a fun game. The puppy will quickly make the association between the command "fetch" and the sequence of moves he must perform in order to continue the "game." You should always keep the command low key, that is, in a soft, low voice, with a pleasant, not harsh, voice. When the puppy does not respond, do not let irritation creep into your voice - better to forget it and go on to another exercise and try again the next day. Eventually the puppy will learn. You will find that you can provide the puppy with plenty of exercise with a minimum of personal effort with this game. Think about it this way. There are 5,280 feet in a mile. If you throw your object 50 feet a throw, you have your puppy running, sprinting, a mile after a little over 50 throws. That may sound like a lot, but it really won't take long.

Turn your Pit Bull in circles with this game - it develops his ability to spin fast and keeps him flexible.

When the puppy gets a little older, you can get him to sprint faster and for a longer time, probably, with a frisbee. You want to be sure the Pit Bull is well trained to retrieve before you start him on a frisbee or any other moving object, so you can begin by rolling it on the ground and letting him pursue it. Give him the command to fetch and have him bring it to you as you excitedly praise him. Then squat down on your knees and wave the frisbee in the air. Most Pit Bulls love to jump and will instinctively jump up to catch it. Gradually stand up, holding the frisbee near the high point of his jump. Let him win easily and get the general idea of catching it in the air. Don't challenge his abilities until he becomes proficient. When he fetches the frisbee and brings it back to you every time when you roll it on the ground and he can also jump up and catch it every time when you hold it in the air, toss it in the air (but fairly low) just a few feet. He may get the idea and catch it in the air at which time you pour on the praise, making like he just did this wonderful thing. He'll think he's great and work harder and harder to catch. If he doesn't get the idea of catching it in the air, but instead chases it and waits until it falls to the ground, try another technique. Get a partner to stand afaout ten feet away and throw it slowly to each other.

This pulling develops jaw strength and the front legs. I always let him win, but he has to work for it. I'm careful not to jerk out a tooth, though.

The pup can't catch it unless he catches it on the way in the air because it doesn't fall to the ground. If he still doesn't catch it, return to rolling it and having him jump up and catch it in your hand. Eventually he'll catch on. If he catches it in the air once, from then on he'll work like the dickens for it and you can throw it further and further and higher also. This is an excellent conditioner because the Pit Bull is using just about every muscle and it is not demanding on the owner. You want to always begin slowly, giving the dog more than adequate muscle warm-up. When I do my roadwork, I almost always start off slow. When I don't give myself an adequate warm-up, I become fatigued much quicker in my run and sometimes strain muscles. If you are interested, the makers of Gaines dog foods and the Whamo Manufacturing Co. sponsor a nationwide Gaines K-9 Frisbee catch and Fetch Contest. The contest is co-sponsored nationwide by local recreation departments, and winners of local contests compete for the title of State Champion. The winners from each state then compete in one of nine regional contests. The winners of the regionals are awarded prizes and an all-expense-paid trip to the Rose Bowl where they compete for the grand championship, which carries, among other things, a $1,000 savings bond. For information on when and where the nearest local event is to be held, write to: Irv Landers, Whamo Manufacturing Co. 5430 Van Nuys Boulevard, Van Nuys, California 91401.

There are various other little things you can do to keep a Pit Bull active and conditioned. There are various toys that most Pit Bulls love to play with. One is the automobile tire. As adults they'll bite it all over, mostly the inside ring area, and pick it up and throw it around. The puppy can play with a bicycle tire, which you can hang from a tree if your Pit Bull is tied up near one. He may love to jump up and grab it and just hang there holding on. Not all Pit Bulls will do this, but most of them will. Also a short 2x4 is a toy many like. They'll pick it up and carry it around, which strengthens their jaw and neck muscles. Some people put a little lead in them to make them heavier. Have a bucket or box where you put a number of miscellaneous toys like old, smelly, leather shoes, sneakers, a broken leather belt (He will like to shake it and hear it flap), a big old wooly sock with a rubber ball stuffed in it (another toy he'll like to shake), pieces of old carpet, etc. Don't give him all the toys at once because, like a child, he'll quickly tire of them. Rotate them, giving him a new toy every morning after feeding. Another suggestion is, beginning with the small pup (around nine weeks old), give him a large shank bone once a week. This is a controversial suggestion because, according to my veterinarian there is always a small chance of the Pit Bull swallowing a bone splinter and getting it stuck in his intestines, which can be fatal if he can't pass it through, and that chance, small as it is, is not worth it. I know several Pit Bull breeders who have fed bones to a yard of Pit Bulls, averaging about a dozen, for over a decade, and have told me they've never had a problem. You must be careful never to let your Pit Bull near any bone that splinters. Shank bones don't splinter. You can often get them free from butchers or other meat stores. Shank bones are often as big as your arm and a Pit Bull loves them. I put bones under the category of conditioning because they are probably the best way to exercise a Pit Bull pup's jaw muscles and to teach him how to use his mouth correctly to get the hardest bite. I read in an article by Bobby Hall (*Pit Bull Gazette*, August, 1979), that that is how a young lion cub in the wild learns to bite correctly, and that if he doesn't get this early development he'll have trouble surviving. I'm sure that bone gnawing does a lot for the development of a young Pit Bull's ability to use his natural biting leverage. The thing to do is to give him the bone once a week while little (and then only once a month after he's grown). On that day, don't feed the pup and give him the bone that evening when he's very hungry. You might think it cruel or unhealthy for the pup to go all day without eating. On the contrary, it is healthy. See the chapter on nutrition for a further discussion of this subject. When you give the Pit Bull his bone, he will gnaw on it all night. Take it from him the next morning. Some people boil the bones so that there will be no parasites in them for the Pit Bull to catch. Some even build a little wooden platform and tie the Pit Bull on it to gnaw the bone so that the bone won't get on the ground and get parasites. Be sure you don't give a Pit Bull a bone more often than once a week. Frequent bone chewing can lead to excessively worn teeth.

  Another popular "toy" is to tie a garden hose to a tree or post near the dog. Most Pit Bulls will grab the end of it, plant their front feet, and pull back. One guy has a garden hose attached to a heavy spring which is attached to a tree. He will flick the hose a couple times and the Pit Bull will pull hard on it. You need a lot of garden hose because it doesn't last long.

I like to make Morochito jump for a tidbit occasionally. He likes it, too. I use his dry dog food – don't believe in pet store high-priced tidbits. He's just as enthusiastic about his regular dog food.

Sometimes I make him reach for it.

Sometimes I toss his tidbit in the air and he jumps up to catch, even if he wraps both of us up in his chain.

I sure do love my Pit Bull

Youll find that your Pit Bull will always be more active and playful in your presence. He may lie around all day doing nothing, but the minute you go out to the yard, even if you ignore him, he'll grab a toy and vigorously play with it or he'll get his bone that's been laying there all day untouched and go chew on it. (We have an apple tree in our backyard and sometimes when we go out, Morochito will go get an apple and eat it!) A good way to provide a little mild conditioning, then, is to have a chair available near the place your Pit Bull is chained up, and whenever you have some reading to do, even if it's only five or ten minutes reading the newspaper, merely go outside, toss your Pit Bull a new toy, sit down, and read! In addition, whenever you do your daily 15 minutes of calisthenics, like jumping jacks, etc., do them in the yard near the place you have your Pit Bull. He'll get excited, jumping around, etc. This is not a lot of exercise, but if done reasonably consistently, I feel that it is an effective adjunct to more strenuous training. If you do not exercise daily, you should. Perhaps you might start now. Pit Bulls are not the only creatures that are healthier and happier if they exercise. People invent all kinds of ways of getting in a little extra exercise. For instance, some make the dog house entrance high so that the Pit Bull has to hop every time he goes into his house. Others delight in periodically having their Pit Bull jump for tidbits (as shown in the pictures).

   I feel a very special closeness to my Pit Bull. We've run together over hills, on forest trails, in the sweltering heat of summer, during snow storms, in the middle of rain storms – we're out on the road together. He gives me peace of mind. He's a perfect running mate. He doesn't run his mouth – can't talk; gives me time to think and clear my mind. Yeah, we've covered a lot of miles together, he and I. If you are not interested in that, however, or if you don't have the time, you might consider hiring someone to exercise your Pit Bull. High school students, especially those who train for track, may be interested, and may not charge much. You can tell them that running a Pit Bull is a real good workout. When he's running at a pace just faster than you, he pulls you along forcing you to go faster and faster and your feet seem to just barely touch the ground. You run like a Pit Bull on a treadmill. When he runs too fast, you have to run tense, always pulling back so he won't throw you. This is contrary to the way a track runner should run. He must run relaxed, but often an athlete trains in odd ways to develop proficiency. For ithe martial arts we practice relaxing by tensing all our muscles, then letting go. In this manner you are better able to discern the difference and you develop more body awareness. You learn what it really feels like to be relaxed. The exercise is designed to help you to be loose under stress of a combat situation, which makes you faster, and you won't tire as quickly as you will if you are tense. Well, I have found that when I run with Morochito, tense because he's pulling me this way and that, I can run very relaxed and flexible when I run without him. For this reason, I think a young man serious about training for track can get some unique, excellent training with a Pit Bull.

I have mentioned doing various things near the place you have your Pit Bull "tied up." Most Pit Bulls need to be kept on a heavy cow chain because of their proclivity for fighting. If they have plenty of early socialization, this is not as much of a problem. You still have to be careful, however, because dogs are like people – there's always a bully - some will even go into a strange dog's yard and pick a fight. Also, males will fight over a female in heat. The Pit Bull that is very friendly with strange dogs will not let another dog pick on him and when squabbles do develop, the Pit Bull will kill the other dog. Even though the other dog is at fault, and even if the incident occurs on your property, you may find you and your Pit Bull being blamed because of the breed's reputation and because of the mess he makes of the other dog. A heavy cow chain is needed because the Pit Bull is a real escape artist. For those who have not owned one before you would really be surprised how adept these dogs are at getting loose. They are very strong and can break, over a period of time, anything short of a cow chain. If you have a fenced-in yard, so much the better, because the Pit Bull can then run free. If you have an aggressive Pit Bull, however, it won't hold him, and eventually, when you least expect it, over the fence he'll go. One day I glanced out our window to the backyard and saw Morochito playing around on top of my son's club house! He had climbed up the children's ladder and then onto the club house. It was one of those quiet afternoons with nothing happening, and I don't know why that crazy Pit Bull decided to go up there. Owners of some aggressive breeds such as Dobermans or Rottweilers, use an electrically charged wire such as that used by farmers to keep cattle within fenced land. I'm told it won't keep an aggressive Pit Bull in when he decides he wants out, however, and eventually he'll find a way. The best thing is to keep your dog on a running cable, which is just a fairly thick woven steel wire, running as long as you want it - some are several yards, some the length of the yard, and I've seen one that was more than 50 yards long - went into a patch of woods on the owner's land. Some people run the cable up high from tree limb to tree limb and some run it along the ground. You attach the Pit Bull's chain to the cable with a round metal ring called an "O" ring, which you can purchase at most any hardware. It looks like an oversized key ring. You want a heavy-duty one. You slip it over the cable so it can run up and down it. The Pit Bull's chain is connected to the "O" ring with a heavy-duty swivel connection so he won't get himself tangled. Keep the cable well greased to reduce friction and wear. The other end of the chain is connected to the dog's collar with another "O" ring by a swivel connection also. You must use the "O" ring at the collar, too, because the Pit Bull has a tendency to pull out the connection sewn into the collar. With the running cable, the Pit Bull can run up and down the length of the cable and get his exercise. It is not known why, but experience shows that a dog will be more active on a running cable than if he runs loose in a fenced-in yard.

After Morochito climbed the ladder to the top of the kids' club house, he was afraid to come down and had to be "rescued."

One of the most popular conditioners is called a fishing-pole - a real long, flexible pole, resembling a fishing pole, around seven feet or so in length. Bamboo is the most popular wood, but any flexible pole will do. You attach a rope or rawhide to the end of the pole and tie an old rag or a piece of leather or hide to the other end of the rope. (I like to use an old rubber bicycle tire tube because it makes a flapping noise when he catches it and shakes it, and I find he shakes it longer than a rag or hide.) The length of the pole and rope can vary according to what you feel is most comfortable. You want to have as long a pole as you can handle because then you can easily hold the "bait" (rag or hide) as far away from him as possible. You jiggle the pole a little so the hide dances enticingly and he'll scoot after it as fast as his legs will carry him. Keep the hide low to the ground and he'll learn to charge things low and utilize his natural leverage to the maximum. Swing the hide away from him - this is easy to do with a real long pole - and when he seems almost ready to snatch it, make it pop up quickly into the air. You'll find that a Pit Bull can jump very high, especially for his size and relative weight.

I haven't trimmed the branches off this pole, but it still does the job. Keeping it low to the ground teaches Morochito to run low with his head down.

Morochito is charging hard here. He's on his running chain - if you look closely you can see the chain attached to his collar, and the cable running along the ground - in the grass.

He'll use just about all of his muscles in this exercise – it's quite demanding. When he is in the air, pull the hide away from him and he'll usually twist and turn in an attempt to get it. This works his flexibility a great deal because, as you can see from the pictures of Morochito, he will twist into all kinds of contortions in an attempt to get that hide. It also helps the Pit Bull maintain his inherent sense of balance, because he must land correctly. In fact, with the pup, you'll want to start off reasonably easy, not making him jump too high. Don't start pulling the hide away from him in the air until he has become quite proficient at landing on all fours. Do not feel disappointed in your pup if he doesn't seem to have balance or the common sense to land correctly - a pup has to develop just like a human child does. At first Morochito was all enthusiasm but no common sense – he'd land on his side, his shoulder, and every way but right. He finally got so he could spin in the air and land on all fours. But be careful with this exercise and, as I said, make aradual demands of your Pit Bull pup. Several Pit Bulls have, in their enthusiasm, broke their shoulder with this exercise. The pattern is to whisk the hide rapidly along the ground away from the Pit Bull, pop it up in the air, then whisk it back in the other direction and repeat. Athletes in track, boxing, martial arts, tennis, football, and many other sports realize that one of the best methods of building stamina and endurance for short, sudden energy demands is to run a series of short sprints. You'll see football players training regularly by sprinting as hard as they can the width (not the length) of the field, pause or rest, sprint back, and repeat. This is exactly what you are doing with your Pit Bull, providing him with a series of short, all-out sprints. This is called interval training, which for human athletes refers to a regulated program in which the rest interval is very short (timed) and generally means going at a slower pace rather than completely stopping and resting. Some athletes stop completely and rest between intervals. This type of training is called repeats. The complete rest allows the lactic acid to deplete. We'll look at these concepts later. Interval training will work better for a dog than repeats, because it takes a dog much longer to recover from strenuous activity than a human.

 To realize the benefits you are giving your animal, you might try it yourself. Take a long run one day and compare your heart rate and exhaustion for a given amount of time to the same amount of time spent doing short sprints. In addition, at the end of each of your sprints, put a chair or something that is slightly difficult for you to jump over. You'll find that it is an extremely exhausting workout. If you work your Pit Bull consistently, every day, with this type exercise, until he is frothing slightly at the mouth and his breathing rate is quite rapid, you'll maintain him in excellent condition. Start slowly and gradually extend the length of time he works the fishing-pole. Sudden, extensive demands won't build up a Pit Bull & will ruin a pup. A sudden, long workout means nothing - a consistent, daily workout that increases slightly each week will build up a Pit Bull. If you can't find something to serve as a fishing-pole or would prefer an alternative exercise, here is one that is similar. Start a young pup jumping over a small hurdle. I used our picnic table bench and worked up to the picnic table itself (turned on its side). Start with a real small hurdle that is easy for the pup to jump over. Put him on a leash and the two of you sprint to it and jump over. (Let him sniff and walk around it before the very first jump.) Every time you jump over it, give him the command you will later want him to respond to -such as "over." Gradually increase the height. By the time it is too high for you to jump over with him, you can run along side of it and he'll jump over it alone. When he's old enough, and if you have obedience trained him, you can run to it and command him to "over" and he'll jump it. Later you'll be able to merely point to it and he'll enthusiastically jump over it on command. I do not consider this to be quite as good a conditioner as fishing-pole work because there is not so much twisting and turning and no hide to shake when you let him catch it. I would suggest that it is a good idea to alternate - fishing-pole one day, hurdles the next - because it will keep the Pit Bull enthusiastic and not bored with the "game" and because you have more of a relationship with your dog with hurdles because he is responding to your command. (In other words, you are getting in some obedience training while you condition at the same time.) If you want to go to the trouble, setting up six consecutive hurdles for him to run and jump over (similar to the steeple chase for horses) would be a good idea.

When you get to the end of your reach, swing the pole back in the other direction. Morochito spins around when I do it. This picture gives you a better view of his chain attached to his collar, and the cable that runs along the ground.

Periodically flip the pole in the air -Morochito goes to great lengths to get his rag.

Change directions in the air and he'll twist in the air.

Make him reach for it. Morochito can't go any higher here because of his chain.

Every once in awhile let him get his prize. That crazy Morochito normally gets the pole instead of the rag/ and breaks my pole!

Before we move on, I'd like to mention an additional benefit that can be derived from fishing-pole work. You can dramatically strengthen your dog's lymphatic system while you concomitantly squeeze out extra muscular strength over and above that which is developed during the regular conditioning routine. In order to understand the benefits, you must understand "G force." The concepts are cited in an amazing little book called *The Miracles of Rebound Exercise* by Albert E. Carter, which much of this discussion is based upon. You can find it in most health food stores. The research and findings in this book are responsible for the current popularity (with athletes as well as housewives, executives, etc.) of rebound equipment (a little trampoline which looks like a round coffee table and is compact enough to fit in your bedroom). A G force is a measure of the amount of gravitational pull on an object at sea level.[30] We are all strengthened by the force of gravity. A baby learns to lift his head against the force of gravity and strengthens his neck muscles. If you add acceleration and deceleration to gravity, the G force effectively stresses the cellular structure of the body and it becomes strengthened. This is accomplished on a trampoline by bouncing up and down. You get a maximum amount of stress for a minimum amount of effort, because while very little effort is required to bounce up and down on a trampoline, the body becomes subjected to changes in atmospheric pressure -accelerating when going up and decelerating when coming down. At the top of the bounce, the lymph flows up as the body starts back down. At the bottom of the bounce, the lymph flows back down, flushing out the cells and cellular tissue. You may wonder what good it does to strengthen the cellular and lymphatic system. We will look at the lymphatic system in a little more detail when we explain the importance of massaging muscles a little later in the chapter. Suffice it to say at this point that a body's overall strength depends upon an efficient circulatory system and that the trampoline-type exercise is the most efficacious means of cultivating a proficient circulatory system. The Rebound book cites instances in which people on a weight-lifting program have increased the rate of increment in strength dramatically when the weight lifting is supplemented by rebound training. In one example a weight trainer's rate of increase in strength improved significantly. In another example a high school wrestler became consistently stronger and had more endurance. It's quite a book, you really ought to read it.

    The knowledge is very useful for conditioning Pit Bulls. Since they are adept jumpers, the thing to do is get them to jump a lot. Some days use the fishing-pole and make your dog jump up several times in succession and do less running with more jumping. When you feed him have him jump up and catch kernels of dog food, say ten or more times, before you give him his dish. If you give him some command like "up" or "get it" when he goes after the treat, he'll eventually jump up on command without the treat.

    At the time of this writing you could pick up a rebounder for around $100 if you shopped around. At the conclusion of each workout, when the dog is exhausted, hold him in your arms and bounce around 100 times (I'd say five minutes.) You'll both benefit. It would seem that merely bouncing up and down would not do much. Not so. The studies (and I believe, research) indicates that in fact it is a stupendous adjunct to any conditioning program. Another way of looking at it is this - a muscle can built up by, for example, lifting weights; but if the circulatory system is not functioning at its maximum level, the muscular strength will fall short of its potential. It's a thought.

By the way, if you want some really dynamite dogs, begin holding the puppy in your arms while you bounce for 20 minutes every day. Recall in the "Pet" chapter the findings of Dr. Pfaffenberger - that Bloodhounds that have been handled and mildly stressed grow up to be more aggressive, more immune to disease, and more durable in general. This with a very docile breed. When you stimulate the lymphatic system you also stimulate the functioning of the adrenal glands. Let me mention at this point that I believe that gameness is partly a function of the adrenal system. Many a game Bulldog that will not quit in the pit even when he's torn to pieces, will yelp when a horse-fly stings or even if a flea is bothering him. It's just like the boxer that has an iron jaw – can't be knocked out - but if the barber yanks his hair, he yelps. The difference is psychological. In the ring the adrenal system is functioning overtime and the pain threshold is high. Notice I said partly. Many a Pit Bull that's been doped (to eliminate pain) has curred out.

You should precede a strenuous workout like fishing-pole with a warm-up of some sort. I recommend general "rough-house" play with your Pit Bull. I'd wear old clothes, and if you plan to have an obedience trained dog or Schutzhund, I'd begin the play session with some remark like "Okay," which in general tells him he's on free time, and perhaps something like "Let's play." You then push him, at which time he'll charge back at you instinctively, tail a-waggin'. You put your hands on his chest and shove him back – he'll keep coming. This will develop his leverage - do it a lot. From time to time, grab him by one leg, up high by his shoulder, and pull his feet out from under him and dump him (gently with that pup, now). This teaches him to be comfortable with sudden loss of balance and surprise. Grab him by the loose skin on his jaw muscles and gently shake or pull to one side, then the other. In resisting, he'll develop his neck muscles. (In this, also, be careful not to harm a pup.) Get a rag or hemp rope rolled into a ball on one end and do the exercises mentioned earlier. At no time is the pup allowed, with you or other members of the family, to "rough-house" like this without that command "Okay, let's play" (or whatever you decide to use). It will take the pup awhile to discern the difference, but every time he starts to rough-house when he's not supposed to (and he will do it – that's a guarantee), sharply bring your knee up into his chest and say, "No" – doesn't have to be a loud "no" - the knee will make him yelp and he'll soon learn that such behavior is going to be no fun unless his master says, "Okay, let's play." A Pit Bull is a manipulator, by the way, and will do anything to half way get by with something. Like he may jump and gently nip instead of a hard bite. Don't give in an inch - if you do he'll be harder to train. Believe me a Pit Bull that is not controlled when he's a pup is one big pain in the neck when he grows up! Same thing with behavior like grabbing your pant leg and making like you are a 200-pound boar that he's just got ahold of. Curtail that stuff early or you are in for trouble. I feel that a warm-up of this nature will mean that the Pit Bull will get more out of a fishing-pole exercise. An alternative warm-up, perhaps a better one, is walking, which, by the way, is an excellent exercise that provides different benefits fxom Cunning. You run your dog for strength and wind. You walk him for long endurance. The question often comes up - what is meant by walking? Does it mean walking slowly at human pace with the dog in a harness or walking at the dog's pace, off leash in a field? The answer is both. If you are walking the dog for just a few minutes to empty out, walk slowly with the dog on leash - if you are walking a few miles or more and have an area free from other dogs, you let him walk free sniffing around.

In boxing history, two champions that trained harder and went into the ring with more stamina than any others for all 15 rounds were Rocky Marciano and Sugar Ray Robinson. Both, but especially Rocky, incorporated into their training a great deal of walking in addition to roadwork. Walking affects your metabolism in such a way that builds endurance, defined as additional strength after a long, strenuous workout. Some folks get a heavy cow chain and attach it to the Pit Bull's collar for the walk, letting him drag it along; others wrap it around his neck. This is done to develop the all-important neck muscles and increase endurance. (It is like people wearing a weight belt when they run.) Use a light chain for a pup and gradually increase the size and weight of the chain each month. I wouldn't start on that until the pup is four or five months old. I didn't put a harness on Morochito until he was about nine months old. Before that I walked him by attaching his lead to his collar. He was constantly pulling on that lead for all he was worth, so much so that he choked himself; but I feel like that helped develop a good strong neck while at the same time developing his driving strength in his rear legs. A pit dog uses his rear legs for 80% of his work and so this is the area that is most important to develop in order to maximize natural conformation. At nine months old, the neck muscles are more or less developed and a harness is better because he can pull harder and work those rear legs. Look at the pictures of Morochito pulling in his harness. You can see how he works those rear legs. This is an excellent conditioner.

Morochito pulls hard in his harness. Notice his slightly crooked tail. I know more than one old timer that claims this to be a throwback to some of our foundation dogs. I do know that Lloyd's Pilot and some of his progeny had such a tail.

If you hold Morochito back, he tries harder to push ahead. This gives him terrific drive.

A 15-foot lead is attached to Morochito's harness and passes underneath me to a couple of tires hanging from a tree. I am not holding him correctly in this picture, however.

    Another way to condition a Pit Bull's rear legs and develop leverage, is to hang an automobile tire from a tree limb, with a chain preferably, because it is heavy. Have the tire touching the ground. Also attach the tire to the Pit Bull's harness with a rope. You then hold the Pit Bull up close to the tire. (In the pictures of Morochito I am not holding him correctly - I wanted you to be able to see more of him.) You should hold your dog with both hands placed in front on his chest muscles. He will have more endurance this way. Holding him underneath as in the pictures, hinders his breathing, especially when he's breathing hard. An alternative would be to grab the loose skin at the scruff of his neck with one hand and place the other hand on his front chest muscle or underneath him just above his groin. Notice I said place not lift near his groin. The groin area is a place of security for a dog - it is akin to placing your hand on a human's shoulder. This is why I prefer the hand-on-the-groin technique. You need something to excite him so he'll charge ahead, picking up the tire as he does so. One dogman works his Pit Bulls this way after he's walked them and put them on the treadmill. The dogs are panting heavily when he brings them to the tire device. He has a little rabbit in a cage just out of reach of the Pit Bull. Pit Bulls are not barking type dogs and so the rabbit doesn't get frightened. He is used to the dogs and calmly sits there munching his cabbage. He also has the rabbit sitting on the ground near the dog's mill and it seems to motivate the dogs to run longer and doesn't bother the rabbit any. He straddles the Pit Bull, holds him as I indicated, and makes a hissing noise like a snake and says, "Sssss - - - get 'em," at which time he releases the Pit Bull who will charge forward, pulling the heavy tire up in the air. When he has reached the end, the owner pulls him back and repeats. Most Pit Bulls will keep this up (if they are in condition and not fat) for a good 10 or 15 minutes after an exhausting mill run. Following this exercise, the Pit Bulls are walked for two to four miles to cool down, are rubbed down, watered, and finally petted and praised.

I picked up that "Sssss - - - get 'em," from that guy I was telling you about. I do that when I'm playing with Morochito, especially with a rag or fishing-pole. It seems to motivate him a bit more and keep him going a little longer - plus, to me, it's fun!

When I release Morochito he charges forward with his head low. This is primarily instinctive because of his breeding, but I maximize his potential with training techniques.

Morochito is moving fast here.

When he reaches the end of the line the weight of the tires pull him back

But his enthusiasm never wanes. He's ready to go again.

    Ideally, the Pit Bull should receive a daily dose of walk, rough-housing, fishing-pole, treadmill, and running twice a day as consistently as possible. Naturally, you probably don't have the time for the complete program; you'll have to choose what you can do.

    When the Pit Bull is around three months old he should be introduced to a treadmill, catmill, or turntable, if you have one. He is much too young for serious training on a mill, but if you get him used to it early, he'll be more likely to run it energetically and enthusiastically when he grows up. You must be careful that the curious pup doesn't hurt himself, falling off the mill or something that might make him shy from a mill later. You can find treadmills for sale in the *Pit Bull Gazette*. They are fairly expensive and some people find ways to make their own. The news media, humane society, etc. get all excited about treadmills, proclaiming them to be the mark of fighting dogs, which is not true. Many of the top pit conditioners do not use the treadmill, preferring other means of conditioning, and to imply that because someone wants a healthy, well conditioned pet, he is training a pit dog, is utterly ludicrous. Yet some dog magazines have been so pressured that they have had to refuse all advertisements for this piece of equipment. There are different types of treadmills - some designed to be a little difficult to run; some very easy so that the dog can really fly, his feet seeming to barely touch the mill; some adjustable for hard or easy running; and some adjustable up to around 30° angles so that the dog is in effect running uphill. I prefer the mill that is very easy to run with as little friction as possible. I'll explain my reasons later. Some prefer a catmill (also called a horsemill) to a treadmill. It is called a horsemill because it is frequently used by horse trainers to exercise horses. It is called a catmill because some people have used a cat as bait to motivate the dog to run it. The mill is a pole cemented into the ground but on a swivel device that allows it to turn. On the top of the pole, another pole crosses it, forming a "T." The dog is put in a harness and attached to one end of the crossbar, and he then runs around in a circle. The track should be filled with lime to provide proper drainage and keep it from getting too muddy when it rains. Some people put a cat in a little cage attached to the other end of the bar to excite the Pit Bull and make him run longer, and some use a raccoon if they can get one because they are less excitable and, after they get used to it, rather enjoy the game. Actually, it's usually not necessary to use a cat or 'coon to run the dogs. An animal may be used to get the dog started if he doesn't catch on or is not interested, but once he gets the idea and gets into shape, most Pit Bulls will run the mill for an hour or more without any animal baiting them -they love to run. If a Pit Bull will run a mill without bait, it is just common sense that the trainer won't want to bother with keeping a cat or 'coon, but whenever someone gets a picture of a Pit Bull being conditioned in this manner, they seem to get the impression that everyone uses it. Some Pit Bulls, just like some people, are just plain lazy and won't run a mill no matter what the motivation. Vindicator, I understand, was that way. Some people will put the dog's water bucket in front of him for him to chase after. (If he gets to drink out of the bucket after his workout, he is more prone to chase it.) In recent years the catmill has become more popular than the treadmill because many of the experienced Pit Bull conditioners that I have talked to say they have found that a Pit Bull conditioned on a catmill has more endurance than one conditioned on a treadmill. I'm not sure I agree, however; I think sometimes something becomes popular because it is a change. People tend to become tired of a method or technique and are psychologically ready to feel something else is better. Other reasons a catmill is preferred are that it is usually cheaper to make and is much easier on the dog's feet. With the catmill, the dog runs on the ground, but with a treadmill, the pads of a dog's feet can get cut to pieces, even with a carpeted run. There are various medicines available to protect and toughen the dog's feet. (See the chapter on medicine for particulars.) It is my feeling that if you begin the Pit Bull early enough as a pup, he will have sufficiently tough pads. I've been told not to run a Pit Bull on a hard surface (like a street) because it will tear up his pads; but I wasn't told that until after Morochito was a year and a half old. He had been doing his roadwork with me almost every day, about three to four miles a day on the street! But I started him on that when he was just a wee little pup, eight weeks old. For myself, I prefer the treadmill to the catmill, for reasons I will disclose later.

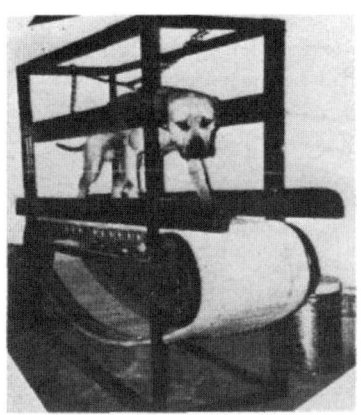

Here's a good treadmill, sold by Boyd McCormick in Hillsboro, TN

This is a particularly well built turntable, homemade by Jack Swinson in Greensboro, N. C. He covered it with carpet to protect the dog's feet and also built the shelter over it. The chain that hangs from the middle attaches to the dog's harness. The wheel is stopped by pressing on the surface with a carpeted piece of board

Another variation for exercise is the turntable. It is a large wheel that spins as the dog runs. It is cheaper to make and the dog can sprint faster than if he's running on the ground because there is less friction. I don't like them because the dog has to run at a kind of angle, leaning to one side slightly as he runs. If exercised on a turntable, he should be turned to run in the opposite direction at intervals so that he'll develop equally. Some dogs just refuse to run in the opposite direction, however.

Before you run a dog on a mill, you should have him empty out. If you walk him before his mill work (and you should), he may empty out on his walk. If he doesn't, moisten a wooden match stick with your lips and stick it into his rectum and leave it there a few minutes. If the Pit Bull has anything in him at all, he'll "get the urge" and go almost immediately.

Another excellent conditioner is swimming. The problem is that most folks do not have access to a swimming pool or lake for a daily swim. Remember in order for a conditioning method to be beneficial, it must be applied on a daily basis, not just sporadically. There's a man in Virginia who uses swimming as his primary conditioning method. He has his own pool which he pops his Pit Bulls into, gradually extending the amount of time they swim around. They can't get out because of the porcelain walls which they can't climb. Their master pulls them out when they are good and tired. This is an excellent way to get a Pit Bull quite leg weary because of the resistance of the water. (Some martial artists who regularly have access to a pool train by performing kicks and punches in the water. They will attest to the fact that one's limbs do indeed become weary, and that after a sufficient training time they can really explode those kicks and punches in the air.) It was also a favorite training method for the undefeated slugger, Rocky Marciano. Swimming also promotes flexibility. If your Pit Bull becomes lame from running, or if his pads get sore, you can maintain his level of endurance by daily swims. Swimming as an adjunct training method is sometimes called hydrotraining by marathon trainers. An article in *Runner's World*, June, 1982, entitled "Peaking" by Brooks Johnson, makes the statement "Hydrotraining is the safest method of cardiovascular overload because there is no risk to the muscloskelatal structure." In addition to roadwork, swimming is included in conditioning programs used by top race horse trainers. The Spendthrift Farm in Lexington, Kentucky provides stables and training grounds for some of the best horses in the country, like the famous Seattle Slew (offered price - $12 million). Affirm (offered price - $16 million - one of only three horses alive today who is a triple crown winner), and Nashua (offered price - $7 million). Because of the money involved, horse racing has become very scientific and owners employ only the best trainers who can produce. Another place that uses swimming and is also recognized as one of the best in the country is San Luis Key Downs Thoroughbred Training Center near Oceanside in Southern California. Here they work seven hours a day, swimming 30 or 40 head per day. Having done it for 18 years, they claim it is especially beneficial for building strong lungs. They also train mules for racing, by the way, using swimming in addition to their roadwork, too. They say that for a horse, 15 minutes of swimming is equivalent to two or three miles of running at full gallop. Young horses are started off with a three-minute swim and gradually work up. A horse or dog uses his front legs a lot when swimming so I believe the front legs get strengthened more with swimming than with running. The utility of swimming is enhanced by the fact that it reduces a dog's weight by using up calories faster than any of the other conditioning methods, because the lower temperature of the water stresses the system at the same time as the dog works (swimming). Research shows conclusively (*Research Quarterly*, Vol. 34, 1963, "The Effects of Short Periods of Physical Training Upon Body Weight of White Mice," research performed at the University of Wisconsin.) that swimming reduces weight significantly greater than treadmill work, while treadmill work provides significantly greater endurance than swimming.

Well, there you have just about all the basic conditioning techniques except for my particular favorites which I saved for last. I want to propose some extensive training methods that will maximize a Pit Bull's potential. Before doing that, however, I want to share with you my storehouse of knowledge regarding conditioning of athletes, including building strength, endurance, stamina, etc., which I have accumulated from my martial arts and boxing experiences and from literature on training for competitive track and also training methods used for race horses. In the mile race, the difference in the average time between a winner and a second-place horse, is less than 1/5 of a second, and between second- and third-place horses, a shade more than 1/5 of a second.[31] The difference is the slight edge provided by the hores's bloodlines (breeding), conformation, and by his training (conditioning).

Actually there is no perfect conditioning program. In fact there seems to be almost as many opinions about the correct way to condition a dog as there are pit dogmen. But the successful ones have certain features in common. Each one calls for lots of running; each begins slow and gradually increases in amount and intensity; each follows a definite plan with enough flexibility for individual differences and unforeseen circumstances. Pit dog men have been conditioning dogs in America since the turn of the century and they do know their business.

I don't want to leave the impression that this chapter is designed to teach folks how to condition a dog for pit fights. Most of those who match dogs already know how to condition. I do draw on their techniques in order to aid in the development of a Pit Bull to his maximum condition. I think if we combine their techniques with my knowledge of athletics, you can put a fine edge on that condition. Of course, you may not care whether or not your dog does get in that fine a shape, but if you intend to compete in Schutzhund or weight-pulling, I believe you'll have an edge. Not only will your Pit Bull be stronger and have more stamina, he'll also be more alert and responsive. Any animal, human or otherwise, is more alert and responsive if put in top condition. In addition, I feel like you'll have a lean, muscular, superbly beautiful dog. I don't believe this is possible without a strenuous conditioning program. You may also notice that I will refer, at times, to the way a Pit Bull utilizes his muscles in a pit. I do so because, genetically, those are the muscles that will give him more drive, and they need to be developed.

It is said by some that running is the king of all exercises. For a dog, this seems especially true. What I want to do is add finesse to a running program. Let's look at some concepts involved in road-work training. There are two states the body can enter when running -aerobic and anaerobic. The aerobic state exists when a dog runs long distances, pacing himself. It is a cardiovascular state and builds endurance and a strong heart. In this state the dog becomes exhausted, experiencing tired muscles, but he doesn't get appreciably out of breath. He pants, of course, but is not hyperventilating. The anaerobic state exists when a dog sprints for short intervals as fast as his legs will fly, as in mill work. His legs do not become tired, but he gasps for breath, panting very quickly. As you can see, the long run at a slow pace and the short, fast sprints are two different training techniques that affect a dog in different ways. When a Pit Bull performs work like running, he burns up body fuels which combine with oxygen to produce the necessary energy. Oxygen from the air is taken into the blood and pumped by the heart to the muscles. Normally, the dog's body is in a state of oxygen balance, with the oxygen supplied by the blood equal to the oxygen consumed in the muscles. As he works harder (or runs faster), the heart beats faster and pumps more blood (and thus more oxygen) to the muscles. When he runs at top speed, the muscles need more oxygen than the blood stream can supply, even though the heart is pumping as fast as it can. But the muscles can "borrow" oxygen temporarily from the body, allowing a top-speed run for a short period of time. When the oxygen is depleted, the muscles are fueled chemically by substances called adosine triphos-phate (ATP) and glycogen that are stored in the muscles and can be rapidly converted to energy. During this time, however, lactic acid is formed in the muscles in conjunction with the process that releases the borrowed oxygen and chemicals. The presence of lactic acid causes the muscles to feel tired. This state is called "oxygen debt" because the muscles need oxygen. The oxygen debt is "paid back" by the blood as soon as the dog stops running. This is why he continues to pant and his heart keeps beating rapidly for awhile after he's finished an all-out run. As the oxygen debt is repaid, the lactic acid in the muscles is neutralized and the heartbeat slows and his breathing returns to normal. In sprinting, nearly all the oxygen consumed is supplied through the oxygen debt process. As the length of a dog's run is increased and he paces himself, oxygen debt becomes less significant and oxygen balance becomes the vital factor. Thus, training with sprinting is very different from training with distance running.

A good treadmill is probably the best method of sprinting a dog. If the mill is a good one, there'll be very little friction and the dog can run so doggone fast his legs will seem like a blur. Most Pit Bull conditioners use either a treadmill (or a catmill), or they don't like this device and prefer long runs either with a bicycle or running next to a car. The Monks of New Skete like to exercise their German Shepherds that way. A pit dog man who likes running as a conditioner will generally condition his dogs to the point where they will run 15 to 20 miles a day. Some like to have them follow a motorcycle up and down hills and some like to tie them to one of those big old three-wheel motorcycles and go up and down real steep hills. Those who prefer long running to mill work have noted that a dog on a treadmill will tend to sprint real hard for a time and then he'll learn to slow down and pace himself. However, he'll tend to run for a longer time on the road or on hills than on the mill and also tend to have more endurance and is better able to withstand stress. On the other hand, they don't get their lungs worked hard like they do on a treadmill, which gives them more drive for short-term bursts of energy demands. I believe that the thing is that many don't use a treadmill for what I see as its primary usefulness, and that is to develop oxygen debt (anaerobic state) so that the dog's ability to use oxygen is increased. A Pit Bull should not be allowed to run on a mill until he slows down. He should sprint all out and be taken off the mill as soon as he slows down even a little and walked until his breathing is normal, then put back on the mill again and repeat. A knowledgeable conditioner uses a catmill this way, walking the dog for two to five miles afterwards. It is a well known fact that you sprint a dog on a mill for strength and walk him long distances for endurances.

One excellent dog man who's over 70 years old and has conditioned Pit Bulls for over 30 years, has a turntable and an electric treadmill which moves at a slow walking pace. His dogs end up walking for long periods of time after completing their sprint work on the turntable, while he watches television. Another very experienced dog conditioner one who has been recognized by the Pit Bull fraternity as one of the best conditioners in the country (now retired) also used an electric treadmill as part of his dogs' keep. He had his dog walk and trot for three to five hours straight. This is equivalent to long slow distance (called LSD). You might think an electric treadmill is very expensive, but it isn't necessarily. I have recently learned of a very inexpensive way of converting a certain item into an electric (slow moving) treadmill. I would love to share it with my readers, but, unfortunately I had to promise I would not disclose it. Probably this device will soon be well known but in the meantime I'm compelled to honor my promise.

As I mentioned, some prefer long-distance running to mill work. They start the dog slow and after he's warmed up, go all out until he's dragging. Then they walk him slowly until his energy has been renewed, then walk briskly for two to five miles. Notice that in all instances, the workout is finished with a long walk. This is excellent exercise for the owner and I highly recommend it. Walking provides the dog with a post-run stretch that helps dissipate lactic acid build-up. A cool-down workout helps improve muscular relaxation and reduce stiffness.

Here are several other ways to run a Pit Bull all out. One, as I mentioned, is to let him run along with a motorcycle in the country. (Sand hills would be perfect.) Of course most people do not have access to reasonably isolated hills to run on. With many Pit Bulls you must find a place where there are no other dogs. Another popular way, and one that I prefer, is to have the Pit Bull pull you around on a bike. With Morochito, I start out, while he's lively, going up a 30° hill. He does most of the work, pulling me along. I pedal every once in awhile when he slacks just a little - this seems to encourage him to pull harder. We go about 200 yards up the hill, then we go downhill while I pedal. Morochito is sprinting at this point, and not pulling at all. When he's sprinting, I want him going all out without pulling, we get to the bottom of the hill and level off. At this point I usually slow the pace a bit. We will go a pretty good distance, varying the pace according to my feel for which pace is best when I want to push him a little. Generally we go at his pace except from time to time I pick up the pace with plenty of verbal encouragement. Varying the pace a great deal and going up and down hills is an excellent conditioner. Many conditioners run their dogs the same distance at the same pace for months on end. They may gradually increase the distance they have time for - still at the same pace though - generally at as fast a pace as the dog can handle. This practice is fairly common because of the mistaken notion that progress is contingent upon duration; that is, as you grow and get stronger you will need more in terms of training. Some trainers do realize that rather than work a certain distance and gradually increase the distance, it is better to work a certain time and gradually increase the distance in that time. Both running programs are one-dimensional, however, and will not provide maximum benefits, the reason being that as the dog progresses, in order to reach the upper limits of his endurance potential, he needs to run up to six or really eight hours a day (in two sessions); and of course you don't have that much time, and I'm sure you don't care that much about your dog's conditioning. Even the masters of dog conditioning, those who condition Pit Bulls for fighting, are generally not going to put that much time into it.

When we begin this roadwork, he's pulling hard. In this picture, he's too fat and so am I. Before we finished, I trimmed 10 pounds off him and 5 off myself. In addition to the lead attached to his harness, I have a lead attached to a choke chain on his neck, because he's thrown me off the bike several times. He still does it, but the choke chain helps.

He's not so enthusiastic when we finish the bike ride, especially when he's fat and it is summer time as it was in this picture. Still, we ran together for another 4 miles after this picture was taken. Notice the barrel-shaped chest Morochito inherited.

Actually, however, at least one man who breeds and conditions Pit Bulls for fighting, having one of the best success records in the country, states that he does run his dogs up to eight hours a day. Most dog fighters have too many dogs to spend that much time on conditioning. They have to have a lot of dogs because so few, even in well bred litters, are really good - so they keep many dogs so they can choose and retain the best. With a large yard it is difficult to find the time.) Most of them will tell you that if you run a dog that long he'll get "stale" (weak from being overworked, and mentally apathetic). They generally feel this way because they don't start their dogs really young and are unaware of the importance of very gradual increases in workout intensity and plenty of rest when needed. My contention is that the few who do run their dogs for long periods of time daily, can accomplish the same results and even better, by spending less time, with more stress during that time. Another way of explaining weakness with the training technique of gradually increasing the distance and time a dog runs without significantly varying the pace, is this: The dog has a limited ability to compensate for the effects of stress. In order to progressively develop endurance, you must increase the intensity of the workout, not merely the duration. If the dog sprints all out he will quickly tire. The answer is to vary the gait. Race horses are trained by running at varied paces and modern champion track runners have proven that they can develop a superior stamina by training with a varied gait. The technique was originated in the 1950's by one of the most famous track coaches in the world, Percy Wells Cerutty. He was a maverick trainer, 20 years ahead of his time. He was ridiculed by his peers at first, but was later to be admired and copied as his athletes chalked up 30 world records. In any event, the three paces for an animal are trot, canter, and gallop. The best conditioning method, in my opinion, as far as the running aspect goes, is to run your Pit Bull with a car. I say this because it is the only method in which you can direct the dog's gait and thus increase the benefits of his roadwork many fold. It would be ideal if you could begin at a trot because that is the best way to warm up. A trot is a gait best described by saying it is a slow pace a little faster than walk in which the dog sort of bobs up and down as he moves along. All four feet touch the ground at a different time. It is a sort of jarring gait and that is why it is a good warm-up. Track runners often warm up with what is called "shake-ups," which involves jogging along similar to an animal's trot, arms held loosely at the sides, bouncing up and down as you go. It has been found that when a runner warms up with shake-ups and also cools down after his run with shake-ups, he will run better and recuperate quicker with less soreness.

 I haven't been able to figure out how to begin with a trot, however, because Morochito is all enthusiasm and drive at first, continuously lunging forward in his harness. I have to "run the dickens" out of him before I can control his gait. We go about half a mile with him pulling ahead hard while I pull back hard. This is excellent for the development of his drive-train power. We then go at a gallop pace which is a reaching-out, running pace. Generally two feet touch the ground at a time. The dog pushes off with his rear legs, reaching out with his front ones, and the front paws come down simultaneously (or nearly so). This builds lung power and stretches the rib cage. It will also establish oxygen debt after awhile. We go for only a short distance at this pace, however, depending on his condition or how I perceive he feels that day. I know my dog pretty well and I pace him according to how hard he worked the day before, how enthusiasticly he's running, and little signs like how strongly he pulls on the lead, and even the expression he has on his face. I then slow down and he'll trot for a good long while until his breathing is nearly normal - I measure his breathing by watching the rise and fall of his rib cage. We then step up a bit to a canter. A canter is a three-step pace in which the front two feet come down at different times. You can imitate the sound a horse makes when cantering in the following manner: slap your left palm with your right palm (like clapping your hands only you are doing all the work with your right one), let your right hand slide immediately down to slap your right knee while your left hand immediately follows and slaps the left knee. Then repeat the sequence. With practice you can rapidly slap left palm, right knee, left knee. The pace of the canter is slightly faster than the trot, slower than the gallop. We canter for awhile, slow back down to the trot, and then it's all-out - everything Morochito can give. This is where running with a car is best, I believe, as the dog will go all-out longer. After the all-out, we walk back, perhaps trotting a little. Don't forget to always gradually bring the dog down from all-out with an extended trot and walk. The trot, canter, and gallop are done on hills as well as on level ground. The all-out is always on level ground. If we have time and I want to get my dog in tip top condition, we repeat the sequence several times after his breathing is back to normal. For us, however, we generally have to call it a day after the first round. The whole point, however, is that varying the gait is much better than the two extremes - going a long, slow distance or several spurts of short-distance speed running. Before I work Morochito on his gaits, he and I run three to four miles at my pace. This suffices as a sufficient warm-up for him. We go up and down hills, stopping periodically for him to empty out or investigate, and we run through fields with real high, uncut grass. In this type of field he lunges forward, almost jumping in the air, working those rear legs. We jump over creeks and fallen trees and go to college campuses and run up and down steps and jump over little brick walls. I used to work on obedience exercises after his run with me and before he ran at the faster pace with the car or bicycle. He was pretty trainable then, less frolicky yet not mentally drained. We've always loved our times together and we both feel relaxed and drained afterwards .

    I would like to add this thought at this point - An additional benefit that a dog gets by running (or jogging) with his master is that he tends to clear out his system better. By this I mean that the dog will eliminate much more frequently (especially the territorial conscious male) when he leaves his own yard and runs in the park or a wooded area like he would in the wild. When I run Morochito, rather than fuss at him and pull him away from every "pit stop" he wants to make along the way, I stop frequently and let him do his thing. I feel this cleans him out better. Actually it doesn't impede my own conditioning because I am, in effect, interval running and varying my own pace. When I'm sprinting, of course, I don't allow him his whims. One other thing gets accomplished at these stops. Sometimes he stops just to sniff around at some spot - I guess he smells another dog or something. Well, when he does this, I pull a little on his lead and he responds by stubbornly bracing himself, pulling back. I then pull just hard enough so that he has to brace and pull back as hard as he can and I let him win several times, but not always. This is an excellent strengthening technique. It strengthens his front legs more than the rear ones and also increases his pulling ability. You might feel that this is not good because he learns to "get his way" and may work against his obedience training if you are into obedience. This has not been my experience, however. When we play this game, I give no commands; I don't even encourage. But if he is on command to heel, he never balks over an enticing spot. He seems to know the difference. It certainly has made him strong. One time I got into my van, closed the door and pretended he wasn't going to be able to go, just to see what he'd do. That crazy Pit Bull got mad, grabbed the side of the front bumper, and pulled back. On my Volkswagen van that portion of the bumper is rubber and it's small enough for him to get in his jaws. Now I guess this is going to sound like I'm exaggerating, but I swear I'm not. He pulled back with a series of jerks and the whole van shook as he rocked it back and forth! You see what I mean about the clownish antics you can often expect from a Pit Bull pet.

In any event, let me reiterate the points I've tried to make. I believe changing gaits varies the metabolism and strengthens the body's ability to cope with stress. I see conditioning as an art to be pursued as a progressive process of improving and polishing. Too much emphasis on distance running without sprinting or speed work (which is best accomplished on a friction-free mill), can siphon off energy, lower the dog's zeal for the road and make him stale. Too much mill work (speed work) doesn't build the inner core of tenacity needed for the kind of endurance that can be accomplished only with long, slow distance. It is the subtle blending of techniques to increase stamina (aerobic training) with an increase in the ability to use oxygen (anaerobic training) that will maximize all over organism power: heart, lung, gland, muscle, and spirit power. It cannot be overemphasized, however, that you must very gradually build up your Pit Bull. It will definitely pay off in the long run. When you have a well conditioned Pit Bull, you can add some finesse to your training.

If you have conditioned your Pit Bull from the time he's a pup, you'll find that he can run 15 miles or so by the time he's nine months old. If you're running him with intervals - short, hard sprints, etc., he'll be in fine condition, but you'll need to run him for long distances at least once a week. The long distance run should, of course, be at a slow pace. Actually, for maximum benefit you should vary the daily distances you run him. You want to maximize his stress. In other words, run his legs off. You run him until he's completely exhausted. Stress should be regular and strong enough to stimulate adaptation, sometimes called overload. You see, when a dog reaches a certain level of endurance, you can increase this level by pushing him beyond his regular training so that he is terribly exhausted - and then let him rest up. His body will respond by building itself up during the rest period, so that it will be able to handle it the next time. In other words, the dog's physical reserves are limited, but his body will enlarge upon its normal abilities so that future assaults of high intensity training won't use them all up. As the dog grows stronger, the same amount of intensity will use up less and less of his reserves. This is adaptation. It is the same principle that weight-lifters use. First they stress their muscles, tearing them down; then they rest them and the muscles grow larger during the rest. It is for this reason that during the muscle growth stage of the weight-lifter's program, he normally lifts only three days a week, resting in between. This provides faster muscle gains than lifting every day. Track runners also use this principle to build endurance. They run hard days, then easy days, not allowing themselves another hard day until they are sufficiently rested. Look at it this way. If you want to have a magnificently conditioned dog, you must continuously build up his endurance. To do that, something about his workouts must progressively increase. If a dog doesn't increase, it is because he has adapted to a particular level of training intensity and further progress will not come until you up the intensity level. If you do not allow the dog to rest, however, you will wear him down and weaken, if not ruin, him. Vary the daily run -a long one, short ones for one or two days, perhaps a day of rest, then a medium run, then a short run, then a long one. This method allows adequate recovery time, provides mental change of pace, and stimulates fast physical improvement. As I stated, then, stress should be regular, and strong enough to stimulate adaptation. It can't be in such strong doses that it overwhelms the adaptation system, though. The secret is finding the proper doses of stress and recognizing the symptoms of over/understressing. Overstressing is recognized by weakness and lack of enthusiasm, and a lowered head and tail during the early stages of roadwork. Understressing is indicated by a dog having his head up and pulling hard in his harness during the post-workout, cooling-down walk - he should be meekly trudging along. I recall one time I gave Morochito a good, hard workout and we were walking in a field, cooling down. It was a hot day and Morochito was panting hard, frothing a great deal and occassionally stumbling. That's the type of exhaustion you need. Anyway, Morochito suddenly saw a flying bug he wanted, and like a flash he lunged and snapped, then snorted and went after another one. That kind of stuff really excites me; I love it. I laughed and gave him a good pat and a rub-down and we went home - both exhausted but entirely happy.

I have made the statement that the best conditioning involves not only a consistent program of running, but daily doses of walking, rough-house play, fishing-pole work, and treadmill. Frisbee workouts and swimming were suggested as either supplementary work or part of the regular routine. I have one more routine to add, however; I've saved my best for last. The training I've outlined has concentrated on endurance and flexibility, but I maintain that there is even more to conditioning. True to my usual form, of course, I'll have to prefix this "special training technique" with a detailed exposition.

There are certain physical factors that affect limb movement and speed. As a martial artist, I have made it a point to study these factors and I'd like to share my knowledge with you because I believe the principles can be applied to the conditioning of a dog.

Physical speed can be enhanced by improving strength, endurance, flexibility, and by general practice. Let's look at each of these components individually.

Strength - It is a physical law that force is equal to mass times acceleration, or $F = M \times A$. By the same token, acceleration is equal to how much force you have per given mass, or $A = F/M$. If you'll look closely at the formulas, you should be able to see that if you increase your force, you increase your acceleration. Force is increased, of course, by muscle strengthening. What is relevant to us is that if you increase a dog's muscle strength he'll be able to run faster and also his initial acceleration will be faster, resulting in a much harder impact if he should charge an object (for example, the sleeve of an antagonist in Schutzhund work). Many current dog men still subscribe to the traditional theory that heavy strength exercises will leave a dog muscle bound. This is a fallacy that once existed with human weightlifters and has since been disproven. If a weightlifter does not exercise a muscle for the full length of its extension, the muscle is disproportionately built and the result can be a muscle-bound person that has difficulty drinking, for example, because the bicep muscle is so large and tight. One method used by weightlifters to obtain a quick muscle "pump" when working on building the bicep muscle, is a technique called "cheating." The cheating technique is to curl heavier weight by supporting the upper arm and elbow at an angle on a device designed to provide such support, and curling the weight, beginning with the arm at a 45° angle. This tends to build a large bicep muscle, but if not combined with proper strengthening of the antagonist (works against) muscle - tricep in the case of bicep -the muscles are disproportionately developed. If a muscle is properly exercised, however, it will not become "muscle bound" and will actually be faster and more flexible. It has been pointed out that boxers, who have to rely on speed as well as effective punching power, generally are not large-muscled people and that weightlifters with large, heavy muscles may be able to lift much more poundage than a boxer of equal height; the weightlifter cannot punch anywhere near as effectively as the boxer, however. The difference is in the way the muscles are exercised and also, of course, that weightlifters don't practice punching. The modern-day boxer does lift weights, but cannot put much emphasis on weightlifting because the demand on his energy from his regular routine is so great. I am of the personal opinion that large muscles contribute too much weight to the arm and can thus slow the speed of a punch slightly. The size of a dog's muscles, however, are pretty much determined by heredity and while a dog's muscle can be strengthened, it cannot be significantly enlarged.

In any event, we want to exercise a dog's muscle with the method that tends to strengthen it for the purposes we want (long distance running, for example). In Jim Mather's tapes[33], he relates the results of recent research by one of the top exercise psychologists in the world, a man named Astrim. Mather attended a seminar conducted by Astrim in which slides were presented showing the differences between muscle fibers of world class distance athletes and world class sprinters. The muscle fibers of the distance runners were almost totally red with a few white specks. Red represented what he called "slow twitch fiber," a more enduring muscle, but slower contracting. The muscles of the sprinters on the other hand were almost totally white (or greyish) with a few red specks. He called the white fiber "fast twitch fiber," which is faster contracting but has less endurance than slow twitch fiber. Astrim said that this is, for the most part, established at birth, so that if you want to go to the Olympics, you must choose your parents well! The same would be true of a dog. He will have either fast or enduring muscles because he is born that way. In the last six years or so, however, European studies have shown that at least a 15% improvement in fast twitch fiber can be brought about with proper training. Traditional weightlifting, particularly for mass, involves a principle called progressive resistance, where you start with a light weight to warm the muscles; then, doing sets of short repetitions, you progressively add weight until you end up with a weight that you can just barely squeeze out one or two reps. There are variations to this method, but the basic principle is the same. In Mather's tape, he mentions that he has found success in developing fast twitch muscle with a principle called decreasing resistance. Actually, weightlifters who train for strength competition (as opposed to body builders who seek massive, defined muscles) have used this principle for years. Mather appears to have been the first to have discovered its applicability to the martial arts in building fast twitch fiber, with the decreasing resistance principle, you start with the heaviest weight you can lift one time. You do one rep and then decrease ten pounds and lift as many times as you can. Keep reducing until you can't lift anymore. In this manner, as the muscle becomes fatigued you are able to run it through the entire range. You exercise the muscle through the entire motion with the heavier weight when the muscle is less fatigued, instead of as you get more tired, being less able to lift and progressively increasing the weight, thus building mass. The main thing is that this decreasing resistance approach builds fast twitch capability (and strength rather than mass muscle). It is estimated that this type of workout will produce an increase in fast contracting fiber, if the exercise is engaged in consistently over an undefined period of time. The key is to decrease or drain glycogen stored in muscle fiber. With heavy weight reps you tend to do this with the first few reps so that the muscle, with the glycogen depleted, must rely on a fast twitch fiber. The equivalent to weightlifting, for a dog, can be weight-pulling. We have a chapter on this subject that gets into its competitive aspect. Here, however, I'm looking at it as a conditioning technique. I think we can apply the principles of decreasing resistance to weight-pulling and who knows how much can be added to a Pit Bull's strength and stamina? I wouldn't start into a heavy weight-pulling program until the Pit Bull is pretty well grown; you might mess him up. I don't know when would be the earliest age, but I would say around a year. You should start him pulling as a pup so that he'll have the idea and will train easier when he's older. But the pup should have a real light load. When you are ready to begin serious heavy training, start with light loads, say a child, and gradually increase the distance. The *Off-Lead* magazine articles referred to in the weight-pulling chapter help you determine the type of cart or wagon you want. I would suggest that the cheapest would be a boy's wooden wagon. I would get the wooden one because you can remove the center handles and screw runners on the sides so that it will look like the diagram below.

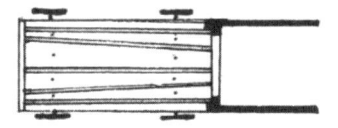

(Sketch provided by my son, Mike.)

You can buy harnesses that will attach to this type of cart, or figure a way of attaching the dog's regular harness to it. I wouldn't begin a pulling program in the summer, but would prefer late fall or winter when it is chilly or even cold. The dogs will be more enthusiastic then and will also fare better since pulling is very strenuous for a dog. I am suggesting a training schedule very similar to that of George Attla, world champion sled dog racer and famous for his 34 superbly conditioned dogs. To give you an idea of the kind of endurance his dogs (and other top competitors) have, the big race they run once a year is in Anchorage, Alaska and consists of three 25-mile dashes on consecutive days. In an article I read somewhere, Mr. Attla lost by 31 seconds to Dr. Roland Lombard of Wayland, Massachusetts. The dogs ran the 75-mile course in a total of 5 ½ hours, the same article related a story about a famous sled dog named Snowbird, who was a Malamute that led a team in 1910 that hauled half a ton of freight over a mountain range. Two weeks later he led Iron Man Johnson's team to victory in the first All-Alaska Sweepstakes. The distance of the race was 408 miles and the team ran it in

72 hours. I don't know if Snowbird would have been able to win a conformation point snow, nor do I know if conformationwise he was even built the way a sled dog is supposed to be. He could run a sled, though; that's for sure.

Anyway, I look at it this way. A Pit Bull has not been bred to have the endurance that a sled dog has, but for over a century they've been conditioned for the stress of pit fighting, so they should have pretty good potential for endurance. If a sled dog can be conditioned to pull a loaded sled over snow for 75 miles in 5 ½ hours, a Pit Bull ought to be capable of at least half that, or more. Let's take a look at Attla's training schedule. First I'd like to mention, by the way, that he has a preference for sled dogs in the 50-pound range. He said he's seen some dogs that were 60 pounds or more that made good racing dogs but they were very few. They had to be really outstanding to be able to carry that much weight in a 25-mile race and win. The smaller dogs, in the 30-pound range can usually outdistance the bigger 50-pound ones - they are more willing to stay with it - but the 50-pound dog, if properly conditioned will last as long as he's needed, for a 30-mile (standard) race, say, and he has a lot more power when you need drive. George said, "With a 50-pound dog that is not tired, when you start driving him you are really going somewhere." This seems to concur with my comments on ideal weight, in the breeding chapter.

George starts his dogs when they are around a year old, generally sometime in October. He begins with short two-mile runs four times a week, gradually increasing the distance so that in two weeks they run up to eight miles. They are allowed to run at their own pace and rest on their days off. Actually he stops a lot to rest the dogs at this stage. He wants to keep them running because they like it, so right from the beginning he establishes a habit pattern of going at a fast pace. The dogs usually start out real fast. While they are going fast, before they slow down to a trot, he stops them. When they take off again, they are going wide open. He keeps doing this and as they become tougher, he lengthens the distance between rest stops until they run four miles wide open - then he starts stepping them up more. The dogs are developing a naturally fast gait that seems comfortable to them and they are always eager for their workouts. If he finds he has a dog that's lazy or goofing off, he just goes ahead and shoots him. His dogs, you had better believe, are in prime condition. Their slowest pace in a race is around 15 miles per hour. From time to time he shifts into high gear and they take off faster and he always places, if doesn't win, every race.

By the beginning of November they are running for 40 minutes each run, regardless of the distance. In the middle of November he runs them every other day for ten miles each day, six days a week and he starts training them to obey commands (to "whoa," move to left, move, to right, and "get up" to speed up). In the middle of December he runs them only three times a week, four if they are looking good, and he runs them wide open the whole time, no resting or slowing of pace. They rest on their days off between runs. By the end of December he has worked them up to 20 miles going at a wide open pace. He then tests them to see how tough they are. He runs the 20-mile course four days straight. In this way he is able to weed out the quitters. They have to run each 20 at their fastest pace. A real good team will do it in an hour and ten minutes for four days straight. The size of the team helps with endurance, but not with speed. A dog can go only so fast, so that a 16-dog team is no faster than an 8-dog team for a short race, say 10 or 15 miles. After the four-day, 20-mile test, he starts training them at varied paces and distances, toughening them up. He tries to keep the dogs off guard so that they never know how far they are going on a given day. He may go up to 40 miles or as little as ten miles. They will then peak (reach their very maximum) about two weeks before the race, at which time he stops training and gives them short attitude runs to keep them mildly warmed up and to build their morale back up. By the time of the race, they are dynamos ready to explode. So, he trains longer to peak for a race (about five or six months) than pit dog men do for a match (about 6 to 8 weeks) and has a longer cooling down after reaching the peak (two weeks) than pit dog men (about three days).

I think we can combine the principles of weightlifting that I have described with George Attla's sled dog training program to come up with a training program for Pit Bulls that is second to none. I would begin with two-mile runs if you have been running and conditioning your Pit Bull as a pup. Then follow Attla's program, although you may not have the time to do up to 20 miles - if not, change your program to suit your own parameters. You can ride a bike and have him follow you pulling the cart.

When you have built up an inner core of toughness and enthusiasm for this pulling game, that is when your Pit Bull will pull the cart with the light load enthusiastically for the distance you have time for, be it five miles, ten, or twenty, and do it at a fast pace, you are ready to work on the principle of decreasing resistance. Now that he's enthusiastic about pulling, he'll probably work like nobody's business in order to be boss of that load when you make it heavy. You will have very gradually increased his load to this point (providing plenty of praise, really getting excited with each success. You can make sure he always wins. I found that if I put my son Mike next to Morochito as he begins to pull a load toward me (best way to begin training for heavy weight-pulling, I think), Mike could help out by giving just a little push when the weight was a bit too heavy for Morochito - just enough help so that he doesn't know he's being helped. At that point I know that I've reached the maximum weight for Morochito for the time being, but he will still make a successful pull. Each successful pull reinforces, I believe, a stronger desire on the part of the dog to keep trying and pulling when the weight gets a bit too heavy. To begin with, these weight-pulling workouts are kept short, successful, and in a light-hearted, playful atmosphere. The Pit Bull should be receiving supplemental running and fishing-pole exercise, but it should be low key so he has plenty of energy for pulling. As he gets the idea and shows plenty of enjoyment with this game, you can start lengthening the workouts by having him pull the real heavy load ten feet, then decrease the load and have him pull say 25 or 50 feet, then decrease the load again and have him pull further, etc. Youll build strength and fast twitch muscle and if combined with a running program, increased stamina. The dog's extra strength will help him run further at a faster pace also. I have found that doing squats two or three times a week definitely increases my ability to run distance at a faster pace.

I think that although some people condition their dogs with pulling, I don't know of anyone who has them pull with a program like I've outlined here. I have given you the principles, but you'll need to experiment with variations in the load and distance in accordance with your own objectives.

Fast twitch muscle is developed two ways: by the principle of decreasing resistance that I outlined, and by moving the muscle fast. Thus a runner can develop fast twitch muscle by sprinting fast, a boxer by working on a speed bag, a Pit Bull by working a treadmill.

I believe a monthly "long one" would allow the dog to be sufficienctly recovered to repeat the doses all year and yet keep a deep resevoir of mental aggression and physical energy. During the month you can set up or experiment with your own routine. You may want to vary pulling, roadwork, fishing-pole work, treadmill work, over five days (leaving two days to rest); or you might want to try circuit trainina. For human athletes, circuit training Involves having the participant go from one exercise station to another - for example:

stretching exercises
jogging
pushups
situps
jump rope
weightlifting
stretching exercises
jumping jacks
broad jumps
isometric exercises
interval running (all-out sprints)

Schematically, a daily circuit training program for a Pit Bull might be as follows:
walk - five minutes and empty out
fishing-pole work - five minutes
obedience work - five minutes
rough-house play - three minutes

frisbee throws/hurdle jumping (on alternate days) - five minutes
treadmill/pulling/roadwork (on alternate days) - 30 minutes
walk - three minutes
rubdown - ten minutes
obedience work - five minutes

This routine takes a little over an hour. If you don't have the time for it yourself, you may find a retired person that has nothing much to do that would be very interested in picking up a little money and might not be too expensive.

Well just in case I haven't given you enough "scientific" conditioning techniques, let me share one more. It's called blood doping, which is very new and there is very little research on it. This section on blood doping is derived from research cited in the May, 1982 issue of *Runner's World* in an article by Barclay Kruse. The research was conducted at New York University in Toronto by some of the top research people in the field of sports.

Blood doping means increasing the hematocrit level (percent of red blood cells in body fluid) so that the blood is viscous (thick). The blood is then said to be "packed," or "packed cell volume" (PCV). The red blood cells carry oxygen to the muscles and when the red blood cells are packed, the oxygen is transported more efficiently - significantly more so as we will see.

The extent of blood doping practiced by marathon runners is really unknown, but there is some speculation and gossip about its use. Here is the method. About six weeks prior to competition, a liter of blood is taken from the athlete and centrifuged (separated - like the process of separating cream from milk) to separate the red cells from the plasma. The packed red cells are then mixed with glycocren and frozen (called high glyceral freezing). The runner then continues to train as arduously as for any race, without interruption. When the runner loses blood, his body immediately begins manufacturing new cells to replace the deficiency. It takes about six weeks for the blood to build up to the original, normal hematocrit level. A few days before the race, the packed red blood cells are "reinfused" back into the system. It takes around four weeks for the hematocrit level to fall back to normal. During this time the athlete's blood is "doped." Does it really increase performance? Well according to the research I mentioned (completely controlled, double-blind), tested athletes showed a 31% increase in run-to-exhaustion tests. The group that received the sham (a solution that appeared to be packed red cells but was merely a harmless solution) showed no increase, but when later tested with real packed cells, a 35% increase resulted. There are several problems with the "scientific" method of blood doping just described. The equipment and facilities are of course not available to the public. Another problem is that if you do not raise the hematocrit level enough, there will not be a significant change in endurance; and if the level is raised too high the blood is too thick and the oxygenation process is dramatically slowed, producing an opposite (sluggish) effect on the athlete. If care is not taken in storing the packed blood it could be toxic or fatal to the recipient - even when trained doctors are performing the work. In fact, one subject in the research indicated above, after reinfusion, suddenly became chilled and passed out. He recovered, but it does show that there are dangers involved. So you're probably wondering why we are discussing blood doping at all. Well there is a natural way of doing this that doesn't have adverse side effects. It is altitude training. You see as you move up higher (above sea level) the body manufactures more red blood cells. At higher altitudes, there is less oxygen content in the air and the atmospheric pressure is lower. At 14,000 feet an athlete produces enough red blood cells to significantly raise the hematocrit level. If a mountain climber scoots up some large mountain, the hematocrit level gets too high, like 60% or more. Thus some climbers will have red blood cells removed before climbing.

The *Runner's World* article enumerated the gossip on a runner named Lasse Viren. He was not generally a winning runner - but won the Montreal Olympics 5,000/10,000 meter double in 1972 - and in 1976 -four years apart! His performance between those races was not impressive. It was claimed that he trained in the Pyrenees Mountains and his blood was doped. This type of blood doping works only wnen there is a change in altitude. When you return to lower ground it takes awhile (presumably around four weeks) for the blood to return to its original hematocrit level. It doesn't work with someone that lives in the mountains and is acclimated to the atmospheric pressure - only when there is a change.

In another experiment, conducted at the University of Washington, white rats were tested. Blood-doped rats significantly outperformed white rats that were not subjected to a change in altitude but had lived for awhile at a high elevation. It was also found that blood doping is effective only with highly trained individuals. Untrained individuals benefit more by simply increasing their conditioning program. Well, I just thought I'd share this information with you and suggest that if you know a dog man that lives in the mountains and you live in the plains, you might want to send your dog to the mountains for a month and see if it works for you.

I believe that if you utilize the techniques outlined in this chapter, you'll have a dog that'll outperform any other Pit Bull where endurance is needed. I think your dog will be a crowd pleaser at weight-pulling contests and in Schutzhund trials, and will be such a beautifully conformed animal that he'll draw many comments from people. You must be careful, however. Early in the chapter I mentioned that you don't want to get your dog run-down and over worked. In fact, some very experienced conditioners will look at the program I've outlined and will say it's unrealistic, that while it may be fine for a sled dog bred for endurance, it'd be too much for a Pit Bull. It might be, if you don't begin the early conditioning with the pup and if you are not gradual enough. Not all Pit Bulls can handle an extensive conditioning program either. The methods I have provided are merely guidelines that must be adjusted for the particular dog as well as the owner's time schedule and facilities.

I want to mention again the importance of walking your dog after a heavy workout - not only because it is bad for a dog to lie down right after strenuous exertion without a gradual cooling off, but because it helps develop flexibility, which is important because lack of it causes resistance to movement and a concomitant reduction in power. Consider the weightlifter who has heavy, pumped-up leg muscles and attempts to kick a football. Although strong, he won't be able to kick the ball nearly so far as a weaker man who has a flexible leg, which will generate much more power. Loose muscles are much less likely to be injured or become lame. They don't tear under sudden stress the way tight, hard muscles do, and they are free to react instantaneously to the needs of the situation. They give agility, strength, and speed. A flexible dog is free to perform at his best.

You also work on a dog's flexibility with a good rubdown. After every workout you should give your Pit Bull a 10- or 15-minute rubdown; many give a 30-minute one. Because of the time constraints in today's fast-paced society, this important aspect of conditioning a dog is often neglected or cut short. Many experienced dog men of the past gave their dogs 30-minute rubdowns daily, because they had the time to spend and they were able to perceive the benefits of their efforts. Today, there is a tendency to place more emphasis on mill work followed by a very brief rubdown or no rubdown at all. I believe we can dramatically increase a dog's daily workload by utilizing a thorough, professional rubdown before and after a strenuous workout.

The importance of the rubdown is perhaps more apparent if we understand what it accomplishes. A proper rubdown puts the animal's body in a balanced metabolic state. Metabolism as defined here is "the bodily process of transforming assimilated food into protoplasm (water, lipoids, carbohydrates, and inorganic salts), breaking down protoplasm into waste mater, producing energy growth, and replacing wornout tissues." The metabolic state is in chemical balance when an animal is not sick and activity is normal. If you understand the chemistry of muscle fatigue you can dramatically alter the negative side effects of grueling roadwork that make a dog stiff and lame. When roadwork becomes demanding, overstressed, fatigued muscles cause a disturbance of the metabolic chemical balance by not allowing the muscles enough time to relax and allow proper inflow of fresh blood to nourish the tissues. Lactic and carbonic acids accumulate in the muscles and surrounding tissues more rapidly than they are eliminated. These acids, particularly lactic, cause muscles to cramp and become painful and the dog will limp. Carbonic acid is carbon dioxide in tissue fluid. Lactic acid is accumulated glycogen in the muscle. The glycogen in eventually flushed out by flowing blood and tissue fluid through the lymphatic system, which is responsible for flushing out toxins and fluid wastes (such as carbonic and lactic acid) that accumulate in muscles, tissue, and blood. After an extremely hard conditioning session, this process can take anywhere from a day to three days, especially if the dog has had two or three days of hard work without a rest break, or at the beginning of a conditioning program for a dog that doesnt receive regular daily exercise. A properly applied and thorough rubdown will expedite the flushing out process and alleviate the pain by relaxing the muscle and stimulating a supply of fresh oxyen-rich blood to the area where it is most needed. A dog instinctively knows this when he vigorously licks his wounds, bruises, or any sore, painful area. The pressure from his tongue stimulates blood flow and reduces the pain. Humans need to prove things, however, and research has accomplished this. In a research project to study the effects of massage on the muscles, rabbits (animals that use their rear leg muscles extensively) were used. Black India ink was injected into their leg muscles after which they were left to their normal daily routine. One group of rabbits had their legs massaged daily while the other group did not. Both groups were fed the same food and interacted together. After a month the legs of all the rabbits were dissected and the muscles studied. The leg muscles of the non-massaged group were stained black in the area around the injection site. The muscles of the massaged rabbits, however, were pink with absolutely no trace of the India ink 35 anywhere in the body!" India ink is used in making tatoos, by the way - it has a lasting stain.

There is also research available on the effects of massage on muscle endurance. In one study a man curled a one kilo (2.2 pounds) barbell to exhaustion, which for him was 840 times without interruption. His arm was then massaged for five minutes after which he lifted the same weight 100 times in the same manner as before without fatigue! Another study found that a person capable of doing 50 pushups will, after a five-minute rest, be able to do about 10 more. The same person, however, can do about 35 to 50 more pushups if the arms are rubbed down during the five-minute rest interval. This indicates a nearly compelte muscle recovery rate in five minutes! These studies were conducted at the turn of the century, but it took many years for the athletic world to pick up on the idea. The East Germans were pioneers in the scientific approach to athletics. Their Olympic track team began using leg massage in the 1950's, I believe it was, and achieved repeated success. Now all track teams of Olympic level use it. Boxers have used rubdowns for years. Many human athletes receive an extensive rubdown just prior to competition. The pre-competition rubdown strengthens metabolism and the athlete has more energy. Some rub or massage an area called "stomach 36," which is a pressure point located four fingers down from the knee on the outside of the leg (side of the calf muscle). Stomach 36 stimulates the adrenal glands and provides energy for exhausting workouts.

One pit fighter confided to me that he gave his dog a 20- to 30-minute rubdown just prior to bringing him to the match sight.

Now to begin the rubdown procedure. Many people who are serious about conditioning will make a little table, about waist high to put the dog on while massaging. Before the rubdown after a workout, get a damp sponge and wipe off the froth on your dog's muzzle (He should have froth if he's been properly exercised) and wipe around his eyes, back of his ears, under his chin, groin area, and the butt. Begin by scratching him behind the ears and manipulating his jaw muscles. I like to rest Morochito's head on my knee while I do this and he loves it. I relax myself during the rubdown. I begin relaxing when I scratch his ears. I breathe slowly using the diaphramic techniques I have learned in meditation. Quite often I hum and this seems to relax both of us. I believe a dog tunes in on his master's attitude and I know of many professional dog men who feel the same. There are several ways to apply the massage:

1. Stroking - This is when you glide your hand smoothly over the fur. Very little pressure is needed. This promotes venous circulation, stimulates the nervous system, and transmits your energy (Believe it or not. to the animal.
2. Friction - With this method you exert more pressure and your hands move in rapid circular motions. It promotes a deeper arterial tissue circulation than stroking, and it starts lymphatic flow.
3. Kneading - A great deal of pressure is used here. You move your hands rythmically over the dog's muscles (Kneading is primarily used when massaging the large muscle areas), squeezing and lifting the fur and muscle. Work in short circular patterns. This method pumps nutrient-fresh blood into the area massaged and flushes out the toxins as I have explained.
4. Pulling and Rotating Joints - This phase helps maintain flexibility, strengthens ligaments and tendons, and boosts production of synovial fluid (lubricating fluid found in joint cavities and in tendon sheaths).

When you and your Pit Bull are relaxed, run your hand slowly from the top of his head down along his vertebrae to his tail, stroking several times. This lets him know for sure that it's rubdown time, not play time. Rub and knead the neck muscles on both sides with circular motions at first, then rubbing back and forth. Work down to the base of the neck where the head meets the first vertebrae and then keep working down the vertebrae. Place your fingers on each side of his vertebrae and massage with small circular movements. Do not lift your fingers as you move down his back. After you have worked the back a few minutes, reach under his right front leg with your right hand and begin with his left shoulder, pulling down across his chest all the way back to the top right stifle up high in the gut, then right down the right side of the right leg muscle. Do this several times, then repeat on the other side, and keep going back and forth -one side then the other. Keep your fingers together, not spread stroking. You are much more effective that way because the heat and energy in your hand becomes concentrated. Try it on yourself and you should be able to discern the difference. You then roll the dog over on his back and scratch his belly. (If the dog is not used to this, he may think it means play and not lie still - start him from a pup, however, and he'll lie still.) Stroke his belly with circular motions, which should keep going up toward the chest. Gradually work up to the chest, and as you get to this area, begin a friction-type massage. This part of the massage, stimulating the abdomen, is very important because it will help clean out your dog - the digestive process becomes more efficient, production of gastric juices is aided, and urination is increased. Medical science experimentation has shown this to be true, by the way. Understand this, the muscles receive no nutrition until the food is digested, assimilated into the blood, and the nutrients then carried to the body parts. It follows then that the quality of nutrition received by the body part depends to a large extent on the quality of the blood and lymph circulation. By massaging the chest, you clear the central lymph node of toxic build-up and open up the system to flush out wastes accumulated in the muscles during heavy conditioning. Spend a good amount of time in this area. Then lay the dog on his side. Take his front paw in your hand and gently rotate it, first in one direction then the other. Pull gently on the paw to stretch the tendons. Sometimes I take each toe between thumb and forefinger and squeeze firmly. Grasp the bottom of his front leg like you would hold a baseball bat and gently squeeze, then rotate your hand back and forth slowly so that the heat of your hand will penetrate. (Always talk to your Pit Bull in a quiet conversational tone while doing this, which will establish rapport with him. I've had many enjoyable moments with my Morochito during his rubdown.) Work your way slowly up his leg kneading and stroking. Most of the traditional dog men start up high and work down the leg - massaging with the fur, the feeling being that this is more comfortable to the dog. Contemporary dog massage technique calls for you to do the opposite. You always massage toward the heart! This squeezes out the lactic acid and other toxins and does it in the most expeditious way. You'll be going against the fur, but my experience concurs with what I have read - the dog enjoys the massage just as much as if you went with the fur. When you get to the shoulder muscle, spend some time kneading. Then hold his leg and rotate the shoulder joint. You can then start on the rear leg. Actually, it is better, theoretically, to begin with the rear leg (furtherest area from the heart). I work the front leg first because Morochito stays relaxed when I do. If I go to his rear leg from the chest, he often starts to wag his tail and wiggle. A few other dogs I worked on had a similar response, so I think the reaction is not a unique one. Start at the bottom of the rear leg just as you did with the front, and massage it in a similar manner. Knead the tibia and metatarsals. (See the conformation standard in the "History" chapter.) This is the area above and below the hock (part of the dog's rear leg that sticks out like an elbow). When you finish, turn the dog over and repeat on the other side.

Do not cut the rubdown short; it is an important aspect of conditioning. Some people use baby oil every third or fourth day for the rubdown, wetting the hands with oil and rubbing them dry on the dog's fur, being careful not to get any in his eyes. I don't agree with using oil, however; I don't feel that it does any good - but I thought I'd mention it because some do use it. Some use Asorbine Junior when the dog has been run a lot. I wouldn't use anything, except if the dog starts to get a little lame, use a horse linament like one indicated in the "Medicine" chapter, and wrap his legs in hot towels and let him rest until the lameness goes away. Rest is always important when the dog becomes exhausted.

Nutrition also plays an important role in conditioning. If a dog is receiving the stressful conditioning outlined in this chapter, he will need considerably more vitamins, minerals, and carbohydrates. You'll need the supplementation outlined in the chapter on nutrition. When the dog is really worked hard, he also needs more water for his tissue than normal. Some people add water to the dry dog food they feed so that the dog gets more fluid than normal. I don't like to do that, though, because I think they need hard food to clean their teeth whereas the soft food leaves deposits that may cause cavities. Most people give the dog a fresh bucket of water every morning. I like a metal bucket - you ever drink water out of a plastic container? -tastes awful! I don't give the fresh water in the morning, however, because he doesn't drink much then. I give it to him right after his workout; that's when he drinks the most. If I were heavily conditioning him and had the time, I'd not keep water in his bucket. To assure that he always drank fresh drawn water, I'd go out and offer- him fresh water several times a day, including after the workout, and not leave any water out there. Ionized well water with no chemicals in it (described in the "Pet" chapter) is best.

Now if you really want to get scientific with your conditioning program, you'll vary the dog's diet with the workout, providing high-carbohydrate food and low-carbohydrate food, depending on the workout. Weight trainers call this rebound training. For a dog, a high-carbohydrate food would be Eucanuba, Science Diet, or other stress-formula diet. A low-carbohydrate food would not include any commercial food and instead consist of chicken livers (1 cup), cottage cheese (1/2 cup), cooked carrots (1/2 cup), cooked green beans (1/2 cup), and vitamin supplements. This diet has been improvised from one I found in the newspaper (*Greensboro Record*, July 2, 1981). It was provided by Hill's Pet Products (makers of Science Diet). The recipe is a reducing diet. I revised it a little. Where he used lean beef, I used chicken livers - even lean beef is striated with fat (can't be seen with the naked eye). He used canned carrots and green beans - I recommend fresh cooked vegetables. I also used lower amounts. I would suggest feeding chicken livers and cottage cheese at one meal and the vegetables at the second meal.

I said you would vary the diet according to the workout. Here is a suggested program for three levels of conditioning:

a. Drain - Follow a program of short treadmill workout, say five minutes, with long runs at varied gaits, including low speed (trot) - keep increasing the distance. This will drain the Pit Bull and deplete the glycogen in the muscles.

b. High Intensity - This is the second stage. The dog enters it reasonably exhausted. You push him for short periods of time. Put him on the treadmill and have him sprint for five minutes, take him off and walk 10 or 15 minutes, treadmill five minutes, etc. Be sure he is going all out on the treadmill - if he slacks down a little and doesn't respond immediately to verbal encouragement, that's enough for the day. The "work five minutes, walk 10 or 15 minutes" is based on modern research on excercise physiology and is called work-to-relief ratio. You might be surprised how much money and quality has gone into modern research on conditioning. It has been found that for every minute of high-intensity work, a low-intensity work (not rest) like walking for two or three minutes (in other words a ratio of 1:2 or 1:3) will maximize the anaerobic effect on the system. This is interval training. If five minutes is too much at first, begin with two minutes and walk four to six minutes. As I mentioned, it's important that the rest periods involve continuous body movement of some kind. You may choose to work on obedience lessons, like heeling. As I have emphasized, continuous movement is important because it expedites the removal of lactic acid, the biochemical reason for fatigue, from the bloodstream and keeps the dog from becoming stiff during the rest period. Alternating periods of exercise and relief trains the anaerobic system and increases the dog's ability to perform in sporadic flurries at high intensity.

c. Power - Power is developed by weight-pulling. You must be sure the dog is enthusiastic about pulling so you gradually increase the distance and weight. There is at least one day of rest between each level.

Now to coordinate the diet with the program, try a 10-day rotation, something like the following one adapted from a research based program in a 1981 *Muscle Mag* article:

Day	Type of Training	Diet (Assuming dog is fed twice a day)
1	Drain	Low Carbohydrate
2	Drain	Low Carbohydrate
3	Rest	Low Carbohydrate
4	High Intensity	High Carbohydrate
5	High Intensity	High Carbohydrate
6	Rest	High Carbohydrate
7	Power	High Carbohydrate
8	Power	High Carbohydrate - morning / Low Carbohydrate - evening
9	Rest	Low Carbohydrate
10	Rest	Fast

(The dog may need a two-day rest between high intensity and power.)

It may be that I've made too much of conditioning. Perhaps a pet doesn't need all that, but I tell you truly - a conditioned Pit Bull is really a beautiful animal. Almost all of the obedience trained Pit Bulls and Stafs that I've seen are much too fat for my tastes. This is just a personal opinion, I guess, but I really like to see a lean, muscular dog. (I try my best to keep myself that way, also. At the age of 42, I am often mistaken for a much younger man and my karate instructor says I look younger every year.) Just this month (July, 1982), there was an article in our local paper about Dr. Roy Walford at the Los Angeles School of Medicine at the University of California who has found that he can extend the life of rats by keeping them thin. He is so excited about his findings that he personally plans to lose 25% of his own body weight over the next three years even though he is already considered to be about 10 pounds underweight by current standards. He hopes thereby to extend his life to perhaps 130 or more, because he and a lot of other longevity experts around the country believe that what works for the mice will work for humans also.

I also don't think that a dog is meant to lay around all day and eat the quantity recommended on the commercial packages of dog food, nor do I think jumping hurdles periodically or heeling exercises even give a dog a cardiovascular effect. I believe you have to look at nature to understand the amount of exercise that a dog really needs. In the wild a wolf or wild dog generally runs about 20 or so miles a day and they are generally quite lean.

I also feel that conditioning an animal is a science and an art that can be a lot of fun and challenge. The pit fighters have been conditioning their dogs basically the same way for almost a hundred years, and they are very good at it. I think, however, that an analogous situation existed in the history of American boxing. For many decades training methods remained fairly standardized. Today's boxers are much, much better than the boxers of the forties and fifties. All of the athletes today are better. Results of modern research studies indicate that tensile strength in the modern athlete has increased tremendously as a result of overload training methods such as I have described. Today's athletes are stronger, faster, and more agile because of today's advanced nutrition, weight training, technique development, and scientific principles. The conditioning of animals does not have to be a stagnated art, it can become as scientific as the training of human athletes.

"Sprinters and long-distance runners used to think of themselves as radically different breeds, but today's exchanges of ideas are benefiting both disciplines." - Bill Dellinger and Bob Wischnice (*Runner's World*, June, '82)

Chapter 8: Scientific Breeding

It is a funny thing about life; if you refuse to accept anything but the best, you very often get it. -Somerset Maugham

This chapter may be the most important one in the book. I say this because all the knowledge in the world about socialization, training techniques, special feeding programs, and conditioning methods are of no avail if the blood is not good; but when you start searching for your puppy you are confronted with thousands of choices. You visit breeders and they show you pedigrees full of famous dogs. You read magazines and find the same confusing mess. Just when you think you've found the pedigree you like, you read about some better pups that are available on the other side of the country and you just can't make up your mind. (I hope this chapter will help you with this problem.) Or, you may be disenchanted because you bought a pup that came from a litter that had an excellent pedigree, yet the pup didn't turn out the way you wanted. This chapter explains why.

In discussing characteristics and specific dogs, you will note that I do refer primarily to combat dogs. This is because the majority of Pit Bulls are combat bred and that is how they become known. After all, this is a book about Pit Bulls. My references should not be construed to intimate, however, that I encourage breeding for the pit. The principles apply, whatever your breeding purposes.

Before we get into the basics of breeding, let's start with the initial selection of the puppy. I suggest that the first step should be to read as much as you can before you talk to breeders and select a puppy. Read historical accounts of the foundation dogs of major strains - like Dibo, Colby Dime, etc., and read the current magazines, like *Pit Bull Gazette*, so that you are aware of current dogs that have developed out of a strain that sounds appealing to you. My bibliography contains suggested literature. It will help you immensely, when you visit a breeder's yard, if you have background knowledge of various strains. What I'm saying is that I think you're better off becoming a semi-expert on Pit Bulls before you buy. Most people learn from many sad experiences. Why not take advantage of others' mistakes and experiences and short cut your route to success by reading about the subject first? In the historical chapter, I mentioned some of the people that are well known. You'll want to read more about them. Find out what dog or dogs they have used as foundation dogs; look at the bloodlines of some of their current stud dogs and females. Many of them advertise their dogs and show part of their pedigree. You'll want to be able to recognize the dogs in the pedigree and be able to determine which breeders are reliable. I'm sorry to say there are many people out there who will advertise pups supposedly out of a particular stud or bitch when in fact the pups are of inferior quality. Every time a combat dog does exceptionally well, you'll find a rash of pups available, all over the country, with his breeding. For example, at the time I'm writing this chapter, the Jeep dog has retired to stud. His last fight is recorded in my "Combat Dog" chapter. That fight was probably one of the best in recent years and Jeep retired a four-time winner. Well, all of a sudden there are litters cropping up all over that Jeep sired or that have the same bloodlines. Understandably, some of these are legitimate litters that perhaps weren't advertised before because the line wasn't so popular. Still, Jeep would have to have had quite a sex life to be responsible for all those litters! Last year it was Zebo - and Bullyson, who was recognized as one of the best producers, but I just don't think all the dogs on the market with Bullyson in their pedigree are truly Bullyson bred – there's a blue zillion of them! If you buy from the well known Pit Bull people mentioned in books and magazines, you are perhaps more assured of correct pedigrees because these folks have pride in their strains and they are competing, not to sell pups, but to develop a superlative strain of Pit Bulls. I do not mean to imply that if you have not heard of a particular breeder, you'll get a bad deal - I merely mean your chances are better with one of the well knowns. There are a good many excellent breeders who do not contribute articles to the magazines and do not actively advertise pups. They don't have to. Dog men know them and buy from them, often ordering a pup from the other side of the country. I am familiar with only some of them in my area, North Carolina, and a few here and there throughout the country.

The second step is word-of-mouth. Look up as many Pit Bull breeders and owners in your area as you can. You'll need to keep a few things in mind, however; Pit Bull owners are much like car owners. In other words, you can talk to some people and they are all hep on Fords – wouldn't buy another brand - owned Fords for the past 20 years - never been disappointed. Yet you turn around and another guy has the same things to say about Chevys and will tell you about people he knows who have owned Fords that were real lemons. It is the same with Pit Bull men. You will also find regional differences of opinion. For example, in my area a dog named Red Boy Tramp is an extremely popular dog. He won all his battles so, of course, everyone wants to breed to him; however, there are a lot of dog men on the West Coast who have never even heard of Red Boy. You will also find fads. At the time of this writing, Zebo, currently retired to stud and owned by Richard S. Johnson of Kentucky, is one of the most popular stud dogs. People all over the country are breeding their dogs to him (and have bred to his brother Vindicator, who many say was an even better dog). Zebo's other brother, Gush, is also a good pit dog. His sister Rosie, is another good one. When you have three good ones in a litter, you know that's good producing. Zebo was a seven-time winner, which is a phenomenal record. It is very difficult to get a champion (a three-time winner of contract matches - should be good contest matches, not prearranged matches the dog should have no trouble winning), and even more rare to get a grand champion (five-time winner). Naturally Zebo has been criticized as not really having won seven. Maybe he did; maybe he didn't - I don't know. I do know that some friends of mine went to one of his fights and related it to me. Zebo demolished his opponent and went four pounds uphill to do it. He also traveled out of state for the match - a decided disadvantage. Whatever his critics say, he was a most excellent and game fighter. He is also a proven producer. Like any Pit Bull, he has produced his share of curs, depending for one thing on who he was bred to; but he has produced some game, quality Pit Bulls also.

    Now let's look at another dog, who was very popular in North Carolina a few years ago. Big Boy was a huge, black dog - so big in fact, that he had difficulty finding matches because not too many fighting dogs were in his weight class. He fought for almost five years and was never stopped except one time, and that was when he had his first roll - he was almost three years old at the time. Not very many people know about that roll. The dog that stopped him was also a huge black dog, named Duke, who was as big and strong as Big Boy. After that, Big Boy killed most dogs he fought. In fact, several years later, Duke and Big Boy were in the same yard and Duke accidently got off his chain and went after Big Boy - a mistake. No one was home and Big Boy killed Duke after an awful fight.

    Anyway, as I said. Big Boy never found a dog after Duke that could stay with him; but he had a fault, and because of that fault many people don't like Big Boy blood, and understandably so. Big Boy's fault - he was a cur. Yep - Big Boy wouldn't scratch. That's right. If a turn were to be called in a fight, Big Boy wouldn't come out of his corner. For that reason, all his fights were country style, which refers to a match in which there are no turns called. The dogs are turned loose and that's it. Because Big Boy was such an awesome fighter, he was bred numerous times, yet many people would not breed to him. Even today, most people do not like Big Boy blood. Many of his progeny have been strong, very hard biters, but they lack gameness. A friend of mine told me he once saw one of Big Boy's sons - a catchweight black dog - in a match. He said this dog was making one heck of a mess of his opponent, that he was as effective a biter as he's ever seen but didn't take a hold and hang on, bulldog style - he would bite (deep), shake, then immediately take another bite. He was an extremely fast biter, with no special preference for ear, leg, or whatever. He would just bite, bite, bite, and in a matter of minutes his opponent was lying on the ground underneath him - at which time he turned and jumped the pit! This type of behavior is fairly common with some of Big Boy's progeny. On the other hand he has produced some game ones and I know of one very well-known Pit Bull man who swears by Big Boy blood. His yard is not built on it, but he has some excellent dogs with Big Boy blood in there. (I withhold the man's name in the interest of discretion, but there isn't a pit dog man in the country who doesn't know him and would not agree he is hard to beat.) Big Boy, by the way, is Morochito's great grandfather.

Zebo's Son, Swinson's Zebo

Zebo weighs about 45 pounds in hard condition, I think. (You might say average weight.) There's nothing at all wrong with his gameness or with any of his littermates that I know of. Big Boy was a huge dog, 68 pounds on the chain I'm told; yet he was a cur. Now, let's look at the pedigrees of both dogs. I think you'll find it an interesting comparison. Here's Zebo's first:

```
                                              Hubbard's Bounce
                         Tudor's Dibo ─────── Heinzl's Bambi
             McCraw's Snowball
                                              Tudor's Red Mike
                         Maness' Cissie ───── Tudor's Lou
    Lonzo's Andy
                                              Tudor's Dibo
                         McCraw's Snowball ── Maness' Cissie
             Johnson's Black Lil
                                              Conklin's Mohawk
                         Red Lady ─────────── Beal's Princess
Ch. Zebo
                                              Tudor's Dibo
                         McCraw's Snowball ── Maness' Cissie
             Beal's Powhattan
                                              Conklin's Mohawk
                         Red Lady ─────────── Beal's Princess
    Lonzo's Angie
                                              McCraw's Snowball
                         Lonzo's Andy ─────── Johnson's Black Lil
             Greg's Lady
                                              Orday's Smokey
                         Lonzo's Fay ──────── Orday's Jet
```

And now, here's Big Boy's:

```
                                              Tudor's Dibo
                         McCraw's Snowball ── Maness's Cissie
             Beal's Powhattan
                                              Conklin's Mohawk
                         Red Lady ─────────── Beal's Princess
Henley's Big Boy
                                              McCraw's Snowball
                         Lonzo's Andy ─────── Johnson's Black Lil
             Greg's Lady
                                              Orday's Smokey
                         Lonzo's Fay ──────── Orday's Jet
```

Very similar aren't they? (Angie is not a littermate of Big Boy, but of a separate breeding. Nevertheless, it's the same blood and Zebo's father Andy was also the same blood.) But one dog is a very, very popular known producer; the other a cur dog, said to produce curs. Zebo is better bred because he is more linebred off Snowball (son of Dibo). Snowball was a dog that could kill another Pit Bull as fast as you set them down in front of him. His story is in the historical chapter. Although Snowball is grandfather to both on the top side and both dogs have him through Lonzo's Andy who was not only a proven pit dog but a proven producer par excellence; still, Snowball had more influence on Zebo than on Big Boy because he appears five times including up close (grandfather) in Zebo's pedigree (Snowball is father to Black Lil so I counted him one more generation than is shown.) and only three times in Big Boy's pedigree. Traits common to both Zebo and Big Boy blood are a very hardy body type - strong, heavily muscled, hard bite - the type that is expensive on watering containers, because they like to play with them and can puncture even galvanized ones. They are usually slow to mature - a Dibo trait.

Vindicator was, I believe, three years old before he was ready to fight. Anyway, the point is that the pedigree doesn't tell the whole story. You need to talk to Pit Bull people as much as possible. If you can't find any in your area, some of the ones who advertise in magazines will correspond, but the majority won't. You just have to write a lot of people. This is the approach I have taken, and I'd say I've had about one in ten letters answered. Those are well worth the effort, though. You can learn much from experienced Pit Bull people. Let me tell you something. I'm a martial artist, among other activities, and karate people can talk the horns off a brass monkey. I mean you go to work out and everyone shoots the bull for an hour and works out for half an hour. You go and compete in a tournament and the topic of conversation is, of course, primarily karate techniques and philosophy. You get with a scuba diving group and all you'll hear is dives they've been on, what's the best buy nowadays in equipment, etc. Same thing with tennis enthusiasts, shooting, knife throwing - you name it. But I never, ever met a group in any activity that could out talk Pit Bull folk. I mean really. I recall one pit fight I attended. We met at midnight, sat around talking about dogs for an hour, then drove all night to go to the fight, had a two-hour wait the next morning while people were getting together – I'm not sure what was going on -watched one dog fight, drove all the way back home - and when we got back to my friend's house and sat down, we got out papers (pedigrees of dogs) and started in on that. But on the whole trip, I don't recall any conversational topic other than Pit Bulls. Those folks can go on and on. They were still talking about Pit Bulls when I finally left. I hadn't slept since the night before last and neither had they, but I kept my ears open and learned a whole lot. They will talk about other breeders - and when they have nothing but good things to say about someone not in the group, I figure that's something to note. I've never heard anyone, for example, have anything bad to say about Howard Heinzl or Bert Clouse, or their dogs. Many of these people have a real library of books, too. I've met people with magazines that go all the way back to the 1950's and earlier.

 From your readings and conversations, you should be able to ascertain characteristics of various strains. It is very rare that any one dog has all the desirable characteristics of a Pit Bull - deep gameness, strength, conformation, wrestling ability, temperament, intelligence, etc. - so you set down your priorities and pick a line that seems closest to what you like. For example, dogs with Zebo blood (which is a Dibo strain) tend to be hard biting, fairly slow to mature, and strong. Those with Dibo blood tend to be more "bulldog-gish," that is stocky, heavily muscled, etc. They tend to be barrel chested (with the concomitant endurance), with powerful hips and a well reached back. Dibo dogs also tend, however, to have a straight hock - in fact they can be almost double jointed. This means they will have less pushing leverage in the back legs and will need to rely on wrestling ability. Some dogs with Dibo blood tend to be sort of a buckskin color (Dibo was a buckskin) and others tend to be black. Those with Zebo and Alligator blood are usually black in color.

Zebo and Alligator blood tend to be dominant and pups from them are likely to carry their characteristics. Of course, we can always complicate the issue. There are many who say Zebo is not bred exactly the way his pedigree shows. Well, this is a problem, I'm afraid to say, that is quite prevalent in Pit Bull breeding as well as other species - not with the top breeders, of course, but otherwise it is so widespread that it's unbelievable. The Pit Bull breed is really hurt by so many who maintain their dog is bred a certain way when, in fact, it isn't. I'm not saying this from personal experience; I hear it from so many Pit Bull people. Many of these complaints may be sour grapes because of a dog that didn't work out or because of a personal grievance against a breeder. A top breeder and active sportsman once told me that one thing about winning all the time is that you get a lot of enemies and a lot of criticism. Anyway, I personally believe Zebo is bred the way his pedigree shows because he resembles his father Andy (son of Snowball) right much, and some of his progeny have had characteristics much like Andy. Anyway, another characteristic of Dibo blood is an occasional blue eye and a tendency to be undershot – Dibo was undershot. A dog who is under- or overshot, can bite just as hard or harder than a dog with a perfect mouth. His ability to bite is more psychological than structural.

Colby dogs tend to have a longer muzzle and many of them are white or mixed white and another color. They are pretty game, some very game. Colby and Dibo blood tend to go well together, especially Dibo and Colby Dime. Traditionally, Colby dogs tend to have squinty, coal black eyes similar to the white show variety Bull Terrier. The Pit Bull on the cover of the February, 1980 *Pit Bull Gazette* looks like the old Colby dogs - as does the picture of "Humbug" on the cover of the paperback novel *Humbug*. (See comments on the book in the "Combat" chapter.) Colby dogs tend to have well bent hocks that gives them plenty of speed, agility, and leverage in the back legs. Perhaps this is why the highly respected breeder of Pit Bulldogs, Howard Heinzl, has extensively bred a cross of Dibo and Colby (primarily Colby Dime) blood - to offset the weak back legs of Dibo dogs.

Carver blood can produce some very game dogs, but like Colby blood, there is a lot of it so you have to be selective and stay with proven progeny. Boudreaux and Bullyson blood (a Dibo strain) tends to be athletic, but I'm told that if the Bullyson is tightly inbred, you tend to get curs. Some say Bullyson was a cur, that he wouldn't go after 30 minutes - but it's just that not many could stay with him 30 minutes. In any event, Bullyson is said to be one of the best producers of our day - but if you inbred too much on a dog like that, you could bring out the cur in him. Bullyson's son Benny Bob (who was the only dog to defeat Bullyson) was dead game. Art, the Dog with a Heart, was known for his ability. Kingfish-bred dogs are generally known for their ability. Well, there is no way I could cover all the characteristics of all the different strains nor do I mean to give the impression that these "characteristics" are definite things - they are only generalities. I want to make that statement clear because some owners of, i.e., quality Dibo-bred dogs may take umbrage, feeling that I am putting down their line by saying their dogs have weak leverage in their back legs, when in fact, their dogs have strong back legs. The characteristics I mentioned are generalities of the original strain. In many cases, outcrosses have corrected inherent deficiencies, and in some cases where the strain is relatively pure, the characteristic just doesn't show up because, again, it's a generality. Moreover, to say a dog is a Colby strain or Dibo strain these days is in a sense misleading. The original strain of Colby dogs was kept pure (by John Colby). I really do not know personally of any dogs that are inbred, pure, original Colby. Dibo was, as the historical chapter points out, an outcrossed dog with some excellent linebreeding - including Colby blood. Today, however, you have Dibo strains through Ironhead, through Snowball, through Alligator, etc. What we do have, is Dibo based or Colby based strains.

The two points I wanted to emphasize are that you want to do your best to learn about a breeder you are considering and that the more you know about the various dogs in a pedigree, the better. If temperament is important to you, you may not want a dog linebred off Cotton's Bullet; he was a people-biter. You will tend to get better conformation, a larger size, and better teeth with American Staffordshires. Temperament, in my opinion, tends to be about the same. Both Pit Bull and Staf people tell me they feel that Stafs have a better temperament, but most of the Pit Bull people I know don't know many, if any, Stafs; and most Staf people I know haven't ever even seen a Pit Bull. Well, all I can say is, most of the Stafs I have seen that were not obedience trained were more aggressive, especially as pups, than most Pit Bulls. The main consideration, however, is the temperament of the parents and, even more importantly, that of the grandparents. Heinzl-bred dogs tend to have an excellent temperament.

As I have suggested, you should study a lot of pedigrees. Many of the serious breeders today have studied pedigrees so much they have them practically memorized. Maybe it's a coincidence, but I have found that when I'm talking to various knowledgeable Pit Bull men, if I mention most any known Pit Bull, they'll say, "Oh yeah, he's off of so and so and is bred so and so." They can practically give you the dog's complete pedigree. You must learn how to study a pedigree. The presumption is, of course, that you can recognize the key dogs at least and are familiar with their strong points and weak points. You study a pedigree from right to left - that is from the oldest generation forward. There is a tendency to study a pedigree beginning with the parents. It's the other way around. Begin as far back as you can. You see, the important thing is to determine the foundation of the dog's line. I'll try to give you an example of what I mean at the end of the chapter when we look at Morochito's pedigree. I would like to make it clear that when I state that you look at a pedigree from right to left, I do not mean that the performance of the parents is of secondary importance. On the contrary, if the parents do not shine in whatever characteristic you consider of primary importance - gameness for instance, then you are ignoring sound breeding precepts. If the parents have not demonstrated the characteristics you seek then you gamble that these characteristics, inherent in the foundation strain, will pass on to the pup you are considering. The whole idea behind planned breeding, however, is to eliminate as much of the gamble as possible - otherwise why even look at the pedigrees? I'm trying to say that in selecting your puppy, you find superlative performing parents that have the foundation you like and want to keep breeding into.

At this point, so that we can communicate, I need to explain some basic breeding concepts, that is, inbreeding, linebreeding, and out-cross (sometimes referred to as crossbreeding). Inbreeding refers to mating a son back to his mother, a daughter back to her father, brother to sister, or half-brother to half-sister (having same father but different mother, or same mother but different father). Inbreeding has been practiced for hundreds of years. It has been severely criticized, particularly within the last 20 years or so, one reason being that it is felt (generally by inexperienced breeders, but also by some "professional" breeders) that inbreeding will produce dogs with nervous disorders, dull intelligence, structural disabilities, and a host of similar problems. It is observed that if humans mate in this manner, there is a high probability of the same thing happening -but it's also true that a genius could be the result. Because of the high probability of a dullard resulting from such a mating, however, it is considered inhumane. Well these feelings have merit - such things do happen. Many experienced dog breeders have found from their own sad experiences that inbreeding produced some very low quality animals for them. In fact, as mentioned in the historical chapter, the second largest dog registering body in the U. S. has made definite pronouncements against inbreeding. The problem is that the mishaps are the result of incorrect inbreeding. As the really top dog men know, in order to be successful, inbreeding must be selective. The whole purpose of inbreeding is to hold onto and control desired characteristics and improve or upgrade all types of animals. It is used successfully with livestock. Mishaps do occur; on the other hand, the best dogs in history, from a performance standpoint as well as from a producing standpoint, have been the result of a selective breeding program that included inbreeding and/or linebreeding. If you recall from the historical chapter, John Colby had only one outcross in 30 years of breeding. The difference is in the way you go about it. Done correctly, it most definitely purifies a strain and is the only way you can control characteristics. Onstott relates in his book, *The New Art of Breeding Setter Dogs*, an experiment with white rats at Wistar Institute. Full brothers and sisters were bred for 20 generations - selecting for breeding only those rats that were the sturdiest and that had the most stamina. At the end of the experiment they had a strain of rats with greater than average size, fertility, longevity, and endurance.

Let's look at a sample pedigree of an inbred Pit Bull who came from the yard of Estes Reece and is the mother of Jack Swinson's (Greensboro, N. C.) dog Tanner. Notice this is a brother-sister mating. In addition, notice Miss Spike appears eight times in the third generation. In other words Miss Spike is the grandmother of both the mother and father. This is heavy inbreeding. All the dogs in the peidgree are proven and as noted elsewhere in the book, both Boomerang and Miss Pool Hall Red were Grand Champions.

```
                                    Hooten's Snake        Carver's Ironhead
                                                          Carver's Miss Spike
                  Wood's Snooty
                                    Art's Missy           Carver's Pistol
                                                          Carver's Miss Spike
   Wood's Bart (Red Devil)
                                    Davis' Ch. Boomerang  Carver's Pistol
                                                          Carver's Miss Spike
                  Wood's Miss Pool Hall Red
                                    Hyde's Mennie         Carver's Ironhead
                                                          Carver's Miss Spike
Swinson's Sandy (Reece's Blond Bomber)
                                    Hooten's Snake        Carver's Ironhead
                                                          Carver's Miss Spike
                  Wood's Snooty
                                    Art's Missy           Carver's Pistol
                                                          Carver's Miss Spike
   Wood's Brandy
                                    Davis' Ch. Boomerang  Carver's Pistol
                                                          Carver's Miss Spike
                  Wood's Miss Pool Hall Red
                                    Hyde's Mennie         Carver's Ironhead
                                                          Carver's Miss Spike
```

When we say "inbreed," the question often arises, which type of inbreeding is best? Brother to sister matings represent the most intense inbreeding. The man currently recognized as the best breeder of sporting Beagles, utilizes heavy, selective, brother-sister matings, and his best dog was the result of a brother-sister mating. Pit dog men have not had much luck with this type of mating, however. Time and time again, this seems to produce very game dogs with little pit ability and who won't bite effectively. I don't know why this is true, but it seems to be the case most of the time. Notice I said most of the time and I mean from my personal observations. There will be some who disagree because they have had good results from brother-sister breedings. If proven game, offspring from these matings can make excellent Breeding dogs, especially if bred back into a highly related line because they tend to intensify the effect of the dog they were inbred from. This will not necessarily be true, though, because a brother and sister may for all practical purposes be quite unrelated, because one pup in a litter may receive a preponderance of his genes from a grandparent on, i.e., the father's side, totally unrelated to another pup in the same litter that receives a concentration of genes from a grandparent on, say, the mother's side. It is true, however, that the brother-sister-bred dog should intensify the effect of his mother and father on subsequent matings - at least moreso than any other type of breeding. Daughter bred back to father (or, not generally as popular, son back to mother - especially if the mother has not been proven) has provided, unquestionably the best results. If the daughter is bred back to the father, say for example Red Boy Tramp bred to his daughter, this is called a double cross. If a daughter from this litter is bred back to Red Boy, this is called a triple cross and the resulting litter is theoretically 87% Red Boy Tramp. This type of breeding is very popular with pit dog men as it has produced some beauties. A triple cross is as tight as you want; any more than this and you start having the problems symptomatic of extensive inbreeding. Inbreeding preserves the excellent foundation blood, but it will not generally strengthen it, whereas linebreeding, if the outside blood used is good, will enhance the foundation blood.

Before we get into selective inbreeding, we need to look at this related concept of linebreeding, which is the mating of animals closely related to the same ancestor. One picture being worth a thousand words. I have permission from Cheryl Petersen of California to use the pedigree of her Pit Bull, Tuff, as an example. (There is a short story about Tuff in the "Introduction.") This is an example of a linebred Dibo dog. Heinzl's Gringo was the last living grandson of Dibo. He died in early 1980 I think. Okay. Notice that Boss is linebred Gringo (his father and grandfather). Gringo is linebred Colby Dime on his bottom side. Ginger's father, Bummy, was a dead-game grandson of Gringo. Ginger is linebred Colby Dime on the bottom side. (All that Colby blood -Barney, Jenny, etc. - is Colby Dime.) This is an example of planned breeding. Heinzl's Gringo.

		Tudor's Dibo	Hubbard's Bounce
	Heinzl's Clancy		Heinzl's Bambi
Heinzl's Gringo		Heinzl's Dutchess	Myer's Mike
			Heinzl's Patsy
	Heinzl's Brindy	Lyon's Pucky	Colby's Dime
			Colby's Margie
Heinzl's Boss (Tuff's father)		Colby's Dolly	Colby's Dime
			Colby's Tibbie
	Heinzl's Gringo	Heinzl's Clancy	Tudor's Dibo
			Heinzl's Dutches
Heinzl's Raquel		Heinzl's Brindy	Lyon's Pucky
			Colby's Dolly
	Heinzl's Millie	Kinard's Mike	Sander's Satan
			Sander's Patsy
		Heinzl's Soda	Arizona Pete
			Heinzl's Polly
	Heinzl's Tex	Heinzl's Ajax	Heinzl's Honcho
			Heinzl's Patch
Heinzl's Bummy		Heinzl's Chris	Heinzl's Musty
			Heinzl's Margo
	Heinzl's Raquel	Heinzl's Gringo	Heinzl's Clancy
			Heinzl's Brindy
Fonseca's Ginger (Tuff's mother)		Heinzl's Millie	Kinard's Mike
			Heinzl's Soda
	Colby's Joey	Colby's Emjay	Colby's Barney
			Colby's Jenny
		Colby's Jill	Colby's Morgan
			Colby's Dolly
Fonseca's Chris		Colby's Prince	Colby's Pumpsie
	Colby's Mink		Colby's Winnie
		Orday's Jet	Orday's Smokey
			Loposay's Monkey

The purpose of linebreeding is similar to inbreeding - to enhance a pedigree and to control characteristics. Tuff and his littermates are much more likely to have the characteristics - personality, conformation, gameness, etc. - similar to Gringo than if Gringo appeared only once in the pedigree - remember this includes faulty characteristics as well as good ones, so you linebreed off a superlative dog of course. Trouble is no dog has it all, and when you do find one that comes close, you might find he is crossbred and therefore a chance in a million combination of mixed genes that culminated in an excellent dog. So when you linebreed, you are likely to have some pups that have his (the dog you are linebreeding from) bad characteristics and none of his good ones - but you are just as likely to get some pups with his good characteristics and none of his bad ones. Most likely, though, there will be a mixture of traits.

As to the question, which is better, linebreeding or inbreeding, I would say to linebreed off a dead game, inbred dog. Linebreeding helps maintain endurance, size, conformation, and intelligence, I believe. The considerations that need to be made are the following: Though linebreeding takes longer to arrive at what you want, you are less burdened with filial degeneration (to be explained later). Selective inbreeding keeps a characteristic and improves quicker than any other breeding, if done correctly - but you must be more selective and cull much more extensively than with any other method. Now, pay attention to this. At times an entire litter may not meet your standards, and you need the faith in the bloodlines to try again and perhaps even a third time. You must be very particular with each litter and with each mating. A great deal of patience and faith are needed. If the dog being inbred is an ace - you know he is and you know his pedigree - then it's there in his blood somewhere to come out again, perhaps even better.

If a dog does not have any dog appearing more than once in his pedigree and he is bred to a bitch who also has no dog appearing more than once in her pedigree and neither dog has any dogs in common in their pedigrees (called an "open pedigree" which is the same as an outcross or a crossbred dog), then you are not breeding for any characteristics, and you are merely trusting to luck - and as any true gambler will tell you, luck fails most people most of the time. An old adage among Pit Bull breeders is "breed best to best to get the best," but many a Pit Bull owner has been disappointed because he purchased a pup whose mother had a large number of famous dogs in her pedigree and whose father also had a large number of famous dogs (but not the same as the bitch's) in his pedigree - and the pup was a mouse. I will have to mention this, however. A good many top dog men today are mixing pedigrees - virtually open pedigrees, by merely breeding "best to best," that is, breeding top quality studs to top quality bitches, without special regard for their pedigrees, culling the ones that don't turn out so good - and getting some really dynamite dogs! I believe this is because they are breeding for qameness. They cannot, therefore, depend on dogs having any particular color, size, ability, or other characteristic. In other words, if a stud dog that is proven game and is Lightner bred, is bred to a bitch that is also proven game but is, say Hemphill bred, the gameness characteristic is not necessarily lost because of there being two different strains involved. Patrick said that it works like this: if you breed for, let's say size, you could breed a St. Bernard to a Bull Mastiff and get a large dog. Breed those pups to a Great Dane and you'll get some funny looking dogs - but they'll be big ones! In other words, if you breed for one trait, like size, you can mix a strain, or breed, and retain the trait.[38] Well that seems to make sense, but there are some problems with the theory. It is true that if you bred different breeds of dogs, all large breeds, you'd probably get large dogs. Some traits, however, involve "quantitative inheritance" and some do not. This means that some traits depend on many different genes combining together. I suspect that the trait gameness is polygenic (also means many genes make up the trait). If this is true, then it is more likely that you'd lose a trait when you mix strains and depend on the nicking (a breeding term meaning that the blood of the two dogs in a mating combines well together and produces animals that are superior in quality) of genes from dogs of different bloodlines, than with line- or inbreeding. It is true that at least half the dogs that have earned Register of Merit (recognition as having produced more pit champions than other dogs - explained in the combat chapter) are outcrossed dogs. So I don't mean to imply that linebreeding and/or inbreeding is the only way to have a successful breeding program, but I do maintain that your chances are much better and you'll be more consistent with line- or inbreeding if done correctly. The thing is that if the famous dogs have no common ancestors in their pedigrees and no one ancestor appears more than once in a pedigree, then theoretically the ancestors' influence is extremely diluted because their individual contribution is so small. Brackett states that "a dog appearing in the fourth generation contributes only 1/256 of the heredity factors in a puppy, and that one can understand that those distant relatives could not have done much to overcome the influence of unrelated and perhaps inferior specimens appearing in the pedigree later. Altogether too many fanciers are misled into feeling they have a worthwhile breeding animal because back in the third or fourth generation there appears one or more outstanding dogs."[39] In other words the closest generations provide the greatest influence even though the foundation is extremely important just as the foundation of a house is important. This concept can be underscored by my sharing an article by Jim Uselton, used with his permission. Breeding The A.P.B.T.

In order to breed intelligently the combat dog owner and breeder should know something about the mechanics of Canine Genetics and heredity, which is the way that certain characteristics, such as size, color, conformation, gameness, etc. are transmitted from one generation to the next.

These traits or characteristics are transmitted through chromosomes. Each parent contributes 39 chromosomes, for a total of 78 to each puppy. If acquiring good proven linebred, or inbred brood bitches from an old and proven bloodline, that has been kept straight and accurate, should then be bred to a proven and compatably bred stud dog of the same bloodline, then a breeder should be able to expect what he is looking for in combat dogs. No breeding is always 100% game, but breeding intelligently and staying with a good proven bloodline and keeping your bloodline straight will improve your percentage greatly.

Keep as many of your best bitch puppies as you possibly can. This is one time where a very small kennel is at a disadvantage. You should watch how the young bitches develop and act, as long as you can, and try them out before culling them, and keeping the best for the future. If you do not do this you will suffer for it in the long run, because the time will come when your foundation brood bitch will get old and you will find them being replaced by dogs that may be inferior, and farther away from the old and proven bloodlines. Also, don't forget—a cur son or daughter of a great sire or bitch is no better than any cur, so remember, if you allow your good stud dog to breed someones inferior bitch, the offspring may receive more bad genes from the inferior bitch, than from your good game stud dog, and produce a litter of curs from your good stud dog and your kennels!

This canine Genetics Table shows the average number of chromosomes that a puppy could possibly receive from any ancestor in a given generation back to the tenth generation. This would compare with the Human Generations back to 1620 A.D. These odds would be cut down considerably by tight linebreeding and inbreeding.

So, you can see how difficult it would really be for anyone to have any pure Colby or any of the other old time bloodlines, therefore, that is why I think we should keep the bloodlines straight that we have now, that was started by the "old timers."

Generation	Number of Potential Ancestors	Average Chromosomes from Each	Odds Against Receiving Even 1 Chromosome
1st (Parent)	2	39	
2nd (Grandprt.)	4	19 or 20	
3rd (Gr. Grp.)	8	9 or 10	
4th (Gr. Gr. Grp.)	16	4 or 5	
5th (Gr. Gr. Gr. Grandparent)	32	2 or 3	
6th (Gr. Gr. Gr. Gr. Grandprt.)	64	1 or 2	
7th - etc.	128	(at least 50 ancestors would be unrepresented.)	4 to 3
8th - etc.	236		8 to 3
9th - etc.	512		5 to 1
10th - etc.	1024		10 to 1

The characteristic most valued by the majority of Pit Bull breeders is gameness, the trait that seems to typify the breed. Genetics is quite complex because very few characteristics are governed by a single gene. We don't really know what genetic factors make up a game dog but most breeders maintain that it is a recessive (as 40 opposed to dominant) trait. Eberhard, in his book *The New Complete Bull*

Terrier, has provided a definition I like of the terms recessive and dominant as they apply to breeding. A dominant trait is characterized by the following:
1. It does not have to skip a generation to show up.
2. A large number of the progeny pick it up.
3. It overcomes recessive traits.
4. It is easy to breed for.

A recessive trait, on the other hand, is characterized by the following:
1. It may skip one or more generations.
2. Only a small percentage of individuals in the strain carry the trait.
3. The trait must come from both sides of the family.

    As I understand it, some characteristics can be both recessive and dominant. A black colored coat is an example of a dominant trait. Black Pit Bulls will produce a preponderance of black pups when mated with lighter colored Pit Bulls. Gameness seems to be recessive and because of this, particular attention needs to be paid to it in the breeding program. If you are breeding for an illusive trait like this, it is difficult to also get a dog that conforms to ideal physical attributes. You may get a dog with a blue eye, pink eye, crooked tail, weak teeth, or whatever. If you want a pretty dog, select pretty dogs in a pedigree and linebreed them. Quite often the line- and particularly the inbred game dog, produces dogs with very poor conformation and with structural problems. A Pit Bull adage is to use an inbred dog for breeding but an outcross to obtain an athlete. More on this concept later. I maintain that with a proper breeding program and with patience, one can obtain both the gameness and the conformation. This can be very difficult to do and requires a great deal of discipline. You just breed for both and you have to be more patient, holding onto your strain; and when you don't get it in one generation, you breed again and sell off the undesirables. It may help if you hold fast to this concept: theoretically, every pup in a litter gets 50% of his genes from his mother, and 50% from his father. Beware of statistical concepts. Statistically, if you flip a coin ten times, it will turn up heads five times and tails five times. We all know it just doesn't work that way. It will, however, if you keep fliping long enough. You've probably had the experience of having straight runs - say five, six straight heads, or tails. Well those straight runs could be a litter of pups - and could be all good ones, or all bad ones. The idea is to keep flipping.

    The dead game dog that has structural problems, like weak hind-quarters, is likely to be fighting from the bottom. He may love it in the pit and may go down happy - breaking your heart, giving you goose bumps up and down your spine to see him crawl when he can't even walk across the pit, because he is not athletically structured. I maintain that you can keep such a dog for breeding, holding onto that gameness, and, if he's bred correctly, also getting some pretty dogs built right.

Don't forget that the inbred dog isn't necessarily poorly structured. You'll see plenty of pictures of inbred Pit Bulls in magazines, and they look fine to me. Of course, you may not be interested in a pit dog, its being illegal and all, but I'm saying there's no question you want the characteristic gameness. If you didn't, you wouldn't be buying a Pit Bull or a Staf, you'd be getting another breed, wouldn't you? So whether you want a pet or a Schutzhund dog, I feel like you should breed for gameness and conformation. I think more people are doing that these days, both consciously and unconsciously. In the old days of pit fighting, the primary emphasis was on gameness, to the exclusion of all else; but, in my opinion, beginning, in the 1950's there was an emphasis put on rough, strong dogs. At one match, Earl Tudor was being intimidated about his dog - this guy was telling him his dog wasn't game. Mr. Tudor turned to him and said he wasn't betting on his dog being game, he was betting on him winning.

Of course the policy of not breeding strictly for gameness has been criticized as being responsible for a lot of curs. I don't think that is the case though. There were still a lot of curs in the 1930's and some of the matches today equal or exceed the famous matches of the past.

There are other breeding endeavors in which multiple charactcristics arc successfully attained - with goats, for- example. I mention them because a friend of mine raises them and I buy milk from him. Goat's milk is better for you (and your dog) than cow's milk. (See the "Nutrition" chapter.) Anyway, he and others breed goats that will produce a larger quantity of milk that is also of a richer quality than other goats, while at the same time breeding for show conformation. Goats are shown just like dogs and have structural conformation standards they must meet, which is supposed to make them stronger and sturdier. Many people have champion show goats that are also champion milk producers. Point made.

Another example, I believe, is the famous King Ranch, named after the original owner, and probably the oldest of the large Texas ranches and certainly the most successful. This section is taken primarily from the book *The King Ranch* by Tom Lea.[41] The ranch survived depressions, loss of market, and changing markets that put other ranches out of business. Its success can be attributed to its breeding program with cattle and horses. The owners developed, through scientific, selective breeding, superlative strains of beef cattle. They did so by intensive linebreeding for the desired characteristics, and outcrossing to maintain hybrid vigor. They always used, as an outcross, a strong bull that had a very mixed pedigree. When mated with a cow that was highly linebred, the desired characteristics would predominate in the offspring. Breeding the offspring of the outcross back to the linebred strain, would in a couple of generations, produce herds that very closely resembled the original stock (from which they had been linebred). Yet they would be larger and hardier. It may be that we could do the same with American Staffordshire and American Pit Bull Terriers - linebreed on one strain, and when quality has leveled out, outcross. In other words, a highly linebred Pit Bull that has structural problems could be outcrossed to an American Staffordshire to give a real good dose of strength, conformation, and healthy teeth. The Staf should have a very mixed pedigree (but with plenty of strong show champions). The puppies should have the gameness of the linebred Pit Bull, but be stronger. On the other hand, if the Staf breeder is concerned with gameness, he should outcross to a Pit Bull with a mixed pedigree (but with plenty of dead game fighters).

I think we can also learn something from the success the King Ranch had in breeding horses. When this ranch was formed in the middle 1800's, a premium was placed on high quality horses from the start because they had large cattle herds and needed quality draft horses for the cowboys. The early Texas frontier ranch horses were Mustangs, an extremely hardy strain you have probably heard of or read about. The Mustang is a short, smaller strain of horse that is strong and wiry. They descended primarily from horses that escaped from or were abandoned by early explorers and Spanish conquistadors. They had to abide by the law of nature - only the fittest survive. They were not bred for conformation or by any human breeding program - the thing is, the strongest stallions lived and got the lion's share of breeding. The result was extremely sturdy mares and crafty, strong stallions.

In the early 1900's the King Ranch[42] decided to experiment with a breeding program to improve their horses. Since the ranch's earliest days, the cow ponies had been selectively bred so as to retain the most efficient horses. They had to have the stamina and spirit for the work demanded of them, and if they didn't measure up, they were sold. The good ones were so efficient that a cowboy merely had to point the horse toward a steer that he wanted cut from the herd, and the horse would do all the work and all the thinking - in fact, he'd do it better than if he were guided by the cowboy. In an attempt to "grade-up" (as it was called), the King Ranch decided to crossbreed the ranch horses with pure Thoroughbred horses. Although they are no good for ranch work, being too big and leggy and not having the tenacious spirit needed for working cattle all day, they have been bred for size and conformation and are the fastest of the horse breeds on long stretches. (The Thoroughbred is the strain used today on the racetrack.) They came from England where they were the result of the British breeding pure Arabian stallions with native English mares. King Ranch managers traveled to Kentucky to get some of the very best Thoroughbreds. In 1916, they selected the very best cattle horse they had ever had on the ranch - Old Sorrel. He was exceptional as to beauty, disposition, conformation, smoothness of action, and fine handling qualities. It was determined to preserve, as much as possible, his wonderful qualities. They bred him to 50 of their best Thoroughbred mares. The most successful mating resulted in a male named Solis, who was mated to his daughters from the same band of Thoroughbred mares, and in a very short time they had a band of about 40 mares and then they mated Solis to 40 of his half-sisters and then they had a strain of horses highly inbred Solis that became champions. In fact, I understand that this breeding program established a new breed - the one we now call Quarter Horse. When they bred Old Sorrel to the Thoroughbred mares, they kept the horses that had the conformation suited for ranch work and sold the rest. If those remaining didn't have the necessary stamina and tenacity, they, too, were sold. So the only horses they kept were those with both ideal conformation and the ability to perform. The King Ranch was fortunate in that it had enough land, cattle, and cowboys to work all those horses under the severest of tests. They kept a written record of each horse, noting its strengths and weaknesses at work and in conformation. By the way, I'd like to mention that they paid top dollar to their cowboys so their horses were worked by the best horsemen available. This makes a difference, I believe. Although some exceptional Pit Bulls will perform well no matter who owns them, such as Morochito's half-brother who has been abused, overfed, underfed, overconditioned, underconditioned, fought long and hard off the chain, and still has demolished every dog set down in front of him, there are many, many Pit Bulls which have been ruined by owners who didn't know what they were doing. I believe there are a lot of well bred Pit Bulls which would have been champions if they had been handled by caring, experienced people. In other words, you don't know if a breeding program is successful unless the performance tests are adequate. If those who train and handle the animals are inexperienced, the animal will not be getting a fair test. Anyway, at the same time that Solis was producing all those horses, six other sons of Old Sorrel were bred to selected mares thought to be best suited to them, and in this way quite a large population of grandsons and granddaughters of Old Sorrel came about. Fairly good results were obtained from these matings, but the best results were obtained from the close breeding employed with Solis. The Solis breeding was more inbred, and brought out and intensified his superior qualities (from his father Old Sorrel). Horses were performance tested and pedigrees were carefully studied so that each stud was placed with a band of mares most likely to nick conformation-wise and performance-wise, because of pedigree relationship.

That was more than 30 years ago. Notice they are saying exactly what this chapter is saying - inbreeding and linebreeding carry no guarantees and you have to be very selective.

In 1940, after 20 years of successful breeding, the Klebergs, who were managers of the ranch and instilled the breeding program, established the American Quarter Horse Association. The Quarter Horse is a breed that has to live on the range and rely on the native grass and shrubs for food, and yet take on enough flesh and muscle to withstand the hard work required of them. They look like small Arabians, but their hind end and rear legs are more muscular. They cannot come close to beating a Thoroughbred on a long run, out there isn't a breed of horse in the world, I'm told, that can beat them at quarter-mile sprints. (That's where their name comes from.) They have unbelievable endurance, a quiet disposition and friendly temperament, are easy to train, have extreme early speed and the strength and sure-footedness to carry heavy weight over any kind of terrain. They stop and turn easily and do not become leg weary or lazy even when asked to stop and start quickly many times in the course of the day's roping, cutting, or other work. The Quarter Horse has the most symmetrical and muscular conformation coupled with the most perfect balance of any of the horse breeds. (Sounds like the horse's equivalent to the Pit Bull to me.) The King Ranch has had grand champions in Quarter Horse shows just about every year since 1941. The horses are both conformation champions and efficient cattle horses. I realize that the principles of breeding cattle horses may not apply when breeding Pit Bulls - but then they are breeding principles and should apply.

I think this is a good argument for experimenting with Pit Bull/Staf crossbreeding. The idea will still be highly criticized by both Staf and Pit Bull people. For one thing, there have been plenty of this type of matings already, and I understand from some pretty authoritative sources that several breeders of combat Pit Bulls have actually bred in Stafs but hid the fact by showing the breeding as being pure Pit Bull. They haven't had much success in that although they got some fair combat dogs, they didn't get any real good ones -no great champions that I know of. The Pit Bulls inherited the strong characteristics of the Staf but lost some gameness. By the same token, outcrosses of champion show Stafs to Pit Bulls have lowered the Stafs conformation. I'll bet in both cases, however, that those outcrosses have not utilized the methods outlined here to intensify the desired characteristics. I do not mean to make an issue of it; I merely threw the idea out as a suggestion for anyone who might want to try it. This type of breeding is not in my personal plans because I want to preserve the original breed - I want as close to dead game Pit Bulls as I can get and I believe I can do it and maintain strong, beautiful animals at the same time. Just about all the dogs in Morochito's family (close up - mother, father, brothers and sisters, and sisters' children - sister bred to brother Jake) are strong, pretty (in my opinion) dogs. Now Morochito's grandmother, Shivar's Beanie was a short, squat, ugly Pit Bull, I'm told, but she sure doesn't produce that way. In any event, the lion's share of Morochito's family lack nothing in strength, conformation (except an occasional "crooked" tail and a few overshot mouths – Morochito's teeth are even - but these are factors that don't concern me - in fact I like the crooked tails). Look at Jeep, Peterbuilt, most of the Sorrells dogs, and many others -they lack nothing in gameness or conformation. In fact I personally think the dogs I just mentioned (just examples that I happen to like) are the most beautiful dogs in the world. Just look at the picture of Jeep from the centerfold of *Pit Bull Gazette*, February, 1981. Is that not one beautiful animal? The gracefulness and lean, racy muscularity displayed emulates that of a champion race horse. He exudes strength, intense attitude, and endurance (the kind that beats one of the best pit dogs in the world in three hours and forty-five minutes) - what can I say? So I say pure Pit Bulls can produce beautiful dogs.

Jeep

On the other hand I have this to say about the Stafs that so many say are not game. I have seen or heard of many of them going the distance against some bad Pit Bulls. Let me relate one example. (Granted this is an isolated example, and I do agree that it is harder to get game Stafs than game Pit Bulls.) This guy whose name is Wayne has a white Staf, nice looking dog. The dog was given to him as a pup. He's a smart dog, follows Wayne around when he's feeding the other dogs, doesn't mess with them at all. I remember when we were looking at him in his pen, one of the men was drinking a can of Budweiser beer. He took a sip, then brought the can down by his side. The Staf was watching the can with a quizical, curious expression on his face. He followed the path of the can - so the guy put the can in back of him - and the Staf turned his head to the side as he circled around to see the can. He made us all laugh. Pretty smart I'd say. Someone had the idea we should sit on the other side of the pit and hold up the beer can when he got tired!

This white Staf looked good when rolled, so he was matched. I don't believe he had any extraordinary conditioning in his keep. People don't really share all their conditioning methods, but I know this guy didn't own a treadmill, just had a wheel for him to run on and not a very good one at that. The Staf met up with a darn good Pit Bull, a brindle that had already won one match and was a pound heavier and a little taller than he was. The brindle was also a hard biter. The Staf turned out to be a nose fighter - a good one, too. He'd get on that nose and hand on. Good maneuvers, too. Turned a complete flip one time, over the back of the brindle and came up with a hold - it brought an "Ohhh ..." of admiration from the audience. The brindle was a good hard biter, hard on that stifle, so they were pretty evenly matched. Several times it looked like one was down for count, just laying there breathing hard while the other shook him all over the pit. Just when it looked like one or the other was done for, he'd get a second wind, get out of hold and the situation would be turned about. At an hour and a half the white Staf had bitten all the way through the brindle's nose. The Staf, however, could hardly hobble - his stifle had been punished so badly. In addition, the side of his mouth was torn up pretty badly. Yes, these fights do on occasion get rough, but I want to report that both dogs are alive and well, now retired to their yards. The Staf's lip has grown back and the brindle's nose healed over. In any event, at one hour, forty-five minutes the Staf was on that Brindle's nose again and hanging on. He kept digging in the same spot and the brindle couldn't get out. The brindle started yelping - generally a sure sign of quit - but not in this case. At two hours a turn was called on the Staf. (This was not the first scratch of the fight.) He went across fine but was soon in trouble. Brindle got him down and he looked dead, he sure did. At two hours, five minutes, however, it was brindle's time to scratch. He couldn't see very well - both eyes were swollen and nearly closed: but he staggered across the pit. One of the young girls at pit side called out his name, cheering him on, and when he got three-fourths across the pit, he turned his head in her direction. At that time the handler of the Staf released his dog - a tremendous mistake. When the dogs are that tired, a handler should never release his dog until the opposing dog is on his. The opposing dog has no momentum anyway and many times they've been known to stop right in front of their opponent, just long enough to be counted out. The handler was experienced, but he just wasn't thinking. The Staf was weak, but he went straight into the brindle - and down again. At two hours, 13 minutes, it was the Staf's scratch and he collapsed in his corner. The Staf people swore that their dog should have won because if his handler had held on, the brindle would have walked over toward the girl that called his name; but the brindle people said no way - he still would have scratched straight. Sportsmanship was high on both sides so it was acknowledged that both dogs were equally very game. Both parties immediately worked on first-aid for their dogs. The brindle was in better shape, still standing, and so when he was fixed up the people on his side went over and worked hard to help the Staf who was unconscious, cold, and his blood was hardly circulating. Just to show you how these pit dog people constantly chase after the elusive trait of gameness — after they had been working on the dogs awhile, the owner of the brindle lifted his dog over and said, "Say, Wayne, would you mind facing your dog, just a moment, see if my brindle will move toward him? We won't let them touch." Wayne said, "Okay," and lifted up the Staf. The brindle couldn't see, though, so they couldn't tell anything. This may seem like the pit dog people are very crass - but if so it's because you don't know the dogs. Just before his last scratch, the Staf's tail was wagging away - weakly, it's true, but still wagging. He was happy as could be. He sure did look a mess and it was a long night for him. But he is now as pretty as ever and doesn't look any more scarred up than a good experienced coon hound. The dogs are tough. Also his owner was practically in tears when he made the mistake and let him go when the brindle was scratching. Kept saying, "I'm sorry I let you down, boy." (Actually he should keep talking and thinking positive - a dog can't understand words sometimes but his instinct for emotions is more advanced than ours.) Anyway, he felt so badly, kept saying he let down his dog because while it is his dog's duty to fight, it's his duty to do the thinking. Not many pit fights last as long, with as much action, and have as much damage done as that one so the Staf really exhibited extraordinary gameness.

I realize that was a pretty long story to illustrate a point, but I wanted to bring out the fact that a Staf sure can act like a Pit. I want to reiterate that I am aware that this Staf was an exception and much less likely to produce game dogs than a Pit Bull cur with more proven game dogs up close in his pedigree. It's just that the game genes are present in the Staf and can be tapped; and the strength and conformation tend to be better. Let me point out something here. One of the greatest pit dogs and a dog recognized by many as one of the best producers is Alvin the Dog, the grandson of a Staf! Richard Stratton recommends him as one of the top twelve stud dogs in the country.

Getting back to the subject of the King Ranch, let me share some more material from the book. Some of it may repeat what I have already related, but I wanted to underscore those items because they are important and because the King Ranch is probably the most successful animal breeding institution in the world. The book is very difficult to locate; I found it in a local university's library. It was recommended to me by my karate instructor, Lawrence McSwain, a former student at the university, and a former breeder of Arabian horses. In the book, they say that "type" (conformation) receives particular attention because of the close relationship between conformation and function and because type is also related, to some extent, to performance. The Kleberg brothers define performance, in horses, as "temperament (the ability to learn the tasks for which they are trained and their desire or will to accomplish the tasks asked of them) and endurance (the power to withstand the physical stresses of performance and action)." They said that "development of performance is of prime importance in breeding, yet difficult of definition because temperament and endurance are not fully discernible on the exterior and are not recorded in pedigrees. Clear decisions as to a horse's worth rests ultimately upon tests of performance. This complicates breeding because performance is greatly influenced by good or bad training."

In 1935 the ranch established a stable of Thoroughbred race horses and is now one of the largest Thoroughbred breeding and racing establishments in the country. Their Thoroughbreds are primarily linebred to the horse that is recognized as probably the best producer of race horses in the country. The King Ranch foundation horse, Bold Venture, foaled in 1891, was linebred Domino on both sides of his family, inbred on his mother's side. He was a Kentucky Derby winner and sired two other Derby winners, a sire record that has never been equaled. In addition, One of his sons was a Triple Crown winner, consisting of the Kentucky Derby, The Preakness, and the Belmont Stakes. The ranch follows a breeding program with its Thoroughbreds that is just like the one suggested in this chapter - that is, inbreeding from an animal that has all the desired characteristics, then outcross, and finally linebreed back on the original animal. Actually they linebreed on two strains - Domino and the famous Man O' War. This is analgous, I would say, for example, to linebreeding Dibo and Colby Dime. Let me give you one example of their pedigree analysis and breeding to accomplish a goal.

Their goal has been to concentrate the combination of Domino and Man O' War lines and not intensify the linebreeding specifically to one or the other line. They had a mare, for example, that was granddaughter to Man O' War. They mated her with a stallion that had Domino in his 6th, 7th, and 8th generations. From that mating they obtained a breeding mare that was genetically equal Man O' War and Domino - equal because of the greater number of times Domino appeared in the father's pedigree. In other words, there was about 30 years difference between Domino and Man O' War, but skillful breeding brought them together as contemporary sires in the mare's pedigree. I think Pit Bull breeders should give considerable thought to that point. Because of the great amount of money in successful race horses, the King Ranch has become wealthy in the business. For overhalf a century, they have raised champion cattle, Quarter Horses, and Thoroughbred race horses. They have used selective inbreeding and linebreeding, but with considerable caution, constantly keeping available top quality outcross females to serve as genetic brakes on any adverse trends that continuous breeding of this sort may provoke.

Here is another good argument in favor of inbreeding and line-breeding if correctly used. Current literature is filled with instances of the successful crossbreeding of working animals with show animals. There is an article in the November, 1979 issue of *Dog World* by a man who breeds working/show cross Cockers, specializing in top quality working ability allied to sound conformation. The working Cockers are highly linebred and produce dogs with brains, courage, hunting instinct, trainability, and sound health - but they don't necessarily look right. He has to cull extensively, selling many of them, and keeping only those who are good performers and are also built right. If hunting instinct can be maintained in this manner, perhaps gameness can, too. I realize that gameness is hard enough to breed for with pure Pit Bulls, but the same is true with a hunting nose in hunting breeds.

You will notice that we emphasized the fact that in order for inbreeding and linebreeding to work, we must, from time to time, effect an outcross. Although selective linebreeding is the best way to successfully develop and maintain characteristics in animals, it is fraught with some peculiar difficulties that the breeder must be aware of. Ironically enough, the combat dog is not usually inbred. The athletic combat dog is usually an outcross. An "outcross" refers to the mating of a strain (line- or inbred) to another strain (not to be confused with the "open" pedigree which refers to a completely random breeding with no line- or inbreeding on either side of the family. Outcross and open pedigree are terms that are often used interchangeably, but outcrossing, strictly defined, mates unrelated dogs, but can include line- or inbreeding on either side. The out-cross that includes linebreeding is much better than the totally open pedigree because it is stronger and more controlable.) The reason an outcross tends to produce a better combat dog is that after several generations (Some say three, some say five or more), there is a tendency to lose size, fertility, and perhaps stamina (adding to the criticisms of inbreeding). This is because of a process called "filial degeneration" (also called "filial regression," or "drag"). The word "filial" means a generation or bloodline and the term "filial degeneration" refers to the tendency of the offspring of any animal to revert to the average of the race or strain. Because of filial degeneration, the children of geniuses tend to be of average, or even below average, intelligence. By the same token, the children of morons also tend to be average. Ever see a real pretty girl who has truly ugly parents? Happens a lot. As a kid in Boston, I remember this girl who lived a few houses down the street. She had dark blond hair, a beautiful complexion, and was tall with long, sexy legs. She came from a poor family. Her father was a short, stocky Italian with a pock-marked face - looked like it had been hacked up by a hatchet and her mother was fat as a tub and had hair that was kind of wiry reddish brown. The thing is, though, the blond probably won't have real pretty children. Well, it works the same way with Pit Bulls. The breeding of two quality ace Pit Bulls will not usually produce ace dogs - might produce good dogs but won't generally be like their mama or poppa. The Fork Farm in North Carolina has a very big yard of excellently bred Pit Bulls of Boudreaux and Carver breeding. I visited them one time and looked at their dogs. These folks are very friendly, chock full of information, and love to talk "Pit Bull." They often have a full-page advertisement in *The Pit Bull Gazette*. I love to read their ads because they explain their breeding program. As they mention, among the greatest producing sires and dams of the modern day was Bullyson and Miss Spike. Bullyson was Boudreaux bred. I present Bullyson's pedigree because it is an example of successful linebreeding and inbreeding and because I want to show some pedigrees of well known dogs. Blind Billy was the most inbred dog produced by Dibo. Blind Billy was bred to his daughter four consecutive times, and the final result was Boudreaux' Scrub, who was the father of Boudreaux' Boze and Boudreaux' Eli, who was a fantastic producer. As you can see from the pedigree, Eli was bred Boudreaux' Spook who was the daughter of Boze. The result was Bullyson, Eli, Jr., and Brendy. All three were excellent dogs and excellent producers. This is just one example of many that would seem to prove that the criticisms of inbreeding and linebreeding are not founded on adequate knowledge. We can continue the story. Bullyson was bred to Tina, another daughter of Boze, to produce Benny Bob, whose famous fight with Jimmy Boots is recorded in my "Combat Dog" chapter. Benny Bob was the only dog that ever defeated Bullyson. Bullyson has been a producer of some of the top dogs in the country for the past ten years, not only in his direct offspring but to the second and third generations. One of his sons, Davis' Midnight Cowboy, won three consecutive matches (and was thus a champion) and won best of show in all three. (At many conventions a prize is given to the dog that is voted to be the best performer.) Bullyson himself was, I think, a beautiful and very athletic dog. Brendy had more than 90 pups born to her, a truly astounding number (*Pit Bull Gazette*, November, 1978). Benny Bob is her grandson.

Jack Swinson's Sandy - inbred Ironhead/Miss Spike

Miss Spike is said by many to be the best foundation bitch of modern times. She was the daughter of Dibo's son Spike (a dog mentioned in the historical chapter, who ranks as one of the best pit fighters of his day). Miss Spike's mother was linebred Dibo on her bottom side (through Carver's Black Widow, Cannon's Black Shine, Amber Girl, and others mentioned in the historical chapter). When bred to Carver's Pistol she produced Davis' Champion Boomerang and Art's Missy in one litter, both superior Pit Bulls. She has produced scores of excellent Pit Bulls and her blood seems to be good for second and third generations. Well when Bullyson was bred to Miss Spike, none of the litter had characteristics like either

Boomerang or Benny Bob. You have to study pedigrees and find blood that "nicks" (goes well together and produces).

```
                                                              Hubbard's Bounce
                                    Tudor's Dibo              Heinzl's Bambi
                         Boudreaux' Blind Billy
                                    Tudor's Minnie            Brown's Arizona Pete
                                                              Heinzl's Bambi
                Boudreaux' Scrub
                                    Boudreaux' Blind Billy    Tudor's Dibo
                         Boudreaux' Lena                      Tudor's Minnie
                                    Boudreaux' Red
                                                              Boudreaux' Blind Billy
        Boudreaux' Eli                                        Boudreaux Gypsy
                                    Tudor's Dibo              Hubbard's Bounce
                         Boudreaux' Blind Billy               Heinzl's Bambi
                                    Tudor's Minnie
                                                              Brown's Arizona Pete
                Boudreaux' Candy                              Heinzl's Bambi
                                    Harrell's Poor Boy        Hanson's Red Man
                         Sherrer's Tammie                     Barker's Roxana
                                    Harrell's Kilarney Kate   Cannon's Black Shine
                                                              Towdry's Linda
Bullyson
Eli, Jr.
Brendy
                                                              Tudor's Dibo
                         Boudreaux' Blind Billy               Tudor's Minnie
                Boudreaux' Scrub
                         Boudreaux' Lena                      Boudreaux' Blind Billy
                                                              Boudreaux' Red
        Boudreaux' Boze
                         Boudreaux' Rascal, Jr.               Trahan's Rascal
                Boudreaux' Kandee                             Boudreaux' Lena
                         Boudreaux' Gypsy                     Boudreaux' Blind Billy
                                                              Boudreaux' Polly
    Boudreaux' Spook
                         Barbee's Rocky                       Braddock's Sailor
                Kinard's Young Rock                           Corvino's Jett
                         Kinard's Frosty                      Braddock's Sailor
        Boudreaux' Penny                                      Tudor's Minnie
                         Boudreaux' Blind Billy               Tudor's Dibo
                Boudreaux' Peggy                              Tudor's Minnie
                         Sherrer's Tammie                     Harrell's Poor Boy
                                                              Harrell's Kilarney Kate
```

In selecting a dog to outcross with an inbred Pit Bull, you look Tudor's Dibo for a Pit Bull that is linebred off a dog that is somewhat related, or you look for a common ace two or three generations back. In this manner you can increase size and vigor, while at the same time maintain the qualities you have inbred, a process called hybrid vigor. This method is used with vegetables - corn, for example. Let's look at an illustration of what I would consider an ideal outcross. In the "Combat Dog" chapter, you will find the record of a modern-day pit fight that lasted three hours and forty-five minutes. The match has been said to be as good, probably better, than any of the famous old-time matches. One dog, Homer, died dead game. He crawled to make his last scratch. He fought just about the whole fight as a down dog, overcome by the stronger, more aggressive Jeep. Yet he put up one heck of a fight and would have stopped a lesser dog than Jeep, whether the dog were stronger or not. Well, Let's look at his pedigree.

	Lonzo's Andy	McCraw's Snowball
		Johnson's Black Lil
Greenwood's Oakie	Lonzo's Fay	Orday's Smokey
		Orday's Jet
Ch. Homer	Grider's Bobby Boy	Davenport's Spike
		Kennedy's Spring
Greenwood's Ms. Holladay	Grider's Chatter	Clayton's Eli, Jr.
		Boudreaux' Spook

Does any of the blood look familiar? This dog is an outcross. Lonzo's Andy is strong Dibo blood. (Snowball is son of Dibo.) Lonzo's Fay is Colby Dime linebred (through both Orday's Smokey and through Jet). On Homer's bottom side you see Bullyson's brother Eli, Jr. bred back to his mother. But now look at Zebo's pedigree earlier in this book. Notice the similarities with Lonzo's Andy and Fay. I would suggest that an inbred female out of Oakie or Zebo should nick real well with Homer. (By the way. Homer has two brothers, Freddie and Mountain Boy, that also earned championships - and in different states with different owners. His brothers do not look at all like him; they look more Boudreaux.) Zebo, as you can see, is linebred McCraw's Snowball, while Oakie has similar breeding and contains inbreeding on the Boudreaux line. The similar breeding, however, is far enough back so that, to me, it is still an outcross, not line-breeding. The blood should nick while at the same time producing some hybrid vigor. I don't know if there are any pups out of Homer or not; I just used these pedigrees to illustrate good breeding techniques.

Actually a proven male with characteristics you desire should be bred to several females to see who he nicks real well with. If you'll recall, when I related the successful plan of the King Ranch, their star Quarter Horse was bred to 50 females. Many breeders have a very large yard. For a combat dog, it is practically a necessity. The male is bred to several females and the best retained from the litters. In this manner you can ascertain which breedings nick. The combat dog breeders always prove their Pit Bulls before mating, but some will prove only the males because the test for gameness is pretty rigorous and they are afraid to subject their breeding females to such stress. To develop the gamest strain, it is really better to prove both the male and the female.

Swinson's Zebo (son of Johnson's Zebo) at three months old. He likes to play on top of his dog house.

Although I do feel that periodic/selective outcrossing should be done, I am of the opinion that this process of filial degeneration that is so pronounced with inbreeding can be overcome by hard-nosed selective inbreeding in which you retain and breed only the best in each litter.

Well, if all this sounds complicated, that's only because it is. Let me summarize what I've said and make some comments, and then we'll look at a sample of pedigree analysis by looking at Morochito's pedigree.

1. You should begin by reading as much as you can about breeders and dogs, fortifying yourself with as much background knowledge as possible. Don't listen to the advice of unsuccessful breeders. Listen to winners.

2. You study a pedigree from right to left, determining the key foundation dogs. Combat dogs should have proven parents. An outcross should be made to dogs with the same foundation.

3. Successful breeding is more likely to be accomplished by line-breeding because it is the best way you can control the characteristics of the progeny. Otherwise it is a hit-or-miss proposition that results in a miss more often than not.

4. Linebreeding should be done "selectively," that is by mating dogs that are linebred off common dogs who have the characteristics you most admire and desire. The more often the central animal you are linebreeding from appears in the pedigree, and the closer that animal is to the puppy, the higher the likelihood that the puppy will have the characteristics of that animal. Linebreed consistently to the best dog in the pedigree until a better one occurs, then line-breed to that one.

5. The low quality animals in the pedigree also play a role in the pup's character, which is strengthened by having as few as possible unproven dogs in the pedigree.

6. Linebreeding means that the desirable characteristics of ancestors are brought out to a higher degree - but so are the undesirable ones. In other words, although correct, selective linebreeding can bring success quicker and with more certainty than merely breeding "best to best" without regard to pedigree, linebreeding done incorrectly can also result in more inferior dogs quicker and more consistently than mere hit-or-miss. Breeding "best to best" without regard to pedigree has at times resulted in some fantastic Pit Bulls, but that fact should not form the basis for a breeder to continue the practice because success is still less likely than with thoroughly planned breeding.

7. The good and bad aspects of linebreeding are intensified by inbreeding. Brother/sister matings, where both have a good air, at least fair bite, gameness, and ability, will sometimes produce pups as good or better than their parents and intensify the characteristics. The mating of grandsons or granddaughters to the grandparent strongest in the desired characteristics, highly strengthens those characteristics and the practice has produced excellent Pit Bulls. The most popular inbreeding practice, however, has been daughter to father (double cross) and, if a female from this litter turns out good, breeding her back to the father again (triple cross).

8. Continuous inbreeding will tend to result, over a period of time (generally after three matings), in a reduction in size, lowered fertility, and loss of vigor. This is because of the tendency of a strain to revert toward the average, a process called filial degeneration, or drag. It is my contention, however, that highly selective inbreeding circumvents this tendency and can result in improving size and vigor while maintaining the gameness of the strain, provided the foundation dogs have a minimum of faults. This can be accomplished by selecting only the best animals from the inbred litter to breed again to the pick of other litters, perhaps an aunt or uncle, and culling those that are inferior. Sometimes an entire litter may prove to be inferior. If the pedigree is sound, be patient, keep breeding. Line-breeding takes longer than inbreeding, but inbreeding entails more ruthless culling.

9. "Hybrid vigor" can be established by outcrossing (mating one strain with another). The best outcross, however, selects a strain that does have common high performers about four or five generations back.

10. I think most Pit Bull/Staf breeders will disagree, but I believe that an occasional outcross from a Pit Bull strain to a quality Staf line that has beautiful conformation can result in "hybrid vigor" without losing gameness. You may not have game dogs in the first generation, but I think if you breed back to the Pit Bull line you will regain the gameness quickly. By the same token, I feel that an occasional outcross from a Staf line that has been bred for show, to a proven Pit Bull will increase the gameness without losing the conformation if successive breedings are selected for the desired conformation. Stated another way, I believe Stafs are a lot gamer than they are given credit for, and Pit Bulls are a lot prettier than they are given credit for.

I think the success of the King Ranch's breeding program should be seriously considered.

11. It's been said that it's not necessarily the ace dog you breed to – it's the parent that produced him; and grandparents are said to contribute more to a pup's characteristics than immediate parents. It is better to have four good grandparents than one ace parent. The influence of a single Pit Bull beyond grandparent, however, is pretty thin. The best policy is to be very particular. Breed to an ace dog with proven parents and four proven grandparents - if you can find one. A male should be bred to several females to see which he is best able to pass his strong characteristics on through, that is which females he nicks best with.

12. Don't credit your own Pit Bulls with virtues they don't possess. Self-deceit is one of the biggest stepping stones toward failure, and objectivity is difficult to obtain.

13. Don't assess the worth of a Pit Bull by its inferior progeny. All Pit Bulls will produce low quality at times. What matters is how well their best performers do.

14. Considering the fact that inbreeding is the strongest "planned" program but results in filial degeneration over a period of time and that outcrossing produces hybrid vigor while linebreeding is a compromise between inbreeding and outcross - I suggest the following breeding program:

Inbreed from the best, most prepotent ace you can find. Inbreed by breeding daughter to father for at least a triple cross, but discard whole litters if you don't find what you want, and try again. Each daughter that is bred back to the father should possess, as close as possible, the characteristics you desire. Be very selective and patient. After the triple cross, outcross to an ace - preferably one that has a related dog (a good one) four or five generations back (which to me is not really linebreeding): then linebreed back to the original animal until you get a better one. When you get a superlative dog, begin the inbreeding again. When you outcross, the male should be the inbred dog, the female the outcross. Outcross to as many proven females as you have the money, time, and facilities for and begin linebreeding back to your original dog only when you have found an outcross that nicks well. The reason I believe the "out-cross" should be "distantly related" is that, in my opinion, a completely outcrossed dog stands a chance of destroying the foundation you have built up (especially if the dog is prepotent). Such an out-cross may work out for a couple of generations, but not in the long run because undesirables from the outcross will slip in. (Every dog has some somewhere in the pedigree.) In other words, the extensive "selective inbreeding" you've built up might be bred out in spite of the individual greatness of the outcross.

We now come to the illustration of a pedigree analysis. We'll use Morochito's pedigree looking at his strengths and weaknesses so far as my goals are concerned, and consider possible breedings. Let me begin by saying that one very important prerequisite in analyzing your own dog's pedigree is objectivity. This is very difficult to achieve. It is very natural for you to be proud of your own dog. If you happen to have a Pit Bull that is above average, or exceptional in one particular - say conformation and overall beauty, or, for example, gameness - there is a tendency to see that dog as being super in all areas - ability, intelligence, conformation, gameness, hard bite, etc. It is a natural human tendency phycologists call the halo effect.

```
                                Colby's Dime          Colby's Tweedie
                      Colby's Texas                   Colby's Penny
                                Colby's Margie        Colby's Rifle
            Loposay's Rusty                           Colby's Gypsy
                                Colby's Texas         Colby's Dime
                      Burkette's Dutch                Colby's Margie
                                Loposay's Monkey      Munday's Grit
      Loposay's Dubs                                  Faris' Red Pepper
                                Colby's Morgan        Colby's Dime
                      Colby's Barney                  Alex. Colby's Tibbie
                                Colby's Maggie        Colby's Old Yellar
            Colby's Chita                             Freeman's Susie
                                Colby's Dime          Colby's Tweedie
                      Colby's Jenny                   Colby's Penny
                                Alex. Colby's Tibbie  Colby's Rifle
Lancaster's Troubles                                  Colby's Connie
                                Loposay's Bullet      Teal's Jake
                      Loposay's Colonel               Loposay's Betty
                                Loposay's Tiger Lilly Loposay's Ace
            Watkins Bull Winkle                       Burkette's Dutch
                                Lonzo's Andy          McCraw's Snowball
                      Greg's Lady                     Johnson's Black Lil
                                Lonzo's Fay           Orday's Smokey
      Lancaster's Lady                                Orday's Jet
                                Loposay's Rusty       Colby's Texas
                      Loposay's Boe                   Burkette's Dutch
                                Colby's Chita         Colby's Barney
            Loposay's Pam                             Colby's Jenny
                                Loposay's Diamond     Colby's Tinker II
                      Loposay's Sylvia                Burkette's Dutch
                                Burkette's Dutch      Colby's Texas
                                                      Loposay's Monkey

                      Captain's Mistress' Father
```

```
                                                    Tudor's Dibo
                           Tudor's Jeff             Gordon's Lady
              Orday's Rol Andow                     Tudor's Black Toddy
                           Tudor's Coffee           Townsend's Pinkie
Loposay's Bully                                     Trahan's Pete
                           Shire's Buster           McCloud's Dinah
              Orday's Pat                           Clavelle's Pimple
                           Trahan's Beauty          Trahan's Cynthia
Sykes' Bull                                         Colby's Texas
                           Loposay's Rusty          Burkette's Dutch
              Loposay's Boe                         Colby's Barney
                           Colby's Chita            Colby's Jenny
Loposay's Hannabell                                 Colby's Tinker II
                           Loposay's Diamond        Burkette's Dutch
              Loposay's Sylvia                      Colby's Texas
                           Burkette's Dutch         Loposay's Monkey
:mith's Lady                                        Tudor's Dibo
                           McCraw's Snowball        Maness' Cissie
              Beal's Powhatan                       Conklin's Mohawk
                           Red Lady                 Beal's Princess
Henley's Big Boy                                    McCraw's Snowball
                           Lonzo's Andy             Johnson's Black Lil
              Greg's Lady                           Orday's Smokey
                           Lonzo's Fay              Orday's Jet
Harris' Lady                                        Colby's Texas
                           Loposay's Rusty          Burkette's Dutch
              Loposay's Boe                         Colby's Barney
                           Colby's Chita            Colby's Jenny
Loposay's Hazel                                     Teal's Jake
                           Loposay's Bullet         Loposay's Betty
              Loposay's Dolly                       Loposay's Ace
                           Loposay's Tiger Lilly    Burkette's Dutch

                    Captain's Mistress' Mother
```

As I mentioned, you begin the study of a pedigree by looking at the foundation dogs, which are very strong with Morochito on both sides. His mother, shown as Captain's Mistress, is nicknamed "Missy," which is how we'll refer to her from here on. I particularly like Missy's breeding, so we'll study it first. I was extremely impressed when I read an article Howard Heinzl wrote in the *Pit Bull Sheet*, September/ October, 1978, in which he made the statement that he would take Colby Dime over any other dog he ever owned - and Howard has owned or bred to probably the best foundation stock in the country. Dibo, you recall, as well as many others, came from his yard. You may remember from the historical chapter, that Colby Dime is linebred off Colby's Galtie, who was imported from Ireland. John Colby had only one out-cross in 30 years of breeding - he thought that much of his strain. Actually I have heard that a few of the old-timers maintain that the Colby strain is the only one that is pure Pit Bull. Anyway. -that one outcross Mr. Colby made was to the Galtie dog. He must have thought a lot of that lot of that dog to use him as his only outcross. Howard said he once saw Dime's father, Tweedie, in Mexico City and that he looked a lot like Galtie. Look at Morochito's sixth generation. Notice that his bottom side is almost exclusively Colby Dime or Dime's grandfather. Rifle. Colby's Barney and Jenny are both Colby Dime, as are Orday's Smokey and Jet. Okay, let's follow some of the pedigrees down. Colby's Texas is very well bred because he is a son of Colby Dime and his mother is a daughter of Colby's Rifle and nearly as good a producer as Dime. Burkette's Dutch, a proven producer, is a daughter of Colby's Texas and Loposay's Monkey. I'm not sure about Loposay's Monkey, but I think she was Colby bred. I do know she was one heck of a good Pit Bull. She was just a little thing. I was told that one day a man brought his Pit Bull to the yard where Monkey was, a fairly big yard with some top quality fighting dogs. He wanted to try out his Pit Bull - a reasonably large female - to see how good she was. The owner of the yard suggested a female that was of equal weight, but the guy, not wanting to destroy his dog's confidence, wanted a smaller dog. He pointed to Monkey and asked if he could use that little one. The owner said, "No, you don't want to put that Pit Bull on her," but the guy insisted, so the owner said okay but that he wouldn't be responsible. Well, that little Monkey was a whirlwind. The bigger Pit Bull never got a hold on her and Monkey threw her all over the place. Monkey was extremely strong for her size and was very game. She also had a lot of wrestling ability. She would grab a dog, even one bigger than she, get an ear or other head hold, and twist and throw her opponent to the ground - hard. Her owner said that she threw that Pit Bull down so hard, with such a large thud, that they were afraid she'd broken the Pit Bull's shoulder. When you read about Pit Bulls being able to defeat much larger dogs of other breeds, the reason most often cited is gameness - the other dog will quit, even if it's winning, as soon as Mr. Pit Bull latches down on him with those punishing Pit Bull jaws. As I mentioned in the introduction, I believe a lot of that gameness is due to the fact that the Pit Bull is inherently able to withstand so much more pain when in a combat situation. What I'd like to bring out here, however is another factor - ability. Through centuries of selective breeding through a strain built for fighting to begin with, the Pit Bull has an instinctive sense of leverage, timing, and combat moves that other breeds do not have. Naturally some Pit Bulls have more ability than others. If you were to watch a match for the first time, you'd probably be impressed with the strategy and maneuvers some of these Pit Bulls are capable of. Like Monkey, many of them can literally throw an opponent over their own shoulder, much like a human judo player. In any event, getting back to Monkey, she had two desirable traits that you do not generally find in combination - strength and ability. I particularly like, as a personal matter, the strength. I believe if you keep breeding gameness and strength, the ability will eventually show up - in combination with gameness and strength. You then have your ace. Monkey has been bred many times so I gather she is a proven producer. Burkette's Dutch (Colby's Texas and Monkey), by the way, appears twice in Finley's Bo's pedigree - third generation, we'll look at Finley's Bo later on. A lot of people liked Monkey. You'll notice she appears many times in Missy's pedigree, both top and bottom. I believe that mating of Monkey and Colby's Texas was a good one. Okay, let's follow the line up closer. Missy's grandfather, top side, was Loposay's Dubs — another plus for-

Morochito. That's fairly close to him. Dubs was a litter brother of Jeep's grandfather! As you may recall, Jeep is one of the more popular stud dogs around, since his retirement from a magnificent fighting career. His match recorded in the "Combat Dog" chapter is said by many to be the best of modern times. Notice that Dubs is linebred Colby Dime and Rifle, and that Loposay's Monkey is in there. By the way, Colby's Barney (grandson of Colby's Dime) and Colby's Jenny (daughter of Colby's Dime) were both excellent producers. Going down below Dubs, you find Bull Winkle who would be considered by many to be a weakness in a pedigree - but not by me. Bull Winkle was himself an awesome dog. He was a large catchweight dog that never met his match. He is said to have been a poor producer, however, since many curs came from him. As is usually the case, there is disagreement about that because there are a few that really like his blood. My position is this - I wouldn't line-breed from him, but I like the idea that he appears once in Morochito's pedigree fairly close. His bottom side is Lonzo's Andy and Fay - very similar to Zebo. His top side is the very best of original Loposay breeding. Mr. Loposay (now dead - his wife has carried on his line and sells dogs all over the country) began his line with probably the last of the good old Colby blood and Colonel was one of Loposay's best producers. Mr. Arrison of Illinois has some Bull Winkle breeding which is of interest to us here. Arrison's Fraser is a proven producer. His father is Bull Winkle and his mother is Bull Winkle's litter sister. Fraser was bred to Arrison's Missy (litter sister to Morochito's father Rip) and produced a dog named Big Boy (not to be confused with Henley's Big Boy in Missy's pedigree). This Big Boy won three contract matches, taking "Best in Show" at the only large convention he appeared in. At that convention one of the most respected of the old-timers that viewed the match made the statement that Big Boy is "one of the best 43-pounders that I've seen in several years." This indicates to me that Bull Winkle's blood can be excellent, especially when bred into Morochito's father Rip's blood. In Morochito's pedigree Bull Winkle was bred to Loposay's Pam. I believe she was unproven, used only for breeding, but I like her blood. She was a litter sister to Loposay's Hannabell, who, as we will see, was dead game. Pam's father is Loposay's Boe - litter brother to Loposay's Dubs (grandfather to Jeep and great grandfather to Morochito) that we've already looked at. Pam's mother is Loposay's Sylvia, a really dynamite producer, very popular. I saw Slyvia shortly before she died. The mating of Bull Winkle and Pam produced Lancaster's Lady. I don't know a thing about her, so she is, as far as I know, unproven - somewhat of a weakness. She is part of a planned pedigree, however, that is very pleasing to me. By mating her to Loposay's Dubs, the excellent producing Colby blood was intensified.

Missy's father, Troubles, was never fought, but he tested game and was a hard biter. He was, however, a people biter and his owner said he had to shoot him when he came after him once - another potential weakness. That does not bother me very much either, though, because I feel that this particular owner is pretty rough on his dogs and early rough treatment as a pup may have been the reason for Troubles' behavior. This may, in fact, be a plus in my book, because if the mean temperament was due to rough treatment, the dog responded aggressively instead of being made into a shy, cowering dog, which is the usual result. This type of blood would be excellent for Schutzhund training (assuming, of course, proper handling). Since my goal is to have a strain of game, proven Pit Bulls with the intelligence and temperament necessary to be highly competent at Schutzhund trials. Troubles' breeding seems to be excellent because I think I am right in my postulations. Morochito's temperament, as we will look into in more depth following his pedigree analysis, seems to me nearly ideal for Schutzhund.

Now let's look at Missy's bottom side. I believe you can see some excellent, planned breeding here. In the sixth generation you see the same Colby blood as you do on Missy's top side, with a splash of Dibo - a bit more Dibo on the bottom side. Let's skip ahead to the third generation. This is in line with Loposay's Dubs on Missy's top side. We see Sykes' Bull, another large catchweight dog that never met his equal. He was very popular and won many matches. One of the top dog men in the country started his strain with this dog, but eventually gave up on it because it didn't produce. Here we have a situation analogous to Bull Winkle. Sykes' Bull has produced some darn good ones, his son Sampson being the best. Sampson was, in his owner's opinion, better than Bull and was the best heavyweight dog he'd ever seen. Sampson was confiscated in a raid after he had won $2,000 in a hard fought match. He died from lack of treatment in the "humane" dog shelter that night. It was either Sampson or, I believe. Bull (I forget which) that won a game match under the following conditions. He was in keep (training) for a match and was being exercised on a catmill. (See the chapter on conditioning.) One of the drawbacks of a catmill is that the dog can wear a track in the ground and when it rains it gets real muddy. Well, as luck would have it, it rained fairly heavily during Bull's keep ana the cotmill track was full of water and he wouldn't run in it. His owner, after waiting almost a week with practically no conditioning, shipped him to a man who would put him in shape. Bull was then exercised on a treadmill, but not properly. When his owner got him back, the pads of his feet were cut up and bloody from running the treadmill. (My vet informed me that one of the most pain-sensitive areas on a dog are the pads of his feet. Morochito got a cut on his hind foot when doing roadwork with me one time (on glass I think) and it took a good while for it to heal. We both thought he'd never get better and ready to hit the road again!) Anyway, Bull's owner went ahead and matched him anyway, for a pretty good sum of money. Bull made a mess of his opponent and won the match when the owner of his opponent conceded. Bull would probably have killed the dog if the match hadn't been stopped. Naturally I think Sykes' Bull, then, is another plus for Morochito, contributing to his size and strength and overall effectiveness. There is the question, again, of gameness, however. I do know that there have been some successful matings of Sykes' Bull progeny with Bull Winkle's progeny, so evidently that blood nicks fairly well. Bull is well bred on his top side – Tudor's Jeff (son of Dibo and just as illustrious a producer). Jeff was one of Dibo's larger sons and the largest pup in his litter. Bull's mother Hannabell was a dead game bitch, a big plus. She was linebred Colby Dime and her father was Loposay's Boe. If you recall, Boe is also in Missy's father's blood, and was a good pit dog; I believe he won two good matches and a large number of back-yard rolls. This makes Missy linebred Loposay's Boe through proven, high performers. Hannabel, you recall, is a litter sister to the Pam in Troubles' blood. So you see, there are a number of tie-ins here so that the mating of Troubles and Smith's Lady must have been a good one. Further down in Lady's pedigree is Big Boy - another large Pit Bull about whom we've already gone into detail. This would also be considered by many a weakness in a pedigree (not a producer of game dogs). You might notice that Big Boy's mother (Greg's Lady) is also the mother of Bull Winkle (on Missy's top side) - so these two dogs are half brothers. Greg's Lady is a half sister to Zebo, Vindicator, and Rosie. Below Big Boy, you see Loposay's Boe again! Boe was mated to Loposay's Dolly who is a litter sister to Bull Winkle's father! Dolly, by the way, is a sister to Jeep's grandmother Loposay's Dot. So you see, you might say Morochito is pretty linebred on his mother's side (on both top and bottom of mother) from the same blood that produced the top side of Jeep.

This completes the analysis of the pedigree of Morochito's mother. We will return to it with an objective appraisal summarization of its strengths and weaknesses following an analysis of the pedigree of Morochito's father, Rip, which appears below.

Carver's Tiger Jack	Carver's Rascal III	Boudreaux' Rascal
		Carver's Maggie
	Carver's Speedy	Hernandez' Nigger
Lancaster's Rip		Bates' Susie
	Lightner's Roughhouse	Lightner's Danny Boy
Shiver's Beanie		Lightner's June II
	Skinner's Rody	Cotton's Bullet
		Sparks' Haley's Comet

As before, we begin as far to the right as we can. Looking at the top side of Rip – Carver's Tiger Jack - all that blood traces back to Trahan's Rascal (Dibo's half brother and just as illustrious a producer). In fact, Tiger Jack was the purest Rascal-bred dog of of his time - and that really pleases me. Rare blood. Carver's Maggie was a full sister to Elias' Pistol who sired Carver's Pistol who was the father of the famous Davis' Champion Boomerang. What better foundation blood can you get! Rip may appear to be an out-cross, but actually he is a result of planned linebreeding. Cotton's Bullet you see was a grandson of Rascal and one of the best, if not the best, producers of Rascal's progeny. There are some people that feel Bullet is the best blood on the east coast. He was a people biter, but has not tended to produce people biters. As a pit fighter he was a hard biter and a real finisher. Now watch this - the Rascal blood is mixed with the very best of Lightner blood. In fact I do not personally know of any purer or better quality blood than Lightner Roughhouse. This dog was a triple cross off Lightner's Citation, who was an undefeated 42-pound champion and about 95% pure Lightner -that goes right back to Lloyd's Pilot. (See "History" chapter.) I counted Citation 14 times in Roughhouse's pedigree. Citation's father (separate from Citation) 12 times, and Citation's mother (separate from Citation) 3 times. Roughhouse was never matched but he died game in an accidental fight in his yard when he got loose. He was an old dog at the time. Roughhouse was bred to Rody to get Beanie. Rody, daughter of Cotton's Bullet was a litter sister to a very popular dog, Kinard's Sad Sack. The same litter produced Teal's Tip, Teal's Doc, Teal's Spud, and Teal's Susie - all good Pit Bulls. When a mating produces that many good dogs, it's excellent blood. Now get this – Rody's mother, Sparks' Haley's Comet is a granddaughter of Lightner's Roughhouse! The late Mr. Loposay called Beanie the best brood bitch he'd ever owned. She was fairly game and an aggressive little fighter. This breeding by the way (Tiger Jack, Beanie, Bullet) produced Arrison's Doc, a dog that fought on the bottom for 50 minutes before coming to the top to win over his opponent who had previously beaten the popular Ch. Red Danger. Doc was awarded "Best in Show" honors at that match. (Footnote: Much of my information on these dogs appears in Mr. Arrison's stud fee advertisement in *Sporting Dog Journal*.)

That brings us to Tiger Jack himself. He was a darn good pit dog in his prime. He lost favor with many dog men, however, because in his last match, when he was pretty old - really too old to match - he quit. He was matched against a young, strong, aggressive Pit Bull that punished his stifle badly. Tiger Jack fought a pretty good while but finally quit and jumped the pit. You really couldn't blame the old dog, and it was the only time he curred out. Still, it does indicate that he was not dead game - another potential weakness in the gameness aspect. I saw a nine-year-old dog fight for 40 minutes one time and he lost the last of his fangs at 35 minutes. He kept right on fighting like nobody's business, tail up and wagging away to beat the band. He was fighting a young dog who was fighting his first match, really a schooling match. The young dog was a real hard biter, who was later to fight a very hard match against a dog named Zeus. (He tore the skin right off the side of Zeus' head and some experienced men there said he was the best ear dog they'd ever seen. By the way, Zeus completely grew back his skin and fur and is presently as good as new; he hardly looks marked up.) Anyway, getting back to the old dog's fight, his owner conceded the match after his dog fought for about five minutes with no teeth, proving his gameness. He was then allowed a courtesy scratch. (You face the dogs in the pit, release the dog who has lost and see if he crosses the pit and attempts to fight. You pick up his opponent at the last minute.) The old dog's tail was still up and he scratched hard. He was as brave as could be. He had been passed around to several owners, had been set down many times, and had been fought several times against dogs much bigger than he, and he had never quit. He was never owned by a real competent pit man and his breeding was questionable and mixed so he probably couldn't pass on anything. A great dog, I think, that no one ever heard of. That was his last of many matches before he retired to his yard. Anyway Tiger Jack didn't have that kind of gameness. One thing about Tiger Jack, however - he was a darn good producer. The best aspect of Tiger Jack and Beanie was their mating - their blood nicked. Every dog in the litter turned out real well and at least two that I know of were good producere.

Most of the dog men in this area prefer the top side of Morochito's pedigree; Morochito's father. Rip was a hellacious fighter. He killed two dogs in his yard when they got loose and went after him. The dog that is tied up is at a distinct disadvantage, by the way. Rip was never matched because he injured his front foot in a roll when he was real young and could not be properly conditioned. He was rolled many times, however, and looked real good. One man said he was the best he'd ever seen. His owner eventually gave him away, however, because he began to turn a lot. Some experienced dog men informed me that he may have developed a habit of turning because he was involved in so many short rolls. (He generally made a mess of his opponent very quickly and his opponent's owner would break them.) Evidently, rolling a dog too often without letting him go the distance can establish a pattern, to the dog, of short fights, and he may start turning. In any event, his owner considered it a sign of possibly thinking about quitting, so he gave him away. Rip died a year later because he wasn't provided with heartworm medicine (a must in this area) and he contracted a terminal case of heartworms. My dog's half brother, Butch, a son of Rip, has been quite popular, although he's been criticized because he turns a lot, like his father. I don't know why he does that, but he comes out of his corner, scratching very hard. He'll knock a Pit Bull clear across the pit and slam him into a side wall. He fights in hard flurries; then he'll rest awhile. His critics have said that he turns because he has quitting somewhere in his mind. He has never actually quit, however, and has won all his fights. He has been fought a large number of off-the-chain (not been conditioned) backyard rolls, some of them long enough to be the equivalent of a match. Although large dogs don't usually have the staying power of smaller ones, Butch, with a pit weight of 55-56 pounds, is an excellent pacer, and his endurance is unbelievable. When he won his second contract match, he was missing one of his top fang teeth, a definite liability. He won, however, in half an hour, when his opponent's owner conceded the match. After the match, his head stayed up and he acted as lively and playful as if he had just been playing fetch with his master (a very unusual thing to see after a pit contest; the dogs are generally exhausted and weak from loss of fluid). When I went to see him the next day, he was energetically playing with a garden hose in his pen, pulling and shaking it. He wouldn't let it go when I went over to play with him. His championship was won over a dog backed by the owner and publisher of the pit dog magazine, Morochito's half brother Butch, *Sporting Dog Journal*. The dog was supposed to be a good one. Butch lost two fang teeth by the 20-minute mark, and continued with virtually no teeth until his opponent finally had had enough and quit in 48 minutes. Butch is now retired to stud, a champion. He's pretty mixed bred and I know nothing about the breeding on his mother's side, although the breeder of his mother has had some excellent Colby Dime dogs, so I suspect that his mother is bred that way. At the time of this writing I haven't found out, but I do intend to because it would indicate that Colby Dime and Rip's blood nicks well.

Morochito's half brother Butch

I should mention another plus for Morochito's pedigree. Rip's brother is a dog named Obnoxious Ox. He is retired to stud, at the time of this writing, in the yard of Mrs. Loposay in North Carolina. Ox was an awesome fighter that thinks style is something you eat, and gameness is something you eventually demolish. His most famous fight was when he beat Wood's (Brewer's) Snooty in an hour and 38 minutes. They had to pick Snooty up or Ox would have killed him right there in the pit. At the time Snooty was conditioned and handled by a man who is considered to be one of the best in the country. I must add that Ox was conditioned by an equally competent man. Snooty is a grandson of Carver's Ironhead. and his grandmother is Miss Spike on both his top and bottom. Snooty's blood is one of the most popular in the country.

The last step in the pedigree analysis is to find out what I can about Morochito's littermates. One brother, the one that looked most like Morochito, was quite easy-going around other dogs until he was around nine months old. Until that time he ran loose in his yard and would play with other dogs. One day, a female in heat came over to visit, and a large English Bulldog, much larger than the Pit Bull pup, picked a fight over the female. The Pit Bull killed the Bulldog, making a gory mess that I wouldn't care to describe. He was uncontrollable around other dogs after that, so his owners sold him to a man who fights them. When he became of age, he was rolled against another young, inexperienced Pit Bull and did very well, overpowering the other dog. He was rolled a second time with the same results. His owner then decided to test his gameness with an older, experienced Pit Bull that had won a contract match and was a veteran of many backyard rolls. Morochito's brother tore him up and at ten minutes had to be pulled off. He was then sold again and I lost track of him. He is, at the least, a good dog.

One sister was a grey brindle that favored her father Rip in appearance. Until she was around three months old, she was a firecracker, one of the more aggressive pups. At that time, however, she became very shy and cringing in her attitude toward people. I believe she must have had some sort of an accident in her yard, maybe someone inadvertently stepped on her. As I mentioned in the "Pet" chapter, sometimes a pup can be ruined by some small, unnoticed incident at an impressionable age. The pup was sold to a family in the country and although I never saw her again, I spoke to a friend of the new owners and he said the Pit Bull had become outgoing and friendly again. This leads me to believe that she did not inherit a shy trait.

Another of Morochito's brothers, Jake, a buckskin like half brother Butch, was the runt of the litter, although he grew to be taller than Morochito but is not so muscular. He's a combat dog with a pit weight of 53 pounds - a pretty big dog. Jake was a very shy, cowering pup and although he was very pretty, he didn't appeal to me because he seemed to be the least game. He still has a shy personality but he's a very game fighter that has been severely game tested, including a two-dog test (matched against a dog of equal caliber- and then, when he's good and tired and weak from loss of fluid, matched against a second, fresh dog). Jake was two-dogged on his first test, not a recommended way to test because it can turn a good dog into a cur. When he went for this test, he had never been exercised, never even been off his chain in the backyard. Also, he was full of heartworms and was so lethargic that he didn't pull on his leash but just slowly walked up the hill to where the pit was located. Yet he didn't show tired while fighting although his first opponent did. He hit that dog so hard the dog kept wheezing. By the way, on the way up the hill that first dog jumped up and nabbed a chicken that was roosting about shoulder high on a tree limb. Jake's second opponent was a hard biter but Jake easily outmaneuvered both dogs and didn't show any lack of gameness or enthusiasm. Jake was tried and schooled several times -once against a very hard biter - and he showed game every time. In 1980 at the age of about three and a half, Jake had his first contract match at 53 pounds. Jake's opponent was a one-time winner. Jake won the match decisively in 48 minutes. The dogs were equal weight and equal in height. Jake, however, was the stronger dog, had superior wrestling ability, and was by far the harder biter. Jake's opponent, a black dog named Scooter, was a game dog, but Jake gave him little chance to get a good hold. He scratched very hard, slamming Scooter to the floor and burying deep into his chest. At 48 minutes it was Scooter's turn to scratch - he took two steps toward Jake and collapsed in his corner. He had received much more damaging punishment than his owner realized and died the next day. The phenomenal thing about the match was that Jake still had heartworms, although obviously not a bad infection! The vet had informed the owner that his heartworm condition was such that he could possibly be cured if he were given a poisonous medicine that would kill the worms - but quite possibly would kill Jake in the process. Jake's owner decided to match him one time before he gave him the poison that might end his life. I think that when a Pit Bull goes out, he'd rather go in a match than from a bottle of poison. (I know I would.) When Jake healed from the match he was given the medicine and he survived. He was then rolled several times to see if anything had been taken out of him - it hadn't been. He curred out several Pit Bulls just in the roll. He can put a hole in a dog's head that you can stick your little finger into. He out-maneuvered a four-time winner in a short five-minute roll.

    In December, 1981, when he was nearly five years old, Jake had his second contract match, again at 53 pounds. His opponent was a large black Pit Bull named Gabby. Now Gabby was a two-time winner and had an excellent reputation. He was a very game dog with superior wrestling ability. He didn't have a very hard bite, but he won by out-maneuvering his opponents and outlasting them. He was a good ear dog (very frustrating to an opponent) and what is called a hold-out artist. (He paces himself very well, laying back in holds and resting and then pouring it on in flurries.) Many of the people on Jake's side morally pulled for Jake to win - but bet on Gabby, proclaiming that they hoped Jake would win but their pocketbooks forced them to bet on the winning dog. Others were loyal to Jake, betting on the dog they liked, but expressed concern that he would probably lose. Jake, you see, like half brother Butch, is somewhat of a hold-out artist himself. He often appears weak with his opponent, lying on his back, resting. When he's ready, he flips over and jerks free of holds and dives in - all in one fluid, beautiful movement. After half an hour of fighting he generally looks pretty weak. It was felt that if he couldn't stop a dog of Gabby's caliber in half an hour, he would be too weak to sufficiently damage Gabby, and Gabby, known for his endurance, would surely outlast him. The match was attended by some well known veterans of the Pit Bull sport, including the editor of *Sporting Dog Journal*. It did not go at all the way it was predicted. Both dogs weighed in right on 53 pounds. Gabby, however, was a good inch taller than Jake, even though Jake is a rangy dog, tall himself for 53 pounds. Gabby was in excellent shape, having been conditioned by two men that are known to have excellent experience. From the very beginning, Gabby dominated the match. Jake had shown himself to be a strong dog - but Gabby was stronger. In the first five minutes, Gabby opened up Jake's leg, coming close to hitting a bleeder, and for the remainder of the match Jake stumbled on that leg. Jake was continually burying himself in Gabby's chest - but he didn't appear to be doing as much damage - not biting as hard as he had been known to heretofore. Gabby always seemed to shake loose from the hold and get on Jake's ear, and they would circle around and around until Jake finally broke loose. Several times Gabby threw Jake to the floor, shaking out his hold. From time to time, Jake would get Gabby's leg and shake it out. At 45 minutes, the match could have been said to be even. Although Gabby had been top dog, Jake had done more damage - he just hadn't done enough. Gabby hadn't slowed down one bit and didn't seem hurt at all. Those who knew Jake felt like something was wrong with him. No one could understand why he wasn't biting harder. The first scratch was at around an hour and ten minutes - it was Jake's. He scratched hard - but stumbled on that leg. It then turned into a scratching contest, with Jake continuing to scratch straight and true, his legs scrambling, but he was still having difficulty with the injured one. At an hour and a half Jake had gone a lot longer than his backers had predicted, and the inevitable seemed to have materialized - the bite seemed to have been taken out of Jake and he looked too weak to continue. Gabby, in excellent condition, still seemed strong, although his tail dipped just a little (for the first time in the match). At an hour and 40 minutes, however, Jake suddenly barnstormed Gabby, shaking leg holds hard and burying deep into his chest. He bit harder than he had the whole match. At an hour and 48 minutes a turn was called on Gabby. He hesitated in his corner, slowly walked toward Jake, then turned and walked to the side as he was counted out. Gabby had gone longer times before, but this time he seemed very weak after Jake's last barrage. In any event he did cur out and his owner gave him away free to someone at pit side for a can of beer and six dollars. Gabby's owner didn't allow Jake a courtesy scratch, but Jake was ready to go. He struggled to get free of his handler when they carried Gabby away. Jake lost a tooth in that match. He's over five years old now, retired to stud. I'm proud to know that dog.

    Another of Morochito's littermates is a large red dog (like Morochito) named, would you believe, Godzilla. He was a pet until age 4 ½ when he was sold to a person in North Carolina. This fellow has been selling his dogs and buying and breeding every dog he can find with Morochito's bloodlines. (He owns Jake and their sister Brandy.) Godzilla was fat as a hog – I'm told he weighed over 70 pounds. His new owner began to gradually trim him down. When he got down to around 60 pounds, he rolled him with a large dog that is a fair pit dog and a hard biter. In five minutes, actually with his first hold, he broke that Pit Bull's leg. This is not hearsay - I saw the broken leg. The dog was taken to a vet and it was indeed broken. This may have been a freak accident, however, because Godzilla has not really turned out to be an especially hard biter. His owner tested his gameness by rolling him against three consecutive dogs, 15 minutes each for a total of 45 minutes, proving him game, probably dead game. All three were good dogs. Godzilla, however, did not bite especially hard in any of the battles nor did he display more than average ability. The important discovery, however, is the gameness. That's two dogs in the same litter that proved themselves, one by being two-dogged and the other by being three-dogged. Godzilla was matched into a two-time winner named Spike. Spike is an good a nose dog as you'll find and he beat Godzilla when Godzilla was picked up game at 49 minutes. Godzilla was allowed a courtesy scratch and he very weakly struggled across the pit. His owner sold him to one of the top breeders in the country, and the last I heard he was going to be sold to a man in Japan - to begin (to my knowledge) that country's first line of American Pit Bulls.

The other littermates were sold as very young puppies and I know nothing about them. The whole litter, however, seemed lively and healthy.

There is one final consideration – Morochito's gameness. When I completed this book, but before we typed it up, he had not been game tested. He had demonstrated ability and awesome bite when he met that 70-pound Pit Bull, but there was no contest and Morochito was not really put to the test. You might notice in the "Conditioning" chapter I have a picture of a treadmill and a wheel but no picture of a catmill. That's because of an accident that occurred one day when I decided to bring Morochito with me to get a picture where a gentleman I know of has a good catmill. There were several dogs in that yard and, on that particular day many well known Pit Bull fanciers were there. I wanted to show off my Morochito, interact with some Pit Bull people, and get some good pictures at the same time. Well, Morochito got loose as I was putting him on the mill and he ran into a one-time contract winner - a very strong nose and head dog. This dog was about four pounds lighter than Morochito, but was rangy so was just as tall. He was very strong. Morochito kept him on the defensive but on this particular day didn't bite like he had in his prior confrontation with a Pit Bull, nor did he demonstrate more than average ability. Also, his opponent was primarily a nose dog and Morochito had no experience with this style of fighter. Well I really don't want to go into any details, but Morochito inadvertently received a more than adequate gameness test that day.

The performances of Morochito and his litter brothers alleviate any concern I have over an unproven grandmother and two unproven great-grandmothers. It's hard to find pedigrees that do not have unproven females anyway.

Morochito's brother Jake has been bred to his litter sister Brandy twice. All of the pups were very well built (excellent conformation). Several dogs, male and female, have been tested from both litters. Every single one was very, very game but none of them demonstrated much ability at all and only average bite. One of them had an above average (but sporadic in his behavior) bite but also had poor ability. They were all willing to fight any dog set down in front or them, for as long as required to do so, and even when the dogs were older and bigger than they were. There was the little female that got loose as a puppy and lit into an older, experienced Pit Bull that was about twice her weight. She bit him very hard but was picked up when she got away from him. She wouldn't fight after that and was sold. I don't count that in my analysis of the gameness of this strain, though, because she was just a puppy.

Okay, that completes the overall analysis of Morochito's pedigree. The next step in a planned breeding program is to summarize your research information and make various incidental observations. By the way, I am suggesting that the potential breeder actually write down his program (including summary and incidental comments) in a manner similar to the analysis I am proposing here.

1. Morochito's foundation is excellent, on both sides. I wouldn't ask for any better. Morochito has proven that he is game and the brother-sister mating of Jake and Brandy produced very game dogs.

2. Morochito is an outcross, there being no relationship between his father's pedigree and his mother's. Should I decide to make Morochito central in my breeding program, I should make a determination as to which side – mother's or father's - I prefer, and look for something as close as possible to that to breed to. As I have mentioned, personally I like the breeding on his mother's side, so I should look for as pure an inbred Colby Dime bitch as I can find. I would breed her to Morochito and then breed daughter to father for a triple cross. When I outcross, I could breed back to something on his father's side later, because it should nick again.

3. Morochito is just the right size for me, and his conformation is right. I place more importance on that trait than most Pit Bull folk do. Most breeders are primarily concerned with gameness, but I want to breed for both gameness and conformation (including size). As I mentioned, I want Pit Bulls in the 50-pound range. I will discuss my reasons after this section. I think Morochito gets his size from the three large Pit Bulls that are up close – Sykes' Bull, Bull Winkle, and Bull Winkle's half brother, Big Boy. He also gets size from his father Rip, who was a 55-pound dog and produced Morochito's half brother Butch who has a conditioned weight of 55 pounds. I know of some linebreeding off both Sykes' Bull and Bull Winkle that I could breed into, but I'm concerned with the gameness aspect.

4. I like an athletic dog and a hard biter. Morochito probably gets his endurance from Rip's side. Morochito has a considerable number of hard biters in his mother's

pedigree. His father was no slouch as a biter. Morochito has a perfectly conformed neck – well muscled, hard, reasonably long. He got this from Rip - looks just like it. I have the personal opinion that a strong neck plays a part in that deep bite aspect. I say this because when I have seen biters at work, I've noticed that they do their number best when, after they've sunk in deep, they shake hard. Well, I notice those neck muscles play an important part. Of course, as mentioned in the introduction, hard biters bite hard because they want to. Still, I maintain that the Pit Bull that both wants to bite hard and has the muscularity to do it, will be the harder biter.

5. Although Morochito has several awesome Pit Bulls in his background and has an excellent, unique pedigree that pleases me greatly, his mother and grandmothers are unproven. His mother has been rolled, however, and looked good.

The next step in analyzing a pedigree is to list your goals and see how your analysis fits into them. My goals are as follows:

1. I want to be able to assume gameness. This is the basic Pit Bull characteristic, the most unique quality of the breed and must be preserved.

2. I want to develop a strain of Pit Bulls that are Schutzhund quality. Therefore, intelligence and trainability are important factors that I must consider.

3. I like my Pit Bulls to be in the 50-pound weight area and I'll tell you why. Those who want a Pit Bull for combat generally prefer the smaller lightweight dogs, who fight faster and longer and are easier to condition because they tend to have more endurance and enthusiasm for working. Although Pit Bulls as a breed have no standard size, I believe the smaller Pit Bulls are closer to the original. The foundation dogs in the U. S. were Lloyd's Pilot (28 pounds) and Calvin's Pup (38 pounds). However, there is no doubt that some of the big dogs in Morochito's pedigree were good, perhaps fantastic, fighting dogs, as were several other large Pit Bulls. Although fighting is not in my plans, I like the idea of having a big Pit Bull that's game and can take the little Pit Bull no matter how game he is. It is more difficult to breed large game Pit Bulls, I believe, than small ones; but I do think it can be done. I do think that the really large Pit Bulls in the 60-to-70-pound range are too slow. This is just a personal opinion and partially based on a few observations, not a valid study. When Morochito had his accidental meeting with that 70-pound Pit Bull, Morochito threw him all over the place. His speed was far superior, and he wasn't so small that he couldn't handle this bigger dog - as a matter of fact, he did far more damage than the other dog. I realize this may be because the large dog was not a good one (I have no idea.), but I do believe there is a principle involved and as unpopular a belief as it may be with the Pit Bull community, I think the well bred Pit Bull in the 50-pound range can take any dog in the world. (Most feel that there is no ideal size.)

4. I have a preference for good Colby Dime blood. I have mentioned the weaknesses as well as the strengths in Morochito's pedigree. I can find many pedigrees that are more popular than these dogs. However I've seen a good many

dogs that were bred from more popular stock and they didn't impress me as being all that exceptional. They produce their share of curs like any breeding. Anyway, I must make a determination - do I want to breed from Morochito, or keep him just as a pet and start fresh? Well I chose to stay with Morochito because he's been game tested, and I personally love his pedigree among other things. Morochito is the prettiest Pit Bull I've ever seen and he has an intelligent air, a personality about him that I like and that lends itself to my Schutzhund goal. He looked exceptional in his accidental meeting with that Pit Bull that outweighed him by 14 pounds. The performance of his brothers, especially Jake and Butch, indicates gameness, hard bite, and superior ability which is carried in his blood and can be passed on. I have no idea if Morochito is prepotent or not, of course, since I have not bred him. He's not an ace pit dog and since he hasn't received obedience, tracking, or protection training, I have no idea if he's an ace Schutzhund dog or not. When I choose Morochito to be central in my breeding program I am postulating more than I have recommended. The program I have outlined is, however, a general guideline, meant to be viable. It's ideal to find a highly intelligent prepotent ace that has beautiful conformation and four excellent grandparents. Since such an animal would be nigh on to impossible to find, Morochito's the closest dog that I can find that fits my personal goals. I feel like I am considering his beauty reasonably objectively because everyone I've spoken to who has seen him says the same. There are certain things I don't believe you can capture with a camera and I don't believe his pictures do him justice aesthetically. I realize that most Pit Bull folks do not believe in breeding for looks or conformation, choosing to breed exclusively for that elusive, said to be recessive, trait, gameness. If I were breeding for a combat dog, I might do likewise, but my aspirations are much higher - a Schutzhund dog that not only has the gameness characteristic of the breed but is exceptionally game, and is exceptionally pretty to boot! I realize that this idea will be laughed at by many of my readers, and will bother those who aspire to keeping the Staf/Pit Bull as a pet, wanting to end its performance breeding, and those who hold to the tradition that these dogs should be bred exclusively for fighting. As I mentioned in the preface, I do not criticize either view, but I think I'll be able to realize my goals. We shall see.

Morochito looks a little mean here. Actually he just wants to play with that funny looking black thing his friend (the photographer) is pointing towards him. The intimidating appearance of Pit Bulls make them excellent protection dogs.

    I said that Morochito seems to have the temperament needed for Schutzhund. He is very alert and does not shy or act aggressively toward sudden, loud noises or strange happenings. His reaction to, for example, a sudden, loud noise is an alert curiousity. He is very friendly with strange people, especially children, but quite protective of his property and allows no strange adult into the backyard. He has absolutely no fear of a human and shows no tendencies toward being a fear biter. For these reasons, I chose to maintain Morochito's characteristics.

    The final step is to plan a breeding that will match his pedigree analysis to my goals. To strengthen and maintain as many of his characteristics as possible, I could breed him to his sister, instead of finding an inbred Colby Dime female. That would be as tight as you can get. This would be one generation inbreeding and not enough to result in a decrease in size, or structural faults other than those that are apparent in Morochito, his sister, or their parents. None of them have any structural faults that would impair performance. Morochito does have the short, crooked tail that he will probably pass on and that would make his progeny ineligible for show purposes. Since showing is not one of my aspirations in developing my strain, I do not care if he passes it on. In fact, as I said, I like the little, crooked tail. Although it is not recognized as characteristic of the breed in show circles, actually Lloyd's Pilot, one of the U. S. foundation dogs (particularly in the Dibo and Colby strains) had a short, crooked tail! I have noticed that in the mating of Morochito's brother Jake to his sister, my pick of the litter would have been the crooked-tail pup. He was the gamest, the usual winner of "King of the Hill" contests when the pups played on a little hill, and was more alert and responsive to humans. You may recall that the man who is recognized as the best U.S. breeder of performance (field trials) Beagles (producer of 140 champions) stated that he gets his best results from brother/sister matings. In fact the best Beagle field trial champion in recent history was the result of a brother/sister mating. The important thing to do with the mating of Morochito and his sister would be to carefully select the best puppies for future matings. I choose not to go this route, however, for two matings of Morochito's brother Jake to sister Brandy did not produce Pit Bulls that I especially liked. There was nothing particularly wrong with them and some of them were very strong and intelligent. It's just that I would like to find an inbred female with blood that should nick. I have found that in some inbred Jeep pups. I examined hundreds of pedigrees and spent Morochito's five-year lifetime planning and preparing. The dog that Richard Stratton calls (in his latest book) "a candidate for the greatest dog of modern time" is Champion Jeep. He has retired a four-time winner and his exploits have been mentioned in this chapter and elsewhere in my book. In addition, his litter sister is a champion that burned up all her opponents and no dog lasted longer than 38 minutes. (She has thus far won four contract matches.) His pedigree fits perfectly to Morochito's. Let's look at it.

```
                                  Loposay's Rusty      Colby's Texas
                   Loposay's Dubs                      Burkette's Dutch
                                  Colby's Chita        Colby's Barney
      Finley's Bo                                      Colby's Jenny
                                  Loposay's Bullet     Teal's Jake
                   Loposay's Dot                       Loposay's Betty
                                  Loposay's Tiger Lilly Loposay's Ace
J. Crenshaw's Ch Jeep                                  Burkette's Dutch
 (Garrett's)                      Boudreaux' Eli       Boudreaux' Scrub
                   Walling's Bullyson                  Boudreaux' Candy
                                  Boudreaux' Spook     Boudreaux' Boze
      J. Crenshaw's Ch. Honey Bunch                    Boudreaux' Penny
                                  Carver's Cracker     Tudor's Dibo
                   Carver's Amber                      Carver's Black Widow
                                  Trahan's Beauty Tee  Trahan's Rascal
                                                       Carver's Black Widow
```

Jeep's father, Finley's Bo, has the same blood that Morochito is linebred from on his mother's side. This has been noted in Morochito's pedigree analysis so there is no need to detail it here except to note that there is a tie-in with both Loposay's Dubs and Loposay's Dot. In addition - and I feel this is super important – Finley's Bo is one of the seven top stud dogs in the country (*Sporting Dog Register of Merit*, January, 1982). This tells me that not only is Bo's blood the same as Morochito's, it is superlative blood.

Jeep's mother Honey Bunch is the real plus. She is a champion -won five matches, but two were not contract matches. There are not very many female champions so she is indeed rare. Add all this to the fact that she is prepotent. She has demonstrated that she can pass on her traits even when outcrossed! When mated to Irish Jerry's Trim Moody, she produced Grand Champion Weehunt. This dog won six contract matches and ranks among the greatest in recent years. Trim Moody, by the way, was the result of three generations of brother-sister matings. Honey Bunch is the best producing Pit Bull female in the world. Only one other Pit Bull has earned more points than she has on the Register of Merit, and that is Patrick's Tombstone - and he's been bred more than she has. In my opinion, Honey Bunch will go down in history as the 1980's equivalent to Dibo. She is also a beautiful dog as you can see from her picture. Let's look at her pedigree (included in Jeep's above). Her father is Bullyson, whom we've already talked about. You can see that he stands a good chance of being able to pass on his high qualities because of his breeding. (He is strongly linebred Blind Billy, the most inbred Dibo dog of his day.) In fact Bullyson has proven that he can pass on his characteristics and his blood is very popular. He is the father of Midnight cowboy, the champion that won "Best of show" in each one of his matches, and also the father of Jeremiah, an excellent pit dog. He's grandfather of the popular Carver's Diamond, and of Grand Champion Joker, whose match is recorded in the "Combat" chapter. He's also the grandfather of another popular dog, Stompanato, who in turn produced Champion Bocefus. Stompanato's father is Black Shine, a dog we'll look at later. Bullyson's brother, Eli, Jr. was a two-time winner and was never defeated. So great was his ability that many rate him on a par with the great ones - Black Jack, Jr., Tudor's Spike, etc. He is the father of Champion Art the Dog with a Heart, the indomitable pit dog that just blew right through his opponents. (We discussed him in the "History" chapter.) Eli, Jr. is also the father of Champion Hurt and is grandfather of Grand Champion Angus! Bullyson's father, Boudreaux' Eli is, in my opinion, one of the best foundation studs of game dogs these days. I believe Eli picked up Dibo's prepotency and passed it down through Bullyson to Honey Bunch. If you peruse the pedigrees of champions in the *Sporting Dog Journal* for the last five or six years, I believe you'll find Eli-bred dogs as often as any other breeding. Eli was a two-time winner, but he is most known for his ability to produce. Honey Bunch's mother. Carver's Amber, is linebred Black Widow, who is a granddaughter of Dibo and is predominantly Williams bred. She is mentioned in the "History" chapter and is the foundation bitch for many successful yards including Don Maloney's dogs. She is the mother of Maloney's Toot, the best dog he ever owned, who produced Patrick's Tombstone. Notice that Black Widow was mated to both Dibo and Dibo's half brother Rascal in Honey Bunch's pedigree. Finally I'd like to point out that Carver's Cracker is a litter brother to Carver's Ironhead's mother -so this is all excellent, producing blood.

My "pick of the litter" from Brandy and Jake

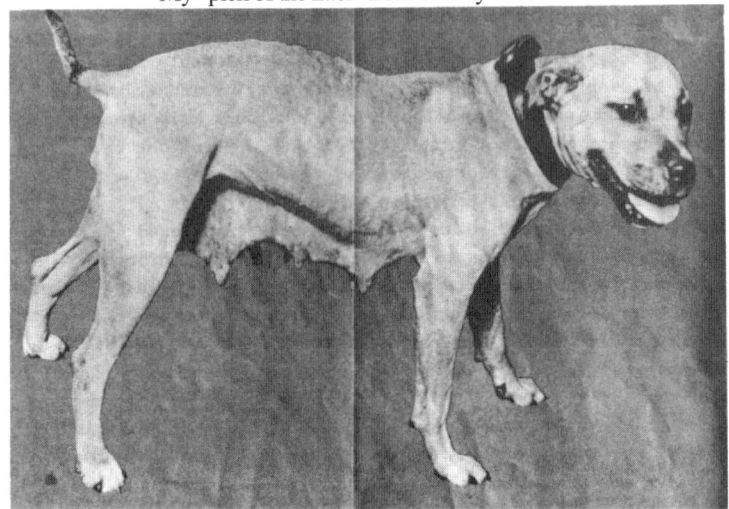

Crenshaw's Honey (Irish Jerry's Ch Honey Bunch)

Now that we have studied Jeep's pedigree and considered his individual performance, we move on to an evaluation of his conformation, temperament, and the integrity of his owner. I have already expressed my opinion on Jeep's conformation - to me it's perfect. He also has an expression, a look in his eyes that I like - reminds me of Morochito. As far as temperament is concerned, Jeep has, outside the pit, a quiet, gentle nature. He dearly loves children and loves to frolic with them. He's never met a person he didn't like. Finally, his owner, Mr. James Garrett, is one of the most respected breeders I know. He's very honest and concerned with the purity of his strain of Pit Bulls, and is not a dog peddler. If you buy a pup from him you know the pup is bred the way it's pedigree shows – that's his reputation.

Sugar – 4 ½ months old

With all that in mind, I have at the time of this writing, just obtained two pups from Mr. Garrett. One is a double-cross on Finley's Bo and a double-cross on Jeep, so I am very pleased with that. Her breeding is a result of Jeep's sister Kate being bred back to her father Finley's Bo and a female from that litter bred to Jeep to produce the mother of the pup I am acquiring. The father is, again, Jeep, so she is a double-father/daughter-Jeep mating. She is a beautiful buckskin, looking like Honey Bunch and Jeep. She was the only pup Mr. Garrett had from that litter when I called him. My heart was broken when he informed me that she has a big congenital hole in her heart. This is the first instance of such a happening in all Mr. Garrett's years of breeding. He didn't feel it fair to sell me the defective pup but offered her to me free with a pup from another litter. My vet informed me that her chances of making it are very slim but I decided to try to pull her through. I named her Sugar. Let me now share with you the pedigree of the other pup I acquired from Mr. Garrett. She ie also a buckskin tnat looks like her father Jeep. I named her Born To Win and we call her Winnie for short.

This pup is bred just right for me. She's a double-cross Jeep up front and double-bred Honey Bunch in the third generation. Bully Bob is a litter brother to Champion Weehunt, that six-time winner I mentioned -a fantastic dog.This was a Honey Bunch breeding that nicked well. Oso Negro is a litter brother to Ch Rascal, who has won 11 matches and lost one (his very first one). He's not a grand champion because only three of his matches were contract matches reported to *Sporting Dog Journal*. The other matches were, however, observed by noted pit dog men. Below Winnie's pedigree is Oso Negro's. It's an interesting one. As you can see, Oso Negro's father, Black Shine, is the result of breeding Eli Jr. to his sister Brendy. Orphan Annie II's father is Eli Jr. Since Bullyson is Honey Bunch's father, that means Sandy is very intensely Eli bred. I think it's interesting to note that

Homer's grandmother, Chatter, is Eli bred. Her father is Eli Jr. Her mother is Eli Jr.'s mother, Spook. Homer, you recall, is the dog that Jeep had his famous match with. I obviously love Eli blood - but with good reason, don't you think?

Born to Win (Winnie) – 8 weeks old

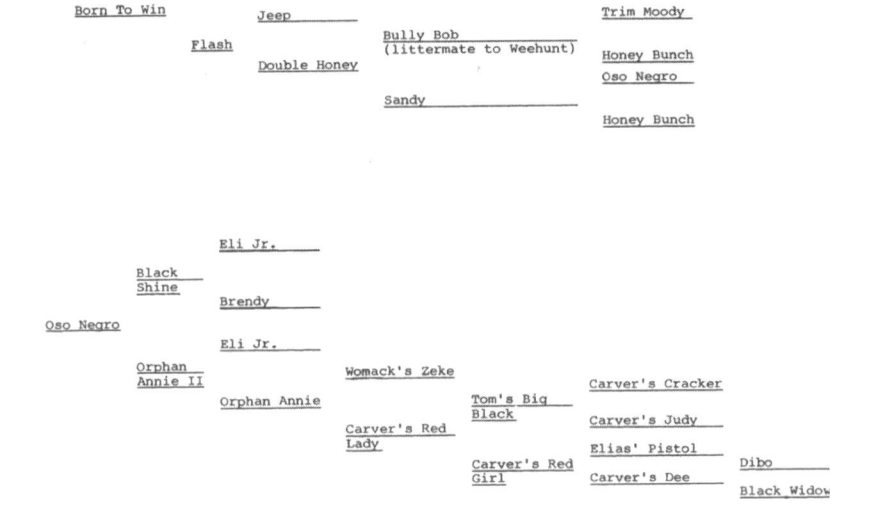

```
                  Jeep
Born To Win                 Jeep                                    Trim Moody
                  Flash                      Bully Bob
                            Double Honey     (littermate to Weehunt) Honey Bunch
                                                                    Oso Negro
                            Sandy
                                                                    Honey Bunch


                  Eli Jr.
         Black
         Shine
                  Brendy
Oso Negro
                  Eli Jr.
         Orphan               Womack's Zeke
         Annie II                                                Carver's Cracker
                  Orphan Annie              Tom's Big
                                            Black                Carver's Judy
                              Carver's Red
                              Lady                               Elias' Pistol
                                            Carver's Red                         Dibo
                                            Girl                 Carver's Dee
                                                                                 Black Widow
```

Orphan Annie's father, Womack's Zeke is also known as Klaus' Zeke. You can see his pedigree on the back of many *Pit Bull Gazette* issues. He's the foundation dog of one of the very best yards - the famous Buckshot Sorrells. Mr. Greenwood, Editor of *Pit Bull Gazette*, thinks enough of this blood that he owns some of these dogs himself - and he settles for nothing but the best! If you look at the pedigree in the magazine, you might notice that Zeke's mother was linebred Black Shine - through Black Widow and a sister of Black Widow! Zeke's father, Goldie, was dead game. Goldie's pedigree goes back to some of the same Lightner blood as Morochito's father's does.

Finally, look at the bottom side of Orphan Annie. It goes back to Carver's Cracker - who is Honey Bunch's grandfather! Carver's Red Girl is a litter sister to Carver's Pistol (father of the great Boomerang). I'm very excited about Winnie's pedigree - I think it's excellent and very well planned.

I traveled to Mr. Garrett's home in Georgia to get Sugar and Winnie and had pick of Winnie's litter. It was easy to pick her. She was the dominant pup in the litter, the biggest one, and by far the prettiest. She had more personality than the others and just seemed to shine. It was a strange coincidence that just about the time I chose her, Mr. Garret said she was the one he'd picked for me before I decided to come down. I like the intense expression in her eyes. To me they look just like Jeep's. She is very strong for her age. She runs close to the ground and has extremely strong leverage in her rear legs - just like Jeep. She also has a natural pose that looks just like Jeep. Breeders of show dogs spend hours training their dogs to pose like that. Jeep (and Winnie) have never been trained to pose nor have they been bred to do so. But Jeep stands like that a lot (when he stands still which is not for long when people come to visit).

I plan to breed Winnie to Morochito. I will then follow my own program and breed daughters back to Morochito to effect a triple cross. I would retain a male from the third mating and look for a female, to outcross to - preferably one that has Jeep or Honey Bunch three or four generations back and is an excellent dog herself. Alternatively, the outcross might come from Mr. Arrison's yard (mentioned earlier) -his dogs are bred just like Morochito, but by then there may be enough other dogs in his breeding process to produce one eligible to be an outcross. I would then linebreed Morochito.

Jeep is, of course, a far better pit dog than Morochito. If my goals were to have a combat dog, I would probably breed back to Jeep instead of Morochito after the first mating of Winnie to Morochito. I am interested in establishing a game Schutzhund strain that could hold its own in any pit contest - but the emphasis for me is Schutzhund.

The program I have outlined can be altered many ways. After breeding Winnie to Morochito, for example, instead of then breeding back to Morochito for a triple cross, I could alternate - breed to Morochito and then a daughter from that litter breed to Jeep, then a daughter from that litter breed to Morochito - then outcross. Winnie is really better bred than Morochito. She also turned out to be much prettier and has far more personality than I expected. I may try the alternate plan if she continues to please me and Jeep is still around. (Quite frankly I have fallen in love with her.)

In summary, my inbred pup comes from as good a pit stock as you can get - and they (Jeep and Honey Bunch) are pretty dogs, and Morochito has all the intelligence, strength, and temperament for high quality Schutzhund. Thus the mating of these two unique animals should eventually fulfill my dreams and expectations.

This completes the analysis of Morochito's pedigree and the chapter on breeding. I want to emphasize that I do not consider my Morochito or Jeep the best bred Pit Bulls in the county, although I have the usual owner's pride. I used their pedigrees, my personal preferences and goals, and the comments as an illustration of a suggested method for a planned breeding program. The planning described in this chapter may seem to simplify breeding, but I don't want to leave you with that impression. The triple cross, etc. program that I outlined is as good as any but is designed to stimulate thinking, not to imply it is the only way or even necessarily the best. There are no guarantees in breeding. Genetics is complex because very few characteristics are governed by a single gene. To my knowledge, it is not known how many genes are in a dog's chromosomes, but is somewhere around 10 or 15 thousand.[43] The possible variations arising from the mating of two dogs then, would be around $2^{15,000}$ - a number uncomprehendingly large. Well it's not really that complicated because most of the genes determine basic structure (one head, two ears, - the basic elements that make the animal a dog). If the traits of a pup were to be determined from only ten genes (for example), however, the number of possible variations of those traits would be a thousand (2^{10}). This is complicated by the fact that Pit Bulls do not pass their characteristics visibly to their offspring. As Eberhard states,[44] "We know how things happen and why they happen, but very little about how to make them happen." I have demonstrated, however, how to increase the possibilities. Pay attention to this - Onstott states that "if a given trait is present in a dog and has been present for five or six generations, it is reasonable to assume that the trait has genetic stability."

I do not claim to be an authority on Pit Bulls and I do not have any breeding experience. I have merely engaged in some extensive reading on the subject, by known and experienced breeders, and have conversed with numerous experienced breeders over the past several years. This chapter can be likened to a rough stone cast into a slow moving pond, setting off an ever widening wave of inquiry. Not perfect, but more polished stones will be tossed into the pond to add to the foundation of knowledge. It is hoped that the extensive bibliography provided in the appendix and from which I gleaned much of the scientific and pragmatic information contained in these pages, will stimulate my readers to further exploration of the relatively new (in national popularity) breed, the Pit Bulldog.

So I would conclude the chapter by noting that the single great characteristic of the most successful breeders in the world, be it Pit Bulls or race horses, or whatever, is - - - patience.

Dean's K.C. Jones

Chapter 9: Medicine Chest And Miscellaneous

> Life is not for science, but science is for life.   - Herbert Spencer

This chapter contains a hodgepodge of practical information that can be useful to owners of Pit Bulls. Some of it is medical because a Pit Bull is often very accident prone. My Morochito is. I've seen that crazy dog chase a squirrel into a pile of abandoned barbed wire laying on the ground, and by the time I pulled him out of there his head and ears were covered with cuts and scratches. He always seems to get into mischief. In addition, some of the information contained here is helpful to those who match their dogs. The fact of the matter is that many people will fight their dogs, law or no law, and if the dog is going to be fought anyway, anything we can do to help him is good. Let me put it this way - I believe that a beautiful dog died unnecessarily in 1979. I think that if proper medication had been available and properly applied, the Snake dog wouldn't have died. There are many other examples.

Let's begin with the Pit Bull's living quarters.
"Construct a Dog House utilizing the maximum of one sheet of Plywood"[45]

FLOOR - The floor is constructed of 2X4's on edge as shown covered with 3 - 2X6's and 1 - 2X8 to give good bottom insulation.
SIDES - Nail strips are kept 2" short of the bottom edge. This will allow the plywood to be nailed to the sides of the floor.
FRONT AND BACK - are cut double the thickness of plywood being used (wider than floor) to allow the edges to overlap. Diagram is made for ½" stock. Cut round or square hole in front 8" from bottom. This will allow 2" for nailing to floor and keeps entry 6" above floor.
TOP - is reinforced as shown and nailed onto strips provided on sides panels.
2 additional 2X3's 21" long are needed. They are to be nailed between the side panels at the top to give full support when nailing top, front and back panels.
I use 1 3/4 galvanized roofing nails to nail the plywood. The large heads and the coating give a longer life to the dog house. I generally give it two coats of paint on all sides and top. Then I creosote the bottom.

If the house is to be used by a female to raise puppies, I would suggest a two-inch thick board be nailed around the inside of the house. This will help her avoid sitting on the pups in the corners or sides of the house. I am told that wheat straw is the best for your dog's bed. Some dogs develop allergic reactions to the fungi found on vegetable matter like hay. Wheat straw is supposed to be non-allergenic. Another reason straw is better is that it has more dead air space in each strand. Some people use wood shavings. Cedar shavings supposedly help keep out fleas. Some stuff a burlap bag with shredded paper, wouldn't work with Morochito - something like that is a play toy for him to tear apart. I put a piece of carpet in his house and he took it out and shook the heck out of it. I nailed one in his house and he ripped it out. Carpet is not good for a dog house anyway because fleas love to live in it.

Notice the dog house opening is six inches up so that the straw can be packed in for a nest and it will not be pulled out by the dog as he goes in and out. The opening should face away from the normal wind direction (especially if you live in a windy plains region). This will make the house warmer in the winter. Some people prefer a flat top because many Pit Bulls love to climb on top and sun themselves during the day which gives them more of the natural vitamin D that sunchine provides. Feeding the Pit Bull on top of such a house encourages this.

If you live in cold country, you may want to put a flap on the doorway. Some Pit Bulls like to play with things like a flap on their house, so it may not work. You might discourage him by coating the flap daily with creosote or tobasco sauce or both. That won't do much for some Pit Bulls, though. Morochito acts like he likes tobasco sauce.

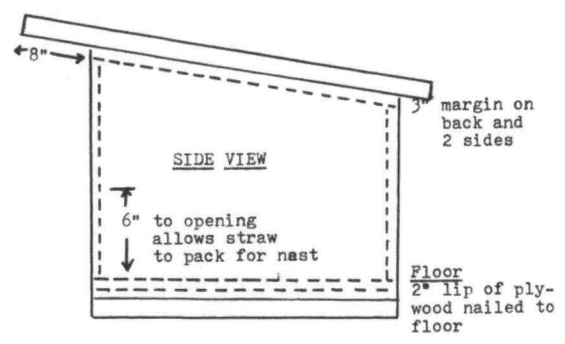

```
 ←8"→
          SIDE VIEW

         ↑
         6" to opening
           allows straw
         ↓ to pack for nast
```

3" margin on back and 2 sides

Floor
2" lip of plywood nailed to floor

PRE-NAIL ALL SUPPORTING NAILING STRIPS

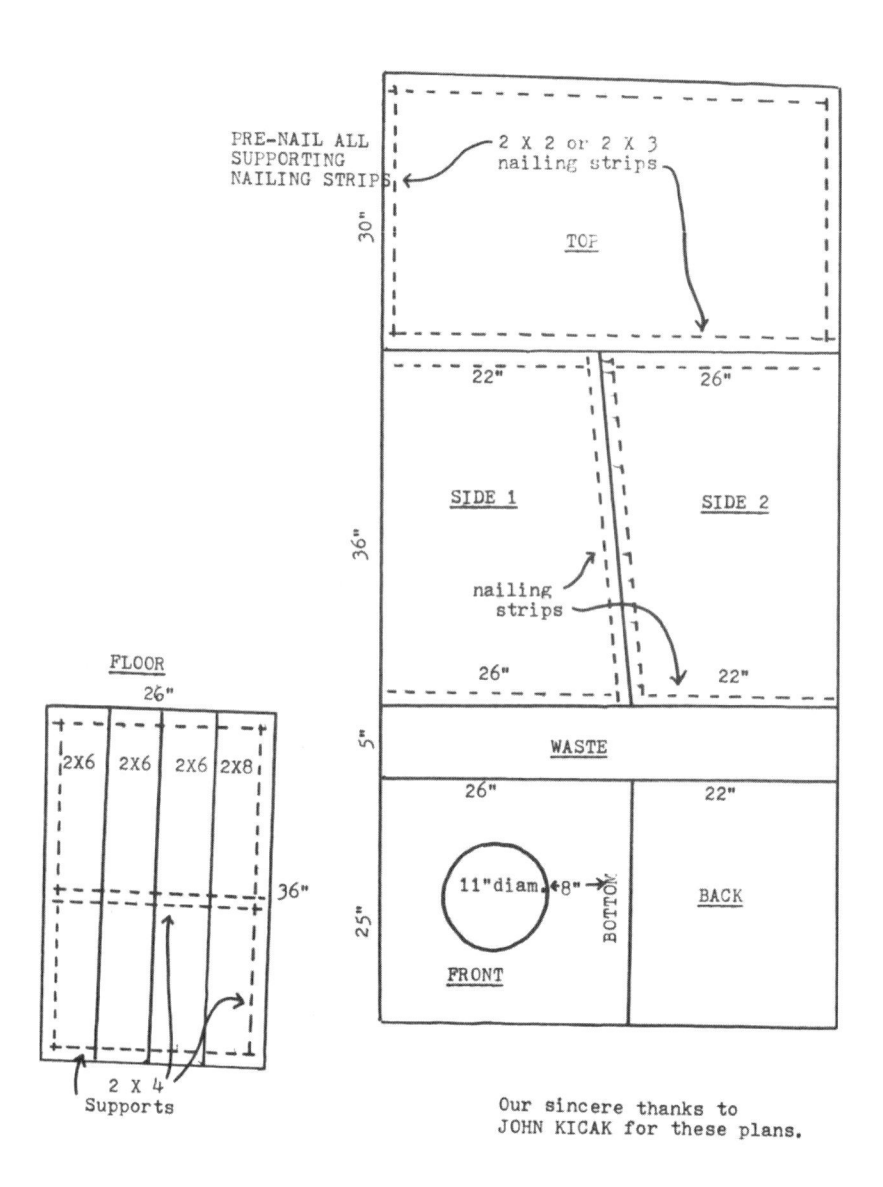

2 X 2 or 2 X 3 nailing strips

30"

TOP

22" 26"

SIDE 1   SIDE 2

36"

nailing strips

26" 22"

FLOOR
26"

2X6 | 2X6 | 2X6 | 2X8

36"

2 X 4 Supports

5"

WASTE

26" 22"

25"

11"diam. ←8"→   BOTTOM

FRONT   BACK

Our sincere thanks to JOHN KICAK for these plans.

Securing the Pit Bull - As mentioned elsewhere, a Pit Bull will exercise himself more on a running chain than in a fenced-in pen. Why this is, to my knowledge, is not known. The running chain is considerably cheaper. I use a 3,000 pound test strength steel strand (cable) that runs about 3/4 of the length of the yard. It is connected to creosoted (treated) posts. I obtained my rig from my friend who works for the telephone company. Most people connect the cable to car axles that are buried in the ground. These can be obtained from junk yards and are very inexpensive. The cable passes through a heavy "O" ring that is connected to a swivel attached to a six-to-ten-foot heavy-duty cow chain. The other end of the chain is attached to another "O" ring that the dog's collar passes through. The collar should be thick. It can be nylon or leather. Nylon is more reliable, lasts longer, and is stronger - but is less comfortable. I like the leather - but you have to be very careful to check it periodically for wear. I apply Neatsfoot oil to it about every two weeks.

Parasites, Disease, and Common Ailments - You can help keep the dog free of parasites (worms, etc.) by laying down a layer of lime around his house and running area. The lime will keep the soil clean and allow proper drainage of urine. The following parasites are common:
1. Hookworms and Roundworms - If you have a persistent problem with hookworms, they are probably in the soil. They don't like lime, however, and you can get a hookworm spray concentrate that will provide additional control. Write The Kennel Vet Corp., P. O. Box 68, Uniondale, New York 11553 (or call 516-292-0430) for a free catalog on this and other items. Of course you can rid your dog of hook and round worms by administering styrid caracide, but the worms will return if they are in the soil around his house. I would suggest you always rely on your veterinarian for treatment of worms. The medicine administered must be specific - for the particular worm - and you can't tell if he's clean unless you examine his feces under a microscope. Always bring two stool samples to the vet - and be sure they are as fresh as possible. Yesterday's stool will show negative. In fact, the reason you bring two stools is that occasionally a positive dog (one that has worms) will show negative in a single stool sample. Pick up stools every day, by the way. Piles of decayed stool attract all sorts of parasites and harmful bacteria.
2. Tapeworms - If you see your dog dragging his butt on the ground, it may be tapeworms - but not necessarily. Do not use that sign as a reason to administer medicine; take him to a vet for examination.
3. Heartworms - Another worm you must watch for is the heartworm. It is the most dangerous today; it is a killer. This worm is transmitted by mosquitoes. When the mosquito bites the dog he transmits infective larva which lives in the dog's muscles for three or four months and then migrates to the bloodstream. They grow to adult heartworms that can be up to a foot in length inhabiting veins, the heart, and the pulmonary arteries of the lungs. Most dogs exhibit the following symptoms: lethargy, coughing, difficulty in breathing. Pit Bulls can be a bit different, however. Many Pit Bulls constantly make snorting and coughing noises all the time anyway. Morochito is always eating grass and coughing when it goes down wrong (It's not

because he's lacking nourishment; he gets more than he needs.) and snorts a lot when he's happy. Every time he comes into the house he goes around snorting for five or ten minutes, investigating. He's excited. Anyway, with many, perhaps most Pit Bulls, you won't know they're infected until it's too late. Pit Bulls are tough and they just don't tend to exhibit the normal symptoms until near the end. I remember one time I decided to help out a freind of mine by exercising his Pit Bull for him for a little while. I went into the yard to get the dog and that feller was all enthusiasm, jumping up and down, jumping up on me. When we started out he almost knocked me down. He ran fine for about a mile; then he started to act like he wasn't interested, wanting to stop and sniff here and there. Finally, at three miles, he laid down and quit. I had to carry him most of the way back. Heartworms. In this instance we caught it in time and he made it through okay. He's completely cured now. I feel real good about that; I think I saved his life. Now the owner gives heartworm medicine to all his dogs. Morochito's father died of heartworms - a waste of a darn good dog and even better producer. The heartworm has killed far more Pit Bulls than all the pit fighting in history. If I accomplish only one thing in this book, I hope I convince every reader who owns a Pit Bull, to be sure to give him heartworm medicine every day that the dog might be subject to infection. In North Carolina, heartworm medicine must be given every day of the year until there are three successive days of temperatures below freezing, and then it must be resumed in the spring as soon as mosquitoes arrive again. As long as mosquitoes are active, there is a danger of heartworm infection. You can give it in liquid form (which is cheaper) or in pill form (which is more convenient). Those who have a yard of dogs usually use the liquid, while owners of a single Pit Bull tend to use the pill. I have read several articles describing how to give a dog a pill - how to hold his mouth open and massage his throat, etc. I can't see going to all that trouble. I just put Morochito's pill in a spoonful of fish flavored canned cat food and he gobbles it down. (We have cats which we feed the canned food to so this is more convenient since I don't use canned food for Morochito.)

4. Fleas - Another parasite, not nearly so harmful and one with which we are all familiar, is the flea, which may be very difficult to control. I personally don't like the flea collar. It is not very effective: it is too close to the dog's nose, providing constant toxin; sometimes it gets worn off, in which case the dog or one of his kennelmates may eat it. The following procedures are much more effective and safe:

a.   Obtain a. "dip" from your veterinarian. It is the most effective way of getting all of the fleas off your dog. You mix the solution with water in a bucket and soak a rag in the solution. Pour the solution on the dog, being very careful to keep it out of his ears (It can cause serious and hard-to-cure infection.), eyes, and mouth. Make sure you apply plenty to the groin area, around his tail and butt, and around his ears.

b. Dust him thoroughly with Sevin Dust, which you can get at the Farmers' Exchange and some hardware and department stores. It is by far the best flea powder you can get and is cheaper than commercial types and is much more effective. Sevin dust will need to be reapplied twice a week for control. Anything that is harmful to fleas has got to be at least toxic to the Pit Bull. For this reason, I don't like to keep on using Sevin Dust or any other flea control on my dog. In the middle of the summer, when the fleas are at their worst, we clean them up, and that's all I do. In any event, you must clean out the fleas in the dog's environment or they will merely jump back on him as soon as the dip and powder has worn off.

c. Sevin Dust the inside of his living quarters and the ground around his house, after thoroughly vacuuming the inside of the dog house.

d. If the dog comes into the house, thoroughly vacuum the house and de-flea any other house pets you have, such as cats.

The above four steps will get rid of any serious flea problem you have. Dogs can develop allergic reactions to fleas and develop redness of the skin and a severe rash sometimes. I wouldn't worry too much about fleas unless they get out of hand,

5. Rabies - You don't have to worry about rabies with most Pit Bulls because they have to stay tied up, generally. Rabies are usually contracted from infected wild animals such as skunks, raccoons, foxes, and bats. If your Pit Bull does get to run around in the woods, there is a potential danger - depending on how widespread rabies is in your area. I don't think rabies is much of a problem these days, but I also don't believe in taking chances. Once a dog catches rabies, he's usually a goner. Prevention is easy - vaccination, which lasts three years. The idea is to bring every pup to the vet and follow a program of required shots which includes rabies.

6. Distemper - This is another killer that is prevented by simply making sure your dog gets his shots.

7. Fly Bites - Sometimes you may find your Pit Bull gets excessively bitten by flies, usually around his ears. In the U.S. these flies are more common in the Southwest region. You can go to your farm supply store and find medicine to apply, which is also used for horses.

8. Skunk Scent - Another accident that can happen to a dog that gets to run loose is Mr. Skunk. If this should happen, clean his eyes with boric acid, since this was probably the skunk's primary target when he sprayed, and then wash him all over with vinegar, which helps destroy the odor, and follow with a good shampoo.

9. Kennel Cough – You'll find that sometimes a Pit Bull can develop "kennel cough." Honey is one of the best things to give for this malady. It will often relieve the symptoms of the cough. It is safest, however, to bring your dog to the vet for an antibiotic, like flocillin, because kennel cough is a virus. One thing about honey - germs can't breed or thrive in it. My advice is to combine the vet's antibiotic with honey and natural vitamin C. (See the "Nutrition" chapter.)

10. Canine Parvo - This deadly disease suddenly increased in the 1970's and although it never reached epidemic levels, it did become very prevalent. As noted in my local newspaper in 1979, 5,263 cases were reported in three months in North Carolina. In the colder regions of the country, parvo nearly disappeared from 1978 through 1980. During the winter of 1981-1982, it increased again, dramatically, all across the country, even through it was an extremely cold winter. This disease is a puppy killer and very dangerous. Statistically speaking, if ten puppies become infected, eight or nine of them will die. Apparently adult dogs between the ages of one year and about eight years do contract parvo but often show no symptoms orbecome only mildly ill. This virus is highly contagious and attacks the gastrointestinal tract, the heart, and the bone marrow. The virus suppresses white blood cell production (opposite from a bacterial infection that causes an increase in white blood cells), thus making it difficult to fight off, especially for a pup.

The symptoms of parvo are depression, acute vomiting, severe diarrhea in the form of grey or yellow/grey stools in the initial stages and bloody, loose stools in later stages, dehydration, and fever. The first sign of parvo is depression and poor appetite. When you see that, watch the pup carefully. A match stick inserted into the puppy's rectum and withdrawn will provide the most convincing evidence of parvo. If it's parvo, the stick will have a very strong odor similar to ammonia. When you detect it, time is of the essence. You must get the pup to the vet as quickly as you can. The earlier the treatment in terms of hours, the greater the chance of survival. There is no better treatment for an infected pup than professional veterinary care. There are many misconceptions about and ineffective (and perhaps detrimental) home remedies for the parvo virus. I have found many, many dog men that swear by the following treatment: Tylan 50 (an antibiotic) - 1 cc per five pounds daily; Sulmet liquid (sulphur) -Ice per pound (orally) daily - or 1 sulphur pill morning and night, and injected fluids. There is no drug that will curb a parvo virus. A good many experienced dog men have a great deal of confidence in the sulphur drug but nevertheless medical studies have proven that sulphur will not affect a parvo virus at all. The instances when puppies survive when given sulphur are all coincidence - they would have survived anyway. The only thing that can be done, at the time of this writing, is to administer supportive fluid for dehydration. The fluid is very important because dehydration can be very severe - the puppy will literally dry up and turn into nothing but loose skin and bones - it can kill him overnight. Most people give intravenous feedings of 250 cc of lactated ringers daily. It is best to have the vet provide the fluids, however, because you have to give enough without giving too much. The puppy will not eat or drink. Starting the second day the vet will usually administer small amounts of fluid every hour all day long. If you force too much fluid into the pup, he will vomit and have more diarrhea and become further weakened. The first positive sign is when the puppy eats a little and is able to hold it down. If he has a firm stool then he is quite sure to make it.

The virus is spread by insects, birds, and by humans that pick it up on their shoes and clothing. Isolation doesn't mean the dog is protected. The virus is resistant to drying, most disinfection, and heat. A pretty fair job of cleaning up a kennel that has been infected can be accomplished by disinfecting the area with a solution of one part Clorox to nine parts water. At the time of this writing, Clorox is the only thing that will kill the virus. Periodically disinfecting your kennel with Clorox is a good idea - but not a conclusive preventative. Many breeders have kept a very clean kennel, using Clorox as a disinfectant, and still have had the deadly parvo strike. The only way you can be protected from parvo is with proper immunization. I underlined proper because it is very important. I found out, like I seem to learn everything in this life, the hard way. My Jeep puppy, Born to Win (described in the "Breeding" chapter) came down with parvo just recently, at age 12 weeks. Mr. Garrett had given her her parvo shot when she was three weeks old and told me to give her another one when she was ten weeks old. The time sort of crept up on me and I hadn't gotten around to it. I didn't realize the danger and figured the shot she had at three weeks probably kept her protected anyway. The first mistake was - get ahold of this now; it is very important - you don't immunize a puppy at three weeks of age. I've written Mr. Garrett and explained it to him - he hasn't had a parvo problem in his yard and probably no direct experience with the disease. The reason you don't give a three-week-old pup a parvo vaccine is that it will negate the maternal immunity the mother naturally gives her puppies to protect them for their first five or six weeks of life. In fact, by innoculating the pup at three weeks old, you make him more susceptible to parvo. A proper immunization program begins with the mother. A parvo shot will provide sufficient antibodies to protect an adult dog for one year - that is if it is a good vaccine. It has to be modified live virus canine cell line origin vaccine. These days most everyone uses modified live canine - but some still use the killed feline, killed canine, or mink vaccine that has proven to be only partially effective and requires more frequent shots. In any event, make sure the vaccine is modified live canine and give it to the mother before breeding or any time up to 30 days afterward. If the parvo shot is her initial one, give her two doses - four weeks apart to be sure. The mother will pass antibodies on to her puppies as they suckle her colostrum. Every nine days the level of immunity given from the mother to the pups decays by one-half until at five or six weeks it is ineffective.[46] You then vaccinate the pups at 6, 10, and 14 weeks of age. After 14 weeks old the puppy is safe and you can give him shots yearly.

Something else I found out is that if a pup has been exposed to parvo, you can still give him a shot. I say this because I would have thought that the exposed pup might contract a worse case of parvo. In other words, I have been under the impression that if you get a flu shot when you have already been exposed to the flu, you end up with a very bad case of it. Well when Winnie (Born to Win) came down with parvo, the other Jeep pup (Sugar, who has a bad heart, and is also described in the "Breeding" chapter) that was living in the same kennel was of course exposed. I hesitated to give her a parvo shot, but my vet assured me that the vaccine can in no way create the disease. The vaccine undergoes several stages of development before it is marketed so that it causes antibodies and never adds virus. If you follow the immunization program I have outlined you will have provided the maximum protection against parvo. You can have your vet vaccinate your dog(s), or if you have a large yard, you can administer the vaccine yourself. If you do it yourself you must be careful that you have a good vaccine, like the one obtainable from the following company:

Vaccines, Inc.
2114 South First Street
P. O. Box 727
Temple, Texas 76503

    I planned - studying dogs, pedigrees, and breeders - for many years for that Jeep puppy. I could have lost that beautiful, unique animal, through ignorance. I know better now and hope I have provided my readers with some useful information.[47]

11. Bee Stings - When your dog gets stung, give him an antihistimine cold pill. Search each swelled bump, and if you see a portion of the bee's stinger protruding, remove it with tweezers. Wipe clean with hydrogen peroxide and apply ice. Wrap the ice in a plastic bag and hold it on the swollen area for five or ten minutes twice a day.

12. Cracked Footpads - Spray with Granulex and apply a healing ointment. 1 have obtained excellent results from cod liver oil ointment (for humans) obtainable from your local drugstore.

13. Elbow Calluses - Rub daily (At feeding time is best.) with vaseline or baby (mineral) oil.

14. Ear Mites - If you notice little dark granules in his ears, it may be mites. Usually the dog will habitually paw at his ears and shake his head. Wipe out the ears with a cotton ball dipped in baby oil and then dip a q-tip in garlic juice and apply the solution liberally over the area twice a day.

15. Heat Stroke - As soon as you can, fill a bathtub with cold water, cold as you can get it, and submerge the Pit Bull. Apply ice packs to back of neck, chest, and groin area. You must lower his temperature and do it fast - heat stroke can kill a Pit Bull.

16. Paint or Grease - If a Pit Bull gets paint or grease on his coat, use kerosene or turpentine to remove it. This is very irritating to the dog's skin and may burn. Therefore apply vegetable oil or vaseline to the area after removing the paint or grease.

17. Poison[48] - The symptoms of poisoning include trembling, panting, vomiting, slimy secretion from the mouth, convulsions, and coma. If your Pit Bull has been

poisoned and you become aware of it early enough, prompt action can save him. Immediately give him an emetic (medicine that causes vomiting) such as hydrogen peroxide and water in egual parts, or soapy water. Force 6 to 12 tablespoons (depending on the size of the dog) down the Pit Bull's throat and he will regurgitate the contents of his stomach. Of course you should bring him to your vet as soon as possible. If you know the source of the poison it will help in finding an antidote. The following household antidotes may be helpful:

Poison	Antidote
arsenic	Epsom Salts
food poisoning (garbage, etc.)	hydrogen peroxide followed by an enema
phosphorus (rat poison)	hydrogen peroxide
strychnine	sedatives (phenobarbital, nembutal)

18. Coprophaqy (stool eating) - This can mean a nutritional deficiency. If the dog is being fed well, however, it is a result of boredom. Always talk to and pat your dogs often. Give them a toy like a tire tube to play with and rotate their toys fairly frequently.

19. Electric Shock - Apply artificial respiration and otherwise treat for shock as explained in section VI-2.

20. Poisonous Snake Bite - Cut a deep "X" over the fang marks and suck out poison (spitting it out); then carry the Pit Bull to the vet. Pit Bulls are tough critters and most of them survive.

21. Automobile Accident - If very far from a vet, treat for shock. In any event, when you carry him to the vet, wrap him in a blanket and be very careful when you move him. Check his gums. If they are white, there is a possibility of internal injury and you'll need to hurry to the vet.

Winnie - after her bout with parvo

If these home remedies do not seem to do the job right away be sure and bring the Pit Bull to the vet. Incidentally, it is well worth your time to ask around (dog breeders, kennels, dog training clubs, etc.) to determine what veterinarians give the most quality service and are the most economical. My vet has an excellent reputation in the community and will give me free advice over the phone, and doesn't charge for an office visit when I bring one of my animals in and it doesn't need treatment, etc. Some of my "free" trips to my vet would have cost me $15 or $20 at many other establishments.

A Few Dangerous Things To Avoid
1.   Painted Toys - Pit Bulls love to chew and the lead in the paint can be very toxic, possibly fatal.
2.   Riding in Cars - When riding in a car, dogs love to stick their heads out the open window. I've read that this is not a very good idea because the wind can cause eye or ear infection.
3.   It is not a very good idea to leave a dog unattended in a car (or tied up in the yard, or in the house) while wearing a chokecollar because the collar may get caught on something and the dog can choke himself - it happens fairly frequently. Pit Bulls and Stafs are particularly vulnerable to this type of accident because they are so active and always getting into things.
4.   It is also dangerous to leave a dog unattended in a car with the windows closed, especially in the summer. A dog does not sweat and can cool his body only

by panting. The temperature inside the car will be much higher than outside. If it is 78 degrees outside, it can get up to 90 or even over 100 inside the car.

5. I have seen people driving around with their Pit Bull in his cage in the back of their station wagon, leaving the tailgate window open to give the dog air. This can make the dog sick because the open window will suck in exhaust fumes from the tailpipe. Keep the tailgate window closed. He'll get plenty of air if you leave a side window open slightly.

6. Bones - As mentioned in the chapter on conditioning, if you give bones to your dog, make sure you give only bones that will not splinter, like marrow bones or knuckle bones. It is best to steam heat the bones because they quite often contain parasites. Don't give bones too often because they can lead to excessively worn teeth. At all costs, you must avoid pork chop bones, steak bones, and especially poultry bones which splinter very easily. More than one dog has died from a gut perforation caused by a sharp bone splinter. It is for this reason (as well as the obvious one) that I bring my breaking stick with me when Morochito and I go for our roadwork. If he spots a chicken bone, he is quick as a flash to snatch it. (As you know, "litter-bugging" is still quite prevalent. We often pass by a discarded box of fried chicken or the like.) More than once I've been able to save him from swallowing an undesirable bone by prying it out of his mouth with my breaking stick.

Shipping Your Dog - Like all dog breeders, Pit Bull fanciers today maintain quality bloodlines by shipping their dogs, often across the country, to be mated. Puppies, of course, are also frequently shipped. This section may provide some useful tips if you haven't shipped a dog before. You can insure the dog for the flight and I think it's a good idea to do so. Quite often the airlines require vaccination or other health papers from a veterinarian before they accept a dog for shipping. They may also require that the dog be checked in an hour or two before flight time. You should call the airlines well in advance and ask for specific instructions and requirements. You will want to take your Pit Bull to the vet early and fulfill whatever requirements are necessary. Don't take a chance and bring the Pit Bull out just before flight time. Do not feed the dog on the day of his flight, and limit the amount of water he drinks. This will help keep him from getting sick. Check on flights well in advance of the planned trip and try to select a nonstop one if at all possible, which is obviously less stressful to the Pit Bull and there is less likelihood of a mix-up and the dog being sent to the wrong destination. Pit Bulls are great chewers, so make sure he's in an adequate crate. Be sure to call the person on the receiving end after the dog is definitely checked in to a certain flight, giving the air-bill or way-bill number assigned by the airline, as well as the flight number and expected time of arrival. The receiver can pick up the dog by referring to the way-bill number. He should phone the shipper when he has the dog in his possession.

The In-jured Pit Bull - This section deals with treatment of the injuries received from catch work, pit fighting, or whatever. As I have stated, I'm not encouraging pit fighting, but many people still indulge in this sport and are sometimes unable to get their dogs to a vet quickly enough for treatment. (Most of the fights are miles out in the country and in the wee hours of the morning or real late at night.) Some well-blooded Pit Bulls have been lost this way and I think that since the dog is going to fight anyway, we might as well do what we can to help him. The following procedures should be of assistance:

1. Wounds. It is extremely rare that a Pit Bulldog is killed in the pit, because with this breed that really takes some doing; but, as stated, it is after the fight, when the dog can't get to a vet quickly enough, that problems occur. Sometimes the dog doesn't appear very badly hurt and in fact is not at the time. Untreated, however, an open wound can become infected. In any event, some on-the-spot work may be called for. Once infection sets in, healing is a long drawn-out process that can result in the dog not making it. A puncture wound is the most susceptible to infection. After a fight, a dog's resistance is likely to be low, increasing the possibility of infection. With a puncture wound, infection is likely to get into the bloodstream. Infection is caused by bacteria. In most instances, the dog's white blood cells and lymph nodes overcome the bacteria and infection is prevented. When the body's defenses are low and/or the wounds are many, the bacteria can get the upper hand. An uninfected wound may swell and become inflamed, but the symptoms should substantially improve in two or three days. If the wound stays red and inflamed or if you find pus, infection has set in. The most effective preventative is an antibiotic shot, the most widely used of which is combiotic. Azium, sometimes given in conjunction with penicillin, is another one. Azium also helps reduce pain and swelling. Give ½ cc once a day for three days. Still another one is flocillin, which saturates the blood with strong antibiotics. Dosage is 1 cc per ten pounds of body weight given every 48 hours. Most Pit Bulls get a shot of combiotic and vitamin B-12 in the upper part of the rear leg. The vitamin speeds recovery and helps the anitbiotic do its work. If the dog can walk, he should be walked around - if he can't walk, roll him from side to side. This will help the medicine circulate through the bloodstream faster. I think vitamin C should be administered immediately. (See the "Nutrition" chapter for a thorough explanation of the healing properties of vitamin C - it expedites the antibiotic work better than anything.) Combiotic, syringes, and other medical supplies can be ordered from the veterinarian supply companies listed at the end of this chapter. Injections are normally given subcutaneous (under the skin) (s.c.) or intramuscular (I.M.). Intramuscular injections are normally used for the more caustic drugs like antibiotics. Subcutaneous injections allow a more rapid absorption of a drug. The common areas for s.c. injection are on either side of the neck or in the flank. Push the hair back to expose the skin as much as possible and rub the skin with alcohol to sterilize. Pinch the skin between thumb and index finger

and inject the needle, which should be long enough so that half an inch of it remains visible after insertion. If it should break at the hub (This happens on occasion), it can be pulled out. The needle should penetrate the entire thickness of the skin. If there is considerable resistance to the flow of the fluid, either the needle hasn't gone through the skin or it has penetrated the muscle. Wiggle the needle slightly, push in a little, then out a little and try again. If you still get no results, withdraw the needle and try again in a different area. Use a different needle; the original one may have become clogged.

Intramuscular injections are generally given in the muscular portion of the hindleg, about half an inch or so deep. Withdraw the plunger slightly to see if a blood vessel has been hit. If it has, it will draw in blood. When the needle is properly placed, the fluid is injected slowly and then the needle is withdrawn.

After the injection, pour hydrogen peroxide in each wound. This is an excellent wound medicine because it is an unstable solution that decomposes to water and oxygen when it comes into contact with tissue. The process involves considerable foaming and bubbling action, which helps spread the solution and its germicidal ingredients deep into the wound, and the foaming action cleans it out. This process doesn't hurt. (I can attest to that because I've had several wounds myself -including a few Pit Bull bites - and I've poured the hydrogen peroxide into the wounds - feels good.) Most Pit Bulls accept the treatment with apparent appreciation. If the wound is deep, you can inject a solution with an eye dropper or bulb syringe. If there is dirt around or in the wound, flush it out thoroughly with the peroxide. The antibacterial ingredients are not very long lasting so you will need more later. I would follow with a spray called Granulex, which also foams and gets down into the wound and facilitates the removal of necrotic tissue and debris, plus its anti-bacterial ingredients are more long lasting. If the wound is a bleeder, you can put a blood stopper powder on it (See the list of sample items that can be purchased from supply houses.) and wrap the wound tightly so as to put pressure on it. If a bleeder gets hit, you will need to apply pressure immediately. This doesn't happen very often - in fact it is very, very rare. Should it happen, though, you must be ready. Fold a towel and press hard against the wound. If the bleeding doesn't clot, you may have to apply a tourniquet by wrapping a bandage, belt, or whatever you can get ahold of, around the limb - above the wound if it is an artery. (An artery wound is indicated when the blood is bright red and pumping out in spurts.) Insert a pencil or other long item into the bandage on the side of the wound nearest the heart. Twist the tourniquet until the bleeding stops, keeping it tight for no more than one minute and then loosening it momentarily to allow slight blood flow. This is very important. Failure to do so can result in the dog's losing a limb. Tourniquets can be very dangerous and should be applied only in extreme cases such as when an artery has been hit (in which case the dog has only a few minutes to live unless the bleeding is stopped). Every ten minutes loosen the tourniquet completely and see if the bleeding has slowed sufficiently so that it can be controlled with hand pressure. A venous wound (where a vein is bleeding) is less dangerous. Such a wound is characterized by an even flow of dark colored blood. You can generally control it with hand pressure. Place a pad of sterile gauze (if you have it) over the wound (a towel or something if you don't) and wrap it with an ace bandage (or whatever is available) and apply pressure with the heel of your hand. Be sure to press hard. Pressure Is the key, as it aids in the formation of a blood clot. When a sufficient clot has formed, it will prevent further hemorrhage. Keep the dog warm by covering him with a coat or blanket, and, of course, get him to a vet as soon as possible.

Apply tourniquet for no more than one minute and then loosen.

When you get the Pit Bull home, you should wash him all over with an antiseptic shampoo, especially the wounds. The most popular one is Betadine Skin Cleanser Antiseptic Degerming Cleaner. It contains providone and iodine. You then spray the wounds with scarlet oil, which contains menthol, carbolic acid, oil of camphor, eucalyptus oil, and tar oil. Finally, you'll want to spread an antiseptic salve or dressing on his wounds. You might want to tape his mouth shut so that he won't lick the dressing off. Later as the wounds begin healing, the dog's licking is good for them as mother nature takes over. In fact, it is the head wounds (ears, nose, etc.) that can be the most dangerous because the dog cannot get to them. Short daily walks also promote healing by increasing circulation.

If the wounds are large, the Pit Bull may have lost fur and skin, but it will grow back in time. If not lubricated, however, the skin will grow back grey and the fur will not cover it very well. Pit fighters generally rub vaseline on the area and the skin grows back with its original color and the fur will grow over it. This will also work for sores a Pit Bull quite often gets from rubbing himself on the ground. Let me tell you what works best for me when Morochito has a wound. In the morning when I feed him, I put vaseline on the wound (only after the healing process has started). In the afternoon I apply Aloe Vera gel to the area. I have found that it will make the fur grow back over a wound faster than anything else I've tried. When I feed him in the evening, I put vitamin E oil on the wound to aid in healing and minimize scarring.

Taping prevents dog from licking dressing off.

    Vitamin C has been recommended as the best food supplement to take for healing wounds. Since a dog (unlike a human) will store vitamin C, feed small units (100 mg. or less). I recommend all natural 30 mg. For an animal this is plenty. If a pill contains more than 30 mg., it is part natural and part synthetic - regardless of what the label suggests. A natural vitamin C pill of more than 30 mg. would be very big, too big to swallow. I recommend feeding a vitamin C pill twice a week and stopping when the dog is healed.

    Another vitamin supplement that is excellent for expediting the healing process is vitamin A, which, like vitamin C, plays a role in collagen formation, and also helps prevent wound infection. The benefits of vitamin A in healing wounds was indicated in very recent research at the University of Illinois' Department of Food Science Study.[49] In this study, rats were wounded and then fed varying diets as the wounds healed. One group was fed a base diet and the other was fed a vitamin A supplement in addition to the base diet. In two weeks the rats were sacrificed and the wounds examined. The wounds of the rats that received the vitamin A supplement healed quicker and tensile strength (resistance to being torn open) increased an astounding 70% over the wounds of rats not receiving vitamin A! You may want to give the Pit Bull aspirin for a few days if he's sore. I've not really heard of giving aspirin to a dog nor have I ever given it to my dogs. (I'm in partnership with another dog man.) I have read that marathon runners swear by aspirin and there is some new research on it. It's long been known that aspirin helps alleviate pain, especially muscular pain. In the past we haven't known why. Now we do. My source for the following information is *Runner's World*.[50]

    Aspirin (Its medical term is acetylsalicylic) reduces inflamation of joints by blocking the synthesis of prostaglandins, which are hormone-like substances that rush blood to an injured area causing it to swell (which is one cause of the pain).

The nerves that carry pain impulses to the brain are stimulated by prostaglandins. Aspirin impedes the work of prostaglandins, thereby acting as a pain killer. This drug should not be used as a pain killer during pit performance, however, because it thins the blood (which is why it's good for people with a bad heart - it prevents clotting of the blood), the reason being that one of the prostaglandins which aspirin impedes is a substance called thromboxane which makes the platelets that help blood clot. If you do give aspirin, be sure you don't give too much. (I would say limit to two pills.) Too much can cause all kinds of problems including bloody stools.

3. Treatment for Shock. Really, it is shock that usually gets a Pit Bull more than anything else. Due to the tenacity that has been bred into the breed for generations, many a Pit Bull keeps on going long after he should stop. Some dead game ones will still go after they are in shock (or at least demonstrate symptoms of shock). Treatment needs to be immediate. You begin by covering the dog with a blanket to keep the body heat in. A dog in shock will be cold and clammy, his eyes will be glazed, and his pulse will be weak. To take a dog's pulse, place two fingers on the femural. A dog's normal resting pulse is between 80 and 120 - larger dogs have a lower pulse. If the dog is in shock, you may need to give a heart stimulant shot. Sometimes cold blood will get into the lungs I've heard. If the dog has stopped breathing, you must work fast. (Delay can be fatal - a dog will be beyond help if he doesn't receive oxygen within approximately five minutes.) You will need to administer artificial respiration. For a dog, this is done by laying him on his side and opening his mouth and making sure his tongue is hanging out. Mucus and blood should be cleared out of his nose by swabbing it out, or an eyedropper should be used if available. Then place the flats of both hands on the dog's side with the fingers over the ribs. Keep your arms straight (elbows locked) and press down firmly. (I forgot to emphasize this to my artist friend, Chris Gallagher, so the illustration with arms bent slightly is incorrect in that respect.) This will empty the lungs. Release the pressure and the natural elasticity of the chest will allow it to expand and bring in oxygen. As you release the pressure, start counting - one one thousand, two one thousand, three one thousand, four one thousand, five - breathe. On the count "breathe" push down again. Keep going until the dog is able to breathe on his own. Don"t give up. You may have to continue for an hour before the dog finally comes around.

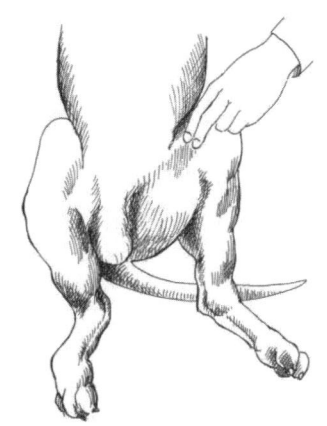

Proper method for taking dog's pulse.

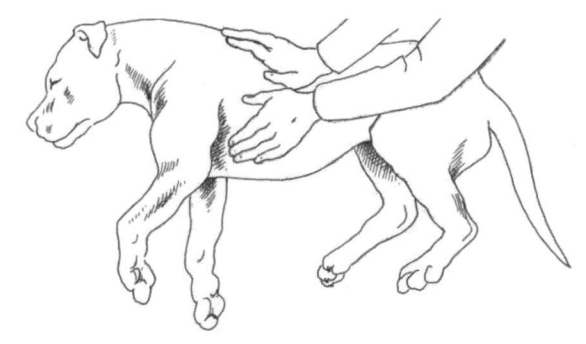

Artificial Respiration - Be sure to keep elbows locked rather than slightly bent as shown here.

    Another method of applying artificial respiration is to hold the Pit Bull's muzzle shut and place your mouth directly over the dog's nose and blow directly into the nose. he breathing count would be the same as indicated for chest pressure.

    If he does come around, keep him covered with a blanket and get him to a vet as soon as you can.

    Generally speaking, the reason the Pit Bull has gone into shock is because he has lost a considerable amount of blood (fluid). To cut down on blood loss, a Pit Bull is generally entered into a match in a state of semi-dehydration. (He is deprived of water for 12 hours before entering the pit.) Some water is also lost from the rapid respiratory rate during fighting. Normal tissue fluids are extremely important in maintaining normal cellular functions. Tissue fluids are composed of water, ions, proteins, and other substances. The signs of dehydration can be undetectable until a water deficit of about 4% of total body weight has taken place. This is dangerous because the dog's owner may be unaware of the importance of replacing lost fluid. If a 50-pound dog loses 4% of his weight in fluid, this is about two pounds, or a little more than a liter. If there is a loss of 8 to 10%, this is very serious dehydration and the dog must be given fluids intravenously within 24 hours or he will die. I know this loss doesn't seem like much, but look at it this way. If a 50-pound dog loses 10% of his weight in fluid, that's five pounds, or about 2 ½ liters, which is quite a lot. With a loss of 12 to 15%, the mouth is dry, the dog cannot urinate, has an erratic pulse, and is near death. If a dog, with a 12 to 15% fluid loss is not given fluids intravenously very quickly (depending on the dog this could be perhaps within an hour or less), he will die. A 50-pound dog with this amount of denyaration will need a liter of fluid immediately and three to four more liters shortly thereafter. The signs of dehydration are as follows:

1. <u>Decreased Elasticity of the Skin</u>. The tissues beneath the skin contain a large portion of the total body water. Since this water compartment is one of the least important to the body, it is drawn upon first in a situation of dehydration. To test for dehydration, pick up a fold of skin along the middle of the back and let it drop. In a well hydrated, normally fleshed dog, the skin spirngs immediately back into place. In a moderately dehydrated dog, the skin moves slowly into place. In severe dehydration the skin may form a tent.

2. <u>Dryness of the Mucous Membranes of the Mouth and Eyes.</u>

3. <u>Sunken</u> Eyes.

4. <u>Circulatory or Vascular Collapse</u> (Shock).

When a Pit Bull goes into shock, he'll lie down. His eyes will be glazed and he'll not be aware of what is going on around him. He'll be cold to touch, especially his lips, which along with his gums will be pale. The pulse will be rapid but weak and the Pit Bull will generally be breathing rapidly.

Mild dehydration and its accompanying ion imbalance can be corrected by administering water and nutrients orally. Gator-Aid or pedialyte are popular oral fluids. If the dog is conscious and will drink, Gator-Aid is especially recommended because it contains glucose which is a stimulant. In more acute dehydration, fluids must be administered either subcutaneously (under the skin), or intravenously (directly into the bloodstream) if especially severe. Lactated ringers is the most popular i.v. (10 cc per pound of body weight is a good rule of thumb). Perhaps Soly-Delta-Cortef, which is a steroid for shock should also be administered.

When a Pit Bull goes into shock, he generally will not drink a sufficient amount or may be in a coma. If he is in a coma, you must work fast to keep him alive. If the dog is real weak, he may not have a sufficient pulse to take the injection. You may want to check the pulse. There is an artery that runs along the inside of the thigh, almost into the groin. Place two fingers on the artery, as indicated, and count the beats per minute.

(Count for ten seconds and multiply by six.) The normal dog's resting pulse is between 80 and 120 beats per minute (slower pulse for bigger dogs, faster for smaller ones). A dog running a high fever can have a pulse rate as high as 160 beats per minute. If the Pit Bull is in shock, the pulse can drop down very low. If it does, you've got to work fast. I've given you the procedures. Do not give up. I know a Pit Bull that was in a coma for at least an hour. His pulse was so weak that no fluid could be injected into a vein. The folks worked desperately on him and when it looked like he might not make it, they slit the skin on his leg and peeled it back looking for a large vein. The dog didn't bleed and the vein would not take any fluid. They finally left in a hurry to find a vet. If ever a dog should have died, I would think it would have been that one. I was overwhelmed when I saw the dog about six months later - completely healed, the fur grown back so that his wounds were barely noticeable, and he was as lively as could be. I heard that he was later rolled with a dog that outweighed him and bit much harder - and he showed game. He eventually became a four-time winner. The point is that you should never give up on your dog. Do everything possible to save him.

When the dog is able to drink he should be given water. Some people give pedialyte (a product generally sold in drugstores for babies that have diarrhea). Good fluid therapy is very important for a dehydrated dog. When an excess of fluids are lost, minerals such as sodium, potassium, magnesium, calcium, and phosphates are lost. These minerals are called electrolytes because when dissolved in water they can conduct an electric current. One important function of these electrolytes is the conduction of messages from the brain along nerve passages to the muscles for proper muscle contraction. When a pit dog goes into shock from loss of fluid and depletion of these important electrolytes, the messages normally carried by the tiny electric currents propagated by the electrolytes do not reach the brain, the dog cannot function and he collapses. If his system does not receive fluids with these electrolytes quickly, he won't live.

When you can provide the minerals in chelated (pronounced kee-lated and means bound to other molecules) form, it will minimize their natural laxative effect. In addition, the chelated minerals are much easier for the dog's digestive system to assimilate so that more of the nutrients are absorbed and less are passed out. Pedialyte is an electrolyte solution as is Gator-Aid. Most of us are familiar with the widespread popularity of Gator-Aid with athletes, especially with marathon runners - particularly in the summer months when more body fluids are lost during hard workouts.

After treatment for shock and wounds, the dog must be delivered as soon as possible to the vet, as I have stated. If the trip is fairly lengthy, turn the Pit Bull from side to side every ten minutes to prevent the possibility of fluid collecting in a lung, causing it to collapse. Be sure to inform the vet as to what type of medicine you have administered and how much.

When the Pit Bull gets home, he should be kept warm, especially if the wounds are serious. By this time the wounds may have started to swell and the dog may feel quite lame. Probably the best treatment for these conditions is the application of ice which works best if applied before the swelling begins. A good way to use the ice is to put a styrofoam cup of water in the freezer, and when it is frozen, you can place the open end of the cup on the wound, exposing the ice directly to the wound, and continuing as long as you have the patience to do so. Reapply often. The wounds, swelling, and lameness will heal quicker if you combine the ice with light exercise. By this I mean short, slow walks - beginning the day after. Apply ice, walk the dog (even if he limps badly) for just a little while, reapply ice, and back to bed. As the swelling and lameness recede, walk him slowly for longer distances. Provide the additional nutrition recommended in the "Nutrition" chapter, particularly nutritional yeast and vitamin C.

The Pit Bull, as a species, is probably one of the healthiest animals in existence and generally heals quickly. Their biggest enemy is infection. If it sets in, it can spread and spell trouble. You must, therefore, keep a close watch on your dog. If you find pus and/or an area of a wound doesn't heal as quickly or cleanly as the rest, bring him to the vet. Infection is not very likely, especially if the wounds are kept clean, but you should be alert to the possibility and the danger.

You have heard that "laughter is the best medicine" - well if a Pit Bull is convalescing, probably the best medicine you can provide is plenty of petting, a positive mental attitude, and talking in a pleasant, happy voice.

Miscellaneous Tips

1. Care of the Old Dog - When the old pit veteran retires to stud the normal policy is to be sure the old boy gets all he wants to eat and is kept nice and fat and happy. Well this just shortens his life span. He will live much longer (and be able to breed many more times) if he is fed less, supplied vitamin-mineral supplements designed for older dogs, continuously exercised, and kept lean. He will thus be healthier and happier. There is an article in an August, 1982 *Greensboro Record* newspaper entitled "Breaking the Age Barrier." It relates the results of research of the University of California, Los Angeles School of Medicine's Dr. Roy Walford. He has experimented with the lifespan of mice and is said to own the oldest mice in the world (over four years old). How did he accomplish this? Dr. Walford elaborated on laboratory work that began in the 1930's that found that mice that survived on a restricted diet lived longer. Dr. Walford practiced "undernutrition without malnutrition" by underfeeding his mice

but providing vitamin-mineral supplements. His mice are scrawny but they live phenominally long lives and stay active and alert longer. Dr. Walford is so impressed with his research that he is following a similar program for himself. At age 57 he is currently considered ten pounds underweight, but plans to lose another 20 or 30 pounds by the mid 1980's.

Morochito a few months after his automobile accident - just as healthy as ever (except for being a little overweight in my opinion)

2. Care of Collar - Every three or four weeks apply Neatsfoot oil to the Pit Bull's collar and check the "O" ring connections for his lead.
3. Sunshine - It was mentioned in an earlier chapter that puppies need sunshine in order to grow properly, but I believe it merits repeating here.
4. Sore Muscles - If the Pit Bull becomes lame from excessive roadwork, apply hot towels to his legs.
5. Insurance - An article in the July 28, 1982 *Greensboro Record* tells of health insurance for dogs that I thought I'd share with you. Veterinary Pet. Insurance Co. of Garden Grove, California offers the coverage which works much like Blue Cross-Blue Shield does. The premiums vary according to the age of the dog - for example, "a 10-year-old unneutered Newfoundland mix male would cost $107 a year, less a $25 deductible because the dog is more than five years old." The owner of a dog less than five years old pays a standard medical coverage premium of $44 a year with a $15 deductible. These rates were stated in the news article and are, of course, subject to change.

Pit Bull Supplies - There are a number of companies that provide vaccines, various medical supplies, vitamins, and miscellaneous equipment for farm animals (cattle, hogs, horses, and dogs). If you write the following company, they'll send you a catalog: Omaha Vaccine Co., Inc., 3030 "L" Street, P. O. Box 7228, Omaha, Nebraska 68107. Some of the items that are listed in their catalog are as follows: (I have listed them in the order of their appearance in the catalog.)

1. (p.5) Procaine Penicillin G Suspension - a sterile suspension for use as an aid in the treatment of pneumonia, wound infection, etc.

2. (p. 12) Amino Acids with B (5% Dextrose and Electrolytes) - a supportive therapy used to stimulate appetites, counteract dehydration, and provide nutrition during severe illnesses wherein the animal does not eat.

3. (p. 12) Vitamin B Complex Solution - an injectable multivitamin containing thiamine, niacin, pantothenic acid, riboflavin, pyridoxine, and B-12

4. (p. 12) Calphosan B-12 Solution - an injectable combination of vitamin B-12 and calcium glycerophosphate and calcium lactate used to aid in the treatment of neuromuscular disorders and anemia

5. (p. 13) Ethereal Camphorated Oil with Guaiacol - a quick acting heart and respiratory stimulant

6. (p. 13) Electrolyte Solution with 2.5% Dextrose, 2.5% Sorbitol - an injectable solution used as an aid in the replacement of vital blood and tissue salts lost by dehydration.

7. (p. 13) Caffeine Sodium Benzoate Solution - used as a cardiac respiratory stimulant

8. (p. 13) Hypodermin - an injectable counter-irritant for the clean, effective treatment of bowed tendons, shoulder injuries, and injuries deep in heavily muscled tendons

9. (p. 22) Sevin 5% Dust - controls external parasites (fleas)

10. (p. 25) Sunbeam Farm 'N' Barn Portable Hanging Scales – four models; can be carried anywhere and features a straight spring balance in telescoping steel cases; dial is recessed for protection and has a compensating adjusting screw for container weight

11. (p. 29) Electrolyte Powder - an oral treatment for dehydration; mix with water

12. (p. 31) Westway Molasses Energi Cube - one or two 1 1/3- pound cubes a day and your horse will improve in appearance and performance

13. (p. 32) Blood Stopper Powder - a powder containing iron sulfate, amonium alum, talc, diphenylamine; used topically as an aid in checking bleeding of wounds

14. (p. 33) Granulex - a liquid spray used in the treatment of wounds

15. (p. 33) Nitrofurazone Soluble Dressing - a topical ointment used in the prevention and treatment of bacterial infections and wounds

16. (p. 34) Horse Liniment - (a) liniment powder (Dr. A. C. Daniels) used for track horses; (b) Absorbine Veterinary Liniment; (c) Esquire Rubdown Solution - a refined stimulating and penetrating rubdown for topical use after workouts

17. (p. 35) Tuff-Pad - This is a substance that is applied to the pads of a dog's feet to toughen them. It is used when dogs are running treadmills or putting in many miles of roadwork. Toughening the dog's pads protects them so that they are not likely to bleed or tear. If a dog has been raised on a chain with very little exercise, his pads are likely to be soft and if he suddenly begins running he's likely to need some "Tuff-Pad."

Another company that stocks excellent supplies for Pit Bulls is Kentucky Bull Dog Supply, 317 Old Morgantown Road, Bowling Green, Kentucky 42101. It carries stress vitamins and supplements, antibiotics, vaccines, collars, harnesses, treadmills, and more. Write them for more information.

Well, this ends the "Medicine and Miscellaneous Chapter. I hope I've been able to provide some helpful tips that will be of use to some folks, and more especially, will help some Pit Bulls.

Mr. James Garrett and that defeater of champions, the great Jeep. He has retired to the yard of Mr. Garrett after many years of fighting. He never met the dog he couldn't demolish - or a human he didn't love.

Chapter 10: The Combat Dog

> It is easy enough to get good lookers and hardfighters, but it takes a game dog to win. - John P. Colby

True words spoken by one of the men responsible for the development of our breed. For 30 years John Colby bred a quality strain. To be sure, he had his share of bad dogs - that can't be avoided. One reason he developed such a good strain, though, is pure mathematics -he had a <u>huge</u> yard. There were others that had large yards, too, though; why were they not nearly so successful? Well, the following article, appearing in *Your Friend and Mine* magazine (Jan.-May, 1973), attempts to answer the question. It was written by the experienced and well known Indian Sonny.

This Here Is A Pure Colby Dog

Mr. John P. Colby was an active breeder for many years and produced some of the best dogs of his time. Much of his foundation stock was from the Gas House and Burke strains as were the dogs of many other breeders.

The difference in quality of the dogs Mr. Colby produced was the result of the breeding principle he employed. Also Mr. Colby possessed (in my opinion) a very important attribute which I refer to as a GIFT. Mr. Colby practiced a simplified version of genetics. BEST TO BEST. In other words selective breeding. Best to Best does not mean performing dogs alone. It entails all aspects of dogs, from performance to pedigree.

The most obvious qualities a dog can possess would of course be gameness, biting power, talent, stamina and a good bloodline. A bloodline is a direct result of a breeder's influence, or breeding principles.

Over the years, dogs bred by Mr. Colby began to exhibit physical and mental characteristics such as conformation, color and gameness which distinguished them.

These dogs were then referred to as COLBY DOGS, and rightly so. Thus we have the Colby bloodline. People were proud to say "THIS HERE IS A PURE COLBY DOG."

I know this sounds simple and it will lead people to ask, why were there not more top breeders? I'll give my version, right or wrong.

Deciding what is Best to Best is the key. I am sure not every dog Mr. Colby bred was dead game. And I am equally sure he did not breed to every dead game dog he owned. This is where the gift comes in. It seems to be an inborn sense or ability. I believe most outstanding accomplishments have been made by men who were endowed with a gift for their respective fields. If a person is lacking in this gift, he can never be as potentially great as one who has it.

There is nothing man can successfully do to achieve the same standards of perfection as the following were able to attain with the gift in their respective fields: - in boxing, Clay, Sugar Ray, Harry Greb. In horses, Man of War, Citation, Sea Biscuit. In dogs, Clark's Tramp, Black Jack, Jr., Tacoma Jack. In dog breeders, Burke, Con Feely, Jim Corcoran, John Colby, Bill Shipley, Joe Corvino. In lions, Fraisor, the stud.

Nor, can a Dallas Cowboy expect to opaaiify for the great and famous Los Angeles Rams???

This is not to say, a person or animal with the gift is automatically better than one who has little or no gift.

There have been many instances where a boxer was thought to be a coming champ and turned out a chump instead because of his lack of dedication. (Check with Heinzl).

I do not believe Man knows enough about genetics at this time to produce great animals and he most certainly didn't know enough in the days of Mr. Colby. Race horse people spend millions of dollars a year trying to produce great horses, and as of now they have had marginal success.

There is no pattern for producing great dogs. Good dogs often produce good dogs and occasionally great dogs. Man does not fully understand greatness and until he does, he will not be able to establish a pattern for producing it in himself or his animals.

The most essential qualities a breeder may possess are. Dedication, a Gift, and a knowledge of Best to Best. (Money might come in handy!). If a breeder combines these attributes, he is likely to produce (with luck) a great strain of pit dogs. It doesn't take much effort to recall the great Colby dogs of the past. These dogs were bred from the pit and for the pit. There is nothing magical about the name Colby. He was the reason his dogs were good and not his name. This brings us to a very important question.

When a strain of dogs that was once highly regarded, such as Colby, stops producing consistently good pit dogs, is this strain still considered to be good?

I have heard people say, "I know he is a cur, but the blood is there." While this is true in many cases, I wonder how long we can continue to breed to curs and hope to produce game pit dogs?

The questions arise, what is good blood and how long will it remain good blood if we continue to breed to dogs who themselves do not possess the good qualities of their ancestors. While great breeders can breed to dogs who themselves do not exhibit good qualities, can the average breeder afford to take this gamble?

Good blood should mean a strain of dogs that consistently produce good game pit dogs. I have seen strains of dogs that have not produced dogs fitting this description for many years and people who are active in the sport refer to them as "Good Blood," or "Good Brood Stock." Many of us seem to proceed under the assumption that once a bloodline is good it remains good forever.

Many well-meaning people have continued to breed Colby dogs exclusively, thinking all that was necessary to preserve the quality of the strain was to breed to a dog who had the name Colby on his pedigree.

I believe we have to continually strive to improve the strain in order to keep it as good as it was, or is, (let alone improve it).

It is an accepted theory that in order for an institution to continue to be productive, it must change with the times and continuously seek to improve. The time to save is when you have something, not when there is nothing to save. To preserve a bloodline there is more required than just breeding to dogs whose pedigree shows a particular name.

It is hard work keeping good blood good, and maybe a little luck. Change is required to prevent change in the quality of the dogs produced. The Colby strain was developed by Change. The best dogs of various strains were used to produce good dogs and keep them good.

I have heard many people subscribe to the theory that the dogs of yesteryear were gamer than these of today. Could it be, in some cases, because we have tried to play Pat, and in doing so, have lost ground?

The people who have bred Colby dogs exclusively for these many years, thinking they were doing what was best, have perhaps underestimated their own ability to breed good dogs. Many of them have bred dogs for forty years or more, and could have perhaps contributed much more to the betterment of their dogs by using their own ideas and experience.

New ideas are necessary in every field in order to keep up with competition and improve the product. Most all sports records have been surpassed in recent years by people who were not satisfied with repeating someone else's performance. Last year's records won't win this year's meet.

I wonder if the dogs of yesteryear were really superior to the dogs of today? Man has a tendency to associate the past with romantic and pleasant memories. The past is when he had his youth and people are prone to think of their time as the best. Things of today are different, they have changed. Man seems to resist change in many forms: perhaps he fears change. I am sure many dog men of the past would think we have it too easy because we don't have to grow secret vegetables and cook our dogs' food or boil their water. Penicillin has replaced many old remedies, making it possible for more people to provide better care for their dogs.

I have read some diets that were used by top dog men. While some were good, none of them could compete with any good commercial dog food (purina) available in countless supermarkets. The poorest feeder of today is able to provide his dog with better nutrition than the best feeder of yesteryear.

Perhaps this accounts, somewhat in the increase in size of today's dogs. We also have a newfangled gadget called a refrigerator. It may not sound like much but stop for a moment and think what it would be like to be without one.

It is not my intention to criticize the methods of the oldtimers or suggest that they were inferior. How many of us would be feeding as many dogs if we had to cope with the same adverse conditions?

I think however, it would be wiser to pick up where they left off. We should try to emulate their objectives rather than their methods, without becomong a carbon copy.

I don't believe everyone is capable of breeding top-notch dogs or of becoming a top-notch dog fighter. If anyone is still in doubt about great dog men having a gift, a talk with Earl Tudor will do much to dispell this doubt, as his vast knowledge is 99 percent self taught. I don't know if Mr. Tudor will agree with me and my theory of a gift, but by listening to him it should become quite obvious that the only way he could have learned the things he knows would be by a great aptitude or a gift for the dogs. I have heard him say, "That Idiot will never be a dog man, he doesn't have enough sense to condition a dog." Indicating the person had no aptitude or gift for the dogs. There is no book you can read or school you can attend to learn the things required to be a good dog man.

The Colby dogs of the past fit the description of good blood as their pit records indicate. The Colby strain was developed on the breeding principle of best to best. It then follows that when the principle of best to best is no longer employed, there is bound to be a drastic change in the quality of the dogs produced.

In a very short period of time, a great strain of dogs can and will be reduced to a strain that can do no more than refer to their pedigree and say, "My great great granddaddy was a pit dog — I think."

Can anyone name any pure Colby dogs of today comparable to the great Colby dogs of the past? Is it then fair to call these dogs of today, pure Colby? The question is, are present day pure Colby dogs to be considered good blood, *regardless of the quality of the dogs which it produces, or is good blood a strain produces game pit dogs, regardless of its name?*

This article is not intended to suggest that I am an expert but merely to express my thoughts as apply to this subject. I hope this article will inspire more knowledgable people than I to contribute their thoughts and experiences to Pit Dog Report, thus inviting an open and beneficial discussion on our favorite subject, Pit Dogs.

Editor's Note:
Nothing I have read in recent years has preyed on my mind as much as this article by Indian Sonny, which we reproduce here as it was originally published in Don Mayfield's *Pit Dog Report*.

I have tried to search my feeble brain for a rebuttal to it, and search as I might, I have not been able to come up with a suitable reply, because I must admit that the greater part of it is *true*!

Being a great believer in the Colby line, and a loyal follower of the line for many years, I just feel that somewhere there must be an answer. But, where and what?

I believe that a great many pure Colby dogs being produced today, fall into the hands of people who want them as companion dogs, watch dogs, catch dogs, or what have you, and many of them may be just as game as the old Colby dogs were reputed to have been, but they just do not fall into the hands of the people who step in the pit to test them out.

There is no doubt about it, there never has been a breeder like John P. Colby. His widow once told me that John P. Colby bred, raised and sold approximately 5,000 dogs during his lifetime. He did not work for a living, spent all of his time with his dogs and fighting chickens. If he produced five thousand dogs over a period of fifty years, that's a hundred dogs a year. If there were ten really good, game dogs out of that hundred, and they made the pit, they were the ones that went down in history, as "Those game Colby dogs." We don't know how many never saw the pit, and never had a chance to prove whether they were any good at all or not. All we see is the records of those that were tested and were proven to be good.

Well that was awhile ago and we know considerably more about breeding today than we did then, but we still have some people that just seem to consistently produce winning Pit Bulls, and others that have just as big a yard, with dogs that have pedigrees that look like they are just as good, but they have many more curs than they have game dogs. Why is that? Well, I think one main reason that Mr. Colby was so successful was that he bred proven dogs more often than not, and he stayed with his strain with hardly any outcrossing. Indian Sonny's point is well taken, however. Some people just seem to have a natural gift. Dedication is also a factor. Nobody wins pit contests all the time, but those who consistently win more than they lose generally have and spend more time with their dogs, have a fairly good yard to work with, and keep the game ones and sell the poor ones. They provide running chains for their dogs, regularly condition them, provide the best housing, the very best feed, play with the puppies, and regularly roll the young dogs, not making excuse for the ones that do not do well. It takes an unbelievable amount of time. What it boils down to is this: You have to genuinely love Pit Bulls and pit contests - the lure of finding out if you have a champion, or a grand champion, or if you get one, can you get another even better one? You love to see the tactical ability and ring strategy that is displayed. You are continually impressed with the awesome strength and biting power that you occasionally witness, compacted in such a relatively small animal. Most of all, you never tire of knowing a dog that has the deep game personality so uniquely displayed by the American Pit Bull Terrier.

Once again I state - I am not promoting or purposely presenting arguments in favor of pit contests - neither am I making negative pronouncements against it. I am trying in this book to objectively "tell it like it is." In other words, this is a book about the American Pit Bull - not what the dog should or should not be. I do want the reader to be aware of the viewpoint of the pit dog enthusiast and I also want to point out some of the inaccuracies in the publicity and "rip-offs" in the fund-raising drives that are supposed to "inform" the public about the "cruelties" of pit fighting and the people involved. Please note that I will also present some of the negative aspects of pit fighting that do exist - without using sensationalism.

From the Netherlands we have a picture of two Pit Bulls owned by Jan Kuiper, Editor of the Holland publication *The Game Dog Magazine,* which deals with American Pit Bull Terriers. The larger, black dog is a 5-month-old male named Country Boy's Patrick. He is Loposay bred. The smaller buckskin dog is a female from the black dog's father's sister.

It is popular for newspaper and magazine reports, articles, exposes´, etc. to present "on-the-scene" reports by inside "undercover" people who claim to have "infiltrated" the pit fighting "organization." The reports are generally pretty gross, replete with pictures and accounts of heavy drinking, drug dealing, prostitution, unbelievably cruel treatment of animals, etc., all based on a semblance of truth but highly exaggerated. To me they are analogous to the following story based on a hunting party, not a pit contest. The story is, of course, ficticious, fabricated by yours truly to illustrate a point.

The Inside Story on Coon Hunting by Sam Snooper

The following account relates a typical weekend spent by American coon hunters. Correspondent Sam Snooper interviewed three coon hunters for the report. One hunter named Pete Savage is an ex-convict. He has spent ten of his 35 years in reform school and prison. Pete had an abnormal childhood, having been raised by his alcoholic grandfather. Pete was deserted by his parents when he was less than a year old and has been on his own most of his life. He has never been able to hold down a full-time job for longer than a year. He, too, is an alcoholic and a hard-core drug user. Another hunter is James Madison. James has never been to prison; however, he has been to court three times for rape and attempted rape charges, but has never been convicted. He never finished grammar school. He ran away from his home in Maine when he was 16 years old. He is now 25. He, also, is an alcoholic and a drug user. The third party is Matt Hendrix, who is 65 years old, a retired farmer. He was never very successful; actually he has been a loser all his life. Matt never attended school and the only fun he seems to get out of life is coon hunting. Mr. Snooper met the three individuals at a poker game and convinced them to invite him along for a hunting trip. Pete did most of the talking for the group. He explained that the reason people hunt coons is because the coon hound is an extension of a man's ego. A coon hound fancier sees himself in the coon hound as it successfully hunts down and kills the coon. Old Matt said Pete's talk was too deep for him, said he hunted coons simply because he liked the dogs, especially a good one, and because it was fun. From time to time one of the men would get up and look out the window at the dogs. If the dogs saw one of the masters they would jump around and bay, drooling at the mouth, tongue hanging out in their lust for the hunt. The men drank and spat huge gobs of tobacco juice at a tobacco urn located in the corner. (They missed most of the time.) They drank their whiskey straight and insisted Mr. Snooper share their "grass" (marijuana) with them. Later in the evening they passed around "speed" pills which they consumed in copious quantities. They had a yard full of top quality coon hounds -

the Redbone strain and some blue ticks also. The best one was a large blue tick. "A real killer, that one," Pete proudly announced. "Never met the coon he couldn't kill, even one-on-one." (Most coons can more than handle themselves one-on-one with a hound dog; it usually takes at least three to kill a coon.) Sam was informed that coon hounds are trained by wounding a coon so his blood runs, tying him in a burlap bag and dragging him for miles over an open field. If a coon hound pup is successful at trailing, he gets to kill and eat the coon. Baby coons are used most frequently. Since a hound won't trail instinctively, the young hound must be "trained" to the hunt and that is why the coon must be sacrificed. Coon hounds do not have much natural endurance and so they must be conditioned on a treadmill. Since most of them won't run a treadmill of their own volition, they must have incentive. This is provided by tying a dead cat or coon in front of them so that they'll keep running. The coon hound is often run to pure exhaustion, so that even if he stumbles on the treadmill, he must keep going.

When the day of the hunt began, the dogs had not eaten for two days so they were wild with hunger and lust for blood. When the masters hooked them up on their leads, they kept growling and snapping their fierce fangs. "We killed almost a dozen coon on the last hunt," announced James, who was a bit groggy from the liquor he had consumed. He hadn't had much sleep either because he had spent the night with a prostitute. Prostitutes often travel to towns where coon hunting is popular because coon hound fanciers are eager for their services. No one knows why this is because coon hunters don't generally have much money - being uneducated and all.

The coon hunters cheered their dogs on as they began the chase. When they caught the coon, they tore him to shreds; blood was slung all over the ground even up to the branches of the trees. The dogs' masters sneered and laughed as the dogs accomplished their duty. Sometimes the dogs would tree the coon and the hunter got a chance to aim at the helpless coon sitting on a branch, pull the trigger, and kill him in cold blood.

Hunting is really an excellent sport, challenging the intellect. The best thing about it is that it is perfectly legal and the Humane Society doesn't bother them at all. It is in fact one of the most popular of all sports in America. There are many magazines that are available for hunters to read and learn and the magazines do not have to be distributed underground. Most of them have pictures of game (coon, birds, etc.) proudly displayed by the successful hunters that killed them.

Does the story seem a bit ridiculous? Of course it does - because most of us are more aware of what hunting is, what goes on in a hunt, and even know some people who are hunters. But the story is no more ridiculous to us than the stories we read about Pit Bull fights are to Pit Bull people. There is a semblance of truth to the hunting story. Hunters tend to be rural people, but of course there are plenty of people who hunt that are in every other occupation, including doctors, lawyers, accountants - you name it. People do not generally train their coon hounds with a bloodied animal - although there are some who do. Actually many bird dog people train their dogs with a dead pheasant carcass. It's accepted practice in many dog magazines and hunting magazines to brag about the number of animals killed. Just one of hundreds of examples - in *Dog World* magazine I found a write-up by an Airedale fancier. I do not want to mention the name of the guy or the article because it may be embarrassing to him or might cause a hassle. In any event, the guy describes his hunts with his Airedale. Said he had several pictures of her exploits - one of her holding a raccoon at bay and one of her "giving the raccoon the"coup de grace.'" Another picture is of the Airedale "with her legs in a mire of mud, her face proud and happy." Her "Scoreboard" is tacked on the wall and the back of the snapshot states "1978-79 record: 100 raccoons, 13 nutria, and 2 muskrats."

Another example. This comes from a very popular book in dog circles, written by a Doctor of Veterinary Medicine, one of the most respected men in the dog business. I respect him quite a bit myself and hope I don't get him or anyone else mad at me for the quotation below. I want to make it clear that I am not criticizing the man or his statement. I share it with the readers because I am pointing out that Pit Bull fanciers cannot understand why something as inhumane as the mass killing of animals for sport receives hardly any publicity, while pit fighting is considered cruel and illegal and causes so much public fervor. They are not aware of any funds being raised or political pressure being brought upon hunters for cruelty to animals. Yet all the uproar over letting two dogs fight, that love to fight, that are perfectly healthy dogs and generally remain healthy and happy into old age. Well anyway, here is the quote: "Dogs are happiest when used for the jobs for which men developed them by generations of selection. Happy too, were these men who used Redbone coon hounds the night before in treeing these raccoons." The quote appeared under a picture of some men displaying some dead raccoons. The statement is so appropos, I just couldn't help sharing it. Name and source omitted, again, in order to prevent altercations.

I have also read that "Coon hound pups generally have to be taken out with killers before they will touch a coon which has been shot out of a tree; yet once he has learned to do so, the pup will enjoy catching and shaking the carcass." (Again I do not wish to footnote the quote.) A training manual for hunting dogs published by *Sports Illustrated* instructs the bird-dog trainer to use pigeons (They are cheaper.) and then to use pheasants or grouse if they can get them. They are told to clip the bird's flight feathers and let the dog sniff it - then shake the bird until it is dizzy so it'll stay in one spot, and have the dog fetch the bird. The hound-dog trainer is instructed to buy a pet rabbit from a pet shop and let the dog run him down. Trainers of retriever dogs use a live duck with the wings and feet shackled by a sock with the toe cut out which has been slipped over his body.

Well, I could go on and on, but I guess that's enough. The Pit Bull fancier just wants to be left alone and is getting disgusted with all the sensationalized publicity.

The fact of the matter is pit fighters tend to be rural people, but there are all kinds of people involved in the sport, just as there are in hunting - professional people as well as blue collar. The media sometimes presents pit fighting as being part of organized crime or mafia run. Organized crime goes where the money is and there is no money to be made at pit fighting. The cost of dog houses, food, vitamins, medicine, and money invested in dogs that do not turn out game or that lack ability is generally greater than pit-side winnings. There are some people who, over a period of time, have developed more consistent winners and they have made money, and a select few have been able to live (but quite modestly) on pit fighting. Even with the best yard of dogs money can buy, you can't make anywhere near the kind of money you can with gambling Vegas style, loan sharking, prostitution, drugs, etc. There is, therefore, very little involvement on the part of organized crime. There is some participation (on a small scale), however, on the part of successful criminals that have extra money to burn and enjoy the sport. Sometimes a joint venture is formed (They may call themselves a syndicate.) to pool resources to buy a dog or yard of dogs to fight - but it's generally for the sport of it, so there isn't any effect on other participants as a result of it. In other words, some criminals invest in stocks and bonds on the New York Stock Exchange. They don't corrupt the stock market by so doing. There is no prostitution at the pit fights, even the large conventions. The people are interested in the dogs. Those who want or need prostitutes engage in all that downtown - not in some deserted farm house 50 miles from nowhere at six o'clock in the morning!

Another fallacy promoted by the news media is that the spectators at pit contests holler and yell for blood and give out lusty cheers when they see a lot of blood. The people cheer on their favorite dog encouraging him on just as a crowd cheers their favorite football team, boxer, or whatever.

Many pit fighters use an animal to motivate the Pit Bull to run a mill. Some will use a coon that they put in a cage and attach to the mill in front of the dog. (Coons are not easy to get, but most of them enjoy the "game" of being chased but not caught.) Some people use a chicken. Some will just stand there and wave a rag or something in the air. Some will attach the water bucket and many use a milk jug half full of water. Some will put a rabbit in cage on the ground near the mill and that is enough to motivate the Pit Bull. The rabbit doesn't pay any attention; he just sits there chewing his lettuce. Some Pit Bulls won't run a mill whether motivated by an animal or not, but many, if not most, Pit Bulls love the mill work and will run it as long as need be without any motivation. Some pit fighters don't use a mill and prefer roadwork. In any event, the dog men are not cruel to animals in conditioning their Pit Bulls.

The pit fights are generally described by news accounts as being bloodier than they really are. The newcomer, seeing the dogs fight for the first time may in fact be aghast at the apparent cruelty as the dogs will in fact often chew each other up very badly. As mentioned many times, however, the dogs love it. Their tails are up and often wagging away to beat the band. They apparently do not feel it unless it's a deep bite and often don't even feel those. Later in the chapter, accounts of some famous fights are detailed and some sample "plain, ordinary, good fights" are presented, too. The fights are not usually as long or hard as the ones I've shared with you. I'd say the average fight lasts 40 to 50 minutes. In many cases there is really not too much action and the dogs are not hurt much at all. Immediately after the match the dogs will, of course, be pretty bloody and cut up if it was any kind of a fight. This is the time that "undercover" people take their pictures (or when the dogs are in holds with deep bite). The thing is, as I have mentioned earlier, most of them heal up just fine afterwards. Look at Butch, Morochito's half brother. This dog has been in numerous battles. He's been fought off the chain countless times. He has amazing endurance and some people say they've seen him go two hours on two dogs off the chain. The picture you see was taken very shortly after he won his second money match on his way to the championship he subsequently gained. Well, as you can see, he looks fine, not at all like he'd look in the middle of a match.

A few hours after a match, a Pit Bull's wounds tend to swell and he looks pretty sorrowful. Those who are against pit fighting would point to the dog and say, "You can't tell me that dog is enjoying himself." The dog may limp around for a few days and then he'll be as frisky as could be. This is similar to a hound dog that hunts all night and comes home limping and sore, bone tired, but happy. Three days later he's ready to go again.

On the other side of the coin, there are a lot of folks who feel like all that analogy between pit fighting and hunting is well and good, but they maintain that on the bottom line the poor dogs are still getting hurt, and many of these people don't care much for hunting either as far as that goes.

Here is a picture of a dog named Tiger after a match. He doesn't look very much up to par.

Here is the same dog (above) three weeks later. There's nothing wrong with him.

In 1981 a lady wrote an expose´ after completing five years with the pit fighting fraternity, as an undercover agent. She had mixed with some of the known experienced pit men. Her article was not full of sensationalism; it pretty much "told it like it is," as I recall. What is impressive is that she was just as convinced of the cruelty (in fact even more so) after the five years as she was when she started. I would have thought that she would have found (to her own conviction) that it is not a cruel sport. It just depends on how you look at it. She observes dogs getting chewed up and feels like they are getting really hurt. She could watch a thousand fights and still not be convinced that, as the Pit Bull fancier maintains, the dogs don't usually get seriously or permanently injured, and that, as mentioned in the old article about Colby dogs, in order to preserve the breed you must prove the gameness and breed only those that prove game. That can be accomplished only when dogs are matched and fight for 30 or 40 minutes. The fact that a dog's great grandfather was game means very little. The problem is, however, pit fighting is illegal. Those who match their dogs obviously disagree with the law and feel that there are many things being done to animals in this country that are more widely practiced and more cruel. In a recent issue of the "Letters from Readers" section of the *Sporting Dog Journal*, the following comment was submitted by a reader:

Even though I doubt you will print this letter, I am writing it because everyone seems to have something to say about dogfighting except Dogfighters. We are not criminals, we are voting citizens like everybody else. We enjoy our sport as much as our dogs enjoy participating in it. Just as many people enjoy the sport of boxing we enjoy similar skills demonstrated in our sport. There is too little freedom in our world for both man and animal. We as a society need more freedom, not less.

I tell you, if you really want to get a good idea of a pit fighter's feelings on the subject (as well as an excellent story about the world of pit fighting in the U.S.), you must read the paperback book *The Life of Humbug* by Fredric Maffei. Humbug was a (fictitious) pit dog. The book was advertised in *Pit Bull Gazette* for awhile, but I haven't seen the ad lately. See if you can order it by writing Manor Book Mailing Service, Box 690, Rockville Center, N.Y. 11571. It used to sell for $1.75.

In past years pit fighting has not really been as widespread, I believe, as it is today. Much of the literature we read today suggests that because of the illegality and increasing pressure of the Humane Society, the sport is fading. I think that the sensationalism of the articles and exaggerated reports of the Humane Society have actually resulted in spreading interest in pit fighting, in many cases to those who do not really know the dogs and who abuse them. In other words; not many years ago, few people really knew what a Pit Bull is - now most everyone does. That means that those wierd people that exist in any society will pick up on it and abuse the dogs. This may be the answer to some of these reports we've read about training dogs to be killers and feeding them kittens, etc. I don't know. I do know there's not very much of that stuff - there aren't many people like that. Pit fighting is not a perfectly clean sport either. Like any other sport, there are some dirty politics involved in the game. The following comment was sent in (and paid for at advertisement rates) to *Pit Pal* in 1978. It gives you an idea of what can (but rarely does) happen.

During the early part of this match a spectator hollered "police!" The dogs were parted and taken out of the pit. After 10 minutes, it was quite evident that this was no police raid, I believe it was done to prevent the defeat of Champion "B." We went back to the pit to continue the fight. But would you believe that S refused to put his Champion back into the pit and that the ref, a son of a prominent dog fancier, and a man who has seen and refereed many contests, refused to declare C the winner, nor would he order S to put his dog in the pit. This man was a guest of S from down South and I believe he didn't want to call S's dog out. I tried to come to some sort of an agreement with S, and even tried to match him at a later date. He also refused. Once he knew that he was matched into us he couldn't wait for us to put up a forfeit, but once the battle started he couldn't wait to grab up his dog and run home! The ref would not declare C the winner, so I declare him the winner and Champion at 35 lbs. Any comments, J.S., don't call, don't come, (one was enough, not in your home town). Send a contract (will fight in 4 to 6 weeks).

Just Our Opinion
B.B.

I must emphasize that the real enthusiasts do not engage in these dirty tricks, although they are aware of them and more than capable of handling them (the experienced ones are, that is). Their primary interest is in developing a game strain of dogs so that if the dog can't win honestly they don't want him. Therefore they tend to have game dogs and don't have as much need to resort to underhanded tactics anyway. They are less interested in the money. (Although if it's a big match for say $1,000, or more, I guess almost anyone is going to be pretty concerned - but those matches are relatively rare.)

The oldest trick is to put something on the dog's coat that will discourage the other dog from biting, or worse, slow poioon that weakens the dog but is not very noticeable during the match, other than the dog's being weak. Sometimes the dog dies later. To prevent this from happening, each handler washes his opponent's dog under the observation of the opponent's friends and the opponent if he is present. (Sometimes the owner may entrust the dog to the handler and may not attend in person.) The washing must be thorough and must be carefully observed. Sometimes milk is used because if the poison is covered with silicone, the soap won't wash it off, but milk, I'm told, will. If milk doesn't cut it, ethyl alcohol will. As an additional precaution, each handler (or an independent party such as the referee) may taste each dog and smell his fur. Primary emphasis is placed on the head, ears, and legs. Some guys will try (during the washing) to get some soap in the dog's ears which might upset the dog's balance or willingness to continue when the going is rough. This is also the time when the person washing the dog or one of his friends may slip a pill to the dog (by putting it in some cheese or something so the dog will eat it). It can be done very quickly, hence the necessity for close observation. In the ring the handler might employ psychological strategy to lower the confidence of the opponent handler, especially if he is the owner of the other dog. For example, when his dog is on top, the handler might keep telling the other handler that he'd better pick up or he will lose his dog. Sometimes an owner will get a bet going on what's supposed to be a fun match, for, say, $100. Many people will test their dog's gameness and ability by simply matching them for $100 instead of rolling them, on the theory that every time the dog fights there is a chance of a tooth being yanked out, spoiling the chances of the dog's being great. They feel like each time the dog fights might as well count. In other words, they are willing to pay $100 to find out if the dog is worth anything in the pit. Anyway, the person proposing a fun match for $100 may intimate he has a young, inexperienced dog he wants to try out, or that his dog hasn't been adequately conditioned - and then show up with an experienced veteran that demolishes the other guy's dog. Some have been known to work their dogs with homemade leather "booties" covering the dog's feet. When this is done the dog's pads will remain soft and his nails will stay long, as if he'd never been worked out. Conditioned dogs, on the other hand, tend to have tough pads and their toenails are worn down - an experienced dog man would pick up on this -but if the dog had been worked with booties, even the experienced man could be fooled. After all, $100 is $100, plus it feeds the insatiable ego of the type of guy who does that or appeals to that type of person's sense of humor.

 In the pit an experienced man will sometimes take advantage of an inexperienced person's lack of knowledge of the rules and bait him into inadvertently breaking one and thereby forfeiting the bet regardless of who has the better dog. Knowing the rules is very important therefore. In some cases the dog cannot hesitate going across the pit and has only 10 seconds to get to the other dog. Sometimes instead of having the first dog to turn be the one that gets to scratch first, and then alternating, the rules state that bottom dog scratches first, and some require top dog to scratch first. A wise owner/handler will not match his dog under rules that do not favor his dog.

One of the oldest tricks (mentioned in Armitage's book - Con Feeley was a master at it) is to pretend that you are going to pick up your dog, either because you are conceding or because there is supposed to be a handle (picking up the dogs and going to respective corners -which never happens unless the referee announces it). Anyway, the trick is to reach down demonstrably toward your dog like you are picking him up. Handles must be fast if the dogs are not in holds. The idea is to snatch the dogs up quickly before they get into each other again. So when the guy reaches down as though he were going to pick up his dog, the other handler may snatch up his dog real quick as a natural reflex without thinking about it - and lose right there.

Another point - the rules generally state that when you face the dogs (See the description of rules and procedures later in the chap-ter), the handler must not make any attempt to cover up his dog. This means that he cannot hold the dog with both arms around the front chest and bend over the dog, covering him up, the reason being that if the opposing dog doesn't see the other dog, he may not come out of his corner; or if he does come out, he may go to the wrong corner looking for the other dog and not get to him in time. If the rules do not state, and the light is dim, a handler may cover up his dog to the extent possible. If the dog seems sure to lose, he might try it anyway hoping no one notices. When a contest turns into an endurance test and it is the other dog's turn to scratch, a knowledgeable handler will try to hold his dog very still and be as still as a rock himself so that the opposing dog may not see them. A dog is much more likely to react to movement. When the dogs are tired sometimes their eyes are a bit swollen and nearly closed - they may not see their opponent for that reason.

When a turn is called, the handlers are to pick up the dogs as soon as they are out of holds (not biting each other). If a turn has been called fairly late in the match, and the dogs are in holds but not biting very hard because they are tired, a handler might make like he thought they were out of holds and start to pick up his dog, sort of pull back on him and then apologize, stating he thought they were out of holds - the rules prevent a handler from touching his dog in the pit except on a pick-up. This will set his dog's bite deeper and sometimes motivate the dog to shake it out (perhaps because he thinks you are taking away his prize).

The following article, submitted by a prominent dog man to *Pit Pal*, illustrates the importance of the rules and is an interesting story about pit fighting.

There comes a time when one must write in and tell it like it is, after he sees what others have wrote in, choosing their own words, so it will sound like they want it to. I am referring to the report sent in to Pit Pal, *Volume I Issue III, page 68, December 1978 match, C Vs. H. Also, the report in the Sporting Dog Journal, page 18, Jan 1979 Feb, South 2nd match, C vs. H. Tell me, how does a dog win after jumping the pit? If these degrading words are used, may I add a few more words to tell you the way it really happened? The way I saw it! C's dog made his first turn at the 7 minute mark, we got a handle at about the 30 minute mark with his dog to go. It was all I could do to hold the little red dog, as he was going wild to get back, and when faced, I could see C's black and white dog was coming for sure! When the referee called out "Pit!" I released the red to meet him in his corner. He made a right turn and headed straight for a long haired young man that was hanging on the pit side. As he went for the man C held his dog. The long haired man tried to get back when he saw the dog coming for him, and the dog went to the air and took hold of the man's shoulder. The man was pulling the dog with him as he went backwards, the red dog working his hold. The good referee was pointing his finger at me and telling me, "You lose." C was still holding his dog, so I told the referee to call a foul on C for not releasing his dog at the word "pit." As by rules he had to, but I could let go anytime till they touch. C released his dog and he went over the pit wall after the red dog that had the young man in his twenties down, working on that shoulder hold. That side of the bleachers had enough room to seat twenty and had fifty on it cleared out, with no one trying to get the dog off of him. As soon as the black took hold, the red released the man and the dogs went to it. We picked them up and put them over in the pit, all of this took place in less than twenty seconds. The man rolled off the bleachers onto the ground, shaking and kicking, thinking the dog still had a hold of him. At this time the good referee was going from one to the other asking, "What should I do?" The one that wrote the reports hollering the loudest, saying "the red dog loses," as he was the only one there that called a bet on the match and he had to be laid 50 to 30. About this time the referee asked Mr. Col. and Mr. Col. told him that when a dog scratches into an object, he is to be brought back into the pit and re-scratched. So the referee got the crowd quiet and told then the fight was still on and a great sound of "no, no, no" came from the crowd.*

A handle was made and the little red dog scratched hard, driving the black into the pit corner, changing his mind about leaving his corner on the next scratch. hus, making the red the winner! I think the best dog in the best shape won, and so does Mr. C, as we talked after the match.

We don't think there was any fault here with the young, long haired man and we are not knocking long hair. The fault lies with these promoters that have these small pits that are set up to handle 100 people, then try and get 300 around them and men getting into the pit acting as referee and not knowing the rules, and reports sent in by one that is still trying to win there bet. Now, I feel better!

P.S. When the red made his scratch the crowd got quiet and no one was leaning on the pit-wall!!

Another negative aspect of pit contests is that for big money fights, drugs like (I think, don't really know - butezology - called "bute" - and lasix, which controls bleeding) may be administered. These are sublimates. Again this is not done by the dedicated pit fighters - they are more interested in breed development than any money that might be invested - at least they are more interested in winning because they have a superior dog rather than due to "tricks." Another reason drugs are not widely used is that they don't give a dog "heart." They can give him endurance (and get him killed staying in there too long) at the expense of slowing down reactions and dulling instinctive fighting behavior. Drugs are extensively used in thoroughbred race horses when they compete and many of the drugs are accepted by the regulations (many of the racing magazines disclose that fact), and drugs are widely used in many human athletic sports, but not that much in pit fighting.

There are some dirty politics involved even in a schooling roll. Generally speaking, the person wanting to roll his dog is looking for a dog of approximately equal, even lower weight. The owner doesn't want to destroy the young Pit Bull's confidence on the first roll. When he finds someone who claims to have a dog that is reasonably aggressive (sometimes you need a dog that'll start the fight), both parties will often agree that their dogs will be rolled "off the chain," which means they won't be conditioned. However, both parties will then undoubtedly proceed to cut back just slightly on the feed (not enough to make the dog battle thin, but enough to provide some endurance), increase the vitamins, and start the dog on daily treadmill work or roadwork coupled with fishing-pole work. This is not the extensive work a dog gets in preparation for a pit fight, but sufficient to let the dog feel good his first time out. Neither party wants to admit to the other that he worked his dog a little.

In any event, there are other rather underhanded policies involved in schooling, such as the fact that many people like to bring their hard-biting roughie-toughies out to school the young dog. One guy I'm told even rubbed the scent of a female in heat all over the dog he brought out to a roll.

Yes, there are some selfish, cut-throat type people involved in pit fighting, but I daresay that that type of thing is no more prevalent in pit fighting than any other sport or endeavor. Actually most of the pit fighters are very friendly and willing to help newcomers -providing advice, etc.

As I mentioned earlier in the book, sometimes Pit Bulls die after a pit fight. In 99% of the cases, when a dog doesn't survive, it is because

(a) his handler did not have enough experience to know he should have picked up the dog earlier, or

(b) the handler (or owner) wouldn't care and would leave the dog in even if he was obviously losing, or

(c) there was inadequate medical attention or

(d) the dog was shot because he curred out or otherwise proved to be inadequate as a pit fighter.

The question is do all Pit Bull people who fight their dogs allow such things to happen, and if not all, then how often does it occur? The answer is that not all dog fighters let their dogs go too long or kill them if they don't work out. The frequency of occurence of direct or indirect killing of inadequate fighters to the total population of people who fight their dogs is just about equal to the relationship between people who kill inadequate field trial (hound) dog performers and total field trial dog owners. Do the top quality pit fighters kill their inferior dogs? Some do, some don't. Some of the best breeders and handlers of quality hound dogs will shoot a hound that doesn't use his nose adequately on his first or second time out -others will sell or give him away.

Now that we've looked at the viewpoints of those who don't like pit fighting and those who do, some of the pros and cons, let's look at the combat dog himslef - how he's raised, schooled, conditioned, fed, etc. We will then look at the pit fight - rules and handling techniques.

Most people who have anywhere near consistent success with pit fighting maintain a "yard" - that is, they keep a plentiful supply of young Pit Bulls to try out, keeping the ones that work out (or females that prove they can produce) and culling the ones that don't. If the bloodlines are good and have produced well, each litter of pups should contain one or two potentially really good combat dogs. The trouble is the owner must wait until the dogs are 15 months or older to find out. As mentioned in the "Introduction" chapter, there is no correlation between aggression and gameness and the pup that dominates the litter may turn out to be a 15-minute cur. Many, many times the runt of the litter that all the pups pick on develops into the most superior pit dog out of the litter. So the pups need to be kept and tried out when they get of age. This means that most owners do not have time to exercise them that much. The dogs are often kept on a running chain as described in the "Conditioning" chapter, allowing them to run and exercise themselves. Some dogs will run and play a lot, but others will rarely run. When people come to visit and look at the dogs, however, most of them get excited, as dogs do, and run around on their chains, jumping in the air, jumping on their dog houses, and play fighting with any "toy" they may have, such as an automobile tire. As the pups get older and closer to being "of age," the owners will often bring an experienced, older Pit Bull close to them so that they can perceive the aggressive behavior of an adult Pit Bull. The behavior of a pup will often tell the owner when he's ready. When he quits trying to play, doesn't bark but lunges enthusiastically on his chain, he's beginning to show signs of being ready for schooling. Some Pit Bulls seem born ready and they will generally get tried first, sometimes as early as nine months. Many owners won't let their dogs "get bitten" (schooled) until they are at least 15 to 18 months old, regardless of how they act and some even wait till two years of age. The basis behind the latter feeling is that many an enthusiastic young pup has been ruined by being schooled too early, finding out the game wasn't what he thought and quit. If the pup is put into a situation where he quits, he usually (although not always) is ruined. Most people do not have the patience to wait two years, however, and prefer to school the young pup early, but go very easy on him. A pup generally begins school with another pup of equal age and weight. They will often play, however, and it generally takes awhile for them to get serious about fighting. At first they are allowed only a few minutes together, just to get the idea. Some will begin school by bringing close to the pup an old pit veteran that has no teeth (meaning no cutting teeth, or fangs) while the pup is on his chain, and letting them go at it for a minute and them breaking them up. It is not a good idea to let the pup's first exposure be with an older dog, however, even if the older dog has no teeth, because the pup knows he's fighting an adult. Sort of like a twelve-year-old fighting a middle-aged boxer with damaged hands. Mentally, if nothing else, the adult has the younger beat.

Bobby Ackel and his famous Nick -winner of best of show at the Gulf Coast Convention in the early 70's

Most pit fighters will not allow their Pit Bulls, particularly young ones near a cur dog because the Pit may perform poorly against a snapping dog - like a cur dog. In other words, if the dog is snapping at him, the Pit Bull may not take hold. I don't know why this is - perhaps the Pit Bull doesn't realize a fight is on, and some Pit Bulls won't fight unless they feel challenged.

In any event, a pup gets plenty of praise and encouragement at this time. I must inject at this point, that this schooling does not make the pup "mean," "bloodthirsty" or "train" the dog to fight. If this were done to another breed of dog, it wouldn't make a pit dog. The term "schooling" is a colloquialism that refers to merely putting the young dogs together and letting them "have at it" - sort of like putting a young hound dog on a trail. The point is, that the young dog is not "trained." Schooling is a process of gradually introducing the pup to what he instinctively wants to do anyway. This cultivation of instincts provides a degree of learning in that he becomes more experienced by finding out what works, what doesn't work, and how to better protect himself, before he gets with a hard-biting veteran. It also helps assure that the Pit will not lose self confidence.

The next step, when the pup seems ready, is to give him his schooling roll. This may be done at a pit (so the pup begins to be familiar with the pit environment) or it may be in someone's backyard. Sometimes the young dogs are brought to pit fights and schooling rolls are held before the regularly scheduled event(s) - especially when there are not many contests scheduled. The wise owner never schools his pup with a dog he hasn't seen fight before (for the reasons mentioned earlier) and some keep a couple of schooling dogs in their yard. These may be dogs that were unable to perform in the pit because they curred out and/or they have a relatively soft bite.

The first schooling roll is normally pretty short (depending on how young the pup is, how much, if any, trouble the pup gets into, etc.). The Pit Bull is praised during the roll and if a good roll dog has been chosen the pup should be top dog. Because of the short duration, nobody gets hurt on these rolls. (Well, there are always exceptions - some pups are naturally born maulers and hard biters.) The dogs are picked up a couple of times and the pup is "scratched" to see if he'll go across and fight. In initial rolls, the pup is often scratched up close where he is more likely to charge into his opponent. Sometimes, if the pup is too far away, he'll sniff around the floor, forgetting about his opponent, or decide to play. On subsequent rolls, he is scratched further and further away. Another technique occasionally used for schooling pups is to initially roll them while they are on a leash. It is said that this will give the pup more confidence. Some people will pick up the opponent dog after the last scratch and run away with him while the pup being schooled is held but praised (for chasing away the dog). More often, though, the roll ends with the pup "scratching" and then immediately being broken off the schooling dog.

Considerable planning may go into the young pup's first roll. Give the pup very little challenge and he may not fight and thus establish poor habit patterns; give the pup too much and he may be ruined. On the other hand, many owners will school their pups with most any dog of comparable weight (barring a real bad news pit winner) and if the pup doesn't work out they sell him; if he does well, they keep him. This latter practice overlooks the fact that some Pit Bulls take longer to mature and do not begin to fight well until one fine day when they are older they suddenly "turn on." Vindicator (brother to Zebo and said to be an even better fighter, although he didn't have as many matches because he was killed in an auto accident early in his career, I understand) wouldn't fight until he was three years old, I'm told. If there is one characteristic a successful Pit owner needs, it's patience.

A lot of people want their dog to go in with no conditioning. They feel that if the unconditioned dog curs out in 15 or 20 minutes, he'll cur out conditioned in an hour - in other words, rolling the young dog unconditioned will indicate to an experienced pit man not only the dog's potential ability, but his probable gameness. Other people openly advocate conditioning a Pit Bull before any roll and will not roll their dogs without it. An experienced person can find out many things from a 20-minute roll. For one, it tells him if the pup is ready or not. If he is not, the experienced owner will break him off early and wait until later. The dog man will also look for an instinctive ability to bite deep in effective places rather than to stay in skin holds. Many young dogs excitedly grab the nearest thing they can - often nothing but loose skin. Some dogs never learn and will continue biting ineffectively as an adult. Often this is a highly inbred dog - inbred for gameness - and the ability has been lost. By the same token, sometimes the young dog will only mouth the other dog and not bite hard. Surprisingly enough this same dog often attacks a piece of hide on a fishing-pole like nobody's business, or will shake a tire all over the place. Sometimes this type of Pit Bull will kill a cur dog (a dog of another breed) but in the pit with another Pit Bull he will just not bite hard. His opponent may be biting deep and shaking hard while he does nothing but mouth the opponent, sometimes just licking him. More often than not, if the dogs are separated, this dog will scratch fine, but continue not biting. A good dog will generally have his tail held high, will learn very quickly even if it is his first time fighting, will unrelentingly pursue the other dog, ride out holds his opponent has on him, and pour it on when the other dog lets up for even an instant. Some dogs will just stand over or hold the other dog, not biting deep or snaking. A real good sign is when a dog instinctively presses hisopponent when he shows weak. This type of fighter is likely to be a finisher, which is a dog that'll win a fight quickly, say half an hour, with little damage to himself. We've talked about the defensive dog, who is almost continually fighting from the bottom in the beginning of the fight, waiting for the other dog to tire and then turning on. This type of dog can be one of the best, but as a young dog is hard to pick out in a schooling roll. Many owners have given up on such a dog, thinking he is no good and then finding out later on that the dog received his championship in the hands of someone else that bought him real cheap. I said that a good dog will learn quickly on the first roll. As an example of this, you will notice that once the other dog lays into the young dog's legs a few times the young dog learns to tuck his legs in quickly any time the other dog dives toward them and also goes right for his opponent's nose if it's close enough. He learns very rapidly to use his rear legs properly, achieving maximum leverage. He'll learn to twist, spin, and vie for position.In addition, the pup will demonstrate his style:

(1) ear dog - You don't have as many ear dogs these days as you did in the past. They used to be considered the best (style) by many. A good ear dog that clamps down hard and won't let go frustrates his opponent because the opponent is tied up and can't get his own hold. This can give a

Pit Bull that's not game a reason to quit. The good ear dog has excellent footwork, good as any boxer. He will let his opponent push him around the pit by giving in to the weight of the other dog and backing away and circling so that he isn't pushed against the pit wall or overpowered. Meanwhile the opponent gets weaker and frustrated, and the harder he pushes the more energy he uses up getting nowhere, while the ear dog is resting. When the ear dog feels the opponent a bit off balance, he'll throw him with the power and leverage of a Judo player. The ability of these dogs is uncanny.

(2) chest dog - In my personal opinion the best style (if there is such a thing) would be the rough, boring-in style of the chest dog. This dog tends to be stronger for his weight class and has more leverage. Wherever his opponent grabs him, doesn't matter, he bores in and buries his snout in that dog's chest or underbelly whenever he can. This type of dog also tends to be a hard biter. The chest bite weakens the muscles there and will tend to weaken the dog's desire to scratch.

(3) nose dog - there are ver few of these dogs today, but to me it is the second best style - if the dog is good at it. By that I mean he is able to maneuver so that he can get to the other dog's nose and when he does he clamps down hard and doesn't let go. The nose is a tender spot on any dog; it is softer, not protected by loose folds of skin or hard muscle, and the dog will bleed more from the nose than most other areas. This means body fluids are lost faster and therefore the dog will weaken or go into shock quicker. The nose dog is protected from counter moves, moreover, if he has a good hold, clamped down hard, because the other dog can't get his mouth onto him. In other words, the opponent can have the same frustrations as an ear dog's opponent and will weaken guicker. The drawback to this style is that the dog has to be quick enough to get to the nose before his opponent counters. If the opponent is a good dog, he will dive under and bury his fangs in the nose dog's chest or make some other countering move. In other words, a dog's nose is a fast moving, small, elusive target. Another drawback to the nose dog's style is there is more of a chance for losing teeth. When the nose dog misses the target a little, both dogs are biting and chewing in the mouth and sooner or later, if they stay there, somebody's tooth generally goes.

This dog is a good ear dog. He bites deep on the ear and twists his opponent to the side.

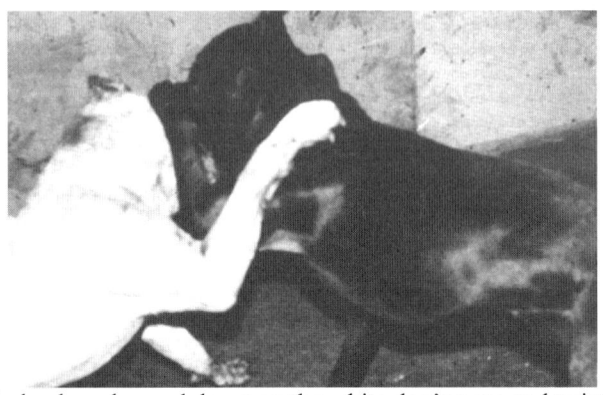

The black dog has clamped down on the white dog's nose and twisted to the side making it difficult for the white dog to use his neck muscles and jerk loose. There is nothing the white dog can do unless he pushes his opponent against the wall and in the process gets him to lose his hold a bit. The white can then jerk free or bore into the black's chest. Other than that, the only thing the white dog can do is wait for the black to let up to change holds.

(4) leg dog - generally rerers to the front legs. This can be the most dangerous style because when the dog dives for those front legs, most good Pit Bulls learn instinctively to tuck them in and grab the dog's nose if possible and we've already mentioned the effectiveness of a good nose hold. We tend to have more leg dogs today than in the past, I believe, perhaps because today's dogs are stronger. A good dog, when he gets his hold on that leg, will shake it like there's no tomorrow, usually throwing the other dog to the ground in the process. The opponent is then off balance and it's difficult to counter. I believe it's worthwhile at this point to relate

a story about a Pit Bull roll that seems relevant. This involves the rolling of a nine-year-old who had never been rolled with another Pit Bull before. I think it should also be mentioned that he was half Staf - X-Pert line I believe. Well, the old dog learned fast. He was rolled with a hard-biting dog that was a pretty good leg dog. At first the old Staf didn't know what to do, but it took him only a few minutes to find out. He learned to tuck those front legs back out of the way and grab his opponent when he dived for them. He fought very well and although he wasn't conditioned and was soon hyperventilating, he didn't show any sign of quit. They rolled him for about 20 minutes and then he scratched good. He didn't show any bad sign. He was too old to match, of course, so he never was, but the point is that fighting ability is an inherited trait, and the instinct can be brought out even in an old dog.

(5) stifle dog - There are a lot of good stifle dogs today and many dog men prefer them. When a hard-biting dog gets into an opponent's stifle, he tends to weaken the muscle the dog relies on to push with, while protecting his own head at the same time.

These are the basic styles. Of course the comments I've made about which is "best" are all generalities; no style is really best - in any given situation the style that wins is best. The owner will not like it if the pup demonstrates that he's continuously favoring one technique to the exclusion of the others - not unless he happens to be one of those rare individuals that's especially good at that technique. In other words, if the dog is continuously going for one area - ear, chest, leg, whatever - the opponent, if he's any kind of Pit Bull, will soon learn countering moves. The following, just one of many examples, may illustrate:

A Pit Bull named Molly was an excellent leg fighter. She always scratched hard and straight - straight for that leg. When she got the leg, she shook it something fierce. It was successful for her when she was young so she always went for that leg. She was a good pit dog, but not a real good one. She looked pretty good in her schooling rolls other than for her proclivity for one technique. She won her first match decisively. When she was matched against a real good one, she couldn't get that leg enough because her opponent was too good. Every time she made her move, her opponent got her nose. Molly never learned; she just kept trying for that leg. She was game. After a reasonably long match, she didn't make her scratch; and her eyes were glazed, and she was in a state of shock and didn't know where she was. Still, she wasn't dead game - some Pit Bulls would go across instinctively, even in a state of shock. She healed fine and in a month felt and looked as good as new. Her owner gave her a short roll to see if she had lost any enthusiasm or vigor and she hadn't -she looked as good as ever. He then matched her against a dog that outweighed her eight pounds. (He knew the dog and figured Molly would make her quit. He shouldn't have. It is very rare that dogs are matched at unequal weight - half a pound makes a considerable difference in a contest that is (if the dogs are game) as much a test of endurance as anything else. But the match was for a small amount of money to see if Molly could make her heavier opponent quit. The dog was too heavy for her, however, and couldn't be hurt sufficiently. Molly evidently knew this and eventually quit. She has a good bloodline and her owner sold her to someone who kept her for breeding. She's produced some good dogs and has some fun once in awhile being used as a schooling dog. She'll teach a young Pit Bull to protect his legs right quick.

A dog's style is partially inherited, partially learned as a pup from the mother (A mother that is an ear dog, for example, will tend to constantly play with the pups' ears, often making them yelp) and partially learned in the schooling roll (when the dog does something that works real well and makes him feel boss, he will always try for that hold ever afterwards. When Morochito's brother Jake was a little pup, one day he grabbed his brother's front leg up high near the shoulder and slammed him down hard on the ground. His brother squalled like nobody's business and their owner had to break them apart. That was always Jake's favorite hold, that and the chest hold. Did he learn it as a pup? Well their half-brother Butch, the one that became a champion, fought the same way, and Morochito showed that he favored the same technique when he got into his accidental hassle with that Pit Bull that outweighed him 14 pounds. I related the incident earlier, but the point is that at first he didn't know what to do, but after he got frustrated and a bit angry, he really threw that big old dog around. He was able to manipulate the bigger dog because he found that when he came in low and pushed up from that position, he had more leverage, and he also found out that if he went for the dog's head and then at the last minute when the other dog went for his nose, he dived down and grabbed the leg up high near the shoulder and shook hard, using those strong neck muscles of his, the result was that he flipped that dog on the ground quick as could be -same technique as his brother and his half-brother. Inheritance seems to be a large part of it. None of the three dogs, Morochito, brother Jake, or brother Butch relied totally on the one technique. They all fought everywhere - head, stifle, you name it. It's just that whenever they saw the opening with their opponent, it'd be a sudden move and bam! - down went the dog and they'd shake the leg like a whirlwind, then bury into the chest. That's a good sign. Some people don't like a dog that will not hold on to their favorite hold for an extended period of time, but lets go to grab some ineffective area, because although this may be merely a show of enthusiasm, this type of dog is generally not a finisher. The real old timers will tell you, though, that Pit Bulls all have such individual unique personalities, that you can never really tell. They never cease to surprise their owners.

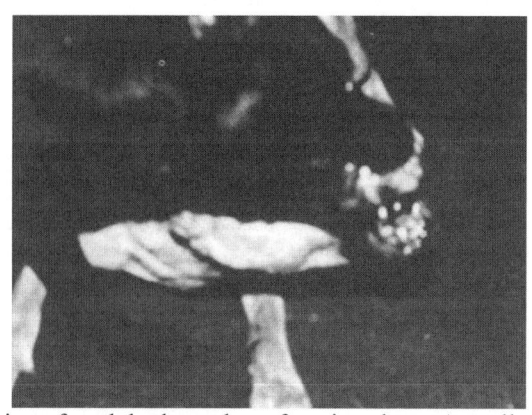

The showing of teeth looks perhaps ferocious here. Actually very little damage is being done. The black has a hold on a corner of the white's nose. The white will soon work his way out.

Anyway, getting back to the young dog's schooling roll, if the dog looks good on the first roll, the owner may decide another easy roll or two may be in order, perhaps exposing the young dog to a dog whose style is generally effective against the young dog's indicated style - i.e., nose dog against leg dog - so that the young dog may learn to deal with it. The best partner for the young dog after hes had a little experience is an old, successful pit dog that has no teeth and is retired. The old boy has a good time reliving the "good old days" and no one gets hurt.

Some people will roll the pup with a much lighter weight dog so that the pup will learn to move faster especially if the pup is or will grow to be a catchweight (heavyweight - generally over 50 pounds). Muhammad Ali (a heavyweight) spent many hours sparring with lightweight boxers. A lot or people will roll a good hard-biting pup with a dog that outweighs him significantly (one that is not really a good fighter and doesn't have a hard bite). If the pup's confidence is not broken, he will learn to use his leverage to maximum potential. It's like karate people - some of us practice our kicks with leg weights. When we take off the weights - look out! Well many karatakas do not like the leg weights because it can be dangerous to the knees if you aren't careful. The trick is to be careful and tense up at the point of extension. In any event the principle is that when you work resisting a heavy weight, you perform better when you subsequently resist a lower weight.

When the dog is ready for a harder test, some people use an experienced dog of equal weight that will put pressure on the Pit Bull. The length of this roll will depend on how well the young dog does. If he looks good in this roll, the owner may decide to go ahead and match him for a small amount of money, say $50 or $100 and figure on investing that much to find out if his dog is game.

Another method occasionally used to test gameness is to roll the Pit Bull fat (a term that doesn't really mean real fat, just not trimmed down to fighting weight and unconditioned). When the dog is not lean, heat dissipation is more difficult and the dog will soon be panting very heavily. If he stays with it for 20 minutes with a good opponent and scratches good even though tired, there is good indication that Pit Bull is game.

Another method of testing gameness without having the dog go the distance is to two-dog him. With this method the young dog is pitted for a good ten minutes with a good, hard-biting dog that'll put him in trouble. The first ten minutes are generally pretty fast paced as the dogs vie for position. After this amount of time, the young dog's opponent is taken out and another good dog replaces him. The new dog will charge in with all the enthusiasm and fervor of a fresh Bulldog. This will tend to make even a Pit Bull quit after a few minutes if he's not too game. This roll should also go for ten minutes and if the young dog still seems eager, doesn't turn (other than in the process of nameuvering) and scratches straight at the end of the roll, chances are very good that this dog is game. Some people will three-dog their Pit, but it's not necessary. Twenty minutes on two dogs should be enough to indicate gameness.

An experienced owner will not generally subject his dog to a gameness test unconditioned. As mentioned earlier, some will game test their dog fat to see if he'll quit in an hour conditioned. Sooner or later, however, if they are observant, they find that this is not necessarily the case. Many times a dog that quit fat in 15 minutes (or just didn't look good at all), later turns out to be dead game and a good dog. A dog will hyperventilate quicker than a human because heat dissipation for him is more difficult. Remember the dog fights because it's fun to him. It's not much fun if he is smothering. The best pit men condition their dogs nearly as well for a roll as they do for a match, although not for as long a period of time.

Lil - A Well Conditioned Pit Bull

The female above is what a conditioned pit dog looks like. Her father is Morochito's half-brother Butch, the champion mentioned in the "Breeding" chapter and whose picture appears elsewhere in my book. Outside the pit Lil is very shy. This picture of her was taken three days before her scheduled match and she is in excellent shape. A great deal of time and planning went into her keep. She is exactly on the weight she is supposed to be which is 36 pounds, if I recall correctly. Notice she is as thin as possible and still not be too weak. She has an ideal conformation for pit fighting. She is tall and rangy. You can get an idea when you see how tall she is (above my knee) and yet only 36 pounds. Those long legs give her lots of leverage. Her mouth is built right for a strong bite.

Here is another picture of Lil. At this angle you can see how thin her waist is. I can almost put my hand around it.

Just previous to Lil's scheduled match, it was cancelled because of a disagreement. The agreement was not written on a contract; it was oral, and the money was not given to a third party to hold. It was to be a $400 match. Two days before the agreed upon date, the owner of Lil's opponent called to say he wanted half the gate to go to the winning side. The other half, of course, goes to the person on whose land the match is held. Lil's owner owned the land and had been responsible for almost all of the observers (about 30 or 40 people) -so he felt that the total gate should go to him regardless of which dog won - especially in view of the late notice. Well, Lil's owner was upset because he had put so much of himself into Lil's keep. She hadn't really had much schooling and hadn't been game tested. The match was, therefore, really a $400 game test. So that evening her owner three-dogged her to see if she was game. She was. Her firstdog bit her very hard and had the best of it for ten minutes. She came up and was doing well at 15 minutes at which time a fresh Pit Bull was put on her. This dog was much heavier than she, outweighing her by seven pounds – that's a lot, about 20% of her weight. It would be equivalent to a 150-pound man fighting a 180-pound man. The big dog shook Lil all over the place but she made a fair account of herself. She was then matched with a dog slightly smaller than she (not sure what the weight was). The smaller dog is an extremely hard biter and very powerful. She was on an exhausted and spent Lil. Lil fought weakly. The smaller dog shook Lil so hard she knocked Lil's shoulder out of joint, or so it appeared. Lil hobbled to make her last scratch, so her owner picked her up and pronounced her as game as any Bulldog needs to be. She is now retired and used only for breeding.

The way a Pit Bull pup is schooled varies with the views of the owner. Some will not fool around. Give the young dog a good hard test - he works out or he doesn't work out. Others will be almost paranoid about not wanting their dog's self-confidence hurt. They'll schedule a roll with some dog then get queasy and come up with some excuse – "Oh my dog is sick," "next month," etc. Finally they'll roll their dog with some dog with no teeth. Most are somewhere in between. Some will have difficulty measuring their dog's potential objectively. If a person knows the blood is there and wants his dog to be a champion, it is difficult to recognize faults. This is particularly true if the owner has only one dog or just a few dogs. A person with a large yard can afford to be more discriminating and will unconsciously be so. Most owners are careful not to over school. Every time a dog fights for any length of time after the initial play fights, it takes a little bit out of him. That is why the stories you read about by the humane society and news media about 20X winners or even 10X winners is hogwash. It is exceptional for a dog to have five contract matches, never mind win five (a grand champion). A dog is generally retired from the game (because he's a loser) or retired to stud (if he's a winner) long before he's had five matches. If he's fought too much, the dog will build up too much scar tissue, his legs (driving power) will become weaker (like an over-fought boxer), and his skin will lose its elasticity and toughness. There is also the danger of losing teeth. The adult Pit Bull is a lot stronger and his bite is a lot harder (for 15 or 20 minutes) when he's rolled, than when he's matched. This is due to the fact that his weight has not been brought down for the roll. So, sometimes the enthusiastic Pit Bull will shake so hard he'll pull out his own teeth. Another reason for not rolling too much or over-schooling a Pit Bull is that he may develop a habit of quitting early. According to several old timers, he may get it into his head he is supposed to fight only for 10 or 15 minutes. After a schooling roll, a dog is generally given at least three to four weeks rest before a second roll.

When a Pit Bull seems ready, the owner will schedule a match at his dog's weight. There are many little factors that make the difference between a consistent winner and an occasional winner. Of course, if someone is lucky enough to own a dog like Boomerang, it doesn't matter - you give him at least adequate conditioning and set him down with any other dog his weight, and he'll win. In most cases, however, considerable planning and experience is necessary to be a consistent winner. For example, it helps if the owner knows the dog that is open to match. Having seen him fight puts you in a better position to evaluate the possibilities. Matching cold against a dog the owner has never seen puts him at a disadvantage. Knowing the handler is an advantage also. The dog that fights on his own territory has an advantage. The one that travels can be drained of energy. If the match is a good distance away, some people will travel the day before and let the dog get there early enough to become acclimated, especially if it is several states away. If they do this the dog will need water, and they will bring a glass jug of local water because drinking water from an area the dog is not accustomed to can make him a little sick or weak, just as it sometimes does people.

One of the most important factors is the establishment of pit weight. The idea is to get the dog down to the lowest weight possible and still not be too weak. The lean dog will have more endurance and heat dissipation will be easier. In addition, since the dogs' matching weight must be nearly identical, your dog must be at his lowest possible weight so that he will be fighting as tall as he can in that weight division. On the other hand if the dog is drawn too fine (too lean), he will not have enough endurance and his bite will be weak. It takes a little experience to be able to determine the dog's best weight and in fact it is somewhat a matter of individual preference. Some would rather sacrifice a little height and let the dog have a bit more weight and be stronger; others bring the dog way down, really too much. Most are in between the two extremes. Obtaining the correct weight is probably even more important than the conditioning the dog receives. Sometimes an owner gets anxious when he can't get a match at the dog's ideal weight and will finally accept a match with a dog at a pound or two above his dog. This is not good practice. Many a good pit dog has had a short career when he might have been a good dog in the hands of a more patient handler.

When the match is set, the money is given to an independent third party who is to act as referee. If the owner (or his appointed handler) does not show up on the agreed upon date and location or if the dog is not right on the weight, the money is forfeited and the third party referee hands the money over to the winner by default. Let me add that the general sportsmanship of the participants in the pit game is really phenomenal. I do not mean that there are no arguments, name-calling, back-stabbing, or cheating. There is right much of it as a matter of fact, as there is in any sport; but for an illegal activity, it is amazing how many honor the informal codes. Many times a loser has to forfeit because of a technicality, such as the dog's not meeting the requisite weight - and then the owners may agree to let the dogs fight anyway to see who's the better dog.

In preparing for a match, the dogs enter their keep (a traditional term referring to the conditioning program), the length of which depends on the personal opinion of the conditioner or owner, the existing condition of the dog, the quality of the dog and his opponent, and such practical matters as the agreed date of the match. Many experienced people keep their dogs, the ones that are open to match, at around four or five pounds above pit weight and in semi-condition. These dogs can, of course, be conditioned quicker, so their keep can be shorter. A keep should be no shorter than four weeks and some insist on ten. Most are somewhere in between. The longer keep is, of course, the better one. Here is where experience makes a great deal of difference, and some people are real artists at putting a dog in peak condition. I have talked with countless pit men from old timers (the real good ones) to those who are relatively new to the game and inexperienced. Everyone seems to have their own preferences and most have their "secret" techniques that they will not disclose. I have been fortunate in that many have shared their techniques with me. The one thing all successful keeps have in common is that they begin slowly, bring the dog to a peak, then taper off so that he has considerable energy at fight date, and they all feed a low-fat, high-protein diet. Some use a treadmill that can be adjusted to slant upward slightly (putting more work on the drive-train rear legs), some use an electric treadmill, and some prefer the old-fashioned straight one. Some do not like the treadmill and prefer to ride a motorcycle in the country, up and down hills while the dog runs along. Some (not many) have facilities for swimming and their "secret" technique is to swim the dog, as mentioned in the chapter on conditioning. Some like to use a three-wheel motorcycle, tie the Pit Bull to the side of it, and go up and down a steep hill. The catmill and the treadmill are the most widely used devices today. Walking is also part of every successful program. The two areas most people cut back on are walking and rubdown. The conditioner that really cares for his dog and loves to condition also, will not quit early on either of these. The longer keeps are better because they build a deeper reserve of inner strength for the dog to draw upon when the match becomes a drain on his energy - that is if the conditioning program is done correctly, bringing the dog to a peak and then tapering down. In a 1981 *Runner's World* magazine I read that the program for many human marathon runners calls for 14 weeks' intensive training (just prior to the race - They really train all year long), of which the last two weeks are the tapering-off period. The dog's conditioning program is shorter as is the tapering off. Most conditioners begin tapering off three days before the match if the keep is a short one, say 4 to 6 weeks, or 5 days for a longer keep, say 10 weeks. Some work their dogs once a day because that is all the time they are willing to put into it. Conditioning a Pit Bull properly is very, very time consuming (one reason the pit fighting fraternity gets very irritated with the implications made by the news media that they are cruel and lack the mental capacity to have feelings for an animal). A person has to really love a dog and love working with him to put in all the time and mental considerations necessary to have a successful pit champion. A conditioning program, to be adequate, entails at least two workouts a day, morning and evening.

    The keep begins with a thorough check-up by the vet. The most important consideration is to cleanse the dog of all worms. Most dogs have at least a few worms, but providing they are under control, they do not visably affect most adult dogs. Under the severe strain of a pit fight, however, the worms will most definitely take their toll on the dog. Most people thoroughly worm, using medicine to cure all types - hook, whips, tapes, and rounds - before taking the dog to the vet. The only way you can really tell for sure if a dog is free of worms is with a microscopic analysis of the dog's stool. The stool must be fresh - if it is not, the worms will die and the test will show negative even if the worms are present. There are different medicines for different worms and there are multi-purpose medicines. In other words, there are different approaches to worming. Most people worm twice - once the day before entering the keep and again a week later. They then take the dog to the vet to see if he is clean. If he is, they may still worm again 2 ½ to 3 weeks before the match, to be sure. Most people discontinue heartworm medicine while the dog is in his keep, unless it is one of the longer keeps in which case they may wait until half way through to discontinue heartworming if they live in an area such as the South, where heartworms are heavy.

Usually the dog in keep is worked out twice a day - morning and evening. The first day is designed to warm the dog up and accustom him to the mill. Thus, begin the first morning workout with a long walk - two to five miles (the longer the better), followed by a 15-minute rubdown, which helps keep the muscles loose and pliable and aids in eliminating soreness and the dog will be more enthusiastic for the workouts. A select few also give the dog a mid-day rubdown and talk with him while patting him. They claim this makes a difference. The person that conditions the dog is almost always the one who handles him in the pit because he and the dog grow very close during the keep. Often it is the handler's verbal encouragement that helps the dog to scratch just one more time and win the match when the other dog quits after the next turn.

The first evening workout begins with the treadmill or catmill. Before putting the dog on the mill, most people walk him ¼ mile, letting him empty out and work out the kinks. (It is important that the Pit Bull empty out before a strenuous workout. If he doesn't before the end of the short walk, the conditioner will insert a wet match stick into the dog's rectum, which will stimulate him to empty out shortly if he has anything in him.) The Pit Bull is generally started with only five to ten minutes on the mill (depending on his condition entering the keep). Following the treadmill the dog is taken for another long walk - about two miles. (Always walk your dog after the mill work so he'll have a slow cool-down.) A 15-minute rubdown will relax him before he is put in his sleeping quarters. He is generally not fed or watered until at least half an hour after the workout. He is given fresh water twice a day. Beginning the second day the walks are gradually increased.

Some people have the time and like to give three workouts a day, the mid-day one being 5 to 15 minutes with a fishing-pole with hide attached. Those who like to supplement the morning and evening workouts with a fishing-pole, will work the dog about five minutes before the treadmill work. As mentioned in the conditioning chapter, the fishing-pole technique involves tying a piece of hide or rag to the end of a long, lightweight pole (Bamboo is best.) and swishing it back and forth in front of the Pit Bull as he runs up and down his chain. The rag is flicked in front of his nose and kept just in front of him down low (teaching him to charge low), and at the last instant, just before he hits the end of his chain you suddenly jerk it around, just out of his reach, and go the opposite way. He charges past the rag when he misses it, puts on the brakes, and twirls around and goes after it in the opposite direction. Periodically the rag (or hide) is flicked up into the air and the Pit Bull jumps up after it -four, five, six feet into the air. This is excellent work and quite popular with conditioners. Some Pit Bulls that refuse to work a mill (often because not exposed to it as a young pup), will work a fishing-pole for an hour or more (pretty tiring and boring for the conditioner, however, and the work often gets cut too short). Other Pit Bulls are not at all interested in chasing after the hide or rag and will just stand there and look totally disinterested (again, usually not exposed to as a pup). Some Pit Bulls will shy away from the dancing rag and put their tail between their legs and quiver. These dogs are by no means necessarily bad pit dogs. Many, many excellent pit dogs are very shy outside the pit. My Pit Bull, Morochito, and his brother Jake have contrasting personalities. Morochito is very outgoing, loves people, very agressive towards animals, enjoys conditioning, and is happy-go-lucky. Jake is very lazy when it comes to conditioning and he is shy and sometimes even cringes when a strange human approaches. Although when he became owned by a pit fighter and began schooling for the pit and later became a winner, his personality was more open and friendly.) Morochito has never fought in the pit; Jake has never lost nor has he met the dog he couldn't demolish, just blow right through him. Anyway, when Jake fought his first match and many in the crowd were cheering him on, his owner asked the referee to request that the spectators please keep it down because Jake is shy of loud noise. (This brought a chuckle from many who didn't know Jake -at the time he was scratching so hard he was literally slamming his opponent down and was barnstorming him to the extent that the dog had a hard time getting a good hold). Another example of shyness is a female who is the granddaughter of Big Boy. She's a two-time winner; they say she's been rolled 17 times - some good hard rolls, too. (As discussed before, this is very unusual and was too hard on her.) She's never been stopped, though. She's a pretty shy one and won't chase a hide or rag on a pole, just lopes doing roadwork and doesn't run a mill very enthusiastically. Anyway, the fishing-pole is an excellent training technique. Some people call it a spring-pole although a spring-pole actually refers to a similar device, a long, heavy, flexible pole with hide hung on the end of it. The pole is attached to a tree or otherwise anchored and the hide hangs in the air. The Pit Bull leaps in the air, catches the hide, and hangs there, the flexible pole bouncing the dog a little. Some Pit Bulls have lost teeth playing this game, however, and not many use it. A similar device is to get a heavy-duty spring and attach a foot of garden hose to it. The Pit Bull will clamp down on the hose and pull. The hose and spring will provide just enough resistance to make it an enjoyable game. If the conditioner talks to the Pit Bull, encouraging him as he does in the pit, his dog will get excited and pull harder. This activity, too, establishes rapport between dog and handler. The handler does the same thing when the dog is on his mill and with other conditioning exercises.

Many, if not most, people keep a daily log of the dog's weight and length of time engaged in each activity (mill, walk, etc.). The dog is weighed after each workout and his weight is a factor in determining the quantity of food provided. If he is losing too much, more food is given. If he gains, the food ration is cut a little. This is part of the art of conditioning a fine athletic animal - keeping him right on the proper weight while exercising him to the maximum without over exercising.

After the half way part of the keep, special care is taken to eliminate over excitement and noise from the Pit Bull's environment. He will need plenty of rest and sleep, and every precaution is taken to see that he is undisturbed. This is when his energy reserves build up and must have quiet, peaceful surroundings.

Some people touch their face (it being more sensitive than the hands) to the dog's nose every day to see if his nose is cool and moist. (A hot, dry nose indicates a sick dog.) When the dog is taken off the treamill after each session, the handler will immediately feel the groin area to see if the dog is hot. (This is an important part of the keep and must be done after every workout.) In the beginning of the keep, if the dog is a little fat and/or unconditioned, the groin area will feel hot. The dog is not ready to match until this area feels the same after intensive mill work as before placing him on the mill.

Mill work can be rough on a dog's feet, and most handlers will apply a foot conditioner to the dog's pads. Some will use a mixture of equal parts turpentine, linseed oil, and burnt motor oil. Others will use a commercial foot-toughener obtainable from farm supply stores or veterinarian supply stores. It is generally applied with a small paint brush. In addition, an antiseptic lubricant is applied before and after the mill work. Beginning with the second day, both morning and evening workouts are gradually extended. The Armitage book, *Thirty Years With Fighting Dogs*, contains Armitage's keep, reflecting his lengthy experience with the dogs. Of course it was written back in the early 1900's. Many of his dogs, however, hit the two-hour mark when matched with a dog that would stay with them. I am not stating that Armitage had dogs that always won or that his conditioning program was superlative. As he relates in his book, he had his share of curs. If one of his dogs lost, though, it was not because he was not sufficiently conditioned. Anyway, each person has his own program for increasing the work. Some will increase the walk or roadwork up to 20 miles and increase the treadmill up to only half an hour (each workout). These folks walk the dog for long distances to build endurance and keep him moving very fast on the mill to build lung power. Electric treadmills (either purchased or homemade) are very populare this days for those who do not have time for the long walks.

Here I am encouraging Swinson's Boss to pick up his speed on a wheel that he's running.

They set the treadmill for a slow, walking pace, place the dog on the mill, and watch t.v. Others keep the walk or roadwork short, down to two to five miles and increase the fast mill work. I think it is interesting to note that Armitage states that "40 minutes is the most any dog needs in a workout on a fast mill." On the other hand, one of the most active and knowledgeable breeders and pit men today says that his keep consists of building the dog up to ten hours a day -five hours each session. Most do not give their dog this much work because, as mentioned in the chpater on conditioning, over-conditioning can make a dog go stale. When questioned about this, the dog man I refer to responded, "How much would you train if you were preparing for an enduring fight where you would lose a lot of blood?" (That is paraphrased, not exactly verbatim.) I believe that those who are able to peak their dogs at three or more hours twice a day, have dogs that are maintained in reasonable condition at all times since puppy-hood, and those that say that giving a dog more than 45 minutes a day or two half-hour sessions a day will make the dog go stale, just keep their dogs on a chain, fat until they put them into their keep." I don't know. I do know that many dogs go well over the hour mark after a keep consisting of nothing more than two half-hour-a-day mill sessions coupled with long walks. Some conditioners increase the mill work five minutes a day and the roadwork a mile or two a day and some increase the mill work 30 minutes a day. In any event the idea is to gradually work the Pit Bull to his limit by three to five days before the match. The Pit Bull should be so tired he doesn't want to come out of his house when he sees his owner or conditioner during the day. At this point the work is gradually cut back. The dog might receive ten minutes on the mill in the morning and the evening. The walks will change from long ones to short ones. The last three days the dog may not receive any mill work, but may be walked short distances four times a day. The programs all differ with each conditioner, but the idea is to gradually bring the dog to an exhausted peak and then gradually reduce the work to short walks so that by the time the dog is set down in the pit, he has recovered from the exhaustion and is now a bundle of pent-up energy seeking release.

Part of the art of conditioning a dog for a match is the feeding program (as touched upon briefly before). By the date of the match, the Pit Bull must be stripped of all fat and right on the pit weight, at which point the dog should be lean with ribs showing. If he is too lean, however, he'll be too weak. His head should appear full with no bones showing, in other words a sign of the weight being too low is a bony appearing head. If the dog's weight is brought down too rapidly, his metabolism will be shocked and it will weaken him. I know of a little white female Pit Bull, Colby bred, who's not very pretty, her conformation is not the best, she's sort of weak, and looks pretty old. (Her pedigree is not known for certain, so I'm not sure how old she really is.) Her owner purchased her for a pretty good price, for breeding, because she is supposed to be dead game and a good dog. Her name is The Rose. She was fat and totally unexercised when he obtained a chance to roll her. He had two weeks to bring her down to pit weight, however, so he fed her nothing but one boiled egg a day. When rolled, she didn't look very good at all. She didn't seem to have any ability, just stood there, and bit whatever came close enough to her; she had no maneuverability. She was also, of course, weak and easily pushed around. She showed no signs whatsoever of quitting, however, so her owner subsequently signed a contract for her to be matched. She was then sent to one of the old timers in the Pit Bull business, a retired man who has the time to spend with a Pit Bull. She entered her keep which included a quality feeding program. It is unbelievable how quickly she became lean, and strong. The Rose won her match, stopping her opponent in 58 minutes, and she looked like she could go for another hour. Her opponent was a good dog, too, but you know that Pit Bull had puppies that night! The word I got was that evidently her owners didn't know she had bred and was pregnant. The puppies are alive and healthy. That shows you how game some Pit Bulls are.

The drooping eyelids of these dogs with tails down indicate they are both exhausted. They do not have the strength to bite adequately and yet they still try to fight. The glazed appearance in their eyes means they are nearly in shock. They have the heart but neither has been sufficiently conditioned. It is cruel to set a dog down and expect him to perform without having given him a proper keep.

Anyway, the feeding program is very important. The dog will need high-quality carbohydrates for energy during the demanding keep, but only enough to satisfy energy needs and no more, because at the same time the Pit Bull must lose weight. Many people begin the keep with the same top-line dry food they have been using, such as Purina Hi-Protein or Wayne's, but on a reduced basis. (Very few are aware of the professional dog foods mentioned in the "Nutrition" chapter.) A 45-pound dog might receive one cup each feeding (morning and evening). Feeding twice a day keeps the energy level up and allows the dog to lose weight easier. Feeding dry food allows the dog to retain fluids better (needed during heavy workouts). In addition to the carbohydrate need, heavy workouts mean that the dog's vitamin-mineral demands will be about triple the normal requirements. The Pit Bull is therefore given - sometimes regularly and sometimes sporadically - (These are approximations, depending on the size of the dog.) ¼ cup wheat germ (provides extra B-complex and helps clean system out), ¼ cup brewer's yeast, dessicated liver pills (7 ½ grains, 15 to 20 a day -Most seem to be unaware that dessicated liver is available in powder form which is far cheaper and about three times more potent), vitamin E pill (400 I.U. for stamina), a natural vitamin C (100 milligrams), ¼ can mustard greens (or spinach) - to be sure the dog gets well cleaned out (Some grow their own greens), two tablespoons of honey, and two of molasses. Some will also give a couple papaya pills (one of the best natural digestive aids you can get), which you can obtain at a health food store. The Pit Bull will need some help with all the extra vitamins and health foods. Occasionally he should fast (skip a meal) or eat nothing but a boiled egg or two for that day. The Pit Bull is weighed after each workout. This is one of the most important parts of the keep and is recorded in the daily log (mentioned before). Also recorded are the number of miles (roadwork) and tne time (mill work), along with comments on the dog's performance (feeling weak, enthusiastic, etc.). The dog must be kept right at two pounds over his pit weight. When he gets too heavy the food must be cut; when he gets overly exhausted, a day of rest is given. About half way through the keep, the dry food is cut in half and lean meat is added. Some people use round steak, seared on both sides, cut into 4-inch cubes, and served raw (Cooked meat loses the nutrients and makes loose stools), but the meat is often bull-neck beef cut into cubes, which is said to provide more strength than other types of meat. Even when visible fat is cut from beef, however, the dog is still receiving fat because beef is slaked with fat, much of it not visible. With many, chicken livers have become very popular in recent years and are, in fact, in my opinion, better than the beef. During the last quarter of the keep, all commercial dry food is cut and replaced with the meat or livers. Also, the mustard greens can be cut the last week. Up until about five days before match time, the Pit Bull is given all the water he can drink. At this time the water is gradually withdrawn so that three days before the match he is given water only once a day. His last food and water is 12 hours before the match. This is so that he will be dried out, which will be explained shortly. Some people keep the dog at two pounds above his pit weight (as previously stated) until the drying-out process in which the weight should drop to right on pit weight. Others keep the Pit Bull two pounds below pit weight until two weeks ahead of the match, at which time the feed is very gradually increased so that a day or two before the match he is half a pound below weight. When his mill work is cut and he is just walked, his weight will go up to ¼ pound below weight. If he puts on too much weight, he is walked longer. Those who use the latter approach feel like the dog will be stronger if he is kept a little below weight and then brought up - that bringing the dog's weight down the last few days would make him weaker. Quality, calibrated scales are mandatory. It can be a heartbreak to put all that time and planning into a dog's keep and have him be overweight at pit side.

The drying-out process is very important. The last food and water is given 12 hours before the match because the dog must be dehydrated and have an empty stomach. The empty stomach is necessary to keep the Pit Bull from getting sick. An athlete can understand this. If you eat a meal before a heavy workout, especially if entering the ring for a few rounds of boxing, you'll get sick, your stomach will cramp, and you'll be weak. It's happened to me several times in karate until I finally learned. Before a heavy workout, I eat nothing but a poached egg and two tablespoons of molasses and some honey (an hour before class). I also drink a cup of ginseng tea. This method provides me with plenty of energy. A dog's digestive system is quite different from a human's, in that it takes a dog about six hours to completely digest a meal. In the past, many newcomers lost a match because they fed their dog a small meal two or three hours before a match to "give the dog energy." Today, almost everyone knows better. A lot of handlers will give their dog a couple tablespoons of honey about two hours before a match. Honey is predigested and will not give the dog cramps, providing you don't give too much. It will also provide energy. I mentioned that the Pit Bull must be dehydrated. The dog will be weaker and you might wonder why it is so important to match him in this condition. It has to do with the red blood cell count, which when the Pit Bull is dehydrated, is said to be high (called PCV-packed cell volume). This is not literally true. If a Pit Bull has, let's say, five million red blood cells when he's had his fill of water, he will still have five million when dehydrated. A high red blood cell count means that the relative number of red blood cells is up - relative to the fluid in the blood. It can be pictured by imagining a test tube filled with fluid and five million red blood cells. Drain out the water so that the test tube is half filled, with the red cells and very little fluid. It will be thicker, more viscous - like 20W oil (used in automobiles) as compared to 5OW oil. When the blood is more viscous, with a high concentration of red blood cells going through the body, the lungs and rest of the body will cool off easier because the rise in hemoglobin concentration of arterial blood produces a higher maximal oxygen content. Since the dog doesn't sweat like a human and relies on panting to cool off, this is especially beneficial. The Pit Bull that is fat and has plenty of water inside him will quickly begin hyperventilating. Another, more important reason for dehydrating the Pit Bull is its effect on bleeding. Naturally when the dogs fight it can get quite bloody (although the dogs are not as bad off as they appear and many of the fights are not really very bloody). It is loss of body fluids through bleeding that causes the Pit Bull to go into shock or become too weak to continue. As explained, the dehydrated dog has thicker blood, so the wounds do not bleed nearly as freely, and they stop more quickly. The Pit Bull that is not dehydrated is almost certain to be beaten if his opponent is half a bulldog. In the past, for a short time, the pit fighters experimented with feeding or injecting high quantities of vitamin K into Pit Bulls just before a match. They picked this idea up from the cock (rooster) fighters. Vitamin K is said to controlbleeding; I'm not sure why. It was found that it doesn't work with dogs and in fact has an adverse effect - the vitamin K can be toxic if too much is given. Old-time cock fighters swore by it, but many of the modern ones, I understand, say it doesn't really control bleeding with chickens either. I think it began with the knowledge (which shows that a little bit of knowledge can be harmful) that vitamin K helps control bleeding (which it does, but modern commercial dog foods and supplements provide more than sufficient amounts of that vitamin). Providing extra, therefore, would not control bleeding better but in fact might cause the dog to bleed easier because it could then interfere with the normal bodily functions. But folks seem to keep trying to come up with something new. More recently, some people have been experimenting with salt. Again, this practice originated from having a little knowledge. The salt program calls for feeding the Pit Bull half a teaspoon of salt two or three days in a row, then going five or six days without it. No salt is given for the last two weeks of the keep. This is supposed to increase the effects of dehydration and therefore produce a higher concentration of red blood cells. It is true that when one takes in extra salt, the body retains fluids, but when one is deprived of salt, the body does not dehydrate to any greater extent than if it hadn't had any salt to begin with. The body needs some salt anyway, which commercial dog foods contain. All that is accomplished by feeding the dog high doses of salt and then depriving him is a tremendous (although not visibly noticeable, especially with a conditioned Pit Bull) shock to the system, that weakens him. Several people have followed this program and their dogs quit just as quickly. It's the heart a dog has that really counts in the long run.

 There are about as many different types of keeps as there are pit fighters, each having its own program and techniques as I mentioned. The sample keep I related is very general and not even representative. For example, not all people begin with dry commercial dog food and gradually cut it out and add meat. For some, the feeding is the same throughout the keep - perhaps all chicken livers, or all round steak, or whatever. Some do not give all the extras like mustard greens, vitamin E, wheat germ, etc. Some work the same amount every day, gradually increasing the work unless the dog shows stale and needs a rest day - others have more demanding schedules (greater work increases) but schedule rest days every two or three days regardless.

The biggest secret of all to a successful keep is not in the specific program or technique - it is in the consistency, regularity, and in not cutting corners. Rain or shine, no workout is cut. Twice a day workouts are doubly effective and the time is never cut short. The successful conditioner will go five extra minutes rather than cut a workout one minute - this includes the rubdown, which, of all aspects of the keep, is the part most often cut, because it is time consuming, can be tedious to those who do not genuinely appreciate a conditioned Pit Bull, and many do not understand its importance. Some use baby oil twice a week when rubbing down the Pit Bull (pouring it on their hands and wiping them dry as they rub down the dog). This is to make the dog's skin tougher, more elastic. Some rub alum on the dog's lips and gums to make them tougher. Some give their dog only half of a particular feeding twice a week and give him a knuckle bone to gnaw on. Before giving the bone to him, they'll put it in boiling water for 20 minutes and then let it cool down. The reason for boiling is to kill any parasites and also to make it even less likely to splinter. (Knuckle bones are given because they don't splinter easily - all others should be kept away from a Pit Bull.) Since it's very important that the Pit Bull be free of all worms and other parasites during his keep, some people build a wooden platform, place it next to the entrance of the dog house, and chain the Pit Bull on the platform (must be shaded) because bones pick up parasites from the ground. The bone is given either late in the evening and taken away the next morning or given in the morning after the workout and taken away in the afternoon. Bone gnawing exercises the jaw muscles.

During the last three to five days when heavy mill and roadwork ends, some people have a large shipping crate that they place the dog in to be sure he stays quiet and some put the crate in their bedroom, letting the dog out four times a day for walks and emptying out, and that's it. A lot of handlers swear that keeping the dog in the bedroom makes a difference.

Next is a description of the match. The Pit Bull is normally weighed several hours before the match to be certain he is right on weight. If he is a little over he is walked until his weight goes down, even a little under to be sure. Some give the Pit Bull a tablespoon of honey at this time. The day of the match the Pit Bull is kept as quiet as possible. On the ride there he stays in a shipping crate in the back of the car, van, station wagon, or whatever. There are generally several riders in the vehicle and they often smoke heavily, which is not at all good for the Pit Bull's lungs. Many experienced handlers, however, will not allow the smoking. Some people leave the back open thinking it will provide the Pit Bull with needed air - another mistake. Experienced dog men realize that carbon monoxide fumes are drawn inside by a rear window and that is bad for the dog. A draft is also created that is bad for him, too. Adequate air is provided by a side window opened just a little. At pit side there is a friendly atmosphere as everyone greets people they have met before but have not seen for awhile. There is a lot of discussion about the dogs involved, talk about other matches, pedigrees, etc. There is very little or no carousing, etc., that the news media reports. There may be some tobacco chewing on the part of the old timers especially, some beer drinking, and some pot passed around by the younger generation - not as much as you'll find at many American parties and get-togethers these days, and many people neither smoke, drink, or chew. After everyone has arrived and the socialization is over, the matches begin. The dogs are brought over to the scales to be weighed. Each Pit Bull is placed in a harness and hung on farm scales that are suspended from the rafters or a tree branch or whatever is available. The referee, both handlers, and other interested parties observe the weigh-in. As mentioned earlier, the dogs must be right on weight. To have a good idea of a pit contest, you should be familiar with the rules. There are several that are used; the modern ones are variations of what used to be called Cajun rules. A detailed set of rules appear in Richard Stratton's second book, *The Book of the American Pit Bull Terrier*. Another sample of rules comes from the now defunct magazine *Pit Pal*, submitted by one of the old timers in the game – he's been involved with the dogs for 40 years now, although he quit fighting them long ago; he still breeds a few. In any event, his suggested rules follow:

This is a great sport and if you expect to be successful, there are several things you must have. First, good dogs, second, good common sense and third, know the rules by which the contest is governed. Be alert, give your dog all the help you can within the rules. Remember, no man ever got rich fighting dogs, and winning is so much better if you do it fair and square.

The following is a set of rules that I have drawn up and feel they are fair to both handlers and dogs.

1. A referee shall be agreed upon by both principals. Both principals and referee shall agree upon a time keeper. Referee's decision to be final.

2. Both dogs shall be weighed in the presence of the referee. If either dog weighs a fraction over the agreed upon top weight or is not present at the agreed upon time for weigh in, he shall then and there forfeit to his opponent.

3. The principals shall toss a coin to determine who washes first; also for choice of corner in the pit. Both dogs shall be washed in the same water with a good soap, then both rinsed in clean warm water. Each principal shall furnish two clean towels for drying his opponent's dog. The dogs shall either be washed in the pit or very near the pit.

4. After each dog is washed and dried, he shall be taken to the pit and kept in his assigned corner until his opponent is brought in. Each principal shall be allowed to name a man or himself to be near his opponent's dog at all times to see that nothing is done to give the dog an unfair advantage. If any handler or watcher sees anything wrong, he shall appeal to the referee, and if the referee finds anything wrong, such as dope, he shall award the fight to the opponent.

5. When both dogs are brought to their corners, there shall be only the two dogs, two handlers and the referee in the pit. The referee shall say "face your dogs." The dogs shall be brought to the score line with both front feet on the floor. The referee shall give the command "Pit." Both dogs shall be immediately released. Both handlers to remain in their corners until dogs are together.

6. This is a scratch in turn contest. A dog who is accused of turning must have turned his head and shoulders from his opponent whether in hold or out. Upon noticing this, either handler may appeal to the referee, and if the referee agrees, he will announce there has been a turn, on whichever dog made the turn. "Handle your dogs when they are free of holds." Each handler must handle his dog as soon as possible without breaking a hold.

7. When the dogs are handled, they shall immediately be taken to their corners and kept behind the scratch line. At 25 seconds the referee shall say "Face your dogs." Both dogs shall be brought to the score line, both front feet on the floor. Both dogs head and shoulders to be shown fair between the handler's knees. Handlers to have both hands on front of dogs shoulders. At 30 seconds, the referee shall command "Pit." The handler of the dog whose time it is to go must take his hands off his dog from the side. Time starts immediately on the command, "Pit." The scratching dog has 10, 15, or 20 seconds to go across and mouth the other dog. The referee shall count the seconds out loud and motion each count with his hand. If, at the end of agreed upon time the scratching dog has not completed his scratch, he shall be declared the loser. The handler of the

dog being scratched to may release his dog anytime after the command, "Pit." He must release his dog when the dogs make contact. Neither handler shall in any way push his dog. If he does, it is a foul and he loses the fight. This must be enforced.

8. There shall be one container of water with two sponges for washing the dogs mouths out. At each handle, the referee shall give each handler a sponge. If there is more than one scratch, the sponges shall be switched each time.

9. After the first scratch, the dogs shall be handled any time they are free of holds and the dog who scratched last may be allowed to remain in his corner until his opponent scratches to him. The contest shall continue in this manner until one dog fails to go.

10. If after the contest has started there comes a time when neither dog is in hold and there has been no turn, either handler may ask for out of hold time. The referee shall say, "Time on for out of hold." If at the end of one minute neither dog has taken hold, the referee shall say, "Handle your dogs." The dogs shall be taken to their corners and at 25 seconds, thereferee shall say "Face your dogs," and at 30 seconds, "Pit," and the handler of the dog who was on the bottom at the time the dogs were handled shall release his dog. If this dog scratches, the contest shall continue. If he fails to scratch, then his opponent must scratch to win. If he fails to scratch, the contest is a draw. If at the end of the one minute out of hold count, neither dog is on the bottom (both free laying side by side) then the dog who had the last hold shall be allowed to remain in his corner and be scratched to by his opponent.

11. If any outsider should attract the attention of a dog by waving something in front of him while he is scratching, the referee shall immediately order the dogs handled, object removed and the dogs scratched over.

12. Should a dog become fanged (his tooth being in his own lip) the handler of the dog may appeal to the referee. If the ref finds that the dog is fanged, he shall order the dogs separated, the dog unfanged, then the dogs to be faced and released within two feet of each other.

13. If during the contest, either dog should jump the pit, the referee shall immediately announce his opponent the winner. Exception to this rule, if either dog should get thrown out of the pit as a result of wrestling close to pit side, the dogs shall be handled and brought to the center of the pit, faced and turned loose two feet apart. The contest shall continue.

14. The handlers shall be allowed to encourage their dogs by voice, snapping of fingers, clapping of hands. They shall not be allowed to touch their dogs until ordered to do so by the ref.

15. Pit Size—Any size acceptable so long as the scratch lines are 14 feet apart and corners are large enough for the handlers to sponge and rub their dog without moving over the scratch line. Floor to be covered with either canvas or carpet. Sides, 30 inches high.

16. If interference of any kind should cause a contest to be stopped or postponed, the two principals shall agree on another location within two weeks. Failing to do so, the referee shall name the time and place. Same weight and rules to apply.

In rule 7 you may notice that the dog cannot be pushed, even a little, when his turn comes to scratch. The handler's hands must visibly move to the side, they cannot move forward. Notice, also, that "the handler of the dog being scratched to may release his dog anytime after the command, 'Pit.' He must release his dog when the dogs make contact." This is where experience comes in. A good handler knows that many times (generally, but not necessarily, when the dogs are tired) a Pit Bull will scratch all the way across the pit -and stop right in front of his opponent. On the other hand, if the handler holds his dog until the last second, he gives an advantage to the opponent dog due to momentum. The handler will generally wait until the opposing dog is half way across, with no sign of changing his mind and then release his dog, if the scratches are near the beginning of the match when the dogs are fresh. Later in the match, if the opponent seems weak or shows any sign of quit. He may wait until the last second to release, hoping the opponent will quit -especially if he doesn't scratch hard. It can work the other way also. When Morochito's brother Jake fought his first match, he was scratching so hard he'd slam his opponent to the ground or against the pit side. Because of this, every time it was scratch time, Jake's handler released him just as soon as the referee said, "Pit," whether it was Jake's turn or not. Jake was the stronger dog, and the handler's policy made the match shorter. There are many tactics a handler should know. He learns to place his body where it will do his dog the most good. He should always stand where the dog can see him. This can really make a difference to the Pit Bull's morale when the going gets rough, knowing that his handler is there providing moral support. The handler also provides verbal encouragement. Sometimes when the dog is down and the handler wants to get him going, he'll slap the ground and say, "Up, (dog's name), up." If he lets his dog lie still too long, his muscles can stiffen up and lead to him quitting. When the Pit Bulls are fighting, they concentrate on each other and tend to avoid the people - referee and handlers. A good handler will place himself where it will benefit his Pit Bull's style. If his dog is an ear or head fighter that likes to hang on and lead his opponent around, he will keep away from the center, giving his dog plenty of room, and try to get in the dogs' way if they get near the pit wall. The ear dog needs room to maneuver. Up against the wall the other dog can bore in. On the other hand, if his dog is the stronger one and is the boring-in, chest-type dog, the handler will establish himself near the center and keep his position so that the fighters can move over toward a corner or the pit wall where his dog will have the advantage.

The handler's hands must come straight up. The dog cannot be pushed.

A handler will often attempt to manipulate turns in his dog's favor if he can. If his dog is getting the worst of a battle and both begin to tire a little so that a turn may be imminent, he may call the opponent's dog by name hoping that he will turn toward him, if it would benefit his dog for the opponent to have to scratch. If the dogs are tired, perhaps lying on the ground vying for position, the handler may snap his fingers near an open area (say for example the stifle if this is one of his dog's favorite holds and he observes that his dog could get to it). This will often cue the Pit Bull to go for it. To catch his dog's attention, the handler may make little noises as he snaps his fingers, as he does during the keep when he's playing with him. He'll snap his fingers and make noises as he gestures to a tire or hide. It is part of the rapport the handler establishes with his dog. A real good handler knows his dog and the opponent's dog. He knows his dog's favorite holds and pace. He knows when to call his dog on, when to provide encouragement when he's tired, and when to be quiet and let the dog rest. You may have noticed that I said good handler rather than experienced handler. Many a very experienced handler will see their dog on the bottom, resting, and holler to him, trying to encourage him to get going. Most Pit Bulls are a heck of a lot smarter than the handler when it comes to fighting. A good handler knows when to let the Pit Bull's instincts dictate the pace and when his Pit Bull needs encouragement. Many times a real good Pit Bull will lay down and relax and let the other dog do what he will, especially if the other dog doesn't have a good hold. It is similar to what Muhammed Ali called "rope-a-dope" when he beat George Forman (not really a new boxing technique as Ali seemed to imply - but an old one). A good handler knows how to maximize the approximately 30 seconds when the Pit Bull is in his corner waiting for scratch time. For one thing he'll be alert to pick up his dog when he is out of holds (neither dog holding on) after a turn is called, and will rush to the corner as fast as he can. The pick-up is best accomplished by grabbing the dog's loose skin around the neck and pulling up as you wrap your arm underneath the dog. If the other handler has not been quick enough to handle his dog, the good handler will be alert to turn around as he picks up his dog and keep turning until the opposing dog is picked up by his handler - because the opponent dog will be quick to jump after your dog and may get a good hold on his leg while you're holding him if you don't keep moving. The first thing he does when he gets his dog in the corner (The dogs must face away from each other in their respective corners) is to spread the dog's legs apart, especially the front legs, so that they won't squeeze in on his lungs, and keep them apart while in the corner. The next thing to do is to check and see if he's been fanged. To be fanged in Pit Bull parlance, means that the dog's fang has penetrated his own lip and is stuck there -this happens fairly frequently. You check for this by running your finger along his gums under his lips, both upper and lower. Next he will sponge the dog down well, talking calmly to him. He'll hold the sponge on the back of his neck, underneath just above his groin, and on his butt. (These three areas are points that will most rejuvenate him.) When the referee calls to face the dogs, some handlers will place one hand on the front chest muscle (holding the dog back) and the other hand underneath the dog on his belly, just above the groin. The area just above the groin is one that to a dog is akin to putting your hand on a person's back. In other words, when a human needs encouragement, you pat him on the back. Dog psychologists state that a dog is encouraged, not with a pat on the shoulders, but with a pat on the belly just above the groin. Some handlers have picked up on this. Good handlers know that you never place your hands under the dog, however, supporting him, lifting up on his belly. This does not help him. How would you like someone to wrap an arm under your stomach and lift you just before going in for the tenth round of a boxing match? The hands are always placed either on muscle (like chest muscle) or holding loose skin (like the loose skin on the Pit Bull's neck). If the handler places his hand on the belly, he just places it there; he doesn't lift up. Some handlers will lift up the hind legs a couple times. (It is said to relieve the strain on the hind legs that are used so much in the contest - similar to the rest a boxer gets when he sits down between rounds.) When the referee says "face your dogs," the good handler will spin around as fast as he can and face his dog toward the opponent. The reason he moves so fast at this point is to maximize the time the dog has to look at the other dog before the referee says, "pit your dogs." You see, a dog has a short attention span and the longer he has to see the other dog the more likely he is to scratch when tired or when his eyes are a bit swollen. In fact, one very experienced and respected handler stands with his Pit Bull on his right in the corner (In other words he doesn't straddle his dog.) and when the referee says "face your dogs" he need only quickly step 90° and his dog is facing. When the referee says "pit your dogs" the handler (if he has a hard scratching barnstormer) will release his dog immediately as soon as the referee says "pit." He does so because he watches the referee, not the dog in the other corner. He'll watch the referee's lips and facial expression. As soon as the referee's lips start to press together to form the word "pit," he's ready to let go of his dog.

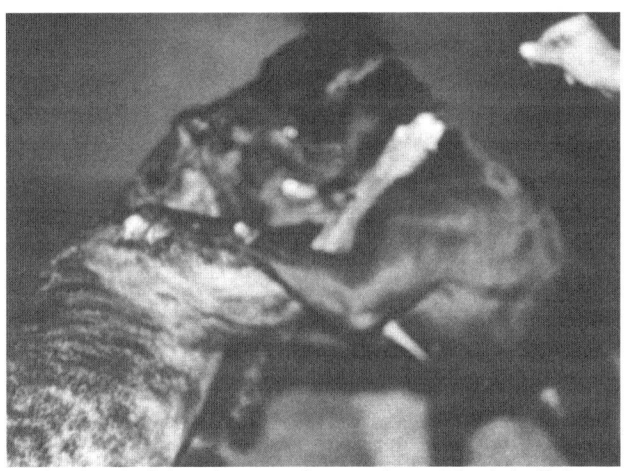

Neither dog is administering any damage here. The brindle's owner is snapping his fingers toward the solid black dog's throat area. The brindle is responding, but has only a "skin hold" which means he is clamping down on the loose fold of skin that protects a Pit Bull. That type of hold will only tire the brindle and won't stop the black dog at all.

Lastly, the good handler never, mentally, gives up on his dog. This handler is convinced in his mind that his dog is going to end up winning no matter how rough the match is going for him. A dog may not have the rationalization or verbal communications powers of a human, but he has much finer developed senses toward feelings and emotions and knows when you are angry, happy, pleased, or discouraged, even when you do not say anything. He senses the confidence - as well as the lack of it in his handler. This fact used to be considered folk lore by many, but modern animal science studies have found that it is really true. A dog can smell changes in another animal's (including human's) "pheromones." I'm really not sure what these are, but I think they are hormones. In any event, pheromones indicate the emotions. To a dog, there is nothing at all miraculous about sensing, or smelling the emotional state of another animal. In addition, a dog will not necessarily look at you when a communication is made, and of course he won't answer back - like "ok," or "thanks." So when you speak encouragingly to him, you won't get the same response you would of a human. The natural human tendency, therefore, is to not genuinely feel like a communication is made. The fact of the matter is, the feeling a handler projects is far more important than the content of his words. You can say, "Good boy, hang in there, boy," etc. all you want - but if you don't really feel like he can do it, your words won't even be half way effective. Of course a good dog will win regardless of who is handling. All things being equal, however, the dog with the better handler will win.

This picture shows a small fight with very few spectators. The dogs are vying for position.

The match is over when a Pit Bull does not make his scratch or when the handler concedes the match, at which time he will often ask for a "courtesy scratch." This means that he will be allowed to face the dogs and release his dog to see if he is game enough to try even though his handler has picked him up. Sometimes the handler of the winning dog will allow them to come together and then break them up. The usual practice is for the handler of the opponent dog to pick up his dog at the last minute (but he should have his dog well away from the corner or the dog continuing to scratch will run head first into the pit wall). Some people will "tail scratch" the losing dog. This means they face the dogs and the losing dog is scratched - but the handler grabs his tail and follows him half way across and stops him by holding back on the tail. This is not a very good practice, however; it is not at all good for the dog. Very few tail scratch.

When the match is over the Pit Bulls are returned to their crates and cared for. If one Pit Bull is excessively hurt, the owner and backers of the opponent dog pitch in to help nurse the hurt one. Sportsmanship is generally very high, much better, really, than most other sports. The loser often congratulates the winner (and means it). Notice I am saying generally. Sour grapes do exist and some will claim their dog was poisoned and all kinds of stuff.

Many of the matches are reported to regional fight magazines like *Sporting Dog Journal*. If a Pit Bull wins three consecutive matches, he is a champion. Below you see a copy of the championship of Morochito's half-brother Butch. (Names blacked out to prevent embarrassment.)

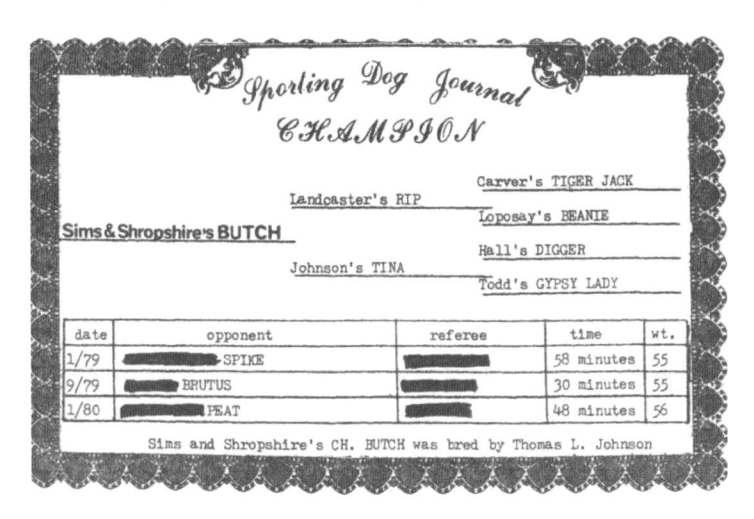

Sporting Dog Journal
CHAMPION

Sims & Shropshire's BUTCH

Landcaster's RIP
    Carver's TIGER JACK
    Loposay's BEANIE

Johnson's TINA
    Hall's DIGGER
    Todd's GYPSY LADY

date	opponent	referee	time	wt.
1/79	SPIKE		58 minutes	55
9/79	BRUTUS		30 minutes	55
1/80	PEAT		48 minutes	56

Sims and Shropshire's CH. BUTCH was bred by Thomas L. Johnson

Just about every person that's seen Butch fight says that he was the best dog at his weight (55 pounds) they had ever seen. *Sporting Dog Journal* has listed in its first issue of each year a list of the champions of the previous year, together with their sires and dams. In the January-

February, 1981 issue, 32 1980 champions were listed (including Butch). In that same year this magazine started a new designation called Register of Merit, in order to recognize the achievements of stud dogs and brood bitches. It was felt that when a Pit Bull is retired from all that hard fighting there should be further honors he can acheive and receive recognition for them. Many champions have not been able to produce match dogs that were nearly as good as they were, and conversely, many dogs, although never matched, have produced quality match dogs.

"In any event, the editors of *Sporting Dog Journal* feel that whether champion or house pet, ace or cur, if a Pit Bull can excell in producing champions, he deserves the recognition. The three best producing sires in the 1970's were Nigger, who, it is believed, was never matched; Tombstone who was matched only once (and won a good one); and Ch. Carlo who was an eight-time winner. In bitches, Ch. Catfish and Pinky were the best producers. Pinky lost her only time out.[52]

The Register of Merit designation is given to any dog or brood bitch that produces three or more champions, and will be referred to in *Sporting Dog Journal* with the initials ROM after his/her name, i.e. Giroux' Ch. Carlo, ROM. The magazine keeps a running account of dogs receiving this particular honor and publishes it in each issue. Each dog or bitch receives one point for each champion produced. Following is the current list of Register of Merit sires and the number of points accumulated:

Patrick's Tombstone   6 pts
Adams' & Crutchfield's Ch. Art   4 pts
Giroux' Ch. Carlo   4 pts
Mayfield's Nigger   4 pts
Giroux' Ch. Gunner 3 pts
Sorrells' Red Jerry 3 pts
Finley's Bo 3 pts

Following is the current list of Register of Merit dams and the number of points accumulated:

Crenshaw's (Irish Jerry's)   5 pts
    Ch. Honeybunch
Lewis' Ch. Catfish 3 pts
Patrick's Red Baby 3 pts
Giroux' Pinky   3 pts

In a situation as we have with Ch. Honeybunch who was owned by both James Crenshaw and Irish Jerry and both have bred champions off her, both names appear on each list.

Most top sires and dams have passed on, but some of them have sons and daughters that could go on to obtain their championships and in so doing add to the number of points of their sires and dams. Many young sires and dams have already produced their first champions and will, in all probability, have other offspring go on to win championships and in so doing add points to their sires and dams. In any event, there is definitely room at the top.

To give you an idea of the fights, I have selected several that were recorded in fight magazines. It is a coincidence that many of them came from 1973 magazines. They just happened to have the best matches I could find. 1973 happened to have been a very good year for pit fighting. I chose some matches of well known, famous Pit Bulls, and others that were not so well known but about which the editor made comments of interest or that were just good fights. The first match is between dogs that were not well known but was a well above average match and I found the comment at the end to be very interesting. It came from *Your Friend and Mine*, June-December, 1973. (Names are omitted to prevent embarrassment.)

J vs B
Males at 38 Pounds
Cajun Rules TS.Ref.

J using a dog he calls Pal, said to be a litter brother to the Gunner dog, out of Orday's Pat bitch and sired by the Killer dog from Mayfield. B is using a dog he calls Ace, a black dog from Loposay breeding.

The buckskin and white dog Pal appears to be the smaller of the two, and the black is leading the fight. The black dog rams the buckskin up against the pit wall and goes in the throat at 20 minutes. Buckskin is taking severe mouth damage, (lips).

30 minutes coming up and the buckskin has a front leg. Black works the cheek to get him off. Buckskin complained and the backers of the black dog roared at 35 minutes.

Dogs swap holds and at about the 50 minute mark the buckskin acts like he is coming to the top.

Black dog acts as though he might turn at 55. One hour and five minutes and dogs are on their feet working mouth and face holds and the black is taking punishment on both front legs. Black works the ear and mouth, Buckskin works the front legs. This is the pattern throughout the fight, at 1:10. 1:30 and the black dog appears to be getting second wind and is giving the buckskin a fit.

1:34, a turn is called on the buckskin. 1:50, both dogs down, in mouth holds. 1:54, pickup, the buckskin to go. Made a hard scratch and both dogs go down. Buckskin gets his favorite hold, a front leg -black has skin hold side of head.

2 hours and a pickup. Black dog came across hard and J released his dog and they met three-quarters of the way across the pit. Black dog gets an ear again and both dogs go down.

2:02, another pickup and the buckskin to go. Went over and made a good scratch.

2:04, pickup, the black dog to go. Came over and hit hard, to complete a good scratch. Dogs go down, the black in mouth holds.

Shift and the black dogs gets an ear. Dogs are resting, and both are down, in holds.

Dogs then come up, with the buckskin on a front leg. 2:10, dogs are still lying in holds.

2:16, Handlers agree to a draw, and both dogs show an eagerness to go across when faced.

We dislike to see a fight like this with a "no decision" end, as both men will go around bragging about their dog had the other one whipped, and the argument will never be settled, but sometimes it is best, to save two good dogs, such as a case like this.

Two good dogs and two good sportsmen.

This match is an indication of deep gameness and ability. The owners need not be concerned with which dog was the winner: they were both as good a dog as any pit fighter would want.

The next fight was said by many to be the greatest of the '70's. The editor stated that those present considered it the best they'd ever seen. It comes from *Your Friend and Mine,* January-May, 1973 and is between Jimmy Boots and Benny Bob, who was the son of Bullyson and the only dog ever to beat his father. Jimmy Boots had won two fights, one over Clark's dog in 40 minutes in Denver, and one against Malcolm X in 17 minutes. His owner had retired from pit fighting but got back in again when he acquired Jimmy Boots. (Jimmy Boots is the dog from Utah, Benny Bob the one from Texas.)

DS vs WB

52 pounds vs 53 ½ pounds
Cajun rules, 20 second count
BP, Referee

In early January of 1973, there was assembled twenty men per side as one of the conditions of the contract, in order to maintain as strict security measures as possible. Also as a part of the agreement was that it was to be held at 300 feet above sea level.

From Texas there was WB, RH, Maurice Carver, to name a few. As their guests from California were Indian Sonny, FJ, Larry McCaw and friends, and PG, plus names but not faces that escape our memory.

The fanciers from Utah included RG with Jimmie Boots, TH, DP, RU, DA, the W brothers - B and D, and each with their entire families which certainly made up their twenty men per side.

EW flew over from Denver to join with those from Utah to see his dog in combat. The strict security was what we got under the direction of DB. It is a lesson we could all follow in any future meetings. It set a relaxed atmosphere on the whole scene.

After a weigh-in of both dogs, the Texans at 53 pounds, and the Utah dog at just a breath above 52 pounds, G had to work in the thirteen minutes he had before pit time to get his dog down two ounces in order to make the weight, which he did.

The rumor that the Texans were going to take the forfeit and that there would be no fight, brought cussing from the crowd, but then – "The fight is on."

Both were tremendous dogs. So evenly matched that only by meeting each other would it have developed into the contest it was.

Benny Bob was true to his reputation as being a hard-biting stifle dog, while Jimmy Boots biting into the shoulders and the chest. They just swapped holds and "bit it out."

The first hour sees Benny Bob with the slight edge, as the end of the hour mark finds Jimmy Boots bit hard in the stifles and his legs are folding under him.

Several scratches by both dogs and then on a scratch by the Texas dog, he carries the Utah dog back into his corner and on top of him, but Jimmy Boots takes hold of the nose and mouth chewing results in the loss of a fang of the Texas dog.

They stay for some time with the Utah dog bunched into the corner and Benny Bob standing over, both chewing it out.

Finally, they chew free of holds, and WB handles his dog off of the top of Jimmy Boots.

He goes after the Texas dog on the pick up and gets hold of the back leg and this helps pull him from the corner and lands on top of Benny Bob as B sets him down again.

The fight seems even again. More scratching by both dogs and then the Utah dog has the odds.

Close to the two hour mark the Utah dog has Texas on the floor and he shakes the shoulder with Benny Bob weakly resisting.

It looks decisive now, but Benny Bob shows his gameness as he goes over on his scratches, two more times before he fails his last scratch.

Jimmy Boots looking straight into the dog and leaning into G's hands, was picked up immediately and taken into the house.

Both sides backed their dogs heavily and sporting gentlemen paid and collected their bets.

> It's not the size of the dog in the fight that
> counts as much as the size of the fight in the dog.
> - Bulow

There are a few things to notice in this match. Benny Bob was ahead for the first hour (An hour is a good, long time.) - so much so that Jimmy Boots' legs were folding under him. For almost another whole hour Jimmy fought as bottom dog. Benny Bob exhausted himself trying to finish his opponent and Jimmy got his second wind. It is an illustration of what is meant by dead gameness.

The next match, also in 1973, is between Butcher Boy and Samson.[53] Butcher Boy was a dog that was considered by those who saw him as one of the best, if not the best, of the heavyweights. You might notice also, reading the editor's introduction, that the people are plain and ordinary, not gangsters, mafia, etc. This match is followed by the one in which Tombstone did so well. It was quite a convention.

The infamous Jimmy Boots - a loveable family pet and one of the best pit fighters ever. Ralph Greenwood has extensively bred his dogs to this great champion.

NH vs S, G & Co.
Males at 57 pounds
Cajun Rules. WD, Ref.

PP conditioned and handled Samson, for the S.G Combine, while N was handling his Butcher Boy dog, which had been conditioned by Maurice Carver. Butcher Boy, a Champion is now six years old.

Two big dogs. 100 to 150 odds being offered on Samson. Samson being a young dog, and winner of one fight, he is a worthy contender over the aging Butcher Boy.

Dogs swap ear holds when they meet in center of the pit.

Butcher Boy is working for the throat, while Samson is content with an ear. Butcher Boy works for the shoulder and front leg but Samson holds him off with the ear hold. Butcher Boy goes for the stifle and his backers roar, but Samson gets him off.

The pit is 16 x 24, with four-tier grandstands on each side. Each side holds about 60 people and each corner is filled with spectators standing. 300 or more.

A turn is called at 15 minutes, with Butcher Boy to go. Butch gets in the shoulder and shakes at 20, and Samson gets a front foot and shakes. Butch going down often and breathing hard. 2 to 1 odds being offered on Samson.

Pickup at 26, Butch to go. Leaped to the attack as Samson met him halfway and got the hold, an ear hold. Butch goes down, age is showing. Butch trying for the throat, Samson, the ear. Butch goes down at 30, but up and walking around the pit with Samson in an ear hold. Samson gets in the stifle and shakes for an instant at 35 but lets go and gets an ear.

Samson sat down and looked at Butch for an instant at 40. Samson in stifle at 44. Butch tries the same hold at 45. Samson gets a front leg at 46, a pickup at 46.

Samson made a good scratch, gets a front leg and shakes. Then back to the ear.

Pickup at 52. Butch to go. And Samson gets a front foot and shakes when dogs come together, then he is back to the ear. At 55, Samson works front leg and then back to the ear. Handlers trying for pickup. Samson goes down and Butch has the ear now. Then back to the shoulder. Samson has an ear, and Butch tries for the shoulder, and a pickup at 57. Good scratch.

Pickup at 59, and a good scratch. Misses though, and hits the wall hard, falls flat and Samson gets the ear, Butch is down in the corner. Pickup at one hour.

Good scratch and Samson gets a front leg but only mouthing. Butch up and he gets a front leg and shakes.

Pickup at 1:02.

Made a good scratch. Pickup a min. later with another good scratch and Samson leads Butch around the pit by an ear. Pickup at 1:05, and a good scratch. Butch made a strong scratch.

H sends Butch into the stifle at 1:08. Samson went down with the Butch dog in an ear hold. H sends Butch into the stifle again at 1:11, then a pickup.

Samson made a good scratch. Pickup at 1:14, and Butch made a good scratch. Samson gets the hold but goes down. Butch with an ear hold.

1:15 and Samson is down against the pit wall and Butch is working the stifle. Samson gets an ear and gets him off and a pickup at 1:16.

Made good scratch but missed his mark. Butch got an ear. Pickup at 1:19, Butcher Boy to go. Butch went over slow and Samson got the hold. Dogs go down. Pickup a minute later and Samson to go.

Went over but did not take hold. Butch got the hold. Another pickup and Butch went over and Samson stood on his line and made Butch come to him. 1:21 and H's backers are encouraging him to let his dog stay.

Pickup at 1:22. Walked over slow and completed scratch, dogs go down. Butch has an ear. Pickup immediately. Butch to go. 1:23, and Butch trots across and his backers roar. Dogs down in corner and spectators on their feet.

Pickup at 1:24. Samson went two steps and fell down and was counted out at 1:25. . . Butcher Boy once again declared the winner. This makes him a four time winner.

The iron will of one stout heart shall make a thousand quail. - Robert Collier

BH VS DM
males @ 55 pounds
Cajun Rules. WD, Ref.

M using a red dog he calls Tombstone. B is using a son of Bullyson, he calls Bullyson, Jr. Dark brindle or black.

The red gets a front leg and the black gets in stifle but ends up in a front leg hold. The red ends up with an ear hold. By the ten minute mark the dogs have established a pattern, front legs and ear holds.

The black tries for the stifle at 12 min. Black works for the throat but the red holds him out with ear hold. Red is in the throat at 15. Red has a bloody front leg. Black gets a hind foot at 20. Red has skin hold in neck. Black gets a front leg and shakes. Red stays in the throat. Mouth fighting at 22. Black gets in the throat at 25. Red goes down, black on top. Red gets on his feet but the black slams him down again in a corner and bores into the throat. Red has a cheek hold. Dogs are on their feet at 30 but the red goes down more often. Red gets a foot and the black has an ear. Black is out of hold catching breath at 31. Red has a front foot hold. 100 to 80 being offered. Dogs trade stifle holds at 32. 34 and each has a hind foot. 36 black is down and breathing hard.

Red is working an ear. Red is down and the black has a front leg at 39.

40, red is down, black in the throat. Red comes up in a flurry of action, then goes down with the black shaking a leg. Red is being called "Toot."

50 and dogs still trading holds. 55, black is working a stifle, red is on his back but has a front leg. Black changes and comes back to the ear. From ear to nose. Dogs trade stifle holds at the hour mark. Red is down, stretched out. Black has a nose hold.

1:18, out of hold count started. Pickup, the red to go. Went over hard to make a good scratch.

At 1:25 minutes, B picks his dog up and calls it quits, to save his dog. The crowd cheered, and DM's Tombstone the winner in one hour and 25 minutes.

You are never beaten until you quit. -Zig Ziggler

The next fight might be interesting to many, especially those who own Pit Bulls with the popular Zebo blood. It is between Zebo and Pete. Zebo's pedigree is provided in the breeding chapter. Jack Swinson's Zebo - named after his father, Zebo. His mother is Beal's Ida Red. Swinson's Zebo looks a great deal like his father - in fact most of those Lonzo-bred dogs have those funny looking ears and are black. The recorded fight may be Zebo's first contract match; I don't know. You may notice the weights are not equal - in Zebo's favor. This inequality is very rare. Zebo would later win a fight in which he had to go four pounds uphill - and win just as decisively. Some of the other fights have unequal weights, also - that is a coincidence, too. I just wanted to record the matches. I must reiterate that this inequality in weight is not usual.

LH VS BF
males at 42 pounds
Cajun Rules JC, Ref.

H using a black called Zebo from Lonzo Pratt. F using his red dog, Pete that he has won two matches with. H weighted in at 41 and one-half while F came in at 39 and one-half pounds.

Red gets the first hold and the black dog gets him off and goes into the chest. Red dog gets an ear with the black still in the chest. Black leaves the chest and goes hard into the shoulder.

5 minute mark and the black is still in the shoulder, with the red trying to get him off with a nose hold. Both dogs fighting the head at eight minutes.

Ten to fifteen minutes the black is doing a job on the red dog's chest. Red dog is weakening from the damage. 20 minutes the red is down and the black dog seems to be getting his second wind.

Turn is called on the red dog at 22 minutes. Red makes a stumbling scratch at 23 with almost no front legs.

Pickup at 24 with the black to go. Black dog runs his scratch.

25 minutes and a pickup with the red dog to go.

Red dog cannot stand on his feet and is counted out. LH and his Zebo dog declared the winner in 26 minutes.

This is Swinson's Zebo. He looks just like his famous father, the seven-time winner, Johnson's Zebo. Swinson's Zebo's mother is linebred from Snowball, the father of Johnson's Zebo.

You can see from the previous contest the damage a good chest dog can do.

Some of the matches that are reported are in very condensed form. Here are a few from *Sporting Dog Journal*, March-April, 1980:

Gamecock Show*
SB vs LJ M 48 Ref HH

JC handling SB's Snake, bred by C out of Ch. Otis and Ch. Honeybunch. J's Pistol Pete a red. Snake doing the driving but Pete holds him out effectively, but not for long. By 20 Snake in control. One scratch each and Pete don't go back at 23 minutes.

Winner JC and SB's Snake.

Snake, by the way, became a champion. He's a fine looking dog.

(*Matches that are part of a "convention" (a relatively large show consisting of several matches - sometimes three, or perhaps as many as ten) are often reported by a certain name, particularly if they are somewhat of an on-going show - examples would be the Gamecock, the Civil War, the Tarheels, Cold Country, Coal Country, etc. - each representing a certain geographical location or a person or group of people.)

This is Jo Lean owned by Jack Swinson. Her father is Jocko and her mother is a daughter of Red Boy Tramp. She is working a piece of hide here. It's very hard to get that hide away from her - you generally have to use a breaking stick to try it out.

DH's Show

D put on his second show in less than a month. Another well run get together. Three good matches and all the sausage and biscuits and coffee you can handle.

FC VS LH
M 48 ½ Ref. RB

WP handling Ch. Jocko a pound light. H handling Bandit a black son of Cables' Ranger (Bullet breeding). Two strong dogs. Bandit on defense trying to keep Jocko out of his back end. When Jocko gets there at 22 minutes it's all over. H picks up at 29.
Winner: P and C's Ch. Jocko.

That Jocko is one hard-biting Pit Bull. I tell you he'll finish a fight very quickly. You may recall the incident related in the medicine chapter, when a dog nearly died right at pit side - his pulse was so low they had to cut open his leg to find a vein to put fluids in. That dog survived and went on to become a four-time winner. He was a good pit dog. Well the dog that nearly killed him was Jocko. I suppose some will disagree with me, but Jocko was the best 48-pound pit dog I know of.

He who has resolved to conquer or die is seldom conquered. -
Robert Collier

DH vs CB
M 45 Ref. JC

H's Zeus, a one-time winner is a double cross off Crenshaw's Ch. Honeybunch. B's Jack a black. Zeus very aggressive and doing the driving but is made to order for Jack, a very strong ear dog. Zeus' ears are real tender by the hour mark, but from time to time he comes to the top for a fast flurry but Jack is in control. The match turns into a scratching contest. Jack can't go at one hour 28 minutes.
Winner: H's Zeus.

I know that dog Jack. He was a good dog and as good an ear dog as you can find. Zeus was just too much for him though.

The Civil War
Mr. T. vs WC

JB handling Mr. T's Reno sired by Stompanoto. C handling a black. Two big ones that didn't bother to weigh in but Reno weighed 79 ½ pounds at the motel and C's black is almost as big. They waltz, fall down, do all kinds of fancy turning without doing any damage, and Reno don't go back at 10 minutes.
Winner: C's black   Rebs 1   Yankees 0

Now this match is an indication of what generally happens with those real big Pit Bulls, especially unconditioned ones. You might be surprised to find that one of those Pit Bulls would probably kill a dog of another breed very quickly and easily - but in the pit with another of their own kind they just do not perform well. Time and time again I've heard of a large Pit Bull that has killed several cur dogs that came into their yard and challenged them while they were on a chain - but when matched with another Pit Bull they don't even break the skin with their bite.

Sometimes (although not very popular) a drop fight may be agreed to. The following match, recorded in *Pit Pal*, May-June, 1979, illustrates:

GL vs FA
M 49

FA conditioned and handled a black dog called Oso for RS. L conditioned and handled a black called Ben. This is an unusual fight. L has a dog that is known as a hard biter but not a scratcher. S had an extremely game dog that took some terrible head biting. This was a drop fight with an hour and 30 minutes time limit. Three judges decide who is ahead at the 1:30 mark. Ben and L were declared the winners. These fights were held April, 1979. We were asked to write up these reports in June so if we got any of the dogs' or peoples' names wrong, we apologize! Jack's Bocefuss was awarded "Best Dog of the Show" trophy. A good time was had by all.

I believe the narratives of many of these matches point out that we are not dealing with a bunch of criminals here - just plain ordinary people that like sportsmanship, have their quarrels and disputes, but on the whole act no different than participants in any other human sport or pastime.

Let me share with you the match in which a Pit Bull named Joker won his Grand Championship. It took place on November 25, 1978 and was reported in *Pit Pal* the following month.

Louisiana
BH vs JU
Males 38 pounds Ref. FB

B with his champion and four time winner, Joker, a red dog, of Bullyson breeding. CF, handling for JU, using a black called Outlaw, a one time winner of Mayfield breeding. Fight starts fast with Outlaw on ears shaking, Joker trying for throat then Outlaw goes back to ears and then on to shoulder. At the 3 minute mark Joker goes into the stifle for a moment and Outlaw gets a hold on the neck. The black dog is a very good wrestler. At the 8 minute mark Outlaw has a neck hold and Joker is steadily trying for the shoulder. Joker gets into shoulder at the 9 minute mark, shaking and the Outlaw dog bites him off with an ear hold. At the 11 minute mark Joker goes to stifle, shaking. Outlaw goes back to the neck and Joker shakes in stifle at 16 minutes. Outlaw on ear and neck at 19 minutes, this seems to be his favorite spot to fight and Joker in stifle, his favorite spot. At the 20 minute mark Outlaw goes to the nose, and Joker goes back into the stifle, shaking hard. Throughout the match the black dog stayed on the nose and ears, with Joker in stifle. At the 32 minute mark Joker is still in stifle with Outlaw on ears. Joker goes from stifle to shoulder, shaking then back to stifle, Outlaw on ears, then nose, then onto eye hold. At around the 40 minute mark Joker is in stifle while black dog is on the bottom with an ear hold. At the 47 minute mark an out-of-hold count, but broken by Joker with a stifle hold. Joker stays in stifle, doing damage, throughout the fight and working hard. U concedes, making B and Joker the winners in 1 hr. 2 min. and also making Joker a five time winner and a Grand Champion. There were no turns called in the match.

The next match is primarily of interest to people in the south-east area of the country. The dog is triple bred Redboy Tramp who was linebred Colby. Redboy Tramp was very popular in the south as he won many good matches and was a crowd pleaser. He was not a hard biter, but won his matches on gameness, a second-wind endurance, and ability. He was a good nose fighter, which will make many opponents go into shock.

RM vs JC
M 43 Ref. VJ

M's Smokey Joe a black. C's Yellow John a red triple bred off of Bass' Redboy. Joe out front from the start, John holding on. After several scratches by each dog Joe decides he's done all he can.
Winner: C's Yellow John.

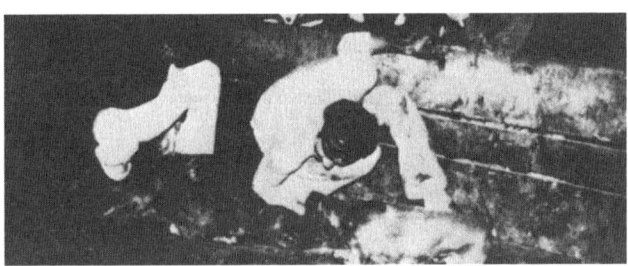

When dogs are evenly matched in ability, if they have true Pit Bull gameness the pit fight becomes an endurance contest after about an hour of fighting. Neither dog does much damage (generally) at this point. It is a question of who quits or is unable to finish before the other. This is when the quality of the keep and professionalism of the handler makes a difference. Here the handler is encouraging his dog. Both dogs are exhausted, just lying there weakly chewing but not willing to quit. The handler may not touch his dog but can get very close and provide verbal encouragement, letting his dog know he is there and supporting him. At 3 hours and 8 minutes the owner of the dog on the left said that he would concede the match if the dog on the right scratched on the next turn. See how weak the dogs are? At 3 hours and 20 minutes the dog on the right (named Pirata) went across like a bullet and won the match and "Best of Show" for that convention. It is very rare for a match to last that long.

The last match has been declared by many, including a very experienced old timer, as the best match of the decade. The old timer (30 years associated with the game) said it was the best match he'd ever seen. There is no doubt, both dogs were rare and unique. A contract was signed between Jeep's owner and backers, and a many-time popular. West Coast winner, Angus, who had defeated that defeater of champions, Ch. Freddie, who, by the way, is Homer's litter brother! The match was called off, however, when Angus couldn't make it. Angus' backers paid the forfeit and offered to bring another dog and Jeep's side agreed. Angus' backers then borrowed Homer, a four-time winner with no opponent lasting an hour with him, and one heck of a dog. Jeep was a champion. He won his championship, beating a darn good dog in two hours and five minutes. Here is the match as recorded in the *Sporting Dog Journal* November-December 1979.

JC conditioned and handled Ch. Jeep. KS handled S's Ch. Homer for BS. Jeep starts out to barnstorm Homer, putting him down at will with shoulder holds. At 20 Homer comes to the top briefly with nose and leg holds but only for a few minutes before Jeep is again overpowering him. By 40 Homer is trying to catch up; he's almost always in hold on the side of the head and ears. The pattern continues the same from the one-hour mark to the three-hour mark. Jeep dominating; Homer coming briefly to the top in flurries. At 3:08 Jeep on a down dog and C calls him into a turn and he flies across. At this point Jeep is ahead but it's still undecided. At 3:22 Homer scratches, stumbling, falling, getting up, falling again to complete a game, game scratch. 3:23 goes with no trouble. The pattern doesn't change; Jeep still stronger with Homer able to come up and shake out his hold. Handled at 3:45, Homer staggers out of his corner but can't make it and is counted out. An outstanding contest; rarely are two dogs of this quality matched into each other. One hundred percent game, hard-biting, talented dogs in absolutely excellent condition. Winner: Jeep

Forcing heart and nerve and sinew to serve your turn long after they are gone, and so hold on when there is nothing in you except the will which says to them: Hold on!   - Kipling

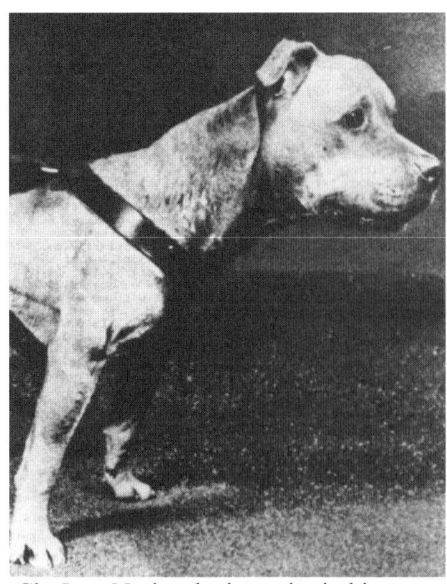

Ch. Jeep Notice the intensity in his eyes.

    The write-up in the Journal did not adequately describe the gameness displayed in that match. Such was the power of the Jeep dog that Homer had his shoulder knocked out of place in the first 20 minutes. Homer continued to fight bravely, however, and periodically he would get a good hold and shake it out good. He actually fought the whole fight on three legs. Although Jeep dominated the match most of the time, Homer always had a hold. Homer was about as hard biting a head dog as you'll find anywhere and he had beaten some darn good dogs. But Jeep, you see, didn't care – he'd just stick his head right in Homer's mouth and let him bite. He'd eventually shake out and then he'd be all over Homer. Homer lost, but I've got to say he did make a mess out of Jeep in the process. Very rarely is as much damage done in a pit fight as in this one. Whenever a match goes for a long time, there is generally a lot of laying around as the dogs catch their breath and try to regain strength, neither one wanting to quit - the fighting comes in flurries. In this match, however, there was no laying around - it was continuous fighting. For almost four hours those Pit Bulls weren't out of holds more than 15 minutes total. After three and a half hours, although Homer was still fighting uphill, it could have still gone either way. But then Jeep got Homer down and was shaking hard. It looked like Homer might have to be picked up or he'd be a goner. He got a handle, however, so he was picked up off the ground where he was stretched out and carried to his corner. He could hardly stand and was very wobbly on his legs - but his eyes and heart were true. His eyes were dead on-on his opponent and when he was released, he headed straight toward him. His body just wouldn't respond to his heart, however. He staggered forward a few steps and fell forward head first - his rear legs tried to stay up but he fell over on his side, stretched out like it was the end. But I'm telling you that Pit Bull just didn't know quit - he just wouldn't stop. He started kicking and wallering around; finally getting his rear legs dug into the floor, he pushed himself forward. His front legs were dysfunctional, and that Pit Bull pushed himself forward with his head on the ground. He was one heck of a Bulldog.

One brief shining moment (from the play Camelot)

The match, of course, could definitely be criticized as being cruel. It is assuredly not, however, representative of most Pit Bull matches. Dogs like either Homer or Jeep pop up about once every 20 years - and they get matched with each other about once every 40 years.They did epitomize what a Pit Bulldog is all about. Jeep is quiet, easy-going, very friendly, and loves children - an ideal house pet as long as he's kept away from other dogs - but if he hadn't been matched, we would never have known him for what he truly is - one of the best pit dogs in history, and dead game. The same could be said of Homer. He, also, was a quiet type of Pit Bull and was great, perhaps greater than Jeep. These dogs are brave because they're bred that way; it's as simple as that. After all, they don't call them Pit Bulldogs for nothing.

> It masters time, it conquers space
> It cows that boastful trickster, chance.
> And bids the tyrant circumstance
> Uncrown and fill a servant's place.
> There is no chance, no destiny, no fate,
> Can circumvent, or hinder, or control
> The firm resolve of a determined soul.
> Gifts count for nothing, will alone is great:
> All things give way before it soon or late.
> What obstacle can stay the mighty force
> Of the sea-seeking river in its course,
> Or cause the ascending orb of day to wait?
> Each well-born soul must win what it deserves.
> Let the fools prate of luck. The fortunate
> Is he, whose earnest purpose never swerves.

Whose slightest action, or inaction serves
The one great aim. Why, Even Death himself
Stands still and waits an hour sometimes
For such a will.
James Marineau
(Cited in *The Secret of the Ages* by Robert Collier)

Ronnie Anderson and his Champion Spade

Chapter 11: Conclusion

> Those who appreciate true gameness in a dog are relatively few, not because they don't like gameness - - because they don't understand it.
> - Bob Stevens

Throughout this book, I have stated that I have tried to be objective in my recounting pit fighting. Many of my readers may say that in fact I am biased and obviously in favor of the sport. I want to state that I have truly tried to be as impartial as possible and that my opinions are a result of much research and observation. I will say, however, that I am not totally opposed to pit fighting. I do not fight my Pit Bull, but he does come from good fighting stock. Let me be more specific in my opinion on fighting Pit Bulls. I feel that, as a practical matter, pit fighting should remain illegal, curtailed -but not strictly enforced. I believe the selectivity necessary to develop top-quality fighting Pit Bulls results in a superlative strain of canines. This is true, however, only when the dogs are bred and handled by those who know what they are doing. I feel that if pit fighting became legal and widespread, breeding would become even less tight than it is today; more people would abuse the dogs; and the strain would be detrimentally affected. I think there have been some incidences of people taking advantage of pit fighting by soliciting thousands of dollars for personal gain. In fact I'm nearly certain of it. I do know that there has been purposeful lying and all the funds solicited certainly weren't used to curtail pit fighting because no noticeable action has been taken. I personally read pamphlets distributed through a leading dog magazine, and they were chock full of sensational, incorrect claims of cruelties involved in pit fighting. The person who showed me the pamphlets told me she was sending in a substantial donation. (She is well off financially.) The person in charge of the solicitation lived in a very high-income-level home and I read about six months later that that person left town, no forwarding address, because of being "threatened by the underworld pit fighters." What happened to all the funds that were donated? No one knows, and pit fighting continued to thrive in the area. This is just one of many examples.

Throughout this book, despite statements to the contrary, I realize that I may have given the impression that although I do not match my Pit Bull, I wholeheartedly support pit fighting. My statement that I feel that it should remain illegal, but not strictly enforced has probably added to that impression. I also realize that statements that there should be a law that is "not strictly enforced" seem quite ludicrous. The general feeling is that something should either be legal or illegal, no middle ground. But I maintain there are some practical aspects to life that do not lend themselves to always "go by the book." Naturally a law that is "not strictly enforced" cannot be legislated in that manner. So far, however, the authorities haven't seemed too concerned with pit fighting because crime fighting is expensive and time consuming and they have their hands full, combating more serious crimes against society. If pit fighting gets too widespread or out of hand, however, they step in. This is what I mean by "not strictly enforced."

In any event, now that I have given my opinion on pit fighting, let me relate what I think should be done with the Pit Bull Terrier breed, hopefully clarifying my position. I feel that the large majority of Pit Bull owners ought to become involved in the legal activities described in this book - obedience, tracking, weight-pulling, and the ultimate challenge, Schutzhund. I do feel, however, these animals should, for the most part, be purchased from the relatively few breeders that breed primarily from and for the pit and that each Pit Bull that is going to be bred be proven game (game tested). I believe that while it may be cruel (Well, that's a strong word - let me say narrow.) to allow dogs of another breed to fight, even if they want to, it is not "redneckish" to game test Pit Bulls, because of their tenacity, ability to heal, and the fact they've been bred that way for so many generations. Under controlled circumstances, particularly where no money is on the line, I don't see how the Pit Bull would get seriously hurt. I don't feel that rolling a Pit Bull for 20 minutes is a sufficient game test - unless a second, more demanding test is planned later on. I feel that the Pit Bull should be allowed to go for a good long time or well two-dogged to determine the strength of the inherited gameness. The Pit Bull will heal up just fine afterwards. As far as cruelty goes, I think that, for a Pit Bull, cruelty is stimulus deprivation (not enough attention) - not occasional fighting. Anyone that knows what he's doing does not fight his Pit Bull often - only when his dog is fully healed. In the arena I will say that perhaps it can be considered cruel to leave a dog in a match too long when he's losing and not pick him up before permanent damage is done. If a gameness test takes place when the Pit Bull is mature, I don't believe it will make him become aggressive toward other dogs (except for that particular dog) after the incident - not if the Pit Bull has had a non-aggressive attitude prior to the test. Witness the talented pit master Peterbuilt, whose favorite pal in his yard is a German Shepherd. In other words, if, during the Pit Bull's puppy and formative years, he has received plenty of obedience training and gobs of canine socialization, off lead, then the gameness test will not change him. (Recall that, in selecting a puppy, various socialization tests can be applied that will indicate whether the puppy has an aggressive attitude toward other dogs or not and that there is absolutely no correlation between an aggressive attitude and gameness. If you want a pet or a Schutzhund dog, select the pup that does not act aggressively toward the other pups.) I have mentioned in the book that I know of many, many Pit Bulls that are quite docile toward other dogs and even other Pit Bulls outside the pit, but are unbeatable in a pit and are as game as could be.

> He who has a firm will molds the world to himself.
> -Goethe

I would like the Pit Bull to be recognized, not as an outlaw, but a respected canine. In fact I do believe the Pit Bull is a superior canine and can be so recognized. Every fictional dog story that I'm aware of and many of the dog magazines emphasize the bravery, intelligence, and affectionate nature of a certain breed or a particular dog. This is because these are the qualities that are generally most desired by dog owners. I would say that most Pit Bulls are at least equal in intelligence to other breeds (although many are perhaps more stubborn and can be difficult to train). As far as affection goes, I believe (again, a generality) that Pit Bulls are more affectionate than most, if not all, other breeds. As far as bravery is concerned, well what breed comes even close to a Pit Bull's bravery? (the result of selective breeding of dogs whose bravery is tested by performance).

In summary, I am of the opinion that a Pit Bull should not be limited to just one activity - tracking, weight-pulling, pit fighting, Schutzhund, or whatever. I do not believe that letting a Pit Bull participate in all of the named endeavors limits his ability to perform any one of these tasks - on the contrary, I feel such wide exposure will enhance the dog's abilities in each area.

I am of the opinion, moreover, that training Pit Bulls can become tremendously "scientific." Take as an example the conditioning aspect. It can be likened to human athletics. Thirty or forty years ago a boxer could shine if he got in top condition, which meant the standard roadwork, light and heavy bag work, and sparring rounds. Everyone had their- "secret" routines, but in reality there wasn't much difference in any of them. Today these techniques are basic, but the conditioning of a boxer has become very scientific (in that advanced research on muscle stimulation, maximization of oxygen consumption, reflexology, etc., is tested and documented) and in order to successfully compete a boxer cannot limit himself to traditional training methods.

Eddie Pickard with Swinson's Lil

This book attempts to stimulate interest in moving beyond the old ways and investigate the fertile area of scientific genetics, nutrition, conditioning, obedience, and working (catch dogs, pit dogs, trackers, weight-pullers, etc.).

Whenever one embarks on such an endeavor, criticism is inevitable. The old, tried and true ways have accomplished objectives and so people will scoff at vitamin E, ginseng, interval training, biomagnetics, etc. I maintain, however, that while some of the unproven and different concepts proposed in this book may not work, they are based upon sound principles, and advancements are made by experimentation.

To that end, I would like to quote Peter Mark Roget in his preface to tne original *Roget's Thesaurus* in 1852 because I believe it is appropos to the writing of this book.[54]

Notwithstanding all the pains I have bestowed on its execution, I am fully aware of its numerous deficiencies and imperfections, and of its falling far short of the degree of excellence that might be attained. But, in a work of this nature, where perfection is placed at so great a distance, I have thought it best to limit my ambition to that moderate share of merit which it may claim in its present form; trusting to the indulgence of those for whose benefit it is intended, and to the candor of critics who, while they find it easy to detect faults, can at the same time duly appreciate difficulties.

Actually, the search for new information is a never ending process. Subsequent to writing the conditioning chapter, for example, I have uncovered research studies which taught me a great deal more about animal conditioning. In addition I have discovered new information that adds further credibility to some of the nutritional supplements I have recommended. A recent study, for example, has disclosed additional benefits to be derived from ginseng. I was also interested to learn that Duk Koo Kim, the Korean boxer that proved to be dead game in his match with Boom Boom Mancini, had consumed copious quantities of ginseng and garlic while training for the fight. (He stayed in the ring taking too many blows to the head and had to have the match stopped even though he was willing to continue. He died that evening in the hospital.) His endurance in that fight (fall of 1982) was stupendous and will probably be considered one of the greatest demonstrations of human tenacity and conditioning in modern boxing history

Well, that's it. I hope you have enjoyed my book as much as I have enjoyed writing it, and the learning involved, and that it has helped you and your Pit Bulldog(s) have a closer association. I know I dearly love my Morochito. We've gone a lot of miles together he and I, and, to me, he is truly a dog of velvet and steel.

Thank you and goodnight!

Bob and Victory's Secret (Vicki) – Morochito's fourth generation

A Wish
I wish for you a courage strong;
I wish you the fibre the valiant need
To hold the fort against the wrong:
I wish you the heart of the fighting breed.
I wish you the best along the way;
I wish you the spirit that lifteth up,
To touch the fringe of a brighter day.
And drink to the full life's loving cup.

—Gordon Richard Higham (from Bob White's Scrap Book Thomas Allen Limited, Toronto, 1953

FOOTNOTES

1. *Bloodlines*, Sept.-Oct., 1976. Reprinted with permission from *Bloodlines*.
2. Eberhard, Ernest. *The New Complete Bull Terrier*, 2nd ed. (Howell Book House, Inc., 1973)
3. *Pit Bull Gazette*, February, 1979.
4. An article by Richard Stratton in *Bloodlines*, Sept.-Oct., 1976
5. The following historical material dealing with the Pit Bull in England prior to being imported to America is adapted from by Col. Bailey C. Hanes, Copyright © 1973, 1966, 1956 by Howell Book House, Inc., by special permission of the publisher.
6. Hammonds, Gary. "A Thought," written April 1, 1977.
7. This ends the material adapted from *The New Complete Bulldog*. P 45 Stratton, Richard F. *This Is the American Pit Bull Terrier*. Copyright 1976 by T.F.H. Publications, Inc. Ltd., page 84. 9
8. Meeks, Jack. *Memoirs of the Pit*, from manuscript published by Pete Sparks, 1967.
9. *Pit Bull Gazette*, November, 1978
10. Brown, Wayne. *History of the Pit Bull*, p. 44.
11. Ibid., p. 45.
12. Reprinted with permission from Ralph Greenwood.
13. Reprinted with permission from Ralph Greenwood.
14. Reprinted from *The New Complete Bulldog* (p. 25-26) by Col. Bailey C. Hanes, Copyright © 1973, 1966, 1956 by Howell Book House, Inc., by special permission of the publisher.
15. *Greensboro Record*. 1/16/80.
16. Fox, Dr. Michael. *Understanding Your Dog*, p. 102.
17. *Prevention*, Feb., 1980.
18. Nutra-Vet Research Corporation, 201 Smith Street, Poughkeepsie, New York 12601.
19. This information was supplied by Hill's Science Diet,
20. Iams Food Company, Iams Breeder Notes, Dept. PBD, This information was supplied P. O. Box 148, Topeka, Kansas 66601. Iams Food Company, Iams Breeder Nc 3622 Delphos Avenue, Dayton, Ohio 45417.
21. Most of my information on vitamin D is taken from a pamphlet that my vet lent me, entitled "Nutritional Aids. Continuing Studies in Animal Nutrition," summer, 1979, published by Ken-L Ration.

22 Shorafa, W. M., et al, "Effect of Vitamin D and Sunlight on Growth and Bone Development of Young Ponies," J. Anim. Sci. 48:882-886, 1979.
23 Nutritional Aids, Continuing Studies in Animal Nutrition.
24 A pamphlet released by General Nutrition Center.
25 Whitney, Leon F. *Dog Psychology.* Dog World, 1006 West Roosevelt Road, Westchester, Illinois 60153
26 Ibid.
27 Goulart, Frances. "Getting High for a Workout, Nature's Drug-Free Uppers," *Muscle and Bodybuilder*, January, 1981.
28 Ibid.
29 Carter, Albert E. *The Miracles of Rebound Exercise.*
30 Lea, Tom. King Ranch, Vol. II, (Little, Brown and Co., Boston, 1957), p. 728.
31 Spino, Mike. *Beyond Jogging.* (Celestial Arts, Calif.).
32 Mather, Jim. Jim Mather is probably the world's leading authority on the speed enhancement of athletes. He holds a black belt in karate and has acted as Chief Instructor for California Karate Academy for many years. He was a major competitor in karate and won many events. His students have included international, national, and state champions. Academically, he holds B.A. and M.A. degrees in Physical Education from Stanford University and is a Ph.D. candidate. He has been a coach in various sports and his clients (He has tutored privately.) have included world record holders and professional athletes. Mr. Mather is most known for his ability to catch arrows in mid-flight. He's performed this feat several times for television and has had the cameras slow down the speed so as to view the catch in slow motion. (This information on Mr. Mather comes from the "Speed Enhancement Newsletter" published by Ultimate Man Enterprises.)
33 Attla, George. *Training and Racing Sled Dogs.* Copyright ©1974 by Arner Publications, Inc.
34 Inkeles, Gordon, G.P. *The New Massage.* (Putnam's Sons, New York, N.Y., 1980).
35 Ibid.
36 Ibid.
37 *Pit Bull Gazette*, May, 1981.
38 Brackett, Lloyd C. *Planned Breeding.* Published by *Dog World Magazine*, Illinois, 1961. 4.0 314   Eberhard, p. 177.
39 Lea.
40 Adapted from *The Development of a Superior Family in the Modern Quarter Horse* by A.O. Rhoad and R.J. Klebera. Jr.,

41 *The Journal of Heredity* (Aug., 1946), contained in The King Ranch, Vol. II, pp. 733 and 734. (Kleberg and his father were managers of the ranch and instilled the breeding program.)
42 Onstott, Phillip. *The New Art of Breeding Better Dogs.* (Howell Book House, Inc., New York, 1971).
43 Eberhard, p. 176.
44 *The Pit Bull Sheet.* Sept.-Oct., 1979. Joan Oilman, the publisher of the magazine, gave me permission to use this plus information from a few other articles in my chapter. The magazine was discontinued and is now merged with *The Scratch Line* published by Dave Reynolds, President of the Society for the Benefit of the A.P.B.T.
45 Vaccines, Inc. pamphlet. 47 The information on parvo is adapted from the advice of my vet, a pamphlet I received from Vaccines, Inc., and a pamphlet by Fromm Laboratories, Inc.
46 Hart, Allan, B.V.S., *A Dog Owner's Encyclopedia of Veterinary Medicine*, T.F.H. Publications, Inc., New Jersey, 1971.
47 Bechtel, Stefan, "Nutrients that Help the Body Heal Itself," *Prevention*, Vol. 34, No. 8, August, 1982.
48 Pearce, Richard, ph.D., "A Simple Solution for Aches and Pains," *Runner's World*, Sept., 1980.
49 Parts of this section were taken from *The Pit Bull Sheet*, Sept.-Oct., 1978.
50 *Sporting Dog Jounal*, January-February, 1981
51 *Your Friend and Mine*, June-Dec., 1973.
52 Cited in *Heavyhands* by Leon and Company, Boston, 1982.)

BIBLIOGRAPHY OF SUGGESTED READINGS

Breeding

Brackett, Lloyd. *Planned Breeding.* Dog World, 1006 West Roosevelt Road, Westchester, Illinois 60153, 1961.

Hutt, Frederick. *Genetics for Dog Breeders.* Freeman and Company, San Francisco, 1979.

Onstott, Phillip. *The New Art of Breeding Better Dogs.* Howell Book House, Inc., New York,

Reid, Ed. *Memories of Staffordshire Bull Terriers and American Pit Bull Terriers.* Stockquest Ltd., London, 1978.

Whitney, Leon F. *How To Breed Dogs*. Dog World, 1006 West Roosevelt Road, Westchester, Illinois 60153.

Bulldog Repair and Supplies
Hart, Allan. *A Dog Owner's Encyclopedia of Veterinary Medicine*. T.F.H. Publications, Inc., New Jersey, 1971.

Schneck, Stephen, with Norris Nigel. *The Complete Home Medical Guide for Dogs*. Stein and Day, 1970.

Write to the following for medical supplies:

Kentucky Bull Dog Supply 317 Old Morgantown Road Bowling Green, Kentucky 42101

Omaha Vaccine Co. P. O. Box 7228 3030 "L" Street Omaha, Nebraska 68107

Vaccines, Inc. 2114 South First Street, P. O. Box 727, Temple, Texas 76503

Wholesale Kennel Supply Co. Drawer 745 Siler City, North Carolina 27344

General

Brown, Wayne D. *History of the Pit Bull Terrier*. PDQ Printing, Dallas, Texas, 1979.

Hanes, Bailey C. *The New Complete Bulldog*. Howell Book House, Inc., 1973.

Lea, Tom. *King Ranch*. Little, Brown and Co., Boston, 1957.

Maffei, Fredric. *The Life of Humbug*. Manor-Book Mailing Service, P. O. Box 690, Rockville Centre, New York, 11571.

Sporting Dog Journal. Conditioning the Pit Dog. This is a booklet that contains nine old keeps beginning with Old Rhody's keep in 1881 and ending with Earl Tudor, in 1973.

Stratton, Richard F. *The Book of the American Pit Bull Terrier*. T.F.H. Publications, New Jersey, 1981.

Stratton, Richard F. *This Is the American Pit Bull Terrier*. T.F.H. Publications, New Jersey, 1976.

Nutrition
Collins, Donald B. *The Collins Guide To Dog Nutrition*. Dog World, 1006 West Roosevelt Road, Westchester, Illinois 80153.

National Academy of Science. *Nutrient Recruirements of Dogs*. National Research Council, 2101 Constitution Avenue, Washington, D.C. 20418.

Write to the following for excellent information concerning dog nutrition:
Hill's Science Diet P. O. Box 148 Topeka, Kansas 66601

Iams Food Company c/o Iams Breeder Notes, Dept. PBD, 3622 Delphos Avenue, Dayton, Ohio 45417

Ross-Wells, Division of Beatrice Foods Co. Berlin, Maryland 21811 (manufacturers of A.N.F.)

Nutra-Vet Research Corporation 201 Smith Street Poughkeepsie, New York 12601

Periodicals
Bloodlines Journal. United Kennel Club, 321 West Cedar Street, Kalamazoo, Michigan.

Off-Lead. Arner Publications, Inc., Box 307, Graves Road, Westmoreland, New York 13490

Pit Bull Almanac. All American Dog Registry, P. O. Box Q, Bellflower, California 90706

Pit Bull Gazette. American Dog Breeders' Association, Box 1771, Salt Lake City, Utah.

Prevention. Rodale Press, Inc., 33 East Minor Street, Emmaus, Pennsylvania 18049

Rare Books

*Armitage, George C. *Thirty Years With Fighting Dogs*. Washington, D.C.: Jack Jones, 1935. Reprint Sparks.

*Colby, Joseph L. *The American Pit Bull Terrier*. Sacramento: The News Publishing Company, 1936.

Davis, Richard Harding. *The Bar Sinister*. Charles Scribner's Sons, New York, 1903

Denlinger, Milo G. *The Complete Pitbull or Staffordshire Terrier*. Washington: Denlingers, 1948.

*Fox, Richard K. (Ed.). *The Dog Pit*. New York: Richard K. Fox, 1888.

*Glass, Eugene. *The Sporting Bull Terrier*. Battle Creek: The Dog Fancier, 1910.

Hanna, L. B. *Memories of the Pit Bull Terrier and His Master*. New York, n.d. (Reprinted by Pete Sparks, Bladensburg, 1955).

*Meeks, Jack. *Memoirs of the Pit*, from manuscript published by Pete Sparks, 1967.

Ormsby, Clifford A. *The Staffordshire Terrier*. Dansville: F.A. Owen Publishing Company, 1956.

Pascoe, H. Richard. *The American Staffordshire Terrier*. Dallas: Williamson Printing Corp., 1977.

**Pit Dog Report*, various Vols. 1-9 (1970-1978).

Sparks, Pete (Ed.). Reprint of *Bloodlines* for 1940. Starke: Pete Sparks.

Sparks, Pete (Ed.). *Your Friend and Mine*, various Vols. 1-22 (1952-1974).

*Note: These may be purchased from Pete Sparks, P. O. Box 716, Starke, Florida 32091

The Armitage book is the best one.

Training and Behavioral Books

Attla, George. *Training and Racing Sled Dogs*. Arner Publications, New York, 1974.

Barwig, Susan. *Schutzhund*. Quality Press, Inc., Colorado, 1978.

Bergman, Dr. Goran. *Why Does Your Dog Do That?* Howell Book House, New York.

Eberhard, Ernest. *The New Complete Bull Terrier*. Howell Book House, Inc., New York, 1971.

Fox, Michael. *Understanding Your Dog*. Coward, McCann, and Geoghegan, Inc., New York.

Johnson, Glen. *Tracking Dogs*; Theory and Methods. Arner Publications, Inc., New York.

Koehler, William. The Koehler Method of Guard Dog Training. Howell Book House, Inc., New York, 1962.

Levorsen, Bella. *Mush! A Beginner's Manual of Sled Dog Training.* Dog World, 1006 West Roosevelt Road, Westchester, Illinois 60153.

Monks of New Skeet. *How To Be Your Dog's Best Friend.* Little, Brown and Co., 1978.

Pfaffenberger, Clarence. T*he New Knowledge of Dog Behavior.* Howell Book House, Inc., New York, 1963.

Whitney, Leon F. *Dog Psychology.* Dog World, 1006 West Roosevelt Road, Westchester, Illinois 60153

Index

Vitamin A, 387, 546
Abady Formula dog food, 383, 392
Acedophilis, 403
Adoption, 67
Aerobic, 452
Alligator, Plumber's, 25-27, 480
Altitude training, 467
American Dairy Goat Association, 402-403
Anaerobic, 452
A.N.F. dog food, 395
Armitage, 142, 165, 177, 213, 229, 234
Arrison, 509
Art, Stinson's, 244
Artificial insemination, 276
Attla, George, 363, 462, 464
B-Complex vitamins, 4-4-405
Badger-baiting, 222-223
Bandog, 220
Earwig, Susan, 285

Beanie, Loposay's (Shiver's), 494, 512-513
Bear-baiting, 220-221
Bee stings, 539
Big Boy, 477-479, 590
Biomagnetics, 277-276
Black Jack, Tudor's, 242-245
Black Jack, Jr., 243
Black Shine, Cannon's, 248, 500
Black Widow, Carver's, 248, 250
Blind Billy, 499
Bloodlines, 254
Blood Doping, 465-466
Blue Paul, 230
Bo, Finley's, 508, 523
Bob, Armitage's, 216
Bob the Fool, 234
Boe, Loposay's 509
Bones, 261-262
Boomerang, 249, 484
Born To Win, 526-527
Boudreaux, Floyd, 67
Boutelle, James, 234
Breeding program (suggested), 483
Breed Standards, 316
Brewer's yeast, 399
Brisbin, Dr. I. Lehr, 47
Brown, Al, 243
Buck, Crenshaw's, 240
Bull-baiting, 221
Bullet, Cotton's, 271, 482
Bull-running, 221-222
Bull, Sykes', 510
Bullyson, Wallings', 247, 524
Bull Winkle, Watkins', 509
Butch (Morochito's half brother), 180, 250, 514
Butcher Boy, 612-614
Vitamin C, 393, 411

Caffeine, 278
Calcium Metabolism, 407
Canter, 455
Carbohydrates, 408
Carnival by James Thurber, 303
Carver, Maurice, 27
Catch Dog, The, 309
Catmill, 446-447
Cerutty, Percy, 412
Chelated, 550
Chicken liver, 471
Circuit training, 464
Cocoran, Jim, 556
Cod liver oil, 398, 406
Colby, John P., 111, 238
Colby Dime, 240, 475
Colby Dogs, 246
Conformation of the Pit Bull, 258
Convention, 509
Copper, 413
Corvino, Joe, 240
Cottage cheese, 402
Courtesy scratch, 211, 512
Cur, 293
Vitamin D, 387, 406
Davis, Ralph, 356-358
Decreasing resistance, 460
Dehydration, 33, 145, 191, 537
Desiccated liver, 397 399, 406, 412
Dibo, 298, 475
Discriminative reinforcement, 410
Distemper, 536
Dog World, 397, 498
Dog houses, 143, 163
Double cross, 485
Drag, 499
Drop fight, 618

Dubs, Loposay's, 508
Dutch, Burkette's, 508
Vitamin E, 387, 393, 398
Egg yolks, 397
Elbow calluses, 539
Electrolytes, 550
Eli, Jr., Clayton's, 27, 526
Esquire article, 266
Eucanuba dog food, 395, 471
Fanged, 297, 601
Fast twitch fiber, 460
Fasting, 408
Feeding schedule, 409
Feely, Con, 216
Fighting Peter, 179, 242
Fighting styles, 142
Filial degeneration, 487, 499
Fishing pole, 433
Fleas, 553
Fly bites, 536
Footpads, 539
Fork Farm, 499
Fo-ti-teng, 416-417
Fox, Dr. Michael, 279, 291
G force, 439
Gallop, 449, 455-456
Galtie, Colby's, 239-242
Gameness, 32
Garrett, James, 106, 554
Gas House, 234, 555
GEO article, 267
Ginger, Fonseca's, 203
Ginseng, 416
Goat's milk, 491
Godzilla, 517
Goldie, Corvino's, 242
Goldie, Fitzwater's, 246

Granulex, 539, 544, 553
Greenwood, Ralph, 21, 174, 209
Grip, McDonald's, 234
Hall, Bobby, 19, 21, 101
Halo effect, 506
Hammonds, Gary, 19
Heartworms, 164, 420, 513
Heinzl, Howard, 26, 28, 203
Hoelcher, Phil, 340
Hold-out artist, 516
Homer, 501-502, 527
Honey, 419
Honeybunch, 103, 250, 523
Hookworms, 534
Horsemill, 447
Humbug, The Life of, 481
Hybrid vigor, 491
Hydrogen peroxide, 539-540
Iams Food Company, 395
Inbreeding, 483
Iodine, 398
Ionized air, 401
Ionized water, 190, 278
Ion Research Center, 401
Iron, 277
Ironhead, Carver's, 248
"Is Fat Beautiful?" by Gary Hammonds, 302
Jack Dempsey, 244
Jeep, Garrett's, 106-107, 161 162, 176
Jeff, Tudor's, 271
Jocko, 618
Joker, Grand Champion, 524, 620
Jimmy Boots, 500, 610
Vitamin K, 597
Kager, Armitage's, 238, 536
Kelp, 398
Kennel cough, 164

King Ranch, 106, 491-492
Knight Crusader, 245, 356
Lactic acid, 435, 451
Lady, Greg's, 511
Lightner, William J., 234-236
Lil, 584
Lime, 447
Linebreeding, 22, 236, 243, 253-255
Lions, 226
Liver, 380
Livingston, Don, 309, 320
Lloyd, Cockney Charles, 171
Loposay, 509
Lymphatic system 439-440, 467
MAGNUM, 383
Mather, Jim, 460
Mastiffs, 219
Mayfield, Don, 246
Mert, Womack's, 249
Midnight Cowboy, 247, 500, 524
Miracles of Rebound Exercise, 439
Miss Pool Hall Red, 249
Miss Spike, Carver's, 217, 246, 249
Missy, Art's, 250
Molasses, 418
Monkey, Loposay's, 508
Monkeys, fighting, 266
Monks of New Skeet, 286
Morochito, 16
Morochito's pedigree, 482, 503, 505
Motorcycle, 452
Mustard greens, 399
Nigger, Mayfield's, 27
Nutra-Vet, 383
Obnoxious Ox, 514
Off-Lead, 288, 341
Off-the-chain, 207, 493

Old family, 234
Old family red nose, 236
Open pedigree, 487, 499
Oso Negro, 526
Outcross, 149, 227, 235
Oxygen debt, 451
Packed cell volume, 140, 142
Kid's Panda Bear, 338, 340
Parvo, 537
Pedialyte, 549-550
Petersen, Cher, 203
Pfaffenberger, Clarence, 279
Pilot, Lloyd's, 235
Pistol, Carver's, 249
Pit Bull Gazette, 98, 117
Pit Bull Sheet, 240, 397
Pit Dog Report, 264
Pit rules, 247
Placer, Joe, 355
Poison, 539
Police Gazette, 235
Polygenic, 487
Prepotency, 217
Prevention magazine, 411
Protein, 277, 379
Pulse, 414
Pup, Galvin's, 234
Purina, 381
Quantitative inheritance, 487
Rabies, 537
Rascal, Trahan's, 247
Rebounder, 439
Recessive traits, 490
Red Boy Tramp, 476
Red Lady, Gordon's, 217
Red Smuts, 231
Register of Merit, 488, 523, 608

Reinforcement in training, 300
Rip, Lancaster's, 519
Rifle, Colby, 240
Roundworms, 534
Rolling Pit Bulls, 154, 288
Rubdown, 465
Ruffian line, 245
Rufus, Hammond's, 27-28, 250
Runner's World magazine, 412
Running chain, 274, 422
Salt, 597
San Luis Key Downs Thoroughbred Training Center, 449
Sarge, Williams', 248
Schooling roll, 215, 575
Science Diet, Hill's (dog food), 381
Selective Breeding, 250
Selenium, 397-398, 405
Sevin Dust, 536
Shipping your dog, 542
Shock, 33, 144
Skin hold, 52
Skunk scent, 536
Slow twitch fiber, 460
Smokey Blue, Brisbin's, 366
Snake, 250
Snooty, Wood's, 27, 514
Snowball, McCraw's, 479
Sorrells, Buckshot, 246
Spendthrift Farm, 449
Spike, Livingston's, 323
Spike, Tudor's, 217
Sporting Dog Journal, 139
Staffordshire Terriers, 230
Stool eating, 540
Stratton, Richard, 23
Super yeast, 399, 403
Supplies, 552

Swimming, 413-416
Swineherd, 243
Swinson, Jack, 448
Tacoma Jack, 244
Tape worms, 534
Thurber, James, 67, 303
Tie-dog, 219
Tombstone, Patrick's, 524, 608
Toot, Maloney's, 150
Treadmills, 169
Trim Moody, 524
Triple cross, 485
Trot, 452
Tudor, Earl, 166
Tuff, Petersen's, 204
Turntable, 448
United Kennel Club, 253
Uselton, Jim, 28, 488
Vaseline, 539
Weehunt, 524, 526
Wheat germ, 393, 399
White Rock, 246
Whitney, Dr., 408
Williams, Jack, 241
Wounds, 543
Yellow John, 621
Your Friend and Mine, 264
Zebo, Johnson's, 52, 107, 173
Zeke, Womack's (Klaus'), 527
Zeus, 512, 619